AMERICAN HOMICIDE

RANDOLPH ROTH

American Homicide

THE BELKNAP PRESS OF
HARVARD UNIVERSITY PRESS
Cambridge, Massachusetts
London, England
2009

Library of Congress Cataloging-in-Publication Data

Roth, Randolph, 1951–
    American homicide / Randolph Roth.
      p.   cm.
    Includes bibliographical references and index.
    ISBN 978-0-674-03520-1 (cloth : alk. paper)
    1. Homicide—United States—History.   I. Title.

  HV6524.R68 2009
  364.1520973—dc22   2009016830

To Allison,
the memory of William Slothrop,
and God's second sheep

Contents

Figures

Preface

This book presents a working hypothesis about why adult homicide rates in the United States are so high. The hypothesis is based on tens of thousands of murder cases from the United States and Europe and includes complete or near-complete data from scores of counties across the United States. Using data I have gathered myself or borrowed from colleagues, I have reconstructed the history of homicide in the colonial and revolutionary periods for New England, New Netherlands, Pennsylvania, Maryland, North Carolina, and eleven counties in Virginia. In the nineteenth century, we have data for five entire states (New Hampshire, Vermont, Louisiana, Florida, and Oregon), seven major cities (New York City, Philadelphia, Cleveland, Chicago, New Orleans, San Francisco, and Los Angeles), and thirty-four rural counties in the Midwest, South, and West. These data have been supplemented by information from the Census Bureau, state health departments, and various law enforcement agencies. Strong patterns have emerged that show correlations between increases in homicide rates and changes in people's feelings about government and society, but the argument here remains a hypothesis. More data will have to be gathered to confirm these correlations, and it is possible that future researchers will amend them or find additional ones.

A full account of my sources and methods appears near the end of this book, but I would like to say a word here about how my homicide estimates were produced. There is only one way to obtain reliable homicide estimates, and that is to review every scrap of paper on criminal matters in every courthouse, every article in every issue of a number of local newspapers, every entry in the death records, and every local history based on lost sources, local tradition, or oral testimony. Although this method is time-consuming, it produces homicide estimates that are far more reliable than those derived from court records alone, which can be too low by a third or more, especially during wars or revolutions. In fact, the data gathered this way are in many instances more accurate than the statistics published in recent years by the Department of Justice and the National Institutes of Health, which suffer from underreporting, coding errors, and a lack of detail on motive and circumstance. Some reporting agencies rule out certain kinds of homicides, such as those committed in self-defense, in the line of duty by law enforcement officers, or during civil disturbances; and some classify deaths caused by criminal negligence as homicides, including automobile-related fatalities. In this book, all deaths resulting from willful assaults are designated as homicides except those occurring in open warfare. They include assaults that were legally justified or not meant to cause death. By including all kinds of homicides, researchers can see which kinds rise and fall together and which don't. Such knowledge is crucial to explaining homicide.

Some homicide estimates are more reliable than others, and for some communities only a minimum count of homicides from a single source survives. But where multiple sources have survived, it is generally possible to arrive at a reliable estimate of the number of homicides that came to the attention of the public, even if those homicides were not recorded at the time or if portions of the original records have been lost. Calculations show that homicides that occurred during wars or revolutions were less likely to appear in surviving records than those that occurred during peacetime, that homicides of African Americans and Native Americans were less likely to appear than those of European Americans, and that homicides were more likely to appear in newspapers after the advent of dailies and penny presses in the 1830s and 1840s. Still, it is possible to measure and to compensate for these differences, using the same matching-list technique that epidemiologists and demographers use to estimate the number of people who have AIDS, for example, or the number of people in a particular census category, such as the homeless.

A common objection to historical homicide estimates is that it is impossible to produce reliable rates for places that have small populations or few homicides. It would certainly be a mistake to make too much of a small community's homicide rate in a particular year: the homicide rate "per 100,000 persons per year" would be high if a single homicide occurred in a given year, while the following year it might drop to zero. But it is possible to produce reliable homicide rates for longer stretches of time, because the cumulative number of people at risk of being murdered for a year becomes large very quickly.[1] The formula for producing such rates is: homicide rate = (number of homicides / population at risk) × 100,000. If study periods are extended far enough, it is even possible to obtain reliable rates for rare kinds of homicide, such as spousal murder, in places where there were very few homicides to begin with, like eighteenth-century New England.

Some historians also object that no one has yet amassed enough statistics on a sufficient number of communities to provide an accurate picture of historical homicide estimates for the United States, particularly in regions like the South or West. That objection is not relevant to the colonial or revolutionary period, because we have data for the majority of the population. But in the nineteenth and early twentieth centuries, before the advent of comprehensive national statistics, there are more gaps in the database. Most states and counties have not been studied yet, and those that have been studied were selected not randomly, but to answer the specific questions of individual researchers. However, the places that have been studied to date have been studied thoroughly. We have reliable estimates or minimum counts of their homicides, and their rates follow robust regional patterns. In the Northeast and the Midwest in the nineteenth century, for instance, all the homicide rates among unrelated adults rose and fell in unison, whether in cities or in the countryside, in areas with many immigrants or few, in poor communities or in wealthy ones. The likelihood that these homicide rates would all go up and down together by chance in every northern jurisdiction studied to date—including places as different as New York City, Williamson County, Illinois (which was settled by migrants from the Upper South), and Holmes County, Ohio (which was heavily Amish and Mennonite)—is virtually nil. The same is true for the Far West and for subregions in the South. That is why it is time to take stock and try to make sense of the patterns in the data.

Of course, there are some things that statistics *cannot* do. It is as difficult to measure people's feelings and beliefs in the past as it is in the present. Historians have created a few good measures, but for the most part we have to gauge the strength of emotions and the popularity of ideas from nonquantitative sources such as diaries, letters, and speeches and from historians' interpretations of those sources. Another limitation of statistics is that too many interrelated changes occur simultaneously in human societies for researchers to measure the impact of a particular variable or to isolate the cause of a specific event. It is impossible for researchers to hold historical circumstances constant while they study the influence of a single factor. Some social scientists claim that they can measure the impact of gun laws or unemployment or the death penalty on homicide rates by controlling statistically for the impact of other variables. Those claims are false.[2]

Explaining homicide requires amassing statistics over long periods and in various social contexts and studying those statistics for robust patterns. Hypotheses derived from such patterns can be evaluated by testing them against new evidence from very similar or dissimilar historical situations to see if they still hold true.[3] For instance, the increase in racial solidarity among white New Englanders after King Philip's War correlated with a decrease in the homicide rate. Would the increase in racial solidarity among whites that accompanied the rise of racial slavery in the Chesapeake correlate with a depressed homicide rate in the same way? Would an area like the Shenandoah Valley, where support for the patriot cause and the new federal government was stronger during the American Revolution than anywhere else in the new nation, see a decrease in its homicide rate while the rate was rising in politically divided communities? Many patterns and the hypotheses devised to explain them have proved less robust than expected. The patterns that appear here and the hypothesis that grew out of them have survived every test so far—a powerful (if nonexperimental) argument on their behalf.

Some readers will want to examine the data on which this study is based. My colleagues and I have founded a collaborative database on the history of violent crime and violent death, sponsored by the Criminal Justice Research Center at Ohio State University. The web address for the Historical Violence Database is http://cjrc.osu.edu/researchprojects/hvd/. The data for *American Homicide* appear there. We have posted our research on the website so that everyone can see complete references for each case, check calculations, remedy errors, test new theories, and find new patterns. We hope that others will contribute their data so that one day we will have a complete picture of homicide in the United States.

I have prepared a statistical supplement to support the quantitative arguments in *American Homicide*. The American Homicide Supplemental Volume (AHSV) is available online through the Historical Violence Database. It contains the calculations for the graphs in *American Homicide* and the tables from which the statistics are drawn.

One final note: murders of children or by children ages fifteen or younger do not follow the same patterns as murders among adults, and the fundamental reasons behind them are not the same. They will be discussed in a separate volume, *Child Murder in America*.

Introduction

On Thanksgiving weekend in 1995, twenty-three-year-old Lamont Galloway was out having a few drinks at the D-2 Nite Club in Columbus, Ohio, when some of his old friends from the Linden neighborhood walked in. Mike Saunders and Willie Meeks, also known as Backdoor and Hundredproof, had come to celebrate their new rap CD with their producer, also an old friend. When they saw Galloway all hell broke loose. Bouncers quickly put a stop to the fight and threw Saunders and Meeks out of the club.

The producer thought everyone would calm down, but Galloway knew better. He called his sister and asked her to bring the family van and park it as close to the door of the club as she could. He also told her to bring his gun. She immediately called her mother. There would be no guns, her mother said, and she would go along to pick up Lamont.

The glass door at the club was opaque, so Galloway and the producer had to poke their heads out every few minutes to look for the van. Unfortunately, when Lamont's sister pulled up to the door, a security guard immediately told her to move. She protested, but he threatened to call the police. As she was backing away, Galloway and the producer peered out and shouted at her to stop. They made a frantic dash for the van, but Saunders and Meeks were waiting behind a parked car, and they leapt out and fired. Galloway fell, mortally wounded, only a few feet from his mother and sister. The producer ran to his own car, but Saunders and Meeks followed him and jumped into the backseat. They told him to drop them off at a nearby gas station. If he said anything to anyone they would kill him.[1]

Galloway's murder affected dozens of people. His mother and sister were traumatized. His five children lost their father, and his girlfriend was left to raise them alone. The producer, fearing for his life, abandoned three successful businesses, including a beauty shop, and fled the state. Seven years later he had to be dragged back to Columbus in handcuffs to testify. Saunders and Meeks, once Galloway's best friends, went to prison, and their families suffered in turn.

Yet no one outside this circle took much notice of Galloway's death. A short paragraph in the *Columbus Dispatch* noted only that he suffered gunshot wounds and was pronounced dead at the hospital. Certainly no one thought to ask why he had been murdered. Most Americans have come to expect young black males to get shot at night in the city. We assume that these murders have to do with poverty, gang culture, and drugs, and we don't concern ourselves with the particulars.

I happened to be on the jury when Willie Meeks and Mike Saunders were tried for murder, so I heard the official explanation of why they killed Lamont Galloway. But that explanation—that Meeks and Saunders felt Galloway had taken more than his share of the proceeds from a recent burglary—doesn't really tell us much. It was only an immediate motive, like all the reasons killers give for murdering people: The guy was messing with my girlfriend. He threatened me. He called me a —— (insert obscenity). She dumped me. She cheated on me. He dissed me. Immediate motives tell us about the trigger that set off the explosion but say very little about what shapes the mindset of murderers, about what ultimately causes men (and for the most part, murderers are now and always have been male) to become killers. Meeks and Saunders could have gone to Galloway and demanded their money. They could have beaten him up. They could have pressured his girlfriend or threatened his sister. They could have stolen his van. But at this time, and in this place, they chose to kill him.

When Americans try to get beyond immediate motives and generalize about why people kill, they commonly attribute murder to a conglomeration of proximate causes: race, ethnicity, poverty, drugs, region, and neighborhood. We blame poor immigrants, blacks, "hot-blooded" Latinos, drunken Irishmen, and Italian mobsters. We put it down to the time or the place: "Forget it, Jake, it's Chinatown." Or it's the Wild West, the inner city, or the South, where, according to one loyal native, there were always "just more folks . . . who needed killing."[2] There may be some truth to some of these generalizations, but they obscure the most important facts about murder, and they don't hold true over time. Most Americans would be surprised to learn, for instance, that black men were once less likely to be killers than white men or that Chinese women were once more likely to be murdered than any other females in the United States. They would be especially surprised to learn that the United States was once one of the least homicidal societies in the Western world, despite its diversity and its history of racial conflict.

Why do homicide rates vary so drastically from one society to another, from one time to another, if murders are so alike in their motives and circumstances? Why, if humans have roughly the same capacity for violence, does murder claim 1 in 10,000 adults in some societies, and 1 in 20 in others? To find out why homicide rates rise and fall over time, we have to try to get beyond generalizations based on proximate causes to discover the ultimate causes of murder. The Centers for Disease Control monitor homicide statistics because homicide rates behave like disease rates. Like cases of the flu, they increase at certain times and in certain places, sometimes very rapidly.[3] To find out what circumstances ultimately foster high homicide rates we first have to go back through history and chart their course, then make the connections between historical circumstances and the human beings who commit murders. It will become evident that homicide rates among adults are not determined by proximate causes such as poverty, drugs, unemployment, alcohol, race, or ethnicity, but by factors that seem on the face of it to be impossibly remote, like the feelings that people have toward their government, the degree to which they identify with members of their own communities, and the opportunities they have to earn respect without resorting to violence. History holds the key to understanding why the United States is so homicidal today.

America's Homicide Problem

No matter where Americans live, their risk of being murdered is higher than it is in any other first-world democracy. From 1965 to 1992 the homicide rate in the United States averaged 9 per 100,000 persons per year. In the mid- to late 1990s the rate declined to 6 per 100,000 per year, but it remains comparatively high and has risen since 2004 (Figure I.1). The next most homicidal affluent democracy, Canada, has had only a quarter of the homicides per capita that the United States has had since World War II (Figure I.2). The others have had from a fifth of the U.S. number per capita (Australia) to less than a tenth (Ireland). The United States still ranks first when populations are compared by gender and ethnicity. Both women and men are far more likely to be murdered in the United States, and Americans of European descent, the least likely victims of homicide in recent decades, were murdered at a rate of 5.5 per 100,000 persons per year from 1965 to 1992.[4] By itself that rate was high enough to make America two and a half to eight times more homicidal than any other affluent democracy.

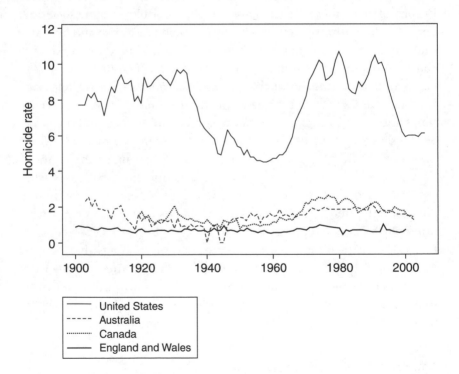

Figure I.1 Homicide rates in affluent democracies, 1900–2006 (per 100,000 persons per year). *Sources:* Eckberg (1995); Archer and Gartner (1984); World Health Organization (1950–).

Americans are exposed to that high annual homicide rate for their entire lives, an expected 78 years for children born today. The likelihood that a newborn American will be murdered if the homicide rate of the recent past persists—as it did for most of the twentieth century—is not 9 in 100,000, but 78 times that. In practical terms, that means 1 of every 142 children born today will be murdered—1 of every 460 white girls, 1 of every 158 white boys, 1 of every 112 nonwhite girls, and 1 of every 27 nonwhite boys.[5] Even if the lower rate of the late 1990s is sustained and the United States has a prolonged period of relative calm, as it did during the middle third of the twentieth century, nearly 1 of every 200 children born today will be murdered.

The risk of being killed is highest in the South, moderately high in the Southwest, and lowest in the North (Figure I.3). It is greatest for the poor, but even wealthy and middle-class northerners run a higher risk of being murdered than do people in other affluent democracies. Their risk is highest when they are in their teens and twenties, living

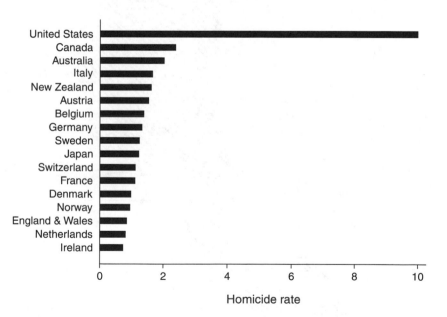

Figure I.2 Homicide rates in affluent democracies, 1950–1990 (per 100,000 persons per year). *Sources:* Gartner (1990: 99); World Health Organization (1950–).

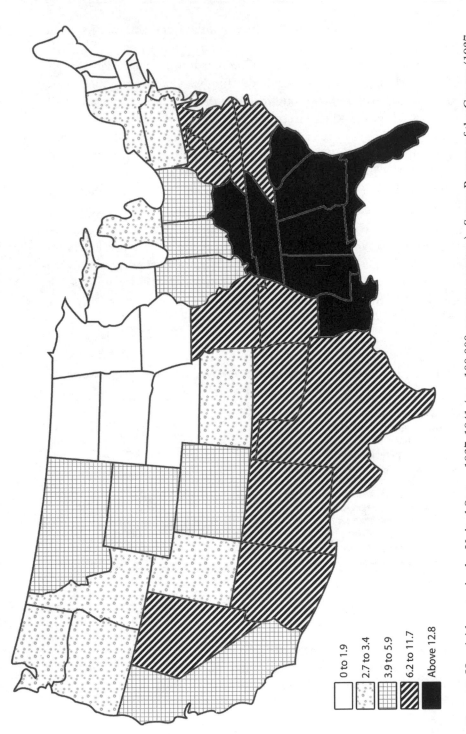

0 to 1.9

2.7 to 3.4

3.9 to 5.9

6.2 to 11.7

Above 12.8

Figure I.3 Homicide rates in the United States, 1937–1941 (per 100,000 persons per year). *Source:* Bureau of the Census (1937–1993).

on their own in apartments, in the military, away at college, or spending a night out on the town.

America's homicide rates are high even by the standards of many less prosperous countries, some with long histories of undemocratic or colonial rule (Figure I.4). Although neonaticide—the murder of newborn children—and the murder of adult women are substantial problems in some of these nations, the total homicide rate has been remarkably low in India, Hungary, Poland, Costa Rica, and Egypt, and was low until the 1970s in Sri Lanka. Of course, there are many countries that have higher homicide rates than the United States, a few four to ten times as high (for example, Brazil, El Salvador, Colombia, and South Africa). And homicide rates soared in the late 1980s in the former republics of the Soviet Union and in Yugoslavia, where there was

Figure I.4 Estimated world homicide rates, late 1900s (per 100,000 persons per year)

Location	Total	Male	Female
Low- and middle-income nations			
Sub-Saharan Africa	22.2	33.4	11.8
The Americas[a]	27.5	51.0	4.8
South Asia[b]	5.8	8.1	3.5
Europe[c]	14.8	23.2	6.8
Eastern Mediterranean[d]	7.2	9.4	4.8
Western Pacific and Southeast Asia[e]	3.8	5.6	1.8
High-income nations			
Canada	1.4	1.9	1.0
Europe	1.0	1.4	0.6
Eastern Mediterranean	4.2	6.0	1.2
Western Pacific and Southeast Asia	1.1	1.3	0.8
United States	6.9	10.7	3.1
The world (high, middle, low income)	8.8	13.6	4.0

Source: World Health Organization (2002: 274–275, 308–313).

a. Includes all nations except Canada and the United States.

b. Includes Thailand and the Democratic People's Republic of Korea.

c. Includes Israel and all Central Asian nations from the former Soviet Union.

d. Includes predominantly Muslim nations from North Africa to Pakistan.

e. Includes the People's Republic of China.

extreme political turmoil. But if future research proves, as it probably will, that China, Bangladesh, and most Arab nations today have moderate homicide rates, then two-thirds of the world's people live in nations that are less homicidal than the United States, and the inhabitants of every other affluent democracy live in nations that rank in the lowest fifth.[6]

The United States' ranking among affluent democracies has persisted throughout the twentieth century despite a decline in its homicide rate from 1934 to 1959 (through the Great Depression, World War II, and the early years of the Cold War) and a rise in homicide in most other industrial democracies since 1965. Homicide rates have followed the same pattern among most affluent democracies during the twentieth century. The differences among those nations emerged earlier.

Hypotheses about American Homicide

Why does America have a homicide problem? Most debates among scholars, policymakers, and commentators have been confined to discussions of recent trends. In the 1960s and 1970s, debate focused on the rise in the homicide rate after 1959, from 5 per 100,000 persons per year to 9 per 100,000; more recently it has focused on the decline in the rate for 1994–2000, from 9 per 100,000 persons per year to 6 per 100,000, and on the uptick since 2004. These debates have produced some important insights, but for the most part, people have stood by their preferred explanations and trimmed the facts to fit them.[7]

One popular strategy has been to look at the latest fluctuation in the homicide rate and try to tie it to a change in society or public policy that happened to coincide with it. Examples include efforts to link the most recent drop in the rate to the relaxation of laws against carrying concealed weapons, which may have deterred assaults by putting more guns in the hands of law-abiding citizens, or to the *Roe v. Wade* decision of 1973, which resulted in a smaller population of juveniles in the 1990s. But such hypotheses cannot explain the ups and downs of homicide rates over long periods or in every era. Concealed weapons were responsible for many homicides in California in the 1850s and in Georgia in the 1890s, for example; and the homicide rate doubled or tripled in the mid-nineteenth-century North even as fertility declined and the abortion rate quintupled. Moreover, both of these hypotheses ignore improvements in wound care and emergency services that have lowered the death rate from penetrating wounds and blunt trauma by about a fifth since 1960. Those improvements, which accelerated rapidly in the 1990s, save about 3,300 assault victims each year and have lowered the homicide rate by more than 1 per 100,000 persons per year.[8]

Similar problems arise with other popular hypotheses about homicide. Urban poverty and unemployment may appear at first glance to be responsible for America's homicide problem, but during the Great Depression of the 1930s, when urban poverty and unemployment were at their worst, homicide rates dropped in most cities, from New York to New Orleans to San Francisco. The crack-cocaine epidemic of the mid-1980s did cost thousands of lives, and had it not ended, the homicide rate would be much higher today. But it is hard to blame America's long-term homicide problem on substance abuse. Drugs and alcohol have been contributing factors in many homicides for centuries throughout the Western world, yet many countries that consume drugs or alcohol at a higher rate than the United States have much lower homicide rates; and in the early nineteenth century, when the United States had the worst substance-abuse problem in its history, and Americans consumed more than twice the alcohol per capita they consume today, the North and the mountain South (which includes the Ozark and Appalachian highlands) had their lowest homicide rates ever.[9]

Deterrence is essential to keeping homicide in check. When law and order break down, as has happened from time to time in parts of the United States and in other nations, homicide rates jump to hundreds and sometimes thousands of people per 100,000 per year. By ending outright lawlessness, effective policing can drive homicide rates down to 10 or 20 per 100,000. But policing and other forms of deterrence can go only so far toward making societies nonhomicidal, and there is not much evidence that America's homicide problem stems from a lack of deterrence. In the 1840s and the 1950s the United States spent more on law enforcement and prisons than almost any other nation on earth, and its systems were models for the world; but when waves of homicides hit in the 1850s and in the 1960s and 1970s, those systems were powerless to stop them. Police and corrections officers were overwhelmed by those waves: many were forced to kill in the line of duty, and many were killed.

Historically, homicide problems have always been more likely to engulf law enforcement officials than to be solved by them. The blunt truth is that homicide is hard to deter even under the best circumstances, and many people who commit murder get away with it, especially if they kill only once, as most do. Forty percent of known homicides in the United States never result in an arrest. Many suspects who are caught are not convicted, so a majority of killers, usually three-fifths or more each year, escape punishment. That pattern has prevailed since colonial times. The primary cause is not poor law enforcement but a lack of evidence: most killers leave little behind. Another problem is that some killers—especially spouse murderers, romance murderers, mass murderers, serial killers, and terrorists—are depressed or suicidal. They may want to kill themselves, or they may want the police or the criminal justice system to do it for them. It is hard to deter people who want to die.[10]

None of this is an argument for ending substance-abuse programs or support for law enforcement. The United States would be a better place if people did not abuse drugs and could always count on their government to protect them. But it would still have a homicide problem, because high homicide rates are caused by other forces. Except for a brief period in the 1950s, America's homicide rate has been stuck between 6 and 9 per 100,000 persons per year for a century. In the late 1990s the United States had full employment, a war on drugs, a million people employed in law enforcement, 1.8 million people incarcerated (11 of every 1,000 adult males), a ban on assault weapons, gun-registration laws, conceal-carry laws, education reform, welfare reform, shelters for battered women, services to protect children from abuse, and the highest rates of church membership and attendance in the Western world. If liberal or conservative hypotheses about homicide were right or if both were right, the annual homicide rate should have been close to 1 per 100,000 persons by the year 2000; but it wasn't, and it has risen since.[11]

Historians have variously attributed the homicide problem to immigrants, the frontier experience, and a patriarchal culture. Each theory seems on the face of it to make sense. Some immigrants did bring violent habits with them, and their homicide rates were initially higher than those for other ethnic and racial groups in America. But circumstances were more important than culture. When the Scots-Irish immigrated to the United States in the eighteenth century, for example, their homicide rate was going down back home in Ulster. They killed at twice that rate in Virginia, and at half that rate in New England. The Irish were four or five times more homicidal in the United States than they were in Ireland in the 1850s and 1860s. Had they continued to kill at the same rate they did in Ireland, they would have been the least murderous of all Americans.[12]

America's frontiers were certainly homicidal, but in most places, such as southern Ohio and the Shenandoah Valley of Virginia, homicide rates fell abruptly at the end of the frontier period.[13] In a few areas, like south Texas, high homicide rates persisted. Why did extreme rates persist in some places and not in others? Why did homicide rates reach frontier levels in certain places only after they had been settled for some time? In Georgia and the Savannah River Valley in South Carolina, for example, rates peaked during the Revolution; in north Texas and southern Missouri they peaked during the Civil War. Were sky-high homicide rates caused by frontier lawlessness or by other forces that emerged there and elsewhere? Understanding frontiers is crucial to understanding America's homicide problem, but they are not the only places where homicide rates have spun out of control in the United States, and frontier violence is not responsible for high homicide rates in most places today.

Changing gender relations have played an important role in America's homicide problem. In the nineteenth century long-term changes in relations between women and men produced an increase in marital and romance homicides that has persisted to this day. But it is hard to explain why marital and romance homicides were so rare in the mid-seventeenth century, when other kinds of homicide were out of control. Nonlethal forms of domestic violence were probably more common in the seventeenth and eighteenth centuries than they are today, and there were fewer formal checks on male power, but men and women in intimate relationships actually killed each other less often. The connections among gender identity, gender relations, and homicide are complex, and higher marital and romance homicide rates cannot be attributed simply to patriarchal culture or other forms of male dominance.[14]

Recently historians have begun to look beyond the bounds of the United States and beyond the past century to explain high homicide rates. But their hypotheses appear increasingly strained as more is learned about the history of homicide in the United States and elsewhere. For example, many European scholars are persuaded that the United States has more homicides because Americans have not made satisfactory progress along the road to civilization. They argue that homicide rates have declined in Europe since medieval times because of the growth of powerful states and criminal courts, which suppressed lawlessness and deterred impulsive behavior, and because of improvements in manners, which encouraged self-control and greater regard for the feelings of others and led to a gradual decline in all forms of interpersonal violence. According to this theory, the civilizing process has encountered reversals from time to time, but the resulting increases in homicides have been always been lower than the increases that preceded them, and the overall trajectory of homicide rates has been downward, even in the United States, where rates remain higher than in other Western nations because of a weaker state, a "premature" democracy, more lenient courts, cruder manners, less regard for others, and a culture that values the defense of personal honor more than self-control.[15]

However, the civilization thesis does not fit the evidence. Once the impact of modern medicine on mortality is taken into account, it becomes clear that homicide rates in Europe were no higher through much of the medieval and early modern period than during the interwar years of the twentieth century or in the United States today. With modern wound care, antisepsis, antibiotics, anesthesia, fluid replacement, trauma surgery, and emergency services, three of every four homicide victims killed before 1850 would probably survive today. Modern people are more successful at saving lives, but they are not less violent. Of course, homicide rates were sometimes much higher in Europe or the United States than they are today, and at times much lower; but those highs and lows cannot be explained by a theory that draws a sharp a line between premodern and modern states and personalities.[16]

Many American scholars believe that an obsession with honor has contributed heavily to violence in the United States, especially among African Americans and southern whites. They contend that high levels of violence are related to "cultures of honor" that codify the ways in which men can earn or lose respect, make them dependent upon the community for their standing, and engender a desperate thirst for popular approval. Cultures of honor, which were the norm in ancient and medieval times, persisted in the clan-based society of the Scottish highlands, the pastoral societies of southern Europe, and the slaveowning societies of the New World, where property and privilege could be defended only by the threat of personal violence. But elsewhere these cultures gave way to "cultures of dignity," in which men were not as likely to respond violently to challenge or insult, because they were taught from birth that they were the equals of others and that they should look only to their God-given consciences for approval. Their sense of their own worth made it easier for them to turn a deaf ear to public criticism.[17]

This theory, however, cannot explain changes in homicide rates within societies that have "cultures of honor," nor can it explain why those societies are not all equally or consistently violent. For example, in the mid-eighteenth century the plantation South did not have a high homicide rate, yet nowhere were men more obsessed with honor. And where honor may have appeared on the surface to be the cause of violence, as it did in many confrontations among Native Americans, in duels among gentlemen, or in bar fights among day laborers, it was actually a proximate cause of violence rather than an ultimate cause—a cultural vehicle for expressing deeper conflicts.

Race and slavery are connected to America's homicide problem, but not in a straightforward way. Before the 1890s, for example, African Americans were far less likely to kill than whites were, and especially unlikely to kill one another. Why, for the past century, has the opposite been the case? Why were Virginia and Maryland no more homicidal than Pennsylvania in the 1720s and 1730s, when they had more slaves and free blacks? Why did slave states become more homicidal after the Revolution, when free states became less homicidal? The answers to these questions hold the key to explaining why America is homicidal today and why some peoples and societies are more homicidal than others.[18]

Every hypothesis about American homicide eventually comes up against the most difficult problem of all: explaining why America was one of the least homicidal societies in the Western world in the mid-eighteenth century and again in the early nineteenth. The mid-Atlantic colonies had a homicide problem in the mid-eighteenth century, and the plantation South developed one after the Revolution, but on the whole, homicide rates in the United States compared favorably then with rates in the rest of the Western world, and homicide rates in the North and the mountain South were probably the lowest in the world after the Revolution. No popular hypothesis about American homicide can explain those low rates or account for the relatively high rates that appeared by the beginning of the twentieth century.

Kinds of Homicide

One of the reasons why homicide is difficult to explain is that not all murders happen for the same reason. Murders involving lovers, spouses, and other adult relatives have followed different patterns from murders involving friends, acquaintances, and strangers. Each relationship has a potential for violence, but those potentials are rarely realized simultaneously. It does happen on occasion. All kinds of homicide soared among Native Americans in southern New England in the mid-eighteenth century and in California in the mid-nineteenth century. Still, historical circumstances are seldom homicidal or nonhomicidal in a straightforward way. They usually encourage some kinds of homicide and discourage others. To understand homicide rates today it is essential to learn why particular relationships become homicidal or nonhomicidal and how the circumstances that tend to generate homicide played out in America before the twentieth century.

The United States has not had a problem with every kind of homicide. Levels of family and intimate violence were not unusually high in America. Homicides of spouses and lovers—which primarily victimize women—are rarely numerous enough to give any society a high homicide rate. Rates of marital and romantic homicides increased in most of the United States in the nineteenth century, but they also increased in England and France. They correlate strongly with changes in family and gender relations that were common in affluent Western societies. Rates of family and intimate homicide were somewhat higher in the United States by the late nineteenth century because of the influence of violence in the society at large on family and intimate relations. The availability of handguns also affected these homicide rates, as did the increasing number of confrontations between romantic rivals and between abusive husbands and intervening neighbors. But marital and romance homicides became a significant problem everywhere in the Western world, so intimate homicides cannot account for the higher homicide rate in the United States.

What elevated America's homicide rate so far beyond the rates of other affluent societies were homicides among unrelated adults—friends, acquaintances, and strangers. But explaining homicides among unrelated adults is much harder than explaining marital and romance homicides. Murder rates among unrelated adults changed abruptly and often. Rates could double or triple in a year or two and fall just as fast. Sometimes they were stable for decades. At times they rose or fell simultaneously in every Western nation, while at other times they changed only in a specific nation or social group. Homicide rates among unrelated adults also had a much wider range than the rates for killing spouses or lovers. They varied from less than 1 per 100,000 adults per year to hundreds and sometimes thousands.

Before the nineteenth century America's homicide rates were remarkably similar to those in Canada and western Europe. Throughout most of the seventeenth century all those areas had high rates. Then rates fell and remained low in most places into the 1760s and 1770s. America's homicide rates diverged from those in Canada and western Europe in the early nineteenth century, but not in a simple way. The rate plummeted in the North and the mountain South but rose in the plantation South and exploded in the Southwest. *The great rift opened in the mid- and late nineteenth century.* By 1900 America had achieved its current status as the most homicidal society in the Western world.

Why did homicide rates among unrelated adults rise and fall so suddenly and steeply? Cultural critics often focus on signature murders peculiar to each era. In the late eighteenth century people blamed dueling. In the 1850s thousands of people, most of them immigrants, died in railroad- and mining-camp brawls. In the 1920s newspapers were full of murders committed by bootleggers and the pioneers of organized crime. In the 1980s even the police would have put the blame on crack dealers. Signature murders certainly contribute to the body count, but there are too few of them to cause large upswings in the homicide rate, and they usually appear after an upswing is already underway. Nor are they truly unique. They are only varieties of the murders that proliferate in every homicidal era: gang murders, vigilante murders, murders over money, status, and territory.

The Causes of Homicide among Unrelated Adults

What ultimately causes the homicide rate among unrelated adults to be high, moderate, or low? Why in some societies is the chance of dying by someone else's hand no more than 1 in 10,000, and in others 1 in 20 or 30? Why at some times and in some places are people quick to come to blows, while at other times and in other places they settle their differences readily, walk away from confrontations, and seek help from friends, family, and institutions when they cannot resolve conflicts by themselves?

The first clue is that historically, only a small minority of murders of unrelated adults have had their origins in long-term, hostile relationships. People who killed nonrelatives within their households—boarders, landlords, slaves, servants, masters, mistresses—had deep-seated, personal reasons for doing so. They may have been driven to distraction by a lazy servant, they may have been feuding with a neighbor in a crowded tenement, or they may have come to hate a greedy landlord. These murders occurred because the relationships between killers and victims became like family relationships. Killer and victim were bound together emotionally, interacted with each other almost daily, and could not easily sever ties. The vast majority of murders committed by women have always been personal.

However, the vast majority of homicides of nonrelatives in both America and western Europe were committed for reasons that were impersonal or abstract. There was no long-term, hostile relationship between murderer and victim. Ninety-five percent of these homicides were committed by men—a proportion that has held steady for four and a half centuries, even though women have become more involved in public life and have taken up more and more jobs outside the home. Why that proportion has held steady is unclear. The rate at which women commit such murders, however, has gone up and down with the rate at which men commit such murders, so it appears that the predisposition to violence or nonviolence outside the household is shaped over time by the same forces for men and women, despite the disparity in their rates.[19]

Homicides among nonrelatives often stemmed from sudden disputes with acquaintances, coworkers, or friends, but they could also be predatory killings that singled out vulnerable strangers and involved rape or robbery. Sometimes these killings targeted people because of their class, race, or politics. Whatever the case, it was not the relationship between the victim and the perpetrator that generated the violence. The killers were already predisposed to violence, willing to prey on others or to view them as enemies or rivals.

The strength and prevalence of that predisposition determines whether men in a given society are homicidal or nonhomicidal, whether they are emotionally prepared to be violent at the slightest provocation or determined to refrain from violence even if they are brutalized or humiliated. Where does that predisposition come from? What causes men to be so alienated that they can kill passersby for money or sex? What causes men to view every encounter with another man as having the potential to be a life-and-death struggle for supremacy or self-preservation? The predisposition to violence is not rooted in objective social conditions. Men who are poor, oppressed, or unemployed can be disposed to violence in one historical situation and to nonviolence in another. The same is true of men who have every advantage. The predisposition to violence is rooted in feelings and beliefs, and the key to explaining it lies in charting the historical fluctuations in unrelated-adult homicide rates and in identifying both the feelings and beliefs that accompanied those fluctuations and the circumstances that fostered changes in them. Criminologist Gary LaFree confirms the fundamental importance of feelings and beliefs when he points out that of all the variables on which social scientists have collected data in the past fifty years, homicide rates among unrelated adults in the United States have correlated perfectly with only two: the proportion of adults who say they trust their government to do the right thing and the proportion who believe that most public officials are honest. When those proportions fell, as they did in the late 1960s and early 1970s, the homicide rate among unrelated adults increased. When those proportions rose, as they did in the 1950s and mid-1990s, the homicide rate fell.[20]

Four similar correlations emerge from an examination of homicide rates in parts of the United States and western Europe throughout the past four centuries:

1. The belief that government is stable and that its legal and judicial institutions are unbiased and will redress wrongs and protect lives and property.
2. A feeling of trust in government and the officials who run it, and a belief in their legitimacy.
3. Patriotism, empathy, and fellow feeling arising from racial, religious, or political solidarity.
4. The belief that the social hierarchy is legitimate, that one's position in society is or can be satisfactory and that one can command the respect of others without resorting to violence.

These feelings and beliefs are closely related—especially the first three; the absence of one usually involves at least a partial absence of another. They also have a synergistic relationship with the homicide rate. When the homicide rate rises, for instance, because of a loss of government legitimacy or a decline in fellow feeling, the rise in homicide itself can undermine the belief that government can protect lives and that citizens care about one another and thereby bring about a further increase in homicide. An increase in homicide can also change the character of a society's social hierarchy and make violence a means of winning respect. Homicide rates can then soar into hundreds per 100,000 adults per year. Alternatively, when nearly all citizens believe that their government is stable and legitimate, when they feel a strong bond with their fellow citizens, and when they believe that their society's social hierarchy is just and violence is not necessary for respect, homicide rates can fall below 2 per 100,000 adults per year. The fact that in most societies these beliefs and emotions have been neither entirely absent nor widely shared explains why most historical homicide rates have fallen between the extremes.

The first correlation, between government stability and homicide rates, is especially evident on contested frontiers and during revolutions, civil wars, and military occupations. If no government can establish uncontested authority and impose law and order, if political elites are deeply divided and there is no continuity of power or orderly succession, men can lose all faith in the effectiveness or impartiality of political, legal, and judicial institutions. They may take up arms on behalf of particular political factions or racial groups and kill without restraint.[21] Some of the homicides committed under these circumstances will be aimed at creating stable regimes by eliminating political rivals. But those homicides are inevitably accompanied by others that may appear to be apolitical but that correlate just as strongly with the lack of political stability. For example, some men become predatory killers, raping, robbing, and murdering as individuals or members of gangs. They may begin killing as political partisans—like Jesse James, for instance—but when they find themselves on the losing side or at odds with an emerging political order, they may begin to prey on former allies and noncombatants, whom they may resent for their weakness, defeatism, or indifference to the cause. They lose their sense of connection with anyone beyond their immediate circle.

Old neighborhood feuds are also likely to turn murderous during periods of political instability. When government breaks down, men kill for what appear to be purely personal reasons, avenging wrongs, settling scores, and simply getting rid of people they don't like. They may be moved to do so by a lack of sanctions (because of weak law enforcement), a fear that their enemies will kill them first, or partisanship (if their personal enemies happen to be on the opposite side in the political struggle). Regardless of motive, these feuds can take on a life of their own and draw in more combatants. Homicide rates can thus reach catastrophic levels during periods of political instability and can remain high for decades. Once learned, homicidal habits are hard to break and can be passed down for generations.

Failures of government stability have had an impact on homicide rates throughout American history, whether they occurred on contested frontiers or during the Revolution, the conquest of the Southwest, the Civil War, or the military occupation of the South after the Civil War. Nearly every American frontier went through a period of lawlessness, but those periods rarely left an enduring legacy, because in most instances governments were able to restore political stability and stop the violence quickly. The political instability of the mid- and late nineteenth century had a more lasting impact on homicide rates because the political hatreds that caused that instability persisted long after the wars and rebellions were over. The aftershocks of that instability are visible on the homicide map today: the areas that stand out are the Southwest, the Border States, and those parts of the former plantation South occupied by federal troops after the Civil War. The violence caused by revolutions, military occupations, and civil wars is harder to end than frontier violence because the contending parties usually remain in place and continue to struggle long after open warfare ends. The political conflicts that arose during the Civil War, Reconstruction, and the conquest of the Southwest continue to this day.

Other Western nations have suffered prolonged periods of political instability. During the late fourteenth century, plague, famine, wars, and revolts by peasants and urban workers crippled local governments and feudal regimes across Europe.[22] In the late sixteenth and the seventeenth centuries England and France were torn apart by religious and civil wars, and it took generations to contain the violence that resulted. But only the United States experienced lawlessness on that scale as recently as the mid- and late nineteenth century.

Government stability and strong legal and judicial institutions cannot by themselves create nonhomicidal societies: they are a prerequisite, but in the absence of other deterrents to homicide, they can only keep homicide rates within moderate bounds, roughly 6 to 15 per 100,000 persons per year. And if political stability—continuity of power, orderly succession, uncontested authority, and rudimentary protection of life and property—is based on force rather than consent, as far as a majority or a large minority of the population is concerned, and if the defense of life and property is viewed as arbitrary or as weighted toward the defense of the ruling majority or minority, homicide rates will get stuck in the middle range, as they were in most of western Europe in the late seventeenth century, in the plantation South in the mid-eighteenth century, and in most of the world's nations in the late twentieth century.

The second correlate of homicide, confidence in government and the officials who run it, plays an important role in determining how men feel about themselves and their society. If men believe that their government shares their values, speaks for them, and acts on their behalf, they feel greater self-respect and gain confidence in their dealings with people outside their families, especially other men. Whether men participate directly in public life, by electing officials and running for office, or indirectly, by deferring to authorities who rule on their behalf, does not matter. What matters is that they feel represented, respected, included, and empowered.

When men doubt the honesty and competence of public officials and question the legitimacy of their government, especially on the national level, they may feel frustrated, alienated, and dishonored. If others share those feelings and act upon them, states can experience power struggles, political instability, and breakdowns in law and order. But such feelings can also lead to an increase in everyday homicides. Feeling dishonored can prompt men to take offense when no slight was intended. Feeling alienated, especially from people who support the government, can lead them to view others as predators or prey. And intense frustration can make men quick-tempered in ordinary disputes. That was the case with Willie Meeks, who conspired to kill Lamont Galloway. Meeks had a strong sense of grievance against the police and the courts. In the months before the murder, the police had been hounding him wherever he went. They suspected him of being involved in criminal activities, so even though he had no record as an adult, they cited him for numerous minor infractions, including jaywalking. Alienated from government (he was twenty-seven at the time of the murder but had never registered to vote) and furious at the authorities, who he thought were out to get young black men, he turned his rage on the friend who betrayed him.

The relationship between the homicide rate among unrelated adults and the legitimacy of government is not as transparent as its relationship with political stability and is rarely visible to contemporaries, who usually associate only politically motivated homicides with weak government or disaffection from the government. But as LaFree has shown, homicide rates rise when men lose faith in public officials and no longer trust their government to do the right thing, and those rates include all kinds of murder, from rape murders to killings in gang fights or barroom brawls.

Every Western government faced challenges to its legitimacy in the nineteenth century, but none of those challenges were as severe or prolonged as those the United States faced. Homicide rates fell in Canada and western Europe as stronger, more responsive, and more popular governments took shape. Homicide rates rose only in the United States, where the federal government faced formidable, disruptive challenges to its authority and failed to establish its legitimacy among a substantial minority of its citizens, especially in the South, the Southwest, and the urban North.

The third correlate of homicide, a sense of patriotism or kinship with countrymen, plays a decisive role in determining whether men will subject other members of their society to violence. Nothing suppresses homicide within a social group more powerfully than a sense of connectedness that extends beyond the bounds of family and neighborhood and forges a strong bond among people who share race, ethnicity, religion, or nationality. If the members of a group identify with other members, even those they do not know personally, the trust, empathy, goodwill, and fellow feeling that result can deter homicide within the group.[23] But solidarity is a double-edged sword: it can deter homicide within a group and at the same time incite homicides among members of different social groups. When men draw the boundary between "us" and "them" in a way that excludes a substantial portion of the population, the potential for homicide is high. Nationalists who question the patriotism of fellow citizens are one group that is likely to turn violent. But men who feel no bond with other members of their society, who are isolated and unable to form close ties with people because of childhood deprivation, are even more likely to become violent. Michael Saunders, who was convicted of murdering Lamont Galloway, had little sense of connection to his family or his neighborhood. Unlike Willie Meeks, he had a lengthy record of arrests for assault, drug trafficking, armed robbery, and domestic violence.

Fellow feeling can grow out of fear or hatred for other groups; traumatic interracial conflicts such as Indian wars or slave rebellions often reduced homicide within racial groups even as they increased violence between them. But patriotism and fellow feeling can also have benign sources, such as pride in a nation's achievements or sorrow at a national tragedy. Such feelings, when shared by a majority of people, can deter homicide at every level of society. Stable and legitimate governments can forge a sense of solidarity among citizens by setting positive goals and fostering national pride in achievements; unstable and illegitimate governments can erode solidarity if they fail to protect life and property or do not govern in a disinterested way. The best predictor of increases and declines in America's homicide rate has been the percentage of new counties named for national heroes—an indirect measure of how Americans felt about their nation and one another. The homicide rate was lowest in the 1820s and 1830s, when the proportion of new counties named for American heroes reached its peak. When the proportion of new counties named for national heroes plummeted, as it did during the sectional crisis, the homicide rate spiked. When Americans stopped identifying with each other through national heroes, they killed each other more often.

When fellow feeling expands to encompass a large portion of the population, it can deter homicide significantly. In most Western nations pride and national loyalty intensified in the nineteenth century. A rebirth of patriotic feeling in Great Britain in the late nineteenth century was accompanied by a falling homicide rate. The same trend emerged when strong central governments were forged in Germany and Italy; life became safer for Germans and Italians, if not for their neighbors or their colonial subjects. But Americans were deeply divided by race, ethnicity, and religion, and homicide rates rose further when those divisions were politicized. There was little to bind Americans together when their sense of political kinship failed.

The fourth correlate of homicide, a legitimate social hierarchy, is a somewhat independent variable. Whereas the other correlates rise and fall in lockstep, it follows its own path. It does not influence homicide as strongly as the three political correlates do, but it can amplify or dampen their effects, especially with regard to nonpolitical homicides. In practice it means that when men feel that their positions in society are satisfactory or that they will be able to earn the respect of others in legitimate ways, they are more likely to turn the other cheek if they are slighted at a social gathering, take it in stride if someone beats them at a game of cards, seek a legal remedy if they are cheated in a business deal, or maintain their composure if they are rejected by a lover or defied by a spouse. Such encounters do not become matters of life or death as long as men's reputations are secure or improving. Unlike the three political correlates, this one has an effect on marital and romance homicides, when it is accompanied by a shift in the balance of power between men and women. When women gain opportunity and men lose it—as happened with Native American women in the mid-eighteenth century, for example, or middle- and working-class white women in the North in the mid-nineteenth century, or black women in the late nineteenth century—an increase in relationship violence is inevitable.

How men secure or improve their reputations depends on the culture of the societies in which they live. In a society that values self-employment, reputations depend on being self-employed or moving toward self-employment in a timely way. In a society based on caste, reputations are contingent on performing the duties required for respect within one's caste and having confidence that others will perform their duties too. As long as ample opportunities for self-employment are available in the first society, and as long as the members of each caste are willing and able to perform their respective duties in the second society, the potential for violence will be low.

However, if men are insecure about their standing (or prospective standing) in society—if they have no hope of winning respect, if they are embittered by a sudden loss of standing, or if the criteria for respect suddenly change or become a matter of dispute—they are more likely to become violent, because every insult, every challenge, and every setback takes on greater significance. Disputes with peers, no matter how trivial they might seem to an outsider, become defining moments in which reputations can be permanently damaged. When men's self-esteem rests on the outcome of such disputes rather than on the normal functioning of a society's social hierarchy, murders of friends, acquaintances, and strangers can proliferate. That was certainly the case for both Michael Saunders and Willie Meeks. In the 1950s their neighborhood was prosperous. Men worked at high-paying factory jobs, over half of all families owned their own homes, and local businesses were thriving. But by 1995 nearly all the manufacturing jobs were gone, and the Linden neighborhood was blighted by high unemployment, empty storefronts, abandoned houses, deteriorating schools, and the toxins the factories left behind. The deindustrialization of Columbus made it impossible for young men like Saunders and Meeks to succeed in the way their parents and grandparents had. They were angry about their lot in life, and it was that anger that made Lamont Galloway's attempt to cheat them intolerable.

Historically, many different kinds of social hierarchies have been capable of deterring or at least containing homicide. Some have been egalitarian and some not. Inequality does not by itself cause high homicide rates, nor do barriers that prevent people from moving to a higher caste or class. As long as citizens accept the justice or inevitability of a hierarchy and believe that they can defend their rights (as they understand them) or resist oppression in nonviolent ways, homicide rates can remain moderate. The degree of inequality and the weight of dishonor that falls upon subordinates by virtue of their caste or class do not matter. Historically, the struggle for position has been contained in many caste- and class-bound societies by the maintenance of relationships between dominants and subordinates that emphasize the duty of the former to protect the latter and the duty of the latter to serve the former.[24] If such hierarchies become unstable, or if they lose legitimacy or have none to begin with, dominant groups may have to keep subordinates in place by force. If dominant groups fail to honor their obligations, if subordinates are unable to protect themselves or their families, or if revolutionary ideas upset the status quo, these hierarchies can become homicidal.

Social hierarchies can be made more or less legitimate by a variety of means: profound economic and cultural changes, emancipation of enslaved people, or relegation of previously free people to subordinate status. These changes usually unfold over a number of years, so their impact on homicide tends to be more gradual than the impact of political events. But when changes in social hierarchies coincide with political events, intensifying or constraining the struggle for position and power, their combined impact can be powerful. Homicide rates reached their lowest point in the northern United States in the decades after the War of 1812, which was a period not only of national unity and patriotism but also of great optimism and achievement. African Americans had seen their rights and freedoms expand in the North since the Revolution, and they were optimistic about the future, despite the persistence of prejudice and discrimination. Territorial expansion had increased self-employment to its highest level in the nation's history. The great majority of adult men were able to win an honored place in the social hierarchy. They had full citizenship, independent households, and ownership of a farm or shop. The struggle for power and position was as muted in northern society as it was in politics, and that conjunction of circumstances held homicidal emotions in check.

The disruption and delegitimation of social hierarchies can encourage homicide. In the plantation South, revolutionary ideas about equality and natural rights undermined the legitimacy of a social hierarchy that was predicated on divisions of caste and class. By the early nineteenth century southerners of both races were refusing to defer to their purported superiors. Slaves were angry because they knew that slavery had been abolished elsewhere in the United States. Free blacks seethed because they would never be treated as equals before the law in the South. Poor and middle-class whites were resentful of slaveowners, who continued to define honor in ways that made it unattainable for anyone but the wealthy. As a result, interracial and intraracial homicides increased as blacks and whites took out their frustrations on each other and defended their honor in violent ways. The social hierarchy also lost legitimacy in the North when self-employment fell from 60 percent of adult males in 1815 to about 33 percent in 1876. As their ambitions were frustrated, northern men became more sensitive about their social standing. The strain on the North's social hierarchy led to deadly quarrels over personal slights and over debts, property damage, and other financial issues. The decline in self-employment also undermined the nation's political stability and became a divisive issue during the debates over immigration and slavery in the western territories. The result was a wave of homicides across the nation. Status hierarchies were in flux throughout the Western world, but nowhere was their legitimacy questioned more than in the United States.

The following chapters chart the course of American homicide from colonial times to the present to show the correlations between changes in American society and increases and decreases in homicide rates among adults. The narrative begins in western Europe in the late sixteenth and early seventeenth centuries, when homicide rates were rising, follows the settlers who brought those rates with them to the North American colonies, and traces the fluctuations in feelings, beliefs, politics, and social structure that eventually combined to make the United States the least homicidal of all Western societies by the early nineteenth century. Various permutations of adult homicide (romance murders, marital murders, and murders of adult relatives) are examined along the way to see how they fit into the pattern created by homicides among unrelated adults. Chapter 7 covers the mid-nineteenth-century watershed, when homicide rates soared, and chapter 8 shows how ethnic, racial, and regional homicide patterns changed dramatically in ways that have persisted now for more than 100 years. The final chapter charts fluctuations in homicide rates in the twentieth and twenty-first centuries, and the conclusion suggests ways of dealing with the terrible legacy our forebears left us.

CHAPTER 1

"Cuttinge One Anothers Throates"

Homicide in Early Modern Europe and America

Throughout most of the seventeenth century, the murder rate among unrelated adults in Europe's North American colonies surpassed the worst rates the United States experienced in the twentieth century. New France, New England, New Netherlands, and the Chesapeake were extremely violent during the early years of European colonization. The violence was not solely a product of the clash between settlers and Native Americans. Non-Puritans killed Puritans; the Dutch killed their fellow Dutch; Englishmen killed Frenchmen; and Frenchmen retaliated. Men died in clashes between rival governments and political factions that fought to control trade and territory. The surviving records indicate that peacetime murder rates for adult colonists— that is, rates that include only killings that took place outside the bounds of warfare—ranged from 100 to 500 or more per year per 100,000 adults, ten to fifty times the rate in the United States today. Peacetime homicide rates for Native Americans were probably higher still, given how frequently they were murdered by Europeans.[1]

As soon as political stability was established on a contested frontier, sometimes by treaty, sometimes by military action, rates for all types of homicide fell. But by today's standards the colonies remained homicidal for decades after the initial years of settlement. Annual rates ranged from 9 per 100,000 adult colonists in New England to 20 to 40 per 100,000 in New France, New Netherlands, and the Chesapeake—

three to five times the rates in those places today. Despite their increased military power and political stability, the new colonial governments were still insecure. They did not have the allegiance of substantial numbers of their own citizens and could do little to foster a sense of solidarity among them. Confronted with riots and rebellions, they relied heavily on force and on prosecutions for sedition, heresy, and treason to keep the peace. The absence of a strong sense of kinship among the colonists, coupled with the adoption of indentured servitude, which reduced thousands of freeborn colonists to the status of near-slaves, bred frustration, contentiousness, and distrust and saddled the colonies with high homicide rates into the 1670s.

Homicide in Europe

The colonies' high homicide rates were in part a consequence of local circumstances. Europeans and Native Americans adapted with mixed success to living with other races and to the hardships of colonial life. But the high homicide rate among unrelated adults was also a legacy of the homicide crisis that engulfed Europe in the late sixteenth and the seventeenth centuries. Homicide rates in England, the homeland of most of North America's colonists, doubled or tripled between the late 1570s and the early 1620s and did not return to level of the 1550s and 1560s until the last decade of the seventeenth century (Figure 1.1).[2] France and the Netherlands, the other nations that sent traders and colonists to North America, were even more homicidal than England in the seventeenth century.

The proximate cause of the surge in adult homicides in England was prolonged economic hardship, which disrupted the social hierarchy and made it impossible for many people to provide for their families or maintain their community standing. Population growth and lagging productivity, especially in agriculture, sent real wages plummeting in the late sixteenth and early seventeenth centuries. The poorest two-fifths of the population saw their real wages fall 30 percent between 1570 and 1620, and wages remained low through the 1670s (Figure 1.1). The decline in wages was compounded by unemployment and by harvest crises brought on by a "little ice age" that lowered global temperatures and shortened growing seasons. Poor harvests and government inaction sent grain prices sky-high in 1573–74, 1586–87, 1590–

91, 1595–1597, and 1600–01. Famine struck, especially in the highlands of northern and western England.[3]

The crisis affected almost everyone. It was commonly said that even a law-abiding citizen had to "pluck his means . . . out of his neighbor's throat." Indictments for theft, burglary, and highway robbery increased as people began to steal to survive. Fear of the poor reached a fever pitch. Vagrancy and homelessness, rooted in unemployment and a chronic malnutrition that left between a tenth and a fifth of the adult population unable to work, were so serious that Parliament passed laws to restrict the rights and movements of paupers. Transients judged to

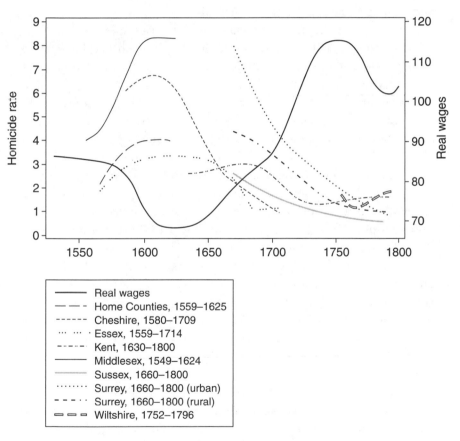

Figure 1.1 Homicide indictment rates and real wages in England, 1549–1800 (per 100,000 adults per year). *Sources:* Roth (2001); Hoffman et al. (2000).

be incorrigible were flogged, branded, or even hanged for the simple crime of vagrancy. In most communities, demographic pressure and economic hardship led to an increase in social stratification and to sharper divisions between the propertied and the poor and between community members and outsiders. Relations among propertied people also became increasingly tense, as evidenced by a real increase in the number of lawsuits involving assaults and property disputes.[4]

Prolonged economic hardship thus diminished fellow feeling in English communities and undermined the legitimacy of England's social hierarchy as people found it increasingly difficult to keep the respect of their neighbors and attain a secure and honorable place in society. The result was a surge in killings among friends, acquaintances, and strangers. The number of homicides that occurred during property disputes, duels, tavern brawls, and robberies increased as relationships among friends and neighbors became more volatile, men became more anxious about their standing in society, and more outsiders became profoundly alienated. The number of homicides that occurred during sexual assaults rose. On the outskirts of London and in southeastern England, a third of victims of nondomestic violence were killed in formal or informal duels. Another 5 percent of homicides occurred in the course of burglaries or highway robberies.[5]

Because relationships among neighbors and between neighbors and outsiders were more prone to violence than they had been in the mid-sixteenth century, there were more murders over debts, boundary disputes, crop damage, poaching, trespassing, and theft. Edmund Riche of Witham, Essex, was killed in 1610 when he and two friends broke into a gentleman's enclosure to kill rabbits. A servant caught Riche and dispatched him with a rapier. At Castle Hedingham, Essex, two young men—one a shoemaker, the other a glover—were stealing peas from Julius Harvie's field when Harvie's servant William Butcher came out to shoo them away. One of the trespassers gave Butcher "a box on the ear," and Butcher struck him on the head with a cudgel and killed him.[6]

The number of murders over slander and insult also increased. Reputation was the lifeblood of the community, the key to good standing and economic success, so there was a lot at stake if word got about that a man was a cheat or a woman was unchaste. Most disputes over insults, especially among people who owned property, were settled in court or in simple fights, which often reached the courts as civil actions for assault and battery. But fights over insults could be lethal. Women, who figured in approximately 6 percent of murder cases beyond the bounds of home and family, used whatever homely implements came to hand. One woman crushed her friend's skull with a wool card; another used a firepan to bludgeon her friend to death; another strangled her neighbor with her bare hands.[7] When men argued over card games or jokes about their wives, they pulled out knives or swords and ran each other through.

Violent confrontations among friends and neighbors increased not only because of a growing obsession with reputation but also because of the newfound popularity of dueling, which appears to have arisen on the Continent and reached England in the late sixteenth century. The dueling code required gentlemen to demand an apology from anyone who had insulted them or damaged their reputations. If an apology was not offered, they were bound to defend their honor in a duel, usually with swords. Initially the code distinguished the violence of men higher on the social scale from the brawls of lesser men; three-fourths of all duels were fought among gentlemen or propertied farmers. But eventually the code was embraced by men from all walks of life. John Lowbery and Hugh Yenans of London, journeymen shoe-makers, were in the kitchen of their master's house one evening when they "quarrelled and abused one another with speech." At dawn the next day they walked to a field outside London, where they fought to a draw, Lowbery with a sword and buckler, Yenans with a pikestaff. Neither would apologize, so they met again that afternoon, and Yenans fatally wounded Lowbery.[8]

Prudence and fashion dictated that men go about armed in late Elizabethan and Jacobean England, so their weapons—daggers, rapiers, swords, and pikes—were ready if anyone gave offense. A third of homicides among unrelated men were committed with these weapons in rural, Puritan Essex, and two-thirds on the outskirts of London. Men often fought on the spur of the moment, in taverns or on the street, and enthusiastic crowds gathered round to watch. Late Elizabethan and Jacobean theater, with its affairs of honor and bloody duels, reflected the stuff of everyday life.[9]

Puritans condemned dueling and encouraged people to resolve their differences peacefully, at law or in church. Homicide rates among Pu-

ritans themselves were extremely low, because they renounced interpersonal violence and walked away from situations that might have led
to murder.[10] They failed, however, to bring about any substantial decrease in the homicide rate outside their spiritual circle, and their hostility toward unrepentant sinners, suspected witches, and Christians
who did not share their commitment to reform created new fissures
in their communities and increased anger and alienation among non-
Puritans. Homicide rates in Puritan-dominated counties rose and
fell with the rates in other counties. Tensions among neighbors and
strangers were too extreme for Puritans to overcome.

The high levels of homicide among unrelated adults correlated not
only with the disruption of the status hierarchy but also with a weak
state that could not command the loyalty and resources of its people.
By and large, Englishmen did not have any special regard for their
fellow citizens or for national values and institutions. Patriotism was
weak by modern standards, although it was probably stronger in England than in most other European nations in the late sixteenth and
early seventeenth centuries. England's lawyers, poets, clerics, and play-
wrights, including Edward Coke, Edmund Spenser, John Foxe, and
William Shakespeare, went to great lengths to persuade their countrymen that they had a common history and shared values and interests
that outweighed class differences. Many Englishmen did believe that
God had chosen them to defend the Protestant faith—an idea reinforced by the miraculous defeat of the Spanish Armada in 1588 and
the last-minute foiling of a Catholic plot to blow up Parliament in
1605. However, England's Protestants were as yet too fractious for their
faith to become a cornerstone of national identity, and patriotic sentiment was not strong enough to bind the English people together. Loyalty to family or to communities of like-minded people far outweighed
national loyalty. As Protestants fell to fighting among themselves and
the cost of England's continental wars escalated, patriotic feeling and
loyalty to the crown and the established church declined. By the 1620s
and 1630s, even patriotic holidays were divisive. Religious dissidents
and critics of royal foreign policy used such holidays to attack the corruption of the Anglican Church and Charles I's rapprochement with
Catholic powers.[11]

The lack of fellow feeling among the English was nowhere more evident than in murders committed by veterans of foreign wars. England
was at war with Spain or France almost continuously from 1585 to

1604. The crown enlisted or conscripted roughly 15 percent of the nation's able-bodied men during that period and trained them in personal combat. Other men fought as mercenaries for foreign governments, especially the Netherlands. Few were motivated by patriotism in the modern sense: their loyalties were to their regiment, their sovereign, or a particular town or region. They had little sense of connection with people who lived in other parts of England and few qualms about brutalizing or stealing from them.[12]

Criminal activity soared whenever these soldiers and sailors deserted or were demobilized in large numbers. Veterans of the force assembled to combat the Spanish Armada and of the wars in Ireland and the Netherlands returned home destitute or disabled and could not find work. They roamed London and the countryside in gangs, robbing, raping, and murdering. Parliament blamed the late-Elizabethan crime waves on the practice of drafting criminals into the service, and it banned the impressment of convicts in 1596, but the post-demobilization crime waves continued. The veterans had been schooled in a brutal and profane military culture that taught contempt for manual labor and sanctioned the bullying of civilians. The hardships they faced when they came out of the service to face the mistrust of an ungrateful nation often made violent criminals of formerly law-abiding men.[13] Veterans of the Elizabethan wars, whether regulars, mercenaries, or privateers, would go on to commit at least a third of the homicides in British North America during the first three decades of settlement.

The impact of demobilization diminished with the accession of James I in 1603. He kept the nation at peace for the next two decades, but political disputes were still directly responsible for many deaths in the late sixteenth and the seventeenth centuries. Aside from casualties related to the English Civil Wars, there were still a substantial number of homicides rooted in bitter disputes over taxation, conscription, religion, or other public matters. Historians have yet to count such homicides, but every history of this period contains stories of lethal confrontations between angry citizens and public officials and among public officials.[14] In all likelihood, the divisiveness of national politics also contributed indirectly to homicides by further undermining patriotism and alienating people from the government, the established church, and one another.

Despite the low level of real wages, homicides and property crimes declined in England in the 1620s and 1630s. Campaigns to help the deserving poor may have played a part in that decline by increasing the legitimacy of the government in the eyes of the disadvantaged. The central government also took steps under the Stuarts to ensure that grain remained affordable to the poor when harvests fell short. Still, homicide indictment rates were much higher than they had been in the mid-sixteenth century and remained relatively high in England through the Civil Wars, the Commonwealth period, and the first years after the Restoration of Charles II in 1660 (Figure 1.1). Actual homicide rates may have been three or four times as high as indictments would indicate in this period, because law enforcement was disrupted during and after the Civil Wars, and politically motivated homicides often went unpunished.[15]

Whether at home or abroad, the English lived in fear of being murdered. Samuel Pepys spent one July night in London in 1664 in "a most mighty sweat" after hearing a noise in his house. "I begun to sweat worse and worse, till I melted almost to water. I rung, and could not in half an houre make either of the wenches hear me, and this mad[e] me fear the more, least they might be gag'd." People who had to travel quailed at the prospect of encountering highwaymen, who prowled the roads to and from London and lay in wait in lonely spots from Sussex to Scotland. Some, like Captain James Hind and Captain Zachary Howard, were royalists who had lost everything in the Civil Wars and turned to robbery to support themselves. Hind robbed every Parliamentarian he encountered; Howard was said to have robbed Cromwell himself. Between them they murdered at least three men. Other highwaymen were less discriminating, robbing and killing anyone who came their way.[16] Tales of their exploits were published in broadsides, written up for the stage, and collected, along with stories about other murderers, in volumes that found their way into nearly every home library in England.

Despite the prevailing atmosphere of fear, England was not the most homicidal nation in Europe in the sixteenth and seventeenth centuries. Research to date shows that rates were far higher in France, where a sharp decline in living standards for the poor put a greater strain on the social hierarchy, and war and civil disruption occurred on a scale unknown in England except during the Civil Wars.[17] France lost a fifth of its population in the late 1580s and 1590s to famine, pestilence, and conflict between Catholics and Protestants. The violence continued in costly wars against Spain and England, in tax revolts, and in feuds among the French nobility that climaxed in the midcentury rebellions known as the Fronde. In Artois, a once-prosperous agricultural province on the frontier between France and the Spanish Netherlands, marauding armies and deserters raped, burned, and pillaged their way through the countryside, and peasants and villagers took revenge on soldiers who fell into their hands. In Haute Auvergne, a pastoral province in the mountains of south-central France, popular revolts and feuds among noble clans reduced the region to near lawlessness, and the weakness of the royal courts and the mounted police (the Maréchaussée) made private justice nearly the only justice.[18]

Records from these regions show that, as in England, most murders in France appeared to have less to do with public affairs than with the defense of property and reputation. But such everyday violence was more prevalent in France than in England because war and civil unrest had made peasants and villagers more hostile to outsiders and the government and more suspicious of their neighbors. National loyalty and patriotic feeling were even weaker than in England, and there was very little empathy or mutual forbearance outside the home. The French crown also did less than its English counterpart to suppress noble feuds and to enlist local elites in the enforcement of the law.

The French were quick to kill anyone they perceived as threatening, whether they were witches, foreigners, soldiers, strangers, religious dissidents, or neighbors who stole cherries or trampled hay while crossing fields. In Artois 92 percent of homicides were rooted in insults to soldiers or foreigners, challenges to honor, jests or pleasantries that "took a bad turn," or property disputes. Tensions ran so high that men carried swords or daggers even on social occasions. Sixty-one percent of homicides were committed with those weapons.[19] Relations among villagers were just as tense in the Haute Auvergne, but because that region was plagued by rebellions, counterrebellions, and criminal gangs, a higher proportion of homicides, rapes, and robberies were committed by soldiers, rebels, or career criminals, and the weapons of choice were pistols and muskets.[20]

The Netherlands did not suffer the same demographic and economic crisis as England or France, at least before the last decades of the seventeenth century. Its economy grew faster than its population because of foreign trade and increased productivity, especially in the dairy, finance, shipping, and textile industries, so the strain on its social hierarchy was less intense. But the Eighty Years' War against Spain (1566–1648) and the social dislocation it created had a disruptive impact on Dutch society. A succession of organized gangs terrorized the countryside from at least the 1650s through the 1730s. Comprised variously of Dutch veterans, foreign soldiers, and gypsies, these criminal bands raided isolated farms in the eastern and southern provinces, beating or murdering people who resisted. Trial records show that in Amsterdam three-fifths of homicides were committed during tavern brawls, street fights, or robberies, and the perpetrators were mostly sailors and laborers with criminal records. Citizens went about well armed, and 80 percent of male victims were killed with swords, knives, or daggers. From 1560 to 1590 the homicide rate in Amsterdam stood at 21 to 24 per 100,000 persons per year. Leiden was equally violent.[21]

It is impossible to know how high homicide rates climbed outside Amsterdam and Leiden during the Dutch Revolt, because nearly all the records from the war years have been lost. But official reports of anti-Catholic and anti-Protestant riots, massacres of civilians by Dutch and Spanish forces, and murders of soldiers by civilians were plentiful before the Twelve Years' Truce (1609–1621). In the 1630s the Reformed Church launched a disciplinary campaign to suppress dueling and fighting, and homicide rates did decline somewhat, but the campaign had little impact on the unchurched or on foreign mercenaries who fought for the Dutch Republic. Homicide rates remained relatively high into the eighteenth century.[22] The French and Dutch colonists who settled in New Netherlands, New England, and New France brought this homicidal behavior with them.

Despite the strength of its legal institutions and a state of peace within its own borders, England experienced a surge in homicides in the late sixteenth and the seventeenth centuries. The increased homicide rate had a profound effect on the Chesapeake and New England as well as New Netherlands, where English settlers intermingled with the Dutch and other colonists from continental Europe. It helps explain why settlers were so concerned about law and order, treason and heresy; why they were wary of soldiers, sailors, and outsiders; and why they were so ready to use violence, individually and collectively. The high homicide rates in Europe also help explain why the homicide rate among unrelated adults was so high in the colonies. Colonial life fostered new kinds of violence and for a time propelled homicide rates far beyond those in Europe, but the roots of America's first homicide problem lay abroad.

Homicide in the Early Years of Colonization

In the earliest years of settlement, European colonists saw far more killing than they ever experienced in Europe. Thousands died fighting with Native Americans and with citizens of rival European powers in conflicts that engulfed the area east of the Mississippi River from the Gulf Coast to Canada in the late sixteenth and the seventeenth centuries. The death rate from warfare was staggering, given the relatively small populations involved. Away from the battlefields, however, the killing continued. Homicide rates among unrelated colonists of the same nationality were initially three or more times those in Europe. Add to those the ordinary homicides that crossed national or tribal boundaries yet occurred outside the bounds of warfare, and the rate was well over 100 per 100,000 adults per year for New England colonists through the Pequot War of 1636–37. The rate in Virginia was more than twice as high, and Maryland's rate was double Virginia's (Figures 1.2 and 1.3).[23]

The ultimate causes of high homicide rates on the frontier were political instability and the absence of unity among settlers. The settlers did not have strong central governments that could protect them from criminals, hostile Indians, or foreigners, especially if they lived away from centers of population. And from the very beginning they were divided. For example, half the people who stepped off the *Mayflower* did not share the Separatists' faith, and many of them were a constant source of disruption. At Jamestown, the gentlemen who refused to perform menial tasks clashed with the men who were feeding and housing them. Everyone was tense and fearful; no one was certain who should lead, what kind of government they should establish, or what strategy they should follow in dealing with the Indians. Dissenters were ordered to submit to humiliating punishments or, in Jamestown, were executed for mutiny.[24]

As time went on, the population became more diverse and the divisions deeper. The English clashed with each other and with the

French, the Dutch, and the Native Americans. Leaders caught up in the struggle for trade and territory used homicide as a tool of public policy: for them, force was a means of achieving political ends, even in times of peace. They recognized that the right to rule depended on military superiority, not on treaty rights or the legitimacy of other colonists' claims. The struggle for trade and territory was also indirectly responsible for many homicides because of its corrosive impact on public morality and social institutions. Whites and Indians, singly or in groups, imitated the behavior of tribes and nations: they took goods, seized land, killed anyone—native or colonist—who stood in their way, and felt justified in doing so. Colonial authorities reported numerous robbery murders, vigilante murders, and revenge murders, which flourished where neither natives nor colonists could gain the upper hand and establish political control. Together such homicides accounted for a third of the known murders of English colonists in the early years of colonization (the other two-thirds were political murders or other kinds of murders among people who knew one another).[25]

Political conflict also weakened institutions that might have re-

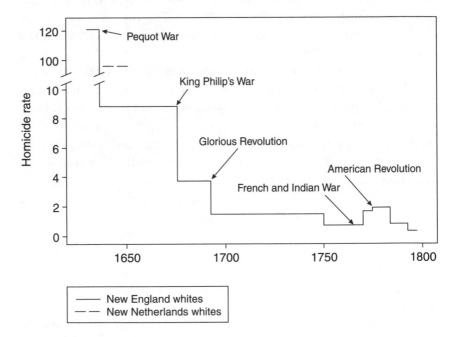

Figure 1.2 Unrelated-adult homicide rates in New England and New Netherlands, 1630–1797 (per 100,000 adults per year).

strained violence. The lack of a common legal or law-enforcement system and the refusal in most instances of rival tribes and nations to accept the legitimacy of one another's systems meant that criminals were
almost certain to get away with murder and that the friends and relatives of murder victims had little hope of obtaining justice. The lack of
security on the frontier also discouraged the migration of families
from Europe, so European colonies during the frontier period had
large contingents of young, unmarried men, who make up the most
homicidal group in the majority of human populations.[26] Many of
them, like John Smith and Myles Standish, were soldiers or sailors and
veterans of foreign wars whose fighting skills were coveted by colony
leaders. Their combat experience and readiness to fight made them a
threat not only to their enemies but also to their friends and neighbors, especially their fellow soldiers and sailors.

Homicides caused directly by political conflict were responsible for
another third of the murders of colonists that occurred on the early

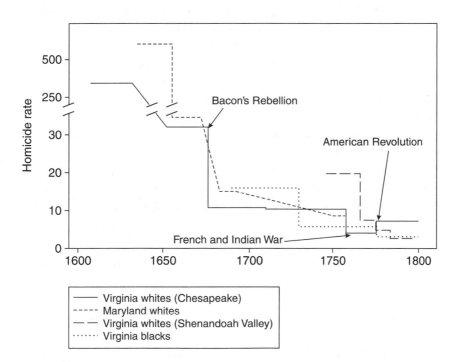

Figure 1.3 Unrelated-adult homicide rates in Virginia and Maryland, 1607–
1800 (per 100,000 adults per year).

seventeenth-century frontier. The English in Virginia, for instance, alarmed by French efforts to colonize Maine, sent two armed vessels north in the summer of 1613 to assert the Virginia Company's rights. The thirty-odd colonists at the new French mission opposite Mount Desert Island refused to surrender when the Virginian vessels appeared. Samuel Argall, the commander of the expedition, ordered his men to fire, even though England and France were not at war. Three Frenchmen were killed, including a Jesuit priest. The survivors surrendered, and Argall destroyed the settlement.[27]

The French, in turn, killed English interlopers. In 1633 Charles La Tour, the governor of Acadia, sent warships to close English trading posts at Machias and Castine. At Castine, La Tour's forces confiscated furs and trade goods, burned the traders' wigwam, and sent the traders packing. At Machias the English traders refused to surrender. La Tour's men killed two of them and took the survivors prisoner. When Thomas Allerton, the owner of the post at Machias, heard what had happened, he sailed to Port Royal. La Tour returned his men to him but refused to return his goods, claiming that they belonged to the king of France, who had title to the territory from Acadia to Cape Cod. He warned Allerton that he would destroy any English settlement north of Pemaquid (near Monhegan Island). When Allerton asked to see La Tour's commission, La Tour replied "that his sworde was Comission sufficient where he had strengthe to overcome: where that wanted he would shewe his Comissions."[28]

English leaders shared that attitude. If they wanted something, they took it by force. When starvation threatened the colony at Jamestown, the English imposed an annual levy of corn on neighboring Indians. In 1617 the Chickahominies refused to give up their corn, and Deputy Governor George Yearley marched against them with 100 men. Twelve Chickahominies were killed and another twelve were kept hostage until the levy was paid. In 1635 the government of Maryland sent ships to attack Virginians who had established a trading post on the Isle of Kent in the Chesapeake Bay. Four people died in the attack. When people on the Isle of Kent again tried to assert their independence in 1638, Maryland crushed the rebellion with an armed force of 50 men and hanged three rebel leaders without benefit of a trial.[29]

The same attitude prevailed in the North. In 1649 the Dutch seized a New England vessel trading in their territory near Manhattan and killed its captain. The owners of the fishing station on the Piscataqua River in present-day New Hampshire were continually at odds with Plymouth Colony over trading and fishing rights on the Kennebec River in Maine. In 1634 the Piscataqua station agent, John Hocking, sailed past Plymouth's trading post on his way to open trade with the Indians. The Plymouth men pursued him; and when they found his ship at anchor a few miles upstream, they began to cut his anchor cables. Hocking shot one of them dead, and a Plymouth man then fired on Hocking, "who fell down dead and never spake a word." Plymouth and Piscataqua appealed to authorities in England and Massachusetts Bay for rulings on their claims, but none was forthcoming. John Winthrop, the governor of Massachusetts Bay, deplored the incident. He told the governor of Plymouth that he "did disavowe the said Action, which . . . had brought us all, & the Gospell under a Common reproache of cuttinge one anothers throates for Beaver."[30]

A substantial minority of peacetime killings of colonists during the early years of settlement were committed by Native Americans trying to defend trade and territory. Native Americans also killed other Native Americans to defend their territory. However, the colonists murdered Native Americans primarily to impress upon them that white men were in charge. In 1633, for example, when the Dutch opened their first permanent trading post on the Connecticut River at present-day Hartford, they forced the Pequots, from whom they had purchased the land, to grant other tribes the right to trade freely at the post, even though it lay firmly within Pequot territory. The Pequots were unhappy. To discourage intrusions onto their land, they murdered a party of unknown Indians who were on their way to trade at the Dutch post. The Dutch retaliated by seizing the Pequots' sachem, Tatobem, and demanding a bushel of wampum for his return. The Pequots paid the ransom, but the Dutch killed Tatobem anyway and handed the Pequots his body.[31]

Native American leaders often used homicide to draw a line between acceptable and unacceptable behavior by their neighbors. Their aim was not to start wars, but to defend rights. Squidragset, an Abenaki sachem, asked Massachusetts Bay officials to discipline Walter Bagnall and John Bray, who ran a trading post on Richmond Island in Maine and were cheating the Indians. The English ignored his request, so Squidragset and his men killed the traders, burned the trading house over them, and "carried awaye their gunnes & what els they liked." Although Governor Winthrop considered Bagnall "a wicked fellowe" who "had muche wronged the Indians," the English authorities hunted down Squidragset's men and lynched one of his leading warriors. They could not tolerate the murder of Englishmen, no matter how justified.[32]

Both Native American and European leaders were willing to use homicide to intimidate allies, deter undesirable behavior, and preempt attacks by potential adversaries. Although the Powhatans had initially formed an alliance with the settlers at Jamestown and helped feed them, they were irritated by the colonists' incessant demands during the "starving time" of 1609–10 and tried to send them a message by killing every settler who left the colony to beg or steal food. One party was found "slain, with their mouths stopped full of bread, being done, as it seems, in contempt and scorn, that others might expect the like when they should come to seek for bread and relief amongst them."[33]

Plymouth Colony also used homicide to send messages to its neighbors. In the winter of 1623 the colonists were afraid that the Massachusetts were about to "cut off" the survivors of Thomas Weston's failing colony at Wessaugusett (in present-day Weymouth, Massachusetts) and that they would "do the like" to Plymouth, "thinking the people here would revenge their death." Weston's men, who had arrived in the spring of 1622 with too few supplies, were starving, and they had angered the Massachusetts by stealing corn and kidnapping the child of a sachem for training in England. Since Weston's beleaguered men were damaging the aura of European invincibility and giving the Massachusetts just cause for war, Plymouth decided to act, especially after hearing rumors that the Massachusetts were preparing to attack. The colonists sent an armed party north under Captain Myles Standish, who had fought as a mercenary in the Dutch Wars and was well schooled in the techniques of terror and intimidation. Standish invited Massachusetts leaders to a feast at Wessaugusett, where he and his men stabbed six of them to death and hanged another. Only one escaped. Standish cut off the head of the most prominent man and stuck it on a post on top of the blockhouse at Plymouth as a "warning and terror" to the Massachusetts. They got the point. Thereafter they called the English "Wotoquansawge, which in their language signifieth stabbers or Cutthroats."[34]

Like colonial and tribal leaders, private individuals did not shrink from killing people to defend their interests or get what they wanted. They adopted the same defensive, hostile, or predatory postures toward acquaintances and strangers that governments showed toward each other. Europeans and Native Americans alike committed robbery murders, singly and in groups. Pecksuot, a Massachusett, told a tale about a French ship that came into Massachusetts Bay before 1620 with "much goods to Trucke." He persuaded his friends to take "all for nothing." They paddled out to the ship with beaver skins to trade, each man concealing a knife in his loincloth. They sold their goods "very Cheap," and when the French lowered their guard, they killed everyone except Finch, the master of the ship, who leaped into the hold wounded. "We bidd him com up, but he would not. Then we cutt thayr Cable & the ship went Ashore & lay upon her sid & slept ther. Finch Came up & we killed him. Then our Sachem devided thayr goods & fiered theyr Ship." In 1638 Arthur Peach, who was fleeing prosecution in Massachusetts for having fathered an illegitimate child by a servant woman, murdered Penowanyanquis, a Narragansett whom he met on his way to New Netherlands. When his accomplices, three runaway servants, balked at his plan to kill and rob Penowanyanquis, Peach, a veteran of the Pequot War, was incredulous. What did the life of an Indian matter? He "had killed many of them." Peach murdered the man and took cloth and five fathoms of wampum from him to finance his journey.[35]

People who had lost family, friends, or property to robbers or murderers sometimes turned to robbery and murder to gain satisfaction, since there was no other means of redress on the frontier. When Richard Killingbeck, a Virginia militia captain, led a small party of men to trade with the Chickahominies in 1617, the Chickahominies killed and robbed them, in part to avenge the killing of the twelve tribesmen by the militia earlier that year during the corn levy and in part because of "the greate quantity of trucke" that Killingbeck was carrying. They then stole some sacred objects from their own village and fled. Similarly mixed motives prompted a Wiechquaeskeck to kill and rob Claes Smit, a Dutch wheelwright who lived near the East River in New Netherlands. The man went to Smit's house to trade for cloth, but when Smit stooped over a trunk to unlock it, the man grabbed an ax and hit Smit in the neck, killing him instantly. The Wiechquaeskeck believed himself entitled to Smit's life because as a young boy he had seen his uncle murdered at Fort Amsterdam by three white men who wanted his beaver pelts. The boy promised himself that one day he would repay the Dutch for the murder, and when the opportunity presented itself, he did.[36]

Even simple thefts spurred homicides. Victims struck at targets of convenience and left more vengeful victims in their wake. Dixy Bull, an English trader on the Penobscot River in Maine, turned pirate after the French stole all his goods in a raid in 1632. He raided not only the French but also the English, because they had failed to avenge his losses. His raids wounded dozens of people and cost the life of at least one of his men, shot dead in a raid on the French post at Pemaquid.[37]

Law and order was compromised on the frontier not only by political conflict but also by the profusion of jurisdictions. Sometimes those jurisdictions harbored killers, but even when rival jurisdictions worked together, it was difficult to agree on an appropriate response to homicides. Most Native peoples believed that they could make amends for homicides with goods or with the blood of the perpetrator's kin or countrymen, if the original perpetrator could not be found. Europeans, on the other hand, believed that perpetrators should be held personally accountable for their crimes and that willful murderers deserved death. In 1634 the Wiscomesses acknowledged that they had killed two Englishmen and five Susquehannas on the Isle of Kent on Maryland's Eastern Shore. A Susquehanna had made fun of a Wiscomesse at a peace parley, and the Englishmen and the Susquehannas had laughed. The victims had been killed to avenge an insult, but ultimately the murder was political: the Wiscomesses were anxious about losing the struggle for control of the upper Chesapeake and had to make it clear to their Native and European neighbors that they were not to be taken lightly. The Wiscomesses tried to compensate Maryland and Virginia, both of which claimed the Isle of Kent, but their offer of *roanoke*, the beads used as currency in the fur trade, was rejected. The English demanded the murderers. The Wiscomesses declined to give them up. The conflict led to years of killings and intermittent warfare.[38]

The clash between Native and European cultures was exacerbated by the presence of so many aggressive young men who were accustomed to violence and knew no other way to command respect. Those of the colonists who had seen service in European wars were likely to reach for a weapon whenever they were challenged or insulted. Edward Stallings, master of a ship that had run aground near Newport News, Virginia, argued with William Epps, the commander of the militia company of Smythes Hundred. Stallings' "uncivill and unmanly wordes" so enraged Epps that he struck Stallings on the head and killed him. George Harrison, a planter at Martin's Hundred, quarreled with Richard Stephens, a Jamestown merchant and fellow militia officer, over a shipment of goods. They agreed to a duel, and Harrison died of his wounds.[39] Such homicides were responsible for a third of the murders that occurred during the early years of colonization.

The violence-prone nature of men who had been schooled in the military made discipline difficult to maintain both in the regular army and in the militia. Officers sometimes had to kill their men to maintain order, and militiamen, who were more fractious than ordinary soldiers, sometimes killed officers who they felt had mistreated them. In 1646 Thomas Cromwell, captain of an English man-of-war that had captured "sundry prizes" from the Spanish in the Caribbean, killed a sailor in Plymouth when the man "reviled his captain with base language" and came at him with a rapier still in its scabbard. In November 1643, at the height of Kieft's War, a Dutch militiaman killed an officer, Captain Daniel Patrick, for refusing to lead a militia company against the Indians in the dead of winter. The man accused Patrick of "treachery," and Patrick spat in his face. As Patrick turned to leave, the man shot him in the back of the head with a pistol. That same year, Maryn Adriaensen, a Dutch militia officer and former privateer who had led several campaigns against the Indians, attempted to kill the colonial governor, William Kieft, in his office at Fort Amsterdam. He felt Kieft was trying to blame him for the war against the Indians, which was causing an increasing number of casualties among the Dutch in New Netherlands. He held a pistol to Kieft's head, saying, "What devilish lies art thou reporting of me?" Kieft was saved when another man grabbed Adriaensen's pistol and let the hammer snap on his thumb. One of Adriaensen's men then fired at Kieft and was in turn shot dead.[40]

Women were not involved in any known homicides outside their families or households in the early seventeenth century, but they were not always a civilizing influence on the frontier. Some of them were as bloodthirsty as the men. One woman jumped for joy when militiamen returned to Fort Amsterdam with a number of severed Indian heads. She began to celebrate by kicking the heads around the compound. A number of other women "upbraided" her, asking her to remember that the Indians would retaliate a thousandfold if they learned that their dead had been treated with such disrespect.[41]

The pattern of homicides that appeared in the early years of colonization—government-sponsored homicides, robbery murders, revenge murders, terrorist murders, and murders among soldiers—reappeared on subsequent frontiers in the eighteenth and nineteenth centuries. From vigilante killings of horse thieves and murders of Indian allies in the Shenandoah Valley of Virginia in the 1750s and early 1760s, to robbery murders of travelers in the Georgia backcountry in the 1790s, to deadly fights among soldiers in the Scioto Valley of Ohio during the War of 1812, the motives and circumstances of frontier homicides were the same. Wherever conflict among rival powers made it impossible to achieve political stability and to agree upon a system of arbitrating legal disputes, private and government-sponsored homicides among unrelated adults were commonplace. What is remarkable, however, is that this frontier violence left no lasting legacy. Once political stability was achieved on a frontier, the homicide rate for colonists fell abruptly, from a third to a tenth of its previous level. The rate on the seventeenth-century frontier, which had stood at 100–500 per 100,000 adults per year, fell in Virginia and Maryland to 30–40 per 100,000 after the Indian treaties of the 1640s and 1650s. In New England at the end of the Pequot War it fell to 9 per 100,000 (Figures 1.2 and 1.3).

Homicide rates dropped regardless of the means by which political stability was achieved. In southeastern New England, stability was achieved because of population loss. The Pawtuckets, the Massachusetts, and the Pokanokets had been militant in defending themselves against the kidnappings, slave raids, and thefts perpetrated by early French and English explorers. At least four dozen Natives and Europeans were killed in the southeastern Indians' encounters with the French and the English between 1605 and 1620. The Indians' ability to defend themselves collapsed, however, in the wake of the great epidemic of 1616–17. Unable to fend off their traditional enemies, the survivors turned to English settlers for protection, especially those at Plymouth. The homicides perpetrated by Plymouth at Wessaugusett brought a measured response from the Massachusetts: they killed three of Weston's colonists who were living with the Massachusetts at Neponset and made a demonstration against Plymouth. But they did not want war and soon renewed their alliance with the English.[42] The English did not really have the upper hand in southeastern New England until thousands of settlers had established themselves at Massachusetts Bay, and Native peoples remained wary of one another. But there were no more frontier-style homicides in southeastern New England after 1623. Once the Natives were not numerous enough to defend themselves, Natives and Europeans stopped killing each other.

In northern New England, stability was achieved by détente. In the early 1630s the efforts of French and English companies to establish permanent trading posts on the Maine coast and the encroachment of English farmers onto Abenaki land in southern Maine resulted in a spate of robbery homicides, revenge homicides, and government-sponsored homicides. But these killings ended abruptly in 1636, when officials at Massachusetts Bay put an end to fighting among rival English companies and agreed with the French to partition Maine. A formal treaty was signed, and years of profitable trade among the French, English, and Abenakis ensued. Many Abenakis moved north, where they were protected by the French and faced no encroachment from European farmers. Once again, political stability led to a decline in both private and government-sponsored homicide.[43]

Stability was more commonly achieved, however, by force. The Pequots were nearly annihilated in the Pequot War of 1636–37, and their Dutch allies were forced to leave the Connecticut River Valley. The English and their allies, the Narragansetts and Mohegans, controlled southern New England, and years of murders over trade rivalries came to an end. In Virginia stability came a decade later. The Powhatans and the settlers had been at peace since 1614, but in 1622 the Powhatans massacred some 400 settlers. After a second massacre in 1644, the colonists counterattacked. They crushed the Powhatans and imposed a harsh treaty on the survivors in 1646. Members of the confederacy were forbidden to set foot on the land between the James and

York Rivers on penalty of death, unless they were official emissaries. The extirpation of the Indians and the creation of a uniform system of law enforcement brought frontier violence and extreme homicide rates to an end.[44]

Homicide rates did not fall as quickly or drastically where political stability remained elusive. Colonists in Maryland found that their Native adversaries were too powerful and they themselves were too few (there were only about 1,000 men, women, and children in 1650) to control the upper Chesapeake. The failure of the colonists to unite in support of Maryland's Catholic proprietary government compounded the difficulty of establishing control. Treaties with Maryland's most powerful Native neighbors in 1651 and 1652 diminished frontier violence but did not eliminate it. In New Netherlands, settlers joined each other sporadically to battle Native Americans for control of the lower Hudson River Valley until the mid-1670s, but the Dutch, the English, and the French were too divided to establish control over the region, and distrust and hatred among groups with disparate religious and national backgrounds made them more likely to prey upon one another. The Dutch found the intrigues of English settlers particularly galling. The English harbored "fugitives and robbers," negotiated treaties with Indians at the expense of the Dutch, and plotted to overthrow the Dutch government. Lawlessness was exacerbated by three Anglo-Dutch wars between 1652 and 1674 and by warfare between the Dutch and the Esopus and Wappinger Indians, who resisted the encroachment of Dutch settlers onto their land.[45]

Of course, homicides between Native Americans and settlers did not disappear altogether in Virginia or New England. The proportion of European homicide victims who were killed by Native Americans fell from three-fourths to one-third in New England after the Pequot War. Most of these postfrontier homicides were rooted in drunken quarrels or property disputes. But through the early 1670s, in areas where settlers had established control, bitter feelings remained and sometimes exploded into terrible violence. In 1644, a year after Dutch and English settlers massacred hundreds of Natives near Stamford, Connecticut, a man named Busshege walked into a farmhouse on the edge of town and smashed a woman's head with a lathing hammer as she stooped to pick up her baby. In 1657 Mesapano attacked a farm in Farmington, Connecticut. He killed a pregnant woman and her maid, beat a small child and left it for dead, and set fire to the house and barn. In 1673 Punneau forced his way into the home of an elderly woman, Lettice Bulgar, and raped her and beat her to death.[46]

Colonists who murdered Indians in the postfrontier period were generally driven by hatred or a desire to get rid of Indians they considered a nuisance. Murders that occurred in the 1650s in Lancaster County, Virginia, for instance, appear to have been part of a loosely coordinated effort to expel the Native population. The treaty of 1646 had promised the tribes of the Powhatan confederacy that no one would encroach on their lands north of the York River and that they could seek redress in Virginia courts for crimes committed against them by settlers; but those promises did not protect the Rappahannocks, who lived between the Rappahannock and Potomac Rivers on land suited to the production of high-grade sweet tobacco. Planters in Lancaster County squatted on Rappahannock land and shot any Indian who "trespassed." The Rappahannocks responded by breaking fences and killing livestock. The planters then persuaded the Virginia legislature to authorize the militia to demand reparations from the Rappahannocks. They met with Taweeren, the Rappahannock *weroance,* or principal chief, and told him he would be tried for damages in county court if he failed to make restitution. The meeting ended in a fight, and Taweeren was killed. Soon afterward a Rappahannock was shot dead for carrying a gun that settlers had lent him. Although the two men who had given the victim the gun were prosecuted, no charges were brought against the killer.[47] When governments abdicated their responsibility to keep the peace, homicide became the means through which settlers and Indians waged an undeclared war against each other.

Homicide among European Colonists in the Mid-Seventeenth Century

The end of outright warfare between colonists and Native Americans and among colonists of different nationalities brought about a decline in homicide rates but did not push them below those of Europe. The decline in murders by Indians and by violence-prone soldiers and sailors did not make the colonies nonhomicidal, because the attitudes and behaviors that settlers had brought with them from Europe persisted. Friends, acquaintances, and strangers continued to murder one another at a high rate by today's standards into the 1670s—6 per 100,000 adult colonists per year in New England, 21 per 100,000 in New Netherlands, 29 per 100,000 in Maryland, and 37 per 100,000 in Virginia.[48] The rate remained high despite better local law enforcement, the creation of county courts, liberal application of the death penalty, and improvement in the economic circumstances of many settlers between the mid-1640s and the 1670s.

As in Europe, politics were contentious, and relationships among friends and neighbors were volatile. The colonists had little sense of a shared religious or national identity, and many outsiders were profoundly alienated from oppressive, unrepresentative, or incompetent colonial governments and the imperial governments that sponsored them. Most disaffected were indentured servants, whose social status was lower than that of any freeborn, law-abiding person in western Europe; but people who did not share the dominant religion or nationality in each colony were also at odds with the controlling governments. Relations between Puritans and non-Puritans in Plymouth, Massachusetts Bay, New Hampshire, Rhode Island, and Maine remained troubled. Ethnic and religious friction was pervasive among the English and the Dutch in New Netherlands, and there was intense conflict between Catholics and Protestants and between masters and indentured servants in the Chesapeake.

The Puritans' case shows how a tightly knit community could actually foster violence. The homicide rate among unrelated adults was lower within the Puritans' closely circumscribed social circle, just as it was in Europe. The persecution they had experienced in England helped them to forge strong bonds among themselves, so that there was less violence within their communities than elsewhere. But in New England the Puritans became the persecutors. They spent much of their time hounding people who seemed to threaten their theocratic experiment: dissenters, sinners, witches, and the wandering poor. They broke up settlements of dissidents, banished heretics, hanged suspected witches, and created so much hostility among non-Puritans that forging bonds across society as a whole was impossible.[49] As a result the society around them became more violent. New England did have a lower homicide rate than New Netherlands or the Chesapeake, thanks to the low rate of violence among Puritans; but the sense of community was not strong enough anywhere in the colonies to push the ordinary murder rate—that is, the rate stemming from murders committed in brawls, property disputes, robberies, or rapes—below the rates that prevailed in seventeenth-century Europe.

Like their contemporaries in Europe, the colonists were profoundly distrustful of government and were likely to take up arms if they felt that their governments were not responsive to their needs. Colonial governments had not yet achieved the legitimacy that would enable them to undertake divisive or unpopular actions without jeopardizing their hold on power, and if they failed to protect the people they were seen as having forfeited their right to rule. In Virginia, for instance, Governor William Berkeley's refusal to wage total war against Native Americans in the Chesapeake was the impetus for a rebellion against him that claimed at least twenty lives. A quarrel in 1675 in Stafford County, Virginia, over a debt owed by a local planter to Indians who lived across the Potomac River in Maryland led to raids and reprisals that soon involved the militias of both colonies and several neighboring tribes, particularly the Susquehannas, who responded to the unprovoked murder of fourteen of their men by the Virginia militia with devastating raids on the Virginia backcountry. At least sixty settlers were killed in the fall of 1675, including the overseer of Nathaniel Bacon's plantation in Henrico County.[50]

Governor Berkeley called for a defensive strategy. He asked for frontier garrisons and patrols to protect settlers and to respond to incursions, and he pressed for a diplomatic alliance with tribes who had lived peacefully under Virginia's jurisdiction since the treaty of 1646, in hopes they would join the fight against the Susquehannas. Bacon wanted to wage war against all Indians, even those who were at peace with Virginia. He and his supporters believed that sooner or later all the tribes would join forces against the colonists. When Berkeley refused to sanction Bacon's effort to raise an armed force to attack the Indians, Bacon and his supporters tried to overthrow the government. At least two of Berkeley's men were killed when they tried to break Bacon's siege of Jamestown with a frontal assault, and at least eighteen men were killed when the governor's forces finally crushed the rebellion in the winter of 1676–77.[51]

The colonial rebellions that occurred during the turmoil of England's Civil Wars were an extreme expression of the rejection of government legitimacy that correlates with high homicide rates. In Maryland, where resentment of the government had produced spectacularly high homicide rates, and where political homicides outnumbered all other kinds of homicides, colonists opposed to the Catholic proprietorship of Lord Baltimore overthrew the government in 1655. Connecticut faced its own revolutionary challenge in 1654 from Thomas Baxter, who had been commissioned by Parliament to fight against "ye Duch and enemies of the Commonwealth of England." England and the Netherlands had been at war since 1652, but New England authorities wanted no part of the war, at least until they could assemble an army large enough to invade New Netherlands. Baxter infuriated local officials by raising his own force. He seized a ship, commandeered arms, and impressed servants. When Parliament finally ordered him to submit to New England's governments, he refused. New England's Puritan regimes were illegitimate, he said. They denied voting rights to men who were not members of Congregational churches—men like Baxter's supporters, who were largely poor and non-Puritan. As Robert Bassett, Baxter's second-in-command, put it, such men were not so much members of the community or "neighbours," "but bond-men & slaves." Basset appealed to the citizens of Fairfield, saying that the Baxterites "would obey no authority but that which was from the State of England. . . . Let us have Englands lawes, for England doe not prohibbitt us from our votes and liberties. . . . Wee can [have] no justice here." Baxter was not a royalist, but since he threatened Congregational rule, he was arrested. His men marched on the Stamford jail to free him, and in the resulting skirmish one of them was killed.[52]

There were dozens of riots, rebellions, and conspiracies in the colonies during the seventeenth century, reflecting widespread resentment of local and royal authorities and doubts about the effectiveness of colonial governments or outright rejection of their right to rule. In 1641, for example, Massachusetts Bay had to send forty soldiers to suppress a heterodox community that Samuel Gorton and his followers had founded at Shawomet, Rhode Island. Gorton's supporters met them with equal force and riddled their flag with shot before surrendering. In 1667 Dutch villagers rioted against an English garrison in Kingston, New York, in an effort to expel their English conquerors from the town. In 1682 some Virginia planters went on a rampage against their neighbors to vent their frustration with glutted markets and low tobacco prices. Tired of the government's refusal to restrict production, they cut down tobacco plants on more than two hundred plantations before they could be stopped. In 1683–84 opponents of the crown's decision to make New Hampshire a royal colony threatened the life of Governor Cranfield, who fled to Boston. They beat up a customs collector, a marshal, and a member of the governor's council. One of the rebels barged into the governor's mansion to protest the taxes that the colony's proprietors were about to impose on land, and he threw two of the governor's men into the fireplace, breaking the ribs of one and singeing the wig and stockings of the other.[53]

The motives behind private homicides among unrelated colonists are less well known, but in a society in which so many colonists felt estranged from their fellow colonists and mistrustful of the courts, it is not surprising that quarrels, property disputes, and ethnic and religious hatreds claimed many more lives than political disputes did (except in Maryland). Killings that resulted from quarrels and ethnic and religious differences were probably responsible for three-fourths of nonpolitical homicides. (Homicides committed during robberies and sexual assaults made up the balance.) As in Europe, men were anxious about their social standing and quick to kill if they were insulted. William Bently, a Virginia tailor, ran aground in a small boat at Merry Point during a storm and cried for help, but people in a nearby house refused to stir. Bently somehow got ashore and staggered into the house, where he found everyone sprawled around drunk. He berated them, and Thomas Godby replied, "Doe you think wee have nothing to doe but to fetch you out of the water?" Matters went downhill from there. Even Godby's friends agreed that he "gave Bently many provoking wordes" before Bently began to beat him. He died of internal bleeding.[54]

Homicides resulting from property disputes reflected the widespread belief that the legal system of the time was unreliable and illustrated how that belief rendered men anxious and trigger-happy in the face of the most insignificant trespasses. Robert Hobbs, a teenager who worked on a tobacco plantation on the shore of Chesapeake Bay in Calvert County, Maryland, confronted the crew of a ship that had spied a pile of oysters on plantation property and was gathering them up. Hobbs "rayled" at the men, but they told him that "hee need not bee soe angry for eating a few oysters, for they cost him nothing." Hobbs retorted that "they cost him his labour, for that hee had beene all the day in getting of them." The plantation overseer, Patrick Due, arrived with his musket and threatened to shoot the sailors if they didn't leave. One of the sailors told Due that if they "had done him any wronge in Eating of his Oysters" they would pay for them, and he "incontiently heaved a Quarter of a peice of Eight on the shoare." Due shot him.[55]

Men had very little respect for the courts and were often unwilling to cede control to them. Thomas Flounders and Walter House were involved in a lawsuit, and one day House walked into Flounders' shop in Wickford, Rhode Island, picked up a piece of wood, and smashed House's skull. Nathan Bedford of Scarborough, Maine, who was engaged in a legal battle with the wealthiest man in town over ownership of a tract of land, was found drowned with bruises on him that convinced the coroner's jurors he had been beaten. And Henry Sherburne, a prominent landowner and former selectmen and clerk in Portsmouth, New Hampshire, was found dead under unusual circumstances shortly after he had filed a complaint against the Bickford family for injuring his cattle and stealing.[56]

Ethnic and religious differences led to homicides because of the lack of a broader sense of solidarity among the colonists. William Becker, a Dutchman, and Richard Colfax, an Englishman, were neighbors in the predominantly English settlement of Middleborough, New Netherlands. They quarreled bitterly over national differences during the first Anglo-Dutch War (1652–1654), and Becker threatened to kill Colfax. Eventually he made good on his word. Like Becker, John Billington was a member of an embattled minority. As an Anglican in Plymouth Colony, he supported a faction led by Reverend John Lyford and trader John Oldham that wanted to reunite Plymouth's Pilgrim churches with the Anglican Church. Plymouth authorities condemned them for their belligerence and profanity and eventually forced Lyford and Oldham to leave. They considered Billington harmless, however, and he was allowed to stay. Deprived of his companions, he came to resent his Separatist neighbors more with each passing day. He conceived a particular hatred for a young farmer named John Newcomen, and one day while he was out hunting he came upon Newcomen in the woods and shot him.[57]

Murders involving rape and sexual assault were rarer than murders among unrelated men, but, as in Europe, they accounted for a large portion of murders of women by nonrelatives. All the female victims of nonfamily, nonhousehold murders for whom the motive for murder is known appear to have been sexually assaulted. Although rape murder is often interpreted as the isolated act of a disturbed man, its rate increased along with the rates for other kinds of murder among unrelated adults; and it was committed with a violence that suggests estrangement from society and a profound malice toward women. These crimes did not fit the pattern of most nonlethal rapes in colonial America and early modern Europe, which stemmed from efforts to blur the line of consent or to coerce sex from children or women of inferior social status. In nearly all of those assaults, violence was used to intimidate and overpower, not to wound or disfigure.[58] That was not the case in lethal sexual assaults. Hannah Willix, a married woman from Exeter, New Hampshire, was found dead in the Piscataqua River in 1648, "her necke broken, her tounge black & swollen out of her mouthe, & the bloud settled in her face: the privy partes swolne &c: as if she had been muche abused &c." The murderer was never found. Mary Sholy, a young indentured servant, was killed (and probably raped) in the woods north of the Merrimack River; her decomposed body, with her clothes "all on a heap" nearby, was found six months after she went missing. Sholy had agreed to pay a man named William Schooler 15 shillings to escort her to the Piscataqua River, where her master lived. Perhaps Schooler was the only man available, but he was certainly a poor choice for the job. He had abandoned his wife in England after wounding a man in a duel, and he had an unsavory reputation.[59]

Another case that may have involved sexual assault was that of Zipporah Bowles, who was killed along with her five-year-old daughter and three-year-old son by a sixteen-year-old named John Stoddard. Stoddard had come to the Bowleses' house late at night, when he knew Mr. Bowles was away. In his confession he said that he had told Mrs. Bowles that he wanted to lodge with her, and she had slapped his face and tried to push him out the door. He picked up an ax and hacked her to death. Initially the murders were blamed on Indians, but six weeks later Stoddard was arrested for trying to kill his one-year-old stepbrother because he was fed up with the child's crying, and he confessed to the earlier killings.[60]

There was nothing extraordinary about the murders that stemmed from property disputes, quarrels, ethnic and religious hatreds, and sexual assaults except the rate at which they occurred. In most cases, the murderers believed their fellow colonists were out to steal their property or had it in for them because of their class, nationality, or faith. The sense that other colonists were adversaries—that society was a war of all against all—put people on their guard and made them reluctant to show weakness under any circumstances. The sense that fellow colonists were adversaries had an even more dangerous impact on men who were deeply alienated or disturbed, like William Schooler and John Stoddard. It gave them license to prey on their neighbors: to take sex, money, or whatever else they wanted from those weaker than they were. Only when colonists came to see one another in a different light—as allies rather than antagonists—would these homicide rates decline.

One of the most telling signs of the wariness and hostility with which men approached one another was the rate at which they killed each other with guns. Colonists were well armed, but, unlike their counterparts in most of Europe, most chose guns over swords or daggers. Probably 60 percent of all households had at least one working gun. Guns were essential tools in the colonies. Men used them to hunt, to control vermin, and to defend themselves against Indians or people of other nationalities. Few men owned handguns; they needed the range and firepower that muskets afforded and the flexibility to fire shot or slugs, depending on the target. Muskets had their limits as murder weapons. They were inaccurate with slugs, impossible to conceal, and difficult to load. But if the would-be murderer had time to prepare his attack or had already loaded his gun for some other purpose, muskets were usually deadly, in no small part because there was no good medical care for the wounds they inflicted. They were the preferred weapons for killing not only Indians but also political rivals, trespassers, and old enemies. Through 1675, 38 percent of homicides among unrelated colonists in New England and New Netherlands were committed with guns; the figure was probably 40 percent in Maryland. Guns were not responsible for violence, which was rife among Europeans everywhere, but their availability may have made that violence more deadly in colonial America.[61]

The homicide problem among colonists was also exacerbated by indentured servitude, which disrupted the social hierarchy more than any other institution in the seventeenth century. It forced formerly free women and men to the bottom of the hierarchy and kept them there for years as near-slaves. In most instances, indentured servants and their owners got along well enough to see their contracts through, but indentured servitude gave mistresses and masters extraordinary power and deprived servants of basic rights. Some owners found ways to lengthen their servants' contracts through fraud or subterfuge. Some deliberately kept servants hungry and then lengthened their terms of service when they caught them stealing food. Some forced themselves upon indentured women and lengthened the terms of women who got pregnant.[62]

The injustices fostered by indentured servitude led servants to try to get back at their owners in many ways: by stealing, burning buildings, and assaulting their children sexually. But all too often the conflicts of interest and expectation that the institution created turned lethal. In the mid-seventeenth century, indentured servitude was responsible for 29 percent of all nonfamily, nonpolitical homicides among colonists in New England, 50 percent in Virginia, and 67 percent in Maryland. Masters and mistresses expected high returns from their investments in servants, tried to wring those returns from servants as quickly as possible, and had no long-term interest in their health or welfare. Testimony from homicide cases also shows that a high proportion of masters and mistresses distanced themselves from their servants psychologically, habitually referring to them as whores or rogues and scoffing at their pretensions to Christianity. Clearly, some masters felt it necessary to dehumanize their servants, to put them beyond the bounds of moral consideration and to deny them the status of civilized human beings. The servants' poverty was another strike against them. As John Smyth, an early immigrant to Virginia, observed, "temporal possessions are the life of a man, and . . . by poverty they grow contemptible." This deliberate distancing of master from servant may have contributed as much to the deadliness of the institution as the conflicts of interest and expectation inherent in it.[63]

Some masters, like John Grammar, a tobacco planter in Maryland, chose to balance their accounts by giving their servants too little to eat. Other masters and mistresses killed servants unintentionally by working them to death. Some servants were singled out for abuse primarily because they were chronically ill—not an infrequent occurrence in colonies plagued by malnutrition, dysentery, malaria, and other disabling diseases. The victims' inability to work infuriated their masters, who felt cheated. Fellow servants testified that Thomas Watson was very sick, but his masters, Thomas and Mary Bradnox, treated him "more like a dogg than a Christean," denying him food and drink and beating him so hard that they broke a vertebra. Alice Sanford was beaten by her master, Pope Alvey, because she was too weak to work. Naturally, the beatings only weakened her further. One day Alvey beat her so badly that she could not walk and then beat her again for not getting up and walking home. A neighbor happened by and asked what was going on. "This Damned whoare," cried Alvey. "I cannott gett her along noe further then I bast her." The neighbor helped him carry Sanford home, where he pried her mouth open with tobacco tongs and shoved hominy down her throat. She died soon afterward.[64]

The violence inherent in the master-servant relationship was such that it often made homicide victims of women, who were usually much less likely than men to be murdered. In New England, where indentured servitude played a smaller role in the colonial economy, European American women were murdered by nonrelatives at a rate of 4 per 100,000 per year at midcentury, a third of the rate at which men were killed. But in the Chesapeake, where indentured servitude played a central role in the economy, European American women were murdered by nonrelatives at roughly the same rate that men were—29 per 100,000 adult women per year in Maryland and 36 per 100,000 in Virginia.[65]

The master-servant relationship also turned women into killers. The wife of planter Thomas Ward felt entirely justified in beating her servant to death, since she was a habitual runaway. A witness testified that "the maid cried out" during the beating and implored her mistress "to use her like a Christian." Ward replied in astonishment, "'Oh! Ye —— you! Do you liken yourself like a Christian?'" Anne Nevell of Calvert County, Maryland, who was fed up with Margaret Redfearne's attempts to run away, "councelld her to drownd herselfe telling her she should not live two moneths." Nevell beat her to death within the year.[66]

The violence was not all one-sided, however. On a few occasions disgruntled servants killed their masters or mistresses. It is impossible to know why individual servants killed their masters, but almost all chafed at their loss of freedom and dignity and felt intensely that indentured servitude was not the natural order of things for Europeans. It created a new niche for them in the social hierarchy and engendered passionate resentments. The situation was especially bad for mistresses and female servants, who worked closely together and could develop a deadly hatred for each other. During the colonial period, females were almost never involved in homicides outside their families or households, but they were involved in one-sixth of killings of masters, overseers, or male servants and in half of the killings of mistresses or female servants.[67]

Male servants who murdered their masters often had escape in mind, and a substantial number were not of the same ethnicity as their master. Robert Driver and Nicholas Favor robbed and murdered their master, Robert Williams, an English fish dealer on the Piscataqua River in New Hampshire, in order to finance their journey back to Europe. Driver was a Scot, and Favor was French. Joseph Emeritt of Charles County, Maryland, beat his Portuguese master to death with a hoe.[68]

The absence of the bond of ethnicity may have facilitated such murders, but other known or suspected murderers did share the nationality of their master or mistress. Some masters were victims of conspiracies, like Mr. Hawkins of Baltimore County, Maryland, who was hacked to death by three of his servants. Others were murdered on impulse by individual servants who later expressed remorse. Murders occurred everywhere, under every conceivable circumstance.[69]

Owners were unrepentant about their harsh treatment of indentured servants. They lived in fear, "pressed at our backs with the Indians [and] in our bowels with our servants," but they were determined to maintain the status quo. In 1661, after servants conspired in York County, Virginia, to rebel against their masters en masse, the House of Burgesses passed a law that made any servant who ran away with a slave responsible for the loss incurred by the absence of the slave as well as for the loss incurred by his own absence. In 1662 the legislature increased the penalty for hog theft to 1,000 pounds of tobacco and an additional year of service for each hog stolen. After a second conspiracy in 1663, the House of Burgesses made the day on which the conspiracy was suppressed an annual day of thanksgiving. And after Bacon's Rebellion, which many servants joined in hopes of securing their freedom through military service, the government returned captured servants to their owners and passed laws that made it harder for former servants to vote and acquire land. It also further increased the penalty for hog theft: second-time offenders would have their ears cut off, and third-time offenders would be hanged. The contest of wills was clear.[70]

Indentured servitude helped make North America a very homicidal place for Europeans by relegating previously free laborers to the status of de facto slaves. Like other murders among unrelated colonists, these homicides were rooted in the violent behavior that seventeenth-century Europeans brought to the New World with them and in the feelings and beliefs about government and society that caused that behavior. Those feelings and beliefs, which arose out of political, religious, and class conflict and the disruption of the European social hierarchy by economic hardship, traveled to the colonies with the settlers and combined with weak and incapacitated colonial governments to produce high homicide rates that persisted even after the frontier period.

CHAPTER 2

"All Hanging Together"

The Decline of Homicide in the Colonial Period

In the final quarter of the seventeenth century the murder rate in the colonies suddenly dropped. The exact timing of the fall in the homicide rate in these years is uncertain because so many court records from the late seventeenth century have been lost, but it appears that between 1675 and 1693 the rate for European adults fell abruptly twice: once after Bacon's Rebellion (1675) and King Philip's War (1675–76) and again in the late 1680s and early 1690s, at the time of the Glorious Revolution in England. The rate remained low by historical and modern standards for nearly eighty years, until the revolutionary crisis of the 1760s and 1770s.

The patterns were very different for African Americans and Native Americans. African Americans were killed by unrelated adults at high rates in the late seventeenth and early eighteenth centuries, when racial slavery replaced indentured servitude as the primary source of bound labor in British North America. Native Americans in New England were killed by unrelated adults at high rates throughout the colonial period, especially between 1720 and 1760.

European American Homicide

The decline in homicide rates among European Americans was dramatic. In Maryland the rate at which unrelated European adults killed each other fell from 29 per 100,000 adults per year to 15 per 100,000 between the mid-1670s and the mid-1690s. In Virginia it fell from 37 per 100,000 to 10 per 100,000, and in New England from 6 per 100,000 to an astonishing 1 per 100,000. By the end of the century, the homicide rate for colonists in the Chesapeake was for the first time within the range of contemporary western European rates—roughly 12 per 100,000 adults per year. The rate in New England may very well have been the lowest in the Western world (Figures 1.2 and 1.3).[1]

Historians have suggested a number of reasons for the sudden drop in homicides among European colonists: the spread of more civilized standards of conduct, a decline in gun ownership, increased prosperity, or improved law enforcement. But none of these suggestions can explain the decline. It was too abrupt to have been caused by an increase in civility, and gun ownership held steady through the eighteenth century. Although the economic circumstances of most free young men and women did improve over the seventeenth and eighteenth centuries, war crippled the New England economy in the late seventeenth century, and in the Chesapeake the economy was decidedly mixed. The General Court improved law enforcement in Massachusetts, but the emphasis was on rooting out "debauchery, irreligion, prophaneness, & atheisme," not on catching murderers.[2]

The character of the colonial population changed during this period, but its growing diversity might have been expected to raise homicide rates rather than lower them. In some places rates did go up, but increases were short-lived and localized. In the late seventeenth and early eighteenth centuries, settlers from Germany, Scotland, and Ireland poured into the colonies. Many were Lutherans, Presbyterians, or Catholics, and their presence was disconcerting to the resident Congregationalists, Baptists, Quakers, and Anglicans. Wherever these new immigrants faced severe discrimination, as Irish Catholics did in New England and the Chesapeake, they were two to four times more homicidal than other colonists. Wherever they were numerous enough to cause a political backlash among the original settlers, as they did in Pennsylvania in the 1720s, the homicide rate tripled. There were few such nativist outbursts, however, and homicide rates for German, Scots, and Irish immigrants moved quickly toward those of other settlers in the colonies where they lived.[3]

The decline of indentured servitude did contribute to the decrease in homicides among unrelated colonists, especially in the Chesapeake, where there had been so many indentured servants. The revival of the English labor market after 1675 lowered the supply and raised the price of indentured servants, forcing New Englanders to rely almost exclusively on free or family labor. Chesapeake tobacco planters turned to slave labor, which became more affordable with the end of the Royal African Company's monopoly of the slave trade and decreased demand for slaves from Caribbean sugar planters (who had seen prices and profits drop). The proportion of white colonists who were bound servants fell in the Chesapeake from nearly half in the mid-seventeenth century to no more than a tenth by the mid-eighteenth century, and in New England from a tenth to near zero.[4]

But these numbers were not the whole story. The proportion of bound servants among homicide victims fell far faster than their proportion in the population. After 1675 masters were suddenly less likely to subject bound white laborers to lethal abuse. By the 1680s and 1690s, the number of murdered servants included in the colonists' homicide rate had fallen from 18 per 100,000 adults per year in Maryland to 2, and in Virginia from 11 per 100,000 adults per year to 3. By the mid-eighteenth century, that number had fallen in Maryland and Virginia to less than 1 per 100,000 adults per year. In New England, only one servant was reported murdered between 1675 and 1692, and none from 1693 to the Revolution. Indentured servitude was not only less common; it was less lethal.

This sudden drop in lethal abuse paralleled the sudden drop in the murder rate of colonists in general. Every kind of homicide became rarer among unrelated European Americans: rape murders, robbery murders, political murders, property dispute murders. Although it is impossible to measure changes in relationships or the emotions they reflected, it appears that empathy, solidarity, and mutual forbearance increased, except where Catholics were concerned. Fear of Indians and slaves, hatred of the French, enthusiasm for the new colonial and imperial governments established by the Glorious Revolution, and patriotic devotion to England drew colonists together. The late seventeenth century thus marks the discernible beginning of the centuries-long pattern linking homicide rates in America with political stability, racial, religious, and national solidarity, and faith in government and political leaders.

In 1675, on the eve of the decline in homicide, the lack of solidarity and goodwill among European colonists was evident in a number of ways. With no serious threat to unite against, they could not find common cause in religion, nationality, or even race. African slaves accounted for only 2 percent of the population in New England and 6 percent in the Chesapeake. Racial consciousness was increasing in British North America, as was the fear that slaves and servants might unite and rebel against their masters; but the fundamental dividing line among the colonists, especially in the Chesapeake, was class, which pitted bound white laborers against their white owners. The presence of Africans could not unite European colonists as long as slave labor played such a minor role in society.[5]

Nor were the colonists united at this time in their feelings about Native Americans. While some held Indians in contempt and would gladly have seen them removed or eliminated, most colonists in the Chesapeake realized that they could not defend their borders without Indian allies. In New England, where settlers and Native Americans had lived in peace for nearly forty years, there were obvious advantages to living side by side with Indians, who made up nearly a fourth of the region's population before King Philip's War. Native Americans provided settlers with furs, corn, labor, and wampum, which was the primary currency for Europeans as well as Indians into the 1660s. New England tribes were the region's first line of defense against the dreaded Iroquois. In addition, settlers who were evangelical Christians saw the Indians as souls in need of salvation, and the spiritual lives of the two peoples were deeply intertwined. One in twenty Indians had already moved to a "praying" town by 1675, and evangelical colonists held out hope for a biracial Christian society. This is not to say that Native Americans were equal partners in New England's social, economic, or spiritual life, or that the two groups were never at odds. But in the interval between the Pequot War and King Philip's War relations were generally civil, and neither group indulged in demonizing the other.[6]

Religion and nationality were also poor grounds for unity. Between 1650 and 1680 the colonists found themselves at war three times with the Netherlands, a Protestant nation, while they had cordial and profitable relations with French Catholics in the Canadian Maritimes and the West Indies and were barely touched by the fighting between England and France in the late 1660s.[7] Quaker and Baptist dissenters in Maryland enjoyed more rights under a Catholic proprietor than they would have in Anglican Virginia or Puritan New England, where they risked being banished or hanged. Certainly, New Englanders were more unified spiritually than colonists in the Chesapeake, because of the dominance of Puritan reformers in Massachusetts, Connecticut, and Plymouth, and of dissenters in Rhode Island. But dominance was not unity, and resentment and alienation were common among the unchurched, who were responsible for most homicides in New England.[8] The wandering poor were denied public charity and warned out of town wherever they went, and the unruly poor—drunks, Sabbath-breakers, fornicators, petty thieves, runaway servants—were fined, whipped, dunked, or pilloried and publicly humiliated. It was hard for many of the poor to see themselves as part of a Christian society.

Governments on both sides of the Atlantic betrayed their insecurity by killing their citizens over political differences. Maryland and Virginia hanged dozens of people for treason. Massachusetts and Connecticut officials showed how precarious they believed social stability to be when they banished scores of colonists for heresy in the seventeenth century and put more than four dozen moral offenders and witches to death. Political conflict and violence were rife, and the colonists were eager to root out internal enemies to ensure the survival of their communities.[9]

Three events changed the way the colonists saw themselves, their fellow colonists, and their governments: King Philip's War, the transformation of the Chesapeake into a slave society, and the Glorious Revolution. These events, which had the potential to destabilize colonial society and divide the colonists in new ways, had the opposite effect. King Philip's War unified colonists who lived on the front line, especially New Englanders. The spread of racial slavery led white property owners, especially in the Chesapeake, to set aside their differences and pull together to defend white supremacy. And an overwhelming majority of colonists came to support the Protestant coup that brought William and Mary to power in 1688, once they were sure of the direction William's reforms would take in the colonies and in the imperial government.[10] Together these events forged a sense of solidarity among colonists that helped them transcend their earlier differences and see one another as allies rather than adversaries. That feeling was a powerful deterrent to homicide, as was the belief that the governments at home and in Britain were *their* governments and would look after *their* interests.

King Philip's War was the most important factor in the decline of homicide in New England. Relations between the colonists and most Native American peoples began to deteriorate in the 1660s and early 1670s, when their roles in the economy changed. As furbearing animals grew scarce and colonists started to raise surpluses of corn and livestock, Native Americans found themselves pushed to the edge of the economy, with little to trade except their land and labor. English currency began to replace wampum as the medium of exchange. Native Americans in western and central New England were bitter about the colonists' failure to come to their aid when they were attacked repeatedly by the Mohawks in the 1660s and early 1670s. Every year settlers and their livestock encroached farther onto Native hunting grounds. Colonial authorities who made an effort to redress Native grievances showed a growing preference for "praying" Indians, who embraced Christianity.[11]

Philip, the Wampanoag sachem who led the rebellion, had good reason to be angry. When the governors of Plymouth compensated Christian Indians at Natick for land lost to settlers, they gave them Wampanoag land—without consulting the Wampanoags. Philip also came into conflict with the colonists over Native ministers who were undermining traditional culture and traditional leaders. He found one of these ministers, John Sassamon, particularly irksome and probably conspired to have him killed. When Plymouth authorities executed the Indians they believed responsible for Sassamon's killing, Philip was furious. The Wampanoags took up arms. Inspired by their early successes, two-thirds of New England's 18,000 Indians joined the rebellion, determined to force the colonists—all 60,000 of them—off their land.

King Philip's War was the most destructive conflict in New England's history and did more than any other event in the seventeenth century to reshape the way New Englanders saw themselves. For nearly all the colonists the war was a race war, pitting whites against Indians, and they urged one another to set aside their differences and join the battle. As contemporary chronicler William Hubbard put it, since the Indians were "all hanging together, like Serpent's Eggs," it was incumbent upon the colonists to do likewise. Benjamin Franklin's grandfather, Peter Folger, who blamed the war itself on the persecution of Baptists, Quakers, and other religious minorities as "Hereticks," called for an end to sectarian hostilities, asking New Englanders:

> Is this a time for you to press,
> To draw the Blood of those
> That are your Neighbours & your Friends;
> As if you had no Foes.

The terrified colonists needed little urging. The specter of Indians lurking in the woods, awaiting the fall of darkness so that they could spring out and bury their hatchets in the skulls of innocents, touched primordial fears. Many colonists abruptly revised their views of Native Americans. They were not primitive souls awaiting the gospel of truth, who might one day evolve into civilized citizens. They were, as Deacon Philip Walker put it, "Incarnat divels sent from the infernall Lake"— the spawn of Satan.[12]

The colonists waged total war. Two thousand Native men, women, and children were killed outright; 3,000 died of exposure or malnutrition after their crops and villages were destroyed. One thousand were sold into slavery in the West Indies, and another 2,000 became permanent refugees in Canada or New York. Captured leaders were hanged. Two were torn to pieces by a mob of women in Marblehead, Massachusetts. By the end of the war, fewer than 4,000 Indians from bands that had supported the rebellion remained in New England.[13]

Although "praying" Indians served in the military campaign against the rebels, they fared little better than their non-Christian brethren. More than 1,000 Indians lived in Christian villages in 1675, but once the war started the colonists viewed them with suspicion. At first they were confined to their villages "on peril of being taken as our enemies, or their abettors." The colonists warned that if they strayed more than a mile from home, "their Blood or other damage . . . will be upon their own heads." But within a few months Massachusetts authorities moved most Christian Indians to a camp in Boston Harbor on Deer Island, where many died of malnutrition or exposure. Those who were not interned on Deer Island ran the risk of being murdered. Two Christian Indians mistaken for rebels in Boston were nearly lynched. White vigilantes suspected Indians from the Christian village of Wamesit of setting fire to barns and haystacks nearby, and they attacked the village, killing a twelve-year-old Indian boy and wounding five women and children. Vigilantes murdered six Christian women and children who were picking berries near Concord.[14]

Missionaries and magistrates who had worked with Christian Indians and dared to stand up for their rights were vilified. An anonymous pamphleteer called them "traytors to their king and Country" and put them on notice: "[S]ome generous spiritts have vowed their destruction. [A]s Christian[s] we warne them to prepare for death, for though they will deservedly dye, yet we wish the health of their souls." Richard Scott threatened to kill the Christian Indians' foremost defender, Captain Daniel Gookin, "calling him an Irish Dog that was never faithful to his country, the son of a whore, a bitch, a rogue, God confound him and God rot his soul." Threats and public ostracism took their toll. Gookin was "afraid to go along the Streets," and when he complained to a neighbor about it, he was told "you may thank yourself." Gookin lost his bid for reelection to the Court of Assistants, and Daniel Henchman, another sympathizer, lost his post as a militia officer when his men refused to fight with him. Missionary activity ceased, and most defenders of the Christian Indians were cowed into silence. By the end of the war, only 500 "praying" Indians remained.[15]

Anyone who sought to deal peacefully with non-Christian Indians was suspect, no matter what his status. In a later phase of the war involving the French, Edmund Andros, who was then governor of the Dominion of New England, ran afoul of public opinion when he tried to return Abenaki hostages who had been seized without warrant by militiamen. Andros, a native of the Isle of Jersey, was accused of treachery; since he was "of a French extract, so [he acted] in the French interests." Someone claimed to have heard an Indian say that "the Governor had more love for them the Indians, then for his Majesties Subjects the English" and that he had "hired Indians to kill the English." Captain John Alden, who had been assigned to act as a government envoy to the Abenakis, was also suspected of treason; he was accused at the Salem witchcraft trials of siding with the devil, the Abenakis, and the French.[16]

New England colonists emerged from the war not only with a clear sense of the need for racial unity, but also with a greater regard for one another that bridged religious divides. Baptists won praise from Congregationalists and Presbyterians for their participation in the war. William Turner, who had been imprisoned in 1668 and 1670 for his Baptist views and had been denied a commission on religious grounds at the beginning of the war, was given command of the garrison at Hatfield, Massachusetts, and the massacre he led against Indians encamped at Peskeompscut, which cost him his life, made him a hero. Roger Williams, the founder of Rhode Island and himself a dissenter, won accolades for his efforts to gather intelligence and keep the Narragansetts out of the war. Massachusetts rescinded Williams' banishment because he had "served the English interest." Benjamin Church, a rough-and-ready frontiersman noted for his wry sense of humor and his irregular church attendance, became the war's greatest hero because of his work with Native allies and his successful guerrilla campaign against Philip. Quakers opposed the war, as they did all wars, but by its end they, too, identified with the "English" cause, as did New England's most notorious sectarian, Samuel Gorton, who delighted in the colonists' newfound ability to pull together in the crisis and to form a genuine "body Pollitique of English in these parts."[17]

This inclusive spirit was at work within orthodox churches as well. Congregationalist and Presbyterian churches relaxed requirements for baptism and church membership and welcomed a broader range of colonists into the fold. Most churches adopted the "half-way covenant," which ended the restriction of baptism to the children of members, and they made standards for receiving communion less exacting. The orthodox majority also made a quiet decision to be more forgiving of everyday sinners, particularly young men and women who had premarital sex. King Philip's War marked the end of whippings for fornication in New Haven County, and elsewhere such whippings declined markedly. No cleric championed these changes more ardently than Solomon Stoddard, a minister from Northampton, Massachusetts, and it is unlikely that any minister outdid Stoddard in his zeal to exterminate Native Americans. He counseled the colonial governor to train dogs to hunt Indians as vermin. "They are to be looked upon as theives & murderers, they doe acts of hostility, without proclaiming war. . . . they act like wolves & are to be dealt withall as wolves."[18]

New England's colonists were not yet as unified as they would be at the end of the century. There were a few orthodox preachers who blamed the war and its attendant horrors on sinners, dissenters, and witches and wanted to persecute those responsible; and the orthodox still discriminated against religious minorities and punished sinners.[19] But when war broke out, the colonists realized that what they had in common as whites, Protestants, and English women and men was more important than sectarian differences or moral failings. Although it stemmed from fear and hatred of Indians, this newfound solidarity lessened the alienation and resentment that had caused so many homicides in the mid-seventeenth century and generated greater tolerance and respect for other colonists and for the social order.

However, Indian wars did not automatically trigger increased solidarity among all the colonists. The war that broke out in the Chesapeake in 1675 galvanized Virginians on the western and southern frontiers, but Virginians who lived far from the frontier did not hate Indians or lust after their land so intensely. Marylanders needed Native allies for protection and resolved to stay out of the war. The conflict in Virginia between the supporters of a total war against all Indians, led by Nathaniel Bacon, and the supporters of a limited, defensive war against hostile Indians, led by Governor Berkeley, led in 1675 to Bacon's Rebellion and to open class warfare. Indentured servants and slaves flocked to Bacon's banner on the promise of freedom in return for military service. Berkeley's assembly debated whether to reenfranchise free, propertyless whites and cut the salaries of wealthy officeholders for the sake of political peace.[20]

The defeat of the rebels did not put an end to political hostility. Berkeley and his supporters were in a vengeful mood. They executed twenty-three rebel leaders and confiscated the estates of many more, and once the rebellion was over, they refused to make more than token reforms in a political system that left most Virginians with no voice in government. They did authorize the county courts to hear the grievances of local citizens, but propertyless freemen were disfranchised again in 1677, and nothing was done to limit public expenditures, the fees of officeholders, or the tax advantages of large landowners. Class hatreds remained fierce, and some colonists still had substantial grounds for resentment and alienation.

What changed the way unrelated adult colonists in the Chesapeake felt about one another was not the Indian war or Bacon's Rebellion, but the rise of racial slavery. Between 1660 and 1700 the proportion of Africans in the population of the Chesapeake rose from 5 percent to nearly a quarter. The vast majority of English migrants who headed to the New World as indentured servants still came to the Chesapeake, where there were greater opportunities for land ownership than in the West Indies, as well as lower mortality rates. But by 1700 indentured servants were no longer the major source of bound labor in the Chesapeake, and those who came were more often skilled craftsmen, seamstresses, domestic servants, or overseers. By 1700 the Chesapeake had become a slave society in which the divide between whites and blacks overshadowed class divisions among whites.[21] The new society increased racial consciousness among whites and placed new importance on white solidarity, much as King Philip's War did among whites in New England. This solidarity was not as intense or heartfelt in the Chesapeake as it was in New England, given the sharpness of class divisions among whites and the more remote threat of slave rebellion. But its impact was still strong. Led by a decline in murders of indentured servants, homicides among unrelated white adults dropped by two-thirds.[22]

At first racial slavery rested on little more than brute force. Slave-owners whipped refractory slaves, hobbled chronic runaways by severing their toes, and executed those who rebelled or committed crimes. In 1669 the Virginia legislature encouraged the use of force by making it only a misdemeanor to cause the death of a slave by "excessive" punishment, and in 1680 the legislature made it lawful to kill runaway slaves who resisted capture. Despite these measures, slaveowners recognized that the system of racial slavery needed the support of nonslaveholding whites. Their help, whether as patrollers, overseers, or vigilant neighbors, was vital to keeping slaves in their place. If they did not acquiesce, or if white servants joined black slaves in rebellion against their owners, slavery would collapse.[23]

Between 1662 and 1705 slaveowners in Virginia and Maryland campaigned to clarify the line between Africans and Europeans. Their goal was to control blacks and to secure the racial allegiance of nonslaveholding whites by fostering contempt for blacks and by punishing those who formed personal relationships with blacks. They passed legislation declaring that African slaves who converted to Christianity would remain slaves and that any slave freed by an owner would have to be transported out of the colony at the owner's expense. Free blacks who already lived in the Chesapeake would not be allowed to purchase white indentured servants, and any slave who struck a white for any reason would receive thirty lashes. It became illegal for white women to give birth to mixed-race children, and white servants who dared to run away with slaves had to compensate owners for their time and the time of the slaves who went with them. In the 1680s and 1690s these laws led to a flurry of prosecutions of whites who helped runaway slaves or had sex with blacks. Together with the stigmatization of interracial relationships and the decline in the number of indentured servants who worked side by side with blacks in the fields, these prosecutions weakened social ties between poor whites and blacks. By the turn of the century, the racial divide was clear.[24]

The campaign for white supremacy and solidarity had terrible consequences for African Americans, but positive consequences for many nonslaveholding whites, especially indentured servants. Deadly abuse of white servants declined not only because their skills were prized during the transition to slavery, but also because masters came to see them first and foremost as fellow whites and as Christians. They no longer referred to servants routinely as "rogues" and "whores." They passed laws to protect their rights and dignity. By 1705 it was illegal "to whip a christian white servant naked, without an order from a justice of the peace." Such treatment was reserved for blacks. Indentured servants had the right to keep and accumulate property, but slaves' "horses, hogs, and cattle" were subject to sale by church wardens for the support of the parish. Former indentured servants had their rights guaranteed by law and were incorporated more fully into white society, both economically and militarily. "Freedom dues"—the property that indentured servants received from masters at the end of their contracts—were increased from three bushels of corn to ten bushels, plus 30 shillings in cash and a working musket. Finally, the burden of the poll tax on men with little property was alleviated at the colonial level by the imposition of an export tax on tobacco and duties on imported liquor, servants, and slaves. The annual tax burden for the average white male fell from forty-five pounds of tobacco in the 1670s to only five pounds in the early 1700s.[25]

Politicians in Virginia and in Maryland also stepped up their efforts to court the votes of small property owners. Competition between candidates was so intense that politicians solicited votes with liquor and other gifts on election days. These competitive elections increased corruption and public drunkenness, but they also heightened cooperation across class lines by rallying all property owners (and prospective owners) to the defense of the tobacco economy, slavery, and white supremacy.[26]

Antagonism toward Indians did play a role in forging white solidarity in the Chesapeake, though not to the degree it did in New England. During Bacon's Rebellion the Virginia assembly overturned a 1670 law that had forbidden the permanent enslavement of Indians. According to that law, captured Indian children could be enslaved only until age thirty and captured adults for twelve years. In 1676, however, the assembly granted Bacon and his men the power to enslave enemy Indians for life, and the postrebellion assemblies of 1677 and 1679 extended that right to all Virginia soldiers. In 1682 the assembly defined slavery on racial grounds. Thereafter all laws that applied to African slaves would apply to Indian and mulatto slaves as well. Like other colonies, Maryland and Virginia also stopped giving new counties Indian names. The proportion of new counties in British North America named for Indian people or places fell from 10 percent in the seventeenth century to zero in the first half of the eighteenth century.[27]

The rise of African slavery had a more limited role in forging white solidarity in New England. Even though the proportion of Africans in New England's population never rose above 3 percent, African slavery was an important institution in New England's ports and on plantations in Rhode Island, and New England merchants and seamen played a major role in the slave trade throughout the colonies. Like their counterparts in the Chesapeake, colonists in New England placed more and more restrictions on Africans and Native Americans and came to view them with similar contempt. In 1686 the Massachusetts assembly forbade the sale of "any strong Beer, Wine, Cyder, Rum or any other strong drink, to any Indian or Negro" without a license from the Governor's Council. In 1693 it banned Indians and Africans from the militia, denied Africans the right to drink in taverns, and imposed harsh penalties on whites who received stolen goods from Africans, Indians, or mulattos. In 1703 it established a curfew for "free blacks, slaves, and Indians" and ordered owners who manumitted African slaves to post £50 in bonds to "indemnify" the colony if their former slaves broke the law or became public charges. And in 1705 it imposed penalties on whites and blacks who had mixed-race children.

Whites and free blacks would be whipped, and slaves would be sold out of the province, as would the mixed-race children of enslaved women. The prohibition on interracial sex did not apply to whites and Indians, but otherwise the legislation treated blacks and Indians the same.[28]

The Glorious Revolution of 1688–89 also had a profound effect on white colonists. By the turn of the century it brought political peace and stability to Britain and British North America, put an end to internecine political violence, and stimulated patriotic feeling among colonists. The great majority found common ground in a commitment to the British constitution, with its putative guarantees of representative government and minority rights, and to the British Empire, which promised to spread British values, British enterprise, and British people throughout the world. They also began to identify with a more tolerant Protestantism that respected the rights of most (but not all) dissenters.

The Glorious Revolution helped restore colonists' faith in the imperial government and in their colonial governments. They had been deeply divided over policies implemented by Charles II and James II. The crown had pressured royal colonies like Virginia and proprietary colonies like Maryland to increase revenues and improve defense, and it had curbed the powers of charter colonies like Massachusetts, Connecticut, and Rhode Island, which had been largely self-governing before the Restoration. James II revoked the charters that had authorized New England's assemblies, forced the colonies to unite as the Dominion of New England, and told the dominion's royal governor, Joseph Dudley, to rule by prerogative. When one New Englander objected, claiming that the colonists' rights had been violated, Dudley told him that he "must not think the laws of England follow us to the ends of the Earth. . . . You have no more privilidges left you, than not to be sold for Slaves."[29]

The crown had also disrupted the economy in the colonies by enforcing the Navigation Acts, thus putting an end to direct trade with the Dutch and other foreign powers. The imperial bureaucracy expanded, as did taxes and fees, and the crown gave generous grants of land, quitrents, escheats, and other financial emoluments to officials who were willing to support the new regime. Charles II and James II also tried to strengthen the Church of England. They sent more ministers to the colonies, sought an end to orthodox Puritan rule in

Massachusetts and Connecticut by extending the franchise to propertied non-Puritans, and pressed for formal recognition of the Anglican Church in Maryland.[30]

A growing number of colonists opposed England's plans. In New England, Puritans, Congregationalists, Baptists, and Quakers resisted the pan–New England government that James had created. They were convinced that his goal was to destroy Protestantism and representative government and establish an autocratic, spiritually lax regime. They were particularly appalled to see Restoration culture take hold in New England. Young people were engaging in bawdy games and maypole dancing, and sexually provocative clothing was in fashion. In Maryland, rumors spread that James planned to use the Indians to help the Catholic minority annihilate the Protestant majority. In Virginia, even moderates who tried to meet the crown halfway were disillusioned. It seemed to them that England was determined to loot the colonies and deprive colonists of their rights as English citizens.[31]

The overthrow of James II by William of Orange in the Glorious Revolution of 1688–89 triggered a chain of events that united colonists politically. News of James's flight and William's victory led to bloodless revolutions by militant Protestants who rejoiced at the news that England had a Protestant king again. In Maryland, rebels overthrew the government of the Catholic proprietor and assumed power as the "Protestant Association." In New England, the government installed by James II was overthrown, and charter government was restored to each colony. The first years of William's reign were anxious ones, however. The status of the new colonial regimes was unclear, the war in New England against the French and their Native allies was going badly, and William and his ministers were preoccupied with armed uprisings in Scotland and in Ireland and a war on the Continent. They told the colonists to be patient, but the uncertainty made it difficult to collect taxes, hold courts, or rein in Protestant zealots, who threatened to destabilize the colonies all over again by persecuting Catholics in Maryland and by trying to disfranchise Anglicans and Baptists and prosecuting suspected witches in Massachusetts and Connecticut.[32]

Gradually, however, William's government took hold politically and militarily. William believed in representative government, and he guaranteed the right of colonial assemblies to make laws, levy taxes, and appoint members of the governors' councils (subject to gubernatorial review). At the same time he believed in keeping a firm hand on the tiller, so he retained the power to appoint governors, deputy governors, secretaries, and, through them, judges and sheriffs. He also reserved the right to veto colonial legislation, appoint revenue officers, and establish vice-admiralty courts to enforce trade laws.[33]

William was a confirmed Anglican, but he sponsored the Toleration Act of 1689, which granted freedom of conscience to dissenting Protestants and made property ownership the only qualification for voting. Although he actively supported the Anglican establishments in Virginia and Maryland, he did not let them run roughshod over dissenters. He disallowed acts that would have subverted his religious program, such as laws the Massachusetts assembly passed against blasphemy and idolatry, but he did allow the Congregational establishments in Massachusetts and Connecticut to stand. Catholics, anti-Trinitarians, and non-Christians were still beyond the pale. They could not hold office or worship in public, and with Parliament's support William denied them the right to propagate their views in public through the Blasphemy Act of 1697.

Few colonists were initially satisfied with William's handling of colonial affairs, but his measures proved effective, and the vast majority of Protestants eventually embraced his policies. Conflict with royal officials was inevitable once William and his administrators made it clear that, like James II, they were determined to enforce the Navigation Acts and integrate the colonies more fully into the British economy. But William's conciliatory stance, together with the colonists' growing appreciation of the military and economic benefits of membership in the British Empire, softened the antagonistic tone of colonial politics. By the early 1700s opponents of James II were working in colonial government alongside former proponents, and the power of the Protestant zealots who had sponsored the revolutions in New England and Maryland had waned. Virtually no one questioned the legitimacy of the government anymore or called damnation down upon their political opponents. The fearful, weak governments of the mid-seventeenth century had relied upon executions to put down treason, religious dissent, and rebellion, but under the more secure governments of the early eighteenth century such executions disappeared.[34]

William's handling of religious affairs was just as effective, at least for Protestants. He won the loyalty of Baptists and Quakers when he guaranteed their basic rights and allowed them to come to England, where there were a number of supportive royal officials and members of Parliament, to plead for an end to the lingering discrimination against dissenters in colonies with established churches. The crown also put an end to executions for witchcraft after learning of the miscarriages of justice in Salem in 1692.[35]

For their part, the orthodox gradually came to terms with the loss of their power to persecute dissenters and suspected witches. Supporters of the Congregational establishments of Massachusetts, Connecticut, and New Hampshire, and of the Anglican establishments of Maryland and Virginia, found new ways to promote Christian piety. They set up ministerial associations and missionary societies. They founded colleges—William and Mary opened in 1694 and Yale in 1701—to educate orthodox ministers, and they sent evangelical preachers to every corner of the colonies to spread the gospel. Religious and political rivalries remained intense, but they became less confrontational and claimed no more lives.[36]

William's political and religious settlement reconciled the colonists with one another, but his status as a Protestant hero was what united them. Royal propaganda portrayed him as the savior of the English people. He had found them "in languishing circumstances; almost quite depriv'd of Liberty and Property; having their Religion, Laws and Lives in utmost hazard; sinking under Arbitrary Power and Tyranny; almost overwhelm'd with Popery and Slavery." Now they were on the offensive throughout the world against Catholicism, corruption, and despotism. Militant Protestants were especially pleased by the progress they saw. "God seems to have begun the Reformation of the whole World, and eminently to appear for the True Reformed Religion," proclaimed one colonist pamphleteer. Another declared that "Earth Quakes" had begun "which shall shake yet until they have shaken the Papal Empire to pieces." William's anti-Catholicism was popular throughout the realm, as was his alliance with the Netherlands and Protestant states in Germany against the French effort to establish a "universal" monarchy; but in the colonies his defense of constitutional government and representative institutions and his commitment to tolerance among Protestants were equally important.[37]

The 1690s marked a turning point in national feeling in the colonies. The proportion of counties named for British heroes rose from

40 percent in the decades before the Glorious Revolution to 80 percent and stayed at that level until the revolutionary crisis of the 1760s and 1770s (Figure 2.1). Celebrations of the king's birthday on 4 November and of Gunpowder Treason Day on 5 November (which marked the date on which the British thwarted a Catholic plot to blow up Parliament) were merged with annual feast days to create a grand patriotic holiday, which became the foremost public event in the colonies. Colonial faith in ecumenical Protestantism and in British values and institutions was at an all-time high.[38]

Of course, anti-Catholicism was poor grounds for unity in Maryland, where a quarter of the population was Catholic. Voters turned the most militant anti-Catholics out of office once the Glorious Revolution was complete, but they did so as much in rejection of Puritan extremism as in a gesture of tolerance to Catholics. The assembly, mindful of the need not to drive Catholics to rebellion, granted Catholics the right to vote—a right they had lost in England under William—but

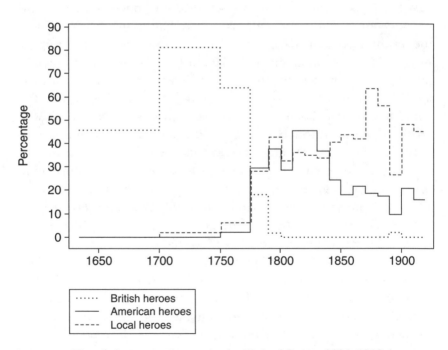

Figure 2.1 Trends in county names in the United States, 1634–1919 (percentage of names of new counties). *Source:* Zelinsky (1988: 124–125).

barred them from holding office or practicing law outside prerogative or chancery courts. Race and a desire for political peace bound Protestant and Catholic colonists together, but it was an uneasy union, and religious antagonism periodically gained the upper hand.[39]

Anti-Catholicism was crucial to the creation of political solidarity in New England. Together with the intense anti-Indian feeling reawakened by King William's War of 1689–1699 and Queen Anne's War of 1702–1713, it helped create the most unified citizenry in the colonies. The struggle against the French and their Indian allies had as powerful an impact on the psychology of New Englanders as any royal propaganda did. It deepened the colonists' sense of religious and racial solidarity and exacerbated their hatred of "savagery" and "popery." People believed that the French and the Indians were conspiring with the devil to destroy them. One of the witches executed at Salem testified that "at their Cheef Witch-meetings, there had been present some French Canadians" and "some Indian Sagamores, to concert the methods of ruining New England." Mercy Lewis, one of the accusers at Salem, reported that French and Indian specters had visited her and shown her the book of Catholic devotions they used. Fears of French encroachment upon New England were not unfounded, of course: in Maine the French fought side by side with the Abenakis, and in 1690 two men from the Isle of Jersey tried to promote the French cause in New Hampshire and Massachusetts by fomenting rebellion among Indian (and African) slaves. They were planning to burn Exeter and Newbury and flee to Canada, where they would free the slaves.[40]

Native Americans, however, remained the primary focus of New Englanders' hostility. After so many years of brutal warfare and so many horrifying atrocities, it could hardly have been otherwise. Mercy Short, who had been taken hostage by a band of Indians, was universally applauded after she killed ten of her captors—six of them children—and brought back their scalps. The Reverend Cotton Mather said of the Indians in 1702 that "the most scrupulous persons in the world must own, that it must be the most unexceptionable piece of justice in the world for to extinguish them." The Glorious Revolution and the war against France confirmed New Englanders in their loyalty to one another, but during this era that loyalty was founded first and foremost on hatred of the Indians.[41]

The impact of the increase in political, religious, and racial solidarity on the homicide rate among unrelated colonists was profound, as was the emergence of political stability in the colonies and in the British Empire at large. Nearly every connection between people—servants and masters, neighbors, and strangers—became abruptly less homicidal in New England and the Chesapeake. Several patterns stand out. First, colonists stopped killing one another over political or religious differences. Politics was still contentious, and rioters expressed outrage from time to time against ministers or public officials who crossed them; but except for a few killings related to land disputes and a quarrel between a Protestant and a Catholic in Maryland, political and religious homicides ceased among European Americans after the Glorious Revolution, not only in New England and the Chesapeake but throughout British North America.[42] These homicides reappeared in the late 1760s and early 1770s as the revolutionary crisis unfolded, but between 1693 and 1765 there was virtually no risk of colonists' being killed in disputes over land, taxes, Indian policy, religion, territorial sovereignty, or constitutional rights.

The sudden disappearance of political homicides played a smaller part in the decline in homicides in the late seventeenth century in Virginia, where political homicides had accounted for a very small proportion of homicides among unrelated colonists to begin with: about 8 percent from the time of settlement through Bacon's Rebellion. In New England, however, political homicides had accounted for 29 percent of homicides among unrelated colonists before 1675, and their disappearance accounted for a third of the decline in homicides that occurred there at the end of the seventeenth century. And in Maryland, where political homicides had accounted for 54 percent of homicides among unrelated colonists before 1675, their disappearance accounted for two-thirds of the decline in homicides. The conflict between proprietary and antiproprietary forces in Maryland still claimed a few lives in this era. In 1690, for example, John Payne, who had been appointed a customs collector by the new antiproprietary government, was shot dead on the Pleasant River when he tried to board a ship commanded by Lord Baltimore's stepson, formerly deputy governor under the proprietary regime and a member of Lord Baltimore's Council. However, the Protestants' victory was so complete by the mid-1690s that Catholics never took up arms again in Maryland.[43]

Another sign of the impact of political, racial, and religious unity on the homicide rate was the disappearance of rape murders and robbery murders among Protestant colonists. From the late 1680s to the revolutionary crisis there are no recorded instances of Protestant colonists in New England or the Chesapeake raping and murdering colonial women, and no Protestant colonist committed a predatory homicide against a fellow colonist. The robbery murders that occurred were committed by outsiders who did not share in the colonists' newfound spirit of solidarity: a free mulatto man, convict servants, Irish Catholic immigrants, or English soldiers and sailors.[44] Protestant colonists now shared too strong an identity to prey on one another as they had done in the early and mid-seventeenth century. Indeed, this sense of identity was so strong that by the late seventeenth century people who were outside the white Protestant mainstream recognized themselves and were recognized by others as outsiders. Irish Catholics, free blacks, and convict servants were not extremely homicidal in the eighteenth century, but their alienation was such that those who were disturbed or desperate could commit acts of violence that Protestant colonists would not.

The decline in robbery homicides and sexual homicides, together with the decline in indentured servitude, had a particularly dramatic effect on homicide rates for women. In Maryland and Virginia those rates fell respectively from 29 and 36 per 100,000 women per year in the mid-seventeenth century to only 1 per 100,000 in the early eighteenth century, and in New England from 4 per 100,000 to 0.4 per 100,000.[45] Those declines—along with the growing proportion of women in the adult population—helped push overall homicide rates to very low levels by the mid-eighteenth century.

As the colonists' homicide rate declined, the contribution of soldiers and especially sailors to the homicide rate became more salient. Together they committed a fifth of all homicides of colonists in New England and in Maryland from the 1690s to the Revolution, even though they accounted for less than a tenth of the population. Sometimes they killed people in the course of carrying out their duties. In New England, press-gangs from the Royal Navy killed at least four "recruits" who were trying to escape, and sentries on the northern frontier shot at least five colonists dead when they mistook them for marauding Indians.[46] But soldiers and sailors were habitual brawlers, and the majority of deaths involving them were the result of fights. English sailors went on a rampage in Portsmouth, Virginia, when several Spanish ships came into port. They chased the Spanish sailors into their boardinghouses and killed two of them before local authorities could restore order. British sailors in Newport, Rhode Island, turned on a couple of local men in a brothel and ran them through with swords. More often, however, sailors turned on their own shipmates in work disputes or drunken fights. Such homicides were confined to the margins of colonial society, on the frontier or in ports or harbors, and only rarely did they involve colonists.[47]

There was little change in the character of other types of homicide, although these too occurred much less frequently. Men still killed each other in drunken brawls or disputes over eviction notices, stolen livestock, or unpaid loans, but these were spontaneous rather than premeditated murders, and few involved guns. The proportion of homicides among unrelated colonists that were committed with guns fell from 38 percent to 13 percent in New England from the late 1670s through the 1760s and from 40 percent to 11 percent in Maryland. As in the seventeenth century, women almost never killed fellow colonists outside their homes or families. Mistresses, landladies, and female servants committed or assisted in a handful of homicides in their households, but except for a couple of shoving matches that resulted in deaths, women did not kill unrelated colonists.[48]

The influx of immigrants from Scotland and Ireland in the eighteenth century raised the homicide rate, though not as much as historians have assumed. Both Scotland and Ireland had high homicide rates. Political instability was the primary cause. Scotland witnessed terrible violence during the English Civil War and during postwar rebellions against the imposition of an Anglican establishment on Scotland. William III reached out to Presbyterian Scots in an effort to restore order, and his successor, Queen Anne, tried to solve the Scottish problem once and for all by establishing the Presbyterian Church in Scotland and by uniting England and Scotland under one government in 1707. The Presbyterian majority was restive, however, because of the loss of political independence, and disgruntled Highlanders, Anglicans, and Catholics launched Jacobite rebellions in 1715 and 1745. Eventually the British government consolidated its power over the Highlands, but many Scots refused to acknowledge the legitimacy of the government. As a people they did not become as unified as the En-

glish in the eighteenth century, and many of them never felt part of
the larger British entity.[49]

The political situation and the homicide problem were even worse
in Ireland. The conquest of Ireland was bloody, especially in the southwest, the seat of rebellion against English colonization, and in Ulster,
where Irish lands were expropriated and handed to Protestant proprietors, who resettled them primarily with Scots Presbyterians. Immediately after the Glorious Revolution the new Scots-Irish were taxed to
support the Anglican Church and were barred from holding office,
voting, celebrating the Lord's Supper, or performing marriages and
burials. Over time, however, the Anglo-Irish regime softened its stance,
and it eventually granted Protestant dissenters the rights to vote and to
hold office. The Scots-Irish became less alienated from the government; some even came to see themselves as part of the ruling Protestant minority. The homicide indictment rate fell gradually in Armagh
and Tyrone, heavily Scots counties in Ulster, from 10 per 100,000
adults per year in the 1730s and 1740s to 7 per 100,000 by the 1760s
and 1770s.[50]

As a whole, Ireland remained more homicidal than England. Agrarian violence was still endemic in the 1760s and 1770s. Vigilantes like
the White Boys (Catholics) and the Oakboys (a coalition of Presbyterians, Anglicans, and Catholics) hamstrung cattle, drove sheep over
cliffs, tore down houses, and burned barns and haystacks. They attacked landowners, middlemen, and collaborators, branding them,
cutting off pieces of their ears, and running wool cards over their
flesh. Catholics remained homicidal wherever they had suffered the
worst violence at the hands of Protestant settlers and the English government. In the southwest their homicide rate was probably at least 14
per 100,000 adults per year. But Irish Protestants were also homicidal,
and outside of Ulster they probably committed homicide at about the
same rate that Catholics did. They, too, felt discriminated against, especially by British trade and tariff policies, which damaged the Irish
economy. Political alienation, ethnic and religious hatred, and disrespect for the courts and other institutions ran deep in Ireland, and all
those factors kept the homicide rate high.[51]

Scots and Irish immigrants brought their homicidal tendencies with
them to North America. They were not numerous enough in New England to raise the homicide rate appreciably there in the colonial

era, although the Scots-Irish, who were largely Presbyterians from Ulster, were more than twice as likely to be murdered or to commit murder as other colonists. However, because they accounted for only 12 percent of the population, they raised the region's homicide rate by only 10 percent. They also appear to have assimilated to New England's nonhomicidal culture fairly quickly. They committed homicide in New England at less than half the rate they did in Ulster in the mid-eighteenth century. That rate might have been even lower had they not been concentrated on New England's northern frontier, where homicide rates were higher for everyone.[52]

In Virginia, where the homicide rate was much higher than in New England, the Scots-Irish had a reputation for extraordinary violence. They appear to have brought fighting techniques like biting and eye-gouging to the colonies, but these were meant to show ferocity and humiliate the victim, not to kill, and they were immediately adopted by non-Scots. The Scots-Irish were 26 percent more likely to be murdered or to commit murder than other colonists, but had they not been concentrated on the frontier, they might have had the same homicide rate as English, Welsh, and German colonists, who killed each other in the Chesapeake at roughly the same rate that the Scots-Irish did in Ulster. When political stability came to the Shenandoah Valley in 1765, its homicide rate fell from over 20 per 100,000 adult colonists per year to 8 per 100,000, despite the continuing influx of Scots-Irish settlers. Scots-Irish homicide rates went down along with everyone else's, and by the end of the century they were almost indistinguishable from those of other white Virginians.[53]

Catholic immigrants from Ireland stood out more than Presbyterian immigrants from Ulster. In Virginia, Irish Catholics were 56 percent more likely than other colonists to be murdered or to commit murder; and in New England they were twice as likely to be murdered and four times as likely to commit murder. Irish Catholics were disproportionately homicidal in part because so many of them were single men who came to the New World as sailors or convict servants, and they felt no kinship with Protestant colonists. They also brought violent ways with them from Ireland. It would take time for them to forge a sense of solidarity with the English or Scots-Irish—or with each other. They were less cohesive across class lines than other ethnic groups and more likely to kill one another, particularly if someone questioned their integrity, their faith, their national honor, or their manhood. Even so, the Irish made up too small a share of the colonial population to raise homicide rates appreciably, and like the Scots-Irish they were less homicidal in New England than they had been in Europe.[54]

The homicide rate among unrelated colonists in the Chesapeake remained much higher than the rate in New England in the early eighteenth century: 9 per 100,000 adults per year compared to only 1 per 100,000. Part of the explanation is that class lines were more significant in the Chesapeake than they were in New England. Although indentured servitude contributed less to the homicide rate in the eighteenth century than it had in the mid-seventeenth, and the decline in murders of bound servants was evidence that planters and overseers had changed how they viewed and treated poor whites, poor whites did not seem to feel any more charitable toward people who were better off than they were, nor were they more resigned to their fate as subordinates in a decidedly hierarchical society. The number of murdered masters, mistresses, and overseers fell by two-thirds after 1675, but that number did not fall faster than the proportion of colonists who owned bound servants. The rate at which masters and overseers were murdered may even have increased: before 1675–76, bound servants in Maryland and Virginia had been three and a half times more likely than masters or overseers to end up as homicide victims, but thereafter masters and overseers were more likely than servants to be homicide victims. The decrease in class feeling associated with the rise of racial slavery and racial solidarity appears to have been one-sided.[55]

The use of transported convicts as bound laborers may have increased the homicide risk for masters and overseers after 1717, when Parliament first gave British courts the power to sentence convicted felons to penal servitude in the colonies instead of hanging them. Between 1718 and 1775, 50,000 convict servants from England, Scotland, and Ireland landed in the Chesapeake. Colonial assemblymen and counselors tried repeatedly to ban the importation of convict servants, but Parliament was eager to shift Britain's crime problem to the colonies. Yet it would be a mistake to blame convict laborers for the continuing violence against masters and overseers. They were almost all property offenders, and they appear to have been only slightly more prone to violence than other colonists, except when they were on the run. The fact that nonconvict servants killed most of the murdered masters and overseers suggests that this homicide problem stemmed from the servant-master relationship itself and the hostility of poor whites toward planters.[56]

Persistent class tension in the South manifested itself in the number of Virginians and Marylanders who killed one another at public events like elections, militia musters, horse races, shooting contests, boxing matches, or sessions of the county courts. Living in a society in which colonists remained divided by caste and class did not instill a yearning for class warfare in freemen of poor or middling circumstances. Instead they felt a desperate hunger for status and prestige and a fear of losing face and falling to the lowest levels of society. For most men suffering acute anxiety about status, it was impossible to walk away from a challenge or an insult. At Dew's Horse Race Ground in Richmond County, Virginia, John Oldham got into an argument with John Hutchins and claimed he could beat him in a fight. A crowd gathered to watch them, shouting, "Well done Oldham," "Well done Hutchins," whenever one of them landed a crushing blow. Finally Hutchins collapsed. Oldham did not mean to kill him, and was sorry that he did; but neither man was willing to stop until one of them was unconscious. Anxiety about status may have intensified in the 1710s and 1720s, when the rate at which male colonists were murdered in Virginia by unrelated colonists rose once again.[57]

Occasionally the gentry were drawn into such contests. George Wortham, a wealthy planter and captain of the local militia in Middlesex County, Virginia, attended a militia muster with Benjamin Davis, a poor young man. The two men retired with other militia members to a tavern in the county courthouse, and both were soon drunk. Davis' pride was already wounded, for Wortham had asked him earlier if he would come and work for him and by doing so had drawn attention to the difference in their social standing. Davis began to take offense at everything Wortham said. When Wortham finally told him to keep quiet and "not to concern himself with that which did not belong to him," Davis drew his sword. Wortham fended him off repeatedly, but Davis persisted, and eventually Wortham had to kill him. Lethal fights on public occasions, especially elections, could occur anywhere in the colonial world. But New England saw fewer such deaths, because most men there believed that they were as good as anyone else and could advance as far as they wanted. In the Chesapeake there was less social mobility because the planter elite had a near-stranglehold on the social hierarchy.[58]

Although the Chesapeake had persistently higher homicide rates than New England, and although Irish and Scots-Irish immigrants did have higher rates for a time, there was an abrupt decline in the homicide rate among unrelated people in the colonies as a whole in the last quarter of the seventeenth century. The decline persisted through the 1760s, in part because of ongoing warfare against France and its Native American allies, which renewed and intensified the colonists' sense of religious and racial solidarity, particularly in New England, and kept them tightly bound to one another and to the British Empire. A third of New England's adult males served in the militia during King George's War (1744–1748) and the French and Indian War (1754–1760). Virginia did not find itself on the front lines until the latter conflict, but it committed a large supply of men and matériel to that war, and the homicide rate in the Chesapeake plummeted to its lowest level in history. Frontier violence remained a problem in the Shenandoah Valley, but the rate in the Chesapeake fell from 9 per 100,000 adults per year to less than 5 per 100,000 as loyalty to Britain grew and hatred of the French and Indians reached a fever pitch (Figure 1.3).[59]

Colonial identity, like British identity as a whole, was shaped by war. British Protestants, colonists included, defined themselves by what they were not; there was little place in their society for Catholics who refused to conform or who persisted in supporting a Catholic Stuart dynasty. Their image of themselves as a people was highly positive. The unprecedented economic success that the colonists and the British Empire enjoyed in the mid-eighteenth century fostered pride in Anglo-American culture, with its enterprise, ingenuity, and enlightened approach to science and the arts. The colonists also took pride in their political system, especially as political stability increased in the eighteenth century. Contested elections and party strife were permanent features of the political scene, but constitutional government, representative institutions, and the orderly succession of monarchs were an improvement over what the rest of the world had to offer. And the British public—active, informed, and opinionated—was itself a source of pride. The political and sectarian controversies of the Civil War and Restoration had produced bitter feelings and social conflict, but they had also laid the foundation at home and in the colonies for national awareness, national feeling, and an empowered citizenry, by producing a profusion of newsletters, pamphlets, and sermons that people from all walks of life could debate at coffeehouses, churches, taverns, and clubs. By the time of the Glorious Revolution, the British public was a force to be reckoned with throughout the empire.[60]

Success bred faith in the system, which bred more success, more trust in political leaders, and greater national solidarity. Eventually British identity encompassed not only the English but also the Scots, the Welsh, and the Scots-Irish. The rise in national feeling may have had an especially strong impact on the way the poor and the middle class saw themselves, by giving them a sense of pride in Britain's accomplishments and a sense of their special destiny. Only Irish Catholics remained wholly beyond the pale, derided, like the French, as a superstitious, indolent, violent people.[61]

Once colonial homicide rates dropped, the culture changed in ways that helped keep rates low. In Virginia, for example, once areas emerged from frontier conditions everyone—even the poor—began to turn to the county courts to resolve personal differences. They filed dozens of civil suits in every county every year for slander, trespass, assault (which included threats and verbal abuse), and assault and battery (which included physical violence). In long-established counties an average of one of every fifty white men were involved in any given year as complainants or defendants in a civil suit for assault or slander.[62] Because very few of the files for these civil suits have survived, it is impossible to know what they were about, but if surviving files from Rockbridge County, Virginia, are any indication, they involved the kinds of disputes that at an earlier date might well have led to murder. Major Alexander Stuart, for instance, sued John Thompson for slander. Thompson had claimed

that a certain Gentleman over heard [Stuart] make an appointment with a negro wench, and that same Gentleman watched sd Stuart until he and the negro wench came to the place appointed or the place of action. Then sd Gentleman returned to a company and asked if they wanted to see Sport and then went back to the place where [Stuart] & the negro wench was, with sundry others with him and found said [Stuart] acting with sd negro wench, that one of the Company took sd [Stuart] by the foot and Disingaged him from off the said Negro wench, and notwithstanding so large a Company was present, [Stuart] Scrambeled and indeavored to Replace him self again on the said negro wench.

Stuart also sued Thomas Paxton, like himself a wealthy planter, for repeating this story.[63]

In the mid-seventeenth century a gentleman like Stuart would have horsewhipped Thompson and challenged Paxton, who was his peer, to a duel. In the eighteenth century the desire for revenge was more often satisfied in court, even though half of all slander suits and three-fourths of all assault suits were settled or dropped before trial, and those that ended in guilty verdicts usually resulted in small damage awards. Most suits were intended merely to demonstrate that the plaintiff was a man who would stand up for his rights. They were not meant to bankrupt the defendant. They thus reflected the less homicidal turn in the culture of Virginia and Maryland as much as they helped shape it.[64]

In New England the decline in homicides was likewise followed by a shift in male culture that helped keep rates low. Changes in genteel manners in the late seventeenth and early eighteenth centuries fostered an appreciation of men who used wit rather than force to triumph over adversaries in politics and in personal disputes. Humor, self-deprecation, control of one's temper, and attentiveness to the feelings of others became the hallmarks of the gentleman. Politics became less combative. Good manners, conversational skills, and a sharp pen were vital to success in a political world that centered upon coffeehouses, soirees, contested elections, and newspapers. There was less fighting and more satirical writing and repartee, skills that were valued not only by the gentry but also by farmers, artisans, and laborers.[65]

Instead of fighting, young men in Connecticut started to play a version of the dozens, which in a patriarchal culture meant running down each other's fathers. Two rival gangs of young men ran into each other on a street in Lebanon in the summer of 1701 and immediately went at it. Eleazer Fitch asked Eleazer Mudge "who made him." Thomas Bernard tried to calm the waters by saying that God had made them all, but Fitch turned to Bernard "and said who made you I know not but who ever he was I wished he had his trident off and you were all Three dam'd together." Bernard asked Fitch "whether his father taught him such Language," to which Fitch replied, "dont tell me of my father. . . . I know who got you my bob Tailed Dog got you and you are all Tail and yet it[']s all ye part of a man y^t belongs to you." As the exchange heated up, the boys' Puritan antecedents came to the fore. One young man called his adversary "the scum of Sodom." Another declared, "I am going to Heaven. . . . You are fire brands of Hell. You are scorched already." This was tame stuff by modern standards, but it still ended up in court. Bernard and his friends brought charges against Fitch for blasphemy, but the court found Mudge guilty of calling Fitch "a Devill Worshiper," and all were found guilty of quarreling.[66]

Using wit against rivals also gave outsiders a nonviolent means of humbling their would-be superiors and had a calming effect on public life generally. The favorite targets of New England satirists were the self-righteous, especially the ministers of orthodox churches. Young Benjamin Franklin, who was too poor to attend Harvard, made fun of Harvard-educated ministers in the early 1720s in the famous "Silence Do-Good" letters written for his freethinking brother's newspaper. The tradition of satire continued through the early 1760s, when a writer for the *New Hampshire Gazette* suggested a remedy for the colony's high taxes and low morals: fire all the ministers and have them open taverns, where they could preach to the individuals who needed their services most. Such satires, which were widely disseminated and repeatedly rehearsed, gave Anglicans, freethinkers, and young journeymen a voice, helped reconcile them to New England's social order, and lessened the chances that alienation would break out into violence.[67]

The continuing low homicide rate among unrelated colonists in New England and the Chesapeake correlated with other changes in colonial society. The fact that a greater proportion of the population was native-born improved prospects for social solidarity. The economy strengthened after 1715, so that poor and middle-income men had a better chance of getting ahead, and their improved prospects helped persuade them that the colonial social hierarchy was legitimate. But like the changes in male culture, these shifts occurred after the homicide rate had fallen. The major changes in homicide rates coincided with the expansion of religious, racial, and political solidarity and the improved stability and legitimacy of government that had occurred in the late seventeenth century.

The decline in the homicide rate came later in North Carolina than in New England or the Chesapeake, but by the mid-eighteenth century it appears that North Carolina also had a low homicide rate, and for much the same reasons (Figure 2.2). North Carolina was far more homicidal than the Chesapeake in the early eighteenth century, because Indian warfare and political strife (including three rebellions against the colonial government) had periodically reduced the colony to lawlessness. But as racial slavery took hold in North Carolina in the 1720s and 1730s, white solidarity increased, and as the colony's government became more effective, the homicide rate declined and was soon comparable to the Chesapeake's—probably 12 per 100,000 adult

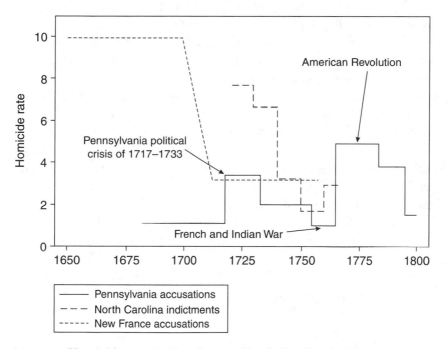

Figure 2.2 Homicide rates in New France, North Carolina, and Pennsylvania, 1650–1800 (per 100,000 persons per year). Pennsylvania, 1775–1783, is extrapolated from 1764–1774. *Sources:* Lachance (1984: 132, 192); Spindel (1989: 57); Marietta and Rowe (1999: 29).

colonists per year on the eve of the French and Indian War and 6 per 100,000 during the war.[68]

Homicide rates followed a more complex pattern in Pennsylvania, but they, too, ended up low on the eve of the French and Indian War, and they fell to an even lower level during the war (Figure 2.2). The colony, which was settled by Quakers, Moravians, and other pietists in the 1680s and 1690s, initially had a very low homicide rate—around 2 per 100,000 adults per year. That rate was largely due to the stability of the Quaker-dominated government, the pietists' solidarity and commitment to nonviolence, and the absence of a staple crop, which almost eliminated the need for slaves or indentured servants. Most of the inhabitants were also willing to live in peace with Native Americans and to abide by the terms of treaties.[69]

However, the homicide rate surged in Pennsylvania from the late 1710s to the early 1730s, to probably 9 or more per 100,000 adults per year—the rate that had prevailed in New England before King Philip's War. The primary cause was a sudden influx of settlers from northern Ireland, Germany, and elsewhere. The arrival of thousands of non-English and non-Quaker immigrants made Quakers and pietists a minority, and the moral and religious solidarity that had prevailed in the colony was destroyed. Quakers and pietists found this new diversity distressing and felt they had been "invaded." They debated whether newcomers should be granted political rights. Relations between established residents and "foreigners" were tense, as they were among newcomers of different nationalities, and many poor immigrants were profoundly alienated from everyone. Germans killed Irishmen, Scotsmen killed Welshmen, indentured servants killed masters or fellow servants, and criminal gangs committed robbery murders. Quakers and other pietists did not themselves become homicidal, but beyond the bounds of their communities Pennsylvania became more so, repeating the pattern that took hold in New England in the mid-seventeenth century, when the society outside the Puritan community became more homicidal.[70]

Matters were made worse in Pennsylvania by an economic recession caused by an act of Parliament that prescribed a uniform rate of exchange for foreign coins to prevent tampering. Pennsylvania obeyed the new law, thanks to the influence of the Penn family and of Philadelphia's Quaker merchants, who were currying favor with the royal government; but other colonies did not. They offered better exchange rates, so Pennsylvania was drained of currency and entered a steep deflationary cycle. The governor of the colony, William Keith, took advantage of the hostility engendered by the monetary policy and organized a rebellion against the mercantile-proprietor party. With the support of non-Quaker immigrants, the poor, and rural pietists, Keith approved issues of paper currency by the colonial government and staged rallies and riots against merchants and assemblymen who refused to support his economic agenda. He accused them of gouging the poor. "We all know it is neither the Great, the Rich, nor the Learned, that compose the Body of the People; and that Civil Government ought carefully to protect the poor laborious and industrious Part of Mankind."[71]

Keith's supporters mobbed the Philadelphia house of James Logan, the leader of the mercantile-proprietor party, destroyed stocks and pillories, and burned the stalls of butchers suspected of overcharging customers. Assemblymen who did not yield to Keith's supporters were harassed and beaten in the streets. Isaac Norris, a member of the mercantile-proprietor party and a defender of the status quo, complained that Keith had "fond us an United Peaceable people & left us by his wicked politicks & Artifice Divided & in partys." Keith fled to England in 1728 to avoid prosecution for sedition, and his political movement crumbled soon afterward. But while it was active, law and order broke down in Philadelphia, and hostility intensified throughout the colony, dividing people along class, ethnic, and religious lines. As a result, homicide and other violent crimes increased.[72]

Pennsylvania also experienced a wave of frontier homicides in the 1720s and early 1730s. Many of the new immigrants flocking to the colony were encouraged to settle on Indian land. The sudden invasion of Europeans led to a rash of murders in the backcountry as settlers and unscrupulous traders skirmished with the Delaware, Shawnee, Conestoga, and other Native peoples who had previously lived in peace with the colonists.[73]

When political calm and prosperity returned to Pennsylvania in the mid-1730s, the homicide rate fell to a moderate level of about 4 or 5 per 100,000 adults per year. The government wrung concessions from Native Americans in 1732, 1736, and 1737 that more than doubled the amount of land open to settlement, and the number of frontier killings decreased as the Indians decamped and moved west. Naturalization laws were liberalized, and the mercantile-proprietary party came to see the wisdom of paper currency. Gradually a new political consensus emerged, and non-Quakers and non-English immigrants began to take part in the political process. Together with the return of prosperity and a flexible monetary policy, the decision to allow immigrants to become citizens helped create a political rapprochement that restored the rudiments of order, although it did not revive the fellow feeling that had prevailed among colonists in the 1680s and 1690s.[74]

During the French and Indian War the homicide rate in Pennsylvania fell to about 2 per 100,000 adults per year as new grounds for solidarity were discovered in a hatred of France and its Indian allies. The colony sent thousands of troops to the front, while Quaker diplomats worked behind the scenes to restore peaceful relations between the colony and its Native neighbors. Pennsylvania's frontiers saw a great many homicides, but away from the frontier, Pennsylvania, like Virginia and North Carolina, became less homicidal during the war.[75] By the early 1760s every colony in British North America, not just those in New England, was either moderately homicidal or nonhomicidal.

The British colonies were not unique in becoming less homicidal in the late seventeenth and the eighteenth centuries. Homicide rates declined in French Canada and throughout western Europe as political instability receded as a result of stronger courts, better law enforcement, more powerful central governments, and (at least in Great Britain and British North America) greater religious tolerance and stronger national feeling. England saw its homicide indictment rate drop by half from the late seventeenth to the early eighteenth century (Figure 1.1), and New France saw its rate drop by two-thirds (Figure 2.2). Data from the Netherlands, France, Switzerland, Sweden, Finland, and Ireland show homicide rates falling there too. No nation had lower rates than Britain or its colonies, but both western Europe and North America were moving in the same direction.[76]

African American Homicide

The homicide rate for African Americans in the Chesapeake and New England was higher than the rate for European colonists in the late seventeenth and early eighteenth centuries—at least 10–15 per 100,000 adults per year (Figures 1.3 and 2.3). The higher rate is not surprising. Slavery and violence were inextricably linked in the years when racial slavery was being established in the colonies. Slaveowners had to use force to persuade newly enslaved people that they no choice but to accept their position at the bottom of a new social hierarchy, and, as with indentured servitude, there was no guarantee that owners or overseers would use force in a rational way or that slaves would submit to it. Whippings and beatings could end in death if the men and women administering them lost control, and slaves could respond violently. It is interesting to note that women of both races were involved in an eighth of the killings of masters, overseers, or male slaves and in nearly a third of the killings of mistresses or female slaves—proportions similar to those that prevailed in murders under indentured servitude.[77]

In the early days of colonial slavery whites who killed slaves often revealed the profound ignorance that lay at the root of racial prejudice. Joseph Lawton, a tenant farmer from Suffield, Massachusetts, seemed to feel that he had been swindled because his young servant, Congo,

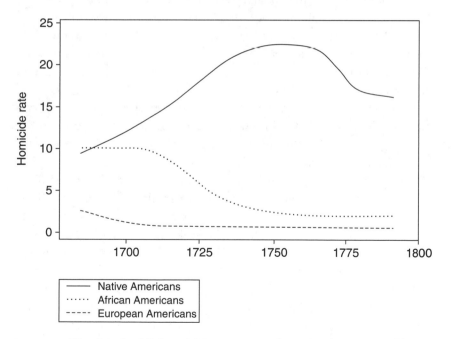

Figure 2.3 Unrelated-adult homicide rates in New England by race, 1677–1797 (per 100,000 persons per year).

newly arrived from Africa, could not understand English. Neighbors overheard him raging at the bewildered boy. When they realized that it had been some time since they had seen Congo, they became suspicious and asked Lawton what he had done with him. Lawton replied that he had nothing to answer for. "Why is it any hurt to kill him? Has he got any soul?" The young man's decomposed body was found in a brook the following spring, the skull crushed.[78]

Most white colonists were determined to dominate a people whom they considered inferior. In 1721 a free laborer named London exchanged friendly barbs with William Ripp, a white laborer, as they unloaded a small boat in the harbor at Newbury, Massachusetts. "In jest," Ripp called London a "Black Rogue." London responded by "telling him He was No more [a] black Rogue than himself." Ripp and London took their "Jocose Speeches . . . in good part," but another white crewman, Ralph Wheeler, asked London "how he dar'd to Speak Such words to a White Man?" London told Wheeler "to mind his Own Business," and Wheeler attacked him. London died of his injuries. In another incident that turned deadly, William Hamilton, an apprentice for a merchant in Salem, shot one of his employer's slaves through the head. Hamilton claimed that his pistol had gone off accidentally while he and the slave were roughhousing, but the grand jury concluded that Hamilton, unable to stomach being beaten by a black man, had shot him deliberately. He was indicted for murder.[79]

In dealing with African Americans whites often behaved as if it was their prerogative to take the law into their own hands, and from the very beginning, agents of the law were overenthusiastic in their use of force against black men. In 1741 three white men in Roxbury, Massachusetts, tried to elicit a confession from a slave suspected of stealing. They tied him to a tree and beat him to death. In Boston in 1746, Jonathan Simpson Jr. ran into the street crying for help. He had tried to whip his father's slave, Bristol, and Bristol had drawn a knife on him. Three watchmen came to his aid; in the course of trying to subdue Bristol they strangled him.[80]

Sources on homicides of Africans by European colonists are far less rich for the Chesapeake and the Shenandoah Valley in the eighteenth century than for New England, so it is impossible to know with certainty if cultural antagonism or conceptions of racial superiority and privilege played as important a role in slave homicides there. But the large number of examinations of owners and overseers who were suspected of beating or whipping slaves to death, and the large number of claims for compensation for rebels, runaways, and felons killed by white posses suggest that colonists in Virginia and Maryland believed they had a harder time than New Englanders did in establishing their authority, maintaining discipline, and curbing resistance. Living in a society that was a quarter black, southern whites also seemed to be more fearful of signs of resistance than northerners were.

And southern whites had good reason to be afraid. If newspaper accounts are any measure, slaves in Virginia and Maryland resisted or rebelled more often than their northern counterparts, perhaps feeling that their chances of success were greater because of their numbers. In Hanover County, Virginia, an aggressive young overseer's assistant who had been hired to get more work out of the field hands on a large plantation got into an argument with a slave who did not get the cooking fire ready before sunrise. The slave took a swing at the assistant with an ax and wrestled him to the ground. Other slaves joined in, and they beat the man badly. Eventually they let him go, but they then tied up the head overseer and an elderly neighbor who came to his aid and beat both of them. The assistant returned with an armed party of twelve men and two boys, and the slaves—forty or fifty in number—rushed them with clubs and staves. The whites opened fire, killing three slaves and wounding five.[81]

In Virginia and Maryland rebellious slaves were routinely killed if they resisted arrest. Such deaths were rare in New England. Virginians and Marylanders also killed a high proportion of runaways and fugitives from justice. Slaves were chased into rivers or ponds, where they drowned, or they were cornered and shot. Jack, a slave of Edmund Scarburgh of Accomack County, had run away after wounding a woman owned by one of Scarburgh's relatives. Scarburgh's overseer found Jack hiding in a cellar, and when Jack rushed him, the overseer shot him in the chest. Scores of fugitives and runaways suffered the same fate. Counting those who killed themselves rather than surrender, and those captured who died in jails from abuse, malnutrition, or exposure, enough fugitive slaves were killed that they alone would have given African Americans a death rate in Virginia of 2 per 100,000 black adults per year—twice as high as the homicide rate for all New England colonists.[82]

Racial slavery was initially less homicidal than indentured servitude had been in the mid-seventeenth century in part because of timing: after 1675 colonial society was probably less homicidal for everyone, including slaves, although the lack of good data on slaves before 1675 makes it impossible to say. The lower initial homicide rate for slaves was also tied to economics. Slaves were more expensive than indentured servants. Crippling or killing a slave ran contrary to a slaveowner's interests: he could earn a return on his investment only if the slave was productive for many years. It was wiser to sell slaves who were troublesome. Even though such slaves sold at a discount, a partial loss was preferable to a total loss.

Murders of blacks by whites began to decline everywhere in the mid-eighteenth century as slavery became more firmly established and whites became more confident of their ability to keep blacks in their place. In New England, the Chesapeake, and the Shenandoah Valley, the homicide rate for blacks fell from roughly 10 to 15 per 100,000 adults per year to 4 per 100,000 between 1730 and 1775 (Figures 1.3 and 2.3). In New England, murders of slaves by owners and overseers simply stopped after 1720. Other kinds of murders of blacks by whites almost disappeared after Bristol's death at the hands of Boston watchmen in 1746, and those that did occur had little to do with racial prejudice or a desire to dominate blacks. The circumstances of the homicides that occurred in the Chesapeake and the Shenandoah Valley are largely unknown, but, as in New England, murders by owners, overseers, and other whites fell sharply.[83]

What would account for the simultaneous decline in the eighteenth century in lethal violence against blacks in New England, the Chesapeake, and the Shenandoah Valley? Similar forces may have been at work in each region. As enslaved Africans adjusted to life in the New World and European colonists accepted the humanity (if not the equality) of Africans, many slaveowners adopted a paternalistic attitude toward their servants. Lethal discipline declined. The routines involved in tobacco production, mixed farming, domestic service, seafaring, and small-scale manufacturing—unlike those in rice or cotton production—required close contact and cooperation between slaves and their masters, mistresses, or overseers. In such circumstances, personal relationships could develop between owners and slaves. However strained, such relationships helped the economic logic of slavery prevail: the destruction of a slave meant the loss of a sizable investment. During the eighteenth century political leaders, newspaper editors, and other influential colonists also changed the face of slavery by emphasizing that abusive owners undermined the institution. Every time they flew into "fits of passion," they sowed the seeds of rebellion in all slaves. Humane treatment and moderate correction were the best ways to ensure loyal service and social peace.[84]

It is more difficult to explain the decline in murders of blacks by other whites. It appears that by midcentury European colonists in New England began to think of Africans as members of their communities—and in most cases as worthy ones, if memorial notices for African neighbors, servants, slaves, and coworkers are any indication. The heedless homicide of blacks became unthinkable. Prejudice, discrimination, and everyday violence persisted, but in ways that did not brutalize most blacks. Efforts got underway during and after the Revolution to abolish slavery and grant blacks basic civil rights. New England colonists did not extend such consideration to Native Americans. They murdered them at an alarming rate through the 1790s.

The reasons for the decline in murders of blacks by whites other than owners and overseers may have been less benign in the Chesapeake and the Shenandoah Valley, although the forces at work in New England may have been at work in Virginia or Maryland too. But in the South whites had to consider the consequences of losing their tempers or taking the law into their own hands when someone else's slave provoked them, because by the mid-eighteenth century slaveowners were more likely to sue whites who injured or killed their slaves. Slaveowners dominated Virginia's and Maryland's courts, and they were quick to hand down judgments against whites who used lethal or disabling violence against other people's slaves without good cause. In addition, because of the decline in slave plots and rebellions, fear had abated in the white community. Whites were less anxious when they encountered black people they did not know on the road or in the woods. In the early eighteenth century, whites who met black men they considered suspicious were more likely to shoot them.

As remarkable as the decline in the rate at which whites murdered blacks was the low rate of black-on-black murder. From the first, African Americans were murdered by other African Americans at only half the rate at which they were murdered by European colonists. Ethnic antagonism among African-born slaves led frequently to quarrels in the late seventeenth and early eighteenth centuries, but on the whole Africans did not bring western and central Africa's high homicide rate with them to North America. Contemporary Africa's high rate was first and foremost a consequence of the slave trade, which had unleashed lethal conflicts over trade and territory. Every African within reach of the slave trade lived on a contested frontier, where rival African and European powers vied for control. Political murders, robbery murders, and murders to capture slaves were endemic, as were murders of male prisoners of war who could not be sold overseas or incorporated safely into their captors' villages. The slave trade also encouraged ritual homicides of slaves in Africa. Among the Bobangi of the Zaire basin, it was common to kill slaves to mark trade or peace agreements between neighboring chiefs or to accompany honored owners to the afterlife. Governments in Dahomey, Benin, and the western Sahel sacrificed slaves to celebrate royal ancestors. The Mangbetu of northeastern Zaire killed and ate slaves (or pretended to eat them) to show off their wealth. Such homicides did not survive the Atlantic passage.[85]

Like European colonists, Africans carried their belief in witchcraft to the New World, but it is doubtful that such beliefs led to many homicides in the colonies. In western and central Africa people often murdered suspected witches, and it may well be that some Africans accused of poisoning other Africans in the New World were actually practicing witchcraft or testing or punishing suspected witches. It is likely, however, that most suspects were falsely accused or were practicing medicine without the permission of their owners (a crime for slaves under colonial law) rather than trying to do harm. There is no evidence that witchcraft had anything to do with fatal or near-fatal poisonings: poison might simply have been the safest and convenient method of killing another slave. In any event, the knowledge of poisons and the customs associated with their use faded relatively quickly in New England and the Chesapeake. Slaves there found it more difficult to preserve their African heritage than did slaves in the Lower South or the Caribbean because there were so few of them. Although most slaves in the Chesapeake came from Upper Guinea, Lower Guinea, or Angola, they rarely lived close to other slaves who came from the same villages and shared their traditions, and their lives were more closely intertwined with those of whites.[86]

After 1730 the rate at which African Americans murdered one another fell in the Chesapeake and the Shenandoah Valley to only a third of the rate at which European Americans killed one another, and such murders all but disappeared in New England, where blacks murdered other blacks at roughly the same rate at which poor whites killed other poor whites. There is only one homicide in the surviving records, and it was a manslaughter rather than a murder. In 1750, Poro, who was owned by a man in Marshfield, Massachusetts, picked a fight with a fellow slave named Gambo, and Gambo struck him on the head with a stick. Poro died the next day. All other black homicide victims in colonial New England were victims of whites.[87]

The patterns are nearly identical in the Chesapeake and in the Shenandoah Valley. The records are not as complete or diverse are they are for New England, but those that survive show a steady decline in the rate at which black adults were murdered by other blacks. In a few instances slaves went on rampages against their masters or mistresses and attacked fellow slaves as well as whites, for reasons unknown. In 1736 a female slave broke into William Cox's house, stole goods, burned his tobacco shed, nearly murdered his son, and killed her children and three of his other slaves before drowning herself. In 1755 a slave of Stephen Watkins murdered one of Watkins' grown children and a fellow slave before hanging himself, and in 1761 a slave on a plantation in Maryland murdered his mistress, his mistress' son, and a female slave and tried to kill a slave child.[88] Most of these slaves appear to have been mentally ill. The actual homicide rate among blacks was probably no more than 2 per 100,000 adults per year.

The decline in homicides of blacks by blacks in the Chesapeake and the Shenandoah Valley was probably a consequence of social and cultural change. By midcentury the size of plantations had increased, the proportion of native-born blacks in the population had risen, there were extended families and kinship networks, bonds among neighbors had intensified, and ethnic divisions among slaves had diminished. The African American experience of banding together to protect one another against abuse coalesced into a shared identity. All those forces forged a racial solidarity among blacks that militated against lethal violence, even among strangers.[89]

Solidarity among blacks may have been even more intense in New England, because there were so few of them and they were concentrated in a handful of towns and counties. In New Hampshire a third of blacks lived in Portsmouth; in Massachusetts a third to a half lived in Boston; in Connecticut nearly half lived in New London or Fairfield County; and in Rhode Island three-fourths lived in Newport or King's County. Cultural prohibitions against homicide may also have been stronger in New England, as they were for working-class whites. Black Yankees adopted the same ironic, self-deprecating humor that white working-class Yankees did. They ridiculed people who put on airs or were holier-than-thou, and they defended themselves or cut others down to size with wit and humor.[90] To this day, African Americans are less likely to commit murder or to be murdered in New England than anywhere else, just as European Americans are.

These cultural adaptations did not mean that slaves in New England accepted their lot. In fact, as soon as masters and mistresses stopped murdering slaves in the 1720s, slaves started murdering their masters, mistresses, and in a few instances white neighbors or strangers. The numbers are small, but they are consistent with those from the Chesapeake and the Shenandoah Valley. Lethal violence against whites, which was almost unheard of during the early decades of slavery, quintupled in the 1730s through the 1750s. Part of that increase stemmed from the increased proportion of blacks in the population, but the rate at which blacks murdered whites increased threefold.[91]

Slaves used clubs, knives, hatchets, and poison to kill whites. In 1731 in Wallingford, Connecticut, Hannah, a slave who belonged to a prominent family, attacked her master's niece and a neighbor with a knife. In 1745, Jeffrey, a slave of a farmer in Mendon, Massachusetts, cut off his mistress' nose and then severed her head with a hatchet. Another slave named Phillis poisoned her master by lacing his gruel with arsenic. There were many similar cases in the Chesapeake and the Shenandoah Valley, but in the South there were also a number of cases that involved two or more slaves who conspired to kill whites. Three slaves beat and kicked their master to death in Strafford County, Virginia, in 1769. In 1753 two slaves struck an overseer with an ax in Accomack County, Virginia, after he beat one of them for being late. They then picked him up and threw him on a pile of burning brush. Still alive, he tried to crawl out of the flames, but they smashed his head with a piece of wood and pushed him back into the fire.[92]

The surge in black-on-white homicides throughout the colonies was in a broad sense political: it represented a decision on the part of a small number of slaves to stage personal rebellions against oppression. In the early days of slavery, many slaves, especially in the Chesapeake, resisted by running away or plotting rebellion with other slaves, but their efforts were so unsuccessful (and so likely to end in death) that by the 1720s and 1730s few blacks were willing to follow that course. Those who were angry, desperate, and willing to risk death had only one option: an individual act of violence against whites. The sentiments that slaves gave voice to when they committed such acts of violence indicated an awareness of their political nature. A black man who beat an apprentice to death in Philadelphia after the apprentice ordered him out of his master's yard expressed feelings that were not often revealed or freely spoken in the nation until the 1960s. A witness had heard him tell the apprentice that where he stood "was no Business of his or any white Dog alive, and that he would not go till he pleased." Another slave who murdered his master in New Jersey hinted at the rebellious feelings stirring in many blacks' hearts. As he was being led to the stake to be burned to death, he told white onlookers that "they had taken the Root, but left the Branches."[93]

These homicides declined as the revolutionary crisis unfolded in the 1760s and early 1770s. The possibilities that the Revolution opened up—rebellion, flight, manumission, or emancipation—may have alleviated the hopelessness and desperation that led some blacks to commit murder. The decline in fatalistic homicides may also have been rooted in increased opportunities for blacks to marry and form families after 1750. Family commitments may have been sufficient to discourage most blacks from killing whites, although the brutal punishments inflicted upon blacks who murdered whites, which included the mutilation and exposure of their corpses, may also have been a deterrent. Whatever the reason, in the early 1760s and 1770s blacks turned to other, milder forms of resistance against whites, such as arson and theft.[94]

Native American Homicide

As a result of the devastation of the Native populations of New England and the Chesapeake by war, disease, and dispossession, by the

1690s there were too few Native Americans left to have a significant impact on the colonists' homicide rates. At that time colonists outnumbered Native Americans ten to one in New England and twenty to one in the Chesapeake. By 1775 they outnumbered Natives in both places by more than 100 to 1. And after the devastating wars of 1675–76, Native Americans who lived near or among the colonists realized that retaliatory violence was futile. A few murders did occur, but from the 1690s until the Revolution every settled or enslaved Indian known to have murdered a white person was caught and put to death. By the eighteenth century even Native Americans who lived farther away from European settlements were reluctant to kill whites except in times of war. The two main deterrents were desire for trade and fear of retribution. Native Americans defended their rights and settled scores on the frontier, but they preferred to do so during wars, when they could count on the help of Indian allies or the French and move their families to safety across the Blue Ridge Mountains or into Canada.[95]

Unlike African Americans and European Americans, however, Native Americans saw their homicide rate increase sharply in the mid-eighteenth century, at least in New England, where documentation is plentiful. There Native Americans were murdered by nonrelatives at a rate of 23 per 100,000 persons per year—more than ten times the rate for African Americans and twenty times the rate for European Americans (Figure 2.3). Indians were murdered by colonists at a much higher rate than colonists were murdered by Indians, even though colonists killed Native Americans for a very narrow range of reasons. On several occasions, Indians and colonists quarreled while hunting together, and the Indian was left dead. In most other known incidents, however, Native Americans were victims of terror or sheer indifference to the value of Indian lives. For sport, a gang of boys in Middleborough, Massachusetts, pushed Patience Seepat off a bridge into a mill pond, where she drowned. Six settlers in Wiscasset, Maine, took revenge on three Abenaki men shortly after the treaty ending King George's War was signed, and during the French and Indian War, thirty-five bounty hunters killed fourteen friendly Penobscots near Owl's Head Bay. Colonists who murdered Indians had little to fear from the law. Few were convicted, and several were freed from jail by friends before they could be tried.[96]

Native Americans were killed most often, however, by their fellow

Native Americans, especially between 1720 and 1760, when most tribes in southern New England lost their remaining lands and political autonomy, and when most tribes in northern New England suffered devastating losses in the three major wars fought there. A few of the murders, almost all of which involved men killing men, appeared to be traditional killings to avenge the deaths of relatives who had fallen in battle. Sam, who was hunting bear in southern Maine with a party of "Eastern" Indians, bragged about having killed a famous chief during Dummer's War. Unbeknownst to him, that chief was the father of one of his companions, who promptly struck Sam down with a hatchet. But Native culture had been transformed; there were no more political assassinations or deaths from ritual combat between rival leaders.[97] Native leaders sometimes found themselves on opposite sides in the struggle between the French and the English for supremacy in northern New England, and many fought against one another in the French-English wars, but political violence among Native Americans was for the most part confined to those wars. Native leaders were so well integrated into the French or English political systems, or so hamstrung by them, that traditional political violence ceased.

Other kinds of traditional homicides were also rare. There are no accounts from the eighteenth century of murders provoked by the desecration of a burial site or by speaking the name of a deceased sachem. In the mid-seventeenth century these affronts had to be avenged because they disturbed the spirits of the departed.[98] The spread of Christianity and the decline of traditional religious practices and of faith in the power of traditional spirits made such provocations less common and the need to respond less urgent.

What increased were homicides over insults, arguments, or gambling debts. Traditional culture had restrained conflict among Native males. Thomas Morton, a non-Puritan settler in Plymouth Colony who befriended neighboring Natives, remarked upon how little they quarreled with each other. They often ignored insults or challenges, especially from men they considered inferior. One sachem explained this forbearance to Roger Williams, saying that there was no reason for him to be concerned about "the barking of a Dog." William Wood, an early settler in Massachusetts, witnessed similar restraint during sporting events and games of chance.[99]

By the mid-eighteenth century, however, such restraint had all but disappeared, at least in southern New England. Native men attacked one another with little or no provocation. Sometimes alcohol played a part in unleashing violence, but most of these homicides stemmed from petty quarrels. Samuel Deerskins and Daniel Jones of Plymouth had been talking civilly for about an hour, when the subject changed to "a meething held among't ye Indians Sometime Before." Jones expressed his opinion; Deerskins told him he was a fool. Jones responded with harsh words and turned to the fire to light his pipe. Deerskins jumped up and stabbed him from behind. Joseph Quasson, who was serving in Maine as a provincial soldier during Dummer's War, got into an argument at camp with another Indian soldier and killed him with a shotgun blast to the testicles. Four Native whalers, also friends, quarreled at sea but decided to settle matters after the voyage because their captain forbade fighting on board. As soon as they docked, they had it out with boat hooks and harpoons. Two of them were killed. The other two quarreled later in their jail cell, so of the four friends only one was left alive.[100]

We can only speculate about why Native American men took out their frustrations on other Indians. There is no record of such petty homicides in northern New England, where Natives retained their tribal autonomy and appear to have developed a greater sense of solidarity across tribal and kinship lines than they had had in the early seventeenth century. Native American men in southern New England were responsible for most reported homicides of Indians by unrelated Indians. Cut adrift from their culture and politically powerless, they had left their families and villages to enter the labor market with whites as fishermen, whalers, farm laborers, and military scouts. It is possible that these men became soldiers and sailors not only because more desirable occupations were closed to them, but also because soldiering and fishing attracted alienated, violent men. The surviving sources do not reveal how the murderers felt about their lives, but the lack of proportion between the violence of their assaults and the immediate causes suggests that, like most beleaguered minorities who have little hope of changing the circumstances of their lives, they carried a great deal of anger with them wherever they went. The loss of their land, their freedom, and traditional ways of winning the respect of their peers unleashed the hostile and defensive emotions that led to murder.

By the end of the eighteenth century the homicide rate among un-related Native American adults had declined in New England. Most Natives regrouped in small settlements after losing their land or inter-married with African Americans to form an inclusive nonwhite caste at the bottom of New England's social hierarchy. Those changes halved the Indians' homicide rate (Figure 2.3), but in 1800 it was still ten times higher than the rates for blacks or whites.

CHAPTER 3

Family and Intimate Homicide in the First Two Centuries

Despite the dramatic surges and declines in the homicide rate among unrelated adults in the first two centuries of settlement, family and intimate homicide rates varied very little from the seventeenth through the early nineteenth centuries. The changing levels of violence among unrelated adults had a modest impact on relations between lovers, spouses, and other relatives, but by and large, family and intimate homicide rates followed a different pattern, because they were driven by forces that had little to do with the feelings and beliefs that correlated so strongly with homicides among unrelated adults.

Family and intimate homicides were extremely rare. In all of New England, for example, only about 35 spouses and 25 adult relatives were murdered before 1800. One or two lovers were killed, and no romantic rivals. The pattern differed only for Native Americans, whose family and intimate murder rate was fifteen to twenty times the rates for African Americans and European Americans. The rate peaked in the mid-eighteenth century, when Native American families came under intense pressure from warfare and the loss of their land to European encroachment.[1]

The character of family and intimate murders remained the same from the colonial period through the Revolution and the early national period. The perpetrators were usually men, and the victims were most often women. Women were killed in roughly 40 percent of homicides of adult relatives (parents, siblings, adult children, in-laws, step-relatives, and so on), in 80 percent of marital homicides, and in 67 percent of romance homicides among lovers in New England and the Chesapeake.[2]

Generally, in the Anglo-American world marriage, kinship, and romantic relationships were almost never lethally violent, in large part because of the mutual dependence that family ties fostered and because of the support extended by relatives, neighbors, and legal authorities to spouses, lovers, and family members who were wronged or abused. However, local conditions and cultural practices caused variations in lethal violence rates. Family and intimate murders were rare in England, yet they occurred there at probably two or three times the rate they did in New England, where the hardships of frontier life and the need for cooperation to keep small farms and family businesses afloat seem to have encouraged family members to pull together more than they did in the Old World. Rates in the Chesapeake were significantly higher than in England or New England. The high murder rate among unrelated adults in the Chesapeake may have had some effect on family and intimate relations, but the evidence also indicates that people in England and New England were more likely than people in the Chesapeake to intervene in family disputes to try to prevent lethal violence.[3]

Marital Homicide among European Americans

Marital murders have historically been a serious problem in many societies, and in some societies they still are, but they were rare in early modern England and in the Chesapeake and rarer still in New England from colonial times into the nineteenth century. Why were they uncommon? And why were marital homicide rates so stable compared to homicide rates among unrelated adults? The answer probably lies in the nature of marriage in the Anglo-American world. Relationships between spouses could be very violent, but they were almost never lethally violent. Extreme violence was usually held in check because of the peculiar balance of power between men and women, the ways wives and husbands depended on each other, and the willingness of friends, neighbors, and legal authorities to intervene in the most troubled relationships.

Although there is no way to tell exactly what proportion of marriages were violent, serious spouse abuse appears to have been widespread in both England and America from the sixteenth through the early nineteenth centuries. The violence also appears to have been proportionately the same in both places. Men committed the vast majority of life-threatening assaults, but there were also cases of aggravated husband abuse and mutual violence. According to court testimony, much of the women's violence was provoked, but some women were habitually violent and abused their husbands from the beginning of their marriages.[4]

Husbands and wives fought to change a spouse's behavior, to silence complaints about their own, and to defend themselves against violence. Arguments over adultery provoked a substantial percentage of marital assaults. Oliver Whipple of Hampton, New Hampshire, an attorney and magistrate, had beaten his wife Abigail on a number of occasions because she complained when he tried to seduce their servant girls. He threw a chair at her when she was seven months pregnant and told her he would "split" her brains out. Abigail fought back, but she was no match for him. When she threw a shoe at Oliver and kicked him, he picked her up and threw her against the stove. Robert Holt of St. Mary's County, Maryland, complained that his wife Dorothy and her lover had abused him so violently that he stood "in fear of [his] life."[5]

But the majority of marital violence stemmed from disputes over more commonplace issues like drinking, money, work, or children. The McNeils of Londonderry, New Hampshire, had once owned a substantial farm but had lost almost everything because of Josiah's drinking. His wife Elizabeth, an "industrious" woman who had "educated her Children well," had endured Josiah's drunken assaults for years, but by the time her children were teenagers, she had had enough. One winter day a neighbor called, and Elizabeth asked if he had come to see "the prisoner." There lay Josiah on the floor, bound hand and foot. On another occasion neighbors saw Josiah fleeing into the woods, his wife and son and daughters chasing him "with Clubs or Sticks in their hands." An hour later Josiah appeared at their door seeking protection. "His head and face was bloddy." The records of every county list hundreds of such assaults, many of them severe.[6]

Given the level of marital violence in the Anglo-American world from the seventeenth through the early nineteenth centuries, it is re-markable that so few spouses were murdered. But most marital vio-lence was not meant to kill; it was meant to punish and to inflict suffer-ing. In this period, most abuse stopped short of murder not only because people were afraid of the consequences if their violence be-came obvious, but also because at some level they knew that they needed their spouses if they were to survive in a struggling economy. Without them, who would keep the household running? Who would tend the shop and do the chores on the farm?

Marriages in the Anglo-American world were partnerships, but the terms of those partnerships differed from region to region. They were probably most nearly equal in New England. New England's Puritans did not believe that men and women were equal, but they did have a strong sense of the reciprocal obligations of husbands and wives and of the mutuality necessary for a successful marriage. And to succeed in New England's economy, couples needed all the help they could get from each other. Acquiring a shop or farm was a goal that New En-glanders achieved to a greater degree than anyone else in the Western world, and to a large extent both the ideal and the reality of indepen-dent proprietorship were born from a struggling regional econ-omy. New England was the poorest region in colonial America, but it had the greatest equality of wealth and the highest levels of self-employment. Survival and success depended on family labor and the production of diverse goods that could meet the demands of changing markets, local and international. In short, the regional economy re-quired husbands and wives to work in complementary ways.[7]

As letters and diaries from happier marriages reveal, most husbands and wives derived enormous satisfaction from establishing farms and businesses together. They may still have been unequal partners in the sense that husbands usually controlled finances and investments, yet a few came close, despite the patriarchal character of the society, to liv-ing as friends and equals. New Englanders typically married in their mid-twenties and brought some property and skills to their marriages. After the Revolution they made great strides toward lessening the in-equality in marriage by committing themselves to the universal educa-tion of both men and women. Female literacy rates soon approxi-mated those of men. As a result, New England had the highest literacy rate in the nation, and wives had a stronger hand in business affairs and in educating their children. American periodicals supported the movement toward greater equality in marriage: after the Revolution the proportion of fiction and nonfiction articles that embraced the idea that men should have power over women fell from 42 percent to 29 percent, and the proportion recommending that men and women should make decisions together rose from 12 percent to 27 percent.[8]

Of course, mutual regard did not always prevail in these domestic partnerships. Yet however angry one or both spouses became, they almost always stopped short of crippling or killing. Although much of the violence recounted in historical documents seems on the surface to stem from unfocused rage, in reality people were often using violence instrumentally, to defend or to change the terms of marital partnerships, or to express frustration over their inability to do so.[9] Mutual dependence could generate violence, but more often it seemed to set limits, especially after the Revolution, when abused spouses had the option of ending marriages that became too violent.

The typical marriage was somewhat different in the Chesapeake and in England. Women who were not indentured servants married earlier in the Chesapeake than in England or New England, so there was a wider gap between husbands and wives in age and experience. Fewer couples were self-employed in England than in the New World, which meant that husbands were more likely to work outside the household and to view their families as a financial burden. The gap in literacy between husbands and wives was also wider in the Chesapeake and in England than in New England. It is important, however, not to overstate the regional differences among marriages in the Anglo-American world. All Anglo-Americans—indeed perhaps all northern and western Europeans—contracted marriage freely, married relatively late, and had some degree of mutual dependence in their marriages. Those who were violent used force primarily to try to make their partners change their ways, and levels of lethal violence were correspondingly low.[10]

Only a handful of the spousal murders that occurred from colonial times into the early nineteenth century appear to have been premeditated—that is, planned rather than committed in an emotional fury. Nearly all the deliberate murders in this era were committed by wives who had fallen in love with other men. There are few records of sane husbands committing premeditated murder in any of the counties studied.[11]

Although nearly all the women who deliberately killed their husbands got help from accomplices, they fell into two distinct groups. One group lived beyond the bounds of respectable society and murdered their husbands just to be rid of them. The other wanted desperately to marry their lovers and retain the advantages of life in society. Martha Newdale, a former indentured servant from Maryland, was one of those women who didn't care what people thought. In 1702 she grew tired of her husband's laziness and drinking and ran off to Richmond County, Virginia, with a lover, Abraham Hannisson. Her husband, missing his meal ticket, tracked them down. Martha told him he could move in with her and Hannisson, and he foolishly agreed. She and Hannisson jumped him when he was drunk and beat him to death with a hammer. In 1778 Bathesheba Spooner of Brookfield, Massachusetts, whose father was a notorious British loyalist, persuaded two paroled British soldiers and her lover, a teenaged Continental soldier she had nursed back to health, to murder her wealthy husband. Her co-conspirators dumped the husband's body into the well in her yard so that she could pass off his death as accidental, but when the body was brought up neighbors saw marks of violence on it. The paroled soldiers were later captured with her husband's clothes, cash, and silver buckles.[12]

Deliberate murders such as these stemmed from the practical difficulties of life in a society that rarely allowed divorce. They stood apart from the overwhelming majority of spousal murders, which were committed either unintentionally, during the course of an assault, or by someone who was mentally ill.

Mentally ill spouses presented a serious danger to family members, especially in the days before asylums. Jeremiah Meacham, a weaver from Newport, Rhode Island, spent his days sitting on the roof of his house or hiding in his room. One evening in 1715 his wife went upstairs to persuade him to come down. Meacham stabbed her with a pen knife and bludgeoned her and her sister to death with an ax. He then barricaded himself in his room and held off neighbors until they broke through the floorboards, whereupon he grabbed a torch from one of them and set fire to the house. He was caught when he jumped from a window.[13]

In New England, where religious fervor was intense, it was not uncommon for mentally ill spouses to translate religious delusions into homicide. Thomas Goss of Barkhamsted, Connecticut, an innkeeper and a veteran of the French and Indian War, believed that evil spirits were tormenting him, and he stopped sleeping with his wife, convinced that she and the devil were lovers. Afraid that she would cast a spell on him, he split her head open with an ax while she slept, smeared her blood over their children, and then waited quietly for his neighbors to come. Goss's delusions had an apocalyptic cast. He warned his neighbors that if they hanged him for killing his wife, "thirty thousand males above fifteen years of age, would be instantly killed by the shock, in North-America."[14]

In the Chesapeake, where the white population lived in fear of slave rebellion, mentally ill spouses were more often obsessed with the idea that their slaves were about to murder them and their families. Colin Campbell, a planter from Surry County, Virginia, stabbed his wife to death in April 1802. In the days before the murder he had exhibited "every Symptom of Insanity," including a "wildness of look," "no inclination to sleep or eat," and "paroxyms" of fear during which he ran to and fro. What turned Campbell violent, however, was the discovery of a plot among slaves in Surry and adjacent counties to rise against whites on the day after Easter 1802. Authorities in Virginia and North Carolina quashed the rebellion, but Campbell believed that "the insurrection of Negroes" was imminent. He claimed that he "had stab'd his Wife at her own request" so that she could die by his hand rather than a slave's.[15]

In almost every case, friends and relatives knew that the person who suffered from mental illness posed a threat to his or her family, and they tried to take preventive measures. A neighbor took in family members who were threatened. A husband sued for custody of his children because his wife had threatened them. Neighbors agreed to look in on a family every two hours after a family member's mental condition took a turn for the worse. Such measures were often ineffective, however, as the Walpole, New Hampshire, *Farmer's Museum* acknowledged in an editorial in 1803. All the cases cited above ended in murder. Without the help of asylums, family and friends were vulnerable to deadly assaults.[16]

The majority of spousal murders that occurred in early New England and the Chesapeake had nothing to do with mental illness, however. They stemmed from attacks that were committed in anger and were not meant to be lethal. In most cases the victims did not die immediately, an indication that the attackers did not set out to kill and stopped when they realized they had inflicted a serious injury. Abigail Thomson of Farmington, Connecticut, threw a pair of scissors at her husband. They pierced his forehead and lodged in his brain, and he died nineteen days later. John Steadman, a Scots laborer from Annapolis, Maryland, beat his wife so badly that she died a day later. Because she had threatened and abused her husband for years, Abigail Thomson was hanged for her crime. John Steadman was executed because he tried to cover up his assault and did not seek medical help. In this era they were the only people who committed manslaughter but were convicted of murder and hanged.[17]

The majority of people who committed similar manslaughters did not even serve time. Israel Ford of Weymouth, Massachusetts, hit his wife in the small of her back with a pair of tongs, and she died thirteen days later. Moses Duty of Haverhill, New Hampshire, struck his wife Elizabeth with a hoe, and she died two days later. Ford and Duty were indicted but never tried. A Mr. Maxfield of Ryegate, Vermont, died a day after his wife pummeled him during a drunken fight. Local authorities jailed Mrs. Maxfield and several acquaintances who were at her house at the time of the assault, but she was later released. Althea Cook, the wife of a gentleman farmer from Calvert County, Maryland, died a day or two after her husband beat her, and Amelia Lamphier of Windsor, Vermont, took seven days to die after she was injured. An inquest determined that George Lamphier had kicked his wife, even though she denied it, as did her husband and mother-in-law. Both Lamphier and the husband of Althea Cook were tried as murderers but were found not guilty. The community certainly did not sanction this brutal behavior, but it was clear that these spouses were not willful murderers. They did not set out to kill, and they called physicians once they realized their spouses' injuries were serious.[18]

Another sign that these assaults were not meant to be lethal is that few were committed with guns. Only 9 percent of marital murders were committed with firearms in New England in the seventeenth and eighteenth centuries, and none in the Chesapeake, even though guns were used in two-fifths of murders of unrelated adults during the early years of colonization and during the American Revolution.[19] Marital murderers seldom used more than their fists or feet. Sometimes they picked up whatever was at hand—a stick, a stone, a tool. Guns required preparation and a degree of premeditation. The absence of guns (and of poison) shows that most murderous assaults, like most nonlethal assaults, were committed on the spur of the moment, with no intent to kill.

Yet people who committed manslaughter were not necessarily less serious abusers than willful murderers. George Lamphier, for instance, was clearly a cold, calculating, vicious man. He struck his wife only on parts of her body that would be concealed by her clothes. Bradbury Ferguson of Exeter, New Hampshire, beat his wife Eliza Ann repeatedly but was careful not to leave scars or break bones. When she told him that she was going to swear a complaint against him, he shrugged and said, "Shew your marks." Benjamin Smart of Concord, New Hampshire, lost his temper at his pregnant wife, Nancy, but he waited until their visitor left before he followed her upstairs to the bedroom, threw her to the floor, and kicked her. These people did not want to kill their spouses, but they relished causing pain and exercising power over them, and they meted out their violence judiciously in part to avoid exposure. Some abusers thumbed their noses at the law, though. Moses Duty and Mrs. Maxfield beat their spouses brutally and expected them to be up and about after prolonged assaults, with their injuries on display for anyone to see.[20]

Courts had a high threshold for interfering in abusive marriages: they were reluctant to intervene unless a spouse had been left black and blue or had suffered broken bones. But when disfiguring, disabling, or life-threatening assaults came to the attention of the authorities, they were likely to step in and warn the offender to stop or face prosecution. The penalties for aggravated spousal abuse in early modern England and in colonial New England and the Chesapeake ranged from warnings after first offenses to fines, confinement in the stocks, and whippings. Most whippings were administered in public—a severe humiliation for women in particular, since offenders were stripped to the waist. One woman in Plymouth Colony was allowed to be "punished at home," however; her husband administered a private, legally authorized whipping.[21]

Courts could order abusive spouses to post bond for good behavior as an alternative to punishment. This expedient was satisfactory to almost everyone, including battered spouses, because families did not suffer financially as long as abusive spouses kept the peace. Friends or relatives would step forward to secure the bond, and the pressure on the abuser was intense: a forfeited bond could mean a loss of £40, which for a poor family could represent several years of income. In contrast, the typical fine of £1 or £2 plus court costs, although it had to be paid immediately, might represent two or three months' pay for a laborer. But courts also handed down multiple punishments. Thomas Wilson of Virginia, a tailor, abused his wife in 1626 while he was drunk. The court put him in the stocks, fined him 20 shillings, and ordered him to post bond for good behavior. More typical was the punishment of Henry Sherburne of Portsmouth, New Hampshire, a wealthy landowner who in 1668 was fined and ordered to post bond for beating his wife several times.[22]

By the early nineteenth century, incarceration had replaced whippings. In the counties studied, the majority of husbands and wives tried for aggravated assault or attempted murder were convicted, and penalties for husbands could be stiff. Once state penitentiaries were opened in New Hampshire and Vermont, two-thirds of the husbands found guilty of attempted murder were sentenced to spend five to ten years in prison. Sentences for aggravated assault could also be severe. One of every seven husbands convicted of a marital assault in New Hampshire and Vermont spent between a month and six months in jail, and those who were fined could also face the loss of two or three months' wages. Threats were harder to prosecute, since there were usually no witnesses other than the victim. Only one in seven of these cases ended in conviction. Prosecutors still had an effective sanction in peace bonds, which by the nineteenth century could cost $100 or more if forfeited. In 1800 that sum represented as much as a third of a poor family's annual income.[23]

It is doubtful, however, that fear of prosecution prompted violent spouses to hide or moderate their attacks. Although the penalties were harsh, the odds of prosecution were slim, because authorities preferred to use moral suasion and threats of prosecution to deter spousal abuse. Even if only 2 to 3 percent of marriages were extremely violent—the average that pertains to the nineteenth century—the numbers would indicate that the state prosecuted no more than a small fraction of spouses who committed life-threatening abuse. Few prosecutions for threat, assault, or attempted murder led to divorce or legal separation,[24] because most cases came at the request of abused wives who hoped that state intervention would force their husbands to re-form. They were de facto civil suits.

Before the mid-eighteenth century, divorce and separation could not have played much of a role in deterring marital violence in the Anglo-American world. England's divorce laws were then more restrictive than those of any other Protestant nation, and the colonies generally followed English precedent. Throughout the colonial period the only permissible grounds for divorce in Virginia and Maryland were adultery, desertion, impotence, or neglect. The courts did not grant divorces on the grounds of cruelty, but they did permit separations in extreme cases. In 1676, for instance, Sarah Gibson was "Left to her Liberty" by the General Court of Virginia "Either to goe for England or Stay with her husband" as she thought "best for her Safety," after her husband beat and maimed her. The same court granted Mrs. Burt "seaprate maintenance" in 1679 because her husband was "a terrible fellow" who "ill treated" her.[25]

The colonial governments of New England were more likely to permit separations on the grounds of cruelty, but they, too, stopped short of granting divorces on those grounds, even when they were afraid that one spouse might kill the other. They viewed marriage, in the tradition of radical or reformed Protestantism, as a civil contract that could be voided by civil authorities if one party failed to live up to the terms of the contract, but the only grounds recognized for voiding the contract were adultery, desertion, and impotence. Marital violence was too commonplace to be considered as grounds for divorce, and, as in England, men were allowed to discipline their wives by beating them, just as they would their children, servants, and slaves. Violence could be prosecuted only as an assault—that is, as a violation of the general civil contract.[26]

By the end of the eighteenth century circumstances had changed. Vermont and New Hampshire were the first states to sanction divorce on the grounds of marital violence. The American Revolution led authorities in northern New England to conclude that spouses had a right to live free from violence and that marriage, like any other civil compact among freeborn citizens, should rest only on consent, not coercion. In 1787 Vermont made "intolerable severity" grounds for divorce, and in 1791 New Hampshire followed suit with a less sweeping but still forceful law against "extreme cruelty." These laws were not dead letters. Abused spouses used them freely to protect themselves against violence, and the courts used them to punish violent spouses by granting victims property, alimony, and child custody.[27]

The Massachusetts and Connecticut legislatures also recognized the need to protect spouses, especially wives, against abuse. In 1786 Massachusetts passed a law that allowed abused spouses to seek legal separation "from bed and board." The law did not permit divorces on the grounds of cruelty, but it allowed victims to leave troubled marriages, taking their children and property with them, and freed them from debts incurred by their spouses after the separation. Connecticut did not officially amend its divorce law, but in 1790 the state assembly began to rule favorably on petitions for divorce on the grounds of cruelty. Equally important, in the late 1760s every jurisdiction in New England began granting a substantially greater number of divorces on the grounds of adultery, desertion, and neglect. Many of the marriages dissolved on those grounds were violent, and public officials were willing to hear testimony about abuse as long as the bulk of the testimony pertained to legal grounds for divorce.[28]

The changes in divorce proceedings in Massachusetts and Connecticut did not protect as many victims of chronic abuse as the antiabuse statutes in Vermont and New Hampshire, but they were indicative of the broad consensus that began to take hold in New England after the Revolution: in marriage as in government, tyranny was unacceptable. The ability of abused spouses to dissolve violent marriages may well have become a deterrent to violence and may even have been the primary reason that the spouse murder rate fell by half in New England after the Revolution.

Abused women in the colonies had other resources besides the state, however: their neighbors and relatives. Public scorn for abusers and the intervention of neighbors to protect victims—both of which had their roots in the culture of early modern England—did more than criminal prosecution or the threat of divorce to restrain marital violence. Intervention by third parties was common not only in the seventeenth century, when families enjoyed little privacy and when friends and neighbors had few qualms about interfering in other people's affairs, but also in the nineteenth century, when modern notions of privacy were emerging. Neighbors, servants, and relatives even stepped in when marital violence was mutual.[29]

In the seventeenth-century Chesapeake, where tolerance for fighting and brawling was high, relatives and neighbors appear to have been more reluctant than their counterparts in England and New England to intervene in troubled marriages. But they did intercede to stop extreme marital violence. In 1625 Mr. Bransbie, a Virginia tobacco planter, and two of his indentured servants stormed into Joseph Johnson's house to make him stop abusing his wife. Bransbie, an officer in the Virginia militia, told Johnson that if "he did beat and abuse his wiefe any more he wold beate him tyghtlie unless ye Governor comanded ye contrary." Bransbie intervened again at a later date, even though Johnson "presented his peece owt at his window" and yelled "W[ha]t have you to do heere, you were best kepe back or I will make ye stande back." Bransbie walked up to Johnson and grabbed the gun right out of his hands.[30]

Such interventions could be dangerous. Matilda Nash of Sullivan, New Hampshire, a seventy-year-old widow, gave shelter to the wife and children of a mentally ill neighbor, Daniel Corey, and when she tried to reason with him he struck her on the head with a gunstock and killed her. But most interventions ended peacefully. Constables and justices of the peace were sometimes called in when there was violence, but they intervened more often as neighbors than as town officials.[31]

Relatives, neighbors, and domestic employees also supported abused spouses when they decided to prosecute, separate, or divorce. In poor areas of the country it was not uncommon for friends and relatives to support abuse victims who left their spouses and remarried without divorcing. The practice was probably most common in the seventeenth and eighteenth centuries, when divorce was largely unavailable. As long as the couple behaved well, everyone embraced the fiction that they were married and the abusive spouse was dead.[32] Similar tolerance was not extended to spouses who deserted their families merely to take up with a new love.

Aggrieved spouses who turned to the courts could not expect much help, and wives had more difficulty than husbands in making their cases. In most jurisdictions, judges and jurors were lenient toward husbands who had extramarital affairs or claimed they used corporal punishment only to discipline their wives. Still, women could use court proceedings to proclaim to the world that their husbands were abusers or cheats, and husbands could bring disgrace upon wives who had been abusive or unfaithful. Taking a spouse to court could thus enhance the aggrieved spouse's reputation and expose the abuser or adulterer to the scorn of the community. That was no small matter in an era when churches were a powerful force in community life. Adultery prosecutions may even have helped prevent lethal violence against women, because they enabled husbands to regain control over their wives and to punish their wives' lovers.[33]

Husbands and wives who wanted to shame their spouses could also appeal to the community for support by posting advertisements in local newspapers. The custom became especially popular after the Revolution, when constraints on public and private expression relaxed. Unhappy spouses, most of them women, accused their partners of drunkenness, indolence, abuse, adultery, and theft. These postings sometimes rehearsed the entire history of a troubled marriage. Mercy Griffis told readers of the *Vermont Gazette* about the suffering she had endured over sixteen years of marriage to Benjamin Griffis. Hannah West asked readers of the Windsor *Vermont Journal* to "Hear the Truth" about her husband, who had absconded and left her penniless after nine years of marriage. He took "all my cloth that I had to clothe my family with, and all my yarn I had spinned. . . . He carried away my flax, wood, and all the provisions which we raised on our farm the last year." He left "five children to cry and sob to see the desolation of my family. Since last winter he had been more cruel, and has abused me and his children in a shameful manner, and jamming me till I was black and blue."[34]

Postings usually marked the end of marriages. They were meant to destroy the reputation of spouses who had failed as husbands or wives, but they may also have deterred violence by giving wronged spouses a means of avenging themselves and defending their honor. In addition, they served as a warning to others about the public humiliation that awaited them if they abused their spouses. Postings appeared in Maryland and Virginia and in other areas of the United States, but they were extraordinarily popular in New England, where high levels of literacy and newspaper subscription meant that more spouses could write them and a wider audience could read them.[35]

The literate culture of New England also preserved many stories about spouses who dealt creatively with marital problems that under other circumstances might have prompted violence. Husbands and wives defied the demands of controlling spouses and flouted convention in minor and major ways. The pressure to meet New England's high housekeeping standards, which was the source of many marital problems, prompted a good deal of defiance. Mary Welch of Two Heroes, Vermont, was clearly unhappy in her marriage. Sometimes she would ride off to stay with friends for several days at a time, leaving her husband Nathaniel alone to care for their three children and tend the farm. She told her brother-in-law that "she would Burn up & Destroy their own House and every thing they had and that she would kill her husband." Mary's in-laws were certain that "it was her real intentions" to murder Nathaniel, but since she tended to become angry only when he asked her to perform some task for him, her "real intentions" may have been to show him how hard it was to keep house, do farm chores, care for young children, and cater to his demands. Disapproving neighbors like Nancy Cade gleefully reported Mary's misdeeds. Cade said that she once heard Nathaniel ask Mary to make a small cake, at which "Mary got up and fetched about a Bushel of good flower and puts it into a Tub about half full of swills which was put by for the Hogs and after swearing an Oath said to her Husband there's a Cake for you." When he asked her to mend his shirts, she took out one of his "Holland shirts nearly as good as new which she cut to pieces." When asked to clean the house, she broke the furniture into kindling and burned it.[36]

Azuba Brooks's husband complained that she "did not manage her household concerns as well as women in general" and that "her manner of cooking and taking care of her household concerns was such that her family could not be decent." She in turn told neighbors he was a "Thumb sucking child" and a "Dirty Mangy Puppy." She answered one of his complaints about her cooking "by taking a cake hot from the Fire and throwing it Spitefully Into his Face," and when he complained about her manners she blew her nose and threw the mucus at him. "God Dam You David Brooks," she would say, "I Know how to torment you and I will Do It."[37]

Men were not exempt from the pressure to adhere to New England's standards, and sometimes they came up with innovative ways of defying it. A man who married a well-to-do widow in Cornish, New Hampshire, was tormented by her constant complaints about the way he managed the farm. Why didn't he do things the way her first husband had? One day he went to the graveyard, dug up the remains of her first husband, carried the coffin home, and set it down in the kitchen, "declaring that if it would make so much difference *he* should be on the farm."[38]

Conduct of this sort, though often admired and considered a sign of strong character in New England, was not universally applauded. Respectable society considered it evidence that the defiant partner was at fault in the marriage. Newspapers declared the grave-robbing husband of Cornish a "monster in human shape." Mary Welch's neighbors, inlaws, and even her own sister advised her husband to "whip her severely if ever he thought to live with her."[39] This unusual advocacy of physical punishment shows that people who behaved as Mary Welch did risked putting themselves beyond the protection of society. Still, such people had their sympathizers, and, more to the point, their avoidance of lethal confrontations with their spouses helped create a culture of nonviolence and may have encouraged others to deal with marital problems in nonviolent ways.

A number of factors thus combined to reduce the marital murder rate in New England after the Revolution: greater access to divorce or separation on the grounds of cruelty, higher levels of literacy, and the use of postings to shame abusive spouses. But marital murder rates had been low in the Anglo-American world even before the Revolution because of the mutual dependence of husbands and wives and the willingness of friends, neighbors, and public authorities to protect spouses who were abused or otherwise wronged.

Marital Homicide among African Americans

Marital homicide figures for African Americans are less certain than the figures for European Americans. Surviving sources from the Chesapeake almost never discuss relationships between enslaved victims and assailants, nor do they record slaves' surnames, so it is difficult to separate marital murders from other murders. Nevertheless, it is clear that marital homicides were rare among African Americans. Only two are known to have occurred in New England in the seventeenth and eighteenth centuries.

The first case involved a free man named Cloyes who murdered his wife with an ax in Stamford, Connecticut, in 1675. He was probably mentally ill, because his case never came to trial. The second murder was committed in Boston in 1720 by Joseph Hanno, also a free man. He, too, killed his wife with an ax. That murder stemmed from a conflict over the degree to which Hanno's wife Nanny was willing to accommodate herself to white society. Joseph, born in Africa, had been in New England forty-four years, the last fourteen as a free man. His owners had raised him as a Christian, and he was proud of his faith. His wife's rejection of white religion weighed heavily in his decision to kill her. He had never considered murder, he said, "till she told me, that she had as liev talk with the Devil, as talk with any of GODS Ministers." When asked by a minister who visited him in jail if he understood the principles of Christianity, Joseph replied, "Yes, Sir, I have a Great deal of Knowledge. No body of my Colour, in Old England or New, has so much." "I wish you were less Puffed up with it," the minister said. No other marital murders occurred among African Americans in New England over the next eighty years.[40]

Because information on African American marriages in the Chesapeake is sparse, the marital murder rate there must be estimated by proxy. The best proxy is the rate at which African American women were murdered by African American men or by unknown assailants. That rate, which correlates well with all forms of intimate and familial violence, was as low as the rate for European American women: 0.3 or 0.4 per 100,000 women per year from the seventeenth into the early nineteenth century. Records note a murder method but rarely identify victims and assailants by more than a single name. In 1726, for example, Ben, a slave in Richmond County, Virginia, cut the throat of Winney, a slave on the same plantation. In Middlesex County, Virginia, in 1771 Abram beat and kicked Sarah so brutally that she died on the spot, and in 1795 Peter strangled Alice with a linen handkerchief. A number of murders occurred because of marital problems but involved other victims. For instance, in 1768 a slave in Williamsburg, Virginia, quarreled with his wife about her relationship with another man and was "so provoked" that he threw a hatchet, which hit an innocent bystander in the forehead.[41]

We can only speculate about the reasons for the low marital murder rate among African Americans. To begin with, it is unclear how many of them were full and willing participants in Anglo-American marriage customs. In New England the pressure to marry was strong, and slaves were punished for fornication, adultery, or bearing illegitimate children. Some African Americans probably took part in Anglo-American marriage ceremonies simply to placate their owners or to avoid prosecution, although most who did so appeared to embrace them wholeheartedly. Religious and secular authorities formally recognized marriages among slaves and between slaves and free blacks and granted free blacks full marital rights.[42]

But many African Americans in New England firmly rejected traditional marriage in favor of unsanctioned marriages that could be entered into or dissolved at will. A few of them practiced serial monogamy, taking new partners as circumstances or preferences dictated. Boston Carpenter, a free black man, owned his wife and threatened to sell her if she misbehaved. Some enslaved African Americans had "abroad" marriages in which husbands lived apart from their wives and children. Abroad marriages, whether sanctioned or unsanctioned, had some advantages over cohabiting marriages. Slaves did not have to see their loved ones abused or have their own humiliations witnessed. Unsanctioned abroad marriages could also be dissolved easily if the partners were unhappy. Men simply stopped their conjugal visits. Women could end their marriages without risk to themselves or their children by asking their owners to bar their husbands from the property.[43]

Although abroad marriage had its advantages, there was still potential for discord. Spouses in abroad marriages rarely saw each other during the week, so there was ample time for infidelity, and competition for female companionship among black men was intense because there were far more black men than black women throughout most of the colonial era. Yet before the nineteenth century there is no evidence that an African American in New England ever killed a spouse or a romantic rival because of jealousy. The legal system may have played a role in suppressing violence in marriages among free blacks because of its willingness to punish adulterers. In many instances betrayed spouses had the satisfaction of seeing their spouses or romantic rivals fined or whipped.

Slaves in sanctioned marriages could also petition for divorce. In 1742 a slave named Boston accused his wife of having an illegitimate child by a white soldier, and the Massachusetts legislature granted his request for a divorce. However, it is likely that the fundamental deterrent to spousal homicide, at least for enslaved African Americans, was the ease with which they could dissolve unsanctioned marriages without recourse to law, simply by telling their owners, friends, and relatives they were no longer married. When slaves were freed some found it a great shock to learn that they would have to abide by the white community's rules. Chatham Freeman of Wallingford, Connecticut, married his wife legally after they and their child were freed in 1782, but he soured on her a few weeks later. He was appalled when he found out that he could not set her aside and take another wife. "I never can stand it to be married to that woman!" he protested.[44]

Enslaved spouses probably spent little time together, especially in New England, where most slaveowners had few slaves; so there was less time for murderous violence to ferment. Many free blacks who married slaves did not live with their spouses either, usually because they did not wish to live as quasi-slaves. Free blacks often tried to purchase their spouses and children, and slaves sometimes tried to persuade their owners to buy their spouses and children from other owners. Venture Smith, an enslaved farmhand who lived in Stonington, Connecticut, prevailed upon his owner to purchase his wife and daughter, who lived with Smith's former master in Rhode Island. But Smith's household was shattered one day when his mistress flew into a "violent passion" and beat his wife. Smith took the horsewhip out of his mistress' hand and threw it into the fire. For this offense he was sold. It took him twenty years to purchase himself and his family, and he was fortunate that the owners were willing to sell.[45] Smith's marriage was precious to him, and when slavery made it difficult to sustain, it took on even greater value. Under such circumstances one would expect low spouse murder rates.

Free blacks had a greater chance of realizing the Anglo-American ideal of marriage. Chloe Spear, who was sold into slavery as a child and carried from Africa to Boston in 1762, married her husband Caesar while both were still slaves, but they were freed soon afterward by the abolition of slavery in Massachusetts. They saved enough money to open a boardinghouse for seamen and day laborers. Their marriage had its ups and downs. Chloe was more devout and ambitious than her husband, who took life as it came, but she accepted that her husband was "of a different turn of mind from herself, and not seriously disposed," and they got on well enough. Determined to get ahead, she joined the Baptist Church, learned to read, took in washing, cleaned houses, and brought home gifts of "cold meat and vegetables" from the families she worked for. Caesar cooked, cleaned the house, and looked after their seven children. Although roles were reversed in their marriage, theirs was an archetypal New England union in every other respect, with both partners working to achieve prosperity and economic independence.[46]

African Americans in the Chesapeake were under less pressure to adopt Anglo-American marital practices. The laws of Maryland and Virginia did not sanction slave marriages, so enslaved spouses were free to abandon unhappy marriages and form new ones. Legal action against wayward spouses was not an option, because, unlike their counterparts in New England, the courts in the Chesapeake refused to defend the sanctity of slave marriages. There were some indications that murderous jealousy was a serious problem within African American marriages and between male romantic rivals. Jealousy may have been especially severe among slaves who lived on small plantations, because it was difficult for them to find mates and to keep their families together when slaves were moved or sold. In Virginia in the mid-eighteenth century, a fifth of all enslaved women on large plantations lived as single parents, but nearly three-fifths of the women on small plantations did so.[47]

By the early nineteenth century there were additional remedies for unhappy marriages available to some slaves and free blacks. Those who belonged to interracial churches could ask that unfaithful spouses be excommunicated, and free blacks could bring charges against adulterous spouses in court.[48] Still, probably the greatest deterrent to marital murders among African Americans was their growing sense of solidarity. By the end of the eighteenth century their awareness of themselves as a people apart, beset by white evil, led to a general decline in the rate at which they murdered one another and an increased reliance on one another for emotional and material support, both inside and outside marriage.

Marital Homicide among Native Americans

The only people in the Anglo-American world to have very high rates of marital murder were Native Americans. In New England, the only place where reliable data are available, the rates for Native Americans who lived in or on the fringes of white society were twenty times those of Europeans and African Americans. The problem was worst in the mid-eighteenth century, when murders of unrelated adults also peaked among Native Americans. The pattern is indicative of the strain that the loss of their remaining lands in southern New England and continuous warfare in northern New England put on Native American families and communities. That strain was compounded by discrimination, especially against Indian men. The only jobs open to them in the white economy were in dangerous occupations like whaling, seafaring, and military service, which kept them away from their families and claimed many lives. The ratio of Native women to men stood at four to three in Massachusetts by 1764, and at three to two in Connecticut by 1774. Poverty, depression, and alcoholism were epidemic.[49]

The rates of every kind of homicide went up among Native Americans during the eighteenth century, but spousal murder appears to have been a persistent problem among Native Americans in colonial New England, with high rates even in the late seventeenth century. Sources on Native Americans seldom speak about the motives behind marital murders, and when they do, they usually reflect white views of Native American character or white misunderstanding of Native marriage, which could take diverse forms. Although most Natives had monogamous marriages for which the approval of kin had been sought and dowries paid, tribal leaders sometimes had polygynous marriages, and some Natives had more informal relationships that were contracted and dissolved by mutual consent.[50]

The accounts of early colonists all agree, however, that marriages among Native Americans were prone to violence. Father Pierre Biard, the first Jesuit missionary to Acadia and Maine, complained in 1613 that Abenaki and Micmac husbands were cruel to their wives. "The husbands beat them unmercifully," he wrote, "and often for a very slight cause. One day a certain Frenchman undertook to rebuke a Savage for this; the Savage answered angrily: 'How now, have you nothing to do but to see into my house, every time I strike my dog?'"[51]

Christopher Levett, an English trader on the coast of Maine, found that his Abenaki friends were incredulous when he told them that his wife had refused to cross the Atlantic alone to be with him and that he would have to fetch her. They "wished me to beate her. I told them no, for then our God would bee angrie. Then they runne out upon her in evil tearmes, and wished me to let her alone and take another, I told them our God would be more angrie for that. Againe they bid me beate her, beate her, repeating it often, and very angerly." William Wood, an early settler at Massachusetts Bay, was appalled by the "customary churlishness and savage inhumanity" of Native husbands in southern New England, but he believed that the arrival of the English only made matters worse, because the Native women, "seeing the kind usage of the English to their wives do as much condemn their husbands for unkindness and commend the English for their love, as their husbands—commending themselves for their wit in keeping their wives industrious—do condemn the English for their folly in spoiling good working creatures." Wood also noted that abused Native American women sometimes fled to English households for protection, and he knew several English women who had threatened to scald Native American men who tried to reclaim their wives.[52]

Although there were probably some differences in marital homicide rates among different groups of Native Americans, no European observer made any attempt to differentiate among peoples or made note of any problems that might have intensified marital violence among particular groups. Yet their testimony about wife abuse is consistent. Marital violence among Native Americans was rampant, and it claimed many lives. Some women were killed with hatchets, but most were beaten to death. Some of the violence was no different from white violence: people attacked their spouses in a moment of anger and killed them without meaning to. In 1786, for example, Sage Combs was beaten to death by her husband as they sold baskets and brooms door to door in Salem, Massachusetts. She stubbed her toe as she stepped over a stone wall and sat down momentarily. Her husband, Isaac, frustrated at having to stop, accused her of "carelessness" and hit her. "I struck her twice on her forehead, with a Walnut Stick with several knots in it. The blood gushed from the wound and I then struck her on her Temple with a Sharp Stone." He tried to staunch the bleeding with grass, dirt, and sugar, but the wound was too deep.[53]

A higher proportion of Native American spousal murders were deliberate, however. One man threw his wife out of a window in 1670, while they were lodging at an Englishman's house in Roxbury, Massachusetts. Josiah, a day laborer in Dartmouth, Rhode Island, beat his wife, Margaret, and then shoved her into the fire and let her burn to death. At least one killing anticipated the kind of brutal violence, some of it sexually charged, that would not appear among whites or blacks in the United States until the mid-nineteenth century, when changing gender roles created deep reservoirs of rage in men who were unable to adapt to the new balance of power between women and men. In 1722 Hannah Ompatawin of Natick, Massachusetts, testified before she died of her injuries that her husband had beaten her so viciously that even as he was hitting her she knew she would not recover from the assault.

> I . . . would do any thing in reason to gratify him which I was able, yet nevertheless he flung me down and rent my thigh open forceably, and held me down & violently puncht or Strook me with his knee in my private parts while he beat me almost off the place where I lay then he pulled me on agin and puncht with his knee agin in ye Same place While he gave me my deaths Wound, I told him them boards we lay on Would be a witness aginst him yt he had kill'd me & give me my deaths Wound.[54]

White contemporaries claimed that Indians had a moral code that dictated their response to marital problems. If a woman committed adultery, for example, many tribes allowed the husband to throw her out of his home and kill her lover. Yet in many cases husbands killed both wives and lovers, with no apparent sanctions. A Penacook who lived on the Merrimack River near present-day Concord, New Hampshire, pursued his wife upriver after she eloped with a tribal chief named Peorowarrow. He discovered them asleep on Sewall's Island. He would not kill them as they slept, so he lay in wait all night and shot them with a rifle as they boarded their canoe the next morning. In 1793 Tobias Cayes and his wife Sarah were visited by a friend from Providence, George Pinny. The three went to a tavern in East Hartford to celebrate Christmas, and by the time they started for home they were drunk. The next morning, Cayes found his wife and Pinny in the barn, "clasp'd in each other's arms." He stabbed them both with a pitchfork.[55]

The surviving sources are either silent about motives or hopelessly prejudiced against Indians, so it is not clear why Native American men who were angry at their wives did not simply leave them. Most Native Americans, even those who were Christians, seem to have believed that marriages could be dissolved at will, without any risk of community censure. Yet a man's honor still rested on his being the dominant partner in marriage and on exacting fidelity from his wife, even though the double standard for men and women where extramarital sex was concerned was not as pronounced as it was in the white community.[56]

The conflict between the idea that women should remain subordinate to men and the customs that gave women a great deal of personal and economic freedom set Native American men and women at odds, and as the white culture became dominant, their relationships were increasingly disrupted. They rarely turned to churches or the courts for help in restraining violent partners or to seek punishment for adulterers, as Europeans and African Americans did, and colonial authorities seldom took an interest in cases of adultery, desertion, or domestic violence involving Native Americans. Missionaries and Native judges tried to fill the gap by adjudicating cases that Native men and women brought before them, but their rulings had only a modest effect, because they were often ignored by the offending party. A near-complete division of labor also led to a lack of mutual dependence among married couples and to greater economic independence for wives. For the most part women had to keep households going by themselves. They gathered food, tended crops, earned wages as domestics, and made baskets for sale. Men were often away from home hunting, earning wages, or fighting wars. For men especially, the arrival of the whites had meant devastation: the encroachment of settlements upon hunting land, humiliating defeats in battle, the deaths and enslavement of friends and relatives, the disappearance of traditional ways to earn status. These losses undermined the status hierarchy among Native Americans so severely that they translated not only into an increase in violence among unrelated men, but into jealousy and violence in men's relationships with their wives. As they lost status in society, men began to feel diminished in the eyes of their wives, who were learning ways of making a living on their own. The more diminished men felt, the more abusive they became.[57]

To make matters worse for Native American men, a growing number of Native American women began to marry African Americans. In part this trend resulted from a relative dearth of Native American men and African American women, but Native American women had also quickly discovered that African American husbands were less likely to abuse them and more likely to live at home and support their families on a daily basis. Of course, not every African American involved with a Native American woman was nonviolent. Samuel Freeman of Ashford, Connecticut, beat his common-law wife to death in 1805. Generally speaking, however, African Americans husbands were substantially less homicidal than their Native American counterparts. The preference of many Indian women for black husbands "created a very bitter feeling among the Indian men against blacks."[58] They also resented African American men because once they became members of the tribe by marriage, they were rival claimants for scarce tribal resources.

Romance Homicide

Homicides in which suitors killed their lovers or romantic rivals were even rarer than marital murders in America and England from the sixteenth through the early nineteenth centuries. Like the marital murder rate, the romance homicide rate did not rise and fall with the rate of murders among unrelated adults, because these homicides did not stem from the same feelings and beliefs that prompted unrelated adults to kill one another. Romance homicides had their own distinctive causes, but they appear to have been deterred by some of the same forces that prevented marital homicides: legal remedies and the support of family and friends.

Before 1800 there were only two known cases of romance murder in New England. In 1719 Reuben Hull, a young farmer from Westerly, Rhode Island, shot and killed Freelove Doliver. He had courted her for several months, and when she ended their relationship he was furious. His jailers remarked upon his lack of remorse: he was "obdurate" even as he made his way to the gallows. Abigail Dent, a seventeen-year-old boardinghouse servant from Portsmouth, New Hampshire, was probably killed by a former lover. The chief suspect was a sailor named Thomas Paschal. She was last seen in his company, and they were arguing about Dent's relationship with another sailor. Her body was found later that week in a swamp about a mile from town. Paschal was the only suspect, but his messmate swore that he had been in their room asleep at the time of the murder, so no charges were ever filed.[59]

In the Chesapeake, only one romance homicide came to public attention. One Sunday evening in 1792 Daniel Yowell, who lived in a remote, mountainous section of Culpepper County, stabbed sixteen-year-old Nancy Clark to death at her home. Her mother tried to save her, but Yowell turned on her and slashed her face to the bone before he cut Nancy's throat and disemboweled her. Yowell tried to kill himself, but he managed only to cut his windpipe.[60]

Contemporary commentary indicates that people were astonished by these murders. Romance homicide was almost unheard of in the early modern Anglo-American world. Certainly young people who were rejected were hurt as deeply as young people are today, and occasionally they reacted violently to rejection. Young women in England were known to "faint, cry in the street, or weep and beg" when young men spurned them, and in Massachusetts it was said that women often became "either melancholy or mad." Young men may have been even more vulnerable to rejection because they were the ones to take the initiative in most courtships and their disappointments were more public. It was common for them to react "with rage, anxiety, or madness." In seventeenth-century London, Sage Pover's suitor threatened to hang himself if she did not accept the ring he had bought her. Thomas Bedle went on a rampage after Margaret Inman rejected his marriage proposal and "did faine himself madd or distempered for the love of hir. . . . He brake one of his neighbours glasse windows and rann a knife at one of the servants of the said house and beat or strock the master of the said house." After his fiancée broke off their engagement, Samuel Truett proclaimed on a public street that "I have done my endeavour as far forth as any man to get Nan Collins . . . with child, and if she proves with child, I will keep the bastard, but let the whore . . . go and be damned."[61]

A few young men sent friends to intimidate their lovers into taking them back, but very few rejected lovers ever made any attempt to kill the person they loved or the rival who supplanted them. Young people usually recovered rapidly from romantic setbacks, in part because of the emotional support they received from friends and relatives. Most of them did not get serious about marriage before their early twenties, and by that time they also had some experience with the emotional ups and downs of romance, thanks to a youth culture that facilitated relationships. Adolescents were encouraged to pair off at dances, holiday celebrations, and informal gatherings, and no one thought the worse of them if they moved from one relationship to another. Friends, siblings, and parents helped young men and women get over their disappointments. John Lee of Virginia told his brother Richard in the 1750s that he was fortunate to have escaped the "inferior" girl who turned him down, and he urged Richard to try again with a more suitable person.[62]

The rituals of courtship were also instrumental in deterring romantic violence. Formal exchanges of words, gestures, and gifts enabled young men to declare their interest in young women without investing too much emotion and gave young women graceful ways to encourage or discourage such interest. No one had to risk too much, at least publicly. If the exchanges continued to the point of intimacy—holding hands, sharing food, drinking from the same cup—their behavior alerted parents and friends to the seriousness of the relationship and was a cue for them to offer guidance and support.[63] Such customs lessened the possibility of violence by giving young people a degree of emotional protection.

If a woman allowed herself to become too deeply involved with a man before the relationship failed, she could seek redress by suing for breach of promise. Promises of marriage were binding and could be upheld in court if there were witnesses to the promise or evidence of a serious courtship (particularly exchanges of gifts). However, young women seldom went to court unless they were pregnant and had been abandoned. Sarah Ward of Middlesex County, Massachusetts, testified that Zechariah Maynard "often showed much love to me and promised to marye me. I did not think he would Runawaye and leave me in this condition." Young women who sued often won financial compensation, and they tarnished the reputations of the young men who had wronged them, but also, and perhaps most important, they defended their own reputations in court by proving that they had slept with a man only on the promise of marriage—a widely tolerated if not commended practice. Going to court was not a happy remedy, but it defused potentially violent situations by exposing them to public scrutiny.[64]

The Romantic movement, which swept across the Anglo-American world in the second half of the eighteenth century, raised the emotional stakes in courtships by encouraging a greater investment in intimacy and more open expressions of love. By the early nineteenth century the proportion of fiction and nonfiction articles in American magazines that glorified the expression of feelings in romantic relationships had risen from 18 percent to 57 percent. Yet there is no evidence, at least through the 1820s, of an upswing in possessiveness or jealousy. Young people were not abruptly persuaded that their happiness might depend wholly on the love of a particular person.[65]

The impact of the Romantic movement was tempered by practicality, and its assumptions were initially regarded with a critical eye. Dwight Foster, a young New Englander, noted in 1780 that "there is something heavenly in the Passion of Love—but the Misfortune of it often makes a Man act in a very ridiculous Manner—even a Man of Sense is frequently unable to command himself when his heart is affected by this Passion." Despite its positive associations, romance was associated with immaturity and a loss of reason. Even the young urged caution around it. One woman advised her friend not to be "so symple to send to her sweet hart and woo him." A young man told a friend that it was "not necessary for him to say that he was in love before he knew whether he was beloved." By the early nineteenth century, 58 percent of all articles in American magazines declared that love and happiness were the most important considerations in choosing a partner. However, 42 percent agreed that young people should still take into account practical considerations such as wealth and status.[66]

Although the Romantic movement celebrated complete candor in intimate relationships, women were still encouraged to remain modest and to be wary of male intentions, and men were advised to be guarded and to conduct themselves at all times with unflappable aplomb. Of course, sometimes that behavior achieved the desired end, and sometimes it did not. James Barnard, a young seaman from Massachusetts, was disappointed when the woman he loved turned down his proposal. "She did not know the strength of my feelings, she could not. I had guarded myself with the utmost care—too proud to let anyone know he or she had the power to mar my peace one moment."[67]

There is no record of African Americans in New England committing any romance homicides from the seventeenth through the early nineteenth centuries. The absence of any evidence of such murders is remarkable, given that more and more African Americans, no longer subject to the arbiters of marital alliance who dictated the terms of courtship in sub-Saharan Africa, adopted the Anglo-American practice of marrying for love and were able to court and marry during that period. Venture Smith proudly proclaimed that he had married his wife Meg "for love." Christopher G., a free man from Newport, Rhode Island, wooed his cousin, Elleanor Eldridge, with walks along the beach and romantic letters. "I have thought of you, almost with one thought, since I left. How strange it is that wherever I look I see nothing but my dear Ellen." He signed his letters "true lover." Such courtships were conducted publicly and with the encouragement of friends and relatives (and, in slave times, owners).[68]

There may have been a wider range of courtship practices among African Americans in the Chesapeake, where a greater number of Africans, enslaved and free, held European culture at arm's length. Whereas most slaves in New England were sold singly and few lived near relatives, slaves in the Chesapeake were sometimes purchased with their families or fellow villagers and were able to sustain a few of their traditions. As a result some young men had to win the blessing of a young woman's mother or a female elder before they could marry. Philip Coleman, a former slave, "took a great fancy" to a young woman, but her mother "put up so strong [an] objection that the wedding was called off." Caroline Johnson Harris said that young couples in her quarters had to get permission to marry from "Aunt Sue," who asked young people to think hard about marrying for a couple of days, because marriage was sacred. The advice and instruction of experienced elders may have helped to moderate violent emotions and deter hasty decisions.[69]

On the whole, however, young African Americans in the Chesapeake, especially those who were enslaved, were not as closely supervised in their courtships as their counterparts in New England, and this lack of oversight may have made romantic relationships more susceptible to violence. The circumstances of homicides among African American adults are largely unknown in the South before the Civil War, so it is impossible to know how many romance homicides occurred, but it is likely that failed suitors committed a number of such murders. In Louisa County, Virginia, for instance, a man named Boatswain murdered Rachel and Will, most likely because Rachel had rejected him and he believed that Will had alienated her affections. In Henrico County, Virginia, a slave named Stephen visited a neighboring plantation and asked a young woman to marry him. She refused. A witness testified that Stephen then declared that he was "determined to murder this night." He returned after dark and found Aaron, another slave, in bed with her and beat him to death. Given the rate at which enslaved African Americans began and ended courtships in the Chesapeake, and the absence of strong mechanisms, formal and informal, to keep jealousy, possessiveness, and premarital sexuality in check, romance homicides may well have been more common among Chesapeake slaves than among free blacks or New England slaves.[70]

Among Native Americans in New England, there was only one known instance of romance homicide in the colonial or revolutionary period. Toomalek was a member of a small band of Coos Indians who lived near the Connecticut River near present-day Newbury, Vermont. A short, powerfully built young man, he was in love with a young woman, Lewâ, who eventually married another Coos named Mitchell. Toomalek decided to kill Mitchell, and one evening he surprised the couple as they sat by their campfire. He fired at Mitchell, wounding him seriously but not fatally. A second shot struck Lewâ. She died of her wounds a few hours later.

Mitchell eventually remarried, but matters did not end there. One day Toomalek, in company with a white man named Ebenezer Olmsted, took a bottle of rum and went to visit Mitchell. They drank together for a while, and then Mitchell and Toomalek argued. Mitchell drew his knife and made a feeble pass at Toomalek, and Toomalek stabbed him through the heart.[71]

There is just not enough evidence to be certain about the number of romance murders among Native Americans. But since jealousy was frequently cited as a motive for murder among married Native Americans, and since the motive behind the majority of Native American murders is unknown, it is possible that murders of romantic rivals were more common among Native Americans than among other Americans. The freedom that most Native cultures in New England gave women to take up and discard lovers and the pressure those cultures placed on men to subjugate male rivals may have made romantic failure both more common and less tolerable for young Native American men, especially as traditional ways to earn status disappeared and all relations among unrelated men became more volatile.

Homicide of Adult Relatives

The homicide rate among adult relatives other than spouses was low both in England and among European Americans in New England and the Chesapeake from the seventeenth into the early nineteenth centuries.[72] People rarely killed their parents, adult children, siblings (including in-laws and step-relations), aunts, uncles, nieces, nephews, or cousins. Relatives almost never killed one another for money or property, and they never killed one another over issues that often led to murder in many other early modern societies: a sexual transgression that threatened a family's honor, a dispute about the person a family member was to marry, or the failure of a relative to meet his or her customary obligations to kin. Because of the dynamism of the nonfarm economy in England and British North America, the greater availability of land in America, and the expectation that family members should make their own way in the world with only the help that their families could afford, Anglo-American families did not control the economic destiny of family members to the degree that families did in most Western societies. And as we have seen, Anglo-American families used the courts and public opinion, rather than violence, to deal with romantic and marital disputes. The family killings that did occur had much in common with spousal murders. They were usually the unintended consequence of mental illness, quarrels over trivial matters, or abuse.

In New England, where the best data are available, there were only three known cases in which a relative killed another relative over property. One of those cases occurred in 1688. Edward Hill of Boston conspired with his wife and neighbors to murder his wife's uncle, William Penn, and take possession of Penn's estate with a forged will. Penn had persuaded the Hills to migrate to Massachusetts to help him run his business and had promised to make them his heirs. Edward Hill turned out to be a ne'er-do-well, however, so Penn left his property to another relative in England. Unfortunately, Penn became ill and was forced to move in with the Hills. Edward abused him, stole from him, and finally killed him. Then he offered three neighbors £10 each if they would swear to the authenticity of the will he had prepared. The scheme worked. Eighteen years later the rightful heirs had the fraudulent will overturned, but Hill was never tried for murder because there was no longer any physical evidence against him and because much of the testimony against him came from co-conspirators.[73]

In the Chesapeake, the data gathered so far include only one murder of a relative for property. John Berry, a down-at-the-heels young gentleman from Joppa, Maryland, thought that his prospects were secure after he married a wealthy heiress. She died soon after they wed, however, and he was afraid that his in-laws would disinherit him if he married the woman he loved, a young orphan who had been raised by his late wife. He therefore conspired with the family's servants in 1751 to murder his late wife's father and mother. He promised the servants cash or release from their indentures if they would kill the couple and conceal his role. On the appointed night, two women servants sneaked into their master and mistress' bedroom and attacked them with an ax. They killed their mistress outright, but their master was only stunned, and they could not bring themselves to finish him off. In a panic they called neighbors and claimed that robbers had been in the house, but their story quickly fell apart, and they and their fellow conspirators were arrested and convicted.[74]

A handful of homicides were committed by mentally ill relatives. But most murders of adult relatives were rooted in spontaneous quarrels between brothers or between fathers and sons. Baker Nason got into an argument with his brother Jonathan while they were paddling a canoe on the Piscataqua River near their home in Maine. Jonathan swung his paddle at Baker, and Baker swung back and accidentally killed him. The teenaged Samuel Frost quarreled with his father while they were digging a ditch in Princeton, Massachusetts, and hit him on the head with a pry bar. Since they were not premeditated, such homicides were adjudicated as manslaughters or negligent homicides.[75]

Of course, there was often more to a fatal quarrel than a sudden fit of temper. Men who were angry and depressed because they had fallen on hard times made up a sizable proportion of family murderers. Because they were often forced to turn to families for help, family members sometimes ended up as the targets of their wrath. Benjamin Tuttle, a middle-aged man, lived with his sister and brother-in-law,

John and Sarah Slawson, a prominent couple from Stamford, Connecticut. No one was happy with this arrangement. In November 1676 Benjamin and his sister got into an argument over a trivial matter. Slawson said that she wished her husband had eaten supper before leaving the house to go on watch. Tuttle replied that his brother-in-law could have eaten supper if he had wished. Slawson told Tuttle not to be "short" with her, whereupon Tuttle stormed outside, leaving the door wide open. Slawson asked her daughter to shut the door, but Tuttle reappeared suddenly and said, "I'll shut the doar for you." He then struck his sister repeatedly with an ax, threw her into the fireplace, and watched her burn.[76]

Thomas Starr's life was also following a downward trajectory. To make matters worse, his fiancée had broken off their engagement because of some "ungentlemanly and capricious" act on his part. Starr was too overcome with "shame and remorse" to show his face in public. One evening he got drunk and stabbed his cousin, Samuel Cornwell, with a penknife. Cornwell had not done anything to cause Starr's troubles: he just happened to be there when Starr snapped.[77]

The colonies saw very few cases like these. Yet homicides among adult relatives can be common in societies where resources are scarce and where kinship largely determines a person's chances for marriage, property, or status. Under those conditions relationships among adult relatives are often explosive. In rural France, where population pressure was intense in the seventeenth and eighteenth centuries, and land was scarce and nonfarm opportunities limited, fathers who owned land controlled the fate of their children. Under the prevailing custom of primogeniture, they chose one of their sons to inherit everything. Sometimes they also burdened the inheriting son with punishing financial obligations before he got control of the property. The custom led to high rates of fratricide and parricide well into the nineteenth century.[78]

Economic opportunities were greater in the Anglo-American world (especially for those willing to migrate), and most parents and kin played a supportive rather than a determining role in the lives of their relatives. The goal of the Anglo-American kinship system was to help each family member create an independent household. Relatives recognized that everyone might need some help to achieve that goal. To ensure that an able-bodied relative did not become a burden and endanger the independence of anyone's household, the system set informal limits on help for those who could not help themselves. Adults were free to marry and to earn a living as they saw fit, but they had to succeed largely on their own. These imperatives created a flexible system of kin relations in which there were few formal obligations but many informal ones.[79]

Because parents and adult children, including in-laws, had the strongest bonds and obligations and often lived in close proximity, they were more likely than other relatives to kill one another. Parents were expected to help their children establish their own farms, shops, and households, and children were expected to contribute to the household while they were young and to help parents in their old age. Parents and adult children were also expected to help one another during crises. Other adult relatives seldom provided direct financial support, although they arranged jobs for relatives, extended loans and credit, facilitated migration, and offered support to relatives who moved into their communities. None of these acts were obligatory, but they gave extended families strong emotional bonds and an economic advantage over families with fewer ties.

Still, the fate of adults, especially outside farming, depended less on blood relatives than on spouses, employers, neighbors, and local governments. And because American society was so mobile, people often found themselves living far away from their families and leading very independent lives. As a result of this mobility, troubled relationships among adult relatives were seldom crippling. They could be abandoned or replaced by relationships with nonkin, especially through dissenting churches and other voluntary associations. The ease with which people formed these new connections diminished the likelihood of violence among adult relatives.

The rate at which European Americans murdered adult relatives in New England, Maryland, and Virginia was not constant. It was always low, but it did increase over time. In New England it rose from zero before King Philip's War to 0.1 per 100,000 per year from the late seventeenth through the mid-eighteenth centuries. In the Chesapeake it rose from zero before Bacon's Rebellion to 0.2 per 100,000 per year.[80] However, the differences are so small and the reliability of the seventeenth-century estimates is so limited that this pattern may not be significant.

Part of the explanation for the absence of homicides of adult relatives in the pre-1675 records is that adults were not as densely interrelated in the early colonial period as they would be later. Most emigrants came to the New World alone or in the company of a few close relatives, rather than as members of extended families, and death rates were initially high. It took several generations to create extensive kin networks. It is also possible that mutual dependence suppressed homicides of adult relatives in the early colonial period. Parents and adult children needed one another if they were to escape the poverty of the initial years of settlement. The same was true of other family relationships on the frontier. A young woman traveling west in 1810 remarked upon how much more important relatives were in the Ohio wilderness. "A cousin in this country is not to be slighted," she wrote. "I would give more, for one in this country, than for 20 in old Connecticut."[81] As interrelatedness increased and as the need for cooperation became less pressing, the possibility of deadly conflict increased, because relatives were treated more like any other adults. In fact, by the mid-eighteenth century the circumstances surrounding murders among adult relatives in southern New England and the Chesapeake made them look much like murders among nonrelatives, and the rates of the two kinds of murder began to go up and down together.

There is no record of African Americans in New England committing murders of other adult relatives in the seventeenth or eighteenth centuries. That fact, too, is remarkable, given the increasing interrelatedness of African Americans by the late eighteenth century. Again, the adoption of Anglo-American kinship practices may have helped prevent violence. Kinship obligations were not as extensive or binding among African Americans as they were among most African peoples. African Americans in New England viewed adult relatives much the way European Americans did: as allies who would help them in times of need. Most African Americans adopted Anglo-American kinship beliefs, especially the idea of bilateral descent (from both the mother and father). Bilateral descent limited the power of kinship. Where descent was patrilineal or matrilineal, as it was in most African societies, many people belonged to each clan or kin group; but where descent was bilateral, only siblings shared a common set of kin, and only parents and children had formal obligations to one another. Initially the transition to bilateral kinship beliefs left many African Americans feeling bereft, but the shift opened the way for them to develop closer relationships with nonrelatives like godparents. By the mid-eighteenth century these ties helped African Americans in New England develop an intense sense of solidarity and fellow feeling that left them unlikely to murder one another whether they were related or not.[82]

It is impossible to know how often African Americans murdered adult relatives in the Chesapeake, because records do not indicate whether victims and assailants were related. Still, murders of adult relatives were probably rare, because lethal violence by men against women—a good proxy for all forms of intimate and familial violence, as noted above—was rare. There were undoubtedly more opportunities to murder relatives, since African Americans, slave and free, built more extensive family networks in the Chesapeake than they did in New England, and family played a larger role in their lives.[83] As in New England, however, there are no signs that family networks determined the fates of individuals as much as they did among many peoples in Africa. Relatives played a supportive role, as they did among European Americans, and so they may not have been the objects of murderous rage. And as in New England, the greatest deterrent to murder among African Americans in the Chesapeake was probably the growing sense of solidarity among them. By the end of the eighteenth century they were no longer an aggregate of disparate tribes cast up on an alien shore, their families dead or dispersed. They had densely interrelated families, and they had an awareness of themselves as a distinct people.

Whether Native Americans in New England were more likely to murder adult relatives during the seventeenth and eighteenth centuries is unclear. Known murders of relatives were rare and do not appear to have been a persistent problem. The five known homicides of adult relatives were confined to the mid-eighteenth century, when marital murders and murders of unrelated adults also peaked. In 1726 an Indian man went on a rampage in Colchester, Connecticut, killing two of his children and his brother before killing himself. In 1728 Jacob Swamp brutally murdered his brother, stabbing him so many times that his own clothes were soaked in blood. In 1769, at a dance in Stockbridge, Massachusetts, two brothers got drunk and beat each other so badly that one died the next day. Suicidal depression, murderous rage, and drunken quarrels were common among Native Americans in the mid-eighteenth century, a further sign that warfare in northern New England and loss of land in southern New England had a disastrous effect on the morale of Native Americans and led to violence both inside and outside families.[84]

CHAPTER 4

"A Sense of Their Rights"

Homicide in the Age of Revolution

Although rates of family and intimate homicide remained low for most people in western Europe and North America well into the nineteenth century, the long decline in homicide among unrelated adults ended amid the revolutionary turmoil of the late eighteenth century. The political stability that had prevailed through most of the Western world since the mid-seventeenth century was shattered by a succession of revolutions, civil wars, and military conquests. National loyalties and faith in government were strained and sometimes destroyed by revolutionary ideas, popular protests, and divisive wars. Some regimes collapsed, and those that survived found it difficult to reestablish their authority and revive patriotic feeling among their citizens. Beset by treasonous plots and rebellions and plagued by threats from abroad, newly emerged governments floundered. Their citizens fell to squabbling among themselves over politics, questioning one another's loyalties and refusing to obey laws or administrations they considered illegitimate. The three most important correlates of homicide were thus in place in much of the Western world during the Age of Revolution: political instability, a loss of government legitimacy, and a decline in fellow feeling among citizens. Together, these conditions created the feelings of anger, alienation, and powerlessness that caused homicide rates to spike.

Nowhere was the rise in homicide greater than in revolutionary

145

France. The collapse of the ancien régime, which had governed with a strong hand since the late seventeenth century, led to a brutal struggle for power that lasted from the fall of the Bastille in 1789 until 1802, when Napoleon ended the French Revolution by establishing a dictatorship. By the mid-1790s the homicide rate probably ranged from 30 to 80 per 100,000 adults per year in eastern, southern, and western France, where the republican government was weak and citizens were divided by the Revolution or openly hostile to it. The homicide problem may have been less severe in and around Paris, where the post-Jacobin government had established its authority. But the actual homicide rate for all of France will probably prove to have been 40 per 100,000 adults per year or more, once government and newspaper accounts of homicides are taken into account.[1]

France was not the only Western nation to experience a dramatic rise in homicide during the Age of Revolution. In England and in Sweden, the two countries for which national statistics are available, homicide rates doubled between the 1780s and the 1830s. According to studies of selected towns, homicide rates also appear to have doubled in Germany, Switzerland, and Italy. The rate rose to 20 per 100,000 adults per year in Geneva after that city-state's elite crushed an uprising in 1782 led by the Représentants, the delegates to the lower house of Geneva's ruling council, who had demanded political equality for lower-ranking citizens. In Leiden the rate rose to 30 per 100,000 adults per year after 1801, when Napoleon imposed an authoritarian government on the Netherlands. Rates fell gradually in Canada, where political calm prevailed until the Patriote uprising of 1837, but they increased everywhere else as political stability, faith in government, and national feeling faltered.[2]

Homicide rates among unrelated adults in the United States did not follow a uniform pattern, but in the states and counties studied intensively the number of homicides soared wherever the Revolution divided people into Tory and rebel camps. In other words, homicide rates were highest where the struggle for power between Tories and rebels—and between the British and Continental armies—was most intense. In the countryside around New York City and Philadelphia, in the Ohio Valley, and in the backcountry from southwestern Virginia to northwestern Georgia, homicide rates reached seventeenth-century levels as governments collapsed, law and order broke down, and neighbor turned against neighbor. For most white Americans, the Revolution was profoundly disruptive and divisive, but in those areas it was a genuine civil war. The criminal justice system disbanded or became the partisan tool of whoever was in power locally. Vigilante and revenge killings ensued, some motivated by politics, some not. As in revolutionary France, the proliferation of politically charged homicides was matched by an increase in garden-variety homicides as individuals adopted the same hostile and predatory attitudes toward their neighbors that political partisans showed toward their opponents. The extremely high homicide rates persisted until the end of the War of 1812, when they finally returned to the levels that prevailed in the rest of the nation.

Homicide rates doubled even in places where the struggle for power between Tories and rebels was intermittent or short-lived and the criminal justice system remained effective, like New England and the Chesapeake. In colonies that experienced political violence during the imperial crisis of the 1760s and early 1770s, like Pennsylvania, Massachusetts, and North Carolina, the increase in homicide began before the Revolution as the withering of British patriotism and the erosion of loyalty to the governments imposed upon the colonies by the crown undermined the fellow feeling that had kept homicide in check since the late seventeenth century. And in most communities within those colonies, the revolutionary movement was too divisive for solidarity to be reestablished while the outcome of the Revolution remained in doubt. But in places like the Shenandoah Valley of Virginia, where the Revolution won broad support and caused little disruption, the homicide rate among unrelated white adults continued to fall in the late eighteenth century. Homicide rates also continued to fall for African Americans in the South and in New England. Blacks were less likely to be murdered by whites and by one another, in large part because of the vitality of the antislavery movement, which freed many slaves and increased humanitarian regard for blacks. The movement also forged greater solidarity among blacks and gave them hope for a better future.

Wherever government broke down, political, robbery, and revenge homicides proliferated. The political upheaval undermined existing loyalties and institutions and made people from all walks of life more impatient with legal and economic restraints and more sensitive to personal slights. Ordinary men were suddenly more likely to kill to defend their reputations, property, or rights. Public men—politicians, military officers, attorneys, and newspaper editors—were particularly vulnerable to the Revolution's disruptive effects. In a republic that had yet to develop strong parties or political institutions, they were at the mercy of public opinion, and a surprising number of them died trying to defend their honor in duels.

The American Revolution might have had an even worse effect on the homicide rate if it had created a long-lasting economic crisis or a deep-seated disruption of the social hierarchy. Life was difficult for the poor in America's largest cities—Boston, New York, and Philadelphia—and the urban poor were especially restive and violent in the late eighteenth century.[3] But in small towns and in the countryside, most people were still able to form households and to buy their own shops or farms, thanks to the British victory in the French and Indian War, which had opened vast tracts of land to settlement. African Americans everywhere looked forward to new opportunities because of the decline of slavery. In the slaveholding South, revolutionary ideas would challenge the social hierarchy and lead to a permanent increase in homicides there, but almost everywhere else the Revolution's impact on homicide was confined to the years between 1764 and 1790, when government broke down and fellow feeling declined.

The increase in all kinds of homicides among unrelated adults began the moment conflict between colonists and the government turned violent. Homicide rates rose in Pennsylvania, North Carolina, and South Carolina after revolts broke out in the backcountry in the 1760s over Indian policy, land policy, and the failure to grant newly settled counties adequate representation in colonial assemblies (Figure 2.2). The turning point in New England was 1770, the year of the Boston Massacre (Figure 1.2). In the Chesapeake politics remained nonhomicidal until 1775, when fighting broke out between loyalist and patriot forces (Figure 1.3). Many of the homicides that occurred were political or war-related. In southern New England and the Chesapeake, where the homicide rate for whites doubled, such homicides were probably responsible for a third of the increase in the 1770s and early 1780s. On the Vermont frontier and in the southern and western backcountry, political homicides were responsible for more than half the increase.[4]

The revolutionary conflict had a direct impact on the homicide rate everywhere, but in most parts of the country its indirect impact on the homicide rate was even greater. By eroding British patriotism, undermining the legitimacy of political institutions and political leaders of all stripes, weakening the legal system, and generally vitiating the social contract that kept the peace, the conflict that gave rise to political homicides generated more hostile, defensive, and predatory behavior and spawned other kinds of homicide, such as robbery and revenge murders.

The Rise in Homicide throughout the Country

British patriotism had been on the wane since the mid-1750s. Colonists who served in the armed forces during the French and Indian War—probably one of every three adult males—saw British soldiers up close for the first time and did not like what they saw. They were stunned by the arrogance of British officers, who considered all colonials their inferiors, and shocked by their brutality toward enlisted men. They found regular British soldiers servile, profane, and impious.[5]

The colonists were further alienated by the Stamp Act, which made it clear that their interests were not safe in British hands. Many of them began referring to themselves explicitly as "American" rather than "British." In colonial newspapers the proportion of references to the colonies as "British" or "royal" fell from 38 percent before the war to only 6 percent by its end; references to the colonies as "American" rose from 20 percent to 43 percent. The share of implicit references to the colonies as American also rose, from 5 percent to 17 percent. The erosion of British patriotism was also evident in the names colonial assemblies gave new counties. The proportion of new counties named for British notables fell from 81 percent in the first half of the eighteenth century to 64 percent in the third quarter of the century as disputes over colonial policies intensified. It then plummeted to 18 percent from 1775 to 1789, and to 2 percent in the last decade of the eighteenth century (Figure 2.1).[6]

In New England anti-British feeling generated political homicides long before the war began, during riots against British officials, soldiers, and sympathizers. Ebenezer Richardson was a Boston customs collector suspected of informing on merchants who were violating Britain's import and export laws. In February 1770 a mob gathered in front of his house and began to break his windows. He fired on them, wounding one young man and killing another. Less than two weeks later a group of young men began pelting British sentries with rocks and ice to protest the presence of British troops in Boston. The sentries opened fire, killing five protesters in what became known as the Boston Massacre. A mob was responsible for the death of John Taylor, a Tory from Washington, New Hampshire. According to local tradition, Taylor was being ridden out of town on a rail. Hoping to make his departure as painful as possible, a number of men grabbed his legs and began lifting him up off the rail and slamming him down again. His scrotum got caught on a splinter, his testicles were torn off, and he bled to death.[7]

Once the Revolution got underway, it became difficult to distinguish between homicide and acts of war. After the British army withdrew from New England in March 1776, many loyalists fled, and the patriots were left in firm control of Massachusetts, New Hampshire, and most of Connecticut and Rhode Island. They posted sentries to apprehend loyalist spies, and they established prisoner-of-war camps. Occasionally sentries shot travelers who refused to identify themselves, sentries were themselves shot by spies, and prisoners of war were shot while trying to escape. Some of these killings ended up being adjudicated as homicides, although in most cases verdicts of manslaughter were returned.[8]

In Vermont, southern Connecticut, and eastern Maine, where the patriots did not have firm control, the situation was much more chaotic, and it was more difficult to prosecute political killings. The British staged raids from New York, Long Island, and Canada throughout the war, sometimes with the help of loyalists, and loyalists staged raids of their own. Both loyalists and patriots ambushed and killed people they knew to be political enemies. When the struggle for control of western Vermont intensified in 1777 in anticipation of a British invasion from Canada, neighbor turned against neighbor. John Irish, a loyalist farmer from Tinmouth, was ambushed and killed near his home by an unknown patriot. David Mallory, a medical student from Arlington, was killed by a group of loyalists led by Mallory's teacher, Dr. Samuel Adams. A few people took advantage of the political situation to settle scores. William Prindle, for example, a farm laborer who claimed to be a loyalist, struck a blow for England by killing his patriot employer and cutting off his head.[9]

Internal divisions also claimed lives in New England during the revolutionary period. Conservative patriots were pitted against more radical patriots. Quarrels that might once have been referred to the courts or to colonial assemblies now led to armed confrontation. For instance, some Vermonters wanted independence from New York, while others had reason to be content with the status quo. In 1775 supporters of New York rule fired into a party of protesters who had gathered to prevent the sitting of a county court created by New York. Two men were killed. In turn Vermont's insurgent militia, the Green Mountain Boys, killed at least one supporter of New York rule while suppressing a pro–New Yorker rising in Windham County in 1784. In 1786–87 farmers in western Massachusetts rose against their own county courts to protest foreclosures and the low commodity prices and tight monetary policies that had caused them. The governor of Massachusetts called up militiamen from eastern Massachusetts to subdue the protesters, who were led by Captain Daniel Shays, a Revolutionary War veteran. In Springfield the protesters tried to seize a state armory guarded by the governor's militiamen, and the militia opened fire, killing five rebels and one of their own officers. The show of force persuaded most protesters to abandon the cause, but small bands continued to clash with the militia and with the governor's local supporters over the next four weeks. Those skirmishes claimed at least ten more lives.[10]

In Pennsylvania political discontent spawned a number of homicides in the backcountry in the 1760s, after the French and Indian War. The provincial government had advanced the interests of the Penn family and other land speculators, but it had not protected backcountry settlers against Indian attacks or given them adequate courts or representation in the colonial assembly. Many settlers, hoping that British rule would be more effective and disinterested, supported a campaign by the Pennsylvania assembly in 1764–65 to replace the proprietary government with a royal government. When that campaign failed, a militant minority took Indian policy into its own hands, determined to expel or exterminate the colony's entire Native population.[11]

The killings began in 1763, when soldiers massacred Moravian converts at Lehigh Gap and Conestoga, and settlers burned a settlement of displaced Delawares, Mohicans, and Shawnees in the Wyoming Valley and assassinated their leader, Teedyuscung. After these attacks, murders of Indians almost became casual. Native Americans retaliated for these and other murders, initiating a cycle of murder and revenge that lasted through the Revolution.[12]

Since racial solidarity generally correlates with low homicide rates, the settlers might have been expected to set aside their own differences as they banded together against the Indians. They did not, however, because Pennsylvania settlers were as divided over Indian policy in the 1760s as Virginia settlers had been at the time of Bacon's Rebellion. Most citizens supported the state's attempts to restore peaceful relations with Native Americans. But settlers who lived on the frontier were furious with the proprietary government for refusing to lift a hand to defend them against Indian attacks. Their anger expressed itself in a complete repudiation of government institutions and officials. They would no longer turn to the state for help; instead they would settle disputes themselves. They soon produced prodigious homicide rates, especially in the Wyoming Valley in northeastern Pennsylvania. In the 1770s and early 1780s settlers from Pennsylvania fought for control of the valley with migrants from New England, who were sponsored by the government of Connecticut and its development arm, the Susquehannah Land Company. Dozens of people died. Settlers also attacked traders and government officials who appeared to be siding with Native Americans. The "Black Boys" of Cumberland County in south-central Pennsylvania attacked westbound pack trains that they believed were carrying arms to the Natives, and they fought British soldiers and Pennsylvania officials who tried to arrest them.[13]

As the Revolution got underway, clashes between Tories and rebels made the bloodshed even worse. Tories and their Native allies massacred over 200 settlers in July 1778. Political killings continued in the backcountry during the Whiskey Rebellion of 1794. At least six men died near Pittsburgh during protests against the federal excise tax on liquor.[14]

Southeastern Pennsylvania saw only a few political homicides during the Revolutionary era. Relations among non-Tories were tense, however, because the Constitutionalists, who controlled Pennsylvania's rebel government during the war, governed in a high-handed fashion, persecuting not only Tories but also neutrals, pietists, and lukewarm patriots. In March 1777 the Constitutionalists passed a Militia Act, which compelled men between the ages of eighteen and fifty-three to serve in the militia or pay heavy fines; and three months later they passed the Test Act, which deprived men of their civil rights if they did not swear allegiance to the state. These acts disfranchised the majority of men in Pennsylvania and threatened to bankrupt Quakers, Moravians, and Mennonites, who could not swear oaths or serve in the military.[15]

Opponents of the Constitutionalists rallied around the Republicans, who favored an inclusive franchise, peaceful relations with neutrals, and waivers from military service for pacifists. They clashed with Constitutionalist militiamen in Philadelphia in October 1779, after the city's Republican leaders put an end to price controls and allowed merchants to charge whatever the market would bear. The militiamen were angry that the wealthy had left the fighting and suffering to the poor, and they attacked a house where Republican leaders had taken refuge. At least six people were killed and seventeen wounded in the showdown between the two factions. Militant neutrals formed neighborhood associations to resist tax collectors and military recruiters. William Boyd, a tax collector in Chester County, was killed on his rounds by such resisters in 1780. Political homicides were less frequent in interior counties than in the southeast or on the frontier, but they occurred everywhere in Pennsylvania during the Revolution.[16]

Unlike New England and Pennsylvania, the Chesapeake did not suffer any political homicides before the Revolution began. The only protests that ended in homicide occurred late in the war, during the British invasion of 1780–81, when Virginia imposed a military draft and requisitioned beef and clothing for its troops. The draft sparked riots in a number of counties. The rioters, most of whom lived on the frontier, the Northern Neck, or the Eastern Shore, had legitimate grievances. They did not want to be paid in Continental currency, which was nearly worthless, and they were afraid their families would be left defenseless against Indians, slaves, and loyalist raiders. County officials did not back down, however, and confrontations between militia and protesters left at least two people dead. The toll could have been much higher, but Governor Thomas Jefferson counseled restraint and told local militia officers to track down individual protesters at night and take them "out of their Beds singly and without Noise."[17]

During the war, however, the Chesapeake saw political homicides wherever British forces were powerful enough to undermine patriot authority and encourage loyalist resistance. Such homicides occurred in 1775–76 in and around the adjoining towns of Norfolk and Portsmouth, where the royal governor, Lord Dunmore, ordered his forces to make their last stand. They also occurred throughout the war wherever the British navy and local loyalists raided patriot ships and plantations, and they appeared again when the British invaded Virginia in 1779 and 1780–81.

Patriots kept the upper hand on the Eastern Shore, another loyalist stronghold, despite constant raids by British and loyalist privateers on patriot plantations near the bay. Realizing that there was no hope of an immediate British landing, the loyalists kept a low profile, spying for the British and destroying patriot property. The patriots, who controlled the local government, found that mild sanctions like fines and peace bonds could keep the loyalists in check as long as the British army and navy focused their attention elsewhere. But the potential for violence was always there. In July 1781 a patriot planter came upon three loyalists trying to persuade one of his slaves to join a loyalist raiding party. The loyalists murdered the planter and fled, but the slave told neighbors what had happened, and the loyalists were hunted down. The posse gave them time to pray and then hanged them.[18]

The proliferation of politically charged homicides during the Revolution was accompanied by an increase in other kinds of homicides, especially robbery murders. The line between political murder and robbery murder was sometimes hard to define. Josiah Philips was already a convicted criminal when he declared himself a loyalist and was licensed by Lord Dunmore to rob patriots in the Norfolk area. His interracial gang, which at its peak had fifty members, stole livestock, burned buildings, and killed whoever tried to stop them. Most robbery murders, however, were committed by men who had no political affiliation or who had lost faith in the cause they were fighting for. They murdered their victims to prevent them from talking or killed the officers who uncovered their operations. The majority of them were never caught.[19]

Public violence weakened law enforcement and had a corrosive effect on personal morality. During the war, young men in particular were more liable to break with ordinary standards of right and wrong as they witnessed the violence erupting around them. Teenaged brothers Barnett and Nicholas Davenport worked as farm laborers for a wealthy couple. One day they clubbed the couple to death, killed their three young grandchildren, looted their house, and set it on fire. Such cold-blooded murders, which had all but disappeared from New England after King Philip's War and from the Chesapeake after Bacon's Rebellion, reappeared once the revolutionary crisis began. Gun violence, where it can be measured, was also more common. In New England the proportion of political and nonpolitical homicides committed with guns rose from 13 percent before the Revolution to 52 percent.[20] The increase suggests that more of these homicides were premeditated.

Retaliatory and vigilante murders also increased, at least among whites. Occasionally these murders occurred among criminals. In 1779 Younger Hardwick apparently killed fellow gang member Erasmus Whitworth in Amelia County, Virginia, because Whitworth had stolen part of Hardwick's share of the loot. But most perpetrators and victims were law-abiding citizens. In Albemarle County, Virginia, a local man stepped into a tavern and imprudently told a table of "gamesters" that he had just collected a debt. When he left, one of the gamblers sneaked out after him. Several men took note and followed the gambler. They found their neighbor dead, his throat cut and his money gone. They tracked the gambler to a canebrake where he was washing blood from his hands and hanged him on the spot.[21]

Pennsylvania suffered a rash of deadly brawls and robberies from the mid-1760s into the early 1790s, most of which occurred among strangers. Travelers were waylaid, sailors stabbed, and merchants terrorized by a floating population of former soldiers, runaway servants, gang members, and war refugees, who had no qualms about cutting throats to steal whatever they could. But even for law-abiding citizens, the violent ways learned during the Revolution died hard. John Lacey was a fervent patriot from Bucks County who had once ordered his men to shoot on sight any farmer caught trading with the enemy in Philadelphia. After the war he got into a business dispute with a man named Joel Cooke, who he thought was trying to defraud him. Lacey shot Cooke dead behind a Quaker meetinghouse.[22]

Revenge homicides, robbery homicides, political homicides, and vigilante homicides had always been common on contested frontiers, where no government or coalition of governments could gain the upper hand; and in effect, the Revolution turned the entire country—even long-settled areas like southern New England, southeastern Pennsylvania, and the Chesapeake—into a contested frontier. The decline in British patriotism, the weakening of white solidarity as the threat from Native Americans diminished, and the rise of democratic, egalitarian protest movements facilitated all types of homicide by eroding civility, mutual forbearance, and fellow feeling among unrelated whites, but the lack of a stable government was what truly opened the floodgates to a torrent of murders. Perhaps no homicides were more indicative of the fear and hostility that government instability engendered among colonists than two senseless killings that occurred during this period in Philadelphia. The first murder was committed in 1776, while the Second Continental Congress was meeting in the State House to debate the future of the colonies. A few people began to taunt a lone woman in the street. Someone called her a witch. Others took up the cry, and within minutes a crowd had stoned her to death. A decade later it happened again. A mob seized an elderly woman, accused her of being a witch, and carried her through the streets, all the while pelting her with stones. She died a few days later.[23]

The homicide rate would probably not have risen as precipitously during the Revolution if revolutionary leaders had been able to set up strong, unified governments in every colony and if allegiance to the new nation had immediately taken the place of allegiance to Great Britain; but every state government had difficulty establishing its authority, and American patriotism grew slowly. Nominal loyalty to the United States was widespread once the Revolution was won, but the depth of that loyalty was questionable. Efforts to create national solidarity in the 1780s and 1790s through patriotic celebrations, oratory, and literature foundered over real differences in values and interests. Most nationalist celebrations were partisan, despite the claims of organizers. Political adversaries—Federalist and anti-Federalist, Hamiltonian and Jeffersonian—used feast days, thanksgiving days, militia musters, Fourth of July celebrations, and tributes to George Washington or the French Revolution to promote their particular visions of the American nation. These celebrations had some success in helping majorities to consolidate their power, nationally and locally. They forged solidarity among party supporters and drew a broad range of men and women into nationalistic partisan movements. That was no small achievement, but it would take time to recreate the sense of unity that had existed under the British Empire and to establish the legitimacy of the new central government.[24]

Race was no more effective than patriotism in binding whites together in the late eighteenth century. Fear of Native Americans declined after the French and Indian War. Indian peoples no longer posed a military threat to most whites, except on the frontier, so the need for white solidarity was less pressing, and a growing number of whites expressed outrage at massacres of friendly Indians and the seizure of Native lands. The campaign against slavery also divided whites. Launched in the 1750s and 1760s by Quakers, evangelicals, and enlightened thinkers, the antislavery movement blossomed during the Revolution, and more whites, especially in the North and the Upper South, began to condemn slavery as inhumane and as inconsistent with revolutionary ideals and a free, mobile society. The rift between the Deep South and other areas of the nation began to widen, and northerners began to look askance at states whose economies were dependent on slave labor. Few whites were willing to incorporate blacks or Indians as citizens into American society, and race remained an important bond among whites, but in the late eighteenth century it was not as powerful as it had been.[25]

Local loyalties were more important than they had been before the Revolution. In the 1790s the proportion of new counties named for local heroes was higher than the proportion named for national figures: 43 percent versus 38 percent (Figure 2.1). Many of those local notables were heroes of the Revolution, and local loyalties were not necessarily incompatible with national loyalties. But as new divisions arose over slavery, economic policy, and the western territories, local and regional loyalties sometimes conflicted with national or interregional loyalties, especially for New England Federalists, southern Republicans, and westerners of both parties, who articulated their own regional versions of nationalism. Only time would tell if national loyalties or amalgams of local and national loyalties would prove powerful enough to rebuild the fellow feeling that had existed before the Revolution.[26]

In the short run, revolutionary ideology weakened the bonds that had deterred homicide among unrelated whites. The increase in murders over property and reputation in the late eighteenth century suggests that whites became more protective of their rights and their good names once the Revolution began. The concern with reputation manifested itself in the sudden resurgence of dueling, which had all but disappeared in British North America in the late seventeenth and early eighteenth centuries. The only colony where duels had persisted into the 1680s and 1690s was South Carolina, where planter "aristocrats" from the West Indies kept the custom alive. One or two isolated instances of dueling cropped up elsewhere in the early to mid-eighteenth century. In 1728, for instance, Benjamin Woodbridge, the son of an admiralty judge from Barbados, was killed in a duel on Boston Common. He and Henry Phillips, a recent graduate of Harvard, had quarreled after Woodbridge asked Phillips to sign a note for a gambling debt he owed him and Phillips refused. The men called each other thieves and liars and, in accordance with the code of dueling, borrowed swords so that they could settle their differences honorably. Their friends thought they were joking and learned that Woodbridge had been wounded only when Phillips ran to a tavern for help. Phillips fled rather than face prosecution.[27]

Bostonians were shocked by Woodbridge's death. Clearly, they felt that society had moved beyond dueling. The Reverend Joseph Sewall captured their feelings in a sermon endorsed by all of Boston's ministers in which he denounced "the Society of Evil Doers" that encouraged young men to fight "Bloody and Mortal Duels." Colonial gentlemen rarely fought or challenged each other—it simply was not done. Émigrés might resort to dueling, but colonial gentlemen settled their differences peacefully.[28]

That pattern changed abruptly during the Stamp Act crisis of 1765. The trust and mutual regard that had existed among elites were shattered, and men began to attack each other furiously over political differences. One Virginian, who lamented the new incivility in public life, tried to explain the extreme reactions of friends whose letters to the editor drew public criticism. "Our writers are generally such as have been very little used to Contradiction, and know not how to bear it from one another; and when they find their Writings not treated with that Respect they have been accustomed to in their private Characters, they grow angry, and sometimes abuse one another." Gentlemen who took Britain's side or who wavered before taking the patriot side were subjected to all kinds of public abuse, verbal and physical. Those who accepted stamp distributorships were branded traitors. Many of them were burned in effigy or had their houses vandalized.[29]

Taken aback by this turn of events, gentlemen defended their reputations and proclaimed their superior status (and their disdain for society's legal institutions) by reviving the custom of dueling. They opposed the leveling force of revolutionary ideology by resuming a practice that made it impossible to command the respect of others without resorting to violence. In doing so they helped to create conditions that strongly correlate with higher homicide rates. Yet most challenges came to nothing or were resolved in other ways. Williamsburg attorney James Mercer, whose brother Richard had accepted a stamp distributorship, challenged Arthur Lee, a young physician whose brother Richard Henry had incited the mob that had sent Richard Mercer scurrying back to England. They agreed to a duel with pistols at a race ground, but their shots went wide, and each accused the other of cowardice. The dispute ended in a coffeehouse, where Lee tried to cane Mercer. The crowd took away their canes and pistols, but Mercer would not give up. He pummeled Lee, bloodying his nose and blackening his eyes. The local paper had the last word:

> To fisty-cuffs go the exalted duelists. O sad, sad! the Doctor [Lee], instead of being handsomely run or fired through the body, which would have given him infinite satisfaction, is bled at the nose, and has his eyes closed, as if he had been no better than a clown or peasant. The poor, abus[e]d, unfortunate Doctor, lifts his discomposed, tumefied, bloody, and sightless head; and, notwithstanding the inconvenience of such a situation for the display of oratory, makes a very fine harangue on the most grossly and shamefully violated laws of honour; for which, as a mischief to society, with a truly disinterested spirit, he expresses more concern than for any injury done to his own person. The Coffee-House world manifest their esteem by laughing.

With that peculiarly American scorn for pretension, the editor savaged the duelists for setting themselves above the common man with their silly rituals and pompous speechifying.[30]

Fear of ridicule, however, was no longer enough to deter duelists. Political passions were simply too intense. Colonel James Bayliss died in 1765 in a duel in Dumfries, Virginia, two days after rioters paraded effigies of the colony's new stamp collectors through town with copies of the Stamp Act wrapped around their necks like halters. The effigies had "receiv'd the Insults of the Congregation, by Caneing, Whipping, (the Mosaic Law) Pillorying, Cropping, Hanging, and Burning." It is not clear which side Bayliss was on.[31]

Dueling resurfaced in the late eighteenth and the nineteenth centuries wherever politics became competitive and democracy reared its uncouth head: in Ireland (where the modern rules of dueling were first codified) during the campaign for home rule in the 1760s and 1770s, in England during the controversy over the Reform Bill, in Belgium after the revolt of 1830, in Italy after the unification of 1860, and in Portugal with the advent of contested parliamentary elections in the 1880s. In these nations, as in the United States, public men who went in for dueling affirmed the democratic revolution by acknowledging the importance of public opinion, but at the same time they were also rejecting the revolution by reviving an aristocratic practice that placed them above the "rabble." Dueling combatants were almost always men in the public eye—politicians, newspaper editors, attorneys, and military officers—who were exposed to harsh criticism as politics became more democratic and more confrontational and as the political structures that had kept the peace among political leaders since the Glorious Revolution were dissolved. No longer insulated by the privileges of their class, these men stood before their readers and constituents as individuals, and since their success depended almost solely on the public's perception of them, they could not let slanderous remarks go unchallenged.[32]

Dueling could enhance a man's reputation; a refusal to fight could tarnish his good name and ruin his career. As a Virginian who wrote an "Essay on Honor" said, "the opinion of mankind, which is as forcible as a law, calls upon a man to resent an affront, and fixes the contempt of a coward upon him if he refuses." This attitude was not confined to southern gentlemen. John Farnham, a Harvard student, declared that "it is in vain to expect or presume that . . . [a] man will ever obtain any consequence & respect who suffers himself to be trodden under foot." Ira Allen, a brother of Ethan Allen and the leader of the faction that governed Vermont in the early 1790s, responded immediately when he was insulted by the leader of the opposing faction, Isaac Tichenor, a Princeton graduate referred to by his enemies as "The Jersey Slick." Tichenor claimed to have "slipped General Allen's nose"—that is, pulled it in an insulting way. Allen went across the Connecticut River to New Hampshire to duel with him. The two faced each other, pistols in hand, and were preparing to fire when spectators rushed in to stop them.[33]

Scores of distinguished men met untimely ends in duels. Button Gwinnett, the leader of the radical patriots in Georgia, and Lachlan McIntosh, a leader of the conservative patriots, were political and personal enemies. When command of the Continental forces in Georgia went to McIntosh, Gwinnett tried to embarrass him by arresting his brother on the charge of being a Tory. The two men quarreled so fiercely during the 1777 military campaign in eastern Florida that they had to cede command to a third man. When they got home, the assembly—which Gwinnett controlled—censured McIntosh and exonerated Gwinnett. McIntosh called Gwinnett "a Scoundrell & lying Rascal" and challenged him to a duel. Both men were seriously wounded, and Gwinnett died three days later. The same fate befell Alexander Hamilton's nineteen-year-old son Philip in 1801. After New York City attorney George Eacker insinuated publicly that Hamilton would not oppose the violent overthrow of President Thomas Jefferson, Philip and his friend Richard Price confronted him, and Eacker called them both "damned rascals." They challenged him to a duel. Price escaped unscathed, but Philip was killed. Hamilton became deeply depressed. Two and a half years later he accepted a challenge from Aaron Burr, even though his friends assured him that he had no need to fight because Burr's reputation was so far beneath his. That so many promising or accomplished men chose to risk death rather than their reputations shows how forceful the homicidal impact of the Revolution was. By undermining the unity and mutual regard of the American people and their willingness to accept the legitimacy of government by their political adversaries, the Revolution had created conditions ripe for homicide, even among elites who shared a commitment to republicanism and revolution.[34]

Homicide on the Southern and Western Frontiers

Public men were not the only ones to experience increased volatility in their dealings with other people. The Revolution made all relationships more violent, especially in the southern and western backcountry, where it took decades to create strong, stable governments and where men created their own justice by killing people who wronged them. From the Georgia Piedmont to the Ohio River Valley, homicide rates were extremely high from the mid-1760s through the War of 1812. Rates of 25 to 30 per 100,000 per year were common for white adults in areas where county governments had been established (Figures 4.1 and 4.2). In the backcountry, where settlers and Indians (and the Spanish and British) were still fighting for control, rates probably reached 200 or more per 100,000. Those numbers had not been seen since the early seventeenth century.

Like previous frontiers that were politically unstable and lacked strong institutions that could uphold law and order, the revolutionary backcountry was plagued by vigilantism, revenge murders, political murders, systematic violence by criminal gangs, and campaigns against peaceable Native Americans who did not move on after they were defeated militarily. During the Revolution more backcountry whites took the law into their own hands and killed to advance their interests or defend their rights, lives, and property. This pattern would reappear later in Florida, the Southwest Territory, the lower Mississippi Valley, Texas, and California.

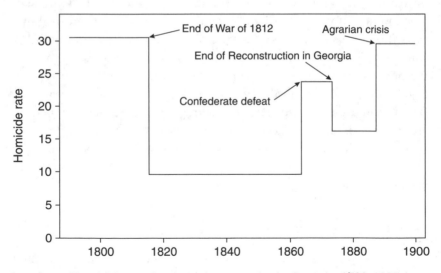

Figure 4.1 Homicide rate in plantation counties in Georgia, 1790–1900 (per 100,000 adults per year). Franklin, Jasper, and Wilkes Counties.

The Revolution came at a difficult time for settlers in the southern backcountry. They lacked the means to govern or defend themselves adequately, and they were divided over whether their interests would be better served by the British government or by patriot governments dominated by coastal elites. Virginia's government took steps before the Revolution to maintain law and order by establishing county governments in the southwest, paying for local improvements, and giving settlers adequate representation in the General Assembly. But the planters and merchants of coastal North Carolina, South Carolina, and Georgia did not want to share power with the frontier population; they deliberately delayed the formation of new counties and refused to give settlers adequate representation in state assemblies or funding for public projects. Their actions compounded the homicide problem in the Lower South by depriving settlers of courts, constables, and militia companies. Settlers in that region had no choice but to take the law into their own hands, and their efforts to protect themselves against criminals and Indian attacks were probably responsible

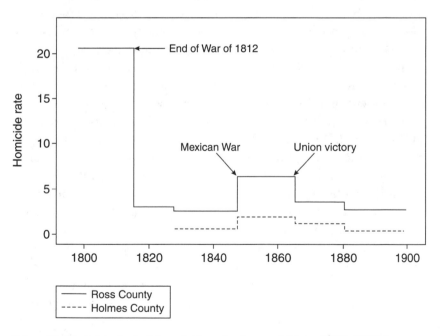

Figure 4.2 Unrelated-adult homicide rates in rural Ohio, 1798–1900 (per 100,000 adults per year).

for as many homicides as political violence was. Jittery farmers gunned down friendly Creeks or Cherokees who wandered near their houses, and residents who tracked down thieves ended up in deadly shootouts. Local vigilantes known as Regulators organized in the 1760s in North and South Carolina to carry out their own brand of justice against criminals. Colonial governments suppressed the Regulators, but fifty lives were lost in a battle between Regulators and state militiamen at Alamance Creek in North Carolina in 1771. Southwestern Virginians fared better, but their county governments were not entirely effective because officials did not have time to establish their legitimacy.[35]

The situation only deteriorated when the British made the southern backcountry a major theater of operations. They invaded the area several times and encouraged loyalists and their Native allies to attack patriots. The battle was joined first in southwestern Virginia. William Campbell, a militia officer in Washington County, stopped a suspicious traveler in 1777 and discovered that the man had been paid by the British to smuggle letters to Cherokee leaders, asking them to attack settlers. Campbell and his friends hanged the man on the spot. Local loyalists, joined by men from North Carolina, attacked patriots and plotted to destroy the lead mines in Montgomery County, which were vital to Virginia's war effort. The outcome of the struggle was in doubt until patriot militia leaders like Campbell, Walter Crockett of Montgomery County, and Charles Lynch of Bedford County (the state superintendent of the lead mines, whose followers allegedly coined the term "Lynch Law" to celebrate his brand of vigilante justice) decided in 1779–80 to fight terror with terror. Tradition has it that during their campaign they shot or hanged a large number of suspected loyalists and forced the British to turn their attentions farther south.[36]

Political violence, including lynchings and murders of prisoners, was most intense in and around Augusta, Georgia, the frontier settlement that held the key to controlling the upper Savannah River watershed. Residents of adjacent areas, including Wilkes County in Georgia and Ninety-Six District in South Carolina, suffered through a six-year reign of terror as British and American forces tried unsuccessfully to establish control over the region. Patriots and loyalists battled back and forth for Augusta and the surrounding countryside. The combatants united briefly in 1779 for a joint expedition against the Cherokees but soon returned to fighting each other.

When the British recaptured Augusta in the spring of 1780, loyalists went on a rampage in the countryside and took revenge on patriots, who had held the upper hand the previous year. A band of loyalists rode up to the farm of Colonel John Dooley, a patriot who had killed a number of loyalists to avenge the murder of his brother, and shot him dead in front of his family. After discovering that the Hart family had once hidden a patriot soldier in their house, loyalists looted the Harts' farm, took Nancy Hart hostage, and ordered her to cook them a meal. As they waited by the hearth, Hart quietly gathered up their muskets and started to push them outside through a chink in the cabin wall. When the Tories saw what she was doing, she took up a musket and threatened to shoot the first man who moved. Two men rushed her, and she shot them both. Meanwhile her daughter had called for help by blowing on a conch shell, and her husband and neighbors came running. They hanged the rest of the group.[37]

Across the Savannah River in Ninety-Six District, South Carolina, loyalists were better organized and more equally matched with patriots, so a greater portion of killings occurred during or shortly after pitched battles. A band of thirty patriots rode out in 1781 in pursuit of a small band of loyalists who had stolen horses. They recovered the horses, but they did not realize that the loyalists were part of a band of 300 under "Bloody Bill" Cunningham, and they made the mistake of camping at Cloud's Creek before completing their journey home. The loyalists surrounded them and refused them terms, because the group included a young man, John Butler Jr., who had killed a loyalist earlier. The young man's father offered to exchange himself for his son, but his son grabbed a rifle and killed a loyalist before he was gunned down. The surviving patriots surrendered, but the loyalists spared only one man, in recognition of the fact that local patriots had spared one of theirs in a recent battle. They hacked the others to death with swords. John Butler Sr. grabbed a pitchfork and defended himself as best he could, but the loyalists chopped off his hands and then killed him.[38]

The next year a band of patriots led by another of John Butler's sons, William, surprised Cunningham's depleted force near Baulknight's Ferry. Cunningham abandoned his men and rode off. Butler gave chase but was unable to catch him. When he returned, he found that one of his men had already killed one of the loyalists. Butler was exasperated: he was not out to avenge Cloud's Creek; he wanted to round up the loyalists and put an end to the killing, now that the war was all but over. His men would not let him punish the killer, however, because the dead man had once tortured the killer's mother in a futile effort to get her to disclose her son's whereabouts. Butler let that killing pass, but later that day they came upon several of Cunningham's stragglers, and another of his men refused his direct order not to shoot. It was clear that no cease-fire could put an end to the enmity between the two camps: it was too strong and too personal, and it would spill past the verges of the war and seep into the lives of the children and grandchildren of combatants.[39]

Harassment of loyalists continued after the war. In Wilkes County, Georgia, where feelings remained bitter, it was not uncommon for jurors deliberating on the courthouse steps to chase down and beat up a loyalist who happened to pass by. Churchgoers forcibly ejected loyalists who dared to show up for services. "Lynch's Law," which referred not just to hanging but to vigilante justice of any kind, became the preferred method of dealing with disputes both personal and political and was celebrated in song and story. This poem appeared in the *Augusta Chronicle* in 1794:

> Some time ago, Augusta acted right,
> To punish one, and put two more to flight;
> Lynch's law, ought still to be in vogue,
> It will rid the town of every cursed rogue.
>
> . . .
>
> The state is robb'd, and plunder'd of its right,
> It'll not be so, if Lynch be kept in sight.[40]

For the most part, vigilante justice stopped short of murder. Men ganged up on people they didn't like and beat them. Twenty armed men stormed the house of Colonel Henry Kerr in Wilkes County in 1793 and carried off Kerr, a friend, and seven of his slaves because of a property dispute. In Augusta, Major Fields Perdue gathered a gang together and went after a former employee, George Tucker, who had had the effrontery to quit and demand his pay. Perdue and his entourage dragged Tucker from his boardinghouse and marched him at gunpoint to the Carolina side of the Savannah River. Tucker reported that they "stripped me naked, and tied my hands with hickory bark, and stood round me with pistols cock'd and sticks" while Perdue gave him thirty lashes. He finally broke free and jumped into the river, where he was rescued by a passing boat.[41]

In more than a few instances this kind of vigilantism did end in death. After a Wilkes County grand jury refused to indict Robert Stewart for murder in 1795, his neighbors got together and killed him. In Richmond County in 1797, a party of drunken men seized a man "on suspicion of several crimes" and hanged him from a tree in the woods. In Franklin County in 1800, John and Julius Neal got a gang together and went after Cormack Higgins, who they believed had robbed and murdered their brother. They brought Higgins to the county seat and took him to the gallows, where another murderer had just been hanged. There they sat him on a horse and put a rope around his neck. Higgins refused to confess, however, even after the Neals shooed the horse out from under him and let him hang awhile, so they cut him down and asked friends to help them take him to their house. John Neal went on ahead. As the rest of the party crossed a river, a single shot from the far bank killed Higgins instantly.[42]

Because the violence between patriots and loyalists had legitimized lynchings, beatings, and revenge murder, vigilante justice gained a measure of approval in the backcountry that it did not have elsewhere. Jurors or grand jurors acquitted all these vigilantes of murder, even the ones in Richmond County whose victim turned out to be innocent. In the eyes of the grand jury, the victim's bad reputation justified the killing.

The movement of settlers into the backcountry also increased the homicide rate after the Revolution by setting up a conflict of interest between settlers and federal, state, and territorial governments. The federal government incurred the settlers' wrath during the Confederation period and Washington's presidency when it tried to enforce the terms of Indian treaties in hopes of preventing violence and building a military alliance with western tribes. The government repeatedly sent troops into the Ohio River Valley in the mid-1780s to tear down homes that squatters had built on Shawnee land. In Georgia the federal government repudiated treaties that the state government had coerced some of the Creeks into signing in the mid-1780s. Those treaties had ceded to the state all the land between the Ogeechee and Oconee rivers in central Georgia. By 1790, however, the flood of settlers into the disputed territory was so overwhelming that Creek leaders accepted the loss of their land east of the Oconee in return for a prohibition of white settlement west of the Oconee, to be enforced by federal troops and by Creek authorities. The Creeks were permitted to arrest or kill any white who set foot west of the Oconee without a pass from Creek or federal authorities.[43]

Washington's administration stationed troops along the Oconee, but the bloodshed continued. Creek warriors who opposed the 1790 cession or were determined to avenge the deaths of friends and relatives defied tribal leaders and raided farms and plantations east of the river. Settlers raided deep into Creek territory, often with the help of the Georgia militia, which the state had garrisoned along the Oconee to protect settlers and to counter federal support for the Creeks. Elijah Clarke, a Revolutionary War hero and a champion of settlers' rights, took matters into his own hands in 1794 and established the "Trans-Oconee Republic" west of the river. He and his supporters declared their independence, set up a government, issued land grants, and built a bustling farm community under the protection of "Fort Defiance" before federal troops forced them back across the Oconee and burned their settlement.

Settlers in Kentucky felt abandoned by the federal government. In the 1780s many considered seceding from the United States and establishing an independent republic. They welcomed federal forces whenever they arrived to fight the Indians, but they railed against the government when it took the Natives' side or tried to mediate the conflict. Like Bacon's Rebels before them, they hated the East Coast elites who had rid themselves of Indians but would not allow settlers in the backcountry to do the same.[44]

Backcountry settlers were also alienated from their state governments, and with good reason. Wherever state governments held title to western lands there was massive fraud, corruption, and claim jumping. The Georgia legislature of 1794 was probably the most corrupt. It gave four land companies—all of which included state legislators as investors—huge land grants for only pennies an acre. Public outrage over the Yazoo land fraud led to the ousting of many of these legislators, but the damage could not be undone, because the courts ruled the grants legally binding.[45]

Virginia's government was less corrupt, but it issued conflicting land grants in the future state of Kentucky and failed to provide for a comprehensive survey. As a result, settlers had to defend their claims in court against well-financed, well-represented speculators, who won almost every case. Settlers who could not afford legal fees had little choice but to sell their land at a fraction of its value to those who could afford to fight in court. The economic consequences of these policies for settlers were disastrous. By the time Kentucky became a state in 1792, two out of three families there owned no land at all, and the numbers were not much better on the Georgia frontier. For most families in these areas, all the hard work they had done and the hardships they had endured went for naught, and all the loved ones they had lost in battles with the Indians died in vain.[46]

In some cases the rage engendered by government actions led directly to homicide. In 1794, when anger against the federal government was at a fever pitch in Georgia because of the suppression of the Trans-Oconee Republic, a Methodist minister named Beverley Allen, who refused to acknowledge the jurisdiction of federal courts in the state of Georgia, shot and killed a U.S. marshal in Augusta. In 1795, when anger over the Yazoo fraud was most intense, Robert Thomas, a state senator who had profited from the fraud, was assassinated by one of his constituents. But antigovernment feeling also increased homicides indirectly by convincing settlers that their governments were illegitimate. It was generally agreed that the "spirit of speculation which seems to have seized hold on all departments, and orders of people, from the man in office to the tiller of the soil," had corrupted government on all levels, and that the right of states to conduct their own affairs where Native Americans or western lands were concerned had been "trampled under the federal foot." In the eyes of many people on the southern and western frontier, governments existed only to swindle the common man out of the fruits of his labor. If they wanted justice, they would have to create it themselves.[47]

In time the federal government did force the Creeks, Cherokees, Shawnees, and other Native peoples out of Georgia, Kentucky, and Ohio, and it established an orderly system for selling federal lands in the Northwest and Southwest Territories. Legislators in Georgia and Virginia tried belatedly to end corruption and ensure that farm families had a fair chance to buy land, and every new state in the trans-Appalachian West empowered poor white men by ending property restrictions on voting. It would take several decades, however, to alleviate the bitter feelings of the 1780s and 1790s, and the hatred of government engendered in the southern backcountry during those decades never truly disappeared.

The frustration of settlers in the postrevolutionary backcountry manifested itself in high homicide rates. Settlers were quick to take the law into their own hands and kill people who appropriated their property or damaged it in any way. Murders occurred over the right to set up fish traps, over attachments for debt, or over hunting dogs that had been shot. Settlers were also quick to kill people who insulted them or failed to show proper respect. Poor people seldom fought duels, but like revolutionary-era public men they felt compelled to defend their reputations and sometimes judged it better to kill or be killed than to tolerate a public affront. Turning the other cheek could be interpreted as a sign of weakness. If a settler did not respond to a challenge, he risked further bullying and intimidation. In taverns and at the saltworks in Ross County, Ohio, for example, men used guns and knives freely and showed no remorse over killing men who had insulted them. After finishing off his victim one murderer declared with satisfaction that "the damned rascal deserved it." Near Augusta, Georgia, a man was stabbed to death in his sleep for having ridiculed another man in front of a crowd, and a man murdered a neighbor for calling him a rogue and a liar at a militia election.[48]

Continuing genocidal violence against Native Americans also boosted the homicide rate in the backcountry after the Revolution. Some men murdered Indians by stealth; others killed them openly and boasted about it to friends. Tom Lion was killed quietly. An elderly Mohican who lived alone in Holmes County, Ohio, Lion made a living by trading game for the supplies he needed, like flour and gunpowder. He enjoyed annoying the settlers, who considered him a harmless nuisance, and he liked to tell stories about all the whites he had killed in his youth. He claimed to have ninety-nine dried human tongues in his cabin. One day he got drunk at a house-raising, and when the conversation turned to the murder of the Hochstetler family on the Pennsylvania border, he bragged that he knew all about the case. A relative of the Hochstetlers overheard him and followed him home that night. Lion was never seen again—murdered, it was believed, his body submerged in a cranberry bog.[49]

Other people killed Natives randomly and without compunction. Three men passing through Lancaster, Ohio, saw an Indian man, woman, and child and decided to kill them on the spot. In 1813 Thomas Griffee of Williamson County, Illinois, was aiming at a bear in a tree when he saw an Indian taking aim at the same bear. He leveled his gun at the man and shot him. Henry Parsons, remembered in Williamson County's history as "a cold, calculating miscreant," shot at least two Native hunters in similar fashion and swore that he would kill any Indian who crossed his path in the woods.[50]

Murders by criminal gangs added to the homicide tally. The cattle and horse thieves who had plagued the southern backcountry before the Revolution were not especially murderous. They had returned fire when cornered but avoided armed conflict whenever possible. They had made money by selling stolen horses and cattle in Chesapeake markets and prospered through speed and stealth, not violence. In the postrevolutionary backcountry many criminal gangs had no qualms about killing hunters, settlers, or travelers for their cash or belongings. When the conflict between settlers and the Creeks was at its height in central Georgia, white gangs took advantage of the situation by murdering and scalping the families they robbed to make it look as if they had been victims of Creek raiders. The practice was so common that by the mid-1780s authorities admitted they could never be sure whether "white or red savages" were at fault.[51]

The most infamous of these criminal gangs were two brothers from a disaffected Tory family. The Harpes terrorized Tennessee and Kentucky in 1798–99, stealing money, clothes, and horses and killing thirty or forty people, some of them children, to eliminate potential witnesses. They were said to have been the sons of a loyalist raider from North Carolina who had fought at Kings Mountain. The family was ostracized after the war, and their neighbors' animosity made a deep impression on the Harpe boys. Before he died, the eldest declared that "he had been badly treated and consequently had become disgusted with all mankind."[52]

Almost as famous as the Harpes, and also a product of the war, was the Cave-in-Rock gang. They robbed and murdered travelers who went down the Ohio River in flatboats in 1797. The leader of the gang, Samuel Mason, came from a prominent Virginia family and had been a captain in the Virginia militia during the Revolution, but his experiences during and after the war had embittered him. As commander of the militia at Fort Henry he had seen more than his share of death. He was the sole survivor when his company of fourteen men was ambushed by Indians in 1777, and the company that rescued him lost all but four men. In 1782 he was trying to carve a farm from the wilderness near Wheeling Creek when Native American raiders stole several of his slaves. Mason and a friend pursued the raiders, but they fell into an ambush, and his friend was shot dead. Within months Mason had turned horse thief, trying to recoup his losses at his neighbors' expense and bitter that, having risked so much for them, he had so much less to show for it. He moved in and out of respectable society for the next few years but turned outlaw for good in the mid-1790s. Like every war in history, the Revolution left behind its share of traumatized or resentful veterans who could no longer function in society. The backcountry afforded these people both a refuge from civilization and nearly unlimited opportunities for criminal activity.[53]

The Revolution left a legacy of violence across the Ohio River Valley and the southern backcountry. It legitimized killing in defense of property, reputation, and rights, but, more important, it transferred authority for life-and-death decisions from the government to ordinary citizens. This legacy fused with the hatred of government across the entire southern frontier. People approached confrontations with the conviction that they had to take full responsibility for safeguarding their rights and reputations. Looking to the despised government for justice was worse than useless: it was shameful. It was up to individuals to see that justice was done.

Homicide on the Northern Frontier

New England's backcountry did not witness as many homicides after the Revolution as the Ohio River Valley or the South, but wherever the government thwarted dreams of landownership or threatened the livelihood of settlers, New Englanders could also be murderous. After the Revolution squatters settled on land in Maine that had been deeded in colonial times to two syndicates of land speculators, the Pejepscot and Kennebec grantees, because they were sure that the speculators' royal charters would be voided. However, the courts ruled in the proprietors' favor. Years of antiproprietary riots and demonstrations ensued, and in 1808 a settler murdered a member of a proprietary surveying party.[54]

A dozen political homicides occurred in northern Vermont during the embargo crisis of 1807–1809 and the War of 1812. Seizures of American ships and sailors by France and Britain during the Napoleonic War prompted Jefferson's administration to prohibit foreign trade in the hope that the denial of American naval stores and foodstuff would force European powers to respect America's right as a neutral power to trade with all nations. The Madison administration set aside Jefferson's unpopular no-trade policy and allowed trade with neutral powers, but depredations against American shipping continued. The embargo and the ensuing war with Britain proved divisive in northern Vermont, where people depended on trading grain, lumber, and livestock with Canada. Political adversaries took up arms against one another. Smugglers killed at least five revenue agents and toll collectors, and at least three smugglers were killed. During the war, a Vermont militiaman who refused to support the invasion of Canada was shot for resisting arrest as a deserter, and two suspected spies were shot by American troops.[55]

Violence against Native Americans persisted in a few areas of the northern backcountry. Some settlers were simply unwilling to live with Indians, many of whom declined to leave after they had been defeated militarily. In Vermont, George Sheldon feuded with Abenakis from St. Francis, Canada, who returned to their home on Vermont's Missisquoi River each spring to hunt and fish. Although the details are hazy, Sheldon apparently believed that the Abenakis had burned his barn, and sometime in the early 1790s he shot two of them dead. Such "ethnic cleansing" kept the homicide rate for Native Americans high long after the backcountry had ceased to be a frontier.[56]

Homicide in the Shenandoah Valley

Homicide was not a problem everywhere during and after the Revolution. In the Shenandoah Valley of Virginia, for instance, where the Revolution had enjoyed broad support, the homicide rate fell, and political homicides were rare (Figure 1.3). Valley patriots never faced an invasion by the British or their Native allies, so their leaders maintained a firm grip on power. They were able to protect residents, provide basic services, and uphold law and order. The valley's residents embraced the Revolution with near unanimity because it promised to protect that order. As a result, patriot leaders had little trouble putting down draft resisters in Augusta County or defeating a small band of local loyalists who gathered at Massanutten in Rockbridge County.[57]

Per capita, the Shenandoah Valley may have committed more men and supplies to the war effort than any other region in the country, sending over 500 officers and thousands of enlisted men into the Continental army. Augusta County alone raised thirty-eight companies between 1776 and 1781. The valley's residents were most interested, however, in carrying the war to the British and their native allies in the Ohio River Valley. Having experienced a devastating Indian war as recently as 1764–1766, and hoping to profit from the opening of new lands in the West, they were particularly supportive of George Rogers Clark's trans-Appalachian campaigns. Valley soldiers were responsible for some of the greatest victories over Native forces and for some of the most infamous massacres, including the murder of the Shawnee chief Cornstalk and other hostages held by Rockbridge County soldiers garrisoned at Point Pleasant on the Ohio River.[58]

The valley's support for the Revolution extended to the new national government. Delegates to Virginia's ratification convention from the valley and from the trans-Allegheny West voted 27 to 1 in favor of the new federal constitution and provided the margin of victory, since delegates from the rest of Virginia voted 61 to 78 against it.[59] Given the almost complete absence of political conflict in the valley, the depth of its citizens' commitment to the Revolution and to the Indian war, and their solid support for both local and national revolutionary governments, it is not surprising that the rate at which unrelated whites murdered each other fell during the Revolution. The rate at which murder suspects were brought in for questioning—the only measure we have of murder activity in the valley—declined from 5.4 per 100,000 white adults in the decade before the Revolution to only 2.2 per 100,000 from 1775 to 1800 (Figure 1.3). Compared to rates from the rest of the slaveholding South or Pennsylvania, which had a similar mix of German, Scots-Irish, and English settlers, that rate was startlingly low. It was comparable to New England's rate during the Revolution, which was the lowest in the nation. Wherever the transition from the old government to the new government and from old loyalties to new loyalties went well, homicide rates among unrelated adults remained low or even declined.

African American Homicide

African Americans also saw their homicide rate decline during the Revolution in New England, the Chesapeake, and the Shenandoah Valley. In New England the rate for blacks dropped to between 1 and 2 per 100,000 adults per year, which was as low as the rate for whites (Figure 2.3). There was only one known case of a black murdering another black, and there were only five known cases of whites murdering blacks. Two enslaved men died of neglect or abuse, but racial hostility played no apparent role in the other three deaths. Crispus Attucks was killed in the Boston Massacre; a suspected thief who attacked his captors with an ax was shot to death; and a man involved in street brawl in Boston was so "disordered in his senses" from a blow to the head that he wandered into the harbor three weeks later and drowned.[60]

In the Chesapeake and the Shenandoah Valley, the rate at which blacks were examined for killing other blacks fell by half, to only 1.2 per 100,000 adults per year, and the rate at which whites were questioned for killing blacks also fell by half, to only 2 per 100,000 adults per year (Figure 1.3). The circumstances of these homicides, where known, were not unusual: a field hand was killed for refusing to be whipped for visiting a woman in the plantation's spinning room; a hired slave was clubbed to death for pocketing wages he had earned by hauling tobacco; and slaves died in fights with other slaves.[61]

Unlike those for most whites, African American homicide rates continued to decline during the Revolution largely because the forces that had depressed the rates in the mid-eighteenth century were still at work. There was growing solidarity among African Americans, and many European Americans had more humane attitudes toward them. It would be a mistake, however, to think that all whites became less violent toward blacks in the late eighteenth century. Where slavery survived, it remained a violent institution. Frustrated or sadistic masters inflicted horrible beatings on slaves. White posses hunted down and killed slaves who took advantage of the lawlessness of the Georgia–South Carolina backcountry to establish maroon communities in swamps along the Savannah River. The same fate awaited slaves who

hid in swamps along the North Carolina coast and raided local plantations. Nervous whites hanged slaves and free blacks suspected of organizing slave rebellions. Prosecutions for "conspiracy" peaked in Virginia in 1775–1777, when slaveholders feared that their slaves might
rise up and join the British. Charleston magistrates hanged Thomas
Jeremiah, a free black harbor pilot, because they believed he was helping the British and organizing a slave revolt.[62]

Many blacks caught up in the conflict itself were killed. During the
British campaign to capture Charleston, South Carolina, patriot soldiers captured four men outside their lines—two whites, a mulatto,
and a black—who they suspected were deserting to the enemy. Governor John Rutledge ordered the soldiers to "hang them up" on the
beam above the fort gate as a warning to others. The British captured a
slave named Ned in Redding, Connecticut, who was fighting with a
band of patriots. After executing the whites, a British officer asked
what should be done with "the negro." His superior said, "damn him,
kill him." The officer stabbed Ned and then cut off his head. When
Cornwallis' soldiers ran low on food at Yorktown, they drove blacks out
of their camp. Dozens were stranded in the no-man's-land between the
British and American forces and were killed in crossfire.[63]

Blacks were far less likely than whites to be victims of political homicides or war crimes during the Revolution. Most did not have an opportunity to choose sides, and many who did were wary of the intentions of both sides. Some 5,000 blacks enrolled in patriot militias or in
the Continental army, and a lesser number in loyalist or British forces;
but they joined in smaller proportions than did whites, even in patriot
New England, which integrated its forces early and relied on slaves and
free blacks to help meet induction quotas for the Continental army.
Outside New England, blacks who enlisted or were purchased or dra-
gooned by military forces usually worked as cooks, servants, teamsters,
or laborers rather than as soldiers. The custom of assigning them support duties probably explains why the British officer in Redding asked
what to do with Ned. Blacks were seldom used or perceived as combatants.[64]

The humanitarian spirit that many whites began to embrace during the Revolution probably helped keep the black homicide rate
low. It was undoubtedly responsible for the continued decline in lethal discipline of slaves and in extralegal violence against all blacks.
Baptist, Methodist, and revolutionary leaders who rejected slavery

did their best in the 1770s and 1780s to increase sympathy for the sufferings of blacks. New Light Calvinists like Samuel Hopkins of Newport, Rhode Island, along with enlightened thinkers like Benjamin Rush of Philadelphia and the Methodist ministers of the Virginia Conference, vilified slavery "as contrary to the Golden Law of God on which hang all the Law and the Prophets, and the unalienable Rights of Mankind, as well as every Principle of the Revolution." Humane attitudes led to the gradual abolition of slavery in the northern United States and the passage of laws in the Upper South that criminalized the unintentional killing of slaves during discipline and allowed manumission of slaves without government interference. The latter laws led to the freeing of 20,000 slaves in Maryland and Virginia.[65]

Among blacks themselves, the decline in homicide was most likely a consequence of a continuing increase in racial solidarity. The rise in the proportion of African Americans who were native-born and the increasing cultural and linguistic unity of African Americans helped enslaved and free blacks form stronger communities. The rapid spread of evangelical Christianity and republican ideology, both of which gained currency among blacks as white Christians and revolutionaries turned against slavery, accelerated the process. Many African Americans formed Christian fellowships and campaigned openly against slavery where they could. Had the opportunity presented itself, it is likely that blacks everywhere would have organized self-help societies like the Free African Union Society of Newport, Rhode Island, or churches like the African Church in Boston. But even where freedom was not yet a possibility, African Americans banded together to improve their lives. For instance, slaves in Granville County, North Carolina, tried to hold an "election" among themselves for justices and sheriffs. They wanted to "have equal Justice distributed so that a weak person might collect his debts, as well as a Strong one."[66]

Although the surviving evidence is slim, it is clear that the dream of freedom and equality that the Revolution created had a profound psychological effect on the black community, making it more unified and less homicidal. African Americans may have taken different sides during the Revolution, or no side at all, but from the beginning they wholeheartedly embraced the idea of freedom. In Charleston, South Carolina, in 1765, during a demonstration against the Stamp Act, a group of slaves started chanting "Liberty." In Maine in 1774 a slave wrote a letter to a prominent citizen to ask for help to secure his freedom, saying, "Yu know the Situation of us poor Slaves, you know what a valuable thing Liberty is to all men leave alone the Poor Unhappy Slaves, we are flesh and blood as much as them of another Colour, but that Cruel yoke of Slavery, hard to be born." Jehu Grant, who ran away from his loyalist master in Rhode Island to join the Continental army, said that "when I saw liberty poles and the people all engaged for the support of freedom, I could not but like and be pleased with such thing (God forgive me if I sinned in so feeling). . . . The songs of liberty that saluted my ear, thrilled through my heart."[67]

When Governor Dunmore of Virginia offered freedom to any slave who fought for Britain and when law and order collapsed in Georgia, slaves ran by the thousands. There were few happy endings for these people. Most of the slaves who escaped to Dunmore perished in the epidemic that swept through his ships. Some Georgia fugitives starved to death in eastern Florida. When Massachusetts abolished slavery, fugitive and free blacks alike were kidnapped and sold.[68] Despite these setbacks, the Revolution raised blacks' hopes that their time was coming. It never had the divisive effect among blacks that it did among whites, nor did it lead initially to more hostile attitudes among whites toward blacks.

The rate at which blacks murdered whites also remained low during the revolutionary period. There was only one known homicide of a white by a black in New England. Pomp, an apprentice, killed his employer, Captain Charles Furbush, after Furbush reneged on a promise to free Pomp from his indentures early and make him his heir. In Virginia, beginning in the 1760s, enslaved men and women sometimes banded together to murder their masters or overseers. Eight slaves conspired to kill Lockey Collier in Elizabeth City County, Virginia. They worked for hours to clean up the scene of the crime but were caught anyway. Blacks who joined loyalist and patriot gangs probably committed some murders, and individual blacks committed murder in the course of armed robberies, but the rate at which blacks murdered whites did not rise.[69]

As in the mid-eighteenth century, the fundamental reason for the low black-on-white homicide rate was the futility of homicide as a form of resistance. Killing whites meant almost certain death for the perpetrator and increased repression for other blacks. Enslaved blacks ran away in great numbers during the Revolution—a third of all slaves fled plantations in Georgia, for example—and blacks were eager to fight for their freedom alongside whites. But it made little sense for them to murder whites or to launch a revolt against them, especially when the abolition movement was making such progress. The Haitian Revolution in 1791 inspired talk of an uprising in the United States, but most slaves appeared to hope that the abolitionists would succeed in bringing a peaceful end to the peculiar institution.[70]

CHAPTER 5

The Emergence of Regional Differences

Homicide in the Postrevolutionary Period

Homicide rates increased in most American communities during and immediately after the Revolution, but as the long-term consequences of the Revolution became clear, they began to fall in the North and the mountain South. By the 1820s rates in the North were at historic lows that ranged from under 1 to just over 6 per 100,000 adults. They would remain at that level through the early 1840s. Those rates were comparable to rates in Canada, Sweden, and the Low Countries, and lower than rates in the rest of Europe. The United States would never see numbers that low again.[1]

In the Ozark and Appalachian highlands of the South, where there were few slaves, homicide rates were as low as those in the rural Midwest by the 1830s and early 1840s. But the populations there were too small to affect the South's overall homicide rate. In slaveholding areas of the South, the homicide rate after 1800 ranged from 8 to 28 per 100,000 adults per year—at least twice what it had been for whites at its low point in the Chesapeake in the late 1750s and 1760s and three times what it had been for blacks in the 1780s and 1790s. After the Revolution homicide rates were thus most strongly linked to the presence or absence of slavery.[2]

It took time for these distinct patterns to take shape in the North, the mountain South, and the slave South. Backcountry violence was an interregional problem until the end of the War of 1812, when homicide rates in Ohio finally fell below those in the Georgia Piedmont (Figures 4.1 and 4.2). Dueling was a national problem until the death of Alexander Hamilton in 1804, after which northerners made it clear that anyone who killed a man in a duel would be drummed out of public life. Homicide rates were high in northern and southern port cities through the War of 1812. Independence opened American ports to ships of all nations, and international tensions created hostility among American and foreign sailors, especially during the Napoleonic era. In Boston, for instance, in the decade after the British occupation, Portuguese, English, American, and French sailors were all involved in murders over women, national honor, or turf. In Savannah, Georgia, thirteen sailors were murdered from 1804 to 1815: a German, a Swede, a Norwegian, two Englishmen, two Frenchmen, two Irishmen, and four Americans. These homicides peaked in 1811–1813, when riots among sailors led to killings in New York, Norfolk, Charleston, Savannah, and New Orleans. The surge in such homicides subsided after the Napoleonic Wars as the maritime economy rebounded.[3]

After the War of 1812 it was clear even to contemporaries that homicide rates in the slave South were diverging from those in the rest of the nation. In the North and the mountain South the homicide rate among unrelated adults fell to its lowest level in American history as loyalist-patriot divisions disappeared and patriotism soared. People in those regions began to boast about America's superiority and to celebrate the unique character of America's political institutions. Edward Tiffin, Ohio's first governor, extolled the transformation of the government from one under which "we [could only] *breathe,* to one under which we may *live.*" The Reverend Samuel Williams of Vermont was confident that Americans had devised the finest government in the world. It was, he said, a government that "reverences the people." He considered the United States "the best poor man's country," a place of opportunity where "the highest perfection and felicity, which man is permitted to hope for in the present life, may rationally be expected."[4]

Widespread self-employment and the removal of many legal and institutional barriers to advancement based on religion, class, or race, including slavery, persuaded the vast majority of northerners and whites in the mountain South that their social hierarchy was becoming more legitimate. A "Citizen of Color" captured the optimism of northern blacks when he wrote in 1814 that "we dwell in safety and pursue our honest callings" with "none daring to molest us, whatever his complexion or circumstances."⁵ Homicide was still a problem in urban neighborhoods where the level of self-employment was low and on frontiers that did not yet have effective governments, and the decline in self-employment that began in the 1820s and 1830s caused widespread anxiety and prompted riots that were responsible for a number of deaths in northern cities. But elsewhere in these regions homicides were rare.

The situation was very different in the slave South. Revolutionary ideas and aspirations wreaked havoc with the status hierarchy of slave society in a number of ways. Poor and middle-class whites were increasingly frustrated by their inability to rise in a society that remained class-bound and hierarchical. Prominent whites were subjected to the rough-and-tumble of democracy and were infuriated by the way they were treated. Blacks despaired over the failure of the abolition movement in the South, and whites were more fearful than ever of black rebellion. As a result, impatience with restraint and sensitivity to insult were more intense in the slave South, and during this period the region saw more than its share of deadly quarrels, property disputes, duels, and interracial killings.

People in the slaveholding South were also less likely than people in the North or the mountain South to trust the federal government and to identify with the new nation. Distrust blossomed in the 1820s and 1830s as proslavery southerners realized that the federal government had turned against them on a number of vital issues, including the admission of new slave states and territories and the suppression of abolitionist speech. The distrust may not have been strong enough to raise the homicide rate, but it was strong enough to nullify the dampening effect that the patriotism of the post–War of 1812 period should have had on the homicide rate among whites. In those decades, when American nationalism reached its nineteenth-century peak, identification with national heroes was weaker in the South than in the nation as a whole. The difference was so strong that a higher percentage of places were named in the North than in the South for the South's national heroes, including Washington, Jefferson, and Jackson. Regional differences in national loyalty would become even more marked in the 1850s, of course, and again in the 1890s. But they were substantial enough in the postrevolutionary period to help raise the homicide rate above the levels of the middle and late eighteenth century.[6] The slaveholding South thus became the first region of the United States to deviate from the long-term trend toward lower homicide rates in North America and western Europe.

None of the correlates of lower homicide rates were present in the Southwest. In the Mexican borderlands rates tripled from the 1820s to the 1840s, probably reaching 40 per 100,000 adults per year in the Rio Grande Valley of New Mexico and in slaveholding areas of east Texas, and 100 or more per 100,000 in California and Hispanic areas of Texas. Mexico's war for independence from Spain (1810–1821) unsettled relations among classes and racial castes, just as the American Revolution had done in the slaveholding South, and led to murders that crossed class and racial lines. Government instability and frontier violence compounded the problem; Mexicans, Americans, and Native Americans killed one another over trade and territory. Mexico's counterrevolution of 1834 set off violent rebellions in nine of Mexico's twenty-seven states and territories, including Texas, California, and New Mexico, which led to a cycle of political killings, robbery murders, revenge murders, and vigilantism. Together, political instability, the failure of the federal and territorial governments to establish their legitimacy, the lack of national feeling, and the delegitimation of the social hierarchy made the Southwest one of the most homicidal regions in North America.

The Decline of Homicide in the North

The turning point in homicide rates in the northern backcountry and in northern ports like New York City was the end of the War of 1812 (Figures 4.2 and 5.1–5.3). Elsewhere in the North, particularly in southern New England and eastern Pennsylvania, the turning point had occurred in the late 1780s (Figures 1.2 and 2.2). Homicide rates declined as soon as political conflict subsided, the Constitution was ratified, and a stronger national government emerged. In Pennsylvania, for example, moderates were determined to build a stronger, more inclusive state government and to lay to rest the divisions of the war years. In 1786 moderate assemblymen altered the Test Act so that pietists could affirm their loyalty without swearing oaths. Two years later they gutted the Militia Act by suspending the fines for refusing

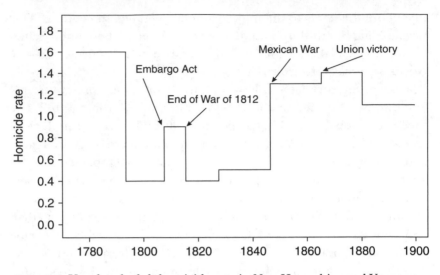

Figure 5.1 Unrelated-adult homicide rate in New Hampshire and Vermont, 1775–1900 (per 100,000 adults per year).

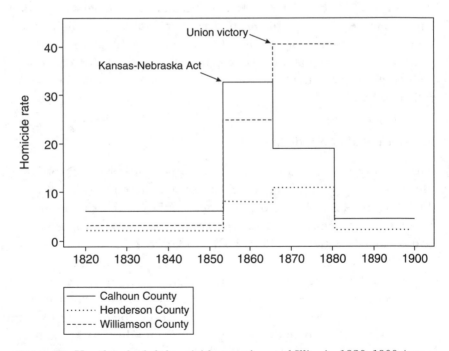

Figure 5.2 Unrelated-adult homicide rates in rural Illinois, 1820–1900 (per 100,000 adults per year).

military service. As their hold on power strengthened in the 1790s, they abolished other unpopular wartime acts and implemented universal male suffrage and a volunteer militia—measures that proved widely popular. The legitimacy of government was rebuilt that way in every state, step by step.[7]

The Revolution had undermined fellow feeling in the North, especially among white Protestants, in ways that would take a generation to repair. Patriotic feeling did not really began to flourish until the 1820s and early 1830s (Figure 2.1), and many northerners still questioned the legitimacy of the central government and the character of the men who ran it. But the Revolution also fostered a belief in the unique promise of the new nation that seemed to help suppress homicide. America would be a country where everyone had a chance to be eco-

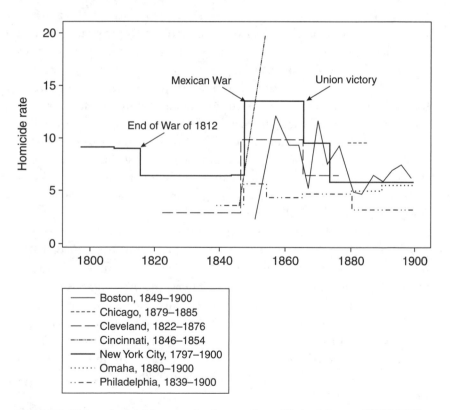

Figure 5.3 Urban homicide rates in the northern United States, 1797–1900 (per 100,000 adults per year).

nomically independent. The abolition of slavery, the extension of voting rights, increased toleration for religious dissenters, and high levels of homeownership and self-employment convinced the vast majority of northerners that they were on their way toward putting an end to the oppression and prejudice that had kept people in abject poverty for centuries in aristocratic and monarchical societies. Obviously there was room for improvement in their society, but most people believed that now everyone could get married, set up a household, and own a shop or farm. The sole requisite for success was hard work. Even the poor, Catholics, and former slaves shared that belief, despite the financial obstacles and social prejudices they faced. The social hierarchy that emerged in the North after the Revolution was thus perceived as far more legitimate than any that had preceded it.

The belief that they had created a society in which everyone had a chance to get ahead did not create the kind of solidarity that fear of Indians, anti-Catholicism, or patriotism had among European colonists in the late seventeenth century. But most northerners believed they had a shared interest in sustaining the social and political order that emerged after the Revolution. The hatred they might have harbored for wartime enemies—many of whom had packed up and left for Canada anyway—was displaced by pride in their extraordinary victory over the British. The hostile, defensive, and predatory emotions that lay behind the murders of friends, acquaintances, and strangers—never as strong in the North as in the South or on the frontier—were supplanted by the feeling that everyone in America could participate in this grand social and political experiment.

For most people this faith in the social and political order of the postrevolutionary North was justified. By the end of the War of 1812, 60 percent of all adult men in the North owned their own shops or farms; the proportion was closer to 80 percent for men in their mid-thirties and older. Most of those who did not own shops or farms at least owned homes or headed independent households. Owning a house or shop or farm was the standard by which people were judged. Those who owned property had a sense of accomplishment, greater resilience in the face of disappointments, and a strong bond with other property owners.[8]

It is impossible to prove that the growing legitimacy of the North's social hierarchy and the respect and satisfaction derived from economic independence were responsible for the decline in homicide in the postrevolutionary North, but it is clear that high levels of self-employment and homeownership were strongly associated with low homicide rates. Of all the areas studied, northern New England and Holmes County, Ohio, where homeownership and self-employment rates were very high, continued to have the lowest homicide rates. Other factors undoubtedly had an impact on rates in the North. The presence of nonviolent pietists like the Amish and Mennonites kept rates low in parts of Ohio and Pennsylvania, for example, whereas the presence of sailors raised the rates of port cities. Like indentured servants, sailors were deprived of rights and wholly at the mercy of their employers, and the humiliation they endured left them predisposed to violence. But self-employment and home ownership were probably the most important deterrents to homicide, because they were the most important sources of respect in a society that judged people by their work ethic and their investment in the community.

Places with the lowest levels of self-employment and homeownership, such as Boston, New York City, and Philadelphia, had the highest homicide rates. The poor, tenement-ridden neighborhoods of those cities were the most homicidal areas of the North. In the first decades of the nineteenth century, these neighborhoods were packed with Scots and Irish immigrants who eked out a living doing work that most natives rejected. They found it very hard to live in such close quarters with others, especially in a society where homeownership was the norm and adult renters were viewed as failures. Crammed together in flats without water or sanitary facilities, they fought constantly to defend their territory and whatever scraps of dignity they still had. Trivial disputes easily escalated into murder. Peter Kain, for example, was driven to distraction by his noisy neighbors in New York City. One Saturday night he smashed all their doors and windows and stabbed one of them to death. Catherine Burney got into an argument with a fellow Scot, Margaret Dix, in their tenement in Boston. She picked up a flatiron and crushed Dix's skull.[9]

Poor urban laborers had less patience than other northerners when challenged or treated with disrespect, and on occasion they fought to the death over card games, elections, and neighborhood turf. After the War of 1812 some of this desperate hunger for respect was channeled into bare-knuckle fighting, which became popular among working-class men in northern cities. Many early prizefights in New York, Boston, and Philadelphia grew out of the same sorts of disputes that everyday murders did. Fighting gave men an opportunity to earn prestige and perhaps a little money as well. Gang fighting offered similar opportunities. Among the first gang fighters were volunteer fire companies, which battled one another for the privilege of putting out fires. In 1839 two New York City companies went at each other with brickbats and sticks for more than an hour. The 1820s and 1830s also saw the rise of gangs engaged in gambling, prostitution, theft, and illegal liquor sales. They fought primarily to protect their businesses and to eliminate rivals, but on occasion they also fought for honor, for a political party, or for ethnic pride.[10]

There were some ominous incidents of collective violence in the postrevolutionary North, but they did not claim many lives before the late 1840s and had virtually no impact on the homicide rate. The nation's large cities, where competition for jobs, housing, and political power was most intense, saw riots that pitted Whigs against Democrats, blacks against whites, natives against foreigners, Protestants against Catholics, capital against labor, and proslavery against antislavery activists. In New York City in the 1820s, striking dockworkers beat up men who crossed their picket lines and attacked employers who refused to meet their demands. In Boston in 1819 sixty blacks mobbed city watchmen who were trying to arrest a fugitive slave. In Providence, Rhode Island, in 1824, whites went on a rampage after a group of blacks refused to make way for whites on a sidewalk; they destroyed twenty homes, taverns, and suspected brothels and ran blacks out of the "Hardscrabble" neighborhood. A weeklong riot in Cincinnati in 1829 drove all blacks out of the city. In New York City in 1824, Catholic weavers attacked Protestant weavers who had gathered to celebrate the Battle of the Boyne.[11]

The worst violence occurred in Philadelphia, where, in a portent of what was to come, riots between Protestants and Irish Catholics in 1844 left a score of people dead. But despite its fearsome reputation, urban collective violence was not usually lethal in this era. For the most part rioters and gang members fought to humiliate their opponents, not to kill them. The goal was intimidation: they wanted to exert control in their communities and show they could not be pushed around. Whenever postrevolutionary northerners began to feel that the government was advocating for a competing group or that they themselves were competing against groups with antagonistic values or interests, lethal violence was possible.[12] But the promise of economic independence for all was still a unifying force. Only in the late 1840s and early 1850s, when the two-party system collapsed and many northerners came to believe that what divided them was far more important than what united them, did lethal violence spin out of control.

Outside cities the failure to achieve or sustain economic independence could have deadly consequences. In small towns and rural communities in the postrevolutionary North, where the majority of people owned shops and homes, almost all intentional homicides were committed by men and women who were socially beyond the pale: bankrupts, alcoholics, convicts, and people who had committed moral crimes. These people were treated with contempt by their neighbors. Otis Cox, for example, was an alcoholic, and when he died, a local man wrote in his diary that "no tears were shed over his remains but [he] was hurried to his grave . . . and in a very few days he will be forgotten."[13]

The effects of such social stigmatization were clear. It is remarkable how often violence erupted when people who had once enjoyed the respect of society suddenly found themselves outcasts. Josiah Burnham of Grafton County, New Hampshire, was well educated, the son of a Congregationalist minister, and a descendant of the Wolcott family of Connecticut. He had done very well as a surveyor and developer, but after a series of questionable property deals he landed in jail. He had been in prison for five years when he was joined by two other respected citizens who had overextended themselves financially: Joseph Starkweather Jr., a militia captain; and Russell Freeman, a former magistrate and town officer. Starkweather and Freeman taunted Burnham for his fecklessness and insinuated that he had cheated on his wife, who had worked tirelessly for years to support their children and pay his debts. Burnham stabbed both men to death.[14]

Like bankrupts, alcoholics were prone to respond violently to perceived injustices and slights, especially in the 1820s and 1830s, when the rural North was becoming increasingly preoccupied with respectability. Ephraim Briggs, a veteran of the Revolutionary War, and Daniel Palmer, once a successful farmer, had lost their good names through public drunkenness. One day at the Red Tavern in Danby,

Vermont, they called simultaneously for a drink. Palmer grabbed the first mug, and Briggs, his elder, ordered him to put it down. Palmer drank anyway, and Briggs slugged him. In the ensuing fight Briggs was killed. Dr. Elias Thomas of Goffstown, New Hampshire, could not abide the humiliation of being escorted home from the tavern every night by Charles Small, a young bartender. One night the drunken Thomas turned on Small and stabbed him. Although alcoholics were primarily a threat to their wives, as homicide rates fell and as they were increasingly marginalized in society they accounted for a growing share of the men who murdered unrelated adults.[15]

People who had flouted society's moral standards also contributed to the homicide rate. Rolon Wheeler, a hardscrabble farmer from Wallingford, Vermont, ran afoul of his neighbors for sleeping with his wife's sister. They came to his house one night to tar and feather him. When they broke into his bedroom, he killed one of them and wounded several others before escaping through a hole concealed under his bed. Jonathan Hall, who worked at a brothel run by the widow Grandy in Vergennes, Vermont, also refused to be run out of town. When a mob of thirty men showed up one night to make good on the community's threat to tear down the brothel, Hall shot the first man to come through the door.[16]

Predatory homicides such as those committed in the course of robberies and sexual assaults nearly disappeared, as did homicides over insults or property disputes. Gun homicides—a good proxy for intentional homicides—declined from 52 percent of homicides among unrelated adults in New England during the Revolution to only 17 percent by the 1820s and 1830s, and from 60 percent in Ross and Holmes Counties in Ohio to zero. Involuntary homicides caused by mental illness or by unlucky blows in ordinary fights accounted for a large portion of homicides among unrelated adults.[17]

By the 1830s and 1840s there were signs that northerners' confidence in their egalitarian social order was waning. Opportunities for self-employment declined after the War of 1812 as the population increased and the economy changed. The creation of integrated regional and national markets made it harder for small or inefficient firms to survive, and more capital was needed to create viable shops and farms. Population pressure further increased costs in the Northeast by raising the price of land in cities and the countryside, and the capital costs of establishing new businesses in the Midwest were so high, especially for farmers, that they offset much of the advantage of cheaper midwestern land. As a result, self-employment declined in the North from 60 percent of all adult males in 1815 to 40 percent by 1860.[18]

The decline in self-employment did not occur overnight, but by the mid-1830s northerners knew it was under way. Per-capita income rose, even for farm laborers and factory workers, because of rising productivity, but incomes did not keep pace with the rising cost of establishing farms or shops, so fewer families enjoyed the prestige and security of self-employment. Few people referred to the decline as a crisis, because its onset was so slow. Most spoke instead of the "pressure of the times" and actively sought ways to cope with diminishing opportunities.

Both the Whig Party and the Democratic Party offered remedies for the decline in self-employment. The Whigs favored greater access to capital and markets, while the Democrats favored greater access to undeveloped land in the West, lower taxes, and limits on the power of banks, corporations, and other potential monopolies. Unions and workingmen's parties in cities like Boston, Philadelphia, and New York City called for shorter hours, a homestead law, and better pay, so that more apprentices and journeymen could rise from the ranks to become master tailors, shoemakers, and mechanics. Young people dealt with the "pressure of the times" in more immediate ways, by delaying marriage and children and saving the money they earned as laborers. They took a few more years to establish their economic independence. Faith in the republic and in prospects for individual success remained strong into the 1840s; but anxiety increased, because the path to home ownership and self-employment had become longer and more difficult.[19]

The fear of failure was palpable among churchgoing northerners, who tried in various ways to improve their children's chances of success. Discipline became stricter, and parents and ministers pressured young people to join temperance societies and to reject sexual temptation. The age at which young people began to worry about their reputations and their futures dropped precipitously. Northerners increasingly praised industry, restraint, and moral zeal, and they expressed scorn for people who failed to toe the line. But their crusade to expand church membership, curb drinking, and improve the moral tone of society ended up being divisive, because it alienated many hard-working people, especially those who drank occasionally, attended church irregularly, and had little use for people who told others how to live.[20]

The moral and spiritual crusades that divided northerners in the 1830s and 1840s did not have an immediate effect on the homicide rate among unrelated adults, in part because homeownership and self-employment remained widespread and because many drinkers and nonchurchgoers steadfastly ignored the reformers and crusaders. Abel Rich, a notorious skeptic from Strafford, Vermont, scoffed when a revivalist confronted him in 1835 before a crowd of neighbors and asked if he had got religion. "None to boast of, I tell ye," he said. Rich, whose fellow townsmen had elected him tithingman, later declared that he bore the preacher no grudge, but if the man "should be mobbed and I was the only witness, I would forget it before morning-g-g, that I would-d-d." In another Vermont town a church committee discovered that one of their members who was an alcoholic had backslid, and they posted a notice at the general store announcing his excommunication. "Whereas Mr. Lyon has not kept his promise to reform, we the Church Committee return him to the outside world from whence he came. By the church committee." The next day another notice appeared. "Whereas Mr. Lyon is so much worse than when he joined the church, we of the outside world refuse to accept him back. By the Outside Committee." The church committee never quite regained the status it had once enjoyed.[21]

Wit was a powerful leveler. It enabled the weak to tweak the noses of the strong, and it defused confrontations that might otherwise have turned violent. The seeds of class conflict were evident in the ongoing battle between Ira Hoffman, a poor farm laborer in Sutton, Vermont, and his employer, a well-to-do farmer who demanded moral rectitude in his employees. Hoffman repeatedly thumbed his nose at his boss, whom he characterized as "mean as cat piss," and infuriated him by using foul language, strutting about town in a fancy satin vest, and, in his most effective move, quitting at harvest time. To make matters worse, he used his quick wit and his thorough knowledge of current events to trounce his employer's beloved Whigs in a local debate over Texas.[22]

The conflict between this young outsider and his employer would have been almost unthinkable in the plantation South. The difference between Hoffman's story and that of George Tucker, the Georgia carpenter who quit his job, asked for his pay, and was stripped naked and whipped by his employer, illustrates how wide the cultural divide was between the North and the slaveholding South. In the North, outsiders like Rich and Hoffman could assert their independence and proclaim their manhood in imaginative, nonviolent ways, whereas southerners were kept in their place by a more rigid class system, and young men who wanted to prove their manhood could do so only by fighting.

In the North, young men who enjoyed tavern life and were not regular churchgoers formed a distinct community in the 1830s and 1840s. They favored the Democratic Party, which appealed to religious dissenters, freethinkers, and antiprohibitionists by supporting the strict separation of church and state and by opposing laws that forced people to quit drinking or observe the Sabbath. The Democrats did not endorse drinking or atheism, as their Whig opponents often charged, but they believed that voluntary support for churches and for reform movements like temperance was the only constitutional way to improve the moral and spiritual tone of society. It may be that the critical turn of mind necessary to resist Christian proselytizing and prohibitionist indoctrination, together with the solidarity that pressure from respectable society created, helped keep the homicide rate low among these men, many of whom were of an age to be predisposed to violence. In the late 1840s and 1850s, however, when it became apparent that the decline in self-employment was not going to reverse itself and that the drinking poor might be fixed permanently at the bottom of the social hierarchy, these factors would not be strong enough to prevent an increase in homicide in this demographic.

Vigilante justice remained popular after the Revolution and was occasionally used against adulterers, brothel keepers, and petty criminals. Though illegal and unpopular with authorities, vigilante justice was not in most instances divisive. It usually reflected the will of the community, and supporters justified it as a direct expression of democracy. Vigilantes typically gathered in groups of fifty to one hundred. Sometimes they tarred and feathered their victims and tore down their houses, but in most cases they simply made noise, broke windows, burned people in effigy, and ordered their victims to change their ways or leave town.[23]

Vigilantes rarely killed people, except on the frontier, where homicide rates were higher and livestock theft endemic, and along major rivers like the Mississippi, Missouri, and lower Ohio, where criminal gangs flourished well into the 1840s, taking advantage of good roads, riverboats, and the proximity of state borders to escape capture. Iowa, for instance, experienced a terrible crime wave after the Black Hawk Purchase was opened to settlement in July 1833. Iowa did not have its own territorial government until 1838, and there were no secure jails, effective courts, or law enforcement until the early 1840s. As a result, Iowans felt they had to take the law into their own hands. They formed vigilance committees and hunted down murderers and horse thieves at considerable risk to themselves. After a mass meeting, citizens in Poweshiek County searched the woods north of Montezuma for members of the "Fox and Long" gang. They caught two, tried them "by a self-constituted jury," and shot them. W. W. Brown's gang plagued communities along the Mississippi River for several years, stealing horses, passing counterfeit money, pirating boats, and murdering witnesses, until residents of Jackson County formed a citizens' army to stop them. The vigilantes cornered the gang at Brown's Hotel in Bellevue. They killed three outlaws and captured all but six of the survivors, but they themselves suffered four dead and seven wounded.[24]

These postrevolutionary northern vigilantes made an effort not to be lawless or vengeful. In Iowa vigilantes executed only seven men in the 1830s and early 1840s, and in each instance they held a trial (a "lynch court") before condemning the accused to death. In every other case, they simply whipped and banished the accused or turned them over to territorial authorities. Their justice was rough—they extracted confessions under threat of death—but it was formal and democratic. At the end of the trial for the thirteen gang members captured after the shootout in Bellevue, the vigilantes voted with beans to decide the men's fate: a white bean for hanging and a red bean for whipping. The red beans prevailed, forty-two to thirty-eight, so the surviving gang members were not hanged, even though they had killed four vigilantes. They were given thirty-nine lashes each, placed on the Mississippi in a boat with three days' provisions, and told not to return on penalty of death.[25]

Despite such violence, homicide rates remained low into the early

1840s, even for African Americans. Blacks were murdered at the same rate as whites in New York City and at only a slightly higher rate in Philadelphia (Figure 5.4)—remarkable statistics given the poverty of most African Americans and the high proportion of African American men who worked as sailors or dockworkers. In Philadelphia several blacks lost their lives in drunken quarrels with other blacks, and a few blacks killed or were killed during robberies or beatings, but on the whole there were few homicides, intentional or unintentional, among blacks. Nor were there many homicides of either type between blacks and whites, except during the "Flying Horse Riot" of 1834, in which two black men died (and another was castrated) after a fight between blacks and whites over who would ride on a carousel.[26]

Homicide rates were also low for blacks in northern New England and in the Midwest. Once the War of 1812 ended, blacks were not in-

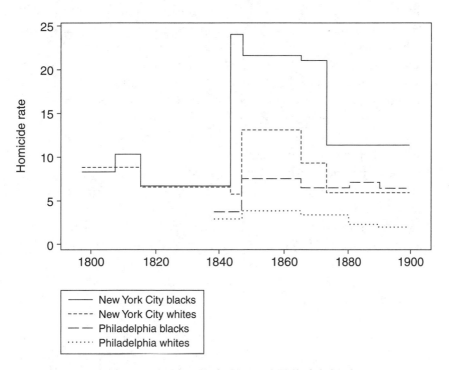

Figure 5.4 Homicide rates in New York City and Philadelphia by race, 1797–1900 (per 100,000 adults per year). New York City: all homicides. Philadelphia: homicides among unrelated adults, indictments only.

volved in a single homicide in the rural midwestern counties studied intensively, or in Cuyahoga County, Ohio, even though several of the counties had substantial black populations. In Vermont and New Hampshire only one African American—an ex-convict—committed a homicide between the late 1780s and the late 1840s, and none were murdered. In short, the patterns that were established in the North during and after the Revolution persisted. Whites seldom engaged in homicidal violence against blacks except during riots, when law and order broke down and assailants had a degree of anonymity; and blacks seldom engaged in homicidal violence against anyone.[27]

By contrast, the long-term impact of the Revolution on homicide rates for Irish Catholics in the North was mixed. Their rates were actually very low in small towns and in the countryside in the early nineteenth century, especially by the standards of contemporary Ireland. In the rural Midwest their homicide rate fell to only 4 per 100,000 adults per year, and in northern New England it fell to 1 per 100,000. That was two-thirds higher than the rates for African Americans or for other whites, but it was much lower than it had been in the eighteenth century. Some of the difference can be explained by proximate causes—that is, by the desperate competition for jobs and by the Irish tradition of recreational violence—but at bottom the higher homicide rate stemmed from a craving for respect, which was all the more powerful in a society dominated by Protestants of English descent who regarded the Irish as "white Negroes."[28]

Irish immigrants were seldom involved in the kind of predatory violence that runaway Irish servants had engaged in before the Revolution. Most Irishmen who were recent immigrants worked as unskilled laborers in mining, canal building, and railroad building. The number of workers usually exceeded the number of jobs, so laborers—many of them desperately poor—often had to fight for employment. Irish laborers were probably no more homicidal than their peers, but their concentration in these competitive occupations increased the likelihood that they would engage in fights or riots that could turn deadly.[29]

The Irish did have a penchant for recreational violence. They considered fighting a sport, and they glorified powerful fighters. But all too often, Saturday night brawls at dances, drinking parties, and brothels ended in death. Clearly, Irish immigrants brought this kind of violence with them to the United States; such killings, usually associated with heavy drinking, made up a large proportion of the homicides that occurred in Ireland in the nineteenth century.[30]

Still, like other rural northerners, rural Irish Catholics saw their homicide rates decline in the early nineteenth century. Optimism about the future probably played a role in moderating violence. Although anti-Irish prejudice and anti-Catholic laws did not die easily, in the late eighteenth and early nineteenth centuries new state laws established religious freedom for Catholics and separated church from state. In addition, America's successful rebellion against Great Britain and its bold stand against British aggression during the Napoleonic Wars fired the imagination of Irish patriots, many of whom came to see the United States as a model and an ally. Immigration to America meant emancipation from British oppression, from Protestant prejudice, from "tyrannous landlords" who worked them like slaves. As laborer John Quinlivan put it, America gave him a chance to be independent and to have "a place to Stop that I can call my own." To many Irish Catholics it was "the land that flows with milk and hon[e]y—the land of work and peace."[31]

But nativism was intensifying even in the rural North in the 1820s and 1830s as Catholics began to outnumber Protestants among Irish immigrants, and many Irish Catholic immigrants had very little hope of bettering themselves. They were simply too poorly paid ever to achieve economic independence, and the only positive recognition they could hope for from the Protestant majority was to be remembered upon their deaths as faithful servants. The newspapers of the period sometimes characterized Irish individuals in passing as "respectable," but such remarks only implied that most Irish men and women did not fit that description. Still, the Irish believed that their achievements in the United States went "far beyont what it was possible for them to have done had the[y] stop[p]ed in Ireland," and they did gain a degree of acceptance in the rural North, at least before the Great Famine.[32] They were a reliable source of cheap labor, and they posed no serious threat to the Protestant majority because they made up less than 5 percent of the population.

In cities like New York and Philadelphia, however, Irish Catholics faced hostility and discrimination from the 1790s through the early

1840s. Wherever they were numerous enough to threaten the jobs and the political power of Protestants, their homicide rate hovered around 12 per 100,000 adults per year—twice the rate for African Americans and three times the rate for non-Irish whites and for contemporary Ireland. They were often killed or implicated in homicides that occurred during riots. They fought and died to defend their neighborhoods, their right to vote, and their right to enter skilled trades. Yet they were far more likely to die in fights with each other.[33] Living in tenements and working for wages had a demoralizing effect on all the urban poor—and Irish Catholics were disproportionately poor. But prejudice and discrimination made matters worse for the urban Irish, some of whom were so angry about their treatment at the hands of the Protestant majority that they turned to gang violence and to predatory crime, which further increased their homicide rate. That pattern would be repeated in the late nineteenth century in cities across the United States: the minority in each city that felt it was losing ground and being pushed to the bottom of the social hierarchy would have the highest homicide rate—the Chinese in San Francisco, for example, or African Americans in Philadelphia, or Hispanics in Los Angeles.

Urban Irish had a powerful ally in their effort to become full and equal members of American society. The Democratic Party courted Irish Catholic voters by opposing anti-immigrant laws and denouncing anti-Irish prejudice. It awarded them patronage jobs, supported their candidacies for state and local offices, and, perhaps most important, gave them a sense of belonging and empowerment. The party also encouraged the Irish to support an antiblack, proslavery agenda and persuaded them to begin thinking of themselves as more deserving than blacks by virtue of their skin color. Given the competition between African Americans and Irish Catholics for jobs and housing in northern cities, the Irish needed little encouragement. As yet they had not clashed with blacks in significant numbers, but clearly there was potential for trouble.[34] Serious violence did not erupt, however, until the late 1840s and 1850s, when the competition between the two groups increased homicide rates both directly—by spawning interracial riots—and indirectly, as disillusionment with politics and frustration with declining economic prospects led to a general increase in homicides of all kinds.

White Homicide in the South

As in the North, homicide rates in the mountain South were probably at their lowest levels in history by the 1830s and early 1840s. Frontier disputes with Native Americans were at times a problem, especially during the forced removal of the Cherokees and other Native peoples to reservations in the West. In Gilmer County, Georgia, for example, several Cherokees murdered a teenaged farm laborer who had encroached on their land, and another murdered an ill-tempered white trader who was selling liquor to the Natives. But those were the county's only reported homicides, and once the frontier period had passed, homicide rates in northern Georgia, in the Ozarks of southern Missouri, and in the upper Cumberland in Kentucky and Tennessee fell nearly to zero (Figure 5.5).[35]

Southern mountain communities were very similar to rural commu-

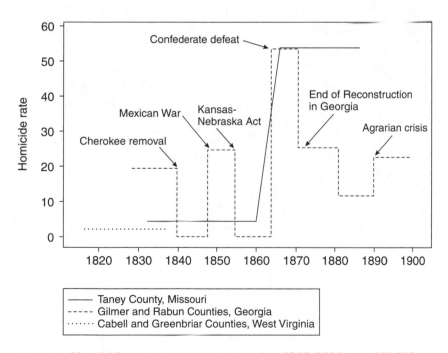

Figure 5.5 Homicide rates in mountain counties, 1816–1900 (per 100,000 adults per year).

nities in the North in the early national period. The land was still fertile, and timber was plentiful. People made a decent living raising hogs, sheep, and cattle, and population pressure was low. Slaves made up less than 5 percent of the population in these rugged counties, so white laborers did not have to compete against slave labor, and farmers did not have to compete against planters for land, political power, or social prestige, at least within their own communities. Land titles were less secure in the mountain South than in the North, and many settlers were still renting or squatting on land owned by speculators in the 1820s and 1830s, but by midcentury roughly two-thirds of adult white males owned at least a house and a small acreage. In plantation counties that figure was 50 percent or less.[36]

People in the mountain South did not need much land to make a good living. Their livestock usually ran free on the land of absentee owners, and without competition from slaves or free blacks, a third of all adult white males were able to earn most of their income outside agriculture, as opposed to a quarter or less in counties where slaves made up a tenth or more of the population. Food was plentiful, and the hazards of urban life were far away. As a result, the white inhabitants of the mountain South were among the tallest, healthiest people in the United States. The sense of empowerment and the expectation of economic independence were as strong in these communities as in the small towns and rural areas of the North. So, too, were patriotism and faith in the new nation, which is one reason why so many people in the mountain South were Unionists during the sectional crisis and the Civil War.[37]

In contrast, by the 1820s the homicide rate in the slaveholding South was at least twice what it had been at its low point in the mid-eighteenth century, and much higher than in the rest of the United States. Although the homicide rate varied widely in plantation counties in Georgia and South Carolina, in the North Carolina Piedmont, and in the Chesapeake and the Shenandoah Valley of Virginia, on the whole it was probably 10 to 25 per 100,000 adults per year for both blacks and whites (Figures 4.1, 5.6, and 5.7). That was double the rate in cities like Philadelphia and New York, which were the most homicidal places in the North. The plantation South was as prosperous as any other region in the United States, so poverty cannot explain the rising homicide rate. Nor can weak criminal justice institutions. The

South built prisons at the same rate as the North, and its cities had the first modern, uniformed police forces in the United States. In rural counties, slave patrols supplemented local sheriffs.[38]

The primary cause of the slaveholding South's higher homicide rate was the Revolution, which had a disruptive effect on slave society and on the relationship between proslavery southerners and the federal government. The Revolution undermined the pretensions of the *soi-disant* aristocracy and increased doubts about the rationale for slavery, but southern society was still firmly controlled by the slaveholding gentry, and many blacks and nonslaveholding whites felt frustrated and aggrieved at not having a share in the fruits of victory. Aware of these feelings, whites were more fearful of blacks, and slaveholders were more wary of nonslaveholding whites. Slaveholders were also distrustful of the federal government. They had been very patriotic during the War of 1812, but their patriotism declined quickly as the national controversy over slavery intensified in the 1820s and 1830s. They had not yet become southern nationalists, but they were rapidly becoming

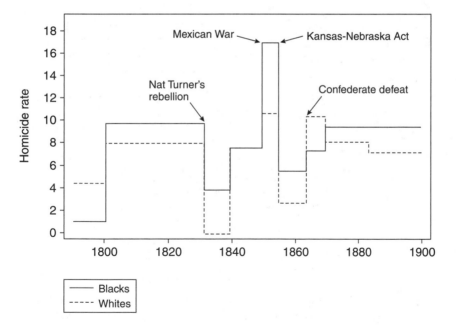

Figure 5.6 Homicide rates in Virginia by race, 1790–1900 (per 100,000 adults per year). Amelia, Lancaster, Rockbridge, and Surry Counties.

alienated from whites in the North and the mountain South, and they viewed the nonslaveholding whites in their midst as actual or potential abolitionists.[39] Together, the loss of faith in federal government, the decline in fellow feeling among whites, the growing fear of blacks among whites, and frustration among blacks and poor whites with the social hierarchy gave rise to the anger and alienation that caused the increase in homicide.

Fear of the antislavery movement was responsible for the initial jump in the homicide rate. Slaveholders were afraid that the success of the movement in the North would encourage blacks to murder whites in the South. For the most part, slaves and free blacks in the South,

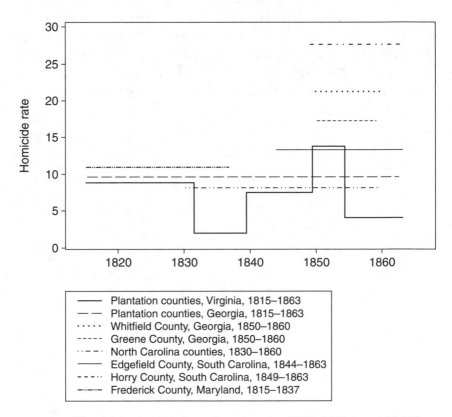

Figure 5.7 Homicide rates in plantation counties, 1815–1863 (per 100,000 adults per year). *Sources:* North Carolina: Bynum (1992: 82); Frederick County, Maryland: Rice (1994: 34, 100); Whitfield and Greene Counties, Georgia: Ayers (1984: 115).

like their counterparts in the North, chose other means to resist slavery and oppression, but whites were increasingly afraid of slaves, especially after the Haitian Revolution in 1791 and the exposure of slave rebellion plots in Virginia and North Carolina in 1800. Determined to do whatever it took to keep the institution alive, white militants used force ruthlessly to suppress abolitionists and to stop the spread of rebellion in the South.

The defeat of the southern antislavery movement was not a foregone conclusion in the 1790s and early 1800s, but southerners knew that their society was at a crossroads. As one anonymous Virginian put it, "The question now is a plain one. Shall we abolish slavery, or shall we continue it? There is no middle course to steer." The abolition of slavery in the North, the disappearance of convict servitude, and the rapid decline of apprenticeship and indentured servitude left southern slavery as the only formal remnant of the hierarchical society of the mid-eighteenth century. There were no longer degrees of servitude in America: only one remained, and African Americans were more impatient than ever to throw off that last form of bondage. George Tucker, a young Virginian from a prominent family, warned in 1801 that slave rebellions were inevitable.

> The love of freedom . . . is an inborn sentiment, which the God of nature has planted deep in the heart: long may it be kept under by the arbitrary institutions of society; but, at the first favourable moment, it springs forth, and flourishes with a vigour that defies all check. This celestial spark . . . is not extinguished in the bosom of the slave. It may be buried in the embers; but it still lives; and the breath of knowledge kindles it into flame. Thus we find . . . there never have been slaves in any country, who have not seized the first favorable opportunity to revolt.

The desire of the slaves for freedom was "an eating sore," rapidly growing worse because of "the very nature of our government, which leads us to recur perpetually to the discussion of natural rights."[40]

John Randolph of Roanoke saw the same dangers: since the Revolution blacks had acquired a "sense of their rights, and contempt of danger, and a thirst for revenge." Whites in the plantation South were divided—and would remain divided—about what course to take. The dangers of slavery, and the moral problems it posed, wore on an increasing number of slaveowners, some of whom manumitted their slaves or let them hire out their own time so that they could save enough money to purchase their freedom. Others thought that they could make slavery safer by Christianizing the institution. They wanted to minister to the souls of slaves and slaveowners, teach generosity and forbearance to all parties, foster respect for slave families, and encourage everyone—especially slaves—to look to heaven for their ultimate reward. Still others, like Tucker and his friend Thomas Jefferson, rejected both positions, certain that blacks and whites could never live as equals in a free society but doubtful that slavery could be preserved, given its inherent dangers and its ability to corrupt the morals of even the most devout Christians. Where slavery was concerned, Jefferson wrote, "We have the wolf by the ears; and we can neither hold him, nor safely let him go. Justice is on one scale, and self-preservation in the other."[41]

The profitability of slavery, prejudice against African Americans, and fear engendered by the Haitian Revolution and slave plots in the United States gave the upper hand to whites who wanted to preserve white supremacy by force. Defenders of slavery scoffed at the naïveté of colonizers, Christianizers, and abolitionists and reminded southerners of the fate of whites in Haiti. Proslavery activists like Edward Clifford Holland warned that blacks would always be on the lookout for opportunities to rebel: they "should be watched with an eye of steady and unremitted observation. . . . They are the ANARCHISTS and the DOMESTIC ENEMY: the COMMON ENEMY OF CIVILIZED SOCIETY, and the BARBARIANS WHO WOULD, IF THEY COULD, BECOME THE DESTROYERS OF OUR RACE."[42]

Defenders of slavery made a special effort to demonize free blacks, who they claimed were fomenting rebellion among the slaves. They also pointed to their poverty and to the property crimes they committed as proof that blacks were unfit for freedom. Blacks had "no moral sensations," they declared, "no taste but for women; gormandizing, and drinking to excess; no wish but to be idle." Some even claimed that blacks were a different species. Their view of black character (which would become the dominant view among white Americans by the 1850s) not only legitimized slavery and racial inequality; it also fed fear and justified violence against blacks.[43]

Proslavery whites used their influence, particularly through churches and the Jeffersonian Party, to prop up slavery. They forced evangelical churches to repeal antislavery resolutions, clamped down on manumissions, and strengthened fugitive slave laws and the slave patrol system. They encouraged prejudice and discrimination against free blacks, fought to admit new slave states and protect slavery in the Southwest territories, and rallied voters across the nation to support white supremacy. But the most militant defenders of slavery were not content with political victory. They were determined to crush black resistance and to silence white abolitionists—or anyone else who expressed sympathy for the suffering of slaves.[44]

The emotions roused by slave plots and the tirades of proslavery whites led to an increase in murders of African Americans by whites. Whenever rumors of a slave rebellion surfaced, proslavery whites responded with overwhelming force. Mass arrests followed by hangings of suspected rebels became routine after 1800. These actions had widespread support, for, whatever their opinions of slavery, southern whites were all deathly afraid of becoming victims of slave violence.[45]

Murders of suspected rebels and white sympathizers escalated after the publication in 1829 of an *Appeal to the Coloured Citizens of the World* by David Walker, a free black shopkeeper and civil rights activist in Boston. Walker threatened whites with violent retribution if they did not "throw away" their "fears and prejudices" and emancipate the slaves immediately. "We cannot but hate you, while you are treating us like dogs." North Carolina was abuzz with rumors that local blacks had read Walker's pamphlet, which was circulated in the South by black sailors and preachers. In Duplin County several slaves gave evidence under torture that they had heard about a conspiracy to rebel on Christmas Day 1830, and sixty-five slaves were arrested. In the countryside it was rumored that the uprising had already started, and 600 whites came streaming into the county seat. They stormed the jail and seized two of the conspiracy's alleged "ringleaders," cut off their heads, and strung up their bodies. The North Carolina legislature lent credence to all the rumors by passing fifteen new laws against blacks, including bans on manumissions and teaching blacks to read or write.[46]

The worst violence occurred in 1831 after Nat Turner's rebellion in Southampton County, Virginia, in which at least 58 whites were killed. Authorities in Virginia and North Carolina charged 91 men and women with conspiracy and hanged 35 of them, including Turner, but militant whites were not satisfied. They went on a rampage, beating, burning, mutilating, and killing suspicious blacks and whites. When a guard unit in Murfreesboro, North Carolina, spied a strange black man walking down a road toward Southampton, they shot him, "cut off his head, stuck it on a pole, and planted the pole at the cross streets." That same day a black carriage driver "behaved imprudently" in the presence of his mistress, and he, too, had his head cut off and stuck on a pole. One militia unit cut off the heads of 15 slaves and put their heads on poles "as a warning to all." In the end, vigilantes killed over 120 men and women, most of whom had nothing to do with Turner's rebellion.[47]

The events of 1830–31 prompted people across the slaveholding South to take preventive measures whenever rumors of insurrection arose, and the nets they cast to capture suspects began to draw in whites as well. In 1835 a woman in Madison County, Mississippi, said she overheard her servants talking about a slave plot on a plantation outside Livingston. Before the scare was over more than two dozen blacks, slave and free, were dead, along with sixteen whites. Two slave preachers were the first victims; they were accused, as slave ministers and conjurors often were, of preaching abolition. Soon afterward a white man was accused of trading with blacks for stolen property. Vigilantes hanged him and his colleague. Then they turned their attention to Angus Donovan, a corn trader from Kentucky, and Ruel Blake, the owner of a slave who had been tortured by the vigilantes. Donovan and Blake had complained of the vigilantes' brutal treatment of blacks. The vigilantes hanged them both. Accusations, forced confessions, and lynchings continued for the next two months.[48]

Proslavery vigilantes were probably responsible for killing between 600 and 700 people in the first half of the nineteenth century. The deaths had a chilling effect on public debate: all but a handful of free blacks and antislavery whites were cowed into silence. But there were not enough of these deaths to affect the overall homicide rate in the plantation South. The rate rose largely because of individual murders of blacks by whites. Whites killed blacks at a rate of 5 per 100,000 adults per year in tobacco- and grain-growing counties in Virginia; 7 per 100,000 in Florida and in Edgefield County, South Carolina, a cotton-growing county; and 23 per 100,000 in Horry County, South Carolina, where the primary crop was rice.[49] These murders might appear at first glance to differ from vigilante murders, but they were caused by the same fears and discontents. Blacks were increasingly determined to assert themselves. Almost every black person who was murdered had at some point refused to do what was asked of him or made a demand that was considered unacceptable. Whites were increasingly determined to keep blacks in their place and more afraid than ever of what might happen if they failed. The individual whites who murdered slaves and free blacks may not have been directly involved in the militant movement to defend slavery, but they were every bit as determined to keep blacks in their place as the vigilantes, politicians, and racial theorists who spearheaded the movement.

As in the eighteenth century, a high proportion of black homicide victims were killed unintentionally by masters or overseers during discipline. Overzealous whippings and beatings claimed the lives of roughly a third of all blacks killed by whites in the Chesapeake, the Shenandoah Valley, and the Georgia–South Carolina upcountry after 1800. But a growing proportion of slaves were deliberately killed by masters or overseers. A third of all blacks killed by individual whites were shot, and another third were stabbed, clubbed, or kicked.[50] This kind of violence, which went well beyond discipline, had not been seen at such levels since the late seventeenth and early eighteenth centuries, when slavery was first established. Clearly, it was part of an effort to underscore the legitimacy of slavery in the wake of the Revolution.

Slaveowners felt that they had to kill slaves who defied them in order to break the increased resistance they were facing from all their slaves. Like their counterparts in the late seventeenth and early eighteenth centuries, they were willing to accept the property loss and the cost of legal fees. Ann Powell, a slaveowner in Amelia County, Virginia, reported that her slave Tom was "a very bad negro." He had run away many times. When her neighbors caught him yet again, he swore that he would keep running away if they returned him to his mistress. They whipped him on the spot for that remark, but the whipping did not satisfy Powell's overseer. He tied Tom to a fence and beat him to death. Drury Moore, an Amelia County overseer whose master was away, sought permission from a justice of the peace to give a slave named Scott more than the usual twenty lashes because Scott had struck him and bitten him on the hand. The justice advised Moore to wait for his employer, but Moore refused. He ordered Scott whipped, but Scott would not cooperate. As he walked away, Moore shot him in the back. Moore told the court that "he had always said he would shoot any negroe th[a]t was under his controll that struck him."[51]

White southerners were not of one mind about killing slaves. Masters and overseers who brutalized their victims were indicted for murder, and witnesses who testified in such cases—all of whom, by law, were white—often expressed horror at what they had seen. Yet none of these witnesses ever came to the aid of an enslaved victim other than to ask the assailant to stop once they thought the slave had had enough, and none of these murderers were convicted. Masters or overseers who killed slaves with less brutality were not even charged. The authorities believed that there was good reason not to interfere, especially if a master or overseer felt the need to use a gun or knife. Taking the side of a slave could undermine discipline and threaten the institution of slavery. Whites who had qualms about the brutal treatment of slaves simply learned to give the worst of their neighbors a wide berth.

Slaveowners and overseers were not the only whites guilty of increased violence against African Americans. In the mid-eighteenth century most men would have been reluctant to destroy someone else's valuable property. Certainly poor whites did not often take it upon themselves to kill a wealthier man's slave. But after 1800 even the poorest of whites felt licensed by the greater social mandate to keep slaves in their place. Robert McCutchen, a farmer in Rockbridge County, Virginia, had hired Harry, a neighbor's slave, to do some work for him. Harry asked for his pay several times, but McCutchen always refused. One Saturday night, Harry happened to meet McCutchen while the farmer was drinking with neighbors, and Harry once again tried to get what was owed him. "You damn'd black Sallymander," said McCutchen. "Clear out, [or] I'll take your life." The neighbors testified that Harry replied civilly, "Mr. McCutchen, I have not said any thing improper to you, nor done you any harm, and you would not go to hurt me." McCutchen said that he would "as soon kill him, as . . . a Lizard," and he grabbed an ax and split his head open.[52]

In the context of widespread fear that society was changing and that slaves were challenging white supremacy, a white man who let a slave embarrass him was seen as acknowledging the validity of the slaves' claims. Adding to the problem was the economic competition that poor whites faced from enslaved artisans. Such competition and the cost of land made it difficult to sustain a small farm or shop and to establish a family, and many whites became mired in poverty. They had no status except that conferred by their skin color, and no way of earning the respect of other whites. As slaves became more aware of the workings of the larger society, they too began to look down upon the white underclass. Poor whites who found themselves competing with slaves for the next-to-lowest rung of the social ladder tried to salvage whatever remnants of pride they could by flaunting their mastery over black men.

Still, men who murdered blacks they did not own did not have the support from the justice system that masters, overseers, and vigilantes did. Slaveowners were not pleased to have their property destroyed for the sake of a poor man's pride. Robert McCutchen was sent to prison. John Hayslet murdered a free black and had to flee the state to avoid prosecution.[53] Proslavery militants confined their antiblack violence largely to their own slaves or to suspected rebels. They viewed murders by nonslaveholders as different from the murders they themselves committed. Yet murders by nonslaveholders were rooted in the same emotions that gave birth to the proslavery movement.

Those emotions also led militant whites to kill people they suspected of favoring abolition. Joseph Samuel confronted James Reynolds in the street in Hamburg, South Carolina, and accused him of having "run negroes to a free State" and "carried them money." Reynolds, who did business with local blacks, replied that "he had never denied earning them money" but that he had never helped a runaway. Samuel beat him to death anyway. Assassins tried several times to kill the South's only noted abolitionist, Cassius Clay. Militants also killed whites from the North who made careless remarks about slavery. An Ohioan standing on a crowded dock on the Mississippi River said in passing that "he would soon be in a free state." Several bystanders jumped him, nailed him up in a pork barrel, and threw him into the river, where he drowned. Governor John Floyd of Virginia applauded such attempts to bring abolitionist "villains" to justice. "The law of nature will not permit men to have their families butchered before their eyes by their slaves and not seek by force to punish those who plan and encourage them to perpetuate these deeds." As sectional conflict intensified, southerners killed northerners more frequently.[54]

In the long run, the Revolution destabilized relations among whites in the slave South as much as it did relations between whites and blacks. After 1800 the homicide rate among whites in the slave South reached 6 per 100,000 adults per year in Virginia; 13 per 100,000 in Edgefield County, South Carolina; and 27 per 100,000 in Horry County, South Carolina.[55] With the spread of revolutionary ideas about equality, the region's caste and class system lost legitimacy in the eyes of the poor, while the well-to-do clung to their ideas about social class and became more obdurate in their efforts to enforce social distinctions.

Southerners from all walks of life also clung to their conception of honor, which was based in part upon the mastery of other men, black and white. By its very nature slave society conferred the greatest honor on men who dominated others. Georgia humorist Augustus Baldwin Longstreet once observed that the worst fate that could befall a man in the South was to be afraid of another man, because fear made a man a slave. And no white southerner could truly be content until he had "understrappers"—white men who worked for a slaveowner. George Keen, a settler in eastern Florida, recalled how much he had wished as a young man that he could have taken part in the "overseer talk" of the local planters he escorted on hunting trips.

> One would say, I've got the best overseer I ever had; another would say, my overseer is a worthless fellow, a third would say I am pretty well satisfied with my overseer, and so on. I would sit there like a bump on a log. You bet I never wanted anything worse in my life than I wanted a plantation of niggers so I could talk about my overseer. I had some niggers, but not enough to have an overseer; that's what worried me. When hunting time come round I was in but when overseer talk was the topic of the day I was ten feet above high water mark on dry land.

Ironically, it was mastery of white men—not slaves—that was the key to self-esteem in the postrevolutionary slave South.[56]

Whites who owned few or no slaves could still take comfort in their superiority to black men, although even that status was under siege. But it was far more difficult for white men to acquire a sense of mastery over other white men. The struggle for dominance among white men had been held in check in the century before the Revolution by the inherently hierarchical nature of British society, which fostered the belief that inferiors (especially indentured servants, convict servants, and apprentices) had a duty to defer to their superiors. The Revolution eliminated that check, even as it heightened ambitions and intensified competition. Poor and middle-income whites who wanted to move up the social ladder in the plantation South had no more opportunity to do so after the Revolution than before because of the inherent economic inequality of slaveholding society and its restrictive definition of honor. They could not compete on an equal footing in a society in which wealth, power, and social prestige were concentrated heavily in the hands of the slaveholding elite. In some states, like Virginia and South Carolina, they could not even look to political participation for a sense of empowerment, since through the 1840s more than half of all white males in those states were still disfranchised by property restrictions.

The situation made relations among poor and middle-income whites more adversarial than in the North or the mountain South. Although many poor and middle-income whites in the slaveholding South tried, like their counterparts elsewhere, to empower themselves through churches, schools, and temperance societies, they did not do so to the degree that other white Americans did, and they turned to violence far more often as a way of venting their frustration. They had the example of southern gentlemen before them, but they embraced personal combat on their own terms as a way to protect their honor, property, or rights. Dominating others was as important to poor and middle-income whites as it was to wealthy whites.

The desire for mastery over others set in motion contests of will that no man felt he could afford to lose. At a husking bee in Rockbridge County, Addison Thompson picked up a rock to throw at a dog then accidentally dropped it. George Rowsey put his foot on it and said, "If you put that rock out of the yard I will put you out." Thompson pulled the rock out from under Rowsey's foot and threw it at the dog, and Rowsey stabbed him to death. A similar contest of wills cost Archer Wingo his life on the day of his father's funeral in Amelia County, Virginia. His mother had invited guests to the family home after his father's burial. A number of people demanded more liquor, but young Archer, who had custody of the key to the liquor cabinet, cut them off. Two neighbors ordered him to hand over the key, and when he refused they threw him to the ground and kicked him to death.[57]

Poor and middle-income men were also notoriously touchy around other people's slaves. Losing face in front of a slave was degrading, and being told by a slaveowner not to touch his slave was a reminder of one's low status. In 1836 in Jasper County, Georgia, Richard Gregory got into an argument in Charles Morgan's store with one of Morgan's slaves and began to beat him. Morgan ordered him to stop, but Gregory ignored him. Another customer, William Nelson, intervened, saying that the slave was too drunk to understand his punishment and that Gregory should at least wait until the slave sobered up. Gregory drew a pistol and shot Nelson. Two years later Jasper County witnessed a similar murder. A slave asked Turner Horton in front of a crowd for a debt he owed. Horton started to beat the slave with a stick, but the slave's owner, Joseph Harrison, ordered Horton to stop. Horton kept beating the slave, so Harrison beat Horton with a stick, compounding his humiliation. That Sunday Horton cornered Harrison at a church service and shot him through the heart.[58]

Even when poor and middle-income whites competed against each other in games of chance or strength, there was potential for serious violence. Men who were eager to prove themselves found losing hard to stomach. Whites killed each other over who was the best at wrestling, who was the best at cards or pitching dollars, who had won more money. The same adversarial psychology led to an increase in homicides over economic disputes. William Johnson, a free black barber from Natchez, Mississippi, wrote a list in his diary of the material causes of murders among whites in that town: "a Barrell of oysters," "Cattle," or "Something about a 20 c[en]t Hat."[59]

Petty disputes had led to homicides in the eighteenth century in the North as well as the South, of course, but the chances of being killed because of a petty squabble were far higher in the slaveholding South in the early nineteenth century because of the changes the Revolution had wrought. It created a struggle for status and preferment that poor and middle-income white men could not win. Petty quarrels took on life-or-death significance. Men became more aggressive and more determined to win respect by dominating others. No one captured this spirit better than Augustus Longstreet. As a judge and a reformer, he was deeply troubled by violence among whites in his native Georgia, but he understood that it grew out of a desperate need for respect. His stories in *Georgia Scenes,* published in 1835, captured the braggadocio of men in the Georgia-Carolina upcountry. They could "knock out the bull's eye" and take any man in a fight, and they ridiculed men who didn't measure up.[60]

The same antagonistic, belligerent spirit was apparent among public men in the slaveholding South. Unlike their northern counterparts, they continued to duel (or kill in ambush) their social and political rivals long after the two-party system took shape and institutionalized political conflict. They murdered one another over insults, slights, or revelations of embarrassing truths. As would-be seigneurs, they had trouble coping with democratic politics. They were used to dominating people and having others defer to them. Such expectations had not posed a problem in the mid-eighteenth century, when the social and political hierarchy was fairly stable and their place in it secure. Except for attacks during the Revolutionary War they had faced no serious challenge since the late seventeenth century, and they had seldom been subjected to public attacks. After the Revolution, however, challenges both real and imagined came from every corner.[61]

Public men with the loftiest political ambitions were the most likely to fight, since they needed to preserve their standing and protect their reputations. When William Crawford, the future U.S. senator and secretary of the Treasury, was an aspiring young politician in Georgia, he was asked by a group of speculators to join their latest venture. He wanted nothing to do with these men, who had been involved in the Yazoo scandal, so he spurned their offer publicly. Peter Van Allen, one of the speculators, challenged Crawford to a duel. Crawford killed Allen and became a political star.[62]

The South produced hundreds of similar stories. John Hampden Pleasants, the former editor of the Richmond *Whig,* became incensed when an essay in the Democratic Richmond *Enquirer* insinuated that he was an abolitionist. The charge stung because Pleasants had in fact supported gradual emancipation briefly in the wake of Nat Turner's rebellion and had published letters from Whigs who thought that slavery hurt Virginia's economy. Yet the *Enquirer*'s editor, Thomas Ritchie, had done much the same by publishing an even-handed account of the legislature's 1832 debate on emancipation. Now Ritchie wanted to claim that he and the Democrats had always been rock-solid in their defense of slavery. Pleasants denied that he was an abolitionist and said that he would like to see "some abolitionist leaders hanged." But with his reputation and his party's standing at stake, he had to challenge the author of the essay, Thomas Ritchie Jr. (the son of the *Enquirer*'s editor) to a duel. Pleasants was mortally wounded. As he lay dying, he lamented the southern obsession with reputation. "What a damned immolation this is to be such slaves to public opinion."[63]

The widely reported duels involving Henry Clay, Andrew Jackson, and John Randolph attest to their popularity among gentlemen with high aspirations. Few men from the backcountry engaged in duels. Duelists were primarily from cities, large towns, or county seats. They followed the rules of the *code duello,* codified for the English-speaking public by Anglo-Irish gentlemen in 1777 and adopted in the United States with some modifications. Usually they claimed to have resorted to violence only after exhausting all other options. Abiding by the rules demonstrated, at least in their own eyes and in the eyes of most fellow southerners, that they were men of restraint as well as passion, of civility as well as courage, tolerant men who nevertheless would not hesitate to cane or kill a man for an affront. Their code of behavior conflated the ideal qualities of statesman and slavemaster in a society that was at once elite-dominated and democratic, and it helped to legitimize slaveowners' mastery of society and politics.[64]

Many gentlemen, however, especially those with less lofty political ambitions, were not interested in following the rules of the challenge and simply went after each other in the street. McQueen McIntosh and Colonel John Hopkins, who were feuding in the local newspapers, ran into each other in Darien, Georgia, pulled out their pistols, and fired away. Hopkins was wounded; McIntosh died. Major John Cooper of Hampton, Virginia, and Thomas Allen, Esq., of York County were parties to a local feud about a school. Allen, who was visiting Hampton for the day with his family, had his two small sons in tow when he ran into Cooper. They exchanged harsh words, and Cooper pulled out his pistol and shot Allen as his children screamed for help.[65]

These killings reflected the persistent difficulty that southern political leaders had in coming to grips with the unruliness of political competition in postrevolutionary America. But the carnage extended well beyond the public realm. Young gentlemen imitated their elders and challenged friends who insulted them or gossiped about them or beat them at card games. They accused them of being "damned liars" or "cheats" or "rogues" and demanded that they fight or be labeled cowards. Some of them even challenged teachers who criticized their work in class. Since the code dictated that men did not have to respond to inferiors, teachers merely had such students expelled.

Some men enjoyed intimidating people and killing those who refused to do their bidding. A farmer and his family were driving their sheep down a road near Florence, Alabama, when a man rode up and demanded that they make way. The road was too narrow for the farmer to turn his flock aside, so the man rode into the farmer's flock "and caused him some trouble to keep it together." The farmer shouted that he would throw a rock at the man if he did not stop. The man ignored him, so the farmer threw a rock. The man dismounted, went into a nearby store, came out with a gun, and shot the farmer. Then he got out his Bowie knife and stabbed him through the heart.[66]

The South swarmed with men who prided themselves on giving in to such violent impulses. Colonel Alexander McClung killed more than a dozen men during his lifetime. As a young man he fought a number of duels, and while he was in the army he killed a general in a duel. After moving to Vicksburg, Mississippi, he got into a feud and killed seven members of a local family. He also killed people frequently on the streets and in taverns. Even his friends shrank from him when he was angry. Yet southerners admired him for his hair-trigger temper and, in the belief that there was something noble about his willingness to kill people who offended him, gave him the sobriquet "the Black Knight of the South."[67]

Men like McClung were the South's conquering heroes. As Longstreet said, "the bully of the county never wants friends," and the more famous the bully, the more friends he had. A number of men like McClung, who were known to have killed men who crossed them, won seats in Congress or their state legislatures: William Yancey of Alabama, Louis Wigfall of Texas, George Tillman of South Carolina. McClung could have been successful in politics too, but he ran for Congress as a Whig in a Mississippi district where being a Democrat was an essential qualification. Longstreet was philosophical about the southern proclivity for electing violent men. He compared southern politicians to hounds that all "jump on the undermost."[68]

It is no coincidence that the culture that condoned this conduct also condoned vigilantism. Southerners admired men who were a law unto themselves. The citizens of Thomas County, Georgia, were plagued by criminals who crossed the nearby state line from Florida Territory to burglarize homes and steal horses. They decided to take matters into their own hands. Anyone who was caught sneaking across the state line at night was shot on sight. After yet another body turned up, a circuit court judge instructed the county's grand jurors to indict the vigilantes. Instead the jurors used the occasion to express their appreciation for a job well done: "We have taken under our serious consideration the inquest upon the body of Mack M. Glass and after making diligent inquiry, we are decidedly of the opinion that the killing of him was a praiseworthy action and that the persons concerned therein are entitled to the thanks of the county for their conduct in executing the laws." Similarly, vigilantes in Vicksburg, Mississippi, decided they had had enough of the riverfront gaming industry. They armed themselves and set out to tear up all the gambling establishments. When some of the gamblers resisted and killed one of the attackers, the vigilantes were infuriated. After overpowering the gamblers they hanged five of them, then gave four others 1,000 lashes each and set them adrift on the Mississippi.[69]

This kind of collective violence was not confined to the plantation South, but it was probably two or three times more common there than in the rural North or the mountain South, and far more deadly. Vigilantism was especially pervasive in the lower Mississippi Valley and on the Gulf Coast. The wealth created by the cotton, sugar, rice, and real estate boom of the 1820s and 1830s attracted gamblers, robbers, horse thieves, slave stealers, and confidence men eager to profit from the region's success. These criminals hid out in swamps and woodlands, traveling up and down the Mississippi River, sailing around the Gulf, and crossing state lines. Vigilantes were confident that they could do a better job at catching these people than law-enforcement officials, since they knew the terrain better and could cross state lines at will; they had few qualms about taking over the law's role and lynching suspects who fell into their hands.[70]

Southerners had a tradition of ruthless vigilantism that went back to the Carolina Regulators and the Revolution. They were accustomed to acting on their own and ignoring the constraints imposed by the legal system. This tradition had been reinforced by slavery, since neighbors often had to band together to patrol the roads for runaways. Like patrolling, vigilante action could also be exciting, especially for young men. They got to saddle up and ride out with friends, often at night, and some of them took pleasure in the suffering and humiliation of victims. Murderers elsewhere in the United States were certainly capable of sadistic violence, like the members of the Philadelphia mob who castrated a black man and raped a black woman during the Flying Horse Riot of 1834.[71] But northern whites rarely tortured other whites. Their peers in the slaveholding South practiced almost every form of sadism on whites, from eye gouging to castration to slow suffocation. The only torment they reserved solely for blacks was burning.

Southern humor in the postrevolutionary period reflected this propensity to cruelty. The plantation South had its share of ironists, like Longstreet, but its humor—of both the published and the everyday variety—more often than not involved physical suffering and humiliation, whereas northern humor specialized in poking fun at pretentious or self-righteous people.

The Tennessee humorist George Washington Harris wrote stories about a young man named Sut Lovingood, who was mean and proud of it. When the family's horse died and his father had to pull the plow himself, Sut thought it "wer pow'ful inturestin, an' sorter funny." He laughed uproariously when his father ran into a hornets' nest "es big es a hoss's head." He also found humor in the death of the kindly Mrs. Yardley. He broke up a quilting bee at her house by tying a line hung with quilts to a skittish horse and setting the horse off with a whack from a fence post. The horse "run plum over Missis Yardley," whose "heart stop't beatin'." Sut thought that was hilarious, but he did help "salt ole Missis Yardley down" afterward so that she could "rotten cumfurtably."[72]

Southern letters from the antebellum period abound with wry comments about victims of murders and brutal assaults. One Virginian described how his friend, John McDermott, had murdered an elderly man: "He sent the poor old fellow to the other country, both drunk and with a pain in his belly, that being the place where John's knife made acquaintance." A South Carolinian spoke of his delight at beating a man and making him beg "like a negro" for mercy. Others recalled with amusement seeing men who had lost an eye or an ear in a fight.[73]

Of course, whites in the slave South were not of one mind when it came to bullying, cruelty, and murder. Many did speak out against the rising tide of murder among whites. Laws against dueling passed in nearly every southern state, and antidueling societies formed in Charleston, Savannah, Vicksburg, and other hotbeds of murder; but they had no impact on dueling or on the murder rate as a whole. Antidueling laws were never enforced, and antidueling societies had trouble even getting their own members to honor their pledges.[74] Some humorists, like Longstreet, tried to discourage violence by poking fun at men with violent tempers and by censuring the bloodthirstiness of those who egged them on, but they were swimming against the tide.

Most southerners wanted to attack the problem of increased violence more directly by outlawing concealed weapons. Few whites had carried pistols or fighting knives in the eighteenth century, but the practice became popular in the plantation South in the nineteenth century as fears of black violence grew and whites became more anxious and belligerent. The proportion of homicides committed with such weapons is uncertain, since most records did not specify the kind of gun or knife used, but guns and knives accounted for a growing share of the known weapons that whites used to kill other whites. After the Revolution, guns or knives were used in 67 percent of homicides among whites in plantation counties in Virginia, Georgia, and South Carolina. According to contemporary observers, a substantial number of those weapons were pistols, dirks, or Bowie knives, manufactured expressly to kill people.[75]

Proponents of concealed weapons claimed that they were necessary for personal defense. Cassius Clay, who carried pistols and knives for protection against antiabolitionist mobs, said that "when society *fails to protect us,* we are authorized by the laws of God and nature to defend ourselves; based upon *the right,* 'the pistol and the Bowie knife' are to us as sacred as the gown and the pulpit." But opponents of concealed weapons believed that men carried concealed weapons for two reasons: to intimidate others and to seize the advantage in spontaneous disputes. In 1834 the grand jurors of Jasper County, Georgia, denounced "the practice which is common amongst us with the young the middle aged and the aged to arm themselves with Pistols, dirks knives sticks & spears under the specious pretence of protecting themselves against insult, when in fact being so armed they frequently insult others with impunity, or if resistance is made the pistol dirk or club is immediately resorted to, hence we so often hear of the stabbing shooting & murdering so many of our citizens." The justices of the Louisiana Supreme Court echoed these sentiments. "Unmanly" men carried concealed weapons to gain "secret advantages" over their adversaries. Those who opposed concealed weapons did not blame them for the slaveholding South's homicide problem, but they understood the psychology of white-on-white violence and believed that concealed weapons made the homicide problem worse by giving bullies and cowards the means to kill anyone they disliked.[76]

Opponents of concealed weapons won the public debate in the South. In an effort to stem the tide of backcountry violence, especially among boatmen on the Ohio and Mississippi Rivers, Kentucky and Louisiana passed the nation's first concealed-weapons laws in 1813. They were joined in the late 1830s by Alabama, Arkansas, Tennessee, Georgia, and Virginia. Whigs and Christian reformers lent the movement its most enthusiastic support in the 1830s and 1840s, but it was extremely popular in most states. It had the support of people who condemned violence outright, but it was also supported by people who believed that there would be fewer deaths if combatants were forced to "fight fair."[77]

Despite their popularity, concealed-weapons laws had no clear impact on homicide rates. They may have discouraged the carrying of handguns and fighting knives, but they were hard to enforce, and they did not address the underlying causes of violence. Men in the North and the mountain South had guns and knives, too, but they rarely used them to kill anyone. Only one free state felt the need for a concealed-weapons law in these years: Indiana, which had been settled predominantly by white southerners. The appeal of violence for men in the slaveholding South—its sporting nature, its excitement, and the opportunity it afforded to prove oneself in front of one's peers—was undiminished, as was the antagonistic spirit that prompted the violence in the first place.

As historian Bertram Wyatt-Brown has observed, a society that was at once a slave society and a revolutionary society could not demand "groveling, obsequiousness, and slavishness" from its freeborn white citizens. It had to give them a chance to prove that they were independent men who could command deference and respect from others. But in a slave society, men had to dominate other men to earn respect, and everyone understood that principle. As a young attorney in Alabama told Alexis de Tocqueville in 1830, men who murdered other men were "always acquitted by the jury, unless there are greatly aggravating circumstances. . . . Each juror feels that he might, on leaving the court, find himself in the same position as the accused, and he acquits."[78] Laws that prohibited the carrying of concealed weapons seemed a better solution than stiff sanctions for the homicide problem. Such laws were not meant to do away with the competition for dominance; they were meant only to lessen its deadliness. But the need to dominate others was what led to murder, and after the Revolution unsettled the social hierarchy and undermined the idea that inferiors should defer to their superiors, whites in the slaveholding South were fated to become entangled in an increasing number of lethal disputes over who could master whom.

In most areas of the slaveholding South, there were mitigating factors that kept homicide rates from rising too far after the Revolution. There were stable state governments that advocated strongly for southern interests, for example, and the federal government had fulfilled at least some of its promises: Great Britain and Spain had been expelled from the Gulf Coast and the lower Mississippi River Valley, as had the Native Americans. But in Florida there were no such mitigating factors, and the feelings and beliefs that correlate with low homicide rates were almost wholly absent, so it remained two to four times more homicidal than the rest of the slaveholding South. Most whites in Florida felt that neither federal nor territorial officials were governing honestly or effectively. Public land was not being distributed fairly. The Seminoles had refused to leave. The banks existed solely to feather the nests of corrupt local officials and to fleece the average citizen, and there was little effort to deter crime. Frontier violence and government instability persisted into the 1840s.

These conditions produced anger and disillusionment with Florida's government and widespread disrespect for the law, especially among poor and middle-income whites, who stood little chance of acquiring prime agricultural land or of getting what they considered their fair share of the proceeds from the cotton, citrus, and real estate booms. Many settlers felt disfranchised and powerless, and they turned to robbery, vigilantism, and other forms of violence. As a result the homicide rate for whites rose to 40 per 100,000 adults per year during the antebellum period and to 70 per 100,000 during the Second Seminole War, 1835–1842 (Figure 5.8).

Florida's homicide problem began during the Patriot War (1812–1814), when American filibusterers tried to oust the colony's Spanish governor and annex the territory to the United States. The homicide rate probably rose into the hundreds per 100,000 adults per year. The fighting was as bitter as any that occurred in the southern backcountry during the Revolutionary War, because the insurgents were opposed not only by Spanish loyalists but also by British merchantmen, runaway slaves, and Seminoles, all of whom had reason to fear an American takeover. Families who lost relatives took revenge, killing or burning out their enemies. After the war, defeated patriots like William Williams, disaffected and inured to violence, formed criminal gangs and robbed and murdered people and kidnapped slaves along the Georgia-Florida border.[79]

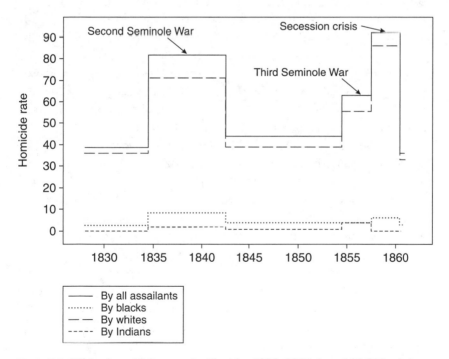

Figure 5.8 White homicide rates in Florida, 1828–1861 (per 100,000 adults per year). *Source:* Denham and Roth (2007).

The homicide rate declined in the early 1820s, when Florida became a territory of the United States and the chaos caused by the Patriot War, the First Seminole War (1816–1818), and campaigns against fugitive slave communities came to an end. But the new territorial government had very little legitimacy in the eyes of many whites, so their homicide rate stayed unusually high—40 per 100,000 adults per year. Control of the government remained in the hands of small cadres of federal appointees, such as the "Nucleus," a faction associated with Andrew Jackson. These factions, unresponsive and unaccountable to the territory's voters, enriched themselves at public expense. They chartered banks that issued hundreds of thousands of dollars in ill-secured loans to faction leaders and their political cronies, then held Florida taxpayers responsible for paying off the bonds that secured the loans if the banks defaulted. Faction leaders also got rich by controlling the survey and sale of land. Under federal law, people who had settled in Florida by 1825 could register and purchase between 80 and 160 acres of the land they occupied for $1.25 an acre before it came up for public auction. It was difficult enough for the poor to come up with the cash they needed, but the faction leaders who controlled land offices made the registration process next to impossible. They dismissed squatters' claims on technicalities, demanded "proof" of occupancy that illiterate farmers found hard to come by, and closed land offices illegally in the weeks before public auctions so that squatters had nowhere to register their claims. The consequences were stark in middle Florida, where land was most valuable: by 1829 only 19 percent of men with fewer than ten slaves owned land in Leon County and 13 percent in Jackson County.[80]

Florida's territorial officials also failed to establish an effective system of law enforcement. Because of penury, indifference, or the misappropriation of funds, territorial officials hired too few constables and deputies, and their jails (where they bothered to build them) were too rickety to hold criminals. As a result, at least a quarter of all homicide suspects jumped bail or escaped from jail. Three of every 100 white murderers were hanged, but because there was no state prison, murderers could not be sentenced to long prison terms, so the rest got no more than thirty-nine lashes, a year in jail, and a $1,000 fine (which was routinely rescinded for those who could not pay). Knowing that there was very little risk of being hanged, outlaws thought little of murdering potential witnesses.[81]

Beset by lawlessness on every side, Floridians felt that they had to take the law into their own hands. They formed vigilante groups and dispensed justice as they saw fit. One in every twenty-five murder victims in Florida was hanged by white vigilantes. Poor and middle-income whites defended what property they had with violence. Neighbors killed neighbors over the placement of a fence, crop damage, the ownership of a canoe, or a contract to supply shingles to the government, usually without first seeking legal redress. Citizens who had their property attached killed the justices of the peace who issued the writs and the deputies who served them. Sectional rivalries between east and west Florida compounded the difficulties of creating a responsive government, and politics became a matter of currying favor with the federal government and of defaming opponents. Calumny led to whippings, duels, and assassinations among political leaders.[82]

Another consequence of the government's inability to establish a legitimate system of law and order was that more people carried guns. Fifty-five percent of the victims of white assailants in Florida (excluding those who were lynched) were shot, compared to 38 percent in antebellum Georgia and South Carolina and 36 percent in Virginia. Having to be ready to fight took its toll.[83]

The homicide rate among whites climbed to 70 per 100,000 adults per year during the Second Seminole War and the depression of 1839–1843, when faith in both the territorial and the federal governments reached a new low. Floridians questioned the federal government's commitment to removing the Seminoles. President Andrew Jackson, furious at criticism of his administration, added fuel to the fire in 1837 by blaming Floridians themselves: "Let the damned cowards defend their country. . . . They ought to have crushed [the Seminoles] at once if they had been men of spirit and character." The financial panic of 1837, which led to the depression of 1839–1843, made matters worse. As Florida's banks failed and poor farmers faced foreclosure, anger at Florida's political establishment finally translated itself into constructive action. Dissidents promising bank regulation and an end to land-office corruption stood for election and won control of the government.[84]

The political crisis finally passed in the early 1840s, and the homicide rate among whites fell once again to 40 per 100,000 adults per year. The end of the Second Seminole War, the arrival of statehood in 1845, and the creation of a more responsive two-party system allayed public anger, and Florida leaders began to behave, at least publicly, as if they were working for the good of the people. But cynicism about the government endured for generations, and Florida's homicide rate remained higher than the rate in the rest of the slaveholding South until the Civil War.[85]

Black Homicide in the South

African Americans in the plantation South were profoundly affected by the Revolution's failure to fulfill its promise of equality and opportunity for all. In the early 1800s it became clear to them that the campaign for emancipation and equal rights had been defeated and that their place in the social hierarchy of the South was fixed. A slave in Southampton County expressed the frustration that all blacks felt when he said, "god damn the white people they have reigned long enough."[86] The end of that reign now seemed further off than ever. Fatalities involving discipline, running away, and insubordination increased, not only because of greater fear and hostility among whites, but also because African Americans resisted the institution on a day-to-day basis with greater fervor than they had in the late eighteenth century, when it appeared that they might gain freedom soon.

There is no sign, however, that black violence against whites had intensified. Blacks murdered whites at a rate of only 1 per 100,000 adults per year in Virginia; 2 per 100,000 in Horry County, South Carolina; and 3 per 100,000 in Edgefield County. With the exception of Nat Turner's rebellion in 1831, African Americans did not stage any organized revolts. Slaves talked about taking up arms, but most recognized the futility of doing so, given the overwhelming force the slave regime could bring to bear on them. Stealth murders of masters or mistresses by small groups of slaves, which had begun in the 1760s and 1770s, were also rare. The chances of escaping detection were poor, and it was almost certain that the innocent would suffer along with the guilty. Even in Florida, where law and order had broken down among whites, blacks murdered whites at a rate of only 3 per 100,000 adults per year, because the odds of escaping were so poor for black offenders. Those odds improved, however, during the Second Seminole War, when the Seminoles encouraged slaves to run away and join their fight, and in those years the rate at which blacks murdered whites jumped to 8 per 100,000 (Figure 5.9).[87]

In Edgefield County, South Carolina, one unnamed runaway did declare a personal war on slavery. He hunkered down in a swamp and decided to kill anyone who came after him. Mason Mosely, a hunter, tried to capture him, but the runaway surprised Mosely with a knife and stabbed him to death. With Mosely's gun he was able to hold off a posse for some time before he ran out of ammunition and was killed. For the most part, however, blacks killed only whites who had wronged them personally or hurt their loved ones. Daniel of Lancaster County, Virginia, dashed out of his cabin and smashed William Mitchell's head with a hoe after he learned that the overseer had forced his son to whip his wife. Malina of Wilkes County, Georgia, believed that her mis-

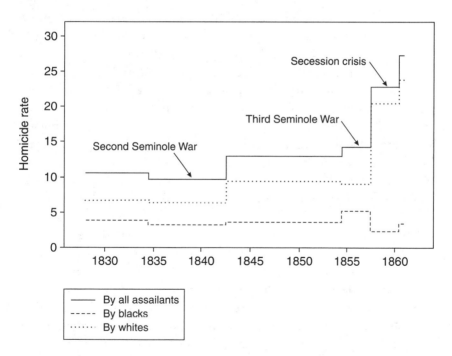

Figure 5.9 Black homicide rates in Florida, 1828–1861 (per 100,000 adults per year). *Source:* Denham and Roth (2007).

tress, Betsy Burns, had killed her infant daughter with an overdose of medicine, so she cut off her head with an ax. Disputes about missing potatoes or poorly sewn garments could end in death if slaves felt that they were being punished unfairly.[88]

Slaves who committed such crimes felt little remorse. Dick of Goochland County, Virginia, who hit his master in his head with an ax for a whipping he considered unjust, believed he would "go to Hell" for his crime, but he was willing to pay that price. "You have killed me," the master said. "Damn you," said Dick, "That's what I intended to do." However, most Christian slaves who committed murder felt that they would not be punished in the afterlife. "They may hang me," said one slave who killed his master, "but I shall go to heaven."[89] Revolutionary and Christian ideas convinced many African Americans of the righteousness of violence against whites. Still, few of them were willing to die for the privilege of killing whites. Like their counterparts in the mid- and late eighteenth century, they resisted oppression primarily through arson and theft.

The frustration of their hopes for emancipation did lead more blacks to kill other blacks in the early nineteenth century. Like whites who were trapped in poor conditions, they took out their anger about their status on each other. The rate at which African Americans killed each other remained at less than half the rates at which whites murdered blacks and whites murdered each other. But for the first time since slavery was established in British North America, the homicide rate among African Americans rose rather than fell. In Virginia it increased to 3 per 100,000 adults per year and in Edgefield County, South Carolina, and in Florida to 4 per 100,000, although no blacks were reported to have killed each other in Horry County, South Carolina.[90]

The failure of the Revolution to free blacks created the same adversarial competition among black men—slave and free—that it did among whites. They competed for respect and prestige in a society that had too little to go around. Like their white counterparts, they were more anxious about their standing among their peers than they had been in the eighteenth century, and they could not tolerate any sign of disrespect from other blacks or any attempt to treat them as a white person would. Being ordered around by whites was bad enough; being pushed around by other blacks was intolerable. Ben and Coon, who worked as waiters at White's Hotel in Monticello, Georgia, had a deadly quarrel about table manners. At dinnertime Ben had started to eat before the rest of the servants were seated. Coon told Bill that he had no manners "and he was afraid he never would." Bill told him to shut his mouth. Coon then made a fatal mistake. He threatened to have Bill whipped. That high-handed remark did not sit well with any of the servants, and Coon immediately realized that he had gone too far. He drew back from the table, but Bill picked up a fork and drove it into his heart, killing him instantly.[91]

Like white southerners, black southerners earned a reputation for killing each other over trifles and for holding lifelong grudges that sometimes ended in murder. A southern humorist made fun of this latter tendency in a story about a slave who was dying. A minister told him that it was time to forgive a man "against whom he seemed to entertain very bitter feelings." The enslaved man said "Yes, sah. . . . If I dies, I forgive dat nigg; but if I gets well, dat nigg must take care."[92]

Like white men, black men also killed their peers for the pettiest of reasons: a 25-cent debt, a 9-cent debt, a hat, a set of lobster traps. Sometimes the killings were accidental; sometimes not. David and Isaac of Harrison County, Virginia, had been digging iron ore and singing hymns together one day when they got into an argument. Isaac broke off a small piece from a chunk of ore, and David told him not to, because the ore would be easier to work when it was intact. Isaac told David that he was merely checking the quality of the ore. Their dispute intensified until Isaac called David a "mean negro." Those were fighting words for David, who threw a mattock at Isaac and killed him.[93]

For blacks in the plantation South, the Revolution thus bore strange fruit: they began to kill one another more often in disputes over respect, property, and rights. The Revolution had lifted their hopes, but by raising expectations and then frustrating them, it intensified their need for respect and weakened the bonds that had held them together without creating new grounds for solidarity. They did not find unity in patriotism because they did not have as strong an attachment to the new nation or their fellow citizens as other Americans did. Northern blacks rallied to the American cause during the War of 1812, but southern blacks did not. In fact in Maryland and Virginia many blacks fled to the British or spied for them during the Chesapeake campaign of 1814.[94]

The alienation and frustration that many black and white men felt manifested itself most clearly in predatory homicides. Although the circumstances of most murders in the eighteenth-century South are unknown, robbery murders and rape murders, like other murders, appear to have become more common in the slaveholding South in the early nineteenth century because so many blacks and whites felt no empathy for fellow southerners, no matter what their race. The shores of well-traveled rivers like the James and the Mississippi were littered with the corpses of men who had been stripped of their possessions and beaten, shot, or stabbed. The vast majority of these killings went unsolved. Highwaymen like Alonzo Phelps, who admitted to killing eight people and robbing sixty more in Mississippi, and James Williams, a "ram-rod swallowing" circus performer who robbed and murdered people on his tours of the South, took their toll; but most robbery murderers were probably amateurs who saw an opportunity to get away with killing someone who was carrying money.[95]

Rape murders, particularly those committed by black men against white women, were rooted in racial hatred as much as in alienation. Lank, a slave from Franklin County, Georgia, raped and murdered a young white girl, Martha Stowe, with the help of his young sons, Jerry and Daniel. Lank grabbed Stowe as she walked down the road and forced *aqua fortis,* a powerful corrosive, down her throat. He then ordered his sons to rape her. They tried but failed, because they had, in their own words, "no courage." Their father "cut her privates" with a knife to make way for himself and raped her "for a good long while." When he finished, he and his sons "stamped her all over" until she was dead, then wedged her body head down between two saplings in a humiliating pose. Lank's sons said that they had "nothing against" Stowe personally, but they confessed that they had planned her murder carefully and that there were "three other families they intended serving the same way." Although rapes and murders occurred elsewhere in the country, the intensity of hatred that it took to plan the torture, rape, mutilation, and killing of a young girl in order to "serve" her family could be found only in the slaveholding South.[96]

The Turner rebellion temporarily suppressed all types of murder in some areas of the South. In the decade after the rebellion, the rate at which whites in plantation counties in Virginia murdered other whites fell to nearly zero, and the rates at which blacks murdered blacks and blacks and whites murdered each other also fell precipitously. Proximity to the rebellion was a crucial factor. Homicide rates were unaffected over most of the slaveholding South, but the seven counties studied to date that were in the vicinity of Southampton County experienced a sudden steep decline in homicides from December 1831 (when reprisals by vigilantes finally stopped) to the early 1840s, when homicide rates returned to their previous levels (Figure 5.6).[97] Ironically, Nat Turner's rebellion probably saved more lives in Virginia than were lost in the rebellion itself. The figures indicate that in the 1830s men of both races in Virginia plantation counties decided that killing members of the other race was imprudent, because it could start another round of rebellion and retribution, and that killing members of their own race over minor differences was foolish when others were all too eager to do the job for them.

White Virginians argued among themselves about the causes of the rebellion and what to do about it. In late 1831 and early 1832, they debated about whether to get rid of blacks altogether by colonization, expulsion, or forced sale to other slave states. Most slaveowners in the Chesapeake and the Shenandoah Valley defended slavery and attributed the rebellion to the religious fanaticism of Turner and his disciples, but others, like Alexander W. Jones, who represented counties across the James River from Southampton in the state legislature, blamed slavery itself. It was "injurious" to the agricultural and industrial development of the state and "dangerous to our tranquility." Future rebellions were inevitable. The "Great Debate" in the legislature in January 1832 ended in a narrow defeat for the gradual emancipationists, but it did nothing to build whites' confidence in slavery.[98]

African Americans were just as divided, at least in Southampton County. Some were angry with the rebels. A number of blacks, especially domestic servants, had thwarted them by warning or sheltering whites. Most blacks were bitter about vigilante killings of innocent people. Nearly 300 free blacks took passage for Liberia rather than risk another day in Virginia. Every sign pointed to deeper divisions among the people of Virginia and suggested that more violence lay ahead.[99]

For the next eight years, however, fear trumped violence. Whites were terrified, and no matter how they felt about slavery, their fear brought them closer together. Governor John Floyd wrote that he "could not have believed there was half the fear among the people of the lower country in respect to their slaves." George Washington's niece wrote that Virginians sat atop "a smothered volcano—we know not when, or where, the flame will burst forth, but we know that death in the most horrid form threatens us. Some have died, others have become deranged from apprehension, since the South Hampton affair." Another Virginian confessed that he and his wife had "not slept without anxiety in three months. Our nights are sometimes spent in listening to noises. A corn song, or a hog call, has often been the subject of nervous terror, and a cat, in the dining room, will banish sleep for the night. There has been and there still is a *panic* in all the country."[100]

Henry Brown, who was living as a slave in Richmond at the time, saw the fear in the face of every white he encountered. "I did not then know precisely what was the cause," he wrote, but

> the whole city was in the utmost confusion; and a dark cloud of terrific blackness, seemed to hang over the heads of the whites. . . . The rustling of "the lightest leaf, that quivers in the breeze," fills [the white man's] timid soul with visions of flowing blood and burning dwellings; and as the loud thunder of heaven rolls over his head, and the vivid lightning flashes across his pale face, straightaway his imagination conjures up terrible scenes of the loud and roaring of the enemy's cannon, and the fierce yells of an infuriated slave population, rushing to vengeance.[101]

By mid-1832 white Virginians had set their course. They stepped up slave patrols, strengthened the militia, and enacted strict laws against potential rebels, especially free blacks and slave preachers. The *Free Press* of Tarboro, North Carolina, a town that lay only fifty miles from Southampton County, warned whites to "keep a sharp lookout for the villains" who were thought to be distributing abolitionist literature among the slaves, "and if you catch them, by all that is sacred, you ought to barbeque them." Whites drew closer to one another, just as they had in New England after King Philip's War, and tried to draw a firmer line between the races. Baptist churches on Virginia's South Shore debated about expelling black church members because they were convinced that black Christians had been complicit in the rebellion and that slave preachers had turned Christianity into a doctrine of rebellion and hate.[102]

Blacks also drew closer together after the rebellion. The vigilante campaign that followed the rebellion terrified blacks almost as much as the rebellion had terrified whites. Charity Bowery, who had been a slave in Edenton, North Carolina, fifty miles southeast of Southampton County, remembered the fear that blacks felt as white patrollers hunted down suspected rebels. "The best and the brightest men were killed in Nat's time. Such ones are always suspected." Harriet Jacobs, who had also been a slave in Edenton, recalled that "colored people and slaves who lived in remote parts of town suffered in an especial manner. In some cases the searchers scattered powder and shot among their clothes, and then sent other parties to find them, and bring them forward as proof that they were plotting insurrection. Everywhere men, women, and children were whipped till the blood stood in puddles at their feet. Some received five hundred lashes; others were tied hands and feet, and tortured with a bucking paddle, which blisters the skin terribly." Henry Brown remembered half-hangings, "a refined species of cruelty, peculiar to slavery," and the whipping of a "colored preacher" who refused to give up his ministry. Allen Crawford, who was born in Southampton shortly after the rebellion, had also heard stories of torture. Patrollers had held the "bare feet" of suspected rebels "to diz blazing fire 'ill you tole all you know'd 'bout dis killing." If a suspect refused to talk, the "white devil" in charge said, "stick him closer!"[103]

These incidents turned blacks more deeply against whites and made them appreciate each other more. Those who were tortured or martyred during the rebellion became heroes, even "old prophet Nat." Henry Brown admired them. He marveled at the tortured black preacher's courage and wondered "how many white preachers would continue their employment, if they were served in the same way?" Blacks refused to obey the new prohibitions on religious services and on reading and writing, and formed secret societies. "On Sundays," Bowery said, "I have seen the negroes up in the country going away under large oaks, and in secret places, sitting in the woods with spelling books." She remembered that blacks were "afraid to pray" openly because "the low whites would fall upon any slaves they heard praying, or singing a hymn, and often killed them before their masters or mistresses could get to them." They prayed together anyway. The renewed closeness among them militated against killing within the community.

There is no surviving testimony to explain why blacks in Virginia killed whites at a lower rate in the decade after the rebellion, but it is not hard to see that the rebellion and its aftermath demonstrated the futility of armed resistance. No African American who wrote about the rebellion blamed the rebels for the terror that whites visited upon local blacks, but no one seemed eager to take up arms. Whites were just as afraid of the consequences of violence against blacks. Killings and hangings might be useful in the short run, but they could not by themselves make whites secure, and, if taken too far, they might incite retaliatory violence. William Parker, who had raised one of the posses that had stopped Turner's rebellion and who had served at the court's request as Nat Turner's attorney, saw matters clearly.

> The excitement having now subsided, which induced many to think wrong, and prevent many who thought right from stemming the tide, it becomes us as men to return to our duty. Without manifesting a fear of the blacks, by keeping a stationed armed force in any section of our country let us adopt a more efficient plan, by keeping up for some time a regular patrol, always under the command of a discreet person, who will not by indiscriminate punishment, goad these miserable wretches into a state of desperation.[104]

In that spirit, whites were more vigilant, but they were also more careful about how they treated blacks, and they reached out to them in small ways, hoping for some sort of rapprochement. In Surry County, which lay next to Southampton, the justices heard credible testimony from a slave named Dick that nearly every slave in his neighborhood had been involved in the Turner conspiracy. A month before the rebellion a man named Mason, who was the alleged leader of the rebellion in Surry County, had told Dick

> that he expected there would be a war this year to set the black people free, that if their masters did not set me free in August, there would be blood spilt, by killing the white people that he expected the St. Domingoes would assist the English people to set them free, that if they come and did not have force enough, he would join and assist them, to kill all the white people as they went, even the women and the children in the Cradle. [Mason] said he was to be one of the rulers or head men over the other black people, that they would have the same laws to govern them that the white people now have.

The justices let matters rest, however, in the hope that peace would continue to prevail in Surry. None of the suspects had taken up arms, and only one of them was considered enough of a threat to warrant transportation out of state.[105]

Churches in the Portsmouth Baptist Association, which ministered to the counties in the vicinity of the rebellion, reconsidered the status of their black members in 1833–34 and at length announced that they were welcome to come back. Black church members returned to the fold. In 1835 the justices of Sussex County, which also bordered on Southampton, recommended that Boson, the last of Turner's rebels to be captured, be transported rather than hanged. Their recommendation was supported by a justice who had sentenced suspected rebels to die in 1831 and by an elder in the local Baptist church, who admitted that the county had condemned many innocent blacks in 1831 and 1832 on the basis of false testimony. "Time has mellowed our feelings, and given full exercise to our reason. We can now view the event freed from that exasperation, which blinded our unbiased judgment." Blacks may have looked askance at this expression of chagrin, but it represented yet another effort by whites to reach out to slaves and free blacks and to curb interracial violence. How widespread that effort was among whites is a matter of debate, but it may have helped to deter murders of blacks by whites, if the fear of violent retribution was not in itself sufficient to give whites pause.[106]

As the memory of the Turner rebellion receded, homicide rates in Virginia plantation counties returned to prerebellion levels (Figure 5.6), jump-started by a robbery murder in Southampton County in 1840, in which a white man named Drake killed another white man named Scott for his money and then murdered Scott's sister, his seven-year-old child, and two of his slaves to cover his tracks.[107] Like the rest of the slave South, Virginia was a more homicidal society than it had been before the Revolution. A traumatic event like the Turner rebellion could mask that fact for a time but could not change it.

The Rise in Homicide in the Southwest

Mexico's northern frontier, which stretched from Texas to California, was even more homicidal than the slave South in the early nineteenth century. As in Florida, conditions were ripe for homicide. The federal and territorial governments of Mexico had little legitimacy; they were widely seen as corrupt and ineffective, unable to provide services or security in the vast, sparsely populated borderlands. The region was politically unstable, wracked by internal rebellions and raids by Indians and filibusterers from the United States. There was racial conflict among the region's inhabitants—Hispanics, Native Americans, African Americans, and Anglos (non-Hispanics of European descent)— and patriotic feelings were in short supply, especially among Anglo immigrants from the slaveholding South. They had moved to Texas to grow cotton, and they were not about to yoke themselves to the Republic of Mexico, which would demand that they become Catholics (a requirement of the 1824 constitution) and free their slaves (as required by the emancipation act of 1828). The social system of Mexico was also in decline. The Mexican War for Independence and the popular insurgency against the colonial elite that it had inspired had introduced radical ideas that marked the beginning of the end for the class- and caste-bound hierarchy.[108]

The borderlands between Mexico and the United States were not as murderous as they would become in the late 1840s, after annexation by the United States, but they already had high homicide rates by the time they entered the Union. In the late 1830s and early 1840s, the rate at which murder cases were heard before justices in Monterey and Los Angeles, California, reached 50 to 75 per 100,000 adults per year. The actual homicide rate in those jurisdictions was probably 100 per 100,000 or more, since murders involving *indios bárbaros* (Indians who lived in traditional communities and were not members of Mexican society) seldom came before the courts. The rate was similarly high among settlers and Native Americans in the lower Sacramento Valley, according to reports from residents of New Helvetia, the immigrant community founded by Swiss entrepreneur John Sutter.[109]

The homicide rate was probably over 100 per 100,000 adults per year in south Texas, which was politically the most unstable and militarily the least secure area in Mexico's northern territories; and probably half that in the Rio Grande Valley of New Mexico and in the slaveholding Anglo-American areas of east-central Texas, which were more stable and secure. But homicide rates were high throughout the borderlands because the contest for power among Mexicans, Americans, and Native Americans destabilized governments, and racially militant settlers from the slaveholding South refused to acknowledge Mexico as their country and Mexicans as their fellow citizens. Most important, the Mexican War for Independence, which had left law enforcement and frontier defenses weak, led in 1835–1837 to violent rebellions against the central government of Mexico in Texas, California, and New Mexico. Those rebellions drastically raised homicide rates over the following decade. The rate at which everyday homicides appeared before the courts tripled, and there were scores of political homicides and robbery murders that never even came before the courts.[110]

Before the migration of southern slaveowners into Texas in 1821, slavery was virtually unknown in northern Mexico, and borderland society as a whole was far more egalitarian than society in central Mexico, where the gap between rich and poor and the social distance between Spaniards, Indians, and people of mixed race were far greater. But borderland society was still hierarchical and racially divided. The *gente fina,* a small class of wealthy landowners, military officers, and government officials, held most of the property and employed most of the workers. They controlled politics through a system of patronage, alliances, and intermarriage. Many of the *gente fina* (or the *ricos,* as poorer Mexicans called them) were of Spanish ancestry, and those who were not claimed it anyway.[111]

Below the *gente fina,* forming an almost separate caste, were the *paisanos*—poor Hispanics of mixed descent who worked the region's farms and ranches. Some owned land, but most were servants or debt peons of the *gente fina.* They usually referred to themselves as *vecinos*—natives or "countrymen" of Mexico—but the *gente fina* continued to call them *paisanos* and considered them rural, rustic, backward, and ignorant. California elites often used an even more disparaging term—*cholos,* or half-breeds—and considered them "thieves and pickpockets scoured from the jails."[112]

Below the *paisanos* were the *indios genízaros*—Indians who lived on missions or worked as servants for Hispanic ranchers, farmers, or townspeople. *Genízaros,* like the *gente fina* and *paisanos,* were considered *gente de razón*—"people of reason" who lived in a civilized way—but they were marginalized people who were no longer members of native societies but not full members of Hispanic society. Not all Hispanics held them in contempt, but *genízaros* were generally treated as inferiors and considered only partly civilized. They had little social status and were sometimes viciously abused by Hispanics.[113]

The struggle for independence disrupted the hierarchy among *genízaros, paisanos,* and the *gente fina* in the borderlands in the same way the American Revolution disrupted relations among whites and blacks in the slaveholding South. The Mexican constitution of 1824 was in some ways more democratic than its American counterpart. It declared everyone a full citizen, equal before the law. However, the gap between rich and poor increased under Mexican rule, in part because the *gente fina* profited most from the trade in cattle, horses, tallow, hides, wine, and silver that developed with the United States and other foreign powers, but also because Mexico's revolutionary governments granted vast tracts of public land to local elites and gave them the opportunity to buy up Catholic mission property at bargain prices when the missions were secularized in the 1830s. The War for Independence and the popular insurgency that accompanied it raised the expectations of *genízaros* and *paisanos* but gave them few opportunities to participate in politics or to improve the material circumstances of their lives and did little to change the way their social superiors treated them. The *gente fina* on the northern frontier supported the war enthusiastically, but most viewed it as an opportunity to dominate their society more completely, free of Spanish interference. The war did little to change their generally contemptuous attitudes toward *paisanos* and *genízaros;* if anything, it made them more determined to control them.[114]

Conflict among the three castes increased. Accounts of the murders that ensued emphasize the part that caste divisions played in generating violence. José María Sebada, a small farmer and soapmaker in the Rio Grande Valley in New Mexico, approached Pablo Salazar, a wealthy sheep rancher, merchant, and militia captain, and demanded his share of water from the local irrigation ditch. Salazar slapped him. Sebada pulled a knife and stabbed him in the stomach. Alférez Manuel García de Lara, a young cavalry officer stationed in New Mexico at San Miguel del Bado, lost his temper when a *paisano*, Antonio Moya, treated him with disrespect at a dance. Moya, who worked as a servant for one of the wealthiest ranchers in the territory, considered himself a cut above other servants. He fell into a conversation with Lara and gave him a peso so that Lara could treat a young lady with whom he had danced. Lara accepted the gift, but he bristled when Moya presumed too much and sat down in Lara's chair. "¡Mil desvergüenzas [what impudence]!" Lara said, turning to a fellow soldier. "You have seen how he has embarrassed me, this *paisano* Moya." Enraged, Moya jumped up and stabbed Lara in the heart with his sword.[115]

Relations between Hispanics (both the *gente fina* and *paisanos*) and *indios genízaros* were equally tense. Most Hispanics were determined to keep *genízaros* in their place, whatever their constitutional rights or their standing as Christians, and were willing to use violence to do so. Don Francisco Real, a rancher who lived near the farming village of Algodones, New Mexico, was incensed when his young servant, Juan José Montoya, failed to return with livestock he had been ordered to corral. Real grabbed his *cabresto*—a horsehair whip—and went after him. When he found him he threw him down, put his foot on his neck, and whipped him so badly that he died three days later.[116]

Individual *genízaros* seldom murdered Hispanics. Like African Americans in the plantation South, they faced terrible retribution if they did. But individual Hispanics felt free to prey on *genízaros*. They raped and murdered *genízaro* women, robbed and murdered *genízaro* men, and killed the livestock and poisoned the waterholes of *genízaro* ranchers. Virtually all Hispanics exploited, bullied, or abused *genízaro* laborers.[117]

Hispanic culture was like the culture of the slaveholding South in yet another way: it celebrated men who were fearless and ready to accept any challenge. It was essential to be *muy hombre* (a man of honor and valor) and a *chingón* (a man who dominated other men). A man who could not stand up for himself was a *chingada* (passive, impotent, homosexual), a *puta* (whore), a *cabrón* (cuckold), a *perro* (dog), or an *hijo de la chingada* (the son of a woman who had been violated). And as in the plantation South, violence was common wherever groups of men gathered. P*aisanos* and *genízaros* murdered one another over card games, debts, and the slightest of personal affronts.[118]

The War for Independence increased homicide in the borderlands not only because of its disruptive effect on class relations and relationships among peers, but because of its destructive effects on public life. The war ended Spanish rule, but Mexico was unable to create a stable, legitimate government or a strong sense of national unity and purpose. The inability of the central government to win public support and govern effectively led to further alienation and rebellion in many parts of Mexico, especially in the borderlands, where political violence was rampant by the mid-1830s. That violence—and the lack of solidarity it reflected—led directly and indirectly to many homicides as private life took on the tenor of political partisanship and citizens engaged in predatory and retaliatory killings.[119]

Rebellions against the central government and its officials occurred throughout the borderlands in the 1820s and early 1830s, but they took an increasingly deadly turn in the mid-1830s, when people across Mexico rose up in opposition to the centralists who had taken control of the national government. The centralists believed that their federalist predecessors had reduced the nation to near-anarchy by weakening the central government, the military, and the Catholic Church. Led by General Antonio López de Santa Anna, they reversed direction, dissolving state legislatures, ruling the former states directly from Mexico City as departments, and abolishing town councils in every frontier settlement except the department capitals (Monterey, Santa Fe, and San Antonio) and the few villages that had had councils before 1808. The centralists also disfranchised the poor by mandating in 1836 that voters have an annual income of at least 100 pesos. In 1843 they raised that requirement to 200 pesos and mandated even higher incomes for representatives to the national or departmental legislatures. They imposed taxes on imports and exports but did nothing to improve frontier defenses or to reform the judicial system, which remained in the hands of poorly trained political appointees. Most criminals never saw the inside of a jail.[120]

People in the borderlands became increasingly alienated from the central government. Mariano Chávez, the president of the New Mexico Assembly, declared in frustration that New Mexico had received nothing more than "hopes and promises . . . from its mother country." Mariano Guadalupe Vallejo, a prominent Californian, echoed Chávez's sentiments. He was disappointed by the government's neglect of his territory. Yet there were worse things than neglect. "When the paternal government of the Mexican Republic remembered us," he observed ruefully, "it did so in such a way as to fill us with dismay." Heavy taxes and tariffs were a drag on the local economy, and interference with local laws and regulations turned the people against government officials. Manuel Castañares, who represented California in the national legislature, urged a return to local government and reform of the judicial system, which "without a doubt . . . would contribute to the growth of a spirit of nationality" that would keep the frontier territories "united to the republic." Tejano petitioners from Béxar, Nacogdoches, and Goliad threatened to rebel if the government did not change course. "We have had enough of these legislators who insult through their very capriciousness" the constitution of Mexico and "the sacred rights" of local communities, they said. "Let the laws be complied with, let's be republicans, let's be men, let's defend our rights, or let's not exist at all." To all these complaints the centralists turned a deaf ear. They were confident of their power in central Mexico and determined to bend the states and territories on the periphery of Mexico to their will.[121]

From 1835 into 1837 rebellions broke out in the departments of Texas, California, New Mexico, Sonora, Nuevo Léon, Coahuila, Tamaulipas, Zacatecas, and Yucatán. In California the territorial assembly met in defiance of the central government and declared California "independent of Mexico until the federal system . . . shall be reestablished." They wanted to free themselves from the "oppressors sent by the Mexican government"—and in particular from Governor Mariano Chico. The *gente fina* detested Chico, who enjoyed insulting federalists and thumbed his nose at genteel society. The California rebels, nearly all of whom lived near Monterey, eventually overthrew Chico, but they soon found themselves battling the *gente fina* of southern California, who were afraid they would be shut out of the new government. Northern and southern Californians fought each other for the next two years as they struggled for control of the new government.[122]

The rebellion in New Mexico in August 1837 was more of a popular rising against both the local and national elite. It was led by *paisanos* and *genízaros*, including Pueblo Indians. They hated the centralist government's tax policy and wanted home rule, especially on the village level. They also hated the militia system, which made the poor shoulder the burden of fighting the Navahos and Apaches. Rebel leader Pablo Salazar complained that militiamen were forced into "serving the ricos" without pay, were abused by officers, and were nearly "dead of hunger." The governor, Albino Pérez, tried to suppress the rebellion, but he had been forced to disband New Mexico's regular army for lack of funds, and at San Ildefonso Pueblo the rebels crushed his volunteer force of poor Hispanics and Indians (many of whom deserted to the rebels). They executed Pérez and mounted his head on a pole, crowing that he would "no longer drink chocolate or coffee!" Then they looted the homes of his supporters and carried their leader through the streets in a sedan chair, chanting "Long live Christ, and death to the robbers."[123]

Calm prevailed for a month as the rebel governor, José Angel Gonzales, a buffalo hunter of Spanish and Indian descent, organized a new government and met with the new assembly, the *junta popular.* The *gente fina* had not taken sides in the rebellion, and many were glad to see the centralist governor overthrown, but they were not willing to be governed by their social inferiors. Afraid that they would become, in the words of former governor Manuel Armijo, "cold victims of the fury of a disorderly insurrection that has no other goal . . . than killing and robbing," the *gente fina* launched a counterrevolution that ended in a bloody assault on the rebels near Santa Cruz. Armijo executed five rebel leaders, including Governor Gonzales, but the new government could not establish its legitimacy or control rebel strongholds in the mountain villages north of Santa Fe. The rebellion, which had already claimed fifty lives, continued.

The rebellion in Texas in 1835–36 also led to a decade of violence and instability. Like the majority of Anglo-Americans, most Tejanos opposed the policies of the new centralist government. They wanted exemptions from federal import taxes, immigration restrictions, land laws, and antislavery laws so that the territory could continue to grow and attract settlers from the slaveholding South. But the majority of Tejanos balked at joining the rebellion, and some opposed it, worried about how they as Hispanics would fare in an Anglo-dominated republic.[124]

Their fears were well founded. When the rebellion began there were 20,000 Anglo-Texans and only 3,000 Tejanos, and many Anglo-Texans were militant white supremacists. They branded mixed-race Tejanos "half-breeds" and "greasers" and took their land by trickery or force. Anglo leader David Burnet was convinced of "the utter dissimilarity of character between the two people, the Texians and the Mexicans. The first are principally Anglo Americans; the others a mongrel race of degenerate Spaniards and Indians." Stephen F. Austin, the preeminent promoter of Anglo colonization in Texas, called the conflict between the Mexican government and the Texas rebels "a war of barbarism and of despotic principles, waged by the mongrel Spanish-Indian and Negro race, against civilization and the Anglo-American race." The Tejanos' Catholicism was also a mark against them. Land agent William Gray referred to Mexicans as "slaves of Popish superstitions and despotism." For militant Anglos, the Texas rebellion was thus "a moral struggle," "a war for principle" fought by "a superior race of men" on behalf of Protestantism and true republicanism.[125]

By the mid-1830s Tejanos had developed their own prejudices against Anglos. They considered Anglos "lazy people of vicious character" who wanted only to steal Tejano property, "money changing speculators" who cared "only for their own well-being." The violence of the Texas rebellion exacerbated tensions between the two groups. The massacre of the defenders of the Alamo, the execution of the entire rebel force captured at Goliad, and the murder of two Anglos in Victoria by centralist vigilantes persuaded Anglos that all Tejanos were enemies of Texas, while the high-handed actions of Anglo rebels—who forced Hispanics to work for them without pay and stole their crops and livestock—deepened the hostility of Tejanos toward Anglos.[126]

The Anglo rebels' victory in 1836 led to hundreds of predatory and vigilante murders in the ensuing decade. South Texas witnessed the worst violence. It became a battleground between Mexico and the Republic of Texas. The Texas government was not strong enough to defend the area against Mexican raiders, military and civilian, and the Mexican government was not strong enough to take the area back. It became a hellish place to live. Anglo bandits known as the "Band of Brothers" roamed from the San Antonio River to the Rio Grande, stealing cattle and robbing and murdering Hispanics. They killed anyone who tried to stop them, including sheriffs and judges. Mexican bandits did the same to Anglos. Contemporaries estimated that at least 200 south Texans were murdered by bandits between 1836 and 1845. Vast stretches of territory were depopulated.[127]

Tejanos fared even worse to the north in Nacogdoches. The town's 600 Hispanic residents were surrounded by Anglos who resented their Tejano neighbors for remaining neutral during the rebellion and used every subterfuge they could to dispossess them. Only a fifth of Hispanic residents were able to patent their land claims under Texas law, and a number were later bankrupted by debt actions and bogus lawsuits filed by Anglos. In 1836 Anglos unsuccessfully petitioned the Texas assembly to disfranchise Hispanics, but local authorities sanctioned illegal detentions of Hispanics and subjected them to whippings and forced labor for minor crimes. Sam Houston, the president of the Republic of Texas, tried to prevent all-out war. He warned Anglo vigilantes "not to adopt any harsh measures towards the Mexicans in the neighborhood of Nacogdoches. Treat them kindly and pass them as tho' there was no difficulty or differences of opinion. *By no means* treat them with *violence.*"[128]

The Anglos did not relent, however, and the Tejanos began to fight back. By the spring of 1838 Anglos were being found murdered north and west of town. That August a number of Nacogdoches Tejanos— joined by a handful of Indian, African American, and Anglo sympathizers—organized a rebel force of 200 men under the leadership of Vicente Córdova, a former militia captain. Córdova proclaimed that they were "tired of suffering injustices and the usurpation of their rights" and were "determined to shed their last drop of blood in order to protect their individual rights and those of the Nation to which they belong." Guillermo Cruz, a supporter of Córdova, told the Anglo rancher he worked for that "they were going to fight for their rights, they had been dogs long enough." The rebels did not receive the support they had anticipated from the Comanches and Cherokees or from the Mexican army, but they held out for eight months before they were defeated. Only a few of them survived, but in the interval they killed or wounded scores of Anglos.

Even without high levels of Tejano-Anglo violence, Texas would have been a very homicidal place because it was a slave state. Slaves made up 30 percent of the republic's population by 1845, and Texas witnessed the same kinds of homicidal violence that other areas in the plantation South did, including insurrection scares, lynchings of suspected criminals and abolitionists, and duels, assassinations, and deadly feuds among Anglo politicians. And like other states in the Mexican borderlands, Texas saw more than its share of violence by and against Indians, which proved deadly for ranchers, hunters, soldiers, traveling merchants, and Native Americans alike.[129] But the ultimate cause of the majority of homicides in the region was the Mexican War for Independence. It destabilized the nation's government and upset the social order that had prevailed among the *gente fina,* the *paisanos,* and the *genízaros*. After the war Mexicans could not create governments or social hierarchies that were legitimate enough, or forge a sense of solidarity among themselves that was strong enough, to prevent the homicide rate from spiraling out of control.

Homicide in the Western World

The long-term effect of the Age of Revolution on homicide rates in the United States was complex, as it was in Europe and elsewhere in the Americas. In terms of both political homicides and everyday homicides, the worst thing that could happen in any area was for international warfare and revolutionary violence to lead to an unending series of revolutions and counterrevolutions. Mexico suffered that fate. So did Italy, where by midcentury the homicide rate was at least 20 per 100,000 adults per year. But when public opinion in France turned decisively against the Republic in 1798–99 in favor of a government that could restore order, it opened the way for the repressiveness of the authoritarian Consulate and its dominant figure, Napoleon. The homicide trial rate fell by half in 1798–1801 as the government used the army, military justice, and a strengthened national gendarmerie with brutal effectiveness. Napoleon lowered the homicide rate by ending the Revolution, eradicating criminal gangs, silencing political opponents, and relentlessly suppressing any resistance to the government or public officials. What happened to the French homicide rate between 1802 and 1825 is as yet unknown, but it fluctuated thereafter with the fortunes of the central government. When a modicum of stability was achieved during the restoration of Louis XVIII and Charles X, the July Monarchy of Louis-Philippe, and the Second Empire of Louis Napoleon, homicide rates were modest; but when those regimes collapsed in 1830, 1848, and 1870, thousands died in the ensuing political violence, and everyday homicide rates spiked until the next regime took shape and restored order. The pattern appeared not only in revolutionary centers like Paris but in remote provinces like Corsica, where the struggle for power was far away and political homicides were few. Whenever nation-building failed and the state remained weak, and whenever no sense of national unity or purpose emerged from political upheaval, homicide rates spiraled out of control.[130]

Most of the United States avoided that fate because there was political peace by the mid-1790s, and a new political system was taking shape and winning support. The return of political stability ensured that the spikes in homicide rates experienced in most of the country during the Revolution were short-lived.

Revolutionary ideas had a subtler effect on homicide rates than political turmoil did, but their effect was nevertheless significant. Where revolutionary ideas gave birth to truly democratic societies, as they did in the northern United States and in the mountain South, or gave genuine hope to oppressed peoples, like African Americans in the North, homicide rates fell to extraordinarily low levels—2 to 3 per 100,000 adults per year. The same low rates appeared in Sweden, Norway, and Canada, societies that developed stable democratic institutions and enfranchised most adult males. Wealth was not distributed as unequally in these societies as in most others, and, more important, self-employment, homeownership, and full citizenship were sources of self-respect and confidence for most people.[131]

The Canadian case is particularly instructive because, like the United States, and unlike democratic nations in Scandinavia, its population was religiously, ethnically, and geographically diverse, and its citizens could not rely on a common language, faith, ethnicity, territory, or historical tradition to help them forge a strong sense of nationality and solidarity. The keys for Canadians were the creation of a successful democratic government within each province and the existence a two-party political system. The rate at which adults in Ontario were charged with homicide fell from a high of 4.5 per 100,000 per year during the War of 1812, when there was significant frontier and military violence, to only 1.7 per 100,000 in the mid-1830s (Figure 5.10).[132]

Canada's homicidal history would have been quite different, however, if the British had frustrated Canada's attempt at self-government. In the late 1830s Canadian reformers, inspired by the political reforms and the democratic movements that had taken hold in Great Britain, demanded greater autonomy for Canadian provinces. Like the Irish nationalists, they wanted home rule rather than full independence. The British government provoked a crisis in 1836–37 by dissolving the reformist assembly in Upper Canada (Ontario), denying the petition of Lower Canada (Quebec) for home rule, and declaring that royal governors had the right to spend monies in the provincial treasuries as they saw fit, without the consent of the assemblies. The British also created forty-four new rectories for Anglican ministers on public land. These high-handed actions in defense of the state and its established church, together with an agricultural depression brought on by the collapse of the international wheat market, led to revolts against the governor and council of Upper Canada in 1837 and of Lower Canada in 1838. London's response was harsh: British troops killed scores of rebels and went on a rampage through rebel areas, destroying crops and burning shops and farms; a dozen rebels were executed and scores more were imprisoned, transported to Australia, or forced into exile in the United States.[133]

Canadians' anger over the actions of the British government spilled over into everyday life: the rate at which adults were charged with homicide in Ontario spiked between 1838 and 1843 to 4.5 per 100,000 (Figure 5.10)—a return to the level during the War of 1812—and it might have climbed higher had not the British government changed course in 1842–43. Britain decided to respect the autonomy of Cana-

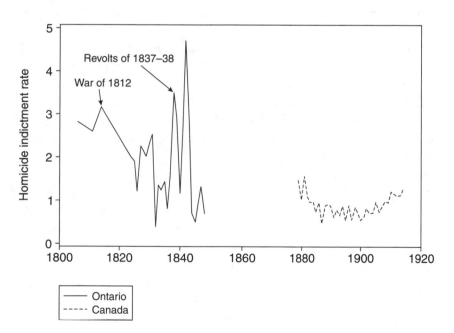

Figure 5.10 Homicide indictment rates in Ontario, 1806–1848, and in all of Canada, 1879–1914 (per 100,000 adults per year). *Sources:* Oliver (1998: 31); Urquhart and Buckley (1965: series Y61).

dian provinces and to support "responsible government" in Canada—government that was, in the words of Canadian patriot William Mackenzie, "responsible to the province" rather than to the royal governors and their cronies. Whitehall limited the powers of royal governors and granted provincial assemblies greater control over public matters, especially taxes and expenditures. It also reaffirmed the rights of Catholics and Protestant dissenters, pardoned former rebels who had not committed murder, and indemnified Canadians for property destroyed by the British during the rebellion.[134]

The victory for reformers had a sudden and dramatic effect on the rate at which adults were charged with everyday homicides. The indictment stream slowed to a trickle, and by the mid-1840s the indictment rate stood at just over 1 per 100,000 adults—roughly equal to the rates in the northern United States and the mountain South. Homicide rates in Canada remained low in the late 1840s and 1850s as its democratic provincial governments took shape. Reformers and Conservatives created a vibrant, two-party system, and a broader sense of Canadian nationalism emerged. The Canadian case shows forcefully that counterrevolutionary movements could drive both political homicide rates and everyday homicide rates to high levels, as surely as successful democratic and nationalistic movements could drive them down.

When revolutionary ideas confronted societies that were inherently antidemocratic, like those of the slaveholding South and the Mexican borderlands, or when economic independence and respectability were increasingly hard to achieve, as they were in northern cities, the frustration, alienation, and conflict that ensued led to increases in homicides. In England and Wales commitments for homicides doubled in the decades following the Napoleonic Wars. The actual homicide rate probably climbed to 5–6 per 100,000 adults by the 1830s and early 1840s—higher than the rates of the 1770s and 1780s and twice the contemporary rate in Canada, Scandinavia, and most of the United States (Figure 5.11). The kinds of homicide that were rampant in mid-nineteenth-century England and Wales—rape murders and robbery murders, murders of employers by servants and laborers, and murders among friends and neighbors at dances, work, taverns, horse races, and card games—reflect the same alienation, the same class antagonism, and the same anxiety over status among poor and middle-income men that caused homicides among whites and blacks in the plantation South and among the *gente fina, paisanos,* and *genízaros* in the Mexican borderlands. In Kent at midcentury, for example, a laborer killed a coworker for calling him a "master's man"; a teamster whose wages had been cut after his employer bought a new plowing machine slashed the throat of his employer's son; a soldier who had been docked a day's pay at an inspection shot his commanding officer, calling him "a tyrant, a rogue, and a thief in his heart." On highways near London, entire families of travelers were murdered and their belongings stolen. Such homicides increased at precisely the time that British nationalism weakened and political frustration increased among middle- and working-class Britons in towns and in the countryside.[135]

Britons of all classes had volunteered by the thousands during the Napoleonic Wars to protect their homeland against a French invasion, and many working-class Britons believed that their loyalty and sacri-

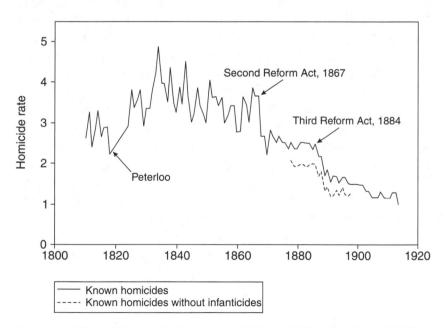

Figure 5.11 Homicide rates in England and Wales, 1810–1914 (per 100,000 adults per year). Known homicides, 1810–1867, are extrapolated from homicide committals. Official statistics first distinguished infanticides from other homicides in 1878. *Sources:* House of Commons (1980–1982); Gatrell (1980).

fices during the war would be rewarded by extension of the franchise and by increased respect for the rights and interests of working people. They were sorely disappointed. The economy slumped badly from 1816 through 1819, depressed by a recession that extended from Europe to the United States and Canada, and by the return of thousands of demobilized soldiers to the labor market. The British government responded by helping the rich: it abolished the income tax and imposed tariffs on imported grain and wool to increase profits for landowners. It spent large amounts on the army and navy, and it tried to stifle dissent with the Six Acts of 1819, which restricted freedom of the press, freedom of assembly, and, temporarily, the right to bear arms. The government also brutally suppressed protests by distressed workers and farm laborers and put down demonstrations in favor of universal suffrage at St. Peter's Fields in Manchester in 1819 ("Peterloo") and at Newport in Wales in 1839. Working-class anger was palpable when the reform Parliaments of 1828–1834 extended the franchise to only the wealthiest middle-class men. Eighty percent of British men still could not vote. In 1834 Whitehall added insult to injury by passing a new poor law that outlawed outdoor relief and forced people seeking relief to live and work in public workhouses, most of which were filthy and disease-ridden.[136]

Although the reformers had touted Britain's commitment to liberty when the government abolished slavery in 1833, their words rang hollow for many poor and middle-class people. The reformers and conservatives who controlled Parliament and the House of Lords had made it clear that they would never grant ordinary Britons the right to vote or help shape public policy. And the older grounds for unity among Britons—militant Protestantism, hostility toward the French—were no longer as strong now that France had declined as an international power and Catholic emancipation had been forced on the government by the threat of civil war in Ireland. As historian Linda Colley has observed, postwar Britain suffered from "a profound loss of direction" and from a "high level" of "malaise and contention" and "alienation."[137]

The economy gradually improved, and by 1850 real wages for the poorest 40 percent of the population were twice what they had been during the Napoleonic Wars. Yet the homicide rate did not drop. Reformers tried to restore law and order by creating modern police forces, first in London in 1829 and nationwide in 1856. Most police departments conducted themselves professionally, compiled impressive felony arrest records, and in time won broad support; but they had virtually no impact on the homicide rate, which was rooted in political anger and alienation. The rate remained high into the mid-1860s.[138]

In both Europe and North America the frustration of personal, national, and democratic aspirations ended in everyday murders among unrelated adults. The links between those murders and the political arena could seem quite distant, but they were not. In the short run, revolutionary violence always increased the number of political homicides and everyday homicides, especially predatory murders and revenge murders. But in the long run, the number of homicides, especially those committed over questions of personal honor or property, depended on the degree to which societies were able to restore law and order, establish stable and legitimate governments, foster a strong sense of nationality, and give citizens—especially the poor and the middle class and members of racial, ethnic, and religious groups that had experienced discrimination—confidence that they were or could become respected members of society. In areas where that happened, such as Scandinavia, the northern United States, the mountain South, and the original provinces of the Canadian Confederation, societies became nonhomicidal. In areas where that did not happen, such as the plantation South, the Southwest, and Great Britain, societies remained homicidal. And where revolutionary upheaval persisted and violent counterrevolutionary movements developed, as in Italy and Mexico, societies became extremely homicidal. The homicidal legacy of the Age of Revolution in Europe and the Americas was thus neither simple nor straightforward, but it was everywhere profound.

The Rise in Family and Intimate Homicide in the Nineteenth Century

Marital homicides, romance homicides, and homicides of adult relatives were relatively rare throughout the nineteenth century, just as they had been in the previous two centuries. The fundamental character of marriage, kinship, and romance did not change. But even though family and intimate homicide rates remained low relative to the rates for unrelated adults, they increased significantly in the late 1820s and 1830s. People in the North who were involved in intimate relationships, including ex-spouses, lovers, and romantic rivals, suddenly faced the real possibility that they might be killed by an estranged spouse or rejected lover.

Murders of wives had nearly disappeared in New England in the four decades after the Revolution, but in the late 1820s the rate of wife murder increased fivefold in New Hampshire and Vermont. The rate at which husbands were murdered by their wives or by third parties who tried to stop them from abusing their wives rose sevenfold in the late 1840s. The murder rate for adult relatives other than spouses increased gradually from the late 1820s through the end of the nineteenth century. By that time it had tripled. Similar increases appeared in rural Ohio and Illinois and in New York City, Philadelphia, Cleveland, and Chicago. Whether these changes were confined to the North is not yet clear. Because the rates of family and intimate murders were low compared to rates among unrelated adults, more research will be needed to determine how widespread the increases were. It appears that marital and romance murders also increased in England and France but did not increase to the same degree in the southern United States, despite the sharp increase in homicides among unrelated adults in the postrevolutionary plantation South.

These patterns suggest that murders of spouses and lovers were not ultimately caused by the first three correlates associated with high homicide rates among unrelated adults. Political instability, distrust of government, and a decline in national feeling coincided with soaring homicide rates among unrelated adults across the United States from the late 1840s into the 1870s, but those developments were not synchronized with homicides of spouses and lovers. They do appear to have made matters worse in the North in the mid-nineteenth century, when men became increasingly likely to kill romantic rivals, abusive husbands, and third parties who intervened in abusive marriages, most of whom were nonrelatives. But rates of spousal and romance murder had already risen in the North, so there can be no causal relationship, and in the South there appears to be even less of a link. In northwestern Europe, spousal and romance homicide rates were rising even as political stability and national feeling were increasing and the homicide rate among unrelated adults was falling.

The increase in spousal and romance homicide rates correlated with a shift in the balance of power between men and women and with changes in feelings and beliefs associated with marriage and romance.[1] In the northern United States young women were becoming more independent economically. Jobs in education, textile manufacturing, the clothing trades, and other fields gave them the ability to delay marriage and to be more selective in the suitors they entertained. Their newfound independence changed the dynamic of romantic relationships, as did the growing economic dependence of young men, whose chances of owning their own farms or shops, especially at an early age, declined because of higher land prices and the rise of large firms. Most young men could offer prospective spouses only a share of a clerk's salary or a laborer's wage, and many were unlikely ever to achieve economic independence. If the declining fortunes of young men had not coincided with the rising fortunes of young women, young men would have taken out their frustrations on one another, as they had during past disruptions of the social hierarchy. Because they did coincide, young men became more likely to lash out at women who rejected them and at male rivals who threatened their chances of marrying.

The increase in murders of lovers may also have been influenced by changes in the ideal of romantic love that led young men and women to invest more of their energies in intimate relationships, especially if they believed they had found their "one and only" true love, and left them at sea when those relationships ended. Most of the perpetrators of romance homicides were respected, well-educated, native-born Protestants who were likely to be well versed in Romantic literature, with its emphasis on passion, self-expression, and the idea that true lovers were destined for each other. Contemporaries often attributed their behavior to the influence of novels.

Yet some of these young people might not have become murderers had it not been for the sudden availability of mass-produced handguns. Romantic disappointment had always stirred strong emotions, even in the seventeenth century; but no generation before the 1840s had access to handguns, and no other kind of murder was committed as exclusively with handguns. It was the perfect weapon for rejected suitors. It enabled them to take their lovers by surprise, kill them quickly without disfiguring them, and then turn the weapon instantly upon themselves.

Technology had little to do with the increase in spousal murders, however. Few spousal murders were committed with firearms before the Civil War. If the perpetrator was an abusive husband, he clubbed, beat, or stabbed his victim. Perpetrators who had no history of abuse and merely wanted to get rid of their spouses usually drowned, burned, or poisoned them. Nonlethal marital violence had always been a problem, but after the 1820s lethal violence escalated, especially in marriages in which the wife embraced any of the new ideals of sobriety, companionate marriage, and domesticity but the husband did not. Such husbands, nearly all of them poor, alcoholic, and socially isolated, a substantial minority of them German, Irish, or French immigrants, brutalized their wives in ways that had been unheard-of in colonial and revolutionary times. Stealth murders of spouses, on the other hand, were the province of respected, native-born Protestants. Their concern with reputation and property made divorce unthinkable. They made the decision to kill out of a desire to improve their lives: to make room for a new lover or to rid themselves of a spouse they no longer loved.[2]

Spousal and romance homicide rates were by far the highest in California, where they probably claimed at least 1.4 men per 100,000 adults each year and 3.9 women per 100,000 during the second half of the nineteenth century.[3] The high rates were probably caused by the same forces that drove up rates in the northern United States, since the great majority of California's Anglo population came from the North. But the increase was exacerbated by intense competition over women, who made up only a quarter of the population in the 1850s and early 1860s, a third of the population in the late 1860s and 1870s, and two-fifths of the population in the 1880s and 1890s. The male cultures of California—Anglo, Asian, Hispanic, and Native American— emphasized male prerogative to a greater degree than the cultures of the North or the South did. But circumstances were such that women, who were in the minority in every ethnic and racial community, felt freer to break off unwanted relationships and start new ones, especially if they led hard lives as prostitutes or servants. The result was an epidemic of jealousy that claimed hundreds of lives.

The increase in murders of parents, siblings, adult children, and in-laws in the northern United States appears to have correlated primarily with the forces that increased homicide rates for unrelated adults. But the increase was largely a native-born Protestant phenomenon: there was no increase among first- or second-generation Irish, French, and German immigrants. Like their English, Scots, Scots-Irish, and African counterparts in the seventeenth and early eighteenth centuries, they almost never killed a blood relative or an in-law. One reason they rarely killed relatives was that they had left so many of them behind in the Old World and they depended heavily, both emotionally and economically, on the ones they had in the New World. For native-born Protestants, however, the homicide rate among adult relatives increased steadily from the early nineteenth century to 1900. The increase suggests that families became more fractious and lethally violent the farther they were from the frontier or the immigrant experience. As with unrelated adults, the number of fatalities among adult relatives stemmed chiefly from property disputes, robberies, sexual assaults, and drunken brawls. Thus relationships among adult relatives appear over time to have become more like relationships among unrelated adults, and they became subject to the same forces that drove homicide rates up or down.

But the fact remains that the actual numbers of people killed in family and intimate homicides were very small—so small that anyone who is not a statistician might dismiss them as meaningless. Over the course of the century, the odds that a spouse or intervening third party would be murdered in a marital dispute or that a lover or romantic rival would be murdered in a romance gone awry ranged from a low of 0.4 to a high of 1.7 per 100,000 adults per year. The rate at which other adult relatives were murdered ranged from 0.3 to 1.8 per 100,000 adults.[4] However, when studies are extended over long periods—in this case, 100 years—small numbers will yield rates that, when adjusted for population, can reveal significant long-range increases or decreases. That is why these rates, low as they are, represented a real increase in lethal family and intimate violence—an increase that has persisted to this day.

Marital Homicide in the North

Marital murders remained relatively rare among European Americans and African Americans through the nineteenth century. The rate at which wives and husbands were murdered varied from place to place, but in the North as a whole it probably stayed below 0.7 or 0.8 per 100,000 adults per year (Figure 6.1). Yet in the late 1820s marital murders suddenly became more common in the northern United States and probably in France and England as well. By 1900 the rate of marital murder in the North was approximately twice the colonial rate and five times the rate of the revolutionary period.[5]

Many marital murders were deliberate and violent. Then, as now, prolonged intimacy could give rise to staggering brutality. Samuel Ackley of New York City came home drunk one day and quarreled with his wife, who wanted him to come straight home after work. He expressed his contempt for her domestic ideals by shoving a curtain rod up her rectum. Peter Crine of Minisink, New York, tried to run his wife through a cotton-seed linter, and when that failed, he stomped on her with his spiked boots and smashed her skull against the fireplace. In Gladstone, Illinois, Isaac Niece hit his wife from behind with an ax while she was cooking; her body fell on the stove, and he let it roast.[6]

To the long litany of brutal spouse murders we should add the murder of neighbors or relatives who came to the aid of battered wives. One particular killing made a deep impression upon people across New England. Ralph Bishop was by all accounts a wonderful young man. In 1861 his best friend (and close neighbor) Woodbury Young was getting ready to go off to war, but before leaving he asked Bishop to keep an eye on his family. Woodbury's father, Brewster Young, had a terrible temper and frequently lashed out at his wife and children. Bishop said he would be glad to help. That year the children summoned Bishop several times by putting a signal in an upstairs window. In June 1862, Bishop was passing by the Young house and heard Brewster Young threatening his wife and his daughter, Emerritta, who was ill in bed. When Bishop walked in, Young ordered him out, telling

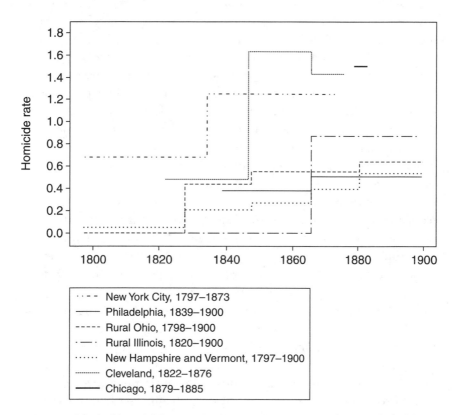

Figure 6.1 Marital homicide rates in the northern United States, 1797–1900 (per 100,000 adults per year).

him that "he had a right to shoot any one that came that he didn't want should come, & the law would bear him out in it." He seized his gun, put it to Bishop's head, and said, "I shot a God Damned rooster through the neck this morning . . . and I will shoot you in the same place." Lowering the gun, he walked into the next room. Mrs. Young told Bishop that he had better go, but he refused to leave. "Law, I ain't afraid of him. He hain't courage enough to shoot any one." They heard Young throwing chairs around in the front room. When Bishop went in to stop him he was met by a shotgun blast to the face.[7]

Willful murders like these produced some modest patterns and hint at why marital homicide rates increased in the mid-nineteenth century. Of the 131 marital homicides that occurred in New Hampshire and Vermont after the mid-1820s, only a fifth resembled the typical marital killings from the colonial and revolutionary periods—an accidental death that occurred in the course of a quarrel or a beating. None of the murders in Holmes or Ross counties in Ohio or in Calhoun, Henderson, and Williamson counties in Illinois stemmed from mental illness or resulted from an unlucky blow. If manslaughter had remained the primary cause of marital homicide, the spousal murder rate would barely have budged, and if mental illness had been the primary cause, the spousal murder rate would have declined, because an increasing number of mentally ill people who were prone to violence were committed to the state asylums that opened throughout the United States in the 1830s and 1840s.[8]

The increase in marital homicides in the 1830s and 1840s stemmed from an escalation of violence within abusive marriages. Two-thirds of the marriages that ended in murder in northern New England and in the counties studied intensively in the rural Midwest had a history of abuse. Husbands, who were the principal abusers in all but four of the cases from this period, used unprecedented violence against their wives. They clearly meant to kill and felt justified in doing so. Most killed their wives at home, but some tracked down wives who had left them. Some were willing to kill or be killed by third parties trying to stop their abuse.

In social terms, abusive husbands who killed their wives or their wives' protectors were not much different from their counterparts in the colonial and revolutionary periods. Most were poor and drank heavily. When they killed their wives at home, they used feet, fists, or heavy household objects, not guns or knives. Half of the abusive husbands who killed their wives at home were Irish, French Canadian, German, or otherwise foreign born, but there is no sign that immigration or immigrant cultures caused the increased homicide rate. It began to rise in the late 1820s and 1830s, when the murderers and victims were exclusively native-born Protestants. The growing proportion of marital homicides that involved the Irish, French Canadians, or Germans after 1840 simply reflected the growing proportion of immigrants and their children among the drinking poor. Furthermore, only four of the twenty-two abusive husbands who killed or were killed by the protectors of wives who had left home were Irish, French Canadian, or German.[9] That number probably reflects how few Irish, French Canadian, and German wives left their husbands to begin with. The Catholic Church's opposition to divorce and the lack of extensive kin networks among recent immigrants undoubtedly kept a greater proportion of abused immigrant women trapped at home.

The problem was not so much that abusive husbands had changed, but that the society around them had changed. Before the 1820s the drinking poor did not stand out from their neighbors. In those years most Americans drank heavily on weekends and holidays, and jobs were plentiful in the frontier and rural economy. Forests needed cutting; land had to be cleared of stumps and rocks. But as these jobs disappeared and as drinking in general declined, a higher proportion of the drinking poor came to be found in the poorest areas of the larger towns of the North, where rents were cheap, taverns were plentiful, and day labor was in greater demand. Neighborhoods like "Hayti" in Rutland, the Water Street area in Burlington, and the Hickory Street area in Chillicothe arose in part because of a decline in independent proprietorship. It took people longer to accumulate the capital necessary to establish their own shops, farms, or households, so more couples in their thirties and early forties were still laborers and rented living space. Most people responded by working harder, drinking less, having fewer children, and joining churches, which conferred a reputation for reliability and gave people more access to credit and good jobs. However, some couples were unwilling or unable to take that course, especially if one or both partners drank heavily. They took up residence in these blighted districts and, unable to see a way out of poverty, became mired in despair.[10]

Newspaper accounts of murders in the North's poor neighborhoods were spare and contemptuous and give few clues about why husbands killed their wives. Charlotte Reindt and her husband Christian, who lived on Hickory Street in Chillicothe, Ohio, were both alcoholics and seemed severely depressed. They rarely spoke or left the house. A former resident of their tenement testified that she had seen Reindt "whip" his wife often "& Strike her with a Stick of wood on the head," but neither she nor anyone else ever intervened. Charlotte's death at the hands of her husband on Valentine's Day in 1864 might not have attracted much notice, but her clothes caught fire when her husband threw her against the stove, and the flames engulfed their room and threatened the rest of the building.[11]

The mixed-race "Hayti" district of Rutland, Vermont, was another dead-end neighborhood where bloody fights and arrests for illegal activity were common. Henry Damon and his wife Sophia lived there with several unrelated couples in a house that had a reputation for problem tenants. One night in 1838 they had an argument about visitors staying in the house, and Henry, who had been drinking, slashed his wife's throat with a razor. Jealousy might have been a factor, since Sophia had been indicted five years earlier for adultery. Evidently Henry still loved his wife, for the *Rutland Herald* revealed that he was in such despair after killing her that he tried to commit suicide. The *Herald* also noted that although several people said they heard Sophia Damon scream for help, no one came to her aid. A couple that "belonged to the house" lay in another bed in the same room at the time of the assault. The husband hid under the covers, and the wife fled the house. A woman in an adjacent room jumped out a window and ran when she heard the "racket." Obviously people had learned that it was safer not to get involved in neighbors' quarrels. In these communities, empathy and fellow feeling were in very short supply.[12]

Most wife murderers were not as abjectly poor as Reindt and Damon, however, and most lived among neighbors who did make some effort to prevent murders. Although poverty contributed to the violent disintegration of marriages, it was not the root cause. Murderers who left a record of their emotional state reported feeling that they had failed in society's eyes—an emotion that correlates strongly with high homicide rates among unrelated adults—and that their spouses had been a constant reminder of that failure.

In the North, feelings of failure stemmed in part from the higher expectations of a society that by midcentury was both prosperous and temperate. Having a house was no longer enough: it had to be a nice house. Having a job was no longer enough: a man had to have a career that followed an upward trajectory. Husbands were also expected to be more than just good providers; they had to be sober, amiable, and respectable. By the late 1840s and 1850s even respectability was not enough in many social circles: men were supposed to be sympathetic, affectionate, and compassionate, especially toward members of their own families. Society had also begun to encourage husbands to share power with their wives and to allow them a say in whether money could be spent on gambling or drinking. In the 1830s and 1840s, the proportion of articles in American magazines that defended the right of women to make decisions in male-female relationships rose from 13 percent to 23 percent. Another 30 percent praised women who used subtle means to guide their husbands to the right decisions, and 17 percent favored having husbands and wives make decisions together. Only 31 percent defended the right of men to make decisions alone, without consulting their wives.[13]

When men could not meet society's expectations or fulfill their own hopes in what was, after all, the land of opportunity, they often turned on their wives, who were a persistent reminder of failure. Henry Mosenbaugh came from Germany to Holmes County, Ohio, found work with German-speaking farmers, and set up housekeeping in a tiny log cabin with his young family. He was a "jovial" fellow who could outdo any man pitching hay, but his lack of skills and his inability to speak English left him no alternative to poor-paying farm labor. Henry began to blame his wife Mary for their circumstances, calling her lazy in front of the neighbors and beating her if she slept in after a long night with their colicky newborn. He also became convinced—for no apparent reason—that Mary intended to leave him for another man. He put an abrupt end to his marriage one Sunday morning in 1876, when he knocked his wife down, beat her senseless with an ax handle, and strangled her as their seven-year-old son looked on and their infant cried on the floor.[14]

Men who drank made failure more certain by wasting money, alienating friends and relatives, damaging their reputations, and upsetting the emotional balance of their households. William Barnet, a fifty-seven-year-old Protestant immigrant from England, worked as a cattle farrier and cleaner of privies. His wife Ann, a thirty-five-year-old Irish Catholic from Canada, took in needlework and made cushions. Together they worked their way up from Water Street, the worst neighborhood in Burlington, Vermont, to Skinner Street, where they lived in a ramshackle one-family house. But their industry was not enough to win them respectability. People kept a wary eye on them because when they had lived on Water Street they had had a row that made the newspapers: they had been drinking, and William had threatened Ann with a knife. She wrenched it from his hand, whereupon he hit her with a flatiron, laying open her skull. He was prosecuted for the assault. At the hearing Ann's employer had to testify that she was "not a common woman," indicating that most people in Burlington might have thought otherwise.[15]

In the weeks before her death in August 1862, the neighbors noted that Ann appeared distracted and disheveled, but she was sober and worked every day. William, on the other hand, was drinking heavily. On the day of her death he went to her employer and demanded her pay, then bought whiskey and tobacco for himself. That purchase may have set off the quarrel that G. N. Isaiah heard that evening. He knocked on the door to see if everything was all right. The couple assured him that they were fine. But by midnight Ann was dead, her throat cut with a rusty butcher knife.

Similar circumstances lay behind Brewster Young's assaults on his family. Young was also a hardworking man in his fifties, affable when sober. He had a respected wife, promising children, and many friends. But he was hard pressed to raise five children on a modest farm, and he was not as prosperous as he thought he deserved to be. After his neighbors testified against him in a civil case about a debt, he became bitter and vowed to get even with them. He drank heavily and began to threaten his wife when she reproached him. Matters grew worse when his daughter got sick and the doctor's bills mounted. He compounded his family's financial problems by destroying furniture and dishes in fits of anger. It was a desperate act for a man who did not have the money to replace the rotten shingles on his roof, but he felt that if he was suffering, his family should suffer, too. Ralph Bishop quickly became the emotional patriarch of a household that longed for an affectionate father, and the intimacy between him and the family infuriated Young, who felt that Bishop was trying to supplant him.[16]

For men who were not doing well financially, the pressure to be sober, industrious, and successful only intensified their sense of themselves as failures, increased the likelihood that they would be unable to leave off drinking, and drove a wedge between them and their wives. But marital unhappiness in such households was probably exacerbated by the spread of misogynist attitudes in the North in the 1830s and 1840s, attitudes that encouraged hostility toward women who asserted themselves in public or private. A number of prominent Democratic newspaper editors railed against female reformers, especially prohibitionists and women's-rights advocates, and ran columns about gossips and busybodies who plagued their innocent husbands and were blind to their own faults. The worst misogyny was less public. Sylvester Corbet circulated a satire of the women's-rights movement surreptitiously in Benson, Vermont, in 1851. He portrayed the town's activists as prostitutes and a physician who lent his support as their pimp, and he detailed the sex acts they were willing to perform and the price they charged for each. Willard Stevens, another Vermont Democrat, denounced women repeatedly in his diary and complained about the control they exercised in society and within the family. No man "that is influenced by a woman," he wrote, "should hold any authority to enact laws for the United States government." Nor should men ever grant women the right to govern, because they would rapidly reduce civilization "to a complete state of degradation." The Democratic Party encouraged such sentiments and provided a supportive home for men who viewed women as the source of their problems.[17]

Marital relationships were clearly changing. Just after the Revolution, two-fifths of husbands petitioning for divorce in Vermont (the first state to grant divorces on the grounds of "intolerable severity") had complained of emotional and physical abuse—an indication that wives were just as likely to lash out at their husbands at the beginning of the nineteenth century as they had been in the colonial period. But by the 1830s and 1840s, complaints by husbands of intolerable severity dropped to less than 10 percent of all petitions. Although a few wives still tried confrontation, ridicule, and violence, both retaliatory and anticipatory, testimony in divorce suits and homicide cases suggests that discontented wives had become less aggressive verbally and physically and that they were trying to change their husbands' behavior in other ways. Nancy Bean believed it "her duty . . . to toil and suffer" with her husband and "cleaved" to him, hoping that the sight of her bruised body would prompt feelings of pity and remorse. Brewster Young's wife kept her children out of her husband's way when he was on one of his "trains," but she also pleaded with him, asking, "Brewster, why do you do so?" Abused wives tried to make their husbands feel guilty or ashamed. They asked their husbands to search their souls, to feel compassion for those they hurt. They were less likely to answer abuse with abuse.[18]

This shift in behavior was probably due to the spread of evangelical and sentimental religion. The great revivals of the 1830s and 1840s encouraged compassion for the fallen, especially men who were drunkards or abusers, and called upon their families to try to redeem them through prayer and moral suasion. Many abused wives came to believe that it was their duty (and best hope) to minister to their husbands and to turn the other cheek if abused. They repudiated physical force and used only moral and spiritual means to change their husbands' ways. Many of these women also adopted the tenets of cultural movements that promoted respectability and domesticity. They believed that they were entitled to husbands who cared about their public image and who were sober, even-tempered, and compassionate.[19]

It might seem logical to assume that religion and the cult of respectability bear part of the responsibility for the deaths of women who refused to fight back or stayed too long in abusive marriages. In fact, however, these movements may have prompted some women—Protestants in particular—to leave husbands they considered morally or spiritually depraved. The proportion of husbands who complained in divorce suits that their wives had deserted them rose from less than a third to half.[20] In any case, physical and verbal aggression on the part of wives did not prevent homicide, nor did leaving abusive marriages. Women who left or stood up to their husbands as forcefully as any revolutionary-era wife had done were murdered, too.

At midcentury there was one notable change in murder patterns in abusive marriages. For the postrevolutionary era, not a single case of separation or divorce leading to murder has surfaced in any of the newspapers or records studied to date. However, during the 1850s hus-

bands began to kill their spouses as they tried to leave abusive marriages or even after they had left. Lorin Ayer's story illustrates the trajectory these marriages followed. Ayer had abused his wife Mary, a
textile worker, for years. Hoping that he would change after they had
children, Mary stayed with him, but Lorin became even more abusive
after their child was born. He also began to drink heavily, and he
threatened to kill himself. In 1871 she filed a complaint and had him
jailed. His sentence was suspended on the promise he would leave
town, which he did; but after a few months he returned, and Mary
took him in. Shortly afterward their baby became ill and died. Lorin
was so despondent that he bought laudanum and arsenic to kill himself, but Mary destroyed them. The next day he showed up at their
boardinghouse drunk. Mary packed her bags and moved out, and
Lorin was evicted. He wandered the streets for a few days and hired an
eight-year-old girl to spy on his wife, convinced that she had been
cheating on him. Although he found no evidence of infidelity, he
bought a handgun anyway and stalked her. One evening he confronted
her on the street and asked her to come back. When she refused, he
said that "she should either live with him or die with him," and he shot
her dead. He held bystanders at bay, then walked around the corner
and shot himself in the head.[21]

Nearly every one of the husbands who murdered their estranged
wives or a person who had given their wives sanctuary or encouraged
them to leave was an economic failure. All but three were forty or
older and had long histories of lost jobs and bad investments. They
also suffered from depression: half of them committed or attempted
suicide after they attacked their wives, something that abusers who
were not estranged from their wives never did. These husbands probably saw themselves as victims of economic forces beyond their control, and they may have been driven to depression and suicide by the
same forces that were raising the suicide rate among middle-aged men
across the northern United States and in western Europe.[22]

Although they were sober at the time of their assaults, most of these
men also had histories of alcohol abuse. Most planned and scripted
their wives' final moments. They asked for another chance, and when
the answer was no, they struck. David Blodgett said, "Oh, Myra! will
you go home with me?" "No, Ed. You have abused me enough." Benjamin Dean asked, "Lizzie, are you coming home with me?" "No, Ben,

never." Louis Castor gave his wife two chances to say yes. When she refused to come back, he asked her if she would return if he deeded all his property to her. She said that "she couldn't do so, if he were worth a million."[23] Each attack came only after the wife made it abundantly clear that the marriage was over. Each husband took that final refusal to mean that he was justified in killing his wife and that the murder was to some degree her own fault.

Unlike abusive husbands who were not estranged from their wives, all estranged husbands used deadly weapons. A quarter of them used knives or razors, and three-fifths used guns, some of which were borrowed or purchased the day before the murder.[24] None of the survivors denied or tried to conceal his crime. They intended to kill, and they were willing to face the consequences.

These murders form a pattern that has persisted in the northern United States to the present day. Support for abused women who sought separations or divorces saved many lives, but abusive husbands saw that support as a threat to patriarchy. By the 1850s the courts had begun to let women keep their children and their personal property, and violent husbands realized that they had nothing to gain by going to court. The law would only legitimize their wives' desertion. Most of them tried to avoid the courts by making some concessions to their wives. Henry Leader of Keene, New Hampshire, had already agreed to give his estranged wife Lucinda a share of their property at the time he tried to kill her. Sylvester Bell of Fairfax, Vermont, had promised his estranged wife that he would allow her to return home to gather her belongings.[25]

The realization that the courts might support their wives may have bred a dangerous fatalism in husbands who had grown up with the expectation that their wives would always serve and obey them. Perhaps they were fatalistic about their crimes and the punishment they would face because they had already lost their dignity. Their wives, in turn, were determined, defiant, and all too incautious on the eve of their emancipation. Mary Ayer was intent on starting her new life and brushed aside her friends' concerns, saying that her husband "had often threatened to kill her, but that was all it would amount to." She talked instead about hiring a lawyer to keep her husband from garnishing her wages and about moving "where she would not have to see him every day." However, estranged wives who took precautions also lost their lives. Emma Bell took the county sheriff with her when she went home to gather her things. Both she and the sheriff were fooled by her husband's civility. The sheriff let Sylvester Bell follow her upstairs, where he killed her.[26]

The changing economic fortunes of women in the North undoubtedly contributed to the increase in murders by abusive husbands. The value of women's labor increased faster than the value of men's labor in the nineteenth century, thanks to improvements in technology and in the marketing of products produced primarily by women, such as textiles and dairy products. Women therefore stood on a more nearly equal economic footing within marriage and could fend for themselves if they left abusive marriages.[27] On the whole, economic change probably decreased everyday marital violence by increasing the value of women and giving them options so that they did not have to stay in abusive marriages; but these same changes undermined the mutual dependence of wives and husbands that had been a hallmark of the traditional household-based economy, and they increased the likelihood that women would be murdered by husbands who squandered their wives' earnings on drink or resented their economic independence. Such conflicts clearly played a role in the murders of women like Mary Ayer and Ann Barnet, who were the primary breadwinners in their households and could fend for themselves. Women's economic progress was a boon to most marriages and most husbands, but not to husbands who were failures.

Economics also played a role in murders committed by estranged wives, although jealousy and rage were probably equally important, since abandoned wives were far more likely to try to kill their husbands' lovers than they were to kill their husbands. In 1848 in Hamilton County, Ohio, Margaret Howard stabbed her husband's mistress, Mary Jane Smith. Howard had been a society wife, and she was left penniless when her husband deserted her. In 1899 Lizzie Provencher, who had been separated from her husband Henry for three years, called at her husband's house in Rochester, New Hampshire, and shot his lover when she opened the door. Lizzie's drinking and abuse had destroyed her marriage, and she led a lonely life after Henry took their only child and left. She worked in a shoe factory and spent her nights alone in a rented room in a flophouse. By contrast, her husband had a small but thriving smithy, had bought a house, and had fallen in love with Annie Cox, a nineteen-year-old textile worker. Henry was so afraid of his wife's threats that he did not dare seek a divorce, so Cox moved in as his "housekeeper." Lizzie was furious about this arrangement and deeply distressed that Cox was raising her son.[28]

Only a few women tried to murder husbands who left them, and those who did were far less likely than men to use a firearm or a sharp weapon. It may have been that women simply lacked experience with guns, large knives, or razors, or it may have been a combination of inexperience and cultural inhibitions. Many of the attempted murders certainly pointed to a lack of expertise. In 1869, for example, a woman in Nashua, New Hampshire, followed her husband to another woman's apartment. She fired four shots at him, but every one missed.[29] The primary reason for the dearth of husband murders, however, is that abandoned wives did not feel themselves to be the failures that men whose wives left them did. Although desertion was humiliating for women, society was more likely to sympathize with wives as the injured parties in a marital breakup. For men, on the other hand, desertion was a public humiliation that struck at their manhood, and murdering their wives was a way of showing the world that they could still control them.

Because of the growing danger of marital homicide, northerners intensified their efforts during the nineteenth century to prevent spouse abuse and to punish abusers. In some instances abusers faced vigilante violence. In the winter of 1824 in Kennebunkport, Maine, three women paid a surprise visit to a habitual abuser. They dragged him by the ears from his house and pushed him face down in the snow. One woman held his head and another his legs while a third "paid him back with interest, the full amount of flagellations, which he had bestowed on his wife." In 1879 in Benton, New Hampshire, the hands at Richardson's mill seized a fellow worker who had bruised his wife badly, carried him into the woods, threatened to hang him, and finally tarred and feathered him. The man ran off and was never seen in Benton again.[30]

A few abused wives decided to take the law into their own hands. In the counties studied intensively in northern New England and the rural Midwest, four wives killed their abusive husbands in the second half of the century. All of these women had a history of resisting their husbands' drunken assaults; all had beaten, clubbed, shot, or stabbed their husbands at least once before killing them. Because of her husband's constant threats, Estella Hunter of Hinsdale, New Hampshire, bought a revolver and kept it under her pillow. Her husband came home drunk and angry three weeks later and warned her about "what would happen to her before morning." She shot him through the head the moment he fell asleep. Like all of these women, Hunter had small children and was abjectly poor. Trapped in a bad marriage, she had nowhere to go and no one to turn to.[31]

A number of abusive husbands were murdered in these counties by their sons, their in-laws, or friends of their wives. Mary Flanders Austin of Bow, New Hampshire, had divorced her first husband on the grounds of extreme cruelty. Yet she then turned around and married a violent drunkard who was only ten years older than her son William. Mary and George Austin led a hard life on her run-down, twenty-acre farm, surviving on the work that George and William did for neighboring farmers. One night George came home drunk and began to beat and choke his wife. William grabbed his shotgun and fired. His stepfather was mortally wounded. On his deathbed he apologized to his wife for treating her so badly and made it clear that the tragedy was his fault.[32]

No matter how straightforward the evidence in these killings appeared to be, the authorities generally took a close look at the circumstances of each death and the motives of those involved. There was evidence of premeditation in the Austin case; William had told his stepfather he would kill him if he beat Mary again, and he kept a loaded shotgun by his bed expressly for that purpose. He was charged with first-degree manslaughter, but a trial resulted in a hung jury. He subsequently pled guilty to second-degree manslaughter and served six months in jail. Another New Hampshire case appeared at first to be a simple matter of a neighbor intervening to protect an abused wife. Richmond Angell of Sunapee was known to have threatened his wife with violence. One day his neighbor, Henry Hayes, refused to leave the Angell house. Angell became enraged and tried to throw him out, and Hayes beat him to death. Hayes later claimed that he had feared for Mrs. Angell's safety. But an investigation turned up evidence that Angell had good reason to be jealous of Hayes' attentions to his wife, and Hayes was eventually found guilty of manslaughter. Alma Smith of Williston, Vermont, a former prostitute, was estranged from her husband, who was apparently weak-minded. She had kicked him out of the house, but one day he came storming back, brandishing a gun and threatening to kill her. Alma and her father killed him before he could get off a shot. But the authorities concluded that father and daughter had financial reasons for wanting the husband out of the way, so the father, who fired the fatal shot, was charged with second-degree murder.[33]

Despite the diligence of law enforcement, however, vigilantism and the right to self-defense may have provided some cover for murders of abusive husbands committed for other reasons. Both vigilante and defensive violence were on the rise throughout the United States in the 1850s, the same decade in which murders of abusive husbands first appeared; the concurrence suggests these murders may have been caused as much by the legitimation of certain kinds of violence in the society at large as by the need to defend abused women against the increasing likelihood that they would be murdered. The fact that 65 percent of these murders were committed with guns—atypical weapons for domestic assaults—also suggests that these murders were rooted as much in the forces that increased the nondomestic homicide rate at midcentury as in the forces that had increased marital violence since the late 1820s.[34]

One more type of marital murder began to increase in the late 1820s and 1830s, well before the increase in homicide among unrelated adults: stealth murders of unwanted spouses. It is impossible to know with certainty how many spouses were murdered by stealth, but it appears from the number of cases confirmed by coroners, prosecutors, forensic scientists, and grand jurors that such murders were more common than they had been in the colonial and revolutionary periods. They accounted for a sixth of known marital homicides between 1828 and 1900.

Stealth murderers were unlike other spousal murderers in several ways. A third were women.[35] Women were much more likely to be stealth murderers than abuse murderers. The weapons used were also different. People convicted of stealth murder in this period tried to avoid or conceal the use of physical violence. Two-thirds of their victims were poisoned. One was drowned, two were strangled, and two were burned to conceal their having been bludgeoned. Only one was shot, in a way that made it appear accidental. Obviously, stealth murderers used such methods because they did not want to get caught. They were not suicidal or fatalistic. They wanted better lives: they wanted access to money or another chance at love, or they simply wanted to unburden themselves of spouses who had become millstones around their necks.

Stealth murders were thus fueled by increasing ambitions. Rebecca Peake of Orange, Vermont, raised a few eyebrows when she married a prosperous widower some years her senior, but she meant to live well, and she did, until her husband, after twenty years of marriage, signed his property over to Ephraim Peake, his son by his first wife, leaving his children by Rebecca nothing. Having title under Vermont law only to the meager property she had brought to the marriage, unable to pass the fruits of her labors to her children so that they might lead better lives than she had, and unable to win a divorce in the absence of cruelty, adultery, desertion, or nonsupport, she was at a loss. After attending a protracted revival meeting she became convinced that in the eyes of God her husband had committed an unpardonable offense. She poisoned him, Ephraim, and Ephraim's sister Fanny to reclaim the property she felt was rightfully hers.[36]

Julius Fox, a young farmer in nearby Tunbridge, Vermont, also found his hopes for marital bliss and a comfortable future dashed. At age twenty he had married his sweetheart, Rosella Ashley, but she died only three or four years later. In his grief he made a hasty decision that he came to regret: he married Rosella's thirteen-year-old sister, Nancy. He needed help on the farm, and perhaps he saw his late wife in her sister. But Nancy was too young to run a household, and after a couple of months she went to visit her parents and did not return. While she was gone, Fox was smitten by a young widow his own age, but he had no grounds for divorce, since his wife had not truly deserted him—she was only staying with her parents. Fox asked Nancy to visit him so that they could "effect a reconciliation," but when she arrived, he lured her into an old barn and beat her to death with a fence rail. He then burned the barn to the ground and left the coroner's jury to make what case it could from her remains.[37]

Most stealth murders were more straightforward. A few of the victims were wives who could not help on the farm as much as their husbands expected: one had become blind, another crippled, another permanently bedridden. Two-thirds of the murderers were adulterers.

Like Peake and Fox, they had no legal grounds for divorce and stood to lose a great deal financially if they left town or if they were found at fault in a divorce proceeding. Like Peake and Fox, they were respectable or wanted to be considered respectable. Unlike abusive murderers, nearly all of whom were heavy drinkers with poor reputations, stealth murderers had or aspired to have some standing in local society. They could have deserted their spouses or forced a breakup. Most spouses who found their marriages intolerable did so, and accepted the damage to their finances and reputations. But as the line between respectable and unrespectable society was drawn more sharply in the 1830s and 1840s, and as the social and monetary cost of disreputability increased, a few unhappily married spouses decided that murder was the cheapest and most logical route to success. Such motives prompted Mrs. Elizabeth Ragan of Piqua, Ohio, to send her children to the store to buy arsenic, which she spooned into her husband's oysters. The same motives led Jeremiah Ricker of Farmington, New Hampshire, to conspire with his housekeeper to give his wife preserves laced with corrosive sublimate. These people wanted it all: to be rid of their spouses, marry their lovers, and maintain their position in society.[38]

Despite the vigilance of relatives and neighbors, the commitment of the mentally ill, the acceptance of separation and divorce, and the development of new forensic tests for poisons, the number of marital murders continued to grow. The numbers increased everywhere—in cities as well as in small towns and in the countryside—but by the late nineteenth century the rate was probably three or four times higher in cities than elsewhere. The character of marital murders in cities was the same as in northern New England and the rural Midwest. Abuse murders, murders of estranged spouses, stealth murders, and murders of romantic rivals predominated. The characteristics of marital murderers were also the same. They were overwhelmingly men in midlife who had been married for some time. Few came from the business or professional classes, except for those who committed murder by stealth. Most lived below or just above the poverty line, because they had few skills or skills for which the demand was decreasing.[39]

It is clear that most of the murderous husbands who lived in Chicago, a city for which there are abundant, detailed records, were not good providers and were unable to control or command the respect of their wives. They could not meet the challenges of the new economy or live up to the new ideals of companionate marriage and domesticity, and they were plagued by a sense of failure and humiliation— again, an emotion that correlates strongly with high homicide rates among unrelated adults. The sense of failure seemed strongest among German American husbands. Many of them had difficulty making a good living because they practiced trades that were in decline, like butchering and shoemaking, and theirs was a more patriarchal culture that made it difficult for them to come to terms with their wives' demands for greater equality and independence. They had the highest spousal murder rates in Chicago.[40]

Throughout most of the nineteenth century, marital murder rates among African Americans in the northern United States roughly paralleled those of whites. In Philadelphia their rates were higher than those for European Americans, but in Chicago they were nearly identical, and no spousal murders occurred among African Americans who lived in northern New England, in Ross or Holmes counties in Ohio, or in Calhoun, Henderson, and Williamson counties in Illinois. The lack of difference overall was in part a consequence of the lower proportion of African American men and women who were married and in part the result of African Americans' greater willingness to leave unhappy relationships and form new ones.

In the late nineteenth century, however, marital murder rates among urban African Americans skyrocketed past those of European Americans. The surge was rooted in the inability of African American husbands to provide for their families. African American men and women began to marry at rates similar to those for European Americans at precisely the time that black political power in northern cities collapsed and discrimination against blacks in jobs, housing, and education increased. African Americans lost influence in northern cities in the 1880s and 1890s as the Republican Party abandoned the cause of civil rights and the political fortunes of white supremacists revived. They also lost ground economically as the influx of immigrants from the South, known as the Great Migration, caused a backlash against black workers among whites who feared for their jobs.[41]

Their stories are sadly alike. In Chicago, Daniel Francis shot his wife Myra, who had left him because of his failure to support her. Henry Russell, an unemployed waiter, grew tired of his wife's complaints about having to take in washing to support the family, and he stabbed her to death. Charles Rollins, a tailor, watched his business collapse in the 1890s, when many white customers stopped patronizing black shops. His wife did not want to live in poverty, and she left him. When she refused to come back home, he shot her.[42]

At the same time, African American women took up arms against their husbands. Their violence was usually defensive. In Philadelphia, Martha Bell, the common-law wife of George Purnell, left him after she discovered that he was seeing another woman. He grabbed her in the street and threatened to kill her if she did not come home. She stabbed him to death. Squire Alexander paid a visit to his former wife, Melinda, after he was released from prison. When he tried to choke her, she hit him in the head with a hatchet. But the violence of African American wives could also be aggressive. May Johnson burned her common-law husband to death with a kerosene lamp when she found him with another woman. Lillie Fisher killed her common-law husband for the same reason. The greater frequency with which African American women killed their husbands was an unforeseen consequence of their greater independence. They were more likely than white women to work for wages and to contribute substantially to the family's income, and therefore they were less fearful of living on their own. They were also better prepared to defend themselves, because they knew that they could not rely on law enforcement and the courts, which were less likely to try to protect black women against domestic violence. These differences did not lead to high rates of husband murder, however, until the 1890s, when African American men fell on hard times economically and the balance of power in marriage shifted decisively toward African American women.[43]

Marital Homicide in the South

There are not yet enough data on southern counties to make a reliable estimate of the rates of marital murders. Most studies understate the incidence of marital murder in the South, either because they rely on a single source, such as newspapers or inquests, or because there are a large number of cases in which the identity of the victim or the relationship between victim and murderer cannot be determined. But the evidence gathered to date suggests that marital homicide rates did not increase much in the South. They had been higher to begin with than northern rates in the seventeenth and eighteenth centuries and were still higher in the nineteenth, but by a smaller margin, because they held nearly steady while northern rates rose.

According to Gilles Vandal's comprehensive study of newspaper reports of homicides, marital murder rates in Louisiana between 1866 and 1884 were comparable to those in the urban and rural North in those decades. The actual rates of marital murder were probably higher than those in the North, but the same patterns appear: higher rates in urban than in rural areas, lower rates for blacks than for whites in rural areas, and roughly the same rates for whites and blacks in urban areas. Data from a variety of sources show that the marital homicide rate was higher for blacks in rural Virginia than in Louisiana, but that whites in rural counties in Virginia had rates that were identical with the rates for Louisiana derived from newspapers alone, and above the rates for northern New England and rural Ohio and Illinois by one or two tenths per 100,000 adults.[44]

Marital homicide rates in rural plantation counties in Georgia and South Carolina were higher than those in Virginia and Louisiana—as high as rates in urban areas—and were roughly the same for blacks and whites. Whether these rates had been higher in the eighteenth century as well is unknown. It is important to note, however, that neither the data for whites in Georgia nor for blacks and whites in Virginia indicate more than a 0.1 per 100,000 per year increase in the marital homicide rate over the course of the nineteenth century, a figure not large enough to be significant. That pattern would make sense, because the pressures that produced more marital murders in the northern United States and western Europe in the mid- and late nineteenth centuries were not as intense in the southern United States. The temperance movement was less robust, and drinking was less stigmatized; separation and divorce were less common; skilled workers faced less competition from industry; patriarchal culture was not under siege to the same extent; and women had fewer alternatives to domestic employment. Such pressures certainly existed, but they were probably not strong enough to raise southern marital homicide rates much during this century.[45]

Some of the homicides that occurred in a marital context but did not involve spousal murder were peculiar to the institution of slavery.

Enslaved husbands sometimes killed owners or overseers who denied them permission to visit their wives, and a number of enslaved (or formerly enslaved) husbands killed white men who were exploiting their wives sexually. For example, a slave in King George County, Virginia, killed a white man who "had had a connection with his wife" by driving a bayonet through the man's head. A slave who lived near Hampton, Virginia, attacked a white man who "startd borthern" his wife right in front of him. He shot the man, hacked him to death with a hoe, and then shot him several more times for good measure. In 1868 Green Pearson of Jasper County, Georgia, killed Reid Leverett, the son of his former master, after the young man began visiting Pearson's estranged wife. Pearson lay in wait outside her cabin one night and surprised Leverett as he crept out of her window. After nearly severing Leverett's head with a knife, he dragged the body into a swamp, beat it and shot it repeatedly, then submerged it in the mud. The violence of these assaults surpassed anything visited on interlopers by husbands who were born free and testifies to the wretched frustration of men whose status in society was so low that other men felt free to impose upon their wives.[46]

Among both blacks and whites, murders involving adultery or allegations of adultery may have accounted for a larger proportion of marriage-related homicides in the South than in the North before the end of the Civil War. Murderous jealousy remained a problem within slave marriages and between enslaved husbands and their wives' male friends because of the informality of slave marriages and the ease with which enslaved women could transfer their affections. White husbands—especially slaveowners—could be equally murderous when confronted with evidence of their wives' infidelity. Given the nature of southern society, with its emphasis on dominating others, cuckolded husbands were often reluctant to accept the public humiliation of suing rivals for alienation of affection, preferring instead to reimpose their dominance and reclaim their wives by murdering their rivals. Dr. Miles Gilmore of Horry County, South Carolina, returned from his rounds one morning in 1863 to find Abraham Causey in bed with his wife. He chased Causey into the yard, grabbed a chunk of wood, and beat him to the ground. He wanted to cut Causey's throat, but, finding his dirk knife missing, he crushed Causey's skull instead and threw his body into a ditch. The number of slaveowning husbands who tracked their rivals down and challenged them to duels or killed them outright is still unknown, but it appears that such murders were much more common in the postrevolutionary South, where men were more anxious about their standing in society, than in the North.[47]

Differences between North and South should not be exaggerated, however. The bulk of marital homicides in the nineteenth-century South were identical with those in the North. Abuse murders, stealth murders, and murders of estranged spouses were the most common forms of marital homicide, and in both regions black women were more likely than white women to murder their husbands.[48] As the marital homicide rate rose and murders of rivals by husbands became more common in the North, as more southern white women began to leave their husbands, and as more African Americans moved North, the incidence and character of marital homicides in the two regions began to converge.

Marital Homicide in the Southwest

The Southwest had by far the worst rates of marital homicide in the second half of the nineteenth century.[49] Homicide rates were high for women and men in the Southwest for every kind of homicide, so violence in the society at large probably contributed to the high rate of marital homicide; but the stories that have been collected to date indicate that the high rate of marital violence, especially between husbands and men who were trying to steal away their wives, was caused in part by intense competition among men over women, who were greatly outnumbered by men in every ethnic and racial group through 1900.[50]

Marriage and marital violence have been studied most thoroughly in California. The imbalance between men and women was far worse there and lasted far longer than on most frontiers. Clearly, men were desperate for female companionship, and women who were dissatisfied with their husbands often took advantage of the situation and took lovers or found new husbands. As a result, California history abounds with stories of deadly confrontations between husbands and their wives' lovers—more so even than the South.

Married women in California were besieged by suitors at every turn, and sometimes they responded. In San Francisco, Charles Drew's wife had a number of admirers. When she told her husband that she wanted a divorce, his suspicions fell on a friend, Dr. Gillis. In a jealous rage, he sought out Gillis and shot him dead in the street. Joseph Hurtado, who piloted a boat on the Sacramento River, was usually away from home, so his wife, feeling lonely and perhaps overwhelmed by their new baby, took one of her suitors as a lover. Hurtado became suspicious and confronted her. She admitted that she had slept with José Estuardo, a neighbor, and they agreed to a trial separation. After a few weeks they reconciled, but Estuardo would not let her alone, and Hurtado found him at the house one day and pistol-whipped him. Estuardo demanded that Hurtado be charged with attempted murder—a felony. Undoubtedly looking forward to spending time alone with Hurtado's wife, he testified in court that his rival was "a dangerous man to be at large." When the hearing adjourned, Hurtado got a gun and shot Estuardo dead.[51]

Because the populations of Chinese and Native American women were small and the number of spousal homicides correspondingly few, it is impossible to know with any certainty why they were killed at a somewhat higher rate than Anglo spouses were. Certainly Chinese and Indian men had a more difficult time economically than most Anglo men did, and most Chinese and Indian women had no way of deterring abuse, since they had few rights as noncitizens under California's legal system. The fact that the Chinese had the highest ratio of men to women of any ethnic group, 14 to 1, helps explain the high level of violence against women and over women among the Chinese. Yet Native Americans had the lowest ratio of men to women of any ethnic group in California—never more than 3 to 2, according to census records— and it is possible that the "missing" Indian women were living in the mountains or in remote canyons while Indian men sought employment in the mines or on ranches.[52]

Known cases of marital homicide among Native Americans in California and Arizona during this period appear to have had more in common with the marital homicides that occurred among Native Americans in southern New England in the mid-eighteenth century than with the ones that occurred among the Chinese, Hispanics, and Anglos. They were caused more often by abuse or drunkenness, and probably stemmed from the demoralization of Indian men over the loss of their land and their way of life. Native men were more likely to lash out at everyone, including their wives. In 1894 Manuel Amayo killed his wife, Luisa Vasilia Escoba, on the Pala reservation in San Diego County. She asked him why he had not bought flour at the store. He said, "If I had had money I would have been drunk." He swore and kicked her, and she hit back, so he struck her with a club and kept hitting her until she died. During a feast in 1852, Bautista, the chief of the Potoyanti, who lived in the foothills of the southern Sierras, got drunk and stabbed his young wife to death. The same pattern appeared among the Apaches who lived on the San Carlos Reservation in Gila, Arizona, where wives were murdered at an extraordinary rate. Some were victims of jealous husbands, who had the right under Apache law to kill unfaithful wives and their lovers; but most were killed when their husbands got drunk on *tiswin,* an alcoholic beverage made from corn.[53]

The marital homicide rate for Hispanics was 63 percent higher in California than the rate for Anglos. Marital homicides were a problem in the Mexican borderlands before the American conquest in 1846–47, so it is hard to attribute the high rate simply to demoralization, alienation, and impoverishment. Hispanic law and culture gave men great power over their wives. Hispanic men had a duty to protect "good" women, especially their mothers, sisters, and daughters; but they had an obligation to punish wives who were disobedient or who flirted with other men. Under Hispanic law husbands also had a right to kill their wives' lovers if they caught them *in flagrante.* Wives could expect little help from family, friends, or the courts in cases of abuse, and they had no right to divorce, so they could not escape abusive marriages.[54]

With virtually no restrictions on their behavior, Hispanic men were often violent and often took violence to extremes. Rafael Montoya, a farmer in La Ciénega, New Mexico, killed his wife in a jealous rage one night, a few hours after they had been taunted on the road by three men. Montoya suspected that his wife was having an affair with one of the men. When she went to the outhouse that night, he concluded that she was going out to meet her lover, so he crept up and stabbed her in the back. Manuel Gallego, who farmed near Santa Fe, had been arrested three times for starting fights with other men before he strangled his wife, María. María had complained to her mother and brother that her husband made her life miserable, but there was nothing they could do. It is not surprising, given how little recourse abused women had, that they often conspired with lovers to murder their husbands.[55]

The Anglo men who settled California, most of whom came from the northern United States, had their own deadly brand of *hombrismo*. Nearly all had forsaken marriage and family for the opportunity to prove themselves as men on the frontier, and many of them spoke disparagingly about getting tied down to women who would try to make them abide by the standards of respectable society. They often fantasized in letters, songs, and diaries about young women who would admire their heroic exploits and be cheerfully subordinate. The Forty-niners were not necessarily out-and-out misogynists; but many of them had gone West because they had not been able to make enough money in the East to marry and have families, and they did not find success any easier to achieve in California, especially where women were concerned. It is likely, therefore, that the gap between male and female expectations of marriage was wider in California than in the rest of the United States and that it contributed significantly to the high marital homicide rate among Anglos in California.[56]

Marital Homicide in the Western World

Wife murders appear to have become more common in England and Wales by the mid-nineteenth century, even though rates of spouse murder as a whole and of other kinds of murder among adults declined there in the late nineteenth century. Homicide trials in England and Wales show a 22 percent increase between 1840 and 1900 in the rate at which men were tried for wife murder. Court records and newspapers show that between 1867 and 1892 the rate in England and Wales was at least 0.2 per 100,000 adults per year, and in Scotland it was at least 0.4 per 100,000 per year. Criminal examinations in northern France also indicate a marital homicide rate of at least 0.4 per 100,000 per year.[57]

That these preliminary rates are comparable to those for northern New England and rural Ohio is not surprising, since the changes in the economy, marriage, and gender relations that led to the rise in wife murders in the northern United States were also felt in England, Wales, Scotland, and northern France. Abuse murders, murders of estranged spouses, murders of abusive husbands, and stealth murders became more common, as they did in the northern United States. Ireland, however, had a slightly lower rate of wife murder: 0.16 per 100,000 adults per year. That rate was in part an artifact of Ireland's low marriage rate and rural character, but it probably also reflected the persistence of more traditional views of marriage and gender roles, a less industrialized economy, greater tolerance of drinking, and less interest in the pursuit of respectability.[58]

There were more murders of husbands and third parties intervening in marital disputes in the northern United States than in England, Wales, Scotland, or northern France. Western Europe did not see as much of the possessive rage and vigilantism that led to such murders. The surge in possessive murders and vigilante homicides of abusive spouses in the northern United States in the late 1840s coincided with the rise in property-dispute murders, robbery murders, rape murders, and fatal tavern brawls and with an increase in the use of guns and knives in disputes. Although there is little doubt that wife murders would have become more common in the northern United States in the absence of a general homicide crisis, as the rise in wife murders in England, Wales, Scotland, and northern France shows, the feelings and beliefs that changed the character and incidence of homicide among unrelated adults in the United States probably made the rise in murders of husbands and third parties intervening in marital disputes much worse.

Romance Homicide

Beginning in the 1830s and 1840s, romance homicides among unmarried men and women also occurred more frequently in the United States, although they remained rare relative to other kinds of homicide. The rate was higher in most urban areas, and rates for blacks and Hispanics were higher than the rate for whites. In Chicago, blacks were nine times more likely to commit romance homicides by the end of the nineteenth century. In Philadelphia, where the indictment rate for romance homicides tripled after 1875, blacks were twenty times more likely to commit romance homicides than whites. In San Francisco, the rate from 1849 to 1900 was 0.8 per 100,000 for Anglos and Asians and 2.7 per 100,000 for Hispanics.[59]

There were exceptions to this rule. In Louisiana, where murders have been categorized by cause, the murder rate from jealousy (a category that included some marital as well as romance homicides) was higher in the countryside than in New Orleans. The rate for the white citizens of rural Gilmer and Rabun Counties in northern Georgia was much higher than the rate in most cities: 2.4 per 100,000 adults. The only certainty is that lovers and romantic rivals were at risk as never before. As the waggish editor of the *Holmes County Farmer* put it, "Murdering for love is getting to be very popular. . . . Perhaps 'tis better to be loved and shot than never to be loved at all."[60]

The romance murders in the counties studied intensively were similar in a number of ways. Like stealth murders, most murders of lovers were committed by respectable, well-educated men. All but two of the murderers in the counties studied intensively in New England, the Midwest, and the South were native-born Protestants of English, Scots, or African descent, and only one had a history of violent behavior. Their victims trusted them, and the women who had rejected them as suitors had tried to remain friends.

W. Seymour Keener, a young gentleman from Rabun County, Georgia, killed his first cousin when she rejected him and then shot her sister for having encouraged her to see other suitors. George Stranahan, a "steady young man" who worked as a tailor for his father in Waterbury, Vermont, was in love with Miss Damon, who was a "well connected" woman of "good reputation." She decided in 1878 that George was not the man for her, and she began to receive other men. Stranahan shot her and then turned the gun on himself. Jim McDonald, a Chicagoan, carefully paid all his debts before killing himself and his lover.[61]

Unlike marital murderers, these men were generally on good terms with the women they killed. Albert McLean, a shoemaker in Henniker, New Hampshire, was a temperate, well-educated young man with an excellent reputation. He and Nettie Belle Douglass got engaged, but since Douglass was only seventeen and McLean had yet to accumulate enough property to support a family, Douglass' parents convinced her to break off the engagement. They did not discourage McLean's visits, however, and assented when McLean asked to take their daughter on a carriage ride. McLean and Douglass spent the day "talking and laughing" and took turns driving his rented rig. But at the end of the day Douglass apparently refused to renew their engagement. McLean pulled a pistol from his coat and shot her three times in the head. Ed Decourcey, a black Chicagoan who worked as a night watchman, was a welcome visitor in Dora Perkins' home. He called on her one afternoon, accompanied by a friend, Thomas Buckner. The three were having a cordial visit until Decourcey asked Perkins, "Whom do you love?" When she said "Tom," Decourcey pulled a revolver from his pocket and shot her.[62]

Why young men began to commit such murders is a matter of speculation, but there were at least three significant developments in American society that were connected with the increase in romance murders. The first was the Romantic movement, which saturated the culture in the 1830s and 1840s and engendered a number of potentially dangerous ideas, especially the notions that people could find fulfillment only through love and that love was as close as human beings would get to the divine. The second development was a change in the economy that left many men discouraged about their prospects and shifted the balance of power in courtship toward young women. The third was the widespread availability of handguns.

In the previous century most Americans had viewed romantic ideals, as they pertained to love, with a degree of skepticism, but in the 1830s and 1840s young people began to invest more energy in the pursuit of romantic fulfillment. Practical considerations gave way to emotional ones in courtship and marriage. The proportion of articles in American magazines that promoted love and happiness as the most important considerations in marriage rose after 1825 from 58 percent to 89 percent, and the proportion that judged wealth, status, or other concerns most important fell from 42 percent to 11 percent.[63]

Romanticism glorified the self and self-expression and celebrated the divine nature of women and men. For many young Protestants, romantic love displaced religion: it gave meaning and purpose to their lives in much the same way that the search for a personal relationship with God did. Steeped in the culture of individualism and dissent, they were more open than Catholics to a movement that glorified the expression of individual personality. Many of them had also begun to believe that death would bring annihilation, not an afterlife in which they would be judged, and that belief may have combined with Romantic ideals to make depressed lovers more dangerous. The idea that everything perishes led many latter-day romantics to hold on to painful memories because they were the only source of meaning in a world that God had abandoned. When their pain became too much to bear, suicidal violence began to seem attractive, because it promised both to end their suffering and to prevent their lovers from ever loving someone else.[64]

At its best, romantic love encouraged compassion, greater intimacy between men and women, more open expressions of love and affection, and greater emotional investment in male-female relationships. Lovers declared that they had completed themselves by mingling their identities and becoming one in heart and mind. Eliza Pattee told her lover, William Onion, that she had found a spiritual refuge in him. "My frail spirit hails with sweet delight every glimpse of hope that promises succor and protection, or in other words, sympathy." But Romantic ideals also encouraged men and women to believe that their happiness depended entirely on the love of one specific person, and that if that person did not return their love, their lives would be meaningless.[65]

The proportion of American magazine articles on romance that embraced the idea that lovers were soul mates, uniquely suited for each other, rose from 18 percent to 33 percent after 1825, and the proportion claiming that love could triumph over any obstacle that class, status, or other differences put in its way rose from 10 percent to 22 percent. In a society that embraced such unrealistic ideas, failure could give rise to dangerous emotions: possessiveness, jealousy, anger, depression, despondency. A well-adjusted young man could still say, "I cannot *cannot* be happy without you" to the woman he loved and not mean it as a threat. But some men took romantic ideas to heart and concluded that if they could not be united with the women they loved in life, "In one another's substance finding food, / Like flames too pure and light and unimbued / To nourish their bright lives with baser prey," they should be united in "one annihilation."[66]

The idealism generated by the Romantic movement even led some men to believe that race might not be an obstacle to true love. Most of them were soon disabused of that notion. Charles Tash was a well-to-do, well-educated young black man of "respectable character," the adopted son of a prominent white family in Exeter, New Hampshire. He courted Sarah Moore for two years, until Moore's parents, who liked Tash but did not consider him son-in-law material, persuaded her in 1831 to tell him that they could only be friends. Tash was beside himself. He threatened twice to kill himself, but Sarah talked him out of it. Instead he signed on as a steward on a ship bound for the South Seas. Three days before he was to set sail, Tash stopped by the Moores' house. They received him cordially, but Sarah gave him no hope. He lingered until eleven, and when Sarah started up the stairs for bed, he pulled out a pistol and shot her, then drew another pistol and shot himself. Miraculously, both he and Moore survived.[67]

Interracial romance homicides were surprisingly common, given the societal strictures against such relationships. Henry Bloomberg of Philadelphia, a white man, had been seeing Emma Otis, a black woman, for some time before he shot her at a friend's house. James Turner, a black Philadelphian, flew into a rage when his lover, a white woman, turned her affections toward other men. He beat her to death. Bud Pullen of Wilkes County, Georgia, a white man, came into a kitchen where his lover, a black woman named Evaline Chenault, was preparing supper for a white family, and shot her in the head. Few of these killings stirred the interest that the Tash-Moore shooting did, so newspapers do not tell us why these women were killed, but the complex feelings that interracial relationships engendered—including a heightened sensitivity to slights and a willingness to ascribe romantic disappointment to racial prejudice—must have made such affairs more volatile than intraracial ones.[68]

Economic frustration may also have played a part in driving men to kill their lovers, no matter what their race. In an era when a man's self-esteem, along with his chances in the marriage market, depended heavily on becoming an independent proprietor or professional, few men who committed romance homicides were self-employed. Such men, however good their reputations, were at a disadvantage when it came to attracting the kind of women they wanted to marry, and they probably knew it. The problem was most severe, of course, for free black men, who suffered terrible economic discrimination, but it affected the majority of homicidal suitors, who seemed to believe that they would have only one opportunity to marry a respectable woman. Most homicidal suitors were also mobile young men, living far from home, so they did not have friends or family to help them find suitable mates or to recover from disappointments.[69] Their desperation, and their anger at rivals who frustrated their plans, was intense.

Meanwhile young women were becoming better educated, and economic change brought them a host of new opportunities in education, textile manufacturing, the clothing trades, and other industries that made them more independent economically. As a result, by the 1830s and 1840s young women appear to have been more selective when it came to entertaining suitors. In fact many young women did not want to marry, fearing the loss of their independence, and as many as a fifth never did—a dramatic increase from the eighteenth century, when all but 2 percent of women married at least once.[70] Their willingness to reject young men who did not meet their expectations, together with the frustration that many young men felt, increased the likelihood of deadly conflict.

Clearly, many of the men who killed or tried to kill their sweethearts were despondent about the turn their lives had taken, and when the women they loved rejected them, they were utterly unable to cope. In their despair they lashed out at everyone, including themselves. William Jewett was well educated, but his first marriage had failed, and he had not done well in his career. He took a job as a traveling salesman and fell instantly in love with Ellen Wood, "a beautiful, promising, Christian young woman" who lived with her parents on a farm in Hudson, New Hampshire. He courted her for several months in 1873, until her parents learned about his divorce and told him that he was no longer welcome at their home. He killed Ellen, tried to kill her father, and killed himself.[71]

Generally speaking, suitors who were not well educated had more in common with estranged husbands who killed their wives than with other romance murderers. They usually had a sense that they were entitled to the women they wanted, and when they were rejected they became enraged. Many of them had been deserted by their first wives, and when they proposed and were turned down it was both an affront and a confirmation that they were complete failures. Rejection evoked a murderous combination of rage, humiliation, and hopelessness. Henry Hatch, a former saloonkeeper, lived in the same boardinghouse as Amelia Batchelder, a textile operative whose estranged husband lived in Boston. Hatch begged her to forget her husband and marry him, but she had no feelings for him and no interest in committing bigamy. He threatened her in front of witnesses several times, then shot her and himself. Harrison Nutting of Mason, New Hampshire, a farmer whose wife had left him a few years before, flew into a rage when his housekeeper, Mary Kezar, refused to marry him. He, too, committed suicide after shooting the woman he loved.[72]

In fact the majority of these men killed themselves. Two-thirds of romance murderers and attempted murderers in northern New England and the Midwest committed or attempted suicide after attacking their lovers. Murder-suicides were common elsewhere as well.[73] Yet rejected suitors were even more likely to commit suicide without killing their lovers first. The number of disappointed lovers who killed themselves in the second half of the nineteenth century was considerable, and in all likelihood the number reported was merely the tip of the iceberg.

It is possible that some of these romance murders might never have occurred had it not been for the sudden availability of mass-produced handguns. Romantic disappointment had always stirred strong emotions, but no generation before the 1830s and 1840s had had ready access to these weapons, and no other kind of murder was committed as exclusively with handguns. If the man was middle-class and if there was any degree of premeditation involved—that is, if the murderer had time to choose a weapon and was already thinking about killing his lover before he met with her—the weapon used was always a handgun. A handgun enabled a young man to take his lover by surprise and to kill her quickly and almost painlessly without disfiguring her or creating too much of a mess. He could then kill himself immediately afterward. And the handgun was a decorous weapon for a man who had never slaughtered farm animals or fought in city streets. It did not require rough work, as a knife or club did. There was no grunting or groaning, no cracking of bone or tearing of flesh, and it minimized the chance that there would be a struggle. Two-thirds of the twenty deadly assaults in northern New England and the Midwest were committed with handguns, as were half the murders of lovers in Philadelphia and three-fifths in San Francisco.[74]

The availability of guns, still the weapon of choice today in romance homicides, may have increased the number of such killings in the United States, but the importance of weapons should not be exaggerated. It appears that murders and attempted murders of lovers were also on the rise in the late nineteenth century in England, where few assaults were committed with handguns. Thomas Horton of County Kent did try to shoot his fiancée before killing himself, and he had bought two revolvers to do so; and Annette Myers, a lady's maid in

London, shot the guardsman who had jilted her; but most homicidal suitors in England used clubs or knives.[75] Handguns undoubtedly facilitated romance homicides, but they were not the ultimate cause of the increase in such murders.

Most of the men who murdered romantic rivals were similar to men who murdered the women they loved. Like murderers of lovers, they were respected, hardworking men who brooded for months before killing. They were also despondent about losing the women who made their lives worth living and convinced that they could never love anyone else. Alphonse Chaquette of Ferrisburgh, Vermont, was a forty-year-old farm laborer, a hard worker with a reputation for sobriety. He had great plans. He had saved enough to purchase a farm, and he had fallen in love with young Minnie Pignon and was ready to marry her and start a family. Minnie, however, was not interested in him; he was far too old. He pleaded with her to marry him, saying that if she refused him he would "lose his soul." He had imbibed enough of the prevailing culture to believe that claim wholeheartedly, but he was also a Catholic, so he enlisted the help of a priest to try to persuade her. But Minnie married a man closer to her own age, and a year later Alphonse walked to their house and shot her husband dead. James Caswell's case was similar to Chaquette's. Caswell had worked for twenty-two years on a farm owned by Willard Cutler in East Montpelier, Vermont. He loved Cutler's daughter, Laura, and she agreed to marry him; but after Cutler died, Laura fell in love with a younger man, George Gould, and married him instead. The Goulds kept Caswell on at the farm, but Caswell could not stand to see them together, and one morning he shot Gould. He had planned to kill Laura and himself as well, but he could not bring himself to shoot her. Impressed by this display of affection, she succumbed to the notion that he might indeed be her one and only, and she married him while he was in jail awaiting trial. However, she came to her senses and hastily filed for divorce when the court sentenced him to life in prison.[76]

Some men killed romantic rivals for the same reasons they would have killed a man in an argument or a property dispute: they did not want to lose a competition with another man. Although it is not possible to gauge the depth of love in a killer's feelings in any precise way, these appeared to be murders that had less to do with love than with the desire to dominate (or not be dominated by) other males. A few men attacked simply because other men showed interest in the women they were interested in. In effect, they considered the other men to be claim jumpers. A Polish farm laborer got into a fight in Hardwick, Vermont, over a girl in a saloon, for example, and broke another man's back. Sometimes race or ethnicity played a part in determining whether a man felt he had a prior right to a particular woman. Charles Morris, a black laborer from Virginia, got angry when a woman he was interested in agreed to spend the night with a white man, Walter Wev, a staff member at the Virginia Military Institute. Morris smashed Wev's skull with a rock. And sometimes a romantic rivalry was an excuse to kill a man who was hated for other reasons. Charles Doherty was a workman on a derrick gang in Waterbury, Vermont. He nursed a grudge against his foreman, Fred Murphy, in part because Murphy had accused him of stealing his newspaper and had had the effrontery to search his room for it. When Murphy appeared to be making a play for his fiancée (who worked at their boardinghouse), he shot him.[77]

Men who were brought up in the South had a habit of turning romantic defeats into affairs of honor. Sometimes they challenged successful rivals to duels, especially if they suspected them of having sullied their reputations to win the girl. Sometimes getting the competition out of the way took precedence over romance. In Gilmer County, Georgia, a railroad station agent and a farmer learned through the grapevine that they both admired the same woman. Neither of them had ever said a word to her, but both considered the prospect of a rivalry over her insupportable and decided to settle the matter with guns.[78]

In Gold Rush California, men fought desperately over the few women available, especially prostitutes, and they killed rivals (and women they considered unfaithful) without compunction.[79] Reports indicate that these murders were spurred more by competition than by thwarted love. The perpetrators focused on their hatred for their rivals and had little to say about the women they were ostensibly fighting over, and in all the cases studied to date there was not one murder that was followed by a suicide. The fact that these killings appeared only in the late 1840s and 1850s, after the homicide rate among unrelated adults soared, suggests that they may have been as much a consequence of the general rise in homicide among unrelated men as of the Romantic movement or the changes in gender relations that made romantic relationships more volatile. However, more research is needed to determine whether murders of romantic rivals stemmed from different causes in the Northeast and the Midwest than in the South and the West, where relationships among unrelated men were more antagonistic.

It is difficult to spot patterns among women who committed murder because there were so few of them. Married women sometimes felt obliged to defend hearth and home from the predations of interlopers by killing their husbands' new loves, but single women almost never attacked romantic rivals. Mildred Brewster was the only single woman in Vermont or New Hampshire to attack another woman in the nineteenth century. Hoping to clear the way for herself, she killed the fiancée of the young man she loved. She was judged legally insane. Whether it was her mental state that prompted the verdict or the singularity of her crime is unknown.[80]

Women who murdered or tried to murder their lovers were very different from the men who did so. They did not try to kill men because they were despondent about being rejected: they attacked because they were furious. They were not suicidal, nor did they care much about their reputations, which were usually not very good to begin with. They simply flew into jealous rages when their lovers strayed. Bertie Milford of Manchester, New Hampshire, was in love with a young man who trained horses at a racetrack in Boston, and she was angry when he paid too much attention to the other girls at a "house of ill-repute." (It is not clear if she worked there, because newspapers did not say anything about her occupation.) She shot him in the chest one day, "so quick," in her own words, that she "hardly knew" what she had done. Julia Sanders of Concord, New Hampshire, whose husband had been "away in Vermont" for a few years, was having an affair with Lyman Roberts, a blacksmith whose wife and children also lived "somewhere" in Vermont. When she learned that Roberts had visited his wife without telling her, she bought a gun and tried to kill him. She failed only because the clerk who sold her the gun suspected that she intended to shoot someone and disabled it.[81]

Prostitutes were especially likely to kill lovers or rivals. Jennie Murray of Concord, New Hampshire, a prostitute with a "chloral habit," shot her lover, Thomas Moran, a boilermaker in the railroad shops, because he paid too much attention to his wife and children. Ida Vanard, who worked in a brothel in Sacramento, took a lover, but when she learned that he was also keeping company with Mary Lee, a prostitute from New Orleans, she was "like a crazy woman." Vanard confronted Lee. Lee apologized and said they had both been drunk, but Vanard did not believe her. She slapped Lee, pulled her hair, threw her to the ground, and stabbed her.[82]

The Romantic movement may have had a "trickle-down" effect on this violence. As publicity about romance murders saturated popular culture, these women may have come to believe that killing a lover who had been untrue or a rival who had stolen a man was an acceptable course of action for a person of passionate sensibilities. They lived in places where few conventions governed courtships and where no one was overly concerned about the social consequences of violent acts. For most of them, the rungs of the social ladder had been sawn away long before, leaving them with no way to escape dead-end careers, so they may have felt they had little to lose by killing the men who insulted them. In doing so they were trying to take control over this one aspect of their lives and reaching for a little respect and perhaps a bit of renown. The lack of hope and satisfaction in their lives that made them greedy for excitement and lured them into unpromising relationships in the first place may also have made them less likely to care about the consequences of their actions.

It is possible, however, that the willingness of these women to use force may have been rooted more in the general increase in lethal violence in those neighborhoods in the second half of the nineteenth century than in changes in customs or feelings associated with romance. That increase, in turn, was rooted in economics. The decline in independent proprietorship had increased the population in poor neighborhoods, and, like the men who killed lovers or rivals, poor women with bad reputations were at a disadvantage in the marriage market. The hardening of the line between respectable and unrespectable society made it impossible for these women to entertain hopes of marrying respectable men, and the rough neighborhoods they lived in, where prostitution, common-law marriage, and extramarital sex were commonplace, made it difficult for them to keep the men they married. Like so many of their contemporaries in the mid-nineteenth-century urban underworld, these women were accustomed to violence as a means of settling disputes, and they were willing to defend their honor and their property, human or otherwise, by force.

Single women who killed their lovers made up a very small proportion of romance murders, however. The vast majority of killings involving unmarried couples were motivated not by jealous rage against a straying lover, but by anger or despair at being denied the love of a particular person. The Romantic movement of the 1830s and 1840s encouraged lovers to think of each other as the ultimate source of all happiness and fulfillment and to consider their bonds indissoluble, and if one partner put an end to the relationship, the other could be inconsolable. Combined with the growing independence of young women and the increasing difficulty young men faced in becoming independent and getting ahead, it changed the way young people thought about relationships and responded to rejection in ways that persist to this day.

Homicide of Adult Relatives

Because homicides of adult relatives are rare, it is difficult to chart their course, but it appears that, unlike the rates for marital and romance murders, the rate for adult relatives continued to increase gradually in the North during the nineteenth century, following a brief decline after the Revolution (Figure 6.2). The data are not as complete or consistent for the South and Southwest, but the evidence suggests that murders of adult relatives became more common in the United States as a whole, despite variations from place to place. By the late nineteenth century, the homicide rate for adult relatives was 0.3 to 0.6 per 100,000 adults per year in the rural North, 0.4 to 1.8 per 100,000 in the rural South, 0.8 per 100,000 in rural California, and 0.6 to 1 per 100,000 in northern, southern, and southwestern cities.[83]

Murders of blood relations, steprelations, and in-laws appear to have increased predominantly among native-born Protestants. In northern New England and the rural Midwest, German, Irish, and French Canadian immigrants and their descendants committed only an eighth of known murders of adult relatives. Like English immigrants to New England and the Chesapeake in the seventeenth century, they had fewer relatives in the New World, and they valued the support of those they had. That was not the case for a growing minority of native-born Protestants, who saw some of their adult relatives as a burden rather than a resource, as antagonists rather than allies. Those who had trouble getting ahead or who found themselves isolated among the drinking poor may also have suffered greater humiliation than immigrants or Catholics, because they faced higher expectations and were more likely to be stigmatized by their relatives for drinking.[84]

In some instances it was obvious that the immediate causes of family murders were financial. As opportunities for self-employment declined, as the cost of owning and operating a shop or farm rose, and as economic ambitions increased, a quarter of northern New Englanders and midwesterners who murdered relatives killed wealthier relatives for their money.[85] Jealousy, resentment, and alienation of affection

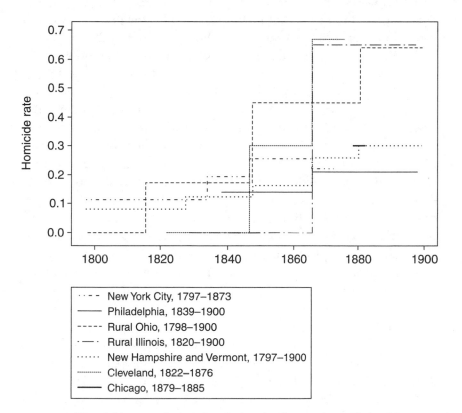

Figure 6.2 Homicide rates for adult relatives in the northern United States, 1797–1900 (per 100,000 adults per year).

contributed to these murders, but they were not crimes committed in the heat of passion. They were carefully planned and executed stealth murders whose object was to remove impediments to inheritance, and, like murders of unrelated adults, they reflected people's growing dissatisfaction with their position in life.

Letitia Blaisdell of New Boston, New Hampshire, was the most ruthless of all these killers. As the adopted daughter of a wealthy family, she had to put a good number of people out of the way before she could inherit any money. She admitted that her adoptive mother, Sarah Blaisdell, had taken loving care of her, but when she turned eighteen, she was pushed gently out the door to make her own way in the world. She worked for six years in textile mills across New England and then, with Sarah's blessing, returned home for a few months to prepare for marriage.[86]

Surrounded by wealth, Letitia grew irritated at the preference Sarah showed for her son and his wife and child, who lived with her. She rebelled by stealing increasing amounts of petty cash. Then one day she decided she wanted the whole lot. She decided to poison her adoptive relatives one at a time, hoping to make their deaths look natural. She killed Sarah in January 1849, and a month later she killed Sarah's grandson by putting morphine in tea or milk. But her impatience was her undoing. She tried to kill her adoptive brother and his wife only four days after their child died, and she botched the job. Their near-deaths alerted the neighbors, and Letitia was arrested and convicted.

In contrast, the majority of murders in which family members killed one another over small amounts of money were committed on impulse and were rooted in long-simmering feuds. People killed abruptly and made no effort to escape. Stephen Pelham of Guildhall, Vermont, killed his brother Martin in 1851 over a harrow their father had left them. Stephen visited his brother's farm one day and claimed the harrow. Martin threatened to beat Stephen with a stick, and Stephen grabbed the stick and struck Martin on the head. Jonathan Nichols, a shoemaker from Newbury, New Hampshire, killed his brother Leonard over a clock. He went to his brother's blacksmith shop in Derry to get the clock, and a scuffle ensued. Leonard said in a fury, "Damn you, I'll fix you; you shall never go back to Newbury." Jonathan responded by throwing a bellows at his brother. The point penetrated two inches into Leonard's skull. Jonathan pulled the bellows out and said, "There, I meant to kill you."[87]

The motives behind the increase in murders of relatives were the same across the nation. Feuds over property rights and inheritance disputes were a sign that family members saw one another increasingly as economic rivals rather than allies. In 1876 in Ross County, Ohio, Philip Galligan killed his sister-in-law with a scythe as they fought for possession of hay cut from a field that both claimed to have inherited. In Jasper County, Georgia, Sidney Lovejoy shot his brother Coley in 1898 in a dispute over the boundary between their farms, and Gene Tyler shot his father over a horse trade. As with homicides among unrelated adults, there was nothing too small or too petty to provoke a murder: a payment for chopping wood, the theft of a pistol, the loss of meat from a smokehouse, the cost of liquor served at a house-raising, the theft of ten cents, crop damage from unpenned hogs, or a request to borrow a nickel.[88]

Along with financially motivated murders, which occurred in considerable numbers among family members in the second half of the nineteenth century, the late 1840s saw dozens of family murders that resulted from senseless arguments, drunken quarrels, chronic abuse, and, in an extraordinary development, sexual assaults. A Mrs. Thomas of Nottingham, New Hampshire, was apparently beaten to death by her drunken son. Thomas Pinkham's son attacked him in Farmington, New Hampshire, with a scythe at the end of an alcohol-fueled wrestling match. In 1872 Maria Van Buskirk of Sandgate, Vermont, was beaten, raped, and strangled by her son-in-law, Samuel Covey. In 1880 Sarah Dillingham of Londonderry, New Hampshire, was strangled, raped, and shot by her nephew, James Dillingham.[89]

Such homicides, much more characteristic of murders among unrelated adults, are an indication that the homicide problem in society at large was spreading to families in the second half of the nineteenth century. Over time, relationships among adult relatives were becoming more like relationships among nonrelatives. The further removed families were from the immigrant experience or the frontier experience, the more likely they were to treat kin like nonrelatives. That was certainly the case for native-born Protestants in New England, whose rates of family homicide went up and down with the nonfamily homicide rate from the late eighteenth century through the nineteenth century. Again, only the Irish and French Canadians had a modicum of protection against the rising tide of family violence, even in the 1880s and 1890s, when they began to build extensive family networks. French Canadians were overrepresented in the number of rape murders and robbery murders they committed against acquaintances or strangers, and the Irish in the number of property-dispute murders and fatal quarrels; but neither group turned that violence against relatives.

The willingness to kill adult relatives was also related to the increase in gun violence, especially among native-born Protestants after the Civil War. Before the late 1840s and 1850s, adult relatives rarely killed one another with guns, even in periods when gun homicides were common among unrelated adults. But in the second half of the nineteenth century, gun use in homicides of adult relatives increased, and by the end of the century it was as common as in homicides of nonrelatives. Guns were used in a fifth of homicides of relatives in New York City, in three-tenths of those in northern New England and the Midwest, and in two-thirds of those in California.[90]

Adult relatives were not all equally at risk in the nineteenth century. Two-thirds of those killed (including in-laws and steprelations) were fathers, mothers, or brothers, and almost all of them were killed by men.[91] Power appears to have been the most important issue: men killed people who had control over them in some way: fathers, mothers-in-law, brothers, and brothers-in-law. These were relatives who demanded deference from them in household decisions, controlled property they hoped to inherit, or interfered in their marriages. Mothers-in-law and brothers-in-law were killed far more often than fathers-in-law, because they took greater responsibility for defending the interests of their married daughters and sisters. Only half as many sons and sons-in-law were murdered as fathers, fathers-in-law, brothers, and brothers-in-law, because they had less power and posed less of a threat. Ties with other relatives may simply have been severed if they became burdensome. Because distant relationships in Anglo-American kin networks were more often a source of short-term than long-term help and of moral rather than material support, they were less volatile, more positive, and more easily dropped and taken up again. It was much harder to sever ties with close relatives or to live without their support, because so much more was at stake.

Whether murders of adult relatives increased in Great Britain or elsewhere in the nineteenth century is not yet known. The rate in England and Wales in the late nineteenth century was probably in the range of 0.1 per 100,000 per year, so it appears not to have increased there as it did in the United States. The rate in France appears to have declined as opportunities for nonfarm employment increased and tensions within farm families over the distribution of land decreased.[92] If future research bears out these preliminary estimates, it would support the hypothesis that the increase in murders of relatives in the United States was caused by the same factors that drove America's general homicide rate, not by any crisis in relationships among blood relatives or in-laws.

In Ireland the rate of those murders that were known to the police was 0.4 per 100,000 outside Dublin. Family homicides in postfamine Ireland were directly related to that nation's economic and demographic crisis. Because of population pressure, poverty, and economic underdevelopment, marriages were delayed, celibacy increased, and more and more men were landless. The result was growing tension within families, especially in the countryside, where a large number of farmers and farm laborers murdered their brothers or fathers in property or inheritance disputes.[93]

It is clear that the rise in property-dispute murders and inheritance murders in the United States was not rooted in a similar economic or demographic crisis. Most Americans, especially white northerners, never experienced the kind of poverty that many Irish experienced in the late nineteenth century. Yet the rise in the price of farm land and the decline of independent proprietorship did put a strain on many American families in the mid- and late nineteenth century. Economic anxiety and ambition were intense, and, more important, expectations among native-born Protestants were higher than in Ireland, and higher than those of Catholic immigrants. More recently arrived on American shores, Catholics may have been less likely to be frustrated by their poverty. In addition to being more dependent on the kin they had in America, they were therefore probably less likely to kill over property issues because they had not yet experienced the economic anxiety or reversals of fortune that some Protestants had.

Adult-relative murders, most of which arose out of the same kinds of small quarrels and property disputes that were causing more homicides among unrelated Americans after the 1830s and 1840s, were thus more likely than marital or romance murders to have been provoked by at least one of the factors that correlate with homicides among unrelated adults. Letitia Blaisdell was an extreme example of someone who was dissatisfied with her position in life and turned to murder because she desperately wanted to be as rich as her relatives were. But many native-born Protestants appeared to feel increasing levels of dissatisfaction with their economic progress, and their frustrated expectations were beginning to produce higher homicide rates not only in the society at large, but within their own families.

CHAPTER 7

"All Is Confusion, Excitement and Distrust"

America Becomes a Homicidal Nation

Between the mid-nineteenth and early twentieth centuries homicide rates fell in nearly every Western nation. Wherever stable, legitimate governments took shape and people developed a strong sense of patriotism and national identity, homicide rates tumbled to historically low levels. The homicide rate in England and Wales fell twice during this period, after 1867 and 1884. Those drops correlate perfectly with two major reforms that changed the nature of the British political system. The 1867 Reform Act gave the vote to all men who were heads of households in incorporated cities and towns, adding just under a million voters to the rolls. The 1884 act enfranchised all male household heads in the countryside, adding six million voters. The homicide rate fell abruptly after each act was passed and then decreased gradually to an astonishing 1 per 100,000 adults per year on the eve of World War I (Figure 5.11).[1] Giving poor and middle-class Britons the vote reduced every kind of murder among unrelated adults, from rape and robbery murders to killings in tavern brawls and in employer-employee disputes.

Homicide rates continued to fall in Canada's core provinces after Canadians won the right to self-government and began to develop strong two-party systems and a clearer sense of identity and nationality. Homicide rates were extremely low in the Confederation provinces that achieved independence from Britain in 1867—Nova Scotia, New

Brunswick, Quebec, and Ontario—despite their ethnic and religious divisions. By the 1880s the homicide indictment rate was less than 1 per 100,000 adults per year (Figure 5.10). But in the 1850s and early 1860s the western frontier of Canada was as violent as the northwestern frontier of the United States. Among white settlers the homicide rate was at least 25 per 100,000 adults per year in British Columbia, and it was much higher among Native Americans. Homicide rates were probably also high in Newfoundland, where conflict persisted between English Protestants and Irish Catholics; and in Manitoba, where mixed-blood Métis twice rebelled against the central government to defend their land against encroachment by English and Scots-Irish settlers. Because of the homicide rates in its outlying provinces, Canada as a whole had a higher homicide rate in the late 1920s than England and Wales, but its rate was still low by historic standards: 2.3 per 100,000 adults per year.[2]

National unification and the emergence of a strong central government sent the homicide rate plummeting in Italy. The data from Germany are far from complete, but the rate at which Germans were tried for homicide also fell rapidly after national unification, dropping by a third between the early 1880s and the beginning of World War I. Only France saw its homicide rate rise slightly in the late nineteenth and early twentieth centuries. The French rate was not very high—perhaps a little more than 2 per 100,000 adults per year, or about the same as Canada's—but it was 50 percent higher under the Third Republic than it had been under the Second Empire of Louis Napoleon. Both regimes had representative assemblies and universal suffrage for men, but Louis Napoleon's constitutional monarchy was more widely popular and would probably have survived had it not suffered a disastrous defeat in the Franco-Prussian War. Conservative and moderate republicans governed well after 1870, but they governed from a narrow middle ground, and only by default, because the monarchist majority could not agree on whether to turn to a Bourbon, an Orleans, or a Bonaparte or to choose a strong man like former general and Minister of War Georges Boulanger. The right consolidated its power over the army and the Catholic Church, while the left turned to radical republicanism, socialism, and anarchism, and both the right and left threatened to overthrow the Republic. Politics became so heated that assassinations and duels among public men reappeared. This constant political turmoil, with ideologues of all stripes warring over what form the government should take, was accompanied by an elevated homicide rate among unrelated adults. By World War I, France's homicide rate was double the rates in more politically stable and unified nations such as England, Wales, Sweden, and Norway.[3]

It was at this time that homicide rates in the United States truly diverged from rates elsewhere in the Western world. In the late 1840s and 1850s they exploded across the nation, not only in the plantation South and the Southwest, where higher rates already prevailed, but also in the mountain South and the North, which had previously had extremely low rates. The least homicidal places in the Western world suddenly became the most homicidal. By the end of the Civil War, homicide rates among unrelated adults were substantially higher in the North than in Canada or western Europe, and higher still by one or two orders of magnitude in the South and Southwest. All kinds of homicide increased: robbery murders, rape murders, and killings over insults, bar tabs, card games, property disputes, and small debts. Ethnically and racially motivated murders increased, as did murders in the workplace and along the nation's roads, railroads, and waterways. Everywhere and under all sorts of circumstances, Americans, especially men, were more willing to kill friends, acquaintances, and strangers.

Immigration, economic hardship, and the conquest of areas populated by Hispanic and Native peoples contributed to the rise in homicide in the late 1840s and 1850s. Irish, French Canadian, German, and Chinese immigrants were well represented both as victims and as perpetrators wherever substantial numbers of them worked as unskilled laborers; and Hispanic and Native peoples in the trans-Mississippi West saw their homicide rates rise because of dispossession, demoralization, and victimization by white settlers. Yet homicide rates also surged among native-born Protestants, and in most areas of the country their rates rose as quickly as those of immigrants or ethnic minorities.[4] Many native-born workers, particularly African Americans, saw their standard of living decline in cities around the nation as masses of immigrants flooded into the country from Ireland, Germany, and French Canada. But native-born murder rates continued to climb even in rural areas, where there was unprecedented prosperity in the late 1840s and 1850s. Immigration, war, and poverty may have contributed to the rise in homicide, but they did not cause it. The rise was too sudden and too widespread. Besides, Canadians and Europeans faced their own problems with immigration, war, and poverty, yet their homicide rates fell.

Ultimately the increase in homicide in the United States occurred because Americans could not coalesce into a nation. As the country struggled through the wrenching and divisive changes of the mid-nineteenth century—the crises over slavery and immigration, the decline in self-employment, and the rise of industrialized cities—the patriotic faith in government that most Americans had felt so strongly after the Revolution was undermined by anger and distrust. Disillusioned by the course the nation was taking, people felt increasingly alienated from both their government and their neighbors. They were losing the sense that they were participating in a great adventure with their fellow Americans. Instead, they were competing in a cutthroat economy and a combative electoral system against millions of strangers whose interests and values were antithetical to their own.

In his inaugural address of 1853, President Franklin Pierce tried to restore faith in America's destiny. He saw "abundant grounds for hopeful confidence." The future was "boundless." It didn't look that way to most Americans. In 1846 the United States had embarked upon a war of conquest to spread slavery into Mexico, a sister republic, and it appeared that slaveholders and proslavery politicians would govern new territory. A flood of immigrants usurped what are now referred to as entry-level jobs, and after three decades of steady decline in self-employment, the promise of opportunity began to ring hollow. Banking monopolies and federal subsidies for special interests fostered economic inequality, and politicians promoted the belief that government corruption was rife (even though the government was no worse than it had ever been). Tenements were overflowing, but more mansions were being built every day. People began to wonder if democracy was a lost cause in the United States. Their fears were exacerbated by the failure of the European revolutions of 1848, which ended in class conflict, socialist uprisings, and military repression. Americans had once hoped, as a writer to the *Southern Literary Messenger* said, that "the rotten and antiquated foundations of every despotic and exclusive institution of the Old World" would "crumble into ruin." Instead, the United States appeared to be recreating old Europe at its worst.[5]

Politics polarized along ethnic, regional, religious, class, and racial lines, and the national polity disintegrated as people argued about whether immigrants, free blacks, Catholics, Hispanics, Asians, and Native Americans should become full citizens and whether slavery would be allowed in the western territories. The rise in homicide coincided with a nationwide decline in patriotism (especially in identification with national political symbols) and with a loss of faith in government and in moderate, mainstream political parties. The proportion of new counties named after national heroes fell from a high of 45 percent in the 1820s and 1830s to only 17 percent in the 1850s and 1860s (Figure 2.1). The Democrats failed as a national party and the Whigs failed altogether, leaving the two-party system in ruins. Parties that were more aggressive ideologically took their place. The leaders of these parties questioned the legitimacy of national institutions and challenged other Americans' morality, patriotism, and right to citizenship. They used extreme rhetoric to generate partisan enthusiasm, and they encouraged righteous and retributive violence, especially in defense of property or rights.[6]

Aggression and vitriolic language invaded personal as well as political relationships and turned everyday encounters over debts or minor offenses like trespassing into deadly ones. More people chose to protect their rights or interests by force, either because they felt that they could no longer count on the government to protect them or because they despised the government so much that they would not seek justice from it. Some even refused to recognize legal decisions that went against them because the government was no longer "their government." And as more Americans became frustrated by their inability to achieve economic independence or anxious about preserving it, the heightened sensitivity about social status and respect that had characterized male behavior in the plantation South and the Southwest spread to other areas of the country. People responded violently not only to threats to their property or person but also to disrespect. They killed over a word, a gesture, a glance. In every region, the majority of murders were everyday homicides—sexual assault murders, robbery murders, property dispute murders, and so on—with no obvious connection to politics. But across the nation, the areas with the greatest political strife had the highest homicide rates.

Homicide in the North

Homicide rates among unrelated adults in the northern United States followed the arc of the nation's political history. They rose in the late 1840s and 1850s, during the Mexican War and the Kansas crisis, remained high through the Civil War, and declined in most places in the late 1860s and 1870s as the nation emerged from chaos and the two-party system revived. Across the northern United States, homicide rates that had ranged in the 1830s and early 1840s from a low of 1 per 100,000 adults per year in northern New England to a high of 6 per 100,000 in New York City, rose to between 2 and 33 per 100,000 in the northern countryside and to between 10 and 20 per 100,000 in northern cities (Figures 4.2 and 5.1–5.3).[7] As with most previous surges in homicide, the increase affected everyone: blacks and whites, the native-born and immigrants, Protestants and Catholics, the rich and the poor. Murders of unrelated adults remained the near-exclusive province of men, but the rate at which women murdered and were murdered by unrelated adults also rose. Victimization and perpetration rates doubled or more than doubled for everyone.

Thousands of homicides that appeared to arise out of class, ethnic, religious, racial, or partisan hostility had an obvious political dimension. Like the killings of blacks by Irish rioters in New York, for example, or of German immigrants by nativists in Chicago, they were caused by conflicts over slavery and immigration and by the fear that the decline in self-employment generated. But the great majority of homicides seemed to have nothing to do with politics. They were the result of tavern brawls, fights over property, and other everyday disputes. Ultimately, however, they stemmed from the same emotions that political homicides did—anger about the government's failure to protect their interests, a decline in fellow feeling, and frustration over the declining opportunities for self-employment that undermined the legitimacy of the North's social hierarchy.

The decline in self-employment was critical. The key to achieving status in the United States was economic independence, but the proportion of adult men in the North who were self-employed fell steadily from around three-fifths in 1815 to two-fifths by 1860 and a third in 1880. By the mid-nineteenth century many Americans faced the prospect of working their entire lives as "wage slaves." In time, the creation of high-paying jobs for skilled and semiskilled workers on railroads and in factories would make wage work more attractive, and Americans would come to consider it honorable for a man to spend his life working for a corporation. That was not yet the case in the mid-nineteenth century. Many Americans were demoralized by their failure to achieve self-employment and despondent about their children's chances of achieving it. It was all well and good for Abraham Lincoln to say that "there is no such thing as a freeman being fatally fixed for life, in the condition of a hired laborer," and that if a man spent his life working for others it was "not the fault of the system, but because of either a dependent nature which prefers it, or improvidence, folly, or singular misfortune." What had been true in the 1820s was no longer true in the 1850s and 1860s. Critics noted that men who thought like Lincoln lived in frame houses, not log cabins. Labor reformer Ira Stewart wondered if Lincoln wanted to be admired because he had once worked with his hands, or because he no longer had to. The Whigs' vision of boundless opportunity was compelling to many poor and middle-income men, but it did not lessen their anger and anxiety about the difficulty of getting ahead.[8]

Although real wages rose, even for the poor, working people experienced their loss of economic independence as a loss of dignity, and they blamed the rich for trampling on their fellow citizens to get ahead. Strikes and other labor conflicts proliferated in coal mining and railroading as workers realized that they would have to fight to improve their wages and working conditions or live like slaves on what their employers were willing to give them.

Mass violence in coal mining and railroading took nearly 200 lives in the 1860s and 1870s, and as workers in small firms grew increasingly frustrated over their wages, working conditions, and prospects, an increasing number of them murdered their employers in disputes over wages, firings, and arrests for disturbances in the workplace. Workers had become more jealous of their rights, and employers were less respectful of people who worked for wages. The relationships between employers and employees were most volatile when they lived together, as they did on ships and on most farms. George Wilson, a sailor on the schooner *Eudora Imogene,* killed both the captain and the first mate after the captain denied him shore leave in New York City. Charles Stockley, a hired hand in Genesee County, New York, killed his employer, John Walker, because Walker did not think Stockley was good enough to court his daughter.[9]

The decline in self-employment would not have caused a general homicide problem in the northern United States, however, were it not for two events that shattered the American polity: the sudden rise in immigration from Europe and the controversy over slavery. Three million immigrants entered the United States in the decade after 1845. More than three-fourths settled in the North. Many of the new immigrants were desperately poor refugees from the potato famine of 1845–1850. Before the famine, 85 percent of all immigrants had worked as farmers, professionals, or skilled laborers. Afterward more than half worked as unskilled or semiskilled laborers.[10]

The American economy was robust in these years, but it could not absorb the vast number of poor immigrants who arrived in the late 1840s and early 1850s. In cities, unemployment rose and real wages fell for a time for all workers, including the native-born. Anti-immigrant feeling ran high among native-born workers in cities. They competed directly against the immigrants for jobs, housing, and political power. Labor leaders promised to defend "our mechanics and working men and women, who had been sorely pressed by the unfair competition and combinations of pauper Europeans." Nativist politicians blamed the immigrants for all of society's ills: rising crime rates, alcoholism, disease-ridden slums, and political corruption. Immigrants were "a noisy, drinking and brawling rabble." They "bring the grog shops like frogs of Egypt upon us." Nativists demanded that the government put a stop to immigration or at least curb the political power of immigrants by requiring them to spend twenty-one years in the United States before they could vote. "Have we not a right to protect ourselves against the ravenous dregs of anarchy and crime, the tainted swarms of pauperism and vice Europe shakes on our shores from her diseased robes?"[11]

Anti-Catholic feeling was even more intense. Before the mid-1840s, three-fourths of all immigrants had been Protestants; after 1845 two-thirds were Catholics from Ireland, Germany, and French Canada. Militant Protestants believed that the pope had sent the immigrants to the United States to subvert American democracy and establish a Catholic theocracy. They were afraid that the Catholic Church, "the child of Satan," was trying to extinguish liberty by "riveting Italian chains" upon the American people. The Catholic clergy lent credence to such fears by opposing the use of the Protestant Bible in public schools, demanding that tax dollars be set aside to support parochial schools, and requiring that all church property in the hands of lay trustees be handed over to Rome. They also spoke about their hopes of making the United States a Catholic nation. In 1850 Archbishop John Hughes told the congregation of St. Patrick's Cathedral in New York City that "everybody should know that we have for our mission to convert the world—including the inhabitants of the United States—the people of the cities, and the people of the country, the officers of the navy and the marines, commanders of the army, the Legislatures, the Senate, the Cabinet, the President, and all!"[12]

Such talk led to a terror campaign against Catholics that peaked in the late 1840s and 1850s. Militant Protestants mobbed Catholic clergymen, desecrated and destroyed Catholic churches, assaulted Catholic voters, and ran riot through neighborhoods populated by German and Irish immigrants. Deadly riots broke out against Irish immigrants in Brooklyn and Philadelphia, against German immigrants in Chicago and Hoboken, New Jersey, and between German Protestants and Irish Catholics in Cincinnati. In the New York City Orange Riots of 1870 and 1871, street fighting between Irish Protestants and Catholics and an assault by the militia on Catholic demonstrators took seventy lives.[13]

Most interethnic homicides were the result of gang fights, turf battles, or personal quarrels in which ethnicity pushed the aggressor over the edge. An Irish immigrant killed an English immigrant in New York City in 1848 simply because he was an Englishman, and he told an English bystander that he would kill him too if he interfered. In 1853 a deadly brawl broke out in the factory town of Rollinsford, New Hampshire, when native-born boys attacked Irish boys who lived in shanties behind the woolen mills. In 1863 Schyler Courier, a native-born, middle-aged cooper in Chillicothe, Ohio, got angry when teenaged German boys pelted him with snowballs. He opened fire with his shotgun, killing Jacob Shears. In 1861 R. T. McHaney, a Scots-Irish farmer in Williamson County, Illinois, learned that an Irishman passing by had insulted his wife, so he got his gun, tracked the man down, and shot him dead.[14]

The anxiety that many people felt about their prospects exacerbated the nativist hostility of the late 1840s and 1850s. Native-born northerners who were disreputable or down on their luck were particularly unwilling to countenance affronts from immigrants. Small indignities that might have been tolerated from other native-born Protestants— being hit by snowballs or having a passerby whistle at one's wife— became unendurable outrages when they were committed by immigrants.

The controversy over immigration also affected homicide rates indirectly, because it damaged mainstream political parties and left everyone feeling victimized. When nativists entered politics on the grassroots level in 1853–1855, they did well, winning state and local races throughout the Northeast. They did poorly to the west of Ohio and Michigan, where immigrants were more welcome and the status of slavery in the western territories was more important to people worried about their economic futures; but they attracted enough support in the nation as a whole to undermine fellow feeling and to contribute to the collapse of the two-party system.

Even more instrumental than immigration and the nativist campaign against it in undermining political stability, patriotic feeling, and faith in government was the conflict over slavery and race precipitated by the Mexican War, or "Mr. Polk's War," as its opponents called it. As it became clear that the purpose of the war was to seize territory and create new slave states, opposition intensified, particularly in the North. "Conscience" Whigs like John Quincy Adams, who were antislavery by conviction, accused Polk and his southern allies of trying to roll back "the happy progress" of Mexico, a sister republic that had abolished slavery, and "afflict her with what has been everywhere the shame of the white man, and the curse of both black and white." Moderate Whigs and Democrats had no quarrel with slavery where it existed, nor did they question the morality of the war, but they believed that the presence of slavery and blacks degraded white labor, and they feared for the future of free workers if newly acquired territories were opened to slavery. David Wilmot, a representative from Pennsylvania, asked in his famous "proviso" of 1846 that slavery and blacks be kept out of any territories acquired by the United States as a result of the war with

Mexico. "The negro race already occupy enough of this fair continent. . . . I would preserve for free white labor a fair country . . . where the sons of toil, of my own race and own color, can live without the disgrace which association with negro slavery brings upon free labor." Regardless of their feelings about blacks, Free Soilers saw the West as "a new country for poor folks," where those who lacked the money to succeed in the East could prosper. The proslavery powers would deny them that opportunity. As Abraham Lincoln said, they would "cancel and tear to pieces even the white man's charter of freedom" in their "greedy chase to make profit of the negro."[15]

Wilmot's proviso was defeated in Congress with the help of northern expansionists, but it became increasingly apparent that a rift had opened between northerners and southerners and among northerners themselves. Each side considered the other to have betrayed American ideals. Centrists like Stephen Douglas and Lewis Cass cobbled together the so-called Compromise of 1850, which admitted California as a free state and gave southerners the right to take slaves into the Utah and New Mexico territories. Southerners also got a tough new fugitive slave law and the de facto repeal of the Missouri Compromise, which quietly opened the door to slavery in Kansas, Nebraska, and other northern territories. But success for Douglas and Cass came at a price. Opening the western territories to slavery outraged most northerners, failed to placate southerners, and shattered the American polity. From that time forward, neither side would accept the legitimacy of a government run by the other, a law passed by the other, or a legal decision handed down by the other. As Ralph Waldo Emerson had predicted at the beginning of the Mexican War, "the United States will conquer Mexico, but it will be as the man swallows the arsenic, which brings him down in turn. Mexico will poison us."[16]

The stage was set for a strong surge in homicides. Naturally, the connection between the political rift and the homicide rate was most obvious where murders involving race and slavery were concerned. All sides in the slavery controversy were furious with the government, and among militants all feelings of kinship with and empathy for Americans who were on the wrong side of the issue evaporated. In the North, the controversy began to claim lives as soon as the Fugitive Slave Law was enacted. Frederick Douglass, a fugitive himself, said in the fall of 1850 that "the only way to make the Fugitive Slave Law a dead letter is to make half a dozen or more dead kidnappers," and abolitionists repeatedly showed their willingness to do just that. Slaveowners and law-enforcement officers were murdered in Pennsylvania and Massachusetts for trying to return fugitives to slavery, and thieves were lynched in the Midwest for kidnapping and selling free blacks into slavery. Most efforts to defend fugitive slaves or free blacks ended without loss of life, but there were enough deaths to exacerbate hostile feelings on both sides of the issue.[17]

The North also saw violence spawned by the campaign for equal rights for African Americans. Antiblack violence was not as intense in the late 1840s or 1850s as it would become in the 1860s and early 1870s, after the Union committed itself to ending slavery and African American men won the right to vote. But militant white supremacists had already gained strength across the nation after the Mexican War, and they used violence to keep blacks in their place. Black workers were mobbed wherever they competed against whites for jobs, especially in northern cities. In New York City in 1847 a black laborer and a black tradesman were killed on their way to work by small bands of whites who wanted their jobs, and in 1858 a group of white paupers in Philadelphia killed a black man because he had a job and they were on relief. Black felony suspects were lynched, and black men who married white women were risking their lives. The California House tavern in Moyamensing, Pennsylvania, was owned by a black man whose wife was white. In 1849 the tavern was attacked and burned, and four people died. Such incidents were almost invariably the work of militant Democrats, for whom they were an integral part of the campaign for slavery and white supremacy. The campaign was tremendously successful in the late 1840s and 1850s. Blacks lost many of the skilled and service jobs they had held to whites. Their health declined, and their life expectancies reached new lows.[18]

Race also played a role in the increase in homicides of blacks by white acquaintances. Some whites murdered blacks for failing to acknowledge their superior status as white men. Captain Diehl of Cleveland, Ohio, got into an argument with an elderly black woman, took offense at her tone, and shot her dead. John Thorner, a German immigrant who worked as a laborer for the wealthiest farmer in Ross County, Ohio, took a dislike to the farmer's trusted African American servant, James Cotton, and during a dispute over payment for goods he had sold Cotton he grabbed a shotgun and killed him.[19]

Racial hostility led to an increase in all kinds of murders of blacks by whites. For the first time since the early eighteenth century, black homicide rates in the North pushed past those of whites, solely because of white violence against blacks. Blacks killed blacks at lower rates than whites killed whites, but whites murdered blacks at roughly twice the rate at which blacks murdered one another in rural areas and at five times that rate in cities.[20]

Occasionally blacks responded in kind to white violence and abuse, further escalating the murder rate. Henry Raymond, a Philadelphian, threw a white man to the ground and cracked his skull when the man tried to interfere in a black political demonstration. Allen Nokes, another Philadelphian, stabbed a white man who had insulted him with racial epithets. In rural areas, such murders ensured that as many whites were killed by blacks as blacks were killed by whites. But in cities, where the surge in interracial homicide was one-sided and politically driven, twice as many blacks were killed in interracial confrontations as whites, even though defensive murders of whites by blacks became more common.[21]

The worst violence of the 1850s over slavery and race occurred in "Bleeding" Kansas, where scores lost their lives in the battle to determine whether the territory would be slave or free. It was a sign of how polarized the nation had become that elected officials were calling upon Americans to murder each other. Among them was Senator David Atcheson of Missouri, who told southerners to "mark every scoundrel among you that is the least tainted with free-soilism, or abolitionism, and exterminate him." He promised to send enough Missourians into Kansas "to kill every God-damned abolitionist in the Territory." Militant northerners responded in kind. The New England Emigrant Aid Company, an abolitionist organization, armed hundreds of antislavery settlers and shipped them off to Kansas. Eli Thayer, who had organized the company and secured its charter from the Massachusetts legislature, thought it "well for the Emigrant to be furnished with his Bible and his rifle; and if he were not protected in his rights according to the principles of the first, let him rely upon the execution of the latter." Antislavery settlers were determined to "fight fire with fire," as settler John Brown put it, and they did. At least 200 people died in the fighting.[22]

Political hatred continued to inspire murders in the North during and after the Civil War. Violence between Unionists and Confederate sympathizers was rampant, particularly in Indiana, southern and western Illinois, and southern Iowa, where many residents came from the South. In 1863 a southerner passing through Henderson County, Illinois, was waylaid by several Union army veterans after a hotelkeeper informed them that the man was carrying a lot of cash. When confronted, he claimed to be looking for a place to live, but the veterans suspected that he was buying horses for the Confederacy. They robbed him, whipped him, hanged him till he was nearly dead, cut off his hands, and left him to die. When they returned the next morning he was still alive, so they shot him. In Keokuk County, Iowa, a prominent pro-Confederate Democrat, George Cyphert Tally, was killed in the Skunk River War in 1863. Tally had gathered a band of southern sympathizers to attack a meeting of county Republicans. Tally began the shooting, but the Republicans returned fire. The Democrats withdrew to the south of town and began to organize for another assault, but Governor Kirkwood sent militia units to disperse them.[23]

Perhaps the worst of this type of violence occurred in Williamson County, Illinois, a farming area in the south-central part of the state that was predominantly Democratic and southern. In 1862 Confederate sympathizers began to murder local Republicans, Union soldiers on leave, and informants who had revealed the hiding places of the county's many deserters and draft dodgers. The killing persisted even after the war. A few Republicans responded by murdering Democrats. By the time the killings and the family feuds they spawned played themselves out in 1875, more than a score of people had been killed.[24]

Political violence triggered a similar rash of homicides in southeastern Pennsylvania, a coal-mining area that was as divided as Williamson County during the Civil War. Most mine owners, foremen, and company store operators were Republicans, but the Irish miners were Democrats and increasingly antagonistic toward the war. They opposed emancipating the slaves, because they were afraid freedmen would move north and take their jobs, and they opposed the draft, which they rightly believed would fall more heavily on poor Catholics like themselves than on the wealthier Protestants they worked for. At a

Fourth of July celebration in Carbon County in 1862, mine foreman F. W. Langdon berated Irish miners who were demonstrating against the war, and they stoned him to death. In the fall of 1863 men with blackened faces burst into the home of mine owner George Smith and shot him dead in front of his family because Smith had been entertaining soldiers who had come to Carbon County to enforce the draft. Anger over the war, the draft, and emancipation led to a wave of murders and robberies of mine owners and their associates. Such killings pushed the homicide rate in coal country to 22 per 100,000 adults per year, a third higher than the rate in New York City.[25]

Racially motivated attacks on blacks also escalated during the Civil War and Reconstruction as the Emancipation Proclamation, the Civil Rights Act, and the Fifteenth Amendment (which gave men the right to vote regardless of race) removed the legal barriers to racial equality. Militant whites blamed blacks and their white abolitionist allies for the suffering caused by the war. The Democratic *Valley Spirit* of Chambersburg, Pennsylvania, proclaimed in the fall of 1862 that the abolitionists had "provoked the present war, and to prolong it to the 'bitter end' the nigger is dragged into the contest by his woolly-head at every turn until it has resolved itself into a war for the special benefit of Sambo, and his abolition admirers." Such attitudes led to deadly antiblack riots. In New York City in 1863, angry Democrats broke up the city's first draft lottery and went on a rampage against Republican officials, the Republican-controlled Metropolitan Police, and blacks, whom they blamed for the nation's problems. They burned an African American orphanage and killed at least thirty blacks, torturing and mutilating many of them. In 1871 Democrats in Philadelphia attacked blacks trying to cast their first ballots. Four died. But most victims of racially motivated violence were killed not by mobs but by individuals acting alone or in pairs.[26]

There is thus no question that the decline in self-employment and the controversies over immigration, slavery, and race were directly responsible for an increase in homicides motivated by class, ethnic, religious, racial, and political antagonism. These murders alone would have made the northern United States more homicidal than Canada or western Europe at midcentury. But the increase in such murders was overshadowed by an even greater increase in vigilante and predatory killings and in homicides over petty differences, turf, and property. Most of these murderers were unaware that their behavior had any connection with political conflict or strains on the social hierarchy. But their behavior shows the impress of broader social and political forces. They were antagonistic toward others because they were anxious about their jobs and about the future, and that anxiety alienated them from others and made them more competitive in their struggle for status. They were also angry at the government and estranged from other Americans, who they felt were indifferent or even hostile to their interests.

Most of the homicides committed by northerners at midcentury stemmed from petty disputes. The victims and perpetrators of these homicides were almost exclusively men, and they came from every ethnic, religious, and racial group. Their quarrels took place wherever working-class people or middle-class people of modest means gathered—in the street, in taverns and dance halls, at work, and in private homes. To contemporaries, the causes of these quarrels seemed insignificant, but in fact men were fighting to retain their self-respect and their position in society. Like southerners in the postrevolutionary period, they were anxious about their standing in the social hierarchy, so they fought over anything that might put them at a competitive disadvantage with another man or show that they could be bullied. They killed each other over card games, races, dogfights, wrestling matches, and raffles. Men were killed for claiming that another country was better than the United States, for throwing a watermelon rind in fun, for teasing a dog, for rattling a door at night and making a ribald speech, for frightening a horse with a lighted pumpkin, for arguing over whose turn it was to unload the grain. One man died because he reminded a friend that he had once been flogged by a Dutch woman.[27]

Any word that touched on a man's work ethic, his faith, his honesty, or his willingness to pay his debts could elicit a lethal response, because these qualities determined a man's social standing in the North. Holmes Perry, a butcher in Lebanon, New Hampshire, was murdered after humiliating a day laborer who did not have thirty-five cents to pay for meat for his family. Addis Hayes, who worked for a small grocer in Philadelphia, was walking out of a tavern with friends when an acquaintance passed by and joked, "There goes another loafer." Hayes beat him to death. Jesse Kendall, the foreman of a road crew in Hillsboro, New Hampshire, slapped one of the paupers in his crew,

Levi Johnson, with the flat of his shovel "in jest" and told him to get to work. Johnson buried the blade of his shovel in Kendall's head. Claude Humphrey of Olmstead, Ohio, reprimanded George Hersnnel, a blacksmith, for working on the Sabbath, so Hersnnel stabbed him.[28]

This heightened sensitivity also showed itself when remarks were made about men's wives. When the wife of James Snow, a hardscrabble farmer, hunter, and fisherman in Walden, Vermont, told peddler John Stanton that she had no money to buy goods, Stanton said, "I guess you have money, as farmers generally have plenty of it." Furious at the insinuation that his wife was a liar, James Snow shot Stanton in the face. When John Gambs, a German farm laborer in Ross County, Ohio, accused farmer George Thacker's wife of stealing meat from him, Thacker beat him to death. These men were defending a northern ideal of personal and family honor—one rooted not in the domination of others, as in a slave society, but in the virtuous reputation needed to succeed in business in a society of free laborers and small businessmen.[29]

For similar reasons, northerners were likely to take offense whenever a proprietor refused them service. The refusal to accept a man's money, whether at a legal or an illegal business, was an affront to his standing in the community. Men killed hotel clerks, boardinghouse operators, tavernkeepers, dance hall bouncers, and brothel owners when they were ejected, refused service, or denied admission. Nearly all of these men were drunk and rowdy at the time, or they had been unruly or unwilling to pay their bills at these establishments in the past. But they did not see their behavior as sufficient reason to refuse them service. Even the dishonorable killed to defend their honor. And tavern and brothel workers, fearing for their lives, raised the death toll further by killing unruly customers.[30]

An alarming number of deadly quarrels had no precipitating causes, or at least none that were apparent to participants or bystanders. They occurred on the spur of the moment on the street, at the railroad station, in taverns and dance halls, at circuses and holiday celebrations—anywhere men came together to amuse themselves and to drink—and they show the degree to which forbearance and fellow feeling had collapsed among men in the North. Sometimes individuals were simply spoiling for a fight. In a remarkable number of cases, a half-dozen or more men, some of them friends, some strangers, joined brawls that ended in the deaths of one or more people.[31]

During this period the North also witnessed another phenomenon previously confined to the slaveholding South: murders committed by bullies. Changing circumstances in the North produced a crop of men who cultivated a reputation for toughness. They challenged people for no reason at all, even women and strangers who had given no offense, and attacked their victims if they did anything other than cower in fear. These dominance displays usually happened in mixed company. Drunken bullies tried to humiliate men in front of women or humiliated women as a way of humiliating the men accompanying them. In Philadelphia Horatio Maloney walked up to a woman in a store and insulted her in front of her companion, Samuel Mangan. Mangan punched Maloney, and Maloney stabbed him to death. William Foster insulted two female passengers sitting near him on a streetcar in New York City. Avery Putnam told him to watch his mouth. Foster killed him. James Rodgers and his friends, spilling out of a Manhattan tavern at closing time, ran into a well-dressed couple, the Swansons, who were on their way home from a social engagement. They insulted Mrs. Swanson repeatedly, and when her husband tried to protect her, Rodgers knifed him.[32]

Gang members turned menacing behavior into an art form. They tattooed their bodies like sailors, adopted nicknames like the "Butcher," "Satan," and "Snake" (Snake was a Vermonter whose real name was Cyrus Putnam). One bare-knuckle fighter named Snatchem, who was a member of New York's Slaughter House Gang, won notoriety as the epitome of the northern bully. He was "a beastly, obscene ruffian" who dressed like a pirate, carried two pistols in his belt and a knife in his boot, and sucked blood from his victims' wounds. He described himself as a "kicking-in-the-head-knife-in-a-dark-room fellow," and he had a friend called Jack the Rat who would bite the head off a mouse for a dime and a rat for a quarter.[33]

This new masculine style had been taking shape in the North since the 1820s, but it was no longer confined to a few large cities, and the new toughs did not stop at fighting. Like their southern counterparts, they fought for the fun of it as well as for bragging rights, but from the late 1840s through the Civil War they killed people frequently and deliberately. Before this period fighting had resulted in only a few deaths in the North, and those were inadvertent.

As nativism gained strength in the 1850s and gangs and volunteer fire companies became ethnically less diverse, more fights pitted the native-born against immigrants and Protestants against Catholics. This was especially true in Philadelphia, where fighting between native-born and immigrant fire companies claimed at least nine lives between the Mexican War and the Civil War. Yet much of the deadly violence of this era had little to do with American-born or immigrant status. Like other northerners, members of gangs and fire companies killed each other to defend their standing among their peers. Bill "The Butcher" Poole was the toughest fighter in New York City and the undisputed champion of its nativist gangs. He became a prime target for anyone who wanted to advance in the ranks of nativist toughs. He was eventually brought down by two native Tammany fighters.[34]

These homicides proliferated as the feelings and beliefs that had restrained lethal violence in the 1830s and early 1840s dissipated. They were not an explicit response to the nation's political crisis or the disruption of the North's social hierarchy, as homicides motivated by racial, ethnic, class, and political hatred were. Men who engaged in such violence left no evidence that they saw beyond the immediate causes of their violent behavior, and although law-enforcement and other government officials were well aware that everyday quarrels caused most northern homicides, they cited nativist-immigrant hostility, drunkenness, and the proliferation of small weapons as the causes of the increase in violence. But alcohol consumption was actually one-half to two-thirds lower in the 1850s and 1860s than it had been in the 1820s, thanks to the temperance movement; and although handguns and knives made quarrels more deadly, together they were responsible for only half of all fatalities, and they were as much a response to the rise in homicide rates as a cause.[35]

Property-related and vigilante murders were also on the rise. By midcentury, strong county and township governments existed everywhere in the North except in Kansas and the Pacific Northwest. Law enforcement and criminal courts were well established. Yet more men —especially farmers—were taking the law into their own hands. Increasingly hostile to governments that did not promote their interests, they rejected or bypassed the courts and enforced their own decisions. Men who had been law-abiding in the 1830s and early 1840s now acted as if they were in a war to decide who would make and enforce the rules concerning life and property.

Property-dispute murders were prompted by a wide range of issues: boundaries, trespassing, vandalism, crop damage, thefts of wood or produce, the ownership of movable property, and trades gone awry. The offenses in question were misdemeanors or civil matters that should have been ignored or decided in court or through arbitration. In a surprising number of cases, contentious parties did turn first to mediators or justices of the peace. But when legal decisions went against them or when they had no proof that their neighbors had broken the law, they were unable to let matters go.[36]

The Plumleys and the Balches of Shrewsbury, Vermont, had feuded for years over insults, boundary lines, and stray livestock. In August 1868 they were at odds again over whether the Balches should pay for damage their cattle had done to the Plumleys' cornfield. They agreed to arbitration. Three neighbors appraised the damage and ruled in favor of the Plumleys. It was the custom for the winner in such disputes to provide refreshments, so Ziba Plumley went to fetch liquor. By the time he reappeared, it was obvious that he had already begun to imbibe, and the restless Balches were wandering over his field. Ziba had had enough. Still angry at having been crippled in a fight with a Balch three years before, Ziba ordered his son Horace to prod a Balch friend, John Gilman Jr., out of the corn at gunpoint. When the frightened Gilman begged Horace to turn the rifle aside, Ziba told Horace to "shoot him." Horace did, and a furious gunfight broke out. The Plumleys hit one Balch in the arm and another in the leg, but the Balches found cover and returned fire. "God damn it," Ziba yelled at his sons, "can't you shoot straight?" The battle raged off and on until the next day, when a brave neighbor walked into the line of fire, berated both families, and took their guns away one by one. The Plumleys and the Balches then surrendered to the authorities.[37]

Legal proceedings often failed to contain hostile emotions in such disputes, now that trust in government had waned. Murder cases often emerged from situations in which large, powerful men who had lost their lawsuits would try to intimidate smaller, less powerful men. The smaller man would pull out a weapon, kill his tormenter, and then claim self-defense. In 1860 in Warren, New Hampshire, for example, Vanness Wyatt's timber was hauled away by James Williams, who had a legal writ attaching the timber for a debt owed by Wyatt's father. Wyatt, a young married man with a ten-month-old child, desperately needed the money the timber would bring in and felt he had been bushwhacked by the courts. He took to carrying a three-foot stick and following Williams around town. One day, while Wyatt was following Williams near the freight depot, Williams, accompanied by a friend, brandished a pistol and said, "Vanness now don't come near me." Wyatt kept following him. Williams stopped and said that if Wyatt "step[p]ed another step he would blow him through," and at that moment he fired. As he lay dying, Wyatt said, "I havent touched you nor want a goeing to." Williams said, "I know you did not but you followed me with a stick." Because Williams had a friendly witness to support his story, he got away with a claim of self-defense. He later confessed that he felt his reputation was at stake. As he told a friend, he "did not like to dodge [Wyatt] & go across lots [to avoid him] & have people laughing at him."[38]

The majority of murders in defense of property were impulsive. They were committed by men who were determined to settle matters on the spot, without resorting to the law. Felix McCann of Sherburne, New York, came home drunk one day and learned that a neighbor who had previously killed two of his stray chickens had now killed a third. McCann grabbed his rifle and shot his neighbor through a window. Sylvester Cone, a farmer in Tamworth, New Hampshire, lost his temper early one Sunday morning when he caught two teenaged boys skinny-dipping in his pond. He told them to get out. They thumbed their noses at him. He returned with a gun and shot one of them dead.[39]

Property-dispute murderers like Cone were often ambitious, upwardly mobile men, deeply concerned about money and economic standing. After the shooting Cone worried about his legal expenses. He had been saving money for a trip to the Centennial Exposition in Philadelphia, and he wrote to his wife from jail, promising that they could still make the trip if she would perjure herself and say that the boys had assaulted him. She was too appalled at his conduct to help him, and he was sentenced to life in prison. Jesse Davenport of Manchester, Vermont, who warned young vandals to stay away from his shop and stabbed the next one who happened by, was obsessed with making money and wrote long letters to his mother and sister about his wheeling and dealing. At one point he had decided that he and his wife did not have enough money to provide for more than three children, so he cut out one of his testicles, thinking that doing so would lessen his chances of having more. Having gone to such lengths to get ahead, he was not about to let neighborhood boys break his windows or carve their initials on his sign.[40]

Property-dispute murderers were utterly convinced that they were within their rights to kill, even if they were defending nothing more than their pride, and they believed, often correctly, that their neighbors would excuse them on the grounds of self-defense. Under English common law, people who were threatened had a "duty to retreat" if they could do so safely. They could use force only if they had their backs "to the wall" and could not get away from their attackers. American law upheld that doctrine in the postrevolutionary period, but at midcentury jurors, judges, and legislators in many jurisdictions moved away from it, arguing instead that people who were threatened had a right to stand their ground and even to attack preemptively if they believed that their lives were in danger. The Ohio Supreme Court finally ceded to lower court practice when it ruled in 1876 that a "true man" had a right to kill in self-defense as long as he did not initiate the hostilities. He had no "duty to retreat." The Indiana Supreme Court concurred in 1877. "The tendency of the American mind seems to be very strongly against the enforcement of any rule which requires a person to flee when assailed." The "no duty to retreat" principle did not become the law of the land until 1921, when it was upheld by the Supreme Court. But by the 1850s it was the de facto law in the North, upheld by prosecutors who declined to prosecute and jurors who refused to convict.[41]

In the middle of the nineteenth century there was also an increase in vigilantism. Vigilantism had nearly disappeared in the Midwest after the frontier period, but it reappeared in a more virulent form in the late 1850s in the wake of Bleeding Kansas, as faith in government and in the impartiality of justice eroded. The Iowa vigilantes of the 1830s had been careful to follow the forms of the law, but their successors launched a reign of terror between 1857 and 1870, shooting or hanging at least forty-six men for murder, arson, or horse theft. These men did not act because there were no sheriffs or jails. Those institutions were obviously effective by the 1850s; nineteen of the vigilantes' victims were already in custody when they were dragged off. The vigilantes simply wanted to bypass the court system, because they no longer trusted it to act swiftly or severely enough to deter crime. They presumed guilt and demanded immediate punishment. Only nine of their victims were tried in lynch courts. The rest were simply put to death.[42]

In 1857 William Barger was jailed in Clinton County, Iowa, awaiting trial for theft, when a mob of forty men led by a postmaster from Jackson County walked in and took him away. The sheriff had opened the cell door for the mob because he did not want them to break the lock. He did break the nose of one of the rioters with the butt of his gun, and he and a half-dozen volunteers grabbed Barger's legs as he was being hoisted into a wagon, but they lost the tug-of-war and left Barger to his fate. The mob made a leisurely progress through the countryside to a tree where previous victims had been hanged and strung Barger up. None of the vigilantes were charged, although the authorities knew them all. That was typical: none of Iowa's vigilante killers were ever convicted of a crime, and only one group of killers had to pay damages to a victim's family.[43]

As in the frontier period, vigilantism was most common along the Ohio, Mississippi, and Missouri Rivers, where many southerners had settled. But it enjoyed widespread support in the North from the 1850s into the 1870s, even after well-publicized incidents in which vigilantes executed men who turned out to be innocent, like Pleasant Anderson of Albia, Iowa. Anderson was accused of killing the son of a local financier in an attempt to steal $12,000. Like many mob victims, Anderson was widely disliked, and the townspeople suspected him of committing other crimes, even though he had never been convicted of anything. The murder was actually committed by the president of the local bank, Samuel Miller.[44]

Even in Vermont and New Hampshire, where no criminal suspect was ever killed by a mob, vigilantes forced confessions from suspects, whipped them, tarred and feathered them, and threatened them with hanging. It was common practice to gather outside jails where suspects in notorious crimes were being held and threaten to lynch them. Mobs were also sending a message to the authorities: if the suspects were not punished, they would be taken by force and killed. The authorities obliged: between 1862 and 1882 they sent half of all the people ever executed in Vermont and a third of those ever executed in New Hampshire to the gallows. Like the vigilantes, they made mistakes: at least two of the condemned were probably innocent.[45]

As in property-dispute homicides, the lack of trust in government led to a widespread loss of faith in the criminal justice system. It was too weak, too slow, and too corrupt to stop crime. H. M. Mott, an Indiana "regulator" who believed that lynching counterfeiters and horse thieves had a salutary effect on society, said in 1859 that he and his compatriots "felt that their natural and God-given rights had been disregarded, and that the arm of the law was too weak to mete out a just retribution to the guilty, under the existing state of society." The editor of the *Tamaqua Courier*, a paper published in eastern Pennsylvania, shared Mott's views. Outraged by the murders committed by the Molly Maguires in the summer of 1875, he spoke out "in favor of a vigilance committee that will make it so hot for those who get the shooting done and those who harbor suspected parties that they can no longer remain among us. . . . Something *must* be done; that something must be *sure*, swift, and terrible."[46]

The increase in vigilante violence was also tied to skyrocketing rates of predatory homicides, particularly robbery murders, which were more closely linked than any other kind of murders to the precipitous decline in empathy and fellow feeling. Beginning in the late 1840s, even relatively nonhomicidal places like New England and the rural Midwest saw the rates of robbery murders rise. Very few of these murders were ever solved. In most cases there was no evidence. Most of the bodies, stripped of identification and badly decomposed, were found along roads, canals, rivers, and railroad tracks or near taverns, brothels, racetracks, shipyards, and factory yards.

A small proportion of robbery murders were the work of the organized gangs that plied the streets and waterfronts of American cities. New York had its Whyos, Bowery B'hoys, Dead Rabbits, and Plug Uglies; Baltimore its RipRaps, Regulators, and Blood Tubs; Philadelphia its Bulldogs, Reedies, and Schuylkill Rangers. Some of the more infamous members of these gangs were rumored to have been responsible for dozens of robbery murders. A few such crimes were the work of thrill killers, like John Capie and Carson Emos, who were caught killing a randomly chosen victim in Philadelphia one Saturday night. Still others were the work of serial killers like Peter Bresnahan, a thief for whom murder was a way of making a living; or the Benders, a German family from Kansas that killed at least twelve unsuspecting travelers who accepted their invitation to stay the night.[47]

The great majority of robbery murderers, however, were probably down-and-out laborers who preyed on targets of opportunity. Not surprisingly, tramps and vagrants were widely feared. They often preyed on the elderly and on farmers or farm couples who lived alone. Charles Williams, a well-educated young immigrant from Bristol, England, had not been able to find steady work. He had been tramping around Vermont all winter, begging and stealing. One day, hungry and depressed, he stopped by a farm in Brandon to ask for a glass of milk and directions to the train station. He told the farmer that he hoped to take a train for Montreal and sail home from there. But he had no money for the trip, and as he cut through the woods on the way to the station, he ran into Frank Brasson, a fifteen-year-old farm laborer who was out hunting. Williams asked to look at his gun and then shot him with it. Apparently he hoped to sell the gun on his way north. He did not get far, however, and when he found himself surrounded by Brasson's neighbors, he turned the gun on himself.[48]

Immigrants like Williams were not as profoundly alienated from society as men who defined themselves by violence, like gang members. However, impoverished immigrants were more likely to kill in these decades than they had been before because they saw themselves not as prospective members of society, but as outsiders who would never have the success that their victims—many of whom were themselves immigrants or children of immigrants—enjoyed. These feelings were not an inevitable result of immigration or desperate poverty. There had been plenty of poor immigrants in the northern United States before the late 1840s, and there was still plenty of poverty and immigration in Canada, England, and other nations where robbery murders were becoming rare. Such feelings were the fruit of the politicized hostility that immigrants encountered in the midcentury North and of the pervasive sense that the path to self-employment and economic success was no longer open to working Americans.

A similar despondency about the future may have seeped into the lives of native-born working men who robbed and murdered their neighbors, employers, or former employers. A few of these killers had had difficulties with their employers, usually over poor performance on the job; but most killed people they knew for money. They were young and ambitious, estranged from their families, and had little in common with their victims, who were usually of a different ethnic group. Perry Bowsher of Ross County, Ohio, was typical of such killers; a young, Ohio-born farm laborer of German ancestry, he desperately wanted to see the world. He had no money, however, so he robbed and murdered an elderly Scots-Irish couple who lived a few miles from his home.[49]

Older farm laborers usually robbed and killed their employers to provide for their own families. However heinous their crimes, these men were just trying to feed their children in a world where there were no safety nets. Hiram Miller, a Vermont-born French Canadian (his name had been anglicized) had served in the Union army, but after the war he had trouble finding work. He hired on with the Gowans in Weathersfield, Vermont, but he kept wandering off in search of more work, so the Gowans refused to pay him his full wages. Miller got into several heated arguments with them and finally quit, but after a couple of weeks he returned to the farm, killed them with an ax, and stole every cent they had.[50]

The attenuation of empathy and fellow feeling among northerners manifested itself most strikingly in the increased willingness of young working men to kill friends and acquaintances or to cozy up to people with money in order to rob and kill them. Anyone who had a substantial amount of cash was a potential victim. William Pendolph, a farmer in Sandgate, Vermont, killed his friend Dave Kinsman because he thought Kinsman had $600 stashed away. He was sorely disappointed to find only $6.[51]

Perhaps the most disturbing manifestation of alienation, however, was the sudden resurgence of rape murder. The number of lethal sexual assaults was not great, but such murders had nearly disappeared in the postrevolutionary period. A young domestic servant died after being gang-raped by six young men at a neighborhood party in Sandgate, Vermont. Charles Scudder, a trusted hostler in Commack, New York, broke into the home of Mary Robbins, tied her to her bed, brutalized her, cut her throat, and left her body in a degrading position. William Fee and Thomas Muldoon, who worked as boatmen on the

Erie Canal, were wandering about on their day off when they met a young woman going from house to house to ask for work. They propositioned her, perhaps offering money, and when she refused they raped her, strangled her, and threw her in a ditch. Annie Morrison was brutalized under similar circumstances by a gang of young men in the woods east of Manchester, New Hampshire.[52]

Like robbery murderers, rapists attacked targets of opportunity: women who were poor and socially isolated. They regarded these women with contempt and assumed they could assault them without sanctions. The Sandgate victim was poor, while her attackers came from respectable families. They had imprisoned her in an upstairs bedroom and invited other men "to go in and have a good time," and only two people were willing to stand up for her when she said she had been "wronged." Like most rape-murder victims, she was beyond the circle of people who mattered. By midcentury the social divide between middle-class and poor working-class women had become wider, and there was a growing presumption that working-class women were not respectable, unless they could prove otherwise. That presumption facilitated the return of rape murders as much as the arrogance and alienation of the rapists themselves.

It was during these decades that the United States also witnessed the appearance of serial killers who murdered young girls and women, subjected them to sexual mutilation, and performed sex acts on their dead bodies. Such killings had never been seen in the nation before. They marked the outer limits of the alienated, hate-filled violence that pervaded American society at midcentury. Such killings reappeared at the same time in Europe, where they had been largely absent since the late sixteenth and early seventeenth centuries, but they remained more common in the United States.[53]

Known serial sexual killers led peripatetic lives, a symptom of their inability to form lasting relationships or to feel themselves part of a broader community. Franklin Evans was a transient who had some success as an herbal doctor and an Adventist preacher. His second and third wives left him because of his violence (his first wife was supposed to have died of natural causes). He apparently began his criminal career in 1850 by murdering a five-year-old neighbor girl in Derry, New Hampshire, although he was not convicted of that crime, because her body was never found. Over the next twenty years he may have killed several other girls, but he was not caught until 1872, when he murdered his teenaged grandniece, Georgiana Lovering. He followed her into the woods, raped her, strangled her, and then took a knife to her belly, genitals, and uterus.[54]

Joseph Lapage was a lumberjack who had fled his native Quebec after raping his sister-in-law. He, too, mutilated his victims, Marietta Ball, a young schoolteacher from St. Albans, Vermont, and Josie Langmaid, a teenager from Pembroke, New Hampshire. His killings were ritualized; he took the women's undergarments and hid them in various locations, cut out their reproductive organs (and probably ate parts of them), and cut off Langmaid's head and threw it into a swamp.[55]

Most of the known sexual serial killers were from the North, the region that also had the greatest increase in rape and marital violence. Although by any definition these men were mentally ill, the social changes that swept across the mid-nineteenth-century North may have helped trigger and shape their violence. The disconnect that they felt from all females (even those in their own families), the rage they manifested in their crimes, and the indifference that they showed to the families of their victims testify to the attenuation of empathy in the midcentury North and to the resultant feeling that the laws and institutions that had bound men in the past did not bind them any longer. Society's preoccupation with respectability, along with the companionate ideal of marriage and romance, which they were too emotionally crippled to attain, would have been both threatening and infuriating to them. They had failed in their relationships with respectable women, and they appear to have singled out their victims—children, students, and schoolteachers—because of their innocence and respectability. The mid-nineteenth-century rise of misogyny and commercialized sexuality may also have encouraged and confirmed their desire to punish and mutilate women.[56]

Sexual assaults and robberies were largely responsible for the increase in nondomestic homicides of women in the mid-nineteenth-century North. Homicide rates for women remained a tenth or less of those for men, ranging from 0.2 per 100,000 adult women per year in New Hampshire and Vermont to 2 per 100,000 per year in Cleveland and rural Illinois. However, they were substantially higher than they had been in the 1820s and 1830s, when there were almost no murders of women by unrelated adults. Apart from robberies and sexual assaults, women were killed in the same circumstances men were. Mary Laker, who farmed with her husband in Petersburg, New York, taunted her hired man, Hiram Coon, about his criminal past. Coon picked up an ax, held it over her head, and warned her not to say another word. She ignored his warning, and he split her head open. Miriam Berry, a widow who farmed in New Durham, New Hampshire, got into a pay dispute with the man who cut her wood, whom she had fired for being "disagreeable," and he shot her. In Calhoun County, Illinois, a Unionist mob fired on the house of a Confederate sympathizer in 1862, killing his pregnant wife. Such violence was so pervasive that it was bound to claim the lives of women as well as men.[57]

Far fewer women killed unrelated adults than were killed by them, but at midcentury women were committing murder more often than before. On occasion, female proprietors of taverns or brothels shot unruly customers, and women sometimes pitched in with male friends or relatives who were involved in brawls. Eliza Rickman, for example, helped her brothers kill William Campbell in rural Ross County, Ohio, because they believed he had stolen a watch; Margaret Kelly helped her husband beat Rose O'Malia to death while they were drinking at the Kellys' home in Cleveland. Women killed unrelated adults for more personal reasons than men did, but female victims were killed for the same reasons and under the same circumstances that male victims were.[58]

Northerners were at a loss about how to stem the rising tide of homicides. States, counties, municipalities, and businesses spent massive amounts on law enforcement. The creation of the North's first municipal police departments in the 1840s, the first private detective agencies in the 1850s, and the National Guard in the 1870s helped ensure that law and order did not break down completely and prevented the return of frontierlike homicide rates, but law enforcement was powerless to prevent high homicide levels and in some instances raised them. Many officers and militiamen were killed in the line of duty, and they were responsible for killing many of the people who died during strikes, robberies, and riots. In New York City in 1849 the militia killed twenty-three people, including an innocent bystander, when it was called out to put down a riot that had broken out at the Astor Theater over a performance by an English actor who had disparaged American audiences. In the 1850s the police gunned down a dozen river pirates in an effort to break up theft rings that operated on the waterfront, and the river pirates retaliated, killing a number of watchmen and police officers. Rioters killed more than a dozen policemen and soldiers in the draft riot of 1863. In Philadelphia at least seven police officers were killed in the 1850s as they tried to stop fights or make arrests. Similar killings occurred in New England and the Midwest, in both cities and the countryside.[59]

The lack of professionalism among law-enforcement personnel contributed to the problem. Many officers were poorly trained, and aggressive or reckless men were rarely weeded out. Some officials turned vigilante. If they got a tip about a burglary or a jailbreak they would lie in wait and shoot the suspects as soon as they came within range. Occasionally they would hand criminals over to vigilante groups rather than take them to jail. But even law-abiding members of thoroughly professional police departments, like Boston's, killed or were killed in the line of duty much more frequently than present-day policemen.[60]

The high homicide rates that prevailed in this era thus affected all northerners, from the poorest members of society to the struggling middle class, and they ensnared law enforcement in a lethal web, as high homicide rates always do. Tasked with lowering the rates and saddled with the blame when they did not fall, law-enforcement officials died in great numbers and often succumbed to corruption or abandoned their mandate entirely. Only in the late nineteenth century, when the political crisis eased and society began to adjust its expectations and accord higher status to men who worked for others would homicide rates begin to decline in the North.

Homicide in the South

Homicide rates did not rise everywhere in the South in the late 1840s and 1850s as they did in the North and the Southwest. In plantation counties in Georgia and South Carolina, where the debate over the status of slavery in the territories annexed from Mexico drew whites together, rates remained steady (Figure 4.1).[61] However, southern cities experienced the same surge in homicides that cities elsewhere did. Conflict between the native-born and immigrants, disagreements over slavery and race relations, and frustration among workers and small proprietors over the decline in proprietorship led to high rates of individual and collective violence.

The violence appears to have been worst in New Orleans, the most ethnically diverse city in the South, where desperately poor Irish and German immigrants clashed repeatedly with equally poor native-born whites. The city's homicide rate soared to 60 per 100,000 adults per year (Figure 7.1). In the municipal election of 1854 the police, who owed their jobs to the Democratic Party, escorted Democratic voters from poll to poll so that they could vote "early and often." In response, members of the nativist American Party attacked the police, killing two Irish patrolmen and wounding Chief of Police Stephen O'Leary. The nativists won the election and appointed a new chief who had once threatened to kill every Irish person in the city. He purged the force of Democratic appointees, whom he called a pack of "damned Irish and Dutch, and a set of thieves," and replaced them with native-born Prot-

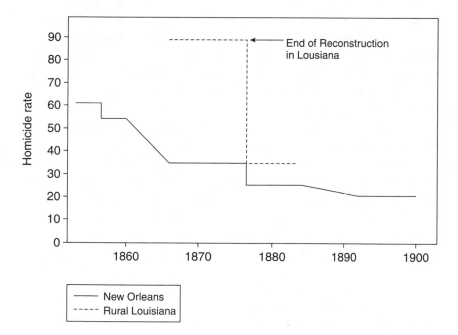

Figure 7.1 Homicide rates in Louisiana, 1853–1900 (per 100,000 adults per year). *Sources:* Rousey (1996: 74, 93, 187n53); Vandal (2000: 21, 23).

estants, who terrorized immigrants and murdered several Irish and German suspects. In June 1858, as voters went to the polls again, there was an all-out brawl between the nativist militia and Democratic vigilantes. Four Democrats died, and many more were seriously wounded. This violence pervaded everyday life. Rapes, robberies, and bar fights involving fatalities were commonplace. The Orleans County sheriff told a British journalist on the eve of the Civil War that New Orleans had become "a perfect hell on earth."[62]

Other southern cities experienced substantial increases in homicide rates. Fifty people died in nativist riots in St. Louis, Baltimore, and Louisville. Some southern politicians actively encouraged violence against immigrants. In 1855 Senator John Bell, a moderate Whig from Tennessee, called for Americans to take up arms against foreigners. "It is better that a little blood shall sprinkle the pavements and side-walks of our cities now, than that the streets should be drenched in blood hereafter." Election riots and riots against suspected abolitionists also claimed lives in southern cities, including Savannah and Augusta.[63]

In the rural Upper South and in the poorer, white-dominated regions of the Lower South there was a brief spike in homicides among whites in the late 1840s and early 1850s. Rates rose in mountain counties in northern Georgia, in the pine-barren counties of southeastern Louisiana, and in plantation counties in Virginia (Figures 5.5 and 5.6). In these areas, divisions over the Mexican War, the question of slavery in the territories, and public policies that favored the rich and disadvantaged the poor and the middle class were initially as great as they were in the North. Planters, merchants, and financiers dominated the South politically and thwarted most democratic reforms, like free public schools and relief for debtors. The poor and the middle class were stymied. They could not get "plain folk" elected to office, and there was nothing they could do about creditors' seizures of tools and livestock, the exemption of slave property from taxation, or the high interest rates charged by banks.[64]

Homicide rates subsided in these counties during the crisis over Kansas. The threat posed by Republicans, abolitionists, and violators of the Fugitive Slave Law reunited white southerners, fostered southern nationalism, and enabled southern elites to represent themselves as defenders of the common people. They were not just protecting their investment in slaves or their potential investment in territorial land; they were defending the white race and the economic independence of southerners.

The proslavery movement was not powerful enough in southern cities to keep the native-born and immigrants from killing each other, but in rural areas it was powerful enough to hold homicide rates steady by 1854–55. Similarly, ethnic and religious hostility among whites, so disruptive in southern cities, was a less significant force in politics and daily life in the rural South, because immigrants largely avoided the area. The Know-Nothing Party attracted considerable support in the Upper South in the election of 1856, but it did so primarily because its supporters viewed it as a potential replacement for the Whig Party and a moderate voice on the issue of slavery in the territories. In all likelihood both factors—the appeal of the proslavery movement and the absence of immigrants in rural areas—contributed to keeping homicide rates in the rural South at 1820s levels.[65]

If southerners had won the national debate over slavery in the late 1850s and early 1860s, those homicide rates might have persisted for decades. But the dissolution of the Union, the Civil War, and Reconstruction changed everything. The formation and ultimate failure of the Confederacy, the efforts by black and white Republicans to reconstruct state governments after the Civil War, and the campaign by conservative whites to "redeem" the South from Republican rule took a terrible toll in human life and had a catastrophic effect on murder rates. Every phase of the process of dissolution and rebuilding led to higher levels of political violence and everyday violence among unrelated adults.

Homicide rates were highest where political divisions among whites and between whites and blacks were deepest. Wherever prewar governments failed under the strain of secession and the war and wherever the struggle to control state governments after the war was most intense, whites began killing other whites as well as blacks, creating the worst homicide rates the South had seen since the early seventeenth century. Wherever white solidarity remained strong and prewar political structures held together, as they did in the Chesapeake and the Shenandoah Valley in Virginia, homicide rates returned to prewar levels. And where new political coalitions formed between blacks and whites during Reconstruction, as they did in New Orleans and in some sugar- and cotton-growing counties in the Deep South, and gave birth to fragile yet more inclusive new governments, neither political nor everyday homicide rates reached catastrophic levels, at least until those governments died a violent death at the end of Reconstruction. In short, where prewar elites remained in power, as they did in Virginia, and where coalitions formed among previously antagonistic groups that allowed them to share power, as they did in parts of Louisiana, homicide rates did not rise to the degree they did elsewhere. In most of the South, however, the transitions from one polity to another were hotly contested, and substantial minorities or majorities of the local population remained hostile to the new governments. Where that happened, the frontier-style struggle for power produced a homicidal disaster.

The drive toward secession after John Brown's raid in October 1859 led to a burst of political violence in the South that lasted until the summer of 1861. Militant whites closed ranks and attacked suspected abolitionists and slave rebels. The violence was worst in Florida and Texas, which had suffered the greatest political instability in the antebellum period. "We sleep upon our arms, and the whole country is most deeply excited," wrote Charles Pryor, editor of the *Dallas Herald*. "All is confusion, excitement and distrust." Reverend Anthony Bewley of Fort Worth, a southerner who supported slavery, came under suspicion because he was a minister in the Northern Methodist Church, which had condemned slavery at its national conference. In 1860 the local authorities charged him with instigating slave rebellion. The charge was ridiculous, Bewley said. "In these times of *heated* excitement, mole hills are raised mountain high." He continued to protest his innocence, but in September he was hanged by a mob. A rash of suspicious fires in north Texas, perhaps caused by a new kind of phosphorous match that burst into flames spontaneously when the temperature rose above 100 degrees, led to the lynching of at least thirty blacks and whites in July 1860. In Florida, militant defenders of southern rights went on a lynching rampage. Statewide, the rate at which whites murdered blacks quadrupled in 1858–1860, from 5 to 20 per 100,000 adults per year, and the rate at which whites murdered whites more than doubled, to 86 per 100,000 adults per year (Figures 5.8 and 5.9). A quarter of those victims, black and white, were lynched.[66]

During the secession crisis, most white lynching victims were immigrants from the North, members of antislavery churches, Know-

Nothing politicians, criminals who formed interracial gangs, or southerners who spoke carelessly about their dislike of slavery. A young watchman on a Red River steamer said that "he would rather die than live in the Southern states," and a group of passengers killed him. J. H. Bell, an officer in the Ninth Texas Cavalry, said something in passing that led his men to believe he had abolitionist sympathies. They strung him up and gave his uniform to a poor soldier. Across the South, Confederate vigilantes killed men and women for passing northern banknotes, peddling copies of the Constitution of the United States, dining with slaves, or wearing the red sash that supposedly marked them as members of the "Mystic Red," a secret abolitionist society. Edward Burrowes, who had moved to Texas from New Jersey, was so frightened that he asked his friends back home not to send him any northern newspapers. "Thair was two men hung in some of the upper counties for takin northern papers, and I might get in the same fix." After a huge mob attacked people at a Northern Methodist meeting in Timber Creek, the *Texas Gazette* proclaimed its lack of sympathy for the victims: "We would rather see a hundred such dogs bleed than one victim of a slave insurrection." The *Matagorda Gazette* went one step further: "The white man who is caught tampering with slaves in this community had better have his peace made with God . . . for if he don't swing, it will be because there is no hemp in the South."[67]

The vigilante violence effectively and emphatically marked the bounds of dissent. The vigilantes were not particular about whom they killed, and this indiscriminate fanaticism intimidated racial moderates and antisecessionists and gave militant whites the upper hand in shaping the Confederacy. A reporter from North Carolina justified the vigilantes' tactics: "The necessities of the times imperatively demand terrible examples." Lynchings put everyone on notice that whatever their personal feelings were about slavery or secession, they had better profess loyalty to Confederate ideals if they wanted to live. That message was meant especially for white dissidents, who were seen as posing the greatest threat to the new Confederacy. To be an "abolitionist," a "submissionist," or a "Black Republican" was to be a traitor to the South and the white race.[68]

Once the Confederacy was up and running, the need for extreme violence diminished. Throughout most of the South, the transition to the Confederacy proceeded smoothly, especially after the attack on

Fort Sumter in April 1861. Initially, at least, the war created a stronger sense of national unity among southern whites, and the vast majority of former Unionists flocked to the Confederate cause. Most of them had supported the Union only as long as it respected southern rights; once the North used force, they joined the fight for southern independence. The prewar power structure remained intact, and support for slavery and white supremacy was as strong as it had been in the late 1850s. Accordingly, during the first years of the Civil War homicide rates held steady throughout most of the South.

Wherever the transition to the Confederacy did not go smoothly, however, and the loyalties of the local population were divided, prewar conflicts exploded into violence. Wherever the Union lost control and the Confederacy failed to gain control, homicide rates rose to 100–200 per 100,000 adults per year. Those circumstances prevailed in the mountain South and in the Confederacy's northwestern borderlands, especially in north Texas, where wheat farmers and cattlemen had long been at odds with the plantation owners who raised cotton in the fertile bottoms along the Sulphur River. The plantation owners, many of whom came from prominent families in the Deep South, looked down upon the farmers and ranchers, most of whom came from the Upper South and were poorer and less well educated. Kate Stone, whose family had come from Louisiana with 130 slaves, found her neighbors repellent. They were low, crude, brutal, lazy, and ignorant. She called north Texas "the dark corner of the Confederacy."[69]

The prejudice of plantation families against the area's ranchers and farmers was exacerbated by differences in religion and politics. Many of the ranchers and farmers belonged to the Church of God or the Northern Methodist Church, which had condemned slavery, and few had any interest in the Confederacy. State representative Robert Taylor of Fannin County asked on the floor of the Texas House, "In this new Cotton Confederacy what will become of my section, the wheat growers and stock raisers? . . . I fear [secessionists] will hang, burn, confiscate property and exile any one who may be in the way of their designs." The markets of ranchers and wheat farmers lay in the North, and the value of their real estate depended on immigration from Missouri and Kentucky. Few owned slaves, and most of them did not want to live in a planter-dominated republic where the rich held all the cards. Thomas Henderson Terry, who enlisted reluctantly in the Confederate army, complained that "the slaveholders stayed at home and let the poor whites fight the war for them." That was not the case in Texas, where the wealthy were overrepresented in the army; but it was a common belief among dissidents in north Texas, who viewed state laws that set a 10 percent tax on produce (not land or slaves) as a way of enabling the wealthy to evade the draft by hiring substitutes.[70]

North Texas farmers and ranchers voted against secession and were never reconciled to it. A good number joined the Union army or moved to California to be out of harm's way, but the majority stayed home and resisted. Young men dodged the draft or deserted from the Confederate army and hid out in thickets along the Sulphur River. The Confederate Home Guard—known by its adversaries as "heel flies" after a pest that plagued Texas cattle—went on the offensive against dissidents. Accompanied by vigilante groups organized by cotton planters, such as the "Sons of Washington" and the "Ten Stitchers," they promised to kill ten Unionists for every Confederate. As the editor of the *Texas State Gazette* put it, "We cannot tolerate in our midst the presence of an internal hostile element, who are treacherously remaining here, to sow the seeds of servile war, and to give aid and comfort to blockading fleets and invading armies." Five north Texas Unionists were lynched by planter vigilantes in January 1862. One had given an antisecession speech during the secession crisis; another had said that "he would lay in Sulphur bottom until the moss grew a foot long on his back before he would go into the Confederate army." A third was condemned because "he put up two pens when he gathered [hogs] in the fall before and, being asked his reason for it, said one pen was for Jeff Davis and the other for Abraham Lincoln."[71]

By the fall of 1862 so many dissidents had been lynched or assassinated that survivors in Cooke County organized a "Peace Party." The Confederates regarded the move as an act of treason. They rounded up forty-two Peace Party members and lynched them all. For north Texas dissidents that was the last straw. Martin Hart, a prominent stockman and prewar politician who had raised a cavalry company for the Confederacy in 1861, turned his back on the Confederacy and took thirty recruits to Missouri, where they formed a Union cavalry brigade to fight the Home Guards in Arkansas and north Texas. Their undersized unit was captured only four weeks into its mission, and Captain Hart and his lieutenant were hanged. But in that brief period they burned towns and robbed and murdered unarmed civilians, doing to supporters of the Confederacy what had been done to them. The Confederates got their revenge. They captured a list of the men whom Hart had sent back to Texas to recruit more soldiers, rounded up five of them, and hanged them.[72]

The violence in north Texas was worse than anything experienced during the settlement years. Confederates and Unionists alike lost their moral bearings. William Quantrill's raiders were among the worst offenders. They began as nominal Confederates and ended up as killers and thieves, robbing and murdering Confederates, Unionists, and neutrals alike. Confederate troops finally drove them out of north Texas after they sacked the town of Sherman, but local Confederate guerrillas like Cullen Baker and "Captain" Bob Lee soon took their place. They made their reputations killing Unionists, deserters, and draft dodgers, but eventually they, too, became little more than common criminals, looting, robbing, and murdering to enrich themselves. Lee boasted that he had personally killed forty-two men, and Baker probably killed fifty or sixty. By the end of their lives killing had become almost a sport for them. A succession of teenagers followed in their footsteps and competed to outdo them. One eighteen-year-old guerrilla boasted that he was going to "kill off . . . every last devil, and they know it. You bet they fly where they hear of me up here—they say I am a d—d sight worse than Quantrill."[73]

From north Texas to Missouri, the Confederacy's borderlands were a hotbed of violence during the Civil War. Slavery had an uneven presence in the region: there were pockets of intense, pro-Confederate sentiment surrounded by large areas in which residents were indifferent or hostile to the Confederacy. That pattern was responsible for the region's internecine violence, which spilled over into everyday homicides. Predatory homicides were common, but so were murders over property disputes, vigilante murders, and revenge murders. Men who hated the Confederate government were unlikely to appeal to it for help, and where government collapsed, even Confederates had no legal recourse, so people got used to settling their own disputes. They took the law into their own hands whenever a friend or relative was bushwhacked, a rustler stole livestock, or a neighbor disputed property lines or refused compensation for crop damage.[74]

Women were also caught up in the violence, even though they were far less likely to kill or be killed than men. Black women were beaten to death for spying or for running away to Union lines. One slave in Pike County, Missouri, was whipped with a band saw "until large blisters formed"; her master then "sawed them open" to punish her for trying to join her husband, a soldier in the Union army. Partisans generally refrained from killing white women, but during the war attitudes toward enemy women hardened, and some men attacked them because they saw it as a way to humiliate their absent husbands. If white women engaged in any war-related activity—if they spied, tore down telegraph lines, harbored guerrillas, provided food to friends and family in hiding, or spoke out publicly—they were threatened, beaten, tortured, and in some instances raped or murdered. They were forced to watch as their homes were burned and their families shot. Six Confederate women in Cooke County, Texas, were rumored to have lynched a woman for saying that she wished the federals would win so that her husband could come home from the army and provide for his family.[75]

In the mountain South the situation was more complex. Whereas differences between Confederates and their adversaries in the borderlands closely followed class, religious, and ethnic lines, allegiances in the Appalachians and the Ozarks were mixed, particularly in those areas where the population owned few slaves and was relatively homogeneous. But generally speaking, people who supported the Union, deserted from the Confederate army, or dodged the draft were less likely to be slaveowners, less likely to be townspeople, less likely to be successful, longtime residents, and less likely to have a stake in the existing order.[76]

Geography and the behavior of regular Union and Confederate forces also played important roles in determining people's loyalties in the mountain South. The Union army lacked the manpower to occupy southern West Virginia, where support for the Confederacy was strong, so it opted for periodic raids against Confederate strongholds and Confederate militias like the Logan County Wildcats. The brutality of the Union raids galvanized support for the Confederacy and resulted in lower levels of internecine violence in southern West Virginia than in north Texas or the Texas hill country.[77]

However, in western North Carolina, eastern Tennessee, and northern Georgia, neither Confederates nor Unionists held the upper hand politically or militarily. Guerrilla, vigilante, and predatory violence were endemic. Future president James Garfield, who was then a Union officer, said that war had turned southern Appalachia into a "black hole" where men killed for "envy, lust, or revenge." In Gilmer and Rabun Counties in northern Georgia, the homicide rate during the Civil War was probably 100–200 per 100,000 adults per year, including political homicides committed by irregulars; and in the upper Cumberland region on the Tennessee-Kentucky border, the rate was at least 600 per 100,000.[78]

People in southern Appalachia were deeply divided over secession and the conduct of the war. A substantial minority remained loyal to the Union, and an even larger proportion of men—perhaps half the military-age population—deserted from the Confederate army or dodged the draft. Many refused to pay their taxes to support a war that would benefit rich slaveholders and leave their own families in need. Andrew Jones, a North Carolinian, declared that slaveowners looked upon "a white man who has to labor for an honest living as no better than one of their negroes . . . these bombastic, high falutin, aristocratic fools have been in the habit of driving negroes and poor helpless white people until they think they can control the world of mankind."[79] By mid-1862 thousands of deserters and draft resisters were hiding in the mountains, some supported by family and friends, others stealing to stay alive. To ferret them out, the Confederates loosed guerrilla leaders like John Gatewood and Champ Ferguson on the countryside, and the dissenters, deserters, and draft dodgers, whether Unionist or not, organized guerrilla bands to defend themselves.

The violence escalated rapidly. It was hard to know, as Mrs. Lou Plemmons of Gilmer County recalled, if any guerrilla band had "a side." They were all dangerous men who were willing to use any means —including terror, torture, and murder—to survive. Even those who had started out fighting for the Union or the Confederacy and were not deserters, criminals, or runaway slaves started to kill indiscriminately, in part because they did not know whom they could trust. John Gatewood operated in largely Unionist territory, so he killed every man he came across. He even shot several Confederate soldiers who were home on leave because he thought their papers might be forged. The governor of North Carolina observed that "the murder of prisoners and non-combatants in cold blood . . . has become quite common, and, in fact, almost every other horror incident to brutal and unrestrained soldiery." Women were brutalized, whipped, or hanged until nearly dead for helping guerrillas. Young boys were taken prisoner and shot.[80]

Such tactics spread fear and distrust throughout the region, and the desire for vengeance led to more political murders, predatory murders, lynchings, and bushwhackings. It was dangerous to go unarmed, even in broad daylight, and it was equally dangerous not to have friends or associates who would avenge a death. Nearly every family in the county armed itself and chose sides. With the number of combatants increasing, the number of deaths mounted steadily.

The violence continued in the mountain South well after the Civil War was over. From the late 1860s through the 1870s, the homicide rate was at least 55 per 100,000 adults per year in Taney County in the Ozarks of southern Missouri and in Gilmer and Rabun counties in northern Georgia, and at least 250 per 100,000 in Fentress and Wayne counties on the upper Cumberland Plateau in Kentucky and Tennessee (Figure 5.5). All these counties had been nonhomicidal before the war. Now they were five to twenty-five times more violent than the slaveholding South had been.[81]

In the first years after the war, men killed mostly for revenge. As journalist Whitelaw Reid observed in November 1865, "men who had been driven from their homes or half starved in the mountains, or hunted for with dogs, were not likely to be very gentle in their treatment of the men who had persecuted" them. Partisan women were just as vindictive. Frank Wilkeson, a private in the Union army who guarded a refugee camp for women and children starved or driven out of southern Appalachia, heard women "repeat over and over to their children the names of men which they were never to forget, and whom they were to kill when they had sufficient strength to hold a rifle." In the upper Cumberland, a former Union guerrilla murdered the Confederate who had killed his father during the war; in turn, he was murdered by his victim's son-in-law. The son-in-law was jailed for that killing, but a mob led by the former guerrilla's family broke into the jail, took him to the top of a mountain, tied him to a horse's tail, and shot him repeatedly as the horse bolted. Most revenge murders ended by the early 1870s, but by then hundreds of people had been killed.[82]

Former Confederates and former Unionists found new reasons to kill each other as postwar Democrats and Republicans. Few mountain

Republicans favored political or social equality for blacks, and none supported the Republicans' radical agenda in Congress; but they were still targets for the militant white supremacists who despised the federal occupation of the South and all that came with it: the Freedmen's Bureau, the enfranchisement of blacks, the Civil Rights Act of 1875, and the effort to suppress the Ku Klux Klan and other vigilante groups. In the upper Cumberland, the Pile gang killed so many Republicans that the Republican governor of Tennessee, William Brownlow, commissioned Clabe Beaty, a former Union guerrilla, to raise a company to end the violence. The Pile gang was captured, but the local sheriff, a Democrat, let the prisoners escape, and the gang's leader made good on his promise to "come back and kill." Democratic "bulldozing"—that is, intimidating or killing political opponents to prevent them from voting—was a significant problem until the late 1870s. At that point it became clear that conservative whites held the upper hand and that the Republican Party would remain a minority party in the South, even though mountain Republicans still had the power to win an occasional state election in the Upper South with the help of blacks or third-party whites.[83]

Property-dispute homicides were also endemic. In the late 1860s and 1870s the economic situation was desperate. Like much of the rest of the South, the region suffered from the wartime loss of crops and livestock, the devaluation of Confederate currency, poor prices for cotton and other staples, and the ruin of the transportation system. Economic necessity, coupled with the predatory emotions born of Civil War violence, drove many mountaineers to steal, and law enforcement proved unwilling or unable to cope. Sometimes local people attacked travelers, but for the most part they preyed on their neighbors, taking honey, hogs, sheep, money, or whiskey.[84]

The thieves killed anyone who got in their way or tried to call them to account. Some killed witnesses; others killed the law-enforcement officers who tried to prosecute them. One thief ambushed and killed a justice of the peace who had served papers on him for sheep stealing. Another, who had stolen sixteen hogs, was furious that his victim had filed suit against him, so he killed his victim's son. At a still in Gilmer County, Wofford Brown accused Anthony Goble of eating meat that Goble's father had stolen. Goble did not deny the charge, and Brown said that he would let the matter pass, since Goble had been young at the time. That assurance did not satisfy Goble, who resented any mention of his family's crimes, so he followed Brown and beat him to death. Goble boasted that Brown "begged like a d—n puppy, and I made him pray manfully." After tormenting him for a while, he tore out Brown's whiskers by the roots, "took a big two pound rock and splashed his d—n brains out, and then jumped on him, and stamped him into jelly." Theft, terror, and brutal intimidation plagued the mountain South for the rest of the century.[85]

The Revenue Act of 1873, which required all whiskey distillers to purchase licenses and pay taxes, made matters worse. Whiskey was one of the few commodities that people in the mountain South could sell for a good price, and the new law hit them hard. Former Confederates and Unionists alike fought the federal government and its local allies, the temperance advocates who blamed the violence of the postwar years on alcohol. But the fight did not unite them. The revenue agents' practice of paying informants for tips destroyed what little fellow feeling was left in the mountains and gave rise to additional feuds and vendettas. In the upper Cumberland, for example, an informant led two revenue agents to a neighbor's still. The distiller killed one of the agents and later hunted down and killed the informant.[86]

One of the worst consequences of the failure of the Confederacy was the intensification of the so-called honorific violence that had plagued the South before the war. In a society filled with mistrust, men could not afford to show weakness or to tolerate disrespect; if they did so, they risked being "run over." They came to believe that swaggering and bullying would deter attacks on themselves and their kin. As often as not, of course, that strategy led to violence. There was no veneer of civilization overlaying mountaineer violence, however: no dueling, no swordplay, no waiting for the other fellow to reload. When mountain people set out to kill, it did not matter how that killing was accomplished. It was perfectly all right to ambush a man, shoot him in the back, or gang up on him. In Rabun County, Georgia, James Bradshaw quarreled with his drunken neighbors and challenged them to fight. They agreed, and one of them held him down while the other smashed his skull with a rock.[87]

After the war the violence also continued unabated in the Confederacy's northwestern borderlands. Confederate guerrillas like the Youngers and the James brothers, who had ridden with Quantrill's rid-

ers, could not stomach returning to postwar society and became outlaws, robbing and murdering from Texas to Minnesota. Yet they continued to claim that they were fighting for the Confederacy and the
plain folk of the South. Guerrillas who stayed closer to home persisted
in trying to settle scores with Unionist neighbors. "I'm not leaving
here," one of them said. "And I'm going to kill every —— Yankee who
crosses me and every —— Negro who won't tip his hat to me." The
guerrillas aligned themselves with the Democratic Party and with terrorist groups like the Knights of the White Camellia and the Ku Klux
Klan and continued their reign of terror. Backed by federal authorities
and the Republican Party, the Unionists responded with violence of
their own.[88]

The Civil War lingered on for decades in the Confederacy's northwestern borderlands. Confederate guerrilla Bob Lee, by then referred
to as the "Man Eater" by friend and foe alike, led his men on the same
sorts of raids in north Texas that he had staged during the war, killing
for profit or politics. He also tried to preserve slavery. He kidnapped a
black child and put him to work, and he refused to pay his black laborers, forcing them at gunpoint to stay on his farm. Hardin Hart, the
county's Freedmen's Bureau agent and brother of Union guerrilla
Martin Hart, took a Republican posse to Lee's farm and liberated his
workers, but Lee escaped, vowing to kill Hart. As fugitives from justice,
Lee and his fellow guerrillas murdered Unionists, ambushed federal
patrols and supply trains, and killed federal judges, tax collectors, and
Freedmen's Bureau agents. They also killed purely for money, murdering a Missouri farmer, for example, who had just sold a load of apples
in Sherman for $500.[89]

Former Confederates in north Texas came down especially hard on
freed slaves. They needed desperately to feel superior to someone, so
they killed black men for talking back, for complaining to the Freedmen's Bureau, for refusing to be whipped, for not giving up their
money quickly when held up. One ex-Confederate claimed that he
killed blacks because they had to be "thinned out." Charlie Hodges,
one of Lee's crew, shot a black child dead because "he had his hands in
his pockets and didn't stand at attention" when Hodges rode past. Any
sign of defiance or disrespect could mean death. Black women did not
have the immunity from violence that white women did. In the eyes of
militant whites, black women did not merit respect, and raping, mur-

dering, and mutilating them was a good way to humiliate black men. Six of Lee's men robbed and murdered freedman Jeremiah Everhart in front of his family and then gang-raped his daughter. Indian Bill English killed a black woman and her child for sport. Elihu Guest shot a pregnant freedwoman and "cut out her womb with its living contents." Freedmen's Bureau agent Albert Evans reported from Sherman, Texas, in February 1867 that four freedmen had been murdered in a single week. "The slaughtering of freedmen still goes on."[90]

Bob Lee was killed by a posse of Unionists and federal soldiers in May 1869, but his men carried on after he was killed. In only six years the fighting between Lee's men and Unionists claimed more than 200 lives and was indirectly responsible for hundreds more in a four-county area with a population of only 40,000. That toll was typical for counties in north Texas, Arkansas, and southern Missouri, all of which were terrorized by former Confederate guerrillas. The Union army could not do much to stop the killing. General Philip Sheridan despaired for freed people and white Unionists in rural Texas: their plight was "truly horrible." But as Lieutenant William Hoffman wrote from Greenville, Texas, in July 1869, the hatred of former rebels for the federals was too deep to overcome. "The coming generation, children and children's children are zealously reared to the one great tenet: implacable hatred to the government." That hatred, which correlates so strongly with high homicide rates in every era, continued to inform life in this region, as it did in most areas of the rural South. In the absence of governments that all parties considered legitimate, and with no sense of national unity that could have strengthened bonds among unrelated men, such violence was inevitable. It did not matter who held the upper hand. The murder rate in the northwest borderlands would not begin to fall until the 1930s.[91]

Homicide rates were not horrific everywhere in the South. In rural Virginia the rates after the Civil War were twice what they had been in the late 1850s, but they were still no higher than they had been on average in the decades before the Kansas-Nebraska Act: 9 per 100,000 adults per year (Figure 5.6). The homicide arrest rate in Richmond was also modest for a southern city in the 1870s: 13 per 100,000 adults per year.[92] Although Virginians encountered their share of hardships during and after the war, their experience was different in crucial ways. Unlike all the other Confederate states, Virginia never saw any guerrilla warfare. Whites in the Chesapeake and the Shenandoah Valley were nearly unanimous in their support for the Confederacy until the final days of the war. The loss of northwestern Virginia in 1861 put most of the state's Unionists behind federal lines, and the decision of the Confederate Congress in August 1861 to seize the property of Unionists who remained in the South forced hundreds of remaining Union sympathizers to flee. The success of the Army of Northern Virginia through the summer of 1864 kept morale high a full year after defeats in Mississippi and Tennessee had undermined morale in the rest of the Confederacy. And, perhaps most important, Virginia's state government, its county governments, and the national government in Richmond were responsive to Virginians who were upset by the government's conduct of the war.

As elsewhere in the Confederacy, many white Virginians who did not own slaves resented the Confederacy's policies on the draft, taxes, and impressments of food and livestock. But the government changed its policies in Virginia in 1863–64. It cut state taxes and increased county aid for the poor and for families of soldiers, enforced price controls to prevent gouging by merchants and speculators, and forced wealthy men into the army by limiting exemptions and outlawing the hiring of substitutes. These policies ensured government stability and popular support for the Confederacy in Virginia and kept homicide rates under control.[93]

There was some support for the Union in Virginia, but most of it came from the poor. Delilah Doggett, a single mother, believed that poor people "had no chance at all" in the planter-dominated Confederacy. Simeon Shaw, a tenant farmer, declared that he "regarded the war as altogether wrong and unnecessary. I considered it was carried on in the interest of slavery. I had no negroes and I told the sesech [secessionists] I was not going to fight for them. If the South had gained their independence, a poor man like me would stand no chance at all here." But the Confederate army and the Home Guard were so powerful that anyone who tried to rebel against the government was crushed. Several hundred Unionists made a stand in the Blue Ridge Mountains in April 1862, but General Stonewall Jackson shelled them into submission. In Franklin County deserters burned three farms, but vigilantes tracked them to a cave and hanged them all. When deserters staged robberies later in the war, Home Guard sentries captured between sixty and seventy of them, ending the crime wave.[94]

The strength of the Union army in Virginia was also a factor. There was little territory not under the firm control of either the Union or the Confederacy, and would-be guerrillas had no room to maneuver. When a Union officer was ambushed in the Shenandoah Valley in September 1864, the Union army burned every barn within a five-mile radius. "The burning," as local residents referred to it for decades thereafter, put an effective end to resistance.[95]

Virginia did see its share of interracial violence during the war. Confederate and Union soldiers lynched or decapitated slaves and free blacks suspected of spying, and Confederate soldiers murdered several hundred black soldiers who had been taken prisoner. But senior officers tried to stop such crimes. General Lee confronted a group of soldiers who were marching black prisoners into the woods to kill them. He placed the prisoners under his personal protection and told his soldiers that he would have them shot if they killed a prisoner of any race. Some slaves who were fleeing toward Union lines or who had been liberated resisted reenslavement violently. In 1862 100 fugitives from Surry County killed 3 whites who tried to prevent their escape. A group of field hands killed planters who tried to reclaim them after Confederate soldiers were routed from the area. For the most part, however, blacks were firmly behind Confederate or Union lines, so occasions for such violence were rare.[96]

During the early years of Reconstruction interracial violence increased. When blacks marched in Norfolk in April 1866 to celebrate the passage of the federal Civil Rights Act, whites attacked them with bottles and brickbats. One marcher was shot by a white man who was in turn killed by angry blacks, and a riot ensued. Union soldiers managed to clear the streets, but four more blacks were wounded and three more whites were killed. Blacks who worked in the tobacco fields were routinely threatened, stabbed, or beaten if they demanded better wages, complained of mistreatment to federal authorities, or tried to find other work. They risked death if they campaigned openly for the Republican Party in 1867–68.[97]

Federal authorities were afraid that Virginia would go the way of the rest of the post–Civil War South. The political situation was unsettled, and law enforcement was weak. Political homicides, predatory homicides, and revenge homicides occurred in many counties, and it appears that homicide rates rose statewide from April 1865, when the war ended, to October 1869, when Virginia elected its first governor and legislature under the revised constitution of 1868. Political polarization and alienation ran deep. Major General Alfred Terry, who supervised military affairs in Virginia at the end of 1865, said that former Confederates, "having failed to maintain a separate nationality . . . desire to keep themselves a separate people, and to prevent, by any means in their power, our becoming a homogeneous nation; second, they desire to make treason honorable and loyalty infamous, and to secure, as far as they may be able, political power." When former Confederates won control of the first government formed under President Johnson in 1866, they rejected the Fourteenth Amendment and passed laws that made de facto slaves of freed people. They even tried to name former Confederate general Jubal Early governor, even though Early, living in exile in Canada, had vowed that "if I were made Governor, I would have the whole State in another war in less than a week."[98]

Blacks and white Unionists turned the tables in 1867, when Congress extended voting rights to blacks, disfranchised former Confederates, and ordered elections for delegates to a convention that would rewrite Virginia's constitution. The constitution they drafted in 1868 guaranteed the right of blacks to vote and hold office, denied those rights to many former Confederates, created a system of tax-supported schools, and permitted the progressive taxation of property. Members of the Conservative Party, formed shortly after the war, were prepared for a showdown with the new government in the gubernatorial and legislative election scheduled for October 1868, and they were just as determined to overturn the new constitution as their Republican adversaries were to uphold it. But General John M. Schofield, the commander of Union forces in Virginia, delayed the election for a year because he wanted both Conservatives and Republicans to accept the right of blacks and former Confederates to vote. That move gave the centrist minorities in both parties an opportunity to come to the fore, which they did, and at length both parties agreed to support universal manhood suffrage.[99]

That decision, more than any other, was responsible for rural Virginia's moderate homicide rate after 1869. The Conservatives won the election of 1869 by a narrow margin, but they did so without fraud or violence, and the defeated Republicans grudgingly accepted the legitimacy of the government, since it represented the will of the majority. But the outcome of the election was as important as the process in deterring homicide. Virginia was one of only two states in the former Confederacy that never elected a Republican governor or legislature during Reconstruction. Prewar elites maintained control, except at the constitutional convention, and white supremacy was never seriously challenged. Conservative Party member John S. Wise of Richmond bragged that in Virginia there had not been "any period in which negroes or alien and degraded whites were in a position to oppress." The Conservatives quickly passed measures to protect white supremacy. They imposed a poll tax, segregated the militia, disfranchised voters convicted of petty theft, preserved the whipping post as a punishment for crimes, and refused to fund the state's public schools adequately, all to keep blacks in their place. But they did not resort to terrorism, because they had a firm grasp on power. The postwar government was not uniformly popular, but it was stable and legitimate in the eyes of most Virginians.[100]

Post–Civil War Virginia was not by any means nonhomicidal, but it saw few political assassinations, lynchings, ambush killings, gang murders, or deadly confrontations involving law-enforcement officers in the late 1860s and 1870s. The Ku Klux Klan made a fleeting appearance in 1868, but it and other supremacist terror groups failed to garner much support, because whites were largely content with their situation. The rate at which rural Virginians were murdered by unknown persons was only 1 per 100,000 adults per year for blacks and for whites. Guns inundated the Chesapeake and the Shenandoah Valley during and after the Civil War, as they did the mountain South and the Confederacy's northwestern borderlands, but gun use in homicides did not increase there during Reconstruction: blacks killed a tenth of their victims with guns and whites a third. There was no increase in gun use in Virginia because there was no sustained increase in intentional violence.[101]

In the late 1860s and the 1870s whites murdered blacks in Virginia at a rate of 2.4 per 100,000 adults per year. That rate was as low as the rate in the early 1830s, after the violence prompted by Nat Turner's rebellion subsided. The rate at which blacks murdered whites also stayed low, at 1.8 per 100,000. Despite the barriers erected to prevent their participation in government, blacks had new ways of asserting themselves, and most could vote or change jobs without being molested. Deadly whippings of servants had ended with emancipation. Of course, powerful deterrents to violence remained; the justice system was still controlled by white supremacists, and any black who raised a hand to a white was certain to be imprisoned or hanged. However, the rate at which blacks murdered one another rose after the war. For the first time it was as high as the rate at which whites murdered one another: 5 per 100,000 per year. The solidarity that had deterred homicides among blacks in slave times was dissipating with freedom.[102]

Virginia society was still hierarchical, and it generated the same discontents and the same spirit of antagonistic competition that it had before the war. Blacks and whites alike feuded over debts, stolen clothes, injured horses, crop damage, or fence rails.[103] But the society was no more antagonistic or homicidal in the late 1860s and 1870s than the society of rural Ohio or Illinois, where homicide rates had risen. And in a further irony, the fact that conservative whites held power through the difficult years of Reconstruction enabled black and white Republicans to make something of a political comeback in Virginia in 1879, and their renaissance probably helped keep homicide rates down by further legitimizing Virginia's polity.

Virginia's Conservatives failed as badly as Republicans in other southern states to meet the basic challenges of rebuilding railroads and factories, restoring agricultural productivity, and educating the workforce at a time when capital was in short supply and global competition was depressing the prices of wheat, tobacco, and other commodities. The Conservatives were not only overwhelmed; they were corrupt and incompetent, and the state government wound up deeply in debt and unable to fund public schools even for whites. White moderates formed the Re-adjuster Party under the leadership of railroad entrepreneur and former Confederate general William Mahone, who wanted to reduce the state debt and increase support for education and transportation. The Re-adjusters were white supremacists, but they reached out to blacks and white Republicans for support on key issues and with their help won the governorship and passed measures in the legislature that helped democratize Virginia society and politics.

The coalition lasted only four years, but it cut the state debt, increased school funding, repealed the poll tax, abolished the whipping post, and gave black teachers the same pay as white teachers. Its success—and the peaceful way in which the Conservatives surrendered power in 1879—kept the homicide rate in check.[104]

Homicide rates were much worse elsewhere in the former slave-holding South, where law and order did break down during and after the Civil War and former Confederates lost power to blacks and white Republicans. The rates in former slave areas did not climb as high as rates in the mountain South or the Confederacy's northwestern borderlands during the Civil War, because the great majority of whites supported the Confederacy (at least until the defeats at Vicksburg and Gettysburg) and refrained from attacking one another. But wherever Union forces established beachheads early in the war, as they did in the lower Mississippi Valley and in the lower Chattahoochee Valley of Alabama and Georgia, and wherever they swept Confederate forces from an area but did not occupy it, as in northern Georgia, homicides became more numerous.[105]

In these contested or unoccupied areas, there was no effective government in the latter years of the Civil War, and the bonds that normally prevented citizens from preying on one another came unraveled. Criminals, deserters, draft dodgers, Confederate Home Guards, and Union patrols engaged in a free-for-all.[106] But homicide rates in these battle-ravaged areas reached their worst levels after the Civil War, when former Confederates lost control to black and white Republicans. Rates were highest where former Confederates were out of power for the longest time and where they fought stubbornly against any sort of compromise with freed people, white Unionists, or federal authorities. In Georgia former Confederates were out of power during the four-year administration of Republican governor Rufus Bullock, but by 1870 they had enough power in the legislature to keep Bullock and his fellow Republicans hemmed in. During that time the homicide rate in plantation counties in the Piedmont rose from 10 per 100,000 adults per year (roughly the same as Virginia's prewar rate) to 25 per 100,000. In Louisiana, where Republicans controlled the state government for eight years, the rural homicide rate reached at least 90 per 100,000 adults per year (Figures 4.1 and 7.1).

The surge in homicides was overwhelmingly the work of former

Confederates. They killed blacks, white Republicans, and one another at an alarming rate. They were responsible for the great disparity between the rates at which blacks and whites committed murder in Republican-governed states. In rural Louisiana, for example, sixteen times as many blacks were killed in interracial confrontations as whites, and whites killed one another at twice the rate blacks did (34 per 100,000 adults per year versus 18 per 100,000). Homicide rates were lower in plantation counties in Georgia and South Carolina, but the disparities between the rates at which whites and blacks committed homicide were similar. The contrast with Virginia, where former Confederates held onto power, was stark. Wherever reactionary whites remained in power, they killed at the same rates they had before the war. Where they lost power, they killed with abandon.[107]

Roughly three-fifths of the nonfamily, nonintimate homicides committed by whites in Louisiana and Georgia during Reconstruction grew out of political or economic disputes. Many of these killings were mass murders of Republicans or black laborers. In Georgia a dozen freedmen died when white militants attacked a Republican rally in Camilla and a polling station in Savannah, and perhaps a dozen more were killed in gang attacks on black farm workers in Henry and Columbia counties. In Louisiana hundreds died in the Colfax Massacre of 1873, the Coushatta affair of 1874, the Caledonia and Natchitoches riots of 1878, and the Bossier and Caddo riots of 1868. The latter two occurred when white militants in the Red River Valley retaliated against local blacks who had tried to arrest a white trader for shooting at a black man.[108]

Some of the violence was spontaneous, but much of it was organized by terror groups like the Ku Klux Klan that were determined to end Republican rule and return white-supremacist Democrats to power. These organizations, led by former Confederate officers and manned primarily by veterans of the Confederate army, were desperately opposed to emancipation, equal rights, and "Negro rule." They wanted to hold on to their cheap, exploitable workforce, but on a deeper level they were terrified of what might happen if black men became full participants in society. Southerners would become "a race of mulattoes . . . another Mexico; we shall be ruled out from the family of white nations. . . . It is a matter of life and death with the Southern people to keep their blood pure." One Georgia Republican observed sharply that "if you talk about equality, they at once conclude that you must take the negro into your parlor or into your bed—everywhere that you would take your wife. They seemed to be diseased upon that subject."[109]

The primary targets of these terror groups were leaders in the Republican Party—preachers, politicians, educators, landowners, militiamen, Union army veterans, and anyone who spoke out about political matters. In the months before state and national elections such people were at grave risk. In October 1868 the Ku Klux Klan killed two freedmen who were politically active in Wilkes County, Georgia, and tried to kill Thomas Allen, a black legislator from Jasper County, but by mistake killed Allen's brother-in-law, Emanuel Trippe. The Klan also killed a friend of Allen's in Jasper County, Malory Cheek, "who had openly denounced the So called *KuKlux*." In the summer before his death, several "Democratic clubs" had visited Cheek and his brother John "to induce us to join them but . . . we refused to have anything to do with them." Malory Cheek went into hiding for months but "gradually became careless of his Safety" and returned home to his wife and children, where the Klan found him one night. John Cheek and his sons fled the state without harvesting their crops.[110]

Blacks bore the brunt of terrorist violence in Georgia, but white Republicans were not spared. George W. Ashburn, an accomplished party organizer, was killed at his boardinghouse in Columbus by a mob of forty men. State senator Joseph Adkins of Warren County, an elderly preacher and farmer and a dedicated Unionist, was murdered as he walked home from the station after a trip to Washington, D.C., to ask for federal aid to stop the violence. State senator Benjamin Ayer of Jefferson County, an elderly physician and a Unionist, was shot dead in the street after he returned from a similar trip. Sheriff Ruffin of Richmond County, who had stood up fearlessly to the Klan, was killed on election day in November 1869. The Klan intimidated Republicans so effectively that Democrats won the legislature in 1870, lessening the need for further violence. The reign of terror lasted another six years in Louisiana, because Republicans held onto power longer there.[111]

Conservative whites also killed fellow Conservatives at an astounding rate. The hostile emotions engendered by political conflict seeped into all social relations and surfaced in a pervasive disrespect for the law and the government, an extreme sensitivity about one's standing in society, a need to dominate others, and a terror of being dominated. Whites who lived in Republican-dominated areas of the former plantation South were far more likely than whites who lived in Conservative-dominated Virginia to kill other whites over insults and property disputes, and to rob and rape. Murders over insults, property-dispute murders, and predatory murders had been common among whites in the slaveholding South, but in areas where Republicans held power they were far more common after the war. Such murders counted for two-fifths of all homicides committed by whites in Louisiana and for fourth-fifths in plantation counties in Georgia and South Carolina, where political homicides accounted for a smaller portion of homicides.[112]

Blacks were also more murderous (though not to the degree that whites were) where state and local governments were too weak to protect life or property. A handful committed robbery, rape, or revenge murders against whites, and a few killed whites who treated them as second-class citizens. In Edgefield County, South Carolina, for instance, a black Union soldier murdered a belligerent former Confederate who ordered him off a sidewalk. But for the most part blacks killed whites to defend their property, their families, their lives, and the freedoms that the Union victory had conferred. They knew they had right on their side, but they also knew the law would not help them. A black man named George Ashley killed a sugar plantation owner after he refused to let Ashley leave the plantation for a better job. A man named Yankee killed Irwin Garrett, the manager of a sugar plantation in Assumption Parish, Louisiana, after Garrett refused to pay him his wages. Perry Jefferson, who was a sharecropper on a cotton plantation in Warren County, Georgia, returned fire when Klansmen surrounded his cabin in November 1868. They had targeted Jefferson because he was prospering and because he had refused to join the county's Democratic club. Jefferson and his sons killed one of the Klansmen and wounded three.[113]

It was inevitable that defensive murders would be more common in Georgia and Louisiana than in Virginia because of the violence and oppression blacks faced there. Nevertheless, blacks attacked whites far less often than whites attacked blacks. The consequences of such murders were as dire as they had been in slave times. Black suspects who did not flee faced certain death, and the chances of escaping were slim. Black suspects in murders of whites were usually hunted by posses of 100 or more men. After Perry Jefferson killed the Klansman, he and four of his sons hid in the woods. He thought the posse would spare his wife and crippled son, but they shot his son eleven times and tortured his wife to get her to disclose his hiding place. Jefferson and his surviving sons surrendered to the Republican sheriff, who jailed them for their own safety until they could catch a train for South Carolina. Klansmen stood watch at every depot, however, and pulled the Jeffersons off the train when it crossed the county line. One son managed to escape, but Jefferson and his other sons were shot. Such cases were all too common.[114]

For that reason, if for no other, blacks refrained from killing whites. They asked the state, the federal government, and moderate whites for protection, but no real help was available, so they defended themselves as best they could through political activism, collective self-defense, and restraint. They campaigned to elect sheriffs and judges who would defend them against violence, and they marched in defense of their rights. They formed militia companies and neighborhood bands of ten to fifteen men to protect themselves against nightriders, and they carried guns with them everywhere: to church, political meetings, stores, fields—anywhere whites might attack them. They resisted arbitrary arrest, but made it clear that they were willing to submit to real justice. The hope was that these measures, together with self-help, greater economic independence, and the creation of their own social and religious institutions, would deter white attacks and give blacks sufficient power to resist de facto reenslavement and to build a relatively free community.[115]

As frustration with their political predicament grew, however, blacks in Republican-dominated states like Georgia and South Carolina began to see more violence in their own communities. They did not have much property to fight over, so feuds were rare; but many of them found it hard to bear any kind of insult, and they were more jealous of their standing within the community than blacks in Virginia were. One man, in jest, asked a friend if he could check his collar for lice. His friend shot him dead. Sam Howard told an acquaintance that he should be "ashamed of himself" for threatening to whip a group of young girls who had sassed him, and his acquaintance stabbed him in the back. Another called a man "a democrat negro" for holding a white man's horse. Three men died in the shootout that followed. Any insult that made someone appear degraded or servile or dishonest could trigger a violent response.[116]

Both blacks and whites were bushwhacked and killed by unknown persons more often than before the war. In plantation counties in Georgia and South Carolina in the late 1860s and the 1870s, unknown persons killed blacks at a rate of 2 per 100,000 adults per year and whites at a rate of 5 per 100,000. In rural Louisiana the rates were 15 per 100,000 for blacks and 12 per 100,000 for whites. Again, the rates were much higher than those in rural Virginia.[117]

As always, wherever the homicide rate rose, so did the percentage of murders committed with guns as more people carried guns to assert or protect themselves. Before the Civil War, blacks in plantation counties in Georgia and South Carolina used guns in 7 percent of the homicides they committed and whites in 38 percent: roughly the same percentages as in pre– and post–Civil War Virginia. But after the war, blacks used guns in 57 percent of the homicides they committed and whites in 80 percent. It is telling that blacks and whites used guns at the same rate whether they were killing blacks or whites. Carrying guns to perpetrate interracial violence or to defend themselves against it also increased the likelihood that whites would kill whites and blacks would kill blacks.[118]

Homicide rates were lower in cities and plantation counties in Republican-ruled states where the prewar elite came to terms with emancipation, civil rights laws, and Republican rule. In Louisiana, for example, sugar counties and cotton counties in the Mississippi Delta had homicide rates less than half those of the rest of the state, even though they were still about four times higher than the rate in Virginia—35 per 100,000 adults per year. The presence of federal troops and the state police in nearby New Orleans prevented the worst violence by the Ku Klux Klan and the Knights of the White Camellia and probably lowered the number of lynchings and mass killings.[119]

Planters in the Delta and the Sugar Bowl quickly realized that productivity would suffer if black workers were too harshly mistreated and frightened away. There was also considerable support among white elites for specific Republican policies: a protective tariff on sugar imports, funds to rebuild levees, and federally subsidized railroad construction. Along with concerns about a stable supply of workers, these policies prompted some former Confederates to break ranks with conservative Democrats in hopes of restoring peace and prosperity. In 1870 General James Longstreet joined the Republican Party and accepted command of the integrated state militia. A number of prominent sugar and Delta cotton planters did likewise and succeeded in electing Republicans from predominantly black districts who were receptive to their interests. Their embrace of Republicanism probably deterred homicide by putting more militant whites on the defensive and by fostering greater trust in government among moderate whites and Republicans.[120]

What happened in New Orleans was more remarkable. Even though deadly antiblack riots occurred in 1866 and 1868 and the city's integrated police force barely survived a pitched battle against white supremacists in 1874 that left 27 dead and more than 100 wounded, the homicide rate dropped to 35 per 100,000 adults per year from a prewar high of 60 per 100,000 (Figure 7.1). The disparities between the rates at which whites and blacks committed homicide were the same as in rural Louisiana, but the rates were far lower. As in rural areas, whites killed half of their unrelated victims for political or economic reasons, and blacks a fifth. Five times as many blacks were killed in interracial confrontations as whites, and whites killed one another at twice the rate at which blacks killed other blacks.[121]

White violence was a serious problem, but it was less extreme than it had been in the 1850s, when nativists and immigrants fought constantly. The city had more than its share of white brawlers, gamblers, and rivermen. But hostility between the native-born and immigrants diminished as the Irish in New Orleans (and other southern cities) rallied to the cause of white supremacy. It helped that the metropolitan police force was integrated and that white merchants and financiers were not wholly averse to Republican economic policies and were eager to revive the productive relationship they had had with the city's free black community before the war. In 1873 General P. G. T. Beauregard organized a Unification movement with some of the city's black leaders that promised a more cooperative relationship between the races, albeit a more unequal one than the Republicans offered. New Orleans remained a very homicidal place. Angry ex-Confederates prowled the streets looking for trouble. Returned soldier Emile Delseriez expressed the hope that one day whites would be able to put blacks in their place again. "We will have no mercy for them. We will kill them like dogs. I [was] never down on a nigger as I am now." But the effectiveness and inclusiveness of the city's Republican government and the conciliatory gestures made by conservative white elites prevented the violence from becoming worse.[122]

Homicide in the Southwest

Because its population was so small, the Southwest did not have a great impact on the nation's homicide rate in the mid-nineteenth century. But the region was staggeringly violent. Homicide rates rose in the late 1840s and early 1850s to the highest levels in the United States—probably 250 per 100,000 adults per year or more. In California rates declined gradually after the mid-1850s but remained high through the 1870s. In counties dominated by immigrants from Europe and the eastern United States they stood at roughly 25 per 100,000, and in mining counties and in farming and ranching counties where Hispanics and Indians made up a substantial minority of the population they were 60 per 100,000 or more (Figure 7.2). In Arizona, Colorado, New Mexico, and south and west Texas, where the mining and cattle booms were just under way in the late 1860s and the 1870s, homicide rates did not decline during this period. They ranged at a minimum from 140 per 100,000 adults per year in Colorado and 250 per 100,000 in New Mexico and in south and west Texas to 600 per 100,000 in Arizona.[123]

The increase in homicide in the Southwest can be attributed in part to the feelings and beliefs that settlers from the North and South brought with them. The same sorts of homicides that plagued the North and South appeared in the Southwest as soon as settlers arrived: murders that stemmed from political, ethnic, racial, or religious conflict, from vigilante or predatory violence, or from personal quarrels or property disputes. In San Francisco, for example, from 1849 to 1880, 6 percent of victims were murdered by mobs, vigilantes, or politically or racially motivated killers, 16 percent by disputants over property, and 25 percent by robbers, rapists, or gang members. Fifty-two percent were killed over insults, gambling disputes, or questions of honor, half of them in brothels, dance halls, or taverns.[124]

The rapid influx of so many settlers during the cattle and mining booms also contributed to the Southwest's homicide problem. The lawlessness of cattle towns and mining camps and the propensity of their largely male population to gamble, drink heavily, and consort with prostitutes made predatory and recreational violence far more common than in the North or South and increased homicide rates for men and women alike. Women seldom became killers themselves, unless they were involved in prostitution or engaged in property disputes alongside their husbands; but they were killed more often by rapists and robbers than women elsewhere in the country, especially if they worked as prostitutes, saloon waitresses, or dance hall girls. In California in the 1850s and early 1860s the rate stood at 9 per 100,000 women per year (the rate for men was 81 per 100,000). The violence was compounded by handguns, which became the weapons of choice for His-

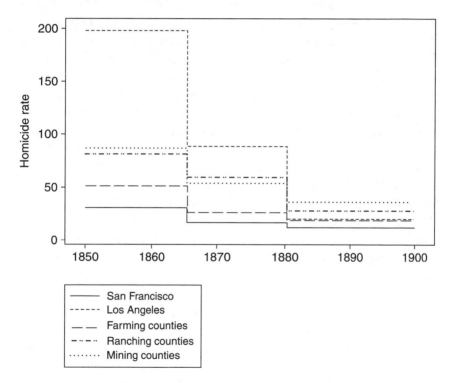

Figure 7.2 Homicide rates in California, 1849–1900 (per 100,000 adults per year). Farming counties: Sacramento and San Joaquin. Mining counties: Calaveras and Tuolumne. Ranching counties: San Diego, San Luis Obispo, and Santa Barbara.

panics and Anglos after the Texas Rangers popularized their use during the Mexican War. From the late 1840s through the 1870s over half of all homicides in California were committed with guns, and probably two-thirds in south and west Texas.[125]

The same conditions that gave rise to the feelings and beliefs associated with high homicide rates in the North and the South were certainly present in the Southwest. It was obvious that there was no stable, legitimate government or reliable legal system. There was a marked shortage of empathy, especially among people of different ethnic backgrounds, and earning status and respect was a struggle. Workers and small proprietors were frustrated, especially in the mining and cattle industries, over economic inequality and the difficulty of achieving economic independence, and ethnic and racial minorities resented the prejudice and discrimination that consigned them to the bottom of the region's social hierarchy. The American conquest of 1846–47 destroyed the territorial governments that Mexico had established and left the region in a state of near anarchy. The lack of effective government and the uncertainty of land titles in Mexico's former borderlands allowed the struggle among Anglos, Hispanics, and Native Americans for control of the region's resources to spiral out of control and led to so many robbery, revenge, vigilante, and property-dispute murders that the region was in a virtual state of undeclared war. California's state and county governments were able to establish the rudiments of law and order in the late 1850s as the influx of settlers slowed and spending on law enforcement increased. But in the rest of the Southwest, especially in the mountains and on the open range, lawlessness persisted into the 1860s and 1870s. State and territorial governments were too weak and unstable to protect lives and property.

It proved difficult to establish legitimate governments in the Southwest. The majority of Hispanics and Native Americans opposed the American occupation and the governments established in its wake, which they quite rightly perceived as hostile; and Anglos disagreed bitterly among themselves over slavery, race relations, immigration, and the distribution of the spoils of conquest. These divisions ran so deep that it was impossible for any government to represent the values and interests of the majority of citizens or to win their trust. The rapid influx of so many alien cultures did little to help foster harmony. Immigrants flooded into the Southwest from Europe, Latin America, and Asia. When Emma H. Adams visited Tucson in 1884, she was astounded to see how many nationalities were represented there: "Americans, Mexicans, Germans, Russians, Italians, Austrians, Frenchmen, Spaniards, Greeks, the Chinese, Japanese, Portuguese, the African, Irishman, and Sandwich Islander."[126] Most of these immigrants were ambitious and aggressive young men who were veterans of the Mexican War or came from violent places like New York City, southeast China, the slaveholding South, or central Mexico. They fought the native-born Hispanic and Indian inhabitants of the Southwest, and they fought among themselves: they were as likely to kill their own kind as to kill across racial or national lines. It would take a generation to create governments that were sufficiently stable and legitimate to end the worst violence, and even then the people of the Southwest were too bitterly divided to forge a sense of kinship strong enough to deter homicide.

The Mexican War set off the initial surge in homicides in the Southwest. The war was inspired by militants from the plantation South who wanted to carry slavery, Protestantism, and white supremacy into the Mexican borderlands, and their conquest of northern Mexico was savage. Soldiers and filibusterers viewed Hispanics and Natives with contempt, and in the absence of effective civil or military government they committed innumerable atrocities. While the regular army did a fair job of deterring assaults on civilians, other units made matters worse. The Texas Rangers, who were sent to northern Mexico by the state government, killed so many unarmed civilians that General Zachary Taylor asked that no more Rangers be attached to his command, since their "atrocities" had intensified Mexican resistance. "The mounted men from Texas have scarcely made one expedition without unwarrantably killing a Mexican," he declared. The Mexicans called the Rangers "los Tejanos sangrientos"—the bloody Texans. As one regular said, "The Mexicans dread the Texians more than they do the devil, and they have good reason for it."[127]

When volunteer units from the South were involved, violence against civilians was the rule rather than the exception. Samuel Chamberlain, a private in a cavalry company that served under General Zachary Taylor, wrote that volunteers from Arkansas and Kentucky believed that "greasers" belonged "to the same social class as their own

Negro slaves." They "plundered and ill-treated them, and outraged the women . . . sometimes in the presence of the fathers and husbands, who were tied up and flogged for daring to interfere in these amusements." They whipped priests, converted cathedrals into stables, and desecrated churches, tearing down crucifixes and dragging them through the streets. They killed innumerable civilians. Men from a Kentucky regiment shot a boy in a field for target practice. Volunteers from another regiment shot an elderly sheepherder "because he objected to the shooting of his sheep." On Christmas Day 1846 several volunteers "insulted" women at Rancho Agua Nueve, and men from the ranch retaliated by killing an Arkansan near his camp. The Arkansan's comrades rode to the ranch, forced sixty men, women, and children into a cave, and started to slaughter them. When General Wool and his regulars heard the gunfire, they rushed to the scene. One Arkansan, holding a bloody scalp, told Wool not to interfere. "We don't a muss with you," he said. Wool ignored him. He and his men were able to rescue forty of the Mexicans.[128]

Mexican guerrillas, who came from areas every bit as violent as the American South, were equally ruthless. Determined to make the American occupation as costly as possible, they routinely picked off soldiers who went to towns or ranches on their days off. They also murdered Mexicans who gave aid and comfort to the enemy. "Yankedoes"—Mexican women who lived with American soldiers—faced the worst violence. One woman in northern Mexico had her ears cut off for fraternizing with an American lieutenant, and another was gang-raped and cut to pieces because she had left her husband for an American soldier. The day that the American army withdrew from the Mexican town of Saltillo, twenty-three "Yankedos" were dragged to the town square. "For hours they were subjected to nameless horrors," including rape by burros. When the guerrillas were done they cut the women's throats.[129]

The politically and racially motivated violence carried into New Mexico and Arizona, where the American occupation had begun peacefully. A new territorial government took shape quickly under Governor Charles Bent, but in January 1847 he and six people traveling with him were murdered under suspicious circumstances near Taos. Over the next few weeks thirteen more Americans were killed in villages north of Santa Fe along the Rio Grande River—the same villages that had staged the 1837 revolt against the Mexican government. The attacks were credited at first to Indians, but they were instigated by the former lieutenant governor of New Mexico, Diego Archuleta, who was angry because General Stephen Kearney had annexed the entire territory after supposedly promising to let Archuleta govern the western half as an independent state. The anti-American insurgency commanded 1,500 troops at its peak—most of them *genízaros* and *paisanos* who were afraid of losing their land. The American army rallied and dispersed the insurgents after intense fighting. More than seventy insurgents died. These killings left a legacy of bitterness in the region.[130]

Bounty hunters—many of them veterans or deserters from the Mexican War—compounded the hostility by killing and scalping nomadic Native Americans. The governor of Sonora, Mexico, wanted to stop Apache raids on Mexican towns and villages along the territorial border and offered a bounty of $50 for each Apache scalp, but he was willing to pay for the scalp of any Indian, man, woman, or child. Dozens of bounty hunters were attracted by his offer, but perhaps the most successful was Joel Glanton, a famous Texas rebel, Ranger, and Indian fighter. Glanton, originally from Edgefield County, South Carolina, thought little of killing men in feuds or barroom brawls, and his work as a "free scout" for the Republic of Texas had prepared him well for "raising the hair" of enemies. After being forced to leave the army for killing a fellow infantryman, he recruited a band of equally unscrupulous men and set off to hunt scalps. Glanton's band murdered scores of Native Americans in southern New Mexico and Arizona, some of them marauders and some not, and they committed rapes and robberies as well. When Indians became too hard to find, they harvested Mexican scalps.[131]

Similar atrocities occurred in California, where the Bear Flag rebels—a motley band of American soldiers, trappers, adventurers, and pioneers—started their own campaign in June 1846 to liberate the territory from Mexico. They loosed a reign of terror against Native Americans and Hispanics from Stockton to San Francisco, looting houses, stealing livestock, and brutalizing the inhabitants. Two of these rebels enslaved a band of Indians at Rancho Nipomo, worked them mercilessly, raped the women, and used the men for target practice. A Bear Flag patrol on the shore of Suisun Bay opened fire on three Hispanic men who were landing in a small boat, not waiting to discover whether they were Mexican soldiers. Ramón de Haro fell first, and when his twin brother, Francisco, tried to shield him, a Bear Flag officer yelled, "Kill the other son of a bitch." Their uncle, José Berreyesa, pleaded with the patrol. "Is it possible that you kill these young men for no reason at all? It is better that you kill me who am old too!" So they did. Pitched battles between American soldiers and Californios took forty more lives before the arrival of 1,500 New York volunteers in March 1847 ended the military phase of the American conquest.[132]

The political instability and racial conflict that followed the Mexican War played out differently in California, south Texas, and the mining and cattle country that lay between and thus had different impacts on homicide rates in the various regions of the Southwest. In California the homicide rate for non-Indians was over 230 per 100,000 adults per year in 1848 and in 1854–55. Most murders in mid-nineteenth-century California were perpetrated by Anglos, who were determined to relegate native-born Hispanics and Native Americans to the bottom of the social hierarchy and to bar Asians, Latin Americans, and free blacks from entering the Southwest and becoming citizens. In the immediate postwar period California's government was simply too weak to prosecute white supremacists, so in most instances murders of minorities went unpunished. Interracial homicides claimed the lives of only 28 percent of Anglos in the 1850s and early 1860s, but because of the great number of minorities killed by Anglos, such homicides claimed 55 percent of Hispanic victims, 56 percent of Chinese victims, 61 percent of black victims, and 66 percent of Native American victims. Most Anglos had never lived in close proximity to free people of different races and nationalities and felt demeaned by having to compete with them. "Amalgamation" was unthinkable. As the editor of the *Californian* said in 1849, "We desire only a white population."[133]

Hispanics, Native Americans, and Anglos killed one another at very high rates during the Gold Rush of the late 1840s and 1850s. In the bonanza year of 1848, gold was plentiful and labor in short supply, so Hispanic prospectors were tolerated and Indian laborers welcomed. But in 1849 nearly 100,000 immigrants arrived in northern and central California, including 80,000 Anglos, 8,000 Mexicans, and 5,000 South Americans. By 1852, 250,000 immigrants had arrived. The goldfields were crowded, and surface deposits had begun to play out. As a result, Anglo miners tried to drive Hispanics and Indians out of the diggings, and Anglos who ranched or farmed drove Hispanics and Indians off their land elsewhere in California so that they could monopolize the market for provisioning miners. That is when the killing began in earnest. Charles Daniell, a Forty-niner, did not stray far from the truth when he told his mother that to "see the elephant" in California meant "to shoot three Indians, hang two greasers, kill a grisly bear, and dig a seven pound lump of gold."[134]

The settlers' war against Hispanics and Native Americans cost thousands of lives. General Persifor F. Smith, commander of the U.S. Army in California, set the war in motion by ruling that "everyone who is not a citizen of the United States, who enters upon public land and digs for gold [is] a trespasser." Across the goldfields, the cry went up: "Down with Foreigners!" Vigilantes at Sutter's Mill drove away Mexicans, Chileans, and Peruvians in April 1849. In July expulsions occurred throughout the Sacramento River watershed. Foreigners were killed and their property destroyed, stolen, or sold at auction. Anyone who was not English, Welsh, or Scots was at risk, including Irish, French, German, Italian, and Basque miners. However, Hispanics were the primary targets. The hostility toward them was so intense that even native-born Californios were expelled. Peddlers from Sonora had been welcome in 1849, when they brought in onions, potatoes, and other goods, and sold them at reasonable prices. But in 1850 they were forced out by Anglo merchants who refused to be undersold.[135]

Miners also expelled slaves or servants working claims for their masters. Thomas Jefferson Green, a slaveowner from Texas, was given the boot when he tried to work his claim with slave labor. Hispanic *patróns* who employed *paisano* and *genízaro* servants were also expelled. A California legislator complained that the laborers brought in by Hispanic contractors from Chile, Peru, and Mexico were "as bad as any of the free negroes of the North, or the worst slaves of the South." The fields were to be reserved, declared Henry Tefft, a delegate to the state constitutional convention, for "intelligent and enterprising white men who, from the want of capital, are compelled to do their own work." The miners attacked Hispanic employers who defied the prohibition on servant labor, whipping them, cropping their ears, or killing them outright.[136]

In 1850 the California legislature tried to discourage foreign immigration (while filling the state's coffers) by passing a bill that imposed a foreign miners' tax of $20 a month. The bill was authored by Thomas Jefferson Green, who had become a state senator. Although he had been kicked out of the mines himself, he was willing to help Anglo miners by keeping Mexican "peons" out. Like most southerners, he hated Mexicans. He once said that he could "maintain a better stomach at the killing of a Mexican" than of a body louse.[137]

The tax was rarely collected from European miners, but they made common cause with Hispanic miners and staged mass protests against it. In May 1850 a protest near Sonora, about seventy-five miles south-east of Sacramento, drew 4,000 miners. A Mexican miner threatened the county sheriff with a knife and had his head nearly severed by a bystander. When they heard about the threat to the sheriff, a band of 150 Anglo veterans organized themselves into a militia company and imposed martial law. They ordered foreign miners to surrender their weapons, forced them to pay the tax, and required them to apply for "good conduct" permits. All Hispanics except "respectable characters" had fifteen days to leave. Between 5,000 and 15,000 foreigners were expelled from the southern mines between May and August. Fake tax collectors also got in on the act. At one mine an Anglo imposter persuaded a posse to help him eject forty Hispanic miners from their claims, and two of the miners were killed before his deception was discovered.[138]

The foreign miners' tax proved so divisive and unproductive that the legislature repealed it in 1851. The repeal did not end expulsions and killings, however. Anglos and Hispanics squared off against each other repeatedly. In 1852 a Fourth of July parade at Rich Bar turned ugly when Anglos began to chant, "Down with the Spaniards!" "Drive every foreigner off the river!" A drunken English brothel owner opened fire, mortally wounding Señor Pizarro, "a man of high birth and breeding, a *porteño* of Buenos Ayres." The Spaniards, in turn, killed a young Irishman. At a gambling house on the Stanislaus River, a dispute over cards led to the deaths of one Anglo and three Mexicans. One of the Mexicans, shot three times and stabbed with his own knife, urged his compatriots on as he lay dying: "Mata! Mata a los chingados Yanquis! [Kill! Kill the fucking Yankees!]" In Downeyville on the night of 4 July 1851 a man named Cannon insulted a Mexican prostitute named Josefa, and she stabbed him in the chest. The town's Anglos seized Josepha, tried her in a lynch court, and hanged her that afternoon. One Anglo who had done his fair share of lynching summed up the general attitude of his countrymen when he said, "To shoot these Greasers ain't the best way. Give 'em a fair jury trial, and rope 'em up with all the majesty of the law. That's the cure."[139]

Relations between Anglos and Hispanics were nearly as violent in San Francisco as they were in the mining country. Many interracial killings occurred in brothels, because so many had both Anglo and Hispanic workers and patrons, but most interracial killings were gang-related. An Anglo gang called the Hounds, originally recruited by the city's businessmen to return runaway sailors to their ships, made a living by stealing and extorting protection payments from Hispanics. In June 1849 two Hounds entered a Chilean shop and demanded a payment. The shopkeeper shot one of them, but the other escaped and brought the rest of the gang back with him. They looted every shop in the neighborhood, raped women, and murdered a man who tried to fight back.[140]

In the countryside, where legal institutions were too weak (or too biased) to defend the property rights of Hispanics, Anglos used every means fair and foul to take the land of Californio farmers and ranchers. Convinced that all Californio titles would be declared invalid, they cut wood on Californio land, stole horses, slaughtered cattle, burned crops, destroyed orchards, tore down fences, appropriated streams and ponds, and chased off ranch hands. When those methods did not suffice, they shot Californio farmers and ranchers in their fields. Hispanic sheriffs who tried to defend Californios were murdered. It is true that some Californio titles were fraudulent or excessive, and wealthy Californios monopolized land to a degree that Americans would not have tolerated anywhere, including the eastern United States. But even if that had that not been the case, Anglos would still have killed Californios, whom they considered "half-civilized black men."[141]

Some Hispanics became bandits and fought back. Bernardo García murdered two Bear Flag soldiers in 1846 and became an outlaw. He robbed and killed Americans until he himself was killed by a posse in 1853. Salomón Pico, a Mexican soldier who had owned a rancho north of Santa Barbara, also turned bandit. He told friends that he "had been cheated out of his property by Americans and in consequence . . . would kill every American falling into his hands." His gang attacked

Anglo traders, miners, and cattle drivers along the coast in the early 1850s. Andrés Fontes joined a gang in 1857 in order to get revenge on the Los Angeles County sheriff, who had jailed him for defending an Indian woman whom the sheriff was harassing. Tiburico Vásquez turned to violence in 1852 after two of his friends were hanged for their role in a fight at a dance in Monterey. Vásquez complained that the Americans had shoved Californio men aside, "monopolizing the dance and the women. A spirit of hatred and revenge took possession of me. I had numerous fights in defense of what I believed to be my rights and those of my countrymen. I believed we were being unjustly deprived of the social rights that belonged to us." He asked for his mother's blessing and began his career as a robber.[142]

Like guerrillas in the Civil War South, most Hispanic bandits lost sight of their original objectives and became predators. They formed alliances with Anglo and Native American bandits when it suited their purpose and attacked non-Anglos, including Hispanics, Indians, and Chinese. They raided mining camps, ranches, stores, taverns, and brothels and killed lone travelers, and they committed rapes as well as robberies and murders.

No incident more clearly shows how murders committed by one alienated group could generate more murders and more brutality than the Ranchería tragedy of August 1855. After robbing Chinese miners camped about forty miles east of Sacramento, a Hispanic gang got drunk and raided Ranchería, a small mining town in Amador County. Screaming "Viva Mexico!," they began shooting at anything that moved. They killed two card players, wounded the hotelkeeper, and killed his wife as she tried to get their children out of harm's way. At the general store, they shot the clerk, severed the head of the owner, and stole $6,000 from the safe. When an Indian came in to see what the commotion was about, they shot him dead.[143]

An Anglo mob accused thirty-six of the town's Hispanic citizens of committing the crime. A motion to hang all of them failed, so they hanged the three who had been identified by a man named James Johnson as the thieves who broke into the store. They were innocent, but Johnson wanted their mining claim. The mob then burned Hispanic homes and businesses and drove the town's Hispanic citizens into Mile Gulch, where eight of them were killed by members of the murdered Indian's tribe. Anglo vigilantes burned the Catholic church and the Chili Flat neighborhood in nearby Drytown, and they lynched one of the bandits, whom they found hiding under a pile of clothes in Gopher Flat. Sheriff Phoenix was killed a week later when he tried to arrest the bandits, but the posse caught most of them. Two were shot dead, two were lynched, and one committed suicide.

The Anglo-Hispanic conflict in California took a very different shape wherever Hispanics remained the majority. Hispanic ranchers prospered along the coast of southern California because of the demand for beef in San Francisco, Sacramento, and the goldfields, and they faced less competition from Anglos, because the area lacked the minerals and the rainfall that had attracted Anglo farmers and miners to northern and central California. Anglo-Hispanic violence was intense in Monterey and San Luis Obispo Counties by the mid-1850s as Anglo ranchers moved in from the north, but in San Diego County, which was too far south to interest Anglo ranchers, there was not a single known homicide in the 1850s or early 1860s involving an Anglo and a Hispanic. Wherever Hispanic power was entrenched and stable, it deterred Anglo-Hispanic homicides.

In Santa Barbara County there was only one known murder of a Hispanic by an Anglo before 1857 and none of an Anglo by a Hispanic. The village of Santa Barbara was home to a small contingent of Anglo businessmen and former officers and soldiers from Stevenson's New York Volunteers, who had been stationed in Santa Barbara during the war, and the county experienced a gradual influx of Anglo ranchers. But the Hispanic population rose simultaneously because of immigration from Mexico, so Hispanics maintained a four-to-one majority. They controlled local government and the courts. When a band of former Volunteers squatted on land that was owned by the Catholic Church, the Hispanic community appealed to the California Supreme Court. The court, dominated by Democrats sympathetic to the Church, ruled that the squatters would have to leave. When a Hispanic posse arrived with the court's order, the squatters opened fire, killing one man, but they were evicted, and their failure sent a message to other would-be squatters: they could not take land by force in Santa Barbara County.[144]

The Anglo businessmen who had settled in Santa Barbara chafed under Hispanic rule. Most of them were deeply prejudiced. Charles Huse, the editor of Santa Barbara's newspaper, complained that the "dregs of society are collected in this town. . . . The greatest part of the population is lazy, does not work, does not pay its debts, does not keep its word, is full of envy, of ill will, of cunning, craft and fraud, falsehood and ignorance." Anglos were particularly upset by the use of Spanish in the town's schools and by the reluctance of Hispanic jurors to convict Hispanics suspected of stealing Anglo property (even though Anglo jurors were just as partial toward Anglo suspects). But the Anglo minority found it difficult to act on its prejudice. When Anglo businessmen formed a vigilante committee to round up Hispanic rustlers, they discovered that they did not have enough horses, and Hispanic ranchers refused to provide them. They tried to establish a separate English-language public school but had to give it up because it was too expensive. When Huse made a stand for the English language and discontinued the Spanish-language page in his newspaper, he lost so many readers that he had to sell—to Hispanics, who transformed it into a successful Spanish-language newspaper. The will to bully and kill Hispanics was there, but not the wherewithal.[145]

Santa Barbara's Anglo minority was emboldened, however, by the Know-Nothing movement, which carried the state in 1855. The *Ignorantes,* as Hispanics called them, hated immigrants, including the Irish, the Germans, the French, and the Chinese, but they disliked native-born Hispanics as well. The Democratic Party was powerless to stop the Know-Nothings' anti-Hispanic legislation, which included a prohibition on the use of Spanish in public schools and a vagrancy law that promised, in its own words, to put "greasers" to work.[146]

The political situation became even less favorable for Santa Barbara's Hispanic majority the following year, when California's Democratic Party embraced the white supremacist, proslavery agenda of the national party and sanctioned its call for the annexation of Mexico and Central America. Negrophobia and Hispanophobia fed off each other. Anglo Democrats in Los Angeles abandoned former mayor Antonio Coronel in the mayoral election of 1856, calling him "el negro." A Democratic newspaper declared that "Californios are a degraded race; a part of them are so black that one needs much work to distinguish them from Indians; there is little difference between them and the Negro race; in the event a Territorial government would be established in the south very soon they would establish friendship with the Negro slaves, would be united with one another, until all would be amalgamated and all would be slaves!" The newly founded Republican Party offered Hispanics little hope. It had close ties to nativists and anti-Catholics, and its presidential nominee was John C. Frémont, the despised leader of the Bear Flag Rebellion.[147]

The changed political climate weakened the Hispanic government in Santa Barbara County and spawned more homicides. The Anglo minority was increasingly resentful of Hispanic rule, especially where the judicial system was concerned. Charles Huse, now the leader of the Know-Nothings, declared that "it would be better to close the doors of the Courthouse. . . . It makes no difference what the testimony is, if the criminal is Spanish or Californian, he is always set free by a jury of 'native sons.'" Spurred by events outside the county, the Anglos decided to dispense justice themselves. In 1857 Anglo vigilantes hanged two Hispanic men on a charge of robbery and murder even though, as one Anglo witness testified, the vigilantes did not know the name of the alleged victim, the place of the alleged crime, or whether there was any evidence against the condemned men. In 1858 an Anglo lawman gunned down a Hispanic suspect, and in 1859 rancher John Nidever and several Anglo neighbors pulled Francisco Badillo and his sixteen-year-old son from their home and hanged them on suspicion of horse theft. Twenty Californios, led by the sheriff, the coroner, and the mayor of Santa Barbara, hurried to the scene. They questioned Badillo's young sons, who had witnessed the murders. When the boys mistakenly identified Nidever's son George as one of the murderers, four Californios went after him and nearly killed him before the other posse members could stop them.[148]

Hispanic authorities jailed the Anglos who had lynched the Badillos and the Californios who had tried to kill George Nidever, but a grand jury comprised of eight Anglos and eight Hispanics deadlocked. The former refused to indict the Anglos, so the latter refused to indict the Californios. With the government hamstrung and incapable of defending life or property, relations between the Anglo and Hispanic communities broke down completely, and the two groups descended into outright war. Troops arrived from Fort Tejon to keep the peace. Major Carleton, their commander, wrote his superiors that "the Americans here will not brook restraint on the part of the Californians, and are exceedingly intolerant of the political as well as official control of any of that people. This sentiment on the part of the Americans seems to have become so intense as now to be almost a monomania. . . . They do not seem disposed to concede to Californians the same civil rights which they claim for themselves." Charles Fernald, another officer, observed that the Hispanic control of the government and the courts in Santa Barbara had left the Anglo minority "morally insane."[149]

Thanks to the federal army and the forbearance of the Hispanic community, the wave of anti-Hispanic violence in Santa Barbara County eventually came to an end. When Anglos voted at a mass meeting to give George Nidever's attackers four days to leave the county, state senator Pablo de la Guerra persuaded the men to do so for the sake of peace, even though the Badillos' murderers remained in the county. Hispanic officials continued to give Anglos half the seats on the grand jury, even though they were entitled to only a fifth. The Hispanic community established a parochial school in Santa Barbara and left the public school to the Anglos. No Anglo was killed by a Hispanic in Santa Barbara County while Hispanics were in the majority. If George Nidever had died from his wounds, a war might have broken out, but fortunately he lived. And because Hispanics seldom responded violently to Anglo violence, there were few incidents in which deaths could occur. In all likelihood, the Hispanic community rejected anti-Anglo violence in part because they were confident of their numerical superiority, but also because they knew that the Anglos would repay any violence tenfold.

The Chinese who migrated to California to work in the mines did not suffer from interracial violence to the degree that Hispanics and Native Americans did, but they, too, were victimized. Arriving en masse in 1851–52 to work for Chinese labor contractors and Anglo mining entrepreneurs, they were attacked from all sides. Anglo miners and laborers drove them out of seven camps in 1852, and they were robbed and murdered by Hispanic bandits and by Natives who demanded fees for permission to live on their land. As mining became more capital intensive, Anglo entrepreneurs were increasingly determined to keep their Chinese laborers, and they were supported by merchants and by government officials, who recognized that the Chinese provided a steady stream of revenue, since they were more likely than the Europeans or Hispanics to pay the foreign miners' tax. Paying the tax also reduced confrontations with the state's revenue agents, although at least two Chinese were killed in attacks on tax collectors in 1855. In the late

1860s and 1870s, however, when the mines played out and the transcontinental railroad was completed, the Chinese moved to cities and to ranching and farming communities, where they were more vulnerable to attack.[150]

The worst violence occurred in Los Angeles in 1871. Anglos and Hispanics went on a rampage through Chinatown after a policeman was killed while trying to stop a fight between rival Chinese gangs. The rioters looted stores, burned buildings, and killed nineteen Chinese, only one of whom had anything to do with the gang fight. Some were shot, some hanged, and others dragged to death. Gene Tong, an elderly doctor, offered the mob several thousand dollars if it would spare him, but the rioters stripped off his pants to get his money, cut off his finger to get his diamond ring, and killed him. Interracial violence was inevitable wherever the Chinese posed a threat to Anglo labor and did not enjoy the protection of Anglo employers. Chinese workers were attacked one night in 1877 on a ranch near Chico, where they had been hired to clear a pasture. Members of the Laborers' Union (an adjunct of the Order of Caucasians, which wanted to end Chinese immigration to the United States) stole onto the ranch, shot the laborers as they slept, and set their bunkhouse on fire.[151]

As in the South, the incidence of interracial homicide was dependent upon the political climate and the will and ability of government and local elites to protect the rights of racial minorities. Political, racial, and everyday homicides were most common where Anglos were battling Hispanics, Native Americans, or the Chinese for control of trade, territory, or jobs. Interracial homicide rates were lower where Hispanics held power, as they did in Santa Barbara and in the deserts of southern California, and where the Chinese were protected by Anglo employers. Homicide rates were also lower where the Anglos displaced non-Anglos rapidly or forced them into small enclaves, as they did by the 1870s in San Francisco and in Sacramento and San Joaquin Counties. None of these places was nonhomicidal, of course. Anglo domination of non-Anglos was not a recipe for social peace, any more than white domination of blacks was in the South. But homicide rates might have been uniformly high in the 1850s and early 1860s if Anglos had coveted southern ranches or jobs in shaft mining or railroad construction.

Interracial homicides were responsible for more than half of the murders that occurred after the American conquest of California, but intraracial homicides alone would have given the Southwest the highest murder rates in the nation. There was little solidarity within any racial group. Chinese immigrants, for instance, who came almost exclusively from Canton and the Pearl River Delta, brought homicidal conflicts with them to California. In the mid-nineteenth century, the delta region was plagued by piracy and banditry, by feuds among clans, villages, and rural districts, and by civil war between the delta's two major ethnic groups: the Punti, the native inhabitants of the region, and the Hakka, who had migrated to the delta from the northeastern provinces in the thirteenth century and spoke a dialect closer to Mandarin than Cantonese. Thousands of murders occurred every year, and the central government was too weak, corrupt, and divided in its loyalties to bring peace and stability to the region. For protection, many people banded together in companies *(kongsi),* which were made up of citizens of particular ethnic, district, and dialect groups. Others turned to secret societies *(hui),* which included people of various ethnicities. Some of these organizations were benevolent, some criminal, and some both, but almost all of them were caught up in the fighting and contributed to the delta's homicide problem.[152]

Since people in the delta were desperately poor, many Chinese men signed contracts with the merchants or criminals who ran the local company or secret society, taking on massive debts in exchange for passage to California. Most companies and secret societies were as well organized in California as they were in China. They controlled the market for Chinese laborers and had the means—usually violent—to force recalcitrant debtors to pay. They did offer their members steady work, burial insurance, health care, and legal representation in California courts, but they also drew people deeper into debt at their gambling houses, brothels, saloons, and opium dens, and many Chinese were killed in feuds among rival companies or societies. Some of these feuds ended in spectacular battles. In Weaverville, for example, two company armies of 200 men or more went up against each other in July 1854. They had trained for the battle for three weeks, at first using clubs, knives, spikes, and spears. But Anglo miners got wind of the battle and lent the combatants rifles, revolvers, and Bowie knives. Between 10 and 20 men died before the companies called a truce. That September, 600 men fought a company war on I Street in Sacramento, and in October 1856, 2,500 men from the Sam Yap and Yan Wo companies battled in Tuolumne County.[153]

Most homicides among the Chinese in California were the result of simple quarrels among rivals. A gunfight broke out in Stockton's Chinatown, for example, after two companies argued over a card game, and three men were killed. But a great many homicides were deliberate assassinations. Companies and secret societies murdered debtors, disobedient prostitutes, or rivals who threatened their interests. Ay Yuen walked into a gambling parlor in Sacramento and shot Ah Cow because he was doing business in another company's territory. Le Chou and three associates killed Lum Sow outside a brothel in Big Oak Flats because Lum Sow had lured away one of Le Chou's prostitutes. Ah Sin, a San Francisco madam, gave one of her prostitutes a fatal dose of opium because she did not turn over her earnings. Prostitutes were frequent victims of homicide, and because a high proportion of the Chinese women who migrated to California worked as prostitutes and were subjected to violence by customers and brothel operators, Chinese women had the highest nondomestic murder rate of any group of women through the 1870s: over 30 per 100,000 adults per year, three times the rate for Hispanic women and ten times the rate for Anglo women.[154]

The Chinese may actually have been less likely to kill each other in California than they had been in the Pearl River Delta. They appear to have had a stronger sense of solidarity overseas than they did at home, and rivalries among companies and secret societies appear to have been less violent because their territories were smaller and more easily defended. But the rate at which the Chinese killed each other in California remained high after the Civil War—at least 33 per 100,000 adults per year—even though the rates at which the Chinese were killed by Hispanics, Native Americans, and Anglos declined. New immigrants from the Pearl River Delta brought homicidal customs with them, making it impossible for California's Chinese to reduce violence within their communities.[155]

Indians living independently or under Anglo jurisdiction killed one another at roughly the same rate as the Chinese—at least 30–40 per 100,000 per year. In the 1850s and early 1860s, 58 percent of the Native homicides in which the circumstances are known involved Indians from different tribes. They fought, as they did before the American conquest, over women, children, and hunting land, and the violence among them, which included murders and family feuds as well as pitched battles, intensified as they tried to make up for the deaths of tribal members and the loss of land. The forms of intertribal violence were traditional, but the threat to tribal survival exacerbated the situation.[156]

Homicides among Indians were also rampant in the towns and mining camps where Native American men went to drink and gamble. Luseños and Cahuillas from San Bernardino County gathered in Los Angeles to play a well-publicized match of peon, but after several intense games and a good deal of drinking, a fight broke out. "Dead Indians were found in every direction. . . . These all had their heads smashed beyond recognition." By one count, at least fifty lives were lost. Alcohol use was obviously a factor in such killings. It played an even greater role in intratribal violence. Of the homicides with known circumstances that occurred within tribes, 93 percent involved alcohol. As time passed, there were more and more homicides involving friends and acquaintances. By the 1870s such killings had eclipsed intertribal homicides. The Native Americans had given up on the effort to maintain tribal prestige and, in complete demoralization, were turning on themselves.[157]

Homicide rates were much higher, however, among Hispanics than among Indians or the Chinese in the 1850s and early 1860s—at least 72 per 100,000 adults per year.[158] That rate was roughly the same as before the American conquest, and indicates that the Hispanic community was as deeply divided as ever. Little is known about the character of those homicides, because to date, research has focused almost exclusively on violence between Hispanics and Anglos. But it is likely that immigrants from Spain, Mexico, Chile, and Peru brought violent habits with them and contributed to the homicide problem. It also appears that most immigrants felt greater loyalty to their nationality than to a broader Hispanic community, and murders across national lines were probably common. However, it is likely that there were fewer fatal confrontations between native Californio *gente fina* and *paisanos* as the power of the former over the latter declined.

Detailed records are available for some cases, and they show that murders among unrelated Hispanics were usually caused by spontaneous disputes. Killings occurred during drunken brawls in saloons and brothels, or at dances or friendly get-togethers on *ranchos*. In San Francisco, 86 percent of Hispanic murders in the mid-nineteenth century were the result of quarrels or feuds. A man named San Miguel, who had escaped from the Sacramento jail, found a cold welcome in San Francisco, where he had been involved in an "affair of honor" with several associates. They surprised him in North Beach and stabbed him twenty times. Diego Sandoval, a bully with a record of violence, demanded money from a diminutive tailor named Álvarez every time their paths crossed. One night, when Sandoval tried to shake him down in public for another $3, Álvarez decided that he had been humiliated long enough, and he shot him. The sensitivity of Hispanic men to insults was well known, but the influx of hostile Anglos and the relegation of Hispanics to the lowest rung of California's social hierarchy clearly increased levels of anger and frustration among Hispanic men.[159]

Bandits and vigilantes also took a toll on the Hispanic population. However, in the late 1860s and 1870s the murder rate among Hispanics fell from 72 per 100,000 adults per year to about 37 per 100,000 adults per year. Hispanic banditry and vigilantism declined as the forces of law and order took hold in California and in northern Mexico, where the bandits had found sanctuary. The closing of mining camps, with their attendant recreations, also saved lives. But Hispanic murder rates remained much higher than Anglo rates. Hispanics were only beginning to form bonds within their community across class and national lines, and anger over the loss of land, status, and political power was intense.[160]

Unrelated Anglos in California murdered one another at a rate of at least 37 per 100,000 adults per year in the 1850s and early 1860s. That rate was four or five times the rate at which whites killed one another in the North and most of the South, and because Anglos were in the majority, those homicides accounted for the majority of homicides in Gold Rush California. The absence of strong government and law enforcement in the first years after the American conquest was a factor in the murder rate, which was highest among Anglos during the early years of the Gold Rush. Immigrants came prepared for violence; without any law enforcement, as one miner put it, "you've got to paddle for yourself." Fear of robbers, claim jumpers, Indians, and Mexicans prompted immigrants to lay in stores of rifles and fighting knives.

Handgun ownership was widespread. "That firearms are necessary in a country like this, no one living here can doubt," said the *Sonora Herald*. "It would not be prudent to travel without them, nor should they be thought useless under the pillow at night." And there were plenty of places to use weapons. Because the mines attracted so many single men, saloons, gambling halls, dance halls, and brothels were everywhere. Hinton Helper said during a tour of California in 1855 that "I have seen purer liquors, better segars, finer tobacco, truer guns and pistols, larger dirks and bowie knives, and prettier courtesans here, than in any other place I have ever visited." Quarrels over women, card games, or careless words quickly led to homicides when men were drunk and well armed. The homicide rate among Anglos declined gradually in the late 1850s and 1860s as law enforcement improved, the pace of immigration slowed, and more families and family-oriented businesses appeared.[161]

Still, the homicide rate for Anglos in California was higher in the late 1840s and early 1850s than on previous frontiers, and it remained high well into the 1870s, two decades after the gold boom had ended. Anglos in California were as homicidal in the decade after the Civil War as whites in most plantation counties in the South, and for some of the same reasons. Settlers from Texas and the slaveholding South brought their violent habits with them and committed more than their share of homicides. Lynchings and gang violence were persistent problems, as were duels among public men. In San Francisco, for example, Senator David Broderick, a Free Soil Democrat originally from New York, clashed with David Terry, a proslavery Democrat, former Texas Ranger, and chief justice of the California Supreme Court. Terry killed Broderick in a duel at Lake Merced in 1859.[162] But Anglo settlers who came from the North, the mountain South, and Europe committed homicide at higher rates in California than they would have back home. The antagonistic, multiracial character of California society, the struggles among Anglos and Hispanics for control of local governments, the polarization of state and federal politics, and the increasing monopolization of California's mines and ranches made all Anglos, not just settlers from the South, more hostile and aggressive toward one another, more concerned about losing face, and more willing to use violence when crossed.

The rate at which Anglos murdered one another fell precipitously in the late 1860s and 1870s, to 15 per 100,000 adults per year, as political and ethnic conflict among them diminished, land titles were sorted out, and they wrested control of California from Hispanics.[163] Even so, California remained one of the most homicidal places in the United States—and one of the most homicidal in all of American history. It had experienced simultaneously a war of conquest against the indigenous inhabitants, a frontier society, and a national political crisis over slavery, immigration, and the decline in self-employment. And the conquest of California was never complete: Anglos never eradicated the indigenous population and continued to rely on immigrant labor from Latin America and China. California remained an embattled, racially divided society, plagued by many of the problems that beset the postbellum South. That is why homicide rates among Anglos in California, like homicide rates among whites in the South, remain elevated to this day.

South Texas was also an embattled society. Despite the American victory in the Mexican War, it remained a contested borderland. In northern Mexico, the struggle between centrists and federalists continued, and local strongmen battled each other for political power and a stake in the booming business of cross-border smuggling. The weak provincial governments were incapable of imposing law and order, since the gangs responsible for the smuggling and raiding that plagued south Texas were protected by the businessmen and politicians who shared in their profits. These gangs, made up of both Anglos and Hispanics, were responsible for hundreds of murders from the end of the war through the 1870s. Apaches, vigilantes, and bounty hunters contributed to the body count. The mayhem did not stop until the late 1870s, when the administrations of Porfirio Díaz and Rutherford B. Hayes secured the border and crushed the Apaches.[164]

Yet ordinary Anglo-Texan citizens perpetrated far more killings than outlaw gangs or Apaches. Many Anglo-Texans—perhaps a majority—were determined to force Hispanics out of south Texas. They did not want to live side by side with "mongrel" and "degenerate" people. "White folks and Mexicans were never made to live together," said one woman from Victoria. Like most other Texans, she believed that "the Mexicans had no business" in Texas, and "the Americans would just have to get together and drive them all out of the country." Gilbert Kingsbury echoed those sentiments when he described his Tejano

neighbors in Brownsville: "These degraded creatures are mere pilfer-
ers, scavengers and vagabonds, downright barbarians but a single remove from Digger Indians, hanging like vermin on the skirts of civilization—a complete pest to humanity."[165]

Anglos were also afraid that Tejanos, being of "mixed blood," would
ally themselves with African Americans and pose a threat to slavery.
When war was declared in 1861, Unionist Hispanics in Zapata County
were ridden down by Confederate troops and killed. But most killings occurred because Anglo-Texans wanted the land, jobs, and resources of the Tejano community. Hispanic ranchers were forced off
their land by foreclosure, legal subterfuge, intimidation, arson, rustling, and murder. In the Cart War of 1857, Anglos killed seventy-five
Hispanic teamsters in an effort to monopolize trade out of San Antonio. In the 1870s Anglo cattlemen organized secret societies to force
Hispanic sheepherders out of south Texas. They killed sheepherders
and destroyed their flocks. In 1877 Anglo entrepreneurs seized control of the salt lakes near El Paso, which had belonged to the residents
of Ysleta and Socorro for generations. Judge Charles Howard, the
agent for the entrepreneurs, told the *paisanos* that the salt was no
longer theirs to sell. The *paisanos* fought back. Six of them died in the
battles with the Anglos; Howard and four of his associates were killed.
Then the Texas Rangers arrived. They put down the rebellion in two
weeks, plundering the homes of Hispanics, raping the women, and
beating the men.[166]

In south Texas, law-enforcement officials reacted to crimes committed by Hispanics in much the same way they would have reacted to
crimes committed by slaves. Dead bodies were put on display to discourage others from committing similar offenses. In 1875 a company
of Texas Rangers shot 15 Hispanic rustlers who were holding 300 cattle on a small island in the Rio Grande River, dragged them back to
Brownsville, and stacked their bodies like cordwood on the street.
Sheriffs and deputies hunting suspects in Hispanic areas sometimes
killed dozens of innocent people to avenge the death of one Anglo.
Near the Nueces River, for example, a single Anglo posse killed 40 Hispanics after a popular rancher was murdered. Anglo vigilantes were
more brutal than law enforcement. They hanged, tortured, burned,
and mutilated Hispanics for crimes ranging from murder and livestock theft to overfamiliarity with Anglo women. Vigilantes lynched at

least 160 Hispanics in the Southwest in the 1850s and another 150 in the 1870s. And of course, Anglos murdered Hispanics regularly in everyday disputes. As the adjutant general of Texas reported in 1875, "a considerable element" of the Anglo community considered "the killing of a Mexican no crime."[167]

The legal system rapidly lost all legitimacy in the Hispanic community. Hispanics armed themselves and attacked Anglo marshals, sheriffs, and Rangers. They joined insurrections and imposed their own rough justice on Anglos. In 1875 thirty Hispanic men set out to punish Anglos for persecuting their people. They raided ranches and small settlements around Corpus Christi, looting, burning, and killing at least five Anglo men. If they had had more men, they would have attacked Corpus Christi itself. Juan Cortina, a young Tejano rancher from Brownsville, led an uprising against Anglos in 1859. Before the Mexican War, he had worked with Anglo rustlers to ship livestock to Mexican ports, and he had been a member of the political establishment in Brownsville, delivering Hispanic votes for its candidates. But he and his men were angry about the anti-Hispanic violence that followed the war, and they wanted to protect the lives and property of Hispanics. "Our personal enemies shall not possess our lands until they have fattened it with their own gore." Cortina got together sixty men and rode into Brownsville. They freed Hispanic prisoners from the jail, looted the stores of Anglo merchants who had mistreated Hispanic customers, and executed five Anglos who had killed Hispanics and had not been punished.[168]

The rebels selected their targets carefully and told Anglos that they had nothing to fear if they treated Tejanos fairly, but Anglos did not take the message kindly. They formed a vigilante group—the Brownsville Tigers—and went after Cortina and his men. The fighting lasted six months and claimed dozens of lives before the rebels were driven into Mexico for good. Such uprisings inspired other Tejanos to resist, individually and collectively, but in the end they probably made matters worse for Hispanics. Militant whites came to believe that Hispanics were preparing to "slaughter the gringo" and that the only way to stop the "gringo hunting expedition" was to strike preemptively.[169]

Because it was mostly interracial, south Texas violence was largely ignored by the rest of the country, but the violence that occurred on the grasslands of the West, an area that stretched from west Texas, New

Mexico, and Arizona in the south to Nevada, Utah, Wyoming, and Montana in the north, captured the imagination of Americans and became emblematic of the violence of the West as a whole. The area was as murderous as California or south Texas after the Civil War, but the violence was primarily due to one factor: the absence of effective government during the rise of the open-range cattle industry. As the demand for beef increased in Europe and the eastern United States, and as railroads and stockyards extended access to markets, the West became cattle country. The cattlemen moved in before the land could be surveyed and parceled out, and few areas were under the jurisdiction of any governing body; as a result every cattleman was "on his own hook" when it came to protecting his range and his livestock. Rustling was endemic, as were fights over water holes and prime grazing land. The arrival of federal land agents, courts, and county governments sometimes made the situation worse by disrupting arrangements that cattlemen had worked out among themselves and by giving large operations the legal power to force small ones off the range. There were hundreds of homicides over trespassing, theft, property damage, claim jumping, and even politics as cattlemen vied for control of local governments and tried to use their power against rivals.[170]

Open-range cattlemen seldom came to blows with farmers. The potential for violence was there: cattlemen did not like it when farmers got in their way, and farmers got upset when cattlemen broke their fences, damaged their crops, stole their cattle, or infected their herds with Texas fever, a tick-borne disease that was fatal to blooded cattle but not to the wild longhorns that carried it. Because farmers could generally muster the power to win these fights, open-range cattlemen preferred to move farther west as the farming frontier advanced rather than have their cattle quarantined or be faced with farmer posses or lawsuits.[171]

However, cattlemen waged a lethal war with sheepherders, whose flocks grazed the same open ranges. Cattlemen claimed that sheep ruined the range for cattle by cutting the turf, cropping the grass too low, and leaving a scent so strong that cattle were unwilling to graze. In fact cattle could ruin the range just as easily as sheep by overgrazing it, but cattlemen were not interested in the facts. The resultant conflict was cultural as well as economic. Most sheepherders in the Southwest were Hispanic or Navaho, and most in the Great Basin were Basque or

Mormon. Southern cattlemen despised all those groups. But sheep-herders did not go quietly. Seventeen men died in Lincoln County, New Mexico, in the Tularosa Ditch War of 1873 and the Horrell War of 1873–74, which pitted Hispanic sheepherders against Texas cattlemen. The herders forced the cattlemen who had been involved in those conflicts back into Texas, but violence against herders and their flocks continued across the West.[172]

Since there were no clear titles to the grasslands, cattlemen also fought one another. Small-scale cattlemen and cowhands who wanted to start their own herds battled large-scale cattlemen, rustling herds and running cattle onto rivals' claims in efforts to gain the upper hand. When large cattlemen hired gunmen to protect their herds and fenced off pastures and water holes, whether they owned them or not, drovers and small-scale cattlemen responded by cutting fences, en-croaching on disputed land, and forming posses to defend themselves. The Fence Cutting War of 1883–84 in west Texas, a general uprising of small-scale against large-scale cattlemen, was one of the most vio-lent range wars. Only six or seven cattlemen were killed, but dozens were wounded. When Texas Rangers entered the fray on the side of the fencers, they became targets themselves. Ranger Ben Warren, a lead investigator, was shot dead through the window of a hotel in Sweetwater, but his fellow Rangers got their revenge a year later, when an undercover Ranger led a band of fence-cutters into a trap and the Rangers shot them down.[173]

The state of Texas tried to end the fighting, lynching, and rustling by dispatching more Rangers to the cattle frontier. The legislature also passed a law that made fence-cutting a felony punishable by one to five years in prison but also mandated that all fences erected on pub-lic land or on another individual's property be removed within six months and that gates be maintained on public roads so that cattle-men could pass through with their herds. The law helped, but the kill-ing persisted for many years.

The homicide rates on the western grasslands were ultimately the re-sult of frontier conditions. Rates were high wherever there was no reli-able government and wherever a group of speculators took control of a county government and imposed its will on an unwilling majority. The cattle frontier was also homicidal because of the kind of men it at-tracted. Most cowboys were poor young men who had few prospects at home, particularly if they came from war-torn parts of the South or Southwest or if they were black or Hispanic. Many hoped to become ranchers, but their wages were usually spent on supplies, clothes, whiskey, guns, prostitutes, and gambling, and the only way they could build a herd was to take up range land without paying for it and stock it with feral or stolen cattle. That was a recipe for violence, especially as wealthy cattlemen and outside investors moved in and used their power to control the land and stock, win supply contracts with the army and Indian agencies, and dictate the terms of trade at railheads.[174]

Many young cowboys had given up (at least for the time being) on self-employment, marriage, and home and land ownership, much as gang members had in the cities of the North, South, and Midwest, or as young Forty-niners did when they signed on for the Gold Rush. They were attracted to the cattle frontier, to its dangers and hardships, because it was an exciting way of life that gave them a chance to prove themselves and command respect. They loved to tell stories about droughts, blizzards, stampedes, Indian wars, and gunfights, all of which involved manly men performing heroic deeds. They admired men who did not retreat in the face of danger or adversity, who had the "grit" or "sand" to stand up for themselves when they were challenged. Oliver Lee, a New Mexico cattleman who had had his share of scrapes, asserted that he never "willingly hurt" anyone "unless they hurt me first. Then I made them pay."[175]

The young cowboy's obsession with proving his manhood and earning respect grew out of the violent culture of the Civil War South, the Mexican borderlands, and American cities, and was reinforced by stories and images from popular culture. Enamored of street fighting, gang fighting, dime novels, and the *Police Gazette*, many young cowboys, like Charlie Siringo and Teddy Blue Abbott, had already knifed or shot people before they became cowboys. Abbott admitted in his later years that he "was really dangerous" when he was young, "itching to shoot somebody in order to prove himself." Young men like Abbott and Siringo were fiercely proud of their macho image and posed for pictures with revolvers, knives, cigars, and whiskey bottles.[176]

Most cowboy violence played out in cattle towns, where young men measured themselves against other cowhands and against the gamblers, saloonkeepers, brothel owners, and bouncers who made a living off them. Young cowboys shot men for cutting in on a dance, cheating at cards, calling them names, or refusing them a drink. Cattle towns tried to curb violence by hiring policemen and by enforcing local ordinances that prohibited the carrying of pistols and dirk knives. Once those measures were in place, the homicide rate in the five major cattle towns in Kansas fell to 60 per 100,000 adults per year in the 1870s—roughly the same as in the mountain South and in ranching and mining counties in California. Before those measures were in place, Ellsworth had eight homicides in a single year and Wichita fifteen—rates of roughly 1,200 and 1,500 per 100,000.[177]

The cattle country of the West was also violent because so many cattlemen were militant whites from the South. The Civil War and Reconstruction left them bitter and alienated. John Selman was a Texan who turned outlaw after deserting from the Confederate army in 1863. Like many other deserters, he turned to crime to survive, but crime soon became a way of expressing his hatred for racial minorities and for the wealthy men who had misled the South into war. The cattle country gave him ample room in which to operate. When the Lincoln County range war reduced southeastern New Mexico to anarchy in the summer and fall of 1878, Selman and his gang moved in. He and his "Wrestlers" cleaned out ranches in the Bonito, Hondo, and Ruidoso valleys, stealing horses, cattle, and clothes. They robbed stores and other businesses. At Bartlett's Mill they forced the wives of two workers into the brush and "used them at their pleasure." At the farm of José Chavez y Sanchez, they found three young men, including two of Chavez's sons, haying in a field, and shot them. When the Wrestlers asked for watermelons at the farm of Martín Sanchez, "his boy, about twelve or fourteen years old, carried the watermelons up for them and before they left they shot him down." They killed all nine members of a Hispanic family and then amused themselves by posing the body of the family's teenage son against a tree with a cigar in his mouth. A petition from the citizens of Roswell stated matters plainly: "Men are shot down like so many dogs in parties of two or three. Women are outraged, and their children driven from their homes. Entire settlements have been compelled to abandon their Ranches, Crops, and flee from the country for safety."[178]

Many cowboy killers, like the Olive brothers and John Wesley Hardin, began their murderous careers during Reconstruction by killing blacks and Union soldiers in north and east Texas, and they thought nothing of killing Native Americans, Hispanics, or African Americans who got in their way on cattle drives or on the open range. Most cattlemen were willing to pay a "toll" of a few lame cattle for safe passage through Indian Territory, but not Hardin. When a band of Indians tried to cut several cattle out of his herd, he shot two of them dead. On another occasion, Hispanic wranglers tried to pass Hardin's herd on the trail. Convinced that they were trying to mix the herds and steal cattle, Hardin killed six of them.[179]

There are hundreds of similar stories from this era. When drover Gregorio Balensuela talked back to Ham Mills, a Texan, and called him a "gringo," Mills shot him dead. Colonel John Chisum, the famous Texas cattleman, brought three black hands with him when he moved his operation to New Mexico. At a Christmas party, one of the black cowboys got "out of line" and was shot dead by several white cowboys. Another talked back to a white cowboy while they were branding calves, and he, too, was shot dead. Beaver Smith, the survivor, was in the habit of singing the praises of Abe Lincoln when he was drunk. The white cowboys voted to hang him, but Ike Smith, one of the white hands, suggested that they brand him instead, because he was an excellent cook. "We laid him on his stomach and I put the Chisum brand on his loin, then jingle-bobbed his right ear, as that was the Colonel's mark." As Teddy Blue Abbott observed, cattlemen were "hard on Mexicans and niggers, because being from Texas they was born and raised with that intense hatred of a Mexican, and being Southerners, free niggers was poison to them." Any black or Hispanic who got "above himself" was likely to be killed.[180]

Many of the gun battles that took place in cattle towns after the war were rooted in the hatred that southern cattlemen, gamblers, and saloonkeepers felt for the northern lawmen and businessmen who dominated those towns. Dyed-in-the-wool Confederate Democrats were pitted against equally militant Unionist Republicans. Phil Coe was a rough and ready Texan and a leader among the Democrats in Abilene, Kansas. He hated the town's Republicans, who owned all the banks and cattle companies and dominated the town council, and Abilene's Republicans hated him. They were especially annoyed by the sign over Coe's tavern, which displayed an anatomically correct bull. The council ordered its lawman, Wild Bill Hickok, to get rid of the sign.[181]

Hickok was the right man for the job. In 1855, at age eighteen, he had moved to Kansas to farm, and when his community was attacked by proslavery forces, he joined an antislavery militia and helped make Kansas a free territory. He fought for the Union in the Civil War and distinguished himself as a scout and a fighter. Abilene's Republican elite hired Hickok because he was a loyal Republican, and they needed someone tough, experienced, and politically reliable to tame the lawless elements in their town.[182]

Legend has it that Hickok and Coe were rivals for the affections of a local prostitute. That may have been so, but they hated each other because of their politics: Hickok had no use for Rebels, and Coe detested Yankees. Coe told his friend John Wesley Hardin that Hickok had it in for southerners, especially Texans. The claim may have been true: Hickok killed mostly southerners.

Hickok went after Coe immediately. He shut down the town's crooked gambling operations, a move that cut into Coe's profits; and, worse, he took a paintbrush to Coe's sign and turned his glorious bull into a steer. Coe threatened Hickok, and Hickok let it be known that he was ready for a showdown. Coe and about fifty followers made a disturbance one day and fired into the air, hoping to draw Hickok out so that Coe could kill him. Hickok demanded an explanation. Coe, gun in hand, said he had shot at a dog. Hickok pulled out his pistols, and both men fired, at a distance of eight feet. Coe missed, but Hickok did not.[183]

The shootout at the OK Corral in Tombstone, Arizona, was a similar affair. The bankers, mine owners, and wealthy cattlemen who dominated Cochise County hired the Earp brothers—fellow northerners, Republicans, and real estate investors—to protect their property against cattlemen-rustlers like the Clantons and McLaureys and outlaws like John Ringo, nearly all of whom were southerners and Democrats. The "war" of 1881–82 killed a dozen men, including Morgan Earp, who was ambushed in a pool hall. But it ended in victory for the Earps and their supporters and led to declines in rustling, robbery, and homicide. Cochise County remained violent, but the days when the Clantons and Ringos could ride into Tombstone and shoot up the town were over.[184]

Politically charged murders occurred everywhere in cattle country where Yankees and former Confederates mixed. It is not a coincidence that 40 percent of the assailants and 15 percent of the victims in cattle-town killings in Kansas were officers of the law—they were mostly Republicans in a hostile, Democratic environment. Teddy Blue Abbott noted that southern cattlemen were always "getting filled up" with talk about killing Yankees.

> Those early day Texans was full of that stuff. Most of them . . . being from Texas and Southerners to start with, was on the side of the South, and oh, but they were bitter. That was how a lot of them got killed, because they were filled full of that old dope about the war and they wouldn't let an abolitionist arrest them. The marshals in those cow towns on the trail were usually Northern men, and the Southerners wouldn't go back to Texas and hear people say: "He's a hell of a fellow. He let a Yankee lock him up." Down home one Texas Ranger could arrest the lot of them but up North you'd have to kill them first.

The problem was that northern lawmen were just as "filled up" about killing them. Politics was deadly business in the mid-nineteenth century, even on the open range.[185]

The political crisis of the mid-nineteenth century did not play out in the same way in the North, the South, and the Southwest. As a result, it had a distinctive impact on homicides in each region. Minorities also experienced the political crisis of the mid-nineteenth century differently, so the homicidal histories of African Americans, Hispanics, Native Americans, and Asian and European immigrants differed from those of native-born whites. America's homicide problem was not caused, however, by regional, ethnic, or racial differences, or by religious or class differences, for that matter. Those differences had not made the United States unusually homicidal in the early national period, and Canada and western Europe had most of the same divisions in the mid-nineteenth century, but they experienced declines in homicide. America became homicidal in the mid-nineteenth century because it was the only major Western country that failed at nation-building. Once the American polity dissolved over slavery, immigration, and the Mexican War, all sorts of disputes, whether political, petty, or personal, were more likely to end in homicide. The homicide problem was made worse by the decline in self-employment, which disrupted the nation's social hierarchy and left many people anxious and fearful about their standing in society, and by the failure of state and territorial governments to establish their authority in the post–Civil War South and on the mining and ranching frontiers of the West. Ultimately, however, it was the federal government's loss of legitimacy and the weakening of patriotism and fellow feeling in the mid-nineteenth century that set the United States on course to become a more homicidal nation.

CHAPTER 8

The Modern Pattern Is Set

Homicide from the End of Reconstruction to World War I

After the nation fell apart over slavery, immigration, the decline in self-employment, and the war with Mexico, national feeling and the empathy, trust, and goodwill that flow from it were never as strong again, except for a brief period during World War II and the Cold War. When the Civil War was over, northern Republicans did their best to revive patriotism and drum up support for the federal government. The Reverend Henry Bellows gave it the "divine" imprimatur and declared it "the great incarnation of a nation's rights, privileges, honor and life." With the war over, he said, Americans should unite to become "a homogeneous, enlightened nation," bound together by patriotic feeling and a commitment to the equality of all, regardless of race, nationality, or previous condition of servitude. Republicans thought that all Americans would eventually endorse that idea.[1] They could not have been more wrong.

Most Americans rejected this homogeneous vision of the Union and remained divided about fundamental questions like the meaning of equality and role of the federal government. Bitterness over the war and Reconstruction, anger over corruption in Congress and the Grant administration, and the continued politicization of racial, ethnic, and sectional hatred made it impossible for Americans to recover the faith they had once had in the federal government.[2] As national allegiances attenuated, the proportion of new counties named for national heroes fell to its lowest level in history in the last three decades of the nineteenth century and the first two decades of the twentieth century: from a high of 46 percent in the 1810s and 1820s, when the nation's homicide rate was low, to only 18 percent. The proportion named for local and regional notables—pioneers, politicians, civic leaders—rose from 35 percent to 54 percent (Figure 2.1). The alienation reflected in those figures is in all likelihood one of the fundamental reasons that America's homicide rate has been high for the past 160 years.

Overall homicide rates did subside in the North, South, and Southwest in the late 1870s and early 1880s as the worst political violence ended, the two-party system revived, and state and local governments reestablished rudimentary law and order. Only the newest cattle and mining frontiers in the West remained extremely homicidal, with rates in excess of 100 per 100,000 adults per year. Rates fell in cities, small towns, and in the countryside. They dropped in Boston, New York, Philadelphia, New Orleans, and San Francisco; in northern New England and the rural Midwest; in mountain and plantation counties in Georgia; and in ranching and mining counties in California. With rare exceptions, the rates remained higher than they had been before the Mexican War, but they were lower than they had been during the Civil War and Reconstruction.

The character of America's homicide problem changed, however, in the late nineteenth and early twentieth centuries, in ways that have endured ever since. The decline in homicide continued in the Southwest through the first decades of the twentieth century, but not in the North, where rates rose gradually from the late 1890s to the eve of World War I, or in the rural South, where rates soared in the late 1880s and 1890s. In those years the South surpassed the Southwest as the most homicidal region in the United States. In addition, homicide rates among blacks surpassed those among whites in both the North and South. They remain higher to this day. Yet in California, homicide rates for blacks did not diverge from those for non-Hispanic whites. Blacks there were less likely than whites to kill one another in the 1880s and 1890s. But homicide rates among the Chinese remained above those of Anglos in San Francisco, as did rates among the Chinese and Hispanics in Los Angeles. High rates of intraracial homicide were thus peculiar to minorities that faced the greatest local prejudice and discrimination. That pattern persists today, except among the

Chinese, whose rate fell after World War I.[3] There are lower homicide rates among non-Hispanic whites in the North, the Southwest, and southern cities, higher homicide rates among whites in the rural South, and a divergence in intraracial homicide rates between non-Hispanic whites and the minorities that are most subject to discrimination (overt or institutional) in each region of the country.

White Homicide in the North, 1877–1917

In the last two decades of the nineteenth century, homicide rates declined across the North (Figures 4.2 and 5.1–5.3), continuing a trend that had begun in most jurisdictions at the end of the Civil War. The rates bottomed out in the late 1880s or 1890s before inching up again in the late 1890s and early 1900s. On the eve of World War I, when a majority of states first met federal standards for death registration, the homicide rate (including family and intimate homicides) for adults of all races ranged from 1 to 4 per 100,000 in New England, 2 to 5 in prairie states, and 3 to 8 in the industrial states. With the exception of a few states with very low rates—Wisconsin, New Hampshire, Vermont, and Maine—the North was more homicidal than Canada or western Europe, but less so than it had been in the mid-nineteenth century.[4]

Homicide rates declined in the North in the late nineteenth century because of a drop in murders among unrelated whites. Labor violence increased, especially on railroads and docks, and around coal mines, steel mills, and logging camps, but it did not claim enough lives to have an appreciable effect on the white homicide rate. Most labor violence was instrumental, aimed at changing the behavior of employers, strikers, scabs, the militia, or the police, so the death toll was surprisingly low. Every other kind of homicide among unrelated whites decreased. Property disputes, tavern brawls, sexual assaults, robberies, and spontaneous quarrels claimed fewer lives than they did in the mid-nineteenth century.[5]

The decline in homicides probably escaped the notice of most northerners. They still read articles in the newspapers each week about murders in saloons and on city streets, and their neighbors could still turn on each other with shocking suddenness in arguments over felled trees, trampled crops, laundry bills, or fishing spots. George Poe, a carriage driver in Chillicothe, Ohio, got fed up with a drunken passenger, pushed him out of the rig, and kicked him to death in the street. James McDuffee of Rochester, New Hampshire, blasted two drunken friends with a shotgun when they stopped by his house one night and refused to go home. A readiness to get rid of people who were annoying or troublesome, or who refused to be bullied or intimidated, was more common than it had been before the Mexican War. But on the whole, northerners were more forbearing and less concerned about dominating others than they had been from the Mexican War through the Civil War, and that change was reflected in the homicide rate.[6]

Robbery homicides were still a problem, especially in cities like Chicago, where they accounted for a fifth of known homicides among unrelated adults. In the seven years for which reliable data are available, Chicago robberies and burglaries claimed the lives of 16 suspects, 6 shopowners, 3 employees, 1 customer, 3 police officers, and 11 homeowners. Thieves were killed trying to steal fruit, shoes, soap, beer, or cash; police officers were killed while trying to arrest them. Elsewhere, however, robbery homicides were in decline and made up a similar or smaller percentage of homicides among unrelated adults in the 1880s and 1890s than they had at midcentury. The proportion fell from 17 percent to 10 percent in New Hampshire and Vermont and held steady at about 9 percent in rural Ohio and Illinois. In small towns and in the countryside, thieves still held up banks, waylaid travelers, invaded the homes of single women, and ambushed farmers on the way home from market. But such encounters—like all encounters among friends, acquaintances, and strangers—were less deadly than they had been at midcentury.[7]

The decline in homicide correlated with the greater sense of unity and purpose that emerged among northern whites after the Civil War. Winning the war reinforced northerners' conception of themselves as a group with shared values, characteristics, and goals. The political divisions of the mid-nineteenth century receded, Republicans and Democrats were gradually reconciled, and the two-party system was restored. Election riots, ethnic riots, and religious riots nearly disappeared in the late 1870s and 1880s as political parties turned their attention to traditional issues—tariffs, the monetary system, temperance, internal improvements—and away from issues that divided whites like race and immigration.[8]

Irish Americans were gradually assimilated into society. Second- and third-generation Irish entered skilled or middle-class occupations in droves, and by the 1880s and 1890s fewer than a tenth of all Irish men were unskilled laborers—a dramatic advance since the 1850s. They and other northern whites began to define themselves by race rather than faith, ethnicity, or national origin. As they entered the main-stream, their absolute homicide rates and their rates relative to those of other whites fell in cities and in northern New England and the rural Midwest. The divisions of the mid-nineteenth century did not disappear entirely, and some new immigrant groups (like the Italians) had high homicide rates. But the return of political peace on the national level and the assimilation of Irish immigrants on the local level reversed the forces that had sent white homicide rates soaring in the late 1840s and the 1850s.[9]

Lower expectations among working people also helped to depress homicide by making wage workers less anxious about their standing among their peers. Self-employment continued to decline, but society had come to accept the idea that wage work was honorable and that a life in service to someone else's business could be a good one. The change was evident in obituaries, which by the late nineteenth century described middle-aged factory workers, railroaders, and clerks as "faithful," "steady," "industrious," and "honest"—words that would never have been used in the mid-nineteenth century to describe middle-aged farm laborers, journeymen, or store clerks, who were implicitly considered failures.[10] Those beliefs were sorely tested in the depression of the mid-1890s, but for the most part, unemployed workers did not turn against corporate capitalism. Most protests were efforts to get better wages and were well organized and nonviolent.

Of course, as skilled jobs became more coveted, it became more painful to lose them. In New Hampshire a former police officer killed a Manchester police sergeant whom he blamed for his forced resignation on charges of intemperance. An electrician killed a fellow worker who got him fired from the electric company in Portsmouth for stealing tools. Such killings were not numerous enough to affect the homicide rate, but they show that the nature of workplace violence changed after certain jobs came to be considered more valuable and became crucial to the employee's identity and self-esteem.[11]

Many historians, especially those with an urban focus, believe that the homicide rate declined in northern cities in the late nineteenth century because compulsory schooling and factory work suppressed impulsive and violent behavior among whites. According to this theory, factory workers, salaried clerical workers, and workers who had stayed in school until their teens were less likely to commit murder because they accepted the discipline that came with those jobs and with year-round education. To succeed, they had to control their tempers, obey orders, cooperate with others, delay gratification, and accept boredom and routine to a degree that skilled craftsmen, farmers, day laborers, and rural schoolchildren did not. Factory and clerical workers also spent more of their leisure time at organized sporting events, in city or amusement parks, or with their families, rather than in taverns, which became the haunts of less respectable whites.[12]

This theory cannot account for the breadth of the decline in homicide in the northern United States in the late nineteenth century. Homicide rates fell not only in industrial cities, like Philadelphia, but also in maritime cities, like Boston, and in small towns and in the countryside, where industrial and clerical jobs were few and schools met for only five or six months a year. And the proportion of white children ages seven through fourteen enrolled in school held steady in the North at 75–80 percent from the 1850s through the 1920s, both in cities and in the countryside, even though the homicide rate among unrelated adults rose and fell and rose again over those years.[13] The decline therefore cannot be attributed to disciplinary forces like schooling, clerical work, or factory work. More instrumental were the changed political climate, the integration of Irish immigrants into white society, and the widespread acceptance of the idea that a majority of Americans would have to work for others.

The impact of modern policing should not be overstated, either. There were few police in small towns or in the countryside, and the number of police who patrolled the streets of northern cities remained stable from the 1850s to the 1920s at roughly 15–20 officers per 10,000 inhabitants. Urban officers did confine unruly enterprises such as cockfighting, dogfighting, gambling, and prostitution to older, poorer, minority neighborhoods, but they were not as professional, apolitical, or honest as reformers would have liked, nor were they much more successful at catching violent criminals than ordinary citizens or rural constables were. And officers were still enmeshed in the violence. One of seven homicides among unrelated adults in Chicago involved a police officer—a third of the time as victims and two-thirds of the time as assailants. Most officers were killed, as might be expected, by people disposed to violence: murderers, burglars, or the mentally ill. But the vast majority of the people whom officers killed were nonviolent offenders: fleeing thieves, drunks who resisted arrest, a saloonkeeper who had violated a zoning ordinance, an innocent bystander near an unruly crowd. The killing of John Shea was all too typical. In 1882 Shea and two of his friends were rolling stolen beer kegs down the street when Officer Walsh happened upon the scene. They abandoned the kegs and fled, but Walsh was determined to stop them, and he opened fire, shooting Shea in the back. By the end of the century the urban police did maintain order on respectable streets and impose a degree of order in rougher neighborhoods. They also had more authority than they had had in the mid-nineteenth century, because they were caught less often in the middle of divisive political battles. But they had little to do with the decline in homicide among northern whites.[14]

The homicide rate crept upward among northern whites from the late 1890s to World War I. Italian immigrants were responsible for a portion of the increase. Italians were murdered by unrelated adults at a rate five to ten times that of other European Americans. They brought much of this violence with them. Italy had the highest homicide rate in western Europe. It was politically unstable in the nineteenth century and had yet to establish an effective criminal justice system from Tuscany south to Sicily, the area most Italian immigrants came from. Italy's homicide rate declined, according to official records, from 14 per 100,000 persons per year in the 1880s to 8 per 100,000 on the eve of World War I, as the central government consolidated its power and national feeling intensified. But the nation was still plagued with feuds, gang violence, honor killings, robbery murders, and revenge murders—the kinds of violence associated with political instability and with governments that fail to inspire trust.[15]

It appears, however, that Italians, like the Irish in the mid-nineteenth century, were more homicidal in the United States than they were in Europe. The high homicide rate among Italians was rooted in the same problems that had caused the high rate among the Irish in the 1840s and 1850s. Many young immigrants traveled from place to place to build railroads, dams, or waterworks, living in labor camps where they fought with fellow workers for jobs or respect. A few made money illicitly and were killed by rival gang members, and many lived in crowded shanties and tenements, where they killed fellow tenants or roommates who trod on their turf. Giuseppi Dorone and Vincenzo Dazane lived in an abandoned labor camp outside Concord, New Hampshire. The camp had been set up for the Italians who had built the city's sewer system years before. Dorone and Dazane slept in a lean-to on a two-foot-wide bunk covered with rags. They had always been "inseparable," but one dark February day they got into an argument. Dazane threw Dorone's belongings out of the lean-to, and Dorone shot him. In Philadelphia, roommates Imogenzo Buno and Giuseppi Resciznuolo quarreled about inviting a guest to dinner. Resciznuolo stabbed Buno in the arm, and Buno shot Resciznuolo in the stomach three times. In Chicago, Carmillo Gentile, a day laborer, ran afoul of his boarders when he held an all-day "carousal" for the neighborhood. The boarders demanded an end to the party, but Gentile was making an excellent profit from the sale of beer, and he sent out for more. In response one of the boarders threw Gentile's beer glass out the window. Gentile grabbed him by the throat, and the boarder stabbed Gentile through the heart.[16]

Like the Irish, whose penchant for recreational fighting left many a Saturday night drinker on the barroom floor, the Italians brought a distinctive form of violence to the United States. Like southerners, Italian men lived by a code that required them to defend their dignity at all costs; and like Hispanics, they were extremely sensitive about anything that touched upon their wives or daughters. Frank Dominito was incensed when a sixteen-year-old boy, James Calderone, spoke to his wife in "disrespectful terms." He went to Calderone's father, Ignazio, to demand that he punish the boy, but Ignazio told Dominito that it was "no concern of his" and asked him to leave. Dominito shot Ignazio dead.[17]

Italians also had the misfortune, like the Irish, to become the targets of nativists and anti-Catholics who wanted to restrict immigration and cull immigrants from the voter rolls. That hostility, and the anger it aroused in the Italians, led to numerous confrontations and casualties on both sides. In Philadelphia, Thomas Carroll taunted a ragpicker, Giovanni Varra, and threw a stone at him. Varra stabbed Carroll with his poker. Frank Sienni, a Chicago barber who was depressed after losing his job, became enraged when a group of young men shouted ethnic slurs at him in the street. He grabbed one of them and slashed his throat from ear to ear. Many of the people who attacked Italians were themselves members of ethnic groups who had been on the receiving end of such abuse a generation earlier. They took a particularly savage pleasure in harassing newer arrivals; doing so confirmed their status as "real" Americans. James Nolan got into an argument with three Italian street cleaners in Philadelphia. He threatened them, and when they had the temerity to call for the police, Nolan clubbed one of them on the head with a broom handle until he was dead.[18]

Violence by Italians increased the homicide rate in the late 1890s and early 1900s. It would take time for them to gain acceptance as part of the broader white community, move out of poverty, and assimilate. But the Italians never constituted a large enough percentage of the population to be responsible for more than a fraction of the increase in homicide among whites in the early twentieth century. They made up, for instance, only 4 percent of the population in Chicago and 5 percent in Philadelphia on the eve of World War I. Other immigrants from southern and eastern Europe—Greeks, Poles, Czechs, Slovaks, Hungarians, Romanians, and Russians—together accounted for a larger portion of the population, but they were collectively no more homicidal than Americans of northern or western European descent, who also saw their homicide rate increase.[19]

Additional research is needed to confirm these patterns, but it appears likely that the general increase in homicide was an indirect consequence of immigration from southern and eastern Europe, which rekindled the kinds of ethnic hatreds and nativist movements that had undermined fellow feeling and divided the North politically in the mid-1840s and the 1850s. The consequences for the homicide rate were not as severe as they had been in the mid-nineteenth century, because the new immigrants did not make up as large a share of the population as the Germans, Irish, and French Canadians did, and because their arrival did not coincide with a political crisis. The two-party system and the stability of the federal government were never threatened. But as tension increased between the native-born (including the Irish, French, Germans, and Scandinavians) and the "foreign-born element," and battles intensified over religion, jobs, neighborhoods, and voting rights, the fellow feeling that had reappeared among whites by the late 1880s and 1890s dissipated. Reformers and stalwarts alike began to challenge the legitimacy of the state and of local political machines that catered to the new immigrants or to more established ethnic groups, and homicides increased, even among members of the same ethnic group.[20]

Black Homicide in the North, 1877–1917

Unlike white rates, black homicide rates followed several different paths in the North in the late nineteenth and early twentieth centuries, depending upon the character of the communities in which African Americans lived. In small towns and in the countryside, the rate at which blacks were murdered by unrelated adults declined in the 1870s and remained at roughly the same level as the white rate through the turn of the century. There were no homicides among unrelated blacks or between blacks and whites in Vermont or New Hampshire, or in Holmes County, Ohio, or in Henderson or Calhoun counties in Illinois. In Ross County, Ohio, blacks suffered only one intraracial homicide, when a drunken man threw a brick at a friend for no known reason at a Fourth of July celebration, and one interracial homicide. In Chillicothe, two teenagers got into a scuffle, and the white boy deliberately killed the black boy. The black community was incensed. Yet when one member of the community rode up and down the streets trying to get a mob together to lynch the white boy, blacks turned their backs on him. They wanted no part of that form of justice.[21]

The dearth of interracial and intraracial murders in the small-town and rural North reflected a lessening of the political tensions that had caused whites to murder blacks in the mid-nineteenth century, as well as the progress blacks had made toward equal rights. By the mid-1870s blacks voted freely across the North, thanks to the Fifteenth Amendment and the Enforcement Acts, which gave the federal government the authority to protect voters against intimidation and to prosecute anyone who harassed voters or stole their ballots. By the turn of the century, grassroots campaigns had integrated the public schools in every state but Indiana. There were signs of progress even there: Indiana law gave local school boards the power to determine the racial makeup of district buildings, and nearly half of black students in Indianapolis attended integrated schools.[22]

Progress toward equal rights was heartening to African Americans. Voting rights and school integration empowered them and intensified their faith in government, especially when the government was run by Republicans. But the feelings of whites were also important factors. Nearly all rural northerners accepted integration of the schools and the polls peacefully, if not enthusiastically, even in places like Ross County, where Copperhead Democrats, still bitter about the Confederate defeat in the Civil War, numbered in the thousands. None of these places had black populations large enough to discomfit whites. Blacks did not enjoy social or economic equality, but they were tolerated and seldom persecuted. They lived and worked on the margins of society, as they had before the Civil War, and for the most part they were unmolested. The older patterns of black life in the rural North continued.

The story was different in cities like Philadelphia. Because Philadelphia had more black residents than any other northern city, African Americans simply by their greater visibility posed a greater threat to white supremacy and faced more open hostility and systematic discrimination than their counterparts in the rural North. But their numbers also enabled Philadelphia's blacks to assert themselves politically in ways that were impossible for blacks in small towns or the countryside. In the 1880s they won several seats on the Philadelphia city council and were well represented on district school committees, and because their votes were crucial to Republican and reform candidates, they won patronage positions as ward heelers, clerks, janitors, and street sweepers. Their influence was limited, however. Although in 1881 Philadelphia became the first northern city to appoint African Americans to its police force, by 1884 they held only 35 of 1,400 positions, and that number declined as soon as the reform mayor left office. Pennsylvania outlawed segregated schools in 1881, but Philadelphia's schools remained largely segregated. And the influence of blacks in Philadelphia politics waned after 1890. At the national level, in response to the rising tide of racism and the party's decline in the South, the Republican Party turned away from its commitment to civil rights, and local Republican leaders followed suit, distancing themselves from their black constituents. They hoped to appeal to white voters who rejected the idea of racial equality but who might support the Republican Party for other reasons. By the end of the century, blacks held only one seat on Philadelphia's city council and five on its school committees.[23]

This loss of political power had devastating consequences for Philadelphia's blacks. Although black children spent as much time in school as white children, their schools were poorly staffed, underfunded, and rundown. African Americans encountered discrimination in housing and employment—even in service occupations that had been open to them earlier. Prostitution, gambling, and organized crime moved into black neighborhoods, where white officials tolerated their presence, and police forces became lily-white and increasingly hostile to blacks. Factory work was difficult to come by, and many blacks were forced into unskilled work, unemployment, or illegal activity such as theft, prostitution, and numbers running. Opportunities were so scarce that one out of eight young African American women worked at least part-time as a prostitute, and many young black men ran with criminal gangs. Because lawlessness was rampant, blacks began to carry knives and handguns for personal protection. It was difficult to start families and hold them together in such dissolute and economically depressed neighborhoods, and there was little that black elites could do to remedy the situation, both because they were powerless within the Republican Party and because the black community as a whole was stigmatized by the vice and crime that overtook its neighborhoods.[24]

The decline of black political power, residential segregation, and the loss of many skilled and domestic jobs had one positive effect in Philadelphia: according to homicide indictments, the rate at which blacks were killed by whites fell from 4.4 per 100,000 adults per year during Reconstruction to 3.3 in the 1880s and 1.4 in the 1890s. Now that society kept blacks so firmly in their place, whites had little occasion and even less reason to kill them. The few killings of blacks by whites that occurred in the 1880s and 1890s took place either during labor disputes in which blacks were employed as strikebreakers or in situations in which whites held the upper hand. Three Irish youths pelted a black store clerk with snowballs on a city street, and when he complained, they beat him to death. A white horseman killed a black stable hand who had had an accident with a horse he was supposed to take to the racetrack. Unlike the murders of skilled black workers and black shopkeepers in the 1850s, or of black voters in the 1870s, these murders were gratuitous. The murderers did not have to kill to get their way; they acted on impulse and killed for emotional satisfaction. Their victims did not pose a threat to white supremacy.[25]

The impact of job loss, segregation, and the loss of political power on the black homicide rate in Philadelphia was startling. The rate at which blacks were indicted for killing one another rose from 2.2 per 100,000 adults per year during Reconstruction to 3.7 in the 1880s and 5.0 in the 1890s—two and a half times the rate at which whites were indicted for killing whites in that decade. For the first time, blacks killed each other at a higher rate than whites killed each other. Frustrated men and women who had lost faith in government and had little chance of finding a satisfactory place in society were extremely sensitive to disrespect, especially if they were denizens of Philadelphia's criminal underworld. Black gamblers, gangsters, and prostitutes did each other in at a frantic pace. In 1895 Hattie Stewart, known as "Better Days," ran a brothel on Lemon Street. William Green, a chiropodist and agent for the State Liquor League, stopped by for his usual services one day, but Stewart refused to accommodate him, saying that he was no longer her "special friend." Green fired several shots at Stewart before she and her employees could calm him down, but all seemed well until another customer took him to task for "shooting at these women all day" and dared Green to try it with him. He did, killing the customer instantly. Five years later Stewart herself was killed by one of her own prostitutes who claimed that Stewart was holding her as a slave. Such killings accounted for most of the increase in black homicides.[26]

Even law-abiding black Philadelphians had their problems with violence, however. In 1901 four men were riding in a carriage in a Republican parade when a stranger jumped on and attacked them with a knife. They threw him off and stabbed him to death. Emma Bond invited friends to her home for a Fourth of July party in 1893. One of her friends took the wrong hat when he left, and she followed him to retrieve it. He thought she was accusing him of stealing it, and he shot her dead. The hypersensitivity to slights that afflicted people for whom respect was a rare commodity led blacks all too often to turn their rage on one another.[27]

Blacks also took their anger out on whites, however. The rate at which blacks were indicted for killing whites rose in the 1890s to a new high in Philadelphia—4.6 per 100,000 black adults per year. For the first time in the nineteenth century, more whites than blacks were killed in interracial homicides in that city. Some of the killings were predatory. Blacks in the criminal underworld were willing to attack any target of opportunity, black or white. And some killings were simply part of doing business in the underworld. Samuel Ramsey, a piano player in a brothel, had to get tough with several white customers who were celebrating Theodore Roosevelt's election in 1900. When they started hitting the prostitutes, Ramsey ejected them, killing one of them in the process.[28]

Most killings of whites were defensive, but Philadelphia records reveal a new fury in the counterattacks. In 1892 John Williams and a friend were sitting on a doorstep when John McGurk walked by and threatened drunkenly to "kill every nigger around here." He then tried to stab Williams. Williams cut him to pieces with a cotton hook. Six Irishmen jumped George Queen in a random street attack, but Queen fought back furiously and killed two of his attackers. A crowd of white youths went to a dance, got drunk, and tried to pick fights. When a brawl broke out, Frank Monroe was outside the hall watching. One of the men tried to punch him, and Monroe made quick work of him with his knife.[29]

Philadelphia records also show that blacks killed whites to defend their dignity. They felt that they had won the right to be treated well, and sometimes they lashed out furiously at people trying to humiliate them. Adam Wilson made fun of Francis Bouchet for selling cream puffs, and when Bouchet asked him to get out of the way of his customers, Wilson threw dirt on him. Bouchet beat him to death. Antonio Salvatore made rude remarks about Jesse Walters' color and grabbed Walters' thumb and bit it; Walters kicked him to death. Emma Logan accused her neighbor, Robert Braxton, of entering her house while she was away. He denied it, and when she called him a liar, he stabbed her.[30]

The worst homicide rates appeared in industrial cities and towns in the Midwest, where the sudden influx of blacks in the late nineteenth and early twentieth centuries led to intense conflict over jobs and housing. The demand for labor was so great in the Midwest that blacks could not be shunted to the side as they were in eastern cities: they had to be integrated into the industrial workforce. Living and working side by side with African Americans was a threatening experience for most whites. In the early 1880s, the rate at which unrelated whites murdered each other in Chicago was comparable to the rates in other northern cities (6 per 100,000 adults per year), but the rates at which blacks and whites murdered one another were substantially higher than in older eastern cities like Philadelphia and New York. Blacks were murdered by whites at a rate of 21 per 100,000 adults per year, and blacks killed roughly the same number of whites. Racial violence and discrimination also took their toll within the black community. Frustrated and demoralized blacks killed one another at a rate of 28 per 100,000 adults per year. Those high rates persisted to the eve of World War I.[31]

Similar interracial and intraracial homicide rates appeared a decade later in Omaha, Nebraska. Blacks became a substantial presence there only in the late 1880s and 1890s, when the city's stockyards and railroads attracted thousands of migrants and increased the city's population from 30,000 to 150,000. Even then blacks accounted for only 3 percent of Omaha's population, but they loomed large in the minds of the city's whites because they held a considerable portion of the city's unskilled jobs and because most of them lived near saloons and brothels in the poor neighborhood west of the railroad yard, and were therefore assumed to be linked in some way to vice. Blacks in Omaha were less likely to kill blacks or whites than whites were in the 1880s and 1890s. But whites, feeling threatened, subjected blacks to considerable violence, just as they had in New York City and Philadelphia during the Civil War and Reconstruction. In the 1890s they killed blacks at five times the rate at which blacks killed one another. Whites murdered blacks primarily in brothels, gambling dens, and bars, but there was also a lynching. In 1891 George Smith, who was thought to have murdered a five-year-old white girl, was taken out of jail by a mob of 15,000, dragged through the streets until his flesh was nearly torn off, and hanged on a streetcar wire. The girl was later found alive, but no one in the white community expressed remorse. Everyone seemed to think that the show of white supremacy had been a good idea.[32]

In the early 1900s, as racially motivated attacks continued and more and more blacks were fired from the railroad, domestic service, or other jobs so that whites could take their place, Omaha's blacks began to take out their frustration on whites and on each other. The rate at which unrelated blacks killed each other jumped from zero per

100,000 adults per year in the 1880s and 3 per 100,000 in the 1890s to 65 per 100,000 in the early 1900s; and the rate at which blacks were indicted for killing whites rose from 5 per 100,000 adults per year in the 1880s and 10 per 100,000 in the 1890s to 30 per 100,000 in the early 1900s. These homicides were identical in motive and circumstance with those that occurred in Philadelphia and Chicago, even though they occurred a decade later.[33]

The use of black workers as strikebreakers exacerbated white hostility across the Midwest. In Williamson County, Illinois, the owner of the St. Louis and Big Muddy Coal Company, Samuel Brush, nearly started a race war when he brought hundreds of black strikebreakers into town in the summer of 1898. The black miners, who had recently been dismissed by a mining company that had settled with its white employees, arrived by train and were immediately ambushed by the white strikers. Brush was ready for trouble, however. He had armed the strikebreakers, and they returned fire until the whites dispersed. The wife of one of the strikebreakers was killed.[34]

The striking miners kept an eye out for blacks who dared to set foot outside the mining compound. Two Welsh miners got into a fight with three black miners at a small Italian saloon on the outskirts of Carterville, the county seat. The blacks were ordered to leave, but a rumor got around that one of them had threatened miner Elmer James, saying, "I'll wash my hands in your blood and ——— your wife before the sun goes down." When word came that armed blacks were marching on the town, white miners rallied and struck out for the station. The black miners were indeed armed, but they were only going to the station to meet friends and travel to a neighboring town for church services. The white miners ordered them at gunpoint to march back down the tracks to Brush's mine. They retreated, but the white miners followed, and when one of the blacks turned and fired to warn them off, the whites responded with a volley that killed five blacks, including the three who had been at the tavern. Incidents like this only deepened animosity toward blacks among whites in midwestern industrial and mining communities in the late 1880s and 1890s, and that animosity flared up into violence all too easily when black and white economic interests came into conflict.

Some scholars have suggested that the criminal justice system contributed to the homicide problem that developed in black neighborhoods in cities and industrial towns. The courts and the police certainly lacked legitimacy in the eyes of many blacks, but the justice system did not turn a blind eye to violence within black communities. Although authorities let vice run rampant in black neighborhoods, they did make an effort to deter homicide. Sometimes that effort was fairly evenhanded. In Philadelphia there was little difference between blacks and whites when it came to the indictment and conviction of homicide suspects. The difference was not dramatic even for interracial murders: 26 percent of whites were found guilty, and 38 percent of blacks. In Omaha, however, the judicial system appears to have gone overboard in its effort to control violence in black neighborhoods, and it showed an undeniable bias when black-on-white violence was at issue. In the late nineteenth and early twentieth centuries, Omaha courts convicted 79 percent of blacks indicted for murdering blacks and 89 percent indicted for murdering whites. Only 38 percent of whites indicted for murdering whites were convicted, and none of the whites indicted for murdering blacks. In any event, there is no evidence that black homicide rates spiraled out of control in northern cities for lack of deterrence.[35]

Other scholars have suggested that the migration of southern blacks, who historically had had higher rates of homicide than northern blacks, caused the higher homicide rate in cities and industrial towns. The rate at which blacks killed whites and each other did go up in Philadelphia as the proportion of black Philadelphia adults who were born in the South rose from 18 percent in 1880 to 56 percent in 1920. But in Omaha, where the proportion of black adults born in the South was never lower than two-thirds, the rate at which blacks killed whites and each other was low until blacks formed a sufficient portion of the city's population to threaten whites. And in Chicago, the rate at which blacks killed each other fell suddenly after 1915, just as migration from the South was peaking. At the time, three-fourths of Chicago's black adults were southern-born, but the intraracial homicide rate decreased there even as it was still rising in Omaha, Philadelphia, and New York City.[36]

The clearest difference between Chicago and other northern cities was not demographic, but political. Blacks in Chicago increased their political power in this era more than blacks in any other northern city. Their South Side neighborhoods supported a formidable political machine, with its own distinctive, militant style. Voters in those neighbor-hoods turned out at a higher rate than blacks in other northern cities. They elected black aldermen and Republican committeemen and sup-ported the city's black newspapers, especially the *Chicago Defender,* a tireless advocate for the poor, which by World War I had a circulation of 125,000. Black ward leaders were known across the city for their skill and cunning, and their support was crucial to the success of white politicians like William Hale Thompson. Thompson was a favorite in the black community because he treated black voters with respect, attended social functions on the South Side, and appointed blacks to powerful positions at City Hall, which Democrats dubbed "Uncle Tom's Cabin."[37]

The rate at which blacks killed one another in Chicago fell from 21 per 100,000 adults per year between 1911 and 1915 to 12 per 100,000 after 1915. That was the year that the *Defender* first appeared, Thomp-son won the mayor's race, and Oscar De Priest, who would become the first black congressman from the North, was elected to the city coun-cil. Chicago's blacks were subject to the same surge in white violence as blacks in other cities were during and after World War I, but they did not turn on each other at the rate at which they had in the past. The intraracial rate was still higher than antebellum rates in cities else-where, a sign that the modest increase in political power had not re-vived the kind of optimism and solidarity that had suppressed homi-cide among northern blacks before the Civil War. But at a time when southern blacks were flocking to Chicago, and the nonwhite homicide rate in the South ranged from 23 per 100,000 adults per year in Mary-land to over 80 per 100,000 in Kentucky, Chicago's rate still fell. Politi-cal empowerment could change homicide rates, even among people with a history of violence.[38]

Homicide in the Southwest, 1877–1917

Homicide rates declined across the Southwest, just as they did in the North. Los Angeles County, which had been the most violent county in California, saw its homicide rate fall the most: from 198 per 100,000 adults per year in the late 1860s and 1870s to 23 per 100,000 in the 1880s and 1890s (Figure 7.2). But substantial declines occurred ev-erywhere in the Southwest. On the eve of World War I, southwestern rates were still high compared to those in the North, but the total homicide rate had fallen to 12 per 100,000 adults per year in California, 15 per 100,000 in Colorado, and probably 20–30 per 100,000 in Arizona, Nevada, and New Mexico.[39]

The parts of the Southwest that were just being taken over by Anglos were still plagued by frontier violence. In Arizona, racial hostility among Anglos, Hispanics, and Native Americans and no-holds-barred competition among Anglo ranchers and miners encouraged an us-versus-them mentality that precluded the development of fellow feeling. Arizona's territorial government, which was controlled by a mercenary group of federal appointees, made matters worse not only because it was corrupt, but also because it had neither the will nor the resources to provide adequate law enforcement. County sheriffs could not hire enough deputies, so most of the territory lacked law enforcement or was policed by cattle, mining, railroad, or express companies, which had the right under Arizona law to hire officers to protect their property and to patrol company towns. Company law was sometimes worse than no law, because company representatives had little regard for the rights of workers. Some Anglo and Hispanic sheriffs had the wisdom to appoint non-Anglo or non-Hispanic deputies to assure local minorities that the law would be enforced impartially, but their deputies could still be caught in the middle of interracial disputes, political feuds, or range wars. The same was true of the Native American police, who tried to enforce the law on reservations. Even if resources had been adequate, it would have been difficult to enforce the law in such a divided, ill-governed society.[40]

The combination of unpopular government, poor law enforcement, racial hostility, and competition for land and mineral rights led to considerable violence in Arizona in the 1880s and 1890s. The homicide rate among unrelated adults in Gila County, for example, was at least 142 per 100,000 per year. Conditions there were particularly conducive to high homicide rates. The Apaches were sent to reservations in the county after their final defeat. They were demoralized and angry and often clashed with whites and with one another. Cattle ranches and copper and silver mines sprang up in the 1880s and 1890s and attracted thousands of young men. Rustling was a problem because of widespread poverty and the proximity to the Mexican border.[41]

The Pleasant Valley War, which pitted local cattlemen against rustlers, claimed twenty-five lives in and around the county between 1885 and 1887. Gila County's remote northern valley provided perfect cover for rustlers. They stole cattle and horses from Mexico, doctored their brands in the valley, and sold them in northern Arizona, southern Utah, and southern Colorado. They then reversed course, stealing cattle and horses from points north and selling them in Mexico. But when they started to prey on the herds of cattlemen who lived near their base of operations, they reaped a whirlwind. In the fighting that followed, all the rustlers were eventually killed or driven out of the country. Of course, they claimed their victims too; the family that led the fight against them lost all but one of its sons.[42]

In Gila's mining towns, which were located along the county's mountainous western border, few people believed that law-enforcement officials would protect life or property. As a result, murders in taverns and gambling parlors, robbery murders, revenge murders, and lynchings were common. Hispanics, Apaches, and European immigrants were recruited to irrigate fields, herd cattle, or work in the mines or construction, and there was violence between them and native-born Anglo laborers. The Apaches had a particularly hard time submitting to Anglo authority. Nah-deiz-az, an Apache who had spent a year at the Carlisle Indian School in Pennsylvania learning modern farming methods, confronted Lieutenant Seward Mott of the U.S. Army, the chief of police on the San Carlos Reservation, after Mott had arrested Nah-deiz-az's father for refusing an order to work. "What did you put my father in jail for?" Nah-deiz-az asked Mott. His father was crippled and could work only for short periods, and then only with one hand. Mott tried to arrest Nah-deiz-az for daring to question him, and Nah-deiz-az said, "Now, you want to put me in jail too? You will not put me in jail." He pulled out his gun and killed Mott.[43]

The Apaches had a nondomestic murder rate of at least 110 per 100,000 adults per year in the 1880s and 1890s. They defended their honor violently and were quick to avenge wrongs done to their families, even if the person at fault was another Apache. Ninety-four percent of Apache victims were killed by fellow Apaches. But Gila County's Anglos were just as proud and vengeful. Their homicide rate was at least 215 per 100,000 adults per year, and 75 percent of the victims were killed by other Anglos. Homicide remained out of control wherever government lacked the legitimacy or resources to enforce the law, and wherever racial hostility or cutthroat economic competition made it impossible to create fellow feeling.[44]

Conflicts between labor and management were also more deadly in the Southwest than in the North. Western mines and logging camps attracted a rough crowd of itinerant workers, who usually lived in camps or towns that were owned and governed by their employers. Cut off from the rest of society, they were at the mercy of their employers and the boardinghouse operators, storekeepers, foremen, and police, who worked for the companies. In the coal mines and company towns of Las Animas County, Colorado, company police were much more trigger-happy than regular police. In many instances they were little more than thugs, hired to take the company's side in labor disputes and keep workers in line both on and off the job. In the late nineteenth and early twentieth centuries, they killed nine people for talking back and resisting arrest. None of those people had posed a threat to anyone; they were only drunk and disorderly.[45]

Company foremen showed a similar disregard for the lives of their workers. In Colorado, mines were twice as deadly as their eastern counterparts, and workers died by the hundreds in accidents, most of which occurred because the foremen and the mining companies ignored the workers' pleas for safer working conditions. Certainly, the mining companies put profits first, but there was more to it than that: among mine owners and mine foremen, there was virtually no empathy for the workers. Many of the Colorado mines were owned by eastern corporations whose officers had no contact with the workers, and by 1905 most of the English-speaking miners had been replaced with eastern and southern Europeans. In the strike of 1903–04, which involved mines all over southeastern Colorado, the mining companies tried to starve the miners into submission, and thirteen people were killed. The strike of 1913–14 was worse; fifty-nine men, women, and children died. Twenty-one of them were killed in the infamous Ludlow massacre, in which company agents turned a machine gun on strikers and burned their camp to the ground. In the late nineteenth century, when Las Animas County was still rural and the mining boom had just begun, its homicide rate was 34 per 100,000 adults per year, equal to rates in ranching and mining counties in California. But in the early 1900s, when the strikes began, its homicide rate rose to nearly 100 per 100,000.[46]

Away from frontier communities and company towns, the Southwest was becoming less homicidal. Anglo homicide rates declined in the late nineteenth and early twentieth centuries for the same reasons that white homicide rates declined in the North. The end of Reconstruction, the revival of the two-party system, acceptance of the decline in self-employment, and the assimilation of European immigrants resulted in the emergence of greater unity among non-Hispanic whites in the late nineteenth century. In San Francisco, the homicide rate for the Irish declined as rapidly as it did for the rest of the white population, and the rates for other non-Hispanic white ethnic groups moved closer to the rate for all non-Hispanic whites.[47] Sectional, ethnic, religious, and class hostility diminished among Anglos and was replaced by a growing sense of racial solidarity. It was not nearly as strong as the solidarity felt by white New Englanders after King Philip's War or by white Virginians and Marylanders during the early years of racial slavery, but it was strong enough to lower the homicide rate among unrelated whites.

The movement away from frontier conditions and frontier homicide rates was most advanced in California and Colorado. In 1900 those states had the largest populations, the most diversified economies, and the lowest homicide rates in the West. The ratio of men to women in their Anglo populations stood at 1.2 to 1. The more balanced gender ratio all but ended the wild, brothel-based culture of the 1850s and 1860s that had claimed the lives of so many men and women. Equally important, the proportion of non-Anglos in the population fell by 1900 to its lowest levels in history: only 7 percent in California and 2 percent in Colorado. Anglo domination reduced the likelihood that minorities would be murdered by Anglos, and because minorities made up a smaller and smaller share of the population, the rate at which Anglos committed interracial murders declined even more steeply. Anglos encountered non-Anglos less frequently than before, and they appear to have been more confident of their dominant position in society. They had pushed the Chinese, Hispanics, and Native Americans so far to the margins of society that minorities had little in the way of jobs or property for Anglos to covet.

The rate at which Anglos perpetrated interracial murders in California fell to 1 per 100,000 Anglo adults per year in the 1880s and 1890s.[48] But the changes that deterred Anglo interracial homicides also appear to have deterred homicides among Anglos. As in southern plantation counties, it was their anxiety over their social standing in a caste society and their need to appear more powerful than minorities that caused them to kill one another. Wherever they held the largest majorities and were most firmly in control, as in cities and farming counties, they killed one another at the lowest rates. Wherever they held narrower majorities and were less firmly in control, as in mining and ranching counties, they killed one another at higher rates. States with the highest homicide rates among Anglos had the highest proportions of non-Anglos in the population: 17 percent in Nevada, 37 percent in Arizona, and 48 percent in New Mexico. California and Colorado were gradually becoming more like northern states in their social and demographic composition, which is why their Anglo homicide rates fell.

In California, where the best data are available, non-Anglo homicide rates in the 1880s and 1890s followed more complicated patterns than Anglo rates. Native Americans continued to suffer catastrophic rates of intraracial and interracial violence. They were killed by unrelated adults at about the same rate as in the late 1860s and 1870s—at least 70 per 100,000 adults per year. Unrelated Native Americans killed one another at a high rate—25 per 100,000 adults per year—and they were still frequently victimized by Anglo, black, and Hispanic assailants. The rate at which the Chinese were murdered by unrelated adults continued to fall, from 49 to 31 per 100,000, but gang violence, which was responsible for 67 percent of homicides among unrelated Chinese in San Francisco in the 1880s and 1890s, kept their intraracial homicide rate as high as that for Indians: 25 per 100,000. They experienced as many assassinations and turf wars over gambling, drugs, loan-sharking, extortion rackets, and prostitution as they did during the Gold Rush. But homicides of Chinese by non-Chinese and by unknown persons fell to low levels, and the rate at which Chinese murdered non-Chinese fell to 1 homicide per 100,000 Chinese adults per year. By the end of the nineteenth century their homicide problem, unlike that of Native Americans, was confined to their own community.[49]

Anglos continued to kill Hispanics at a fairly high rate in the 1880s and 1890s. Hispanics were five times more likely than the Chinese to be killed in interracial homicides. They held a wider range of jobs than the Chinese did, moved more freely in society, and enjoyed full civil rights if they were citizens, so they came into contact with Anglos more often and posed a greater threat to them. They also responded in kind to Anglo aggression, killing Anglos at eight times the rate the Chinese did. But the Hispanic community, unlike the Chinese community, was becoming less homicidal.[50]

Outside Los Angeles the Hispanic community did not suffer from systematic gang violence, as the Chinese community did, and, probably as important, class tensions declined within the Hispanic community as the economic decline of the *gente fina* continued. Hispanics also developed a stronger sense of community and national feeling in the late nineteenth century. That feeling was nurtured by parochial schools, Hispanic festivals, and Spanish-language newspapers, and it reflected pride in the apparent progress of Mexico under the administration of Porfirio Díaz. It would be a mistake to exaggerate the solidarity of the Hispanic community and to neglect the demoralizing impact of discrimination and land loss, which forced the majority of Hispanics to work at low-paying, unskilled jobs and to live in impoverished neighborhoods. Some Hispanics did turn to crime, and some barrios, like the one in Los Angeles, were vice-ridden. But in most places Hispanics made the best of their exclusion from Anglo society and built communities that had a greater sense of solidarity and lower homicide rates than had prevailed when the area was under Mexican control or during the Gold Rush.[51]

In Los Angeles, however, where discrimination was most intense and Hispanics were forced into the worst neighborhoods, a considerable gap opened in the 1880s and 1890s between Hispanic and Anglo homicide rates. Hispanics in Los Angeles killed one another at a rate of 30 per 100,000 adults per year, as opposed to only 11 per 100,000 for Anglos, who benefited from decent urban schooling, better policing, and higher-paid factory jobs and salaried work. Outside Los Angeles the homicide rate among Hispanics had fallen so far that they killed one another at roughly the same rate that Anglos did. A similar gap opened between Chinese and Anglo homicide rates in San Francisco and Los Angeles, where the Chinese faced the worst discrimination and were confined to dangerous, crime-ridden neighborhoods. But like Hispanics, the Chinese killed each other at the same rate that Anglos did in mining, ranching, and farming counties.[52]

The experiences of Hispanics in Los Angeles and of the Chinese in Los Angeles and San Francisco were identical with the experiences of blacks in Philadelphia, Omaha, and Chicago, and they had homicide rates to match. Hatred of the Chinese was so intense in these two cities that it played a pivotal role in securing a nationwide ban on Chinese immigration in 1882; and discrimination against Hispanics was so intense in Los Angeles that many Mexicans went home in the 1880s and 1890s, and few immigrants came to take their place. But where Hispanic and Chinese Californians were not forced by discrimination into deteriorating, crime-ridden neighborhoods, they did not kill one another at higher rates than whites did.

Ironically, African Americans did relatively well in California in the 1880s and 1890s because they were not the focus of Anglo hatred. They accounted for a smaller share of California's population than Hispanics or the Chinese did—less than 1 percent—and they benefited from the rights won during Reconstruction, especially the right to vote and the right to attend integrated public schools. California blacks were not numerous enough to gain much influence within the Republican Party, but because they posed less of a threat to Anglos than Hispanics or the Chinese did, they held on to coveted jobs in the service economy—domestic service, barbering, catering—and in some skilled and semiskilled crafts. Blacks were spared the need to get deeply involved in the criminal underworld in San Francisco and Los Angeles, and those who wanted to get involved had a hard time doing so, because Hispanic and Chinese criminals preferred to deal with their own people. As a result, by the 1880s and 1890s blacks were no more likely to kill one another than Anglos were, and they did not murder Chinese, Hispanic, or Anglo Californians. Like everyone else, however, they did kill Native Americans. Blacks were still occasionally victimized by hostile Anglos or Hispanics, who murdered nearly half of all black homicide victims. Those interracial homicides pushed the total homicide rate for African Americans somewhat higher than the rate for Anglos.[53]

The black experience in urban California is a strong indication that the surge in homicide among blacks in the urban North in the late nineteenth and early twentieth centuries was not caused, as some still argue, by a defect in black culture or black family life or by violence-prone migrants from the South. It was caused by political impotence, economic discrimination, and racial prejudice. Wherever those forces shut minorities out of mainstream urban society, undermined their faith in government, and pushed them into criminal occupations and vice-ridden neighborhoods, minority homicide rates rose. Which minority had the highest homicide rate depended on which was most persecuted. In San Francisco, it was the Chinese, and in Los Angeles, the Chinese and Hispanics.

Homicide in the South, 1872–1887

Homicide rates declined through much of the South from the mid-1870s to the late 1880s, just as they did in the North and the Southwest. They held steady in Virginia at 8 per 100,000 adults per year (Figure 5.6), but they fell drastically elsewhere as soon as white conservatives returned to power in states that had been politically turbulent during Reconstruction. When Redeemers—the coalition of white conservatives who wanted to "redeem" the South from the evils of Reconstruction—took charge in Louisiana in 1877, the homicide rate fell in rural counties from 89 to 35 per 100,000 and in New Orleans from 35 to 25 per 100,000 (Figure 7.1). When former Confederates returned to power in Georgia in 1872, the homicide rate fell in mountain counties from 53 to 12 per 100,000 and in plantation counties from 24 to 16 per 100,000 (Figures 4.1 and 5.5). These declines were caused by a sudden drop in the rates at which whites killed blacks and one another. Arrest rates for homicide also fell in southern and border cities in the late 1870s and 1880s, just as they did in northern cities.[54]

These declines were abrupt. Once conservative whites regained power, the need to kill blacks diminished, and antagonism among Unionist, moderate, and conservative whites receded. White murders of "uppity" blacks and black murders of overbearing whites fell off rapidly. So did political homicides. When former Confederates returned to power, white supremacists no longer felt a pressing need to enforce the color line violently, because they could use poll taxes, registration laws, felon disfranchisement laws, and gerrymandered districts to suppress the black vote; and blacks recognized that challenging white supremacy was no longer an option. The rate at which blacks murdered whites fell from 8.6 to 6.5 per 100,000 in rural Louisiana, from 2.4 to 1.7 in New Orleans, and from 3.4 to zero in Edgefield County, South Carolina.[55]

Deadly conflicts between whites and blacks played out on a smaller, more personal scale than they did during Reconstruction. A black sharecropper who attacked a white landowner was still a dead man. In 1885 Jack Hopkins was shot through the window of his jail cell in Monticello, Georgia, before he could stand trial for stabbing his landlord with a knife. But violence between black sharecroppers and white landowners was rare, unless one tried to steal from the other. One morning in 1879 sharecropper Cary Ashley found his corn being harvested and hauled away by his landlord, Benjamin Jones. Ashley asked Jones what he was doing, and Jones replied that he was taking the crop and "would do as he damd pleased" with it. He then pulled out a pistol and said, "You came here for a fuss and I'll fix you." Ashley gave up, but his wife Jane continued to protest. Jones said later that he didn't shoot Jane Ashley, because two other sharecroppers standing nearby "begged so hard" for him "not to do it," but that he had to kill Cary Ashley to demonstrate his right to take what he wanted from his croppers. Nightriding against sharecroppers declined as whites became more confident of their power, but attacks by individual landlords still took the lives of blacks.[56]

Conflicts among whites also played out on a more intimate scale than they did during Reconstruction. The rate at which whites murdered one another did not fall as sharply as the rate at which they murdered blacks, but the conservative whites' return to power seemed to have a soothing effect on relations among all whites. They felt relieved and empowered by the restoration of a prewar-style order. Anxiety and anger over the standing of poor and middle-class whites in southern society and the nation as a whole diminished, and skeptics rallied to the supremacist cause.

Political homicides among whites did not disappear, however. Deference and respect were still important to southern gentlemen, and in public life they were always encountering people who refused to defer to them. W. E. Bland, a physician, challenged one man's right to vote in an 1880 election in Edgefield County. The man had paid road taxes, but election officials had agreed that the man could not vote if he lived outside the town's corporate limits. A. A. Clisby, a merchant, rose to get a copy of the town plat. "We will prove that he does live in the incorporation," he said. "You will prove it like you prove a dam sight of other things," Bland retorted. Clisby then uttered those time-honored words that always set off deadly violence in the South. He asked Bland "if he intended to call him personally a liar." Bland jumped up and shouted that "he meant to call him a liar and he could construe it as he dammed please," and he struck Clisby in the face. Guns were drawn, and Bland was killed.[57]

If a political official deviated from popular policy, white southerners were not always patient enough to wait for the next election to throw the miscreant out. Many of them still mistrusted government and still believed that taking the law into one's own hands in the service of a just cause was an honorable course of action. In Breathitt County, in the mountains of eastern Kentucky, the county court nullified a state railroad construction tax and returned it to citizens as "refunds," which went to support local schools. The decision was popular among the county's voters, especially farmers, who opposed tax-supported railroads; but when newcomer J. W. Burnett won the presidency of the court as a Unionist-Republican in 1878 he tried to reverse the policy, believing that government-subsidized transportation was the key to Appalachia's economic development. He failed, but the effort made him so unpopular that he was shot dead in the street a few days later. The governor had to send in troops to restore order.[58]

Strictly speaking, most of the differences that whites fought over in the late 1870s and 1880s were personal rather than partisan. Whites did kill federal revenue agents, especially during the Hayes administration, when the federal government stepped up efforts to collect excise taxes from distillers. Hayes, a temperance man, wanted to discourage the liquor trade, but he also wanted to establish federal authority in the South without challenging the South's treatment of blacks, and the collection of liquor taxes enabled him to do so. Revenue agents quickly became the most hated figures in the South. But moonshiners more often turned their wrath against the friends and neighbors who had told revenue agents about their stills.

Wyllis Dyar, a paid informant in the remote Gum Log and Red Hollow districts of Franklin County, Georgia, had been working with federal agents for six months when he was shot through the head as he returned home in his oxcart. Moonshiners also attacked neighbors who refused to support them when they were prosecuted. Robert Woody, a former Confederate soldier from Gilmer County who had switched sides during the Civil War and had been mustered out as a lieutenant in the Union army, signed a petition opposing a pardon for Walter

Webb Findley, an unreconstructed Confederate who was in prison for attacking a federal revenue officer. Woody and Findley had been friends, but they fell out when Findley and a band of twenty men burned the revenue officer's barn and storehouse in retaliation for the destruction of fourteen local stills. A few days after his release from prison, Findley confronted Woody at church. They opened fire on each other and accidentally killed a fellow parishioner.[59]

The convict labor system routinely produced homicides among whites in the years that followed Reconstruction. Redeemer governments used convict labor primarily to keep African Americans in their place and to exploit the labor of black vagrants and petty criminals, but poor whites were also forced to serve short sentences, and few of them could abide the indignity. Some were shot dead trying to escape, like J. W. Hammond, who made a run for it as his crew was grading a rail line in Gilmer County. Others, who were put out to work in the community, turned on their employers. Frank Sanders' time had been purchased by the Swillings, who owned a plantation in Franklin County. Sanders killed the Swillings and their three children with an ax, stole their valuables, and burned their house to the ground. Treating white petty criminals like blacks was dangerous, since it undermined efforts to forge a sense of solidarity among whites. The fact that the convict labor system produced so many homicides shows how important racial solidarity and a secure sense of mastery over blacks were to deterring homicide among whites.[60]

Homicide among Blacks in the South, 1872–1887

Southern blacks lost the Reconstruction battle, and, much like former Confederates after their defeat in the Civil War, homicide rates among them rose. For the first time, blacks killed one another in the southern countryside at nearly the same rate as whites. In rural Louisiana, the annual rate at which blacks killed each other rose slightly, from 18 to 20 per 100,000. Edgefield County, South Carolina, saw a similar increase, from 5 to 7 per 100,000. But in New Orleans, blacks began to kill each other at three times the rate whites did. The rate soared, from 11 to 30 per 100,000.[61]

For blacks the post-Reconstruction urban experience in New Orleans was a disaster. Poor policing, unemployment, inferior schools, political powerlessness, and dangerous neighborhoods made their lives hellish. They may have been the first African Americans to experience the full gamut of urban problems, because their political defeat was so sudden and complete. The Redeemers refused to provide public services for blacks and laid off more than half the city's police officers, leaving the residents of poor, mixed-race neighborhoods inundated with trash, deprived of access to schools, and almost completely defenseless against crime. The number of officers per capita fell from 34 to 15 per 10,000—a common trend in southern cities after Reconstruction—and the proportion of blacks on the police force fell from 27 percent to 7 percent. Blanket arrests of striking black workers and of black patrons of saloons and gambling parlors were routine. White officers, nearly all of them Democrats, had no qualms about breaking up peaceful, legal meetings of black Republicans. White officers even killed two black Republican voters at the polls in 1883.[62]

In the 1880s white officers treated blacks brutally, and blacks lost all faith in them. Two white officers shot and killed a black man simply because he refused an order to "move on." When officers ran into a gang of whites who were mugging and stabbing a black man, they arrested the victim. Police Sergeant Thomas Reynolds tried to arrest teamster James Hawkins, a "law abiding, peaceful man" of "Christian character," but Hawkins' neighbors attacked Reynolds with fists and frying pans. Reynolds stopped the crowd by shooting the innocent Hawkins dead. Indifferent or corrupt officers allowed vice and crime to flourish in black neighborhoods, sometimes profiting by it, and black New Orleans descended into lawlessness. Of course, the New Orleans police also did a poor job of protecting whites. As one editor said, "The wonder is that thieves don't pick up the town and carry it off."[63] The city's homicide rate in the 1880s was twice as high as San Francisco's, four times as high as Boston's, and six times as high as New York City's. Only Los Angeles had similar rates—for non-Hispanic whites. In New Orleans, blacks made up the majority of homicide victims.

The situation was nearly as dire for blacks in the countryside at the end of Reconstruction. After the dispiriting defeat of the Republican Party, they were threatened by white vigilantes and burdened with the injustices of the white-dominated legal system. They also had a very hard time making a living, both because of low commodity prices and because of a crop-lien system that overcharged them for seed, tools, and dry goods and underpaid them at the end of the year for their crops. Thousands of blacks left Louisiana and east Texas for Kansas, hoping to establish safe, independent communities on the prairie. Blacks also left other areas of the South in droves. A freedman from Edgefield County, South Carolina, who had been a probate judge said he had had enough of "the miserable county of Edgefield" after the Hamburg Massacre of 1876, in which white vigilantes attacked the county's black militia company. He helped hire a steamship to take freed people to Liberia. Five thousand more blacks left Edgefield and surrounding counties for Arkansas, where public land was available. "We have tried to make money and have not been able to do so. We are poorer now than when we began. . . . We have exercised all the economy we knew how to use and we are going further down hill every day. There is no help for us here."[64]

Under such conditions, it is not surprising that the rate at which blacks killed one another rose at the end of Reconstruction. Black men were already angry about their treatment at the hands of white society, and they could be dangerous when friends or neighbors betrayed them to whites or made disparaging comments about them. Edgefield County saw dozens of assaults and murders that stemmed from such remarks. Tom Dorn asked Bill King why he had told their landlord, Mr. Miner, that Dorn "cursed him behind his back" every time Miner "called him out to work." Dorn certainly had good reason to curse his landlord; Miner still treated his sharecroppers as slaves and expected them to work his home farm without pay. Still, Dorn denied having cursed him, and King denied betraying him to Miner. They fought, and Dorn beat King to death.[65]

Many of these murders took place at social gatherings like dances or suppers, because these occasions offered rivals a chance to face off in front of their peers. At one Sunday gathering in Edgefield County, Andrew Harris shot a friend for "telling tales" about him. Cato Butler had resolved to kill Henry Turner for a similar affront, but he waited several weeks for the right occasion: a party at which everyone in the neighborhood could watch Turner die.[66]

Under the circumstances it seems remarkable that the homicide rate rose so little among rural blacks. The mindset of Aaron Bosket, an Edgefield County freedman who became a sharecropper after the war, sheds some light on how so many blacks managed to cope with having their hopes for a better life dashed repeatedly. A decade after the Civil War, Bosket was still desperately poor. He had tried to make a living in the state capital, but there were no good jobs for blacks there, so he came home and tried farming, with little success. He and his family lived in a one-room shack that was not much better than slave quarters. But Bosket had seen great advances in his forty years, and he believed that one day he would see more. When whites called him "boy" or "uncle," he didn't show his feelings. He reminded himself that despite setbacks, blacks could now vote, hold office, attend school, bear arms, and move about freely. He just tried to "live lowly and humble" and have faith that God would make things better. W. E. B. Du Bois heard that faith in the words of every freedman he met. He noted that whatever happened, good or bad, their reaction was the same: God would "bring all things right in His own good time."[67]

In Jasper County, Georgia, blacks took advantage of their new freedom and formed a branch of the Judson Society, a Baptist missionary and benevolent society that cared for the sick, buried the dead, and financed the education of black children. They established a school, staffed it with black teachers, and taught themselves and their children to read and write. The editor of the county's Democratic newspaper took note of their efforts and advised whites to emulate them. "The colored people are wide awake on the subject of education, and are taking advantage of all the chances, while the white citizens are inactive and careless. Now, we think it is time for our people to wake up on this subject." The same editor also told whites to let go of their animosity toward free blacks. "The decree of Providence has thrown us together, and it is the duty of both races to so act and cooperate as to get along together harmoniously."[68]

In communities across the South blacks were looking beyond politics for a way out of poverty and ignorance and searching for ways to coexist with whites. They formed cooperative schools and Sunday schools in the 1870s and 1880s, determined to progress despite the refusal of Redeemer governments to support black education. "It was a whole race trying to go to school," as Booker T. Washington said.[69] Their efforts may have deterred some violence within the black community, but as conditions worsened it would prove difficult to persuade young blacks in particular—the majority of whom were literate by the end of the century—that patient resolve and trust in God were the solutions to their predicament.

Homicide in the South, 1888–1917

The uneasy political peace that had settled upon the South after Reconstruction came to an end in the late 1880s and early 1890s, when the southern economy faltered and whites fell to bickering among themselves. It was a time of opportunity in politics for blacks and for poor and middle-class whites. They challenged the rule of conservative Democratic elites at mass demonstrations, at the polls, and through new voluntary organizations like the Farmers' Alliance and the Colored Farmers' Alliance. But it was also a time of anger, alienation, and bitterness. Conservative white-supremacist elites lost power briefly in a number of states, but they regained ascendancy in the late 1890s and early 1900s and created a political regime that was more brutal, corrupt, and nakedly antidemocratic than any the nation had seen since slave times. The consequence of political upheaval and the reaction that followed was once again a rash of lynchings, vigilante killings, and everyday murders.

The challenge to white conservatives came in part from the Republican Party, which was an unstable coalition of white Unionists, black civil rights advocates, temperance and educational reformers, and entrepreneurs who believed that the party's policies on banking, transportation, and other economic issues would spur the development of railroads, coal mines, textile mills, and lumber mills across the South. The Republicans were strong in the Upper South and parts of the Lower South. In the presidential election of 1892, they got over 30 percent of the vote in most counties in North Carolina and Tennessee and in nearly every county in Virginia, West Virginia, Kentucky, and Missouri. They were strongest in the mountain counties of eastern Tennessee, eastern Kentucky, southern West Virginia, western North Carolina, and northern Georgia, but they had pockets of strength in predominantly black counties in Louisiana and along the coasts of Texas, South Carolina, and Georgia.[70]

The Populist Party also challenged Redeemer rule. The party grew out of two farm groups, the Farmers' Alliance and the Colored

Farmers' Alliance, that wanted to emancipate farmers from the crop-lien system and help them remain independent. In the 1880s the two alliances represented three million farmers, yet neither the Republicans nor the Democrats would incorporate their proposals into party platforms. Frustrated with their inability to effect change, some members of the alliances founded the Populist Party.

In the South the Populists drew most of their support from farmers, who faced rising costs and falling prices for their crops. Many of them, black and white, had fallen into the ranks of tenants, sharecroppers, and farm laborers, and even those who were still independent were hamstrung by problems that were beyond their control: international competition, volatile markets, and lower prices for cotton and other commodities as efficiency and output increased. The Populists believed they could help by creating agricultural cooperatives to market crops on favorable terms and by forming exchanges to purchase fertilizer and other supplies at lower cost. They also favored establishing government subtreasuries that would extend credit to farmers at lower interest rates, and they wanted to nationalize the railroads and telegraph companies to eliminate price-gouging by rail barons and commodity speculators. The Populists realized, too, that the farmers' lot would never improve unless they were better educated, so they advocated establishing free public schools for blacks and poor whites.[71]

The Populists did well in a few places in the presidential election of 1892—the upper Piedmont and eastern plantation belt in Georgia, southwestern Missouri, central North Carolina, and parts of Florida, Mississippi, and Texas. Their appeal appeared to be increasing, and conservative Democrats considered them a real threat because so many of the South's dispirited farmers were flocking to them. As historian C. Vann Woodward put it, "The annual defeat of the crop market and the tax collector, the weekly defeat of the town market and mounting debt, and the small, gnawing, daily defeats of crumbling barn and fence, encroaching sagebrush and erosion, and one's children growing up in illiteracy—all added up to frustration. The experience bred a spirit of desperation and defiance in these people."[72]

Conservative Democrats faced challenges from within as well. Although white Democrats were not divided by faith or ethnicity as they were in the North and Southwest, they were divided by class and by their views on revenue laws, temperance, economic development, and other political issues. The party had alienated its rural, white-supremacist base by failing to protect moonshiners from the federal government, and it had collaborated with home-grown and foreign capitalists in the same way the Republican Party did, increasing taxes and giving away public land to subsidize railroads and other corporations. And self-employment did not die an easy death among poor and middle-class white supremacists in the South, because wage work and tenancy were associated with being black. Working alongside blacks as sharecroppers, railroad laborers, coal miners, or convict laborers was utterly humiliating for southern whites. They wanted a government that would help them while keeping blacks in their place.

The Democrats had plenty of schemes to help people get rich, but those schemes were expensive, and they brought prosperity only to those few citizens who had the wherewithal to join the scramble to control coal, timber, and farm land. Those who were too poor or who lacked the entrepreneurial drive to participate became sharecroppers or wage laborers. The middle ground was shrinking. By the time the bottom fell out of the cotton market in the late 1880s, the Democrats were in disarray. The post-Reconstruction political settlement had finally failed, and with it went the political stability that had kept homicide rates in check.[73]

This political upheaval was responsible for the rash of lynchings that hit the South in the late nineteenth and early twentieth centuries. Terrorists and vigilantes did not kill as many people as they had during Reconstruction, but in the 1890s and early 1900s lynchings claimed at least 0.24 whites and 2.4 blacks per 100,000 adults per year across the South. Rates for everyday homicides also rose, from 12 to 23 per 100,000 in the mountains of north Georgia, from 16 to 30 per 100,000 in former plantation counties in the Georgia Piedmont, from 27 to 71 per 100,000 in South Carolina, and from 125 to 800 per 100,000 in the upper Cumberland of Kentucky and Tennessee (Figures 4.1, 5.5, and 8.1). These places were more violent than most, but by the late 1920s and early 1930s homicide rates had reached 15 to 25 per 100,000 in most border states and 25 to 40 per 100,000 in the Deep South. Those rates were much higher than they had been before the Civil War or in the late 1870s and early 1880s. Arrest rates for homicide also rose in cities in the South and the border states between the late 1880s and World War I. Homicide rates held steady only in Virginia, where white conservatives did not face a serious challenge from Republicans or Populists or dissident Democrats (Figure 5.6). The South was not as homicidal as it had been during the Civil War or Reconstruction, but in these decades the South surpassed the Southwest as the most homicidal region of the United States.[74]

In northwestern Georgia, the authors of the renewed violence were frustrated Democrats, who turned to vigilantism to express their anger at the federal government's revenue laws and at violations of the color line. Some lived in the mountains; some lived in and around Dalton, a railroad town of 4,000 inhabitants that served as the metropolis of the area. The vigilantes had prominent spokesmen, but the rank-and-file were below average in wealth, and, like many southern farmers, they were trapped by the crop-lien system and low cotton prices, and they could not find a commodity other than liquor that could get them

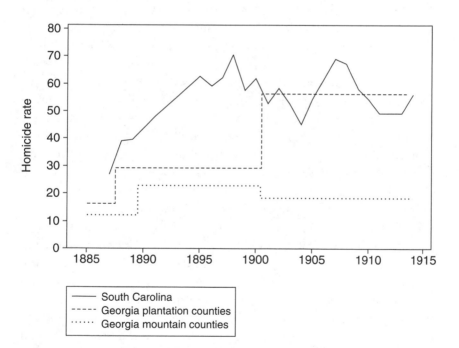

Figure 8.1 South Carolina homicide indictment rate and Georgia homicide rates, 1885–1914 (per 100,000 adults per year). Georgia plantation counties: Franklin, Jasper, and Wilkes; Georgia mountain counties: Gilmer and Rabun. *Source:* South Carolina: Moore (2006: 130–131).

out of debt. They murdered people sporadically in the mid-1880s. In 1885, for example, nightriders gave notice that they would protect the "good people" of Dalton against thieves, prostitutes, and miscegenationists. They burned five suspected brothels in Dalton and killed Tom Tarver, a black man who lived with a white woman. In northern Georgia in 1886 moonshiners killed two federal deputies and four guides who had been helping revenue agents, and in Rabun County in 1888 the Hopkins brothers stoned to death a temperance man as he came out of a service at Mount Carmel Church.[75]

The violence escalated in 1888–89, when the vigilantes decided to put their activities on a more organized footing. In Murray County they began to work through the Distillers Union; in Gilmer County, through the Working Men's Friend and Protective Organization; and in Gordon County, through the Grange. John L. Edmondson, a wealthy landowner who supported the vigilantes, assured the public that they were "all good democrats, every one of them, and they voted all right, too." Nevertheless, these groups felt that the party had not gone far enough to protect white farmers and their families, and they were determined to take control of their communities. They horse-whipped prostitutes and shot three blacks in Dalton who were organizers for the Populist Party. They also used their organizations to settle personal scores. But most of their targets were people who interfered with the moonshine business. Henry Worley had been a moonshiner himself, but when he was indicted for whipping an informant, he cut a deal with federal agents and gave up his friends. Thirty men grabbed him, strung him up in a tree, and told him to leave town. He refused, and they shot him dead in his field two weeks later.[76]

The vigilantes launched at least sixty-six raids in northwestern Georgia between 1889 and 1894, but they could not withstand the combined opposition of the Republican Party, the Populist Party, the Farmers' Alliances, and Democratic merchants and townspeople who felt that lawlessness was bad for business, especially when it came to attracting outside investors. With the help of federal prosecutors, the principal vigilantes were brought to justice and their societies forced underground. However, the killing continued. Moonshiners continued their reign of terror against people who cooperated with law enforcement. Andrew Wilburn of Rabun County fired his Winchester into the home of Joseph Crumpton a few nights after his still was destroyed. The bullet passed through Crumpton's body and killed his daughter Sallie. The Morrow brothers, who had belonged to the White Cap Club in Gordon County, discovered that although vigilantism was enjoyable, it was not very profitable. They graduated from killing informants to robbing trains, stores, and post offices.[77]

Ministers and temperance advocates wrestled with the moonshine culture, with very little success. The Reverend Jim Kimmons went on a crusade against moonshining in the neighborhood around Mount Pisgah Church in Gilmer County, and the moonshiners paid him back by drinking and rioting around his church on Sundays. The hostilities went on for five years, until Carter Lingerfelt, a teenaged moonshiner, returned from a few weeks in jail in Dalton. Kimmons had helped secure his early release, but Lingerfelt was convinced that Kimmons had informed on him. He made a grand entrance into Kimmons' church on Christmas Eve, then waited for him by the door. When Kimmons emerged, flanked by his brother, words were exchanged, and Lingerfelt took a swing at Kimmons. Kimmons and his brother pulled out their guns and opened fire. The wounded Lingerfelt tried to run, but the Kimmons brothers went after him and shot him until they were sure he was dead.[78]

The revenue war took dozens of lives in northern Georgia in the 1890s and early 1900s. It also reinforced hatred of the federal government and bred a backcountry lawlessness that still exists today. People died in feuds and revenge killings, many of which had originated years before in disputes over liquor. Similar conflicts broke out elsewhere in the South, although not all of them involved moonshine. In Cumberland County, Kentucky, near the Kentucky-Tennessee border, battles erupted between Republican farmers and the descendants of Democratic planters. The planters who lived in the fertile bottomlands had supported the Confederacy, but the farmers who lived in the uplands and made up the great majority of the county's population had supported the Union. After the war the county was firmly Republican, but frustrated Democrats fiercely contested every election, and confrontations between Republicans and Democrats were common.[79]

Cumberland County's Democratic minority could never defeat the white Republican majority, but some of them tried to reclaim a piece of the good old days by tormenting the county's blacks. Former slaves had purchased a colony called Coe Ridge, where they got along by logging, farming, moonshining, and performing seasonal labor for whites. They lived without incident until the late 1880s, when young men from Democratic families—the Taylors, Shorts, Capps, Pruitts, Longs, and Vaughns—started to harass them. Most of the whites were related to a noted Confederate guerrilla, and they all lamented the Lost Cause. They had not prospered since the Civil War, and they resented the fact that the Coe Ridge blacks were doing well. They had also heard a rumor that Calvin Coe, a leader of the black community, had courted the wife of a Taylor who had been in prison. Coe denied that accusation, but the Taylors and their friends were determined to run Coe and the other Coe Ridge blacks out of the county and reestablish white supremacy.[80]

The whites began by harassing the Coe Ridge children. They stole chestnuts that the children had gathered. They vandalized the Coe Ridge school and destroyed the children's books and slates. Then they caught some of the children and tortured them, skinning their faces and burning their feet. Finally, in the summer of 1888, Will Taylor, Pat Pruitt, Ike Short, and Charles Short hiked up the ridge to kill Calvin Coe. They shot at Coe and his friends, wounding Oleson Wilburn. The blacks did not have guns, but they charged the whites with knives. Coe stabbed at Taylor and knocked down his gun every time he tried to fire, and when Taylor refused to give up, Coe cut his throat. Coe surrendered to the sheriff, claiming self-defense. He was released because Will Taylor's friends refused to testify: they wanted to kill Coe themselves.

One hundred whites planned to attack Coe Ridge later that month to "finish" the settlement. All but three Coe men and three teenaged boys were away on the Cumberland River rafting logs, but they were warned of the attack by a white neighbor. They immediately bought up all the ammunition at the local store and set up an ambush. When the firing began, all but fifteen of the whites fled. The battle went on for nearly twenty-four hours, until the whites finally rode off, their losses unknown.[81]

Emboldened by this victory, Calvin and Little John Coe began courting two white girls, Molly Ballard and Nan Anderson. The Coe Ridge colony had always been a place where "fallen" white women—unwed mothers, prostitutes, petty criminals—could find a home. But Ballard and Anderson were respectable young women who were simply attracted to the Coes. The couples eloped in July 1889, but they were caught at a station just up the line. Vince Ballard, Molly's father, ambushed Calvin Coe, and Bill Irvin tried to kill Little John Coe, but they shot Oleson Wilburn and Joe Coe by mistake.[82]

Ballard and his friends gave up, but the Taylors tried one more time to kill the Coes. On election day in November 1892 George Taylor walked up to Calvin Coe, put a pistol to his head, and fired. The bullet failed to penetrate his skull, however, and Yaller John and Little John Coe ran after Taylor and shot him down. Yaller John, who had bent the barrel of his gun crushing Taylor's skull, grabbed Little John's gun and said to the whites who had gathered round, "Here's another one just as good. Do you take it up? If you do, step in his shoes. Any man here on the ground wants to take it up, let him step in his shoes." Calvin, who had just regained consciousness, asked, "did you kill the —— man?" "Yes," replied Yaller John, "we landed the son-of-a-bitch in hell."[83]

The Coes were vindicated in the county court. Little John was acquitted, and Yaller John was sentenced to two years in prison, not for murder but for abusing a corpse. Living in a county dominated by white Republicans, they had the sympathy of most whites. In most southern counties, blacks were not so fortunate.

Militant Democrats also went after white Republicans and Populists during these years. Over 700 blacks and whites were lynched in the South between 1889 and 1893, the peak years for such crimes, and the numbers remained high for the next two decades as conservative whites fought for control of the South. Lynching victims were almost always accused of murder, attempted murder, arson, or rape, but the purpose of the lynchings was political. These crimes could have been handled by the criminal justice system, but vigilantes did not want justice to take its course: they wanted to send a message about who was really in charge to blacks and to whites whose actions they disapproved of. They did not lack faith in the government's ability to impose justice; they saw lynching as the only way to forestall change, maintain their position in society, and command respect from blacks.[84]

Anyone who threatened the conservatives' social order was a potential target: black landowners, interracial couples, and Republican and Populist politicians. Lynchings of blacks were most common in counties with the highest proportion of whites working as tenants or farm laborers. They were also common in cotton counties, where landowners were determined to control and exploit black labor. When cotton prices were high, the number of lynchings fell, but when prices were low, and at times of the year when the demand for black labor was high, the number of lynchings rose. Lynchings were rare in counties along the coast of South Carolina and Georgia that were dominated by black Republicans and in mountain counties dominated by white Republicans. They were also less common in counties where the Populist Party flourished. But wherever the Democratic Party was strong, white militants vented their frustrations without fear of retribution.[85]

Much of the fight for control of the former Confederacy in the late 1880s and 1890s was overtly political. Fort Bend County, which like most of east Texas was firmly within the plantation South, saw eight political killings in 1888–1890. The county was divided between the Woodpecker faction, which had the support of blacks, who made up 85 percent of the population, and the Jaybirds, who had the support of most whites. It should have been impossible for whites to take over county government. But young white militants, led by "Red Hot" Frost, the owner of the Brahma Bull and Red Hot Bar, took up arms, paraded through the streets of the county seat, and threatened civil war if the Woodpeckers did not surrender. In the weeks before the election of 1888, a wealthy planter who had pressured blacks to vote for the Jaybirds was killed by a black man whom he had caught stealing cotton. Spurred on by that killing, the Jaybirds ran influential blacks out of the county, including the county clerk, two county commissioners, two schoolteachers, and two successful businessmen. The Woodpeckers tried to make peace by electing an all-white slate of officeholders, but the Jaybirds were not satisfied. The feud blew up again in June 1889, when the county assessor, Kyle Terry, killed a Jaybird, Ned Gibson. The Texas Rangers were sent to keep the peace, but in August a full-scale battle broke out in front of the county courthouse. Red Hot Frost was killed, along with two Woodpecker lawmen and a young black girl who was caught in the crossfire. Kyle Terry won a change of venue to Galveston, but it did him no good. He was murdered in the Galveston courthouse. Woodpecker leaders fled, and the Jaybirds took control. One Texas Ranger summed up whites' satisfaction with the outcome of their campaign: "The negroes thereafter stayed on the plantations, worked and kept out of politics."[86]

Democratic militants terrorized and murdered Populists as well in the last two decades of the century. In the gubernatorial election in Georgia in 1892, Democrats murdered fifteen Populists and threatened others in an effort to keep Populist voters away from the polls. The Democrats won the election only because they controlled local election boards and committed massive voter fraud. In Hall County, in the Texas Panhandle, the Democratic cattlemen were pitted against Populist homesteaders. The governor once again sent the Texas Rangers to stop the killing, but the Rangers simply sided with the cattle barons. In San Saba County, in the hill country, Democratic vigilantes ran blacks and sheepherders out of the county in a running battle that took between twenty and fifty lives before it finally ended in 1896. In Orange County, located in the plantation belt of east Texas, Populists and Republicans together controlled the courts, the sheriff's office, and the county commissions. In 1899–1900 Democrats used every means at their disposal, including arson, lynching, assassination, and armed assaults, to cripple the Populist and Republican leadership, drive blacks out of the county, and restore white rule.[87]

In Grimes County, another plantation county in east Texas, Democrats organized the White Man's Union in 1899 to disfranchise blacks and restore Democratic rule. Waxing poetic, one of its members wrote that

> Twas nature's laws that drew the lines
> Between the Anglo-Saxon and African races,
> And we, the Anglo-Saxons of Grand Old Grimes,
> Must force the African to keep his place.

The White Man's Union took control of the county militia unit and simply assassinated the county's leading black politicians: Jim Kinnard, a Republican who had long served as country clerk; and Jack Haynes, a Populist farmer. After the killings, blacks and white Populists fled the county by the hundreds, leaving the county's Populist sheriff, Garrett Scott, to fend for himself. Scott told a Union leader to "go and get your Union force, every damn one of them, put them behind rock fences and trees and I'll fight the whole damn set of cowards." But

Scott and the remaining Populist leaders could not protect their constituents, and the Union triumphed in the election of 1900, garnering over 1,400 of the county's 1,800 votes (4,500 had voted in the election of 1898, before the terror began). The day after the election, the Union men rode into the county seat and started shooting. The gun battle lasted five days. Finally a light infantry company from Houston rescued the wounded sheriff and his deputies and escorted them out of town. The sheriff's brother and a Populist shopkeeper had been killed, as had the Union leader who had shot them. Similar fighting broke out in dozens of communities across the South where Democratic minorities tried to seize power.[88]

All southern Democrats wanted to avoid federal intervention in elections, and some hoped to lessen the need for fraud and violence at the polls. In pursuit of those goals they introduced new measures to maintain the color line and to suppress voting by political adversaries. Conservatives had passed an array of state laws since Reconstruction, all of which were carefully worded so as not to run afoul of the Fourteenth and Fifteenth Amendments or the Civil Rights Acts of 1866 and 1875. Redeemers in Louisiana, for instance, had simply repealed the 1869 law that banned segregated schools and left it to school boards appointed by their state superintendent of education to establish separate schools for blacks and whites. Virginia's conservatives passed a poll tax that effectively disfranchised the 20–40 percent of voters in predominantly black counties in the Tidewater and the area south of the James River who failed or were unable to pay the tax. By the end of the century, however, militant Democrats grew bolder. Henceforth, in the interest of ensuring peace and racial purity, blacks would be segregated from whites in all public places. To "improve the tone" of politics—that is, to check the power of poor voters—blacks (and in some states poor and illiterate whites) would be permanently disfranchised. Militant Democrats wanted to ensure that blacks and poor whites would never again be able to form a political coalition.[89]

Democrats passed a number of laws between 1889 and 1908 that brought them closer to that goal. Mississippi enacted an election law in 1890 that required voters to live in the state for two years prior to voting (and in the election district for one year), to register four months before an election, to pay a poll tax of $2 for two years before an election, and to "give a reasonable interpretation" of any passage of the state constitution—requirements that made it difficult for the poor and transient to qualify and that allowed registrars to reject any applicant they wished by applying the "understanding clause" arbitrarily. A Louisiana law respected the federal government's right to regulate interstate commerce but required railroad companies to maintain separate passenger cars for blacks and whites on intrastate routes. The Supreme Court allowed such laws to stand, the former because it did not bar citizens from voting on the grounds of race, color, or previous condition of servitude, the latter because it merely provided separate facilities as a matter of public policy and did not stamp blacks "with the badge of inferiority," in the words of Justice Brown in *Plessy* v. *Ferguson* (1896).[90]

Civil rights activists tried to overturn such laws, but Congress had not been able to pass a civil rights bill since 1875, thanks to lukewarm support among some northern and western Republicans and implacable opposition from congressional Democrats, not one of whom had voted for a civil rights law since 1865. When the Democrats won control of Congress in 1892, they repealed the election laws of 1870–1872, making it impossible for federal officials to police elections or suppress political terrorism in the South. With the federal government stymied, southern Democrats were free to forge ahead with their agenda of disfranchisement and segregation.[91]

Republican leaders would not get very high marks for their efforts to protect voters and candidates from violence and to ensure that elections were fair, and Populist leaders contributed to their party's defeat by fusing with the Democratic Party in the presidential election of 1896 and giving up their platform in return for a promise to issue silver coins that could ease the credit crunch. But it is difficult to see how either party could have defended itself and its voters without launching another civil war, or how either party could have defeated the white-supremacist campaign. Too many blacks and whites still feared and distrusted each other, even when they had common interests, and too many whites were determined to kill rather than share power with blacks.

The impact of the Democrats' victory on homicide rates among whites in the South was complex. Militant Democrats certainly concocted the perfect recipe for higher homicide rates. They tolerated lynching and terrorism against white criminals, dissenters, miscegenationists, and moral reprobates. They humiliated poor whites by making it more difficult for them to vote, and they crushed middle-class dissidents by stealing the votes they cast. They opposed policies that could have benefited poor and middle-class farmers and workers, and most of the time they were openly corrupt. Their governments were illegitimate in the eyes of many whites, and they made it impossible for many men to achieve the standing in society they felt they deserved. But militant Democrats accomplished one thing that had the power to deter homicide among whites: they created a caste society in which it was an honor simply to be white, and they invited poor and middle-class whites to help them enforce caste boundaries through racial terrorism. Men did not have to vote to feel the power that came from being white in a caste society, or to feel a kinship with other whites, regardless of class. These factors probably explain why the homicide rate declined modestly among whites in the first two decades of the twentieth century after peaking in the late 1880s and 1890s.

The impact of the militant Democrats' victory on homicide rates among African Americans was anything but modest. The violence, the denial of rights, the loss of life, the destruction of the black community's political leadership, and relegation to the bottom of the social hierarchy as de facto slaves left many blacks, especially young men, feeling angry, powerless, humiliated, and hopeless. They knew full well that southern governments were illegitimate, that they were supported by fraud, murder, and the denial of basic rights. They were also aware that they had been abandoned by the federal government.

Blacks who had grown up in slavery, like Aaron Bosket of Edgefield County, submitted humbly to such oppression, but their sons, to whom slavery was but "a dim recollection of childhood," reacted very differently. Du Bois observed that they either "sank into listless indifference, or shiftlessness," or swaggered with "reckless bravado." Aaron's son Pud was one of the reckless ones. Determined to win respect by being "bad," he cultivated a tough, menacing exterior and demonstrated repeatedly that he was willing to use violence. He and his contemporaries carried pistols and knives to protect themselves against white bullies and predators, but they were more likely to use those weapons on other blacks as they fought for scraps of dignity within their communities. Too many died trying to prove their manhood at each other's expense. A few of them gave vent to their frustrations by going on rampages against whites, which almost invariably ended in their own deaths.[92]

On Coe Ridge, Calvin, Little John, and Yaller John Coe had reason to be proud of their victory over the Taylors on election day in 1892. They had fought bravely, and they believed that they would succeed in the end by being fearless, working hard, educating their children, and trusting in God. Younger men, however, took a different lesson from violence of that day and others like it. Racial oppression and the killing of innocent men like Oleson Wilson and Joe Coe convinced the next generation that they had no hope of changing southern society. The triumph of white supremacists across the South confirmed that conclusion and persuaded many young blacks that trying to live by their fathers' rules—work hard, go to school, trust in God—was pointless.[93]

Once the timber on the Coes' land was cut and the rocky soil on their mountain farms played out, they were forced to rely on gambling, prostitution, and moonshining, and young black men soon learned that the way to succeed in those businesses was to intimidate and prey on others. They didn't wait for trouble—they went looking for it, even within the black community. One Coe Ridge youth, Sherman Wilburn, tried to kill a teacher who had disciplined him, and when his father punished him for the attempt he ran away. He found work as a rafter guiding logs down a river, but the timber entrepreneur who purchased the logs from Wilburn's employer refused to keep him on, in violation of local custom. Two days later the man reconsidered and offered Wilburn the job, but Wilburn was so angry about being dismissed that he shot him. The fellow returned fire and killed Wilburn.[94]

Another Coe Ridge youth, Jesse Coe, got into an argument with a riverboat captain in Celina, Tennessee, in 1896. The captain pulled a pistol and shot him, but Coe wrenched the pistol from the captain and shot him dead. He did his time in prison, and when he came home he was "like a wild Indian," so full of rage that even his friends shied away from him. He left the Ridge for Indianapolis in 1901. There he quickly earned a reputation as a dangerous character. He carried a pistol with him at all times and boasted that he would "burn" any police officer who harassed him. One night two police officers asked him where his friends were, and he shot them both dead. He fled to Coe Ridge and hid in a cave for months, but a neighbor who feared reprisals from whites revealed his hiding place, and local law officers crept up on him and killed him.[95]

Alienated young black men posed a problem everywhere in the South. Law enforcement responded by hounding young blacks, trying to stamp out rebelliousness when the first signs appeared. But police harassment drove some young black men to commit suicidal acts of aggression against whites. Centuries of white violence against blacks had convinced them that every black man was "born under a sentence of death," and they resolved that if they were ever caught in a situation in which they felt they might be killed, they would take as many whites with them as they could. In 1900 Robert Charles, a young Mississippian, was being bullied by a group of New Orleans police officers. He pulled a gun and started shooting. He killed seven whites (four of them police officers) and wounded twenty before he was killed. In revenge, white mobs killed six blacks and wounded seventy. Hundreds of similar incidents occurred across the South. In 1915 J. P. Williams, the police chief in Monticello, Georgia, raided a "blind tiger" (an illegal saloon) in the home of Dan and Matilda Barber. The Barbers and their customers jumped Williams, and they were beating him when Williams pulled a gun and shot Matilda Barber in the face. Dan Barber seized Williams' pistol, but it misfired, and he yelled to his son to bring his shotgun. Williams grabbed his gun again and fired twice, wounding Matilda again. At that point reinforcements arrived to rescue Williams and arrest the Barbers. Matilda survived, but a lynch mob came to the jail that night and hanged her husband, son, and daughters.[96]

Every kind of murder increased within the black community as the frustration of young black men intensified. Killings occurred when men faced off over a debt, a card game, or a point of honor. Abe Banks of Franklin County, Georgia, owed Orange Rucker a quarter, and Rucker owed Banks a dollar. One Saturday night Rucker asked Banks's wife for the quarter, and, not knowing about the dollar owed her husband, she paid him. Banks was furious when he found out about the quarter. He pounded on Rucker's door at midnight, demanding his money, and when Rucker wouldn't open the door he broke it down; Rucker grabbed his gun and shot Banks. Someone threw a bottle during a party in Machen, Georgia, hitting Tink Thompson. Thompson had no idea who had thrown the bottle or if it had been aimed at him, but he was furious at having been treated with dis-respect. His friends told him to put away his pistol, but he worked his way through the crowd, determined to find the man who had hit him. He picked King Johnson, a section hand on the railroad, and shot him in the head.[97]

Young men began carrying handguns everywhere—even to church. On the way home from a Sunday evening service in Jasper County, Georgia, Fred Nolley decided to make the boys walking behind him "hop" by firing his new, nickel-plated pistol at them. Unfortunately, his aim was poor, and he killed one of them. By 1905 this kind of recre-ational shooting had become extremely popular among both blacks and whites in the South. They shot off their guns after church, at re-vival meetings, at picnics, and at neighborhood dances. Unheard of in the rural North, the custom gave young men an opportunity to show off their guns, practice their marksmanship, impress women, and—perhaps most important—make other men lose face when they flinched. The authorities fined dozens of blacks and whites for carry-ing concealed weapons at each term of the county court, but these ef-forts had little effect: too many men felt the need to impress others. When asked about the custom, they claimed that they needed guns to protect themselves. Arms ostensibly carried for self-defense, however, were used most often against friends and acquaintances.[98]

Older members of the black community deplored the recklessness and viciousness of the new generation. To them it seemed that young men had lost their moral bearings, and events all too often seemed to confirm that belief. Katherine Curry, an elderly black woman who ran a kitchen in Lavonia, Georgia, had a reputation for kindness. She was up all hours, fed people whenever they needed a meal, and charged just enough to keep herself and her business going. Moot Teasley, a sixteen-year-old boy who chopped stovewood for her, decided that she must have lots of money, since her business was good, and one day he beat her to death, burned her body, and took all the money she had, which turned out to be $30. No one could explain why he did it—not even Teasley himself. He came from a good home, and Mrs. Curry had always treated him well.[99]

Segregation, disfranchisement, and lynching darkened the lives of young African Americans in ways that their elders could not always un-derstand. Although the reversals of the late nineteenth and early twentieth centuries did not completely destroy a sense of progress among those old enough to remember slavery, they crushed the hopes of blacks born free or freed at an early age. They were outraged at being treated like slaves. They could not abide being forced back down the social ladder and having their destiny controlled by outside forces. The reversals they suffered, like the persecution and discrimination that minorities endured in the urban North and Southwest, fostered resentment and alienation, led them to divert their energies into criminal enterprises, and created a heritage of anger and violence that was passed down through successive generations. The growing homicide problem among black southerners was not caused by slavery or by the failure of Reconstruction to create a racially egalitarian society. It was caused by the hopelessness and rage that the political disaster of the 1890s and early 1900s engendered. Only the frontier, the Revolution, the Mexican War, and the Civil War produced conditions that were more conducive to homicide than those that were created by turn-of-the-century white-supremacist governments.

CHAPTER 9

The Problem Endures

Homicide from World War I to the Present

Unfortunately, the kinds of homicide statistics that are available for colonial times through the nineteenth century are not yet available for the twentieth century. The official data gathered by state and local governments and collated by the Census Bureau, the National Center for Health Statistics, and the Federal Bureau of Investigation should have made it relatively easy to carry the story of homicide in the United States down to the present day. State departments of vital statistics have collected data on homicides since the early twentieth century. However, the data record only the number of victims, not the circumstances of their deaths. The FBI has tried to address that problem since 1976 with its Supplementary Homicide Reports, but some law-enforcement agencies have not reported their data to the FBI, and those that have reported have been reluctant to specify motive and circumstance in cases that have not been closed by arrest or conviction.[1] Thus the data cannot be used to determine rates for specific kinds of homicides, like marital or robbery murders, or rates for specific demographic groups, like Hispanics or the Irish. Nor can they be used to determine homicide rates for minorities below the national level, because before 1968 the state and local data classified African Americans, Asian Americans, and Native Americans jointly as nonwhite. A comprehensive history of homicide since World War I will require the use of multiple sources to reconstruct individual cases, just as the history of the past three centuries has, and may take several more decades.

It is possible, however, to create an overview of the history of homicide over the past century in the United States and in other Western nations. Vital statistics and homicide reports offer reliable counts of the number of homicides from year to year and can be used as proxies for the number of homicides among unrelated adults, since only a minority of homicides involved relatives, lovers, or romantic rivals. Both types of records do specify gender, and the nonwhite homicide rate can be used as a proxy for the African American homicide rate on the state and local levels before the Immigration Act of 1965, since blacks accounted for the overwhelming majority of nonwhites. Details will remain sketchy, but there are enough data to show that homicide rates among unrelated adults in the twentieth century still correlate with the same forces that they correlated with earlier.

The aggregate homicide rate in the United States has been remarkably stable since World War I. There were a few years during the 1950s when the rate was lower, but generally it has oscillated between 6 and 9 per 100,000 persons per year, while rates in most other Western nations have fluctuated wildly. Between 1914 and 1945, homicide rates remained within narrow bounds only in countries that did not experience a civil war, a government collapse, or a brutal occupation—like the United States, Great Britain, Australia, and Canada (Figure I.1). As in the nineteenth century, the highest murder rates correlated with political instability. Ireland had a terrible homicide rate during its civil-war years from 1919 to 1923. Russia saw its homicide rate spike during the Revolution of 1905 and again between 1917 and 1923. Belgium, one of the most pacific nations on earth, suffered a catastrophic breakdown of law and order toward the end of World War II, and its homicide rate spiked to at least 25 per 100,000 persons per year. Many killings were politically motivated, aimed at resisting or supporting the German occupation, but many others were predatory or revenge homicides prompted by the chaos and deprivation of war. France also saw its homicide rate increase in 1944, to at least 18 per 100,000 persons per year—twenty-one times its prewar rate.[2]

Sociologist Roger Gould has observed the same relationship between homicide and political instability in Italy. Italy saw its homicide rate (including attempted homicides) fall to 3 per 100,000 persons per year on the eve of World War I as its central government consolidated power and citizens began to take pride in the nation. In the early 1920s, however, its homicide rate tripled as the prewar political system collapsed and the Fascists seized power. Once Mussolini was firmly in control and his nationalist program gained popularity, Italy's homicide rate fell, despite the hardships of global depression and war, to its lowest level in recorded history—only 1 per 100,000 persons per year. But when the Fascist regime collapsed in 1943–1945, the homicide rate spiked to at least 25 per 100,000.[3]

Statistics are available only for homicide trials in Germany, but its homicide rate appears to have followed the same erratic course as Italy's. The rate of homicide trials declined in the late nineteenth century after the unification of Germany, the end of the cultural clash (*Kulturkampf*) between Catholics and Protestants, and the creation of a popular nationalist government. The rate doubled, however, with the defeat of Germany in World War I, the collapse of the constitutional monarchy, and the imposition of a fragile democratic government. Throughout the Weimar regime Germany was plagued by political and everyday homicides. The government faced substantial challenges to its legitimacy from both the right and the left and was never able to reunify the German people. The rate of homicide trials peaked in 1931–1934, the most politically turbulent years of the regime, but fell by half after 1934, when Hitler consolidated his power. Hitler's regime forged a very strong sense of solidarity among the great majority of the German people, at least in its early years, and gained legitimacy in their eyes by stressing racial unity, obedience to the state, and an end to class warfare. As a result, the homicide trial rate was as low by 1938 as it had been on the eve of World War I. After 1938, however, as its reign of terror escalated and as it tried to cope with breakdowns of law and order both in Germany and in its occupied territories, the Nazi regime ceased to report homicide statistics.[4]

The United States did not experience such wide variations in its homicide rate in the twentieth century, because its governments, state and federal, remained stable. The rate was moderately high from the end of World War I through the early years of the Great Depression, varying between 8 and 9 per 100,000 persons per year and peaking in 1931–1933 at 9.7 per 100,000 (Figure I.1). Homicide rates declined in the West and in New England from 1918 to 1933, but those declines were offset by a 50 percent increase in homicides of southern blacks and a 100 percent increase in homicides of southern whites. The rise in homicide that began in the South in the late 1880s and early 1890s continued as blacks and poor whites were pushed to the bottom of the social order, disfranchised, and ensnared in crippling debt.[5]

The declines in the West and New England were also offset by a 25 percent increase in homicide in the large industrial states of the Northeast and Midwest.[6] The proximate causes of that increase appear to have been immigration, labor agitation, racial conflict, and anger over America's entry into World War I. The ultimate cause was in all likelihood the widening rift among Americans, black and white, immigrant and native, and anger at the government for acting against what citizens believed were their best interests. Conditions were ripe for an increase in homicide. Fellow feeling had decreased markedly among Americans, and workers and immigrants were alienated from the government.

In 1919 whites tried to reclaim jobs and neighborhoods that had been taken by blacks during the war, and race riots erupted in more than twenty northern cities. The Chicago riot, in which twenty-three blacks and fifteen whites died in three days of fighting, was sparked by the stoning death of a black child who had drifted accidentally into a swimming area that whites laid claim to, but in reality it was the culmination of two years of violent clashes between blacks and whites over territory and jobs.[7]

Equally disruptive for northern cities was the rift between native-born whites and immigrants, especially those from southern and eastern Europe. The government's campaign to suppress the labor movement and the Socialist Party stirred up hatred of immigrants, who were seen as the driving force behind unions and left-wing political parties. Animosity toward these immigrants contributed to the passage of the Eighteenth Amendment, which prohibited the manufacturing and sale of alcohol, and prompted the Emergency Immigration Act of 1921 and the Immigration Act of 1924, which set strict limits on immigration from areas other than northwestern Europe. The Ku Klux Klan rededicated itself to "100 percent Americanism" and staged a comeback after World War I as an anti-immigrant, anti-Catholic, and anti-Jewish organization. The founder of the revived Klan, William

Simmons, told his followers that immigrants had turned the United States into "a garbage can! . . . When the hordes of aliens walk to the ballot box and their votes outnumber yours, then that alien horde has got you by the throat." By 1924 the Klan had enrolled somewhere between three million and eight million members, mostly in the industrial Midwest, where hostility to foreign influence in labor, religion, and politics was most intense. Feelings ran so high that when an American sailor repeatedly shot a man who refused to stand for the "Star-Spangled Banner" at a gathering in Chicago, the crowd erupted into applause.[8]

The violence quickly spread beyond cities. There was trouble wherever blacks and immigrant workers tried to organize. In 1919, when black farmers tried to form a tenants' union near Elaine, Arkansas, white vigilantes went on a rampage and killed more than 100 union supporters. On Armistice Day in Centralia, Washington, a lumber town, American Legionnaires shot it out with members of the International Workers of the World. The Legionnaires lost 4 men when they stormed the Wobblies' union hall, but they succeeded in capturing union leader Wesley Everett. They castrated him and hanged him from a railroad trestle over the Chehalis River.[9] As postwar changes in society made it clear to native-born whites that they were in danger of losing control of what they thought of as their society, Americans became increasingly divided along racial, ethnic, and political lines. Those divisions were as deep in some parts of the country as they had been in the mid-nineteenth century.

Alienation from the government worsened in the first years of the Great Depression. The poor and unemployed hated the Hoover administration for its apparent indifference to their suffering. That sentiment was most evident in 1932, when thousands of unemployed veterans decided go to Washington to lobby for the bonuses that Congress had promised them for their service in World War I. They traveled hobo style, some of them with wives and children. Conductors accommodated them by adding empty boxcars to trains; townspeople cheered them on, passed the hat for them, and treated them to free food. When they got to Washington, Hoover refused their request, and when they didn't respond to orders to leave, he called in the army to evict them. Two of the veterans were shot by Washington police on Pennsylvania Avenue. General Douglas MacArthur pursued the rest with tanks, infantry, and tear gas and set fire to their camp. While Americans recoiled in disgust at newsreel footage of soldiers striking veterans—some of them disabled—with bayonets and sabers, Hoover congratulated himself on a job well done. "Thank God we still have a government that knows how to deal with a mob," he said.[10]

The homicide rate rose to 9.7 per 100,000 persons per year in 1931–1933. It began to decline soon after Roosevelt took office and fell to only 6 per 100,000 by the beginning of World War II (Figure I.1). The end of prohibition and the imposition of new immigration quotas probably contributed to the decline by taking the issues that had polarized Americans in the 1920s off the political table, but Roosevelt's efforts to inspire confidence in the country's future and to restore the legitimacy of the government in the eyes of the working class and the poor were more important. It is difficult to overstate the effect that Roosevelt had on the American people. Even those who did not like his policies believed that he might be able to help them. His appeal was immediately apparent: during his first week in office 450,000 letters poured into the White House mailroom. Staffed by one person during the Hoover administration, the mailroom had to hire seventy people to keep up with the flow. Polls showed that two-thirds of Americans who were "lower middle class" and three-quarters who were "poor" approved of Roosevelt's performance and of his economic goals. They wrote more than half the letters that Roosevelt received; they saw him, in contrast to Hoover, as a friend of people who had fallen on hard times.[11]

The homicide rate dropped 0.6 per 100,000 persons per year every year from 1934 to 1937 as the government began to provide the unemployed with jobs and relief, recognized the right of unionized workers to bargain collectively with their employers, issued loans to small businesses, and granted subsidies and incentives to farmers. The administration's policies did not end the Depression, and relief payments were so meager that many families remained hungry and homeless. But the administration itself, and President Roosevelt in particular, won the loyalty of most voters and convinced them that government had a role to play in regulating and subsidizing the capitalist economy. Roosevelt recalibrated Americans' expectations. He declared that they had a "right" to "decent homes to live in," to "productive work," and to "security against the hazards and vicissitudes of life," and he promised that the government would help them secure those rights. A steady decline in homicide rates thus coincided once again with the stabilization of the federal government, the reestablishment of its legitimacy, and the gradual restoration of Americans' faith in the country, their leadership, and one another.[12]

Initially, at least, the administration's appeal was not as strong for Hispanics, Asians, Native Americans, and blacks as it was for whites. Minorities associated the Democratic Party with white supremacy, and they received less than their fair share of federal aid. These factors probably help to explain why between 1933 and 1941 the homicide rate fell by 53 percent among whites but only by 20 percent among African Americans (Figure 9.1). Asian American and Native American rates fell by 33 percent. The decline in the nonwhite homicide rate was particularly meager where minorities faced the greatest hostility: only 13 percent in the South and in California (the areas for which state-level data on nonwhites are currently available back to 1933).[13]

Many blacks were ambivalent about the New Deal. They nicknamed

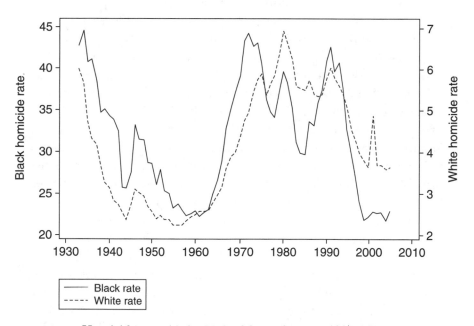

Figure 9.1 Homicide rates in the United States by race, 1937–2005 (per 100,000 persons per year).

the National Recovery Act the "Negro Removal Act," because it encouraged industrial cartels to raise the price of manufactured goods by cutting production and laying off workers. The Agricultural Adjustment Act also raised the ire of African Americans, because it tried to raise commodity prices by paying farmers to cut production and leave land fallow. Landowners in the Cotton Belt pocketed the payments and kicked tenants and sharecroppers off their land. The Social Security Act excluded workers in agriculture and domestic service. Two-thirds of all blacks were left without unemployment, retirement, or disability insurance. And some agencies, like the Works Progress Administration and the Civilian Conservation Corps, refused to give blacks their fair share of jobs, especially skilled jobs. In Chicago, the WPA would not hire black engineers. In Savannah, black painters were shut out. In Salt Lake City, a black writer complained that he and his friends were "hardly able to get a pick and shovel job."[14]

The union movement also benefited African Americans less than it did whites during the Great Depression. The Wagner Act, which Roosevelt supported only reluctantly, gave workers the right to bargain collectively, but it did not prohibit racial discrimination or protect black workers from violence, especially in the South. In Memphis in 1939, when black and white longshoremen struck the city's barge lines, the police (with the support of the barge owners and the mayor) kidnapped and tried to kill the president of the black longshoremen's local, who narrowly escaped being shot to death and had to flee the city. The strike was successful, but the hostility of whites toward blacks made it impossible to unionize the city's other workplaces. At the Memphis Firestone tire plant, white workers joined a whites-only union affiliated with the American Federation of Labor. Their top priorities were maintaining a white monopoly on skilled jobs and keeping lunchrooms, restrooms, and drinking fountains segregated. By refusing to form a united front with black coworkers, they undercut their own bargaining power, and pay for both whites and blacks remained at half what it was in the company's Akron plant. The United Rubber Workers organized Firestone's black workers, but without the support of white workers they had virtually no clout. URW organizers were routinely beaten "and left for dead by the riverfront," and black workers were locked in the most onerous, dirty, and dangerous jobs. Hillie

Pride, a black unionist, said, "You were just like mules and hogs, you weren't hardly counted."[15]

Despite its limitations, the union movement gave blacks a sense of pride and hope, especially in urban areas of the Jim Crow South, where it enabled working-class blacks to assert themselves in ways that had been unimaginable in the 1920s. Most efforts to organize unions in the rural South failed in the face of violence and intimidation, but in cities like Memphis black workers voted in union elections, ran for union offices, and fought openly for their rights. Their successes may have contributed to a localized improvement in the homicide rate: during the 1930s the rate for blacks fell four times faster in Memphis than in the South as a whole.[16]

African Americans made other substantial gains under the New Deal. The Farm Security Administration set up clean, safe labor camps for black farm workers who had nowhere else to live and distributed aid without regard to race to farmers and tenants who desperately needed loans. Congress also funded public housing that was open to all, although it was segregated in southern cities. Vernon Jordan's family moved into Atlanta's first public housing project, dedicated by Roosevelt himself in 1937. Carl Stokes, then a child in Cleveland, remembered how he felt when his family left their run-down duplex where they had "covered the rat holes with the tops of tin cans" and set up housekeeping in a brand new public housing project. "The day we moved in was pure wonder—a sink with hot and cold running water, a place where you could wash clothes with a washing machine, an actual refrigerator. And we learned what it was to live in dependable warmth. For the first time, we had two bedrooms and two beds. My mother for the first time had a room and a bed of her own."[17]

Blacks sent thousands of letters of thanks to the White House. A farmer in Kentucky wrote that his home had been saved from foreclosure. A mother from Memphis declared that she and her children would have "starved this winter if it was not for the Presenent." A woman from Columbus, Ohio, said that she and her family had been "able to live through the depression with food shoes clothing and fuel all through the kindheartness thoughtfulness and sane leadership of Roosevelt."[18]

Still, for African Americans, admiration for the president and his policies did not translate immediately into faith in the Democratic Party or the government. Millions of blacks, having fled the South for the urban North in the Great Migration, found a Democratic Party dominated by Catholic immigrants who felt that their interests were diametrically opposed to those of blacks. In the South, blacks knew the Democratic Party as the power behind Jim Crow. The forces that African Americans encountered in their daily lives militated against putting their trust too easily in a Democrat-controlled government.[19]

Gradually, however, blacks began to feel less alienated from the federal government. By 1940, 42 percent of African Americans identified themselves as Democrats, and that percentage rose quickly as blacks saw their opportunities expand dramatically during World War II. Roosevelt implemented federal job-training programs and opened skilled and white-collar jobs in defense industries to blacks. His 1941 executive order establishing the Fair Employment Practices Committee prohibited discrimination by unions or companies with government contracts. In cities like Memphis, the new edict (together with expanded production in war-related industries) opened thousands of factory jobs to black men and women and led to the successful unionization of a number of local industries, including the Firestone plant, where the United Rubber Workers finally succeeded in bringing whites and blacks together into one union in 1942. Discrimination did not end overnight. It was not until 1956 that skilled positions at the Firestone plant were opened to blacks, and black workers had to sue both the union and the plant to achieve that goal. It would be another fifteen years before separate restrooms and water fountains were eliminated. But because of the union, blacks had better wages, better working conditions, and even better treatment at local stores. As Irene Branch said, "Before we got the union, they'd do you any kind of way. . . . It was better when we got the union, 'cause when they didn't treat you right, you could go to the union. Then we had a right and somebody to protect us."[20]

President Truman continued Roosevelt's policies, opening additional government jobs and services to blacks. He integrated the armed services, the federal bureaucracy, and public housing by executive order. As a result of low unemployment, the shift from agriculture to industry, and union membership, especially in the auto, rubber, and steel industries, black family income increased rapidly, from 41 percent of white family income in 1941 to 57 percent in 1952.[21]

The progress that they made during the final years of the Roosevelt administration and into the Truman administration persuaded a majority of African Americans for the first time since Reconstruction that they could trust the federal government and that it might at long last help them to participate in the American dream. The impact of that belief on the black homicide rate was substantial. The white rate fell 26 percent between the final years of the Great Depression and the early 1960s, from 3.1 per 100,000 persons per year to 2.3, but the nonwhite rate fell 35 percent, from 34.3 to 22.3 (Figure 9.1). The rate fell even faster for Asian Americans, particularly the Chinese and Filipinos, who also benefited from war-related work and the advance of civil rights. They assimilated rapidly into American society once racial barriers began to fall, and their homicide rate fell 72 percent, from 11.1 to 3.1. Only the rate for Native Americans remained where it had been at the end of the Great Depression, at roughly 14 per 100,000 persons per year.[22]

The enduring impact of America's divisive history was still evident in the nation's first comprehensive homicide statistics, which the federal government gathered on the eve of World War II. At that time, Asians, Native Americans, Hispanics, and African Americans together accounted for only 12 percent of the population. The white homicide rate rose sharply as the proportion of minorities in each state's population rose from zero to 10 percent, and more gradually as the rate moved from 10 percent toward 50 percent (Figure 9.2). It did not take a large minority population to send homicide rates soaring among European Americans. Whites had learned violent habits in the fight to control minorities, and they competed intensely with one another wherever caste and class lines were more rigid, as they were (and still are) in much of the South, the Southwest, and the urban North. In Kentucky, Tennessee, and West Virginia the white homicide rate was much higher than each state's racial composition would have predicted, but those were the states that had experienced the most internecine violence during the Civil War. Rates were much lower than expected in Delaware, Maryland, and the District of Columbia, where white power had not yet been challenged despite the presence of large minority populations. A history of political division, instability, and challenges from minorities prompted whites to kill one another. A history of political unity, stability, and dominance over minorities made whites less homicidal.[23]

Similar patterns appeared for nonwhites, although their homicide rate rose more steeply as the minority population moved toward 10 percent, and it stabilized at a very high level (Figure 9.3). The nonwhite homicide rate was higher than expected in Kentucky, Tennessee, and West Virginia, just as it was for whites; but it was also higher in Florida, where blacks were lynched at the highest rate (1.8 per 100,000 adults per year between 1882 and 1930, a rate 50 percent higher than the next highest) and where race riots claimed the most black lives in the 1920s. The homicide rate for blacks, Asians, and Native Americans was lower than expected in New Mexico and Arizona, where Hispanics

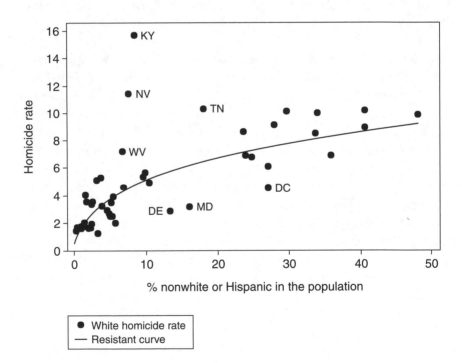

Figure 9.2 White homicide rate in the United States versus percent nonwhite or Hispanic in the population, 1937–1941 (per 100,000 adults per year).

bore the brunt of Anglo hostility. The intensity of persecution, oppression, and vigilantism still determined the rate at which nonwhites were killed by whites and by one another.[24]

The impact of urbanization on whites and nonwhites in the late nineteenth and early twentieth centuries was also evident in the national statistics. On the eve of World War II the white homicide rate was no longer higher in cities than in the countryside, as it had been in the mid-nineteenth century. In the South, the median rate for whites was 9 per 100,000 adults per year in both rural states and the most urban states (Florida, Tennessee, and Kentucky). Outside the South that rate was 3 per 100,000. The urban-rural difference was negligible for whites because both urban and suburban life offered them the benefits of factory work, salaried work, and decent schools.[25]

The nonwhite homicide rate was far higher where a high proportion of the nonwhite population lived in urban areas. In the South the

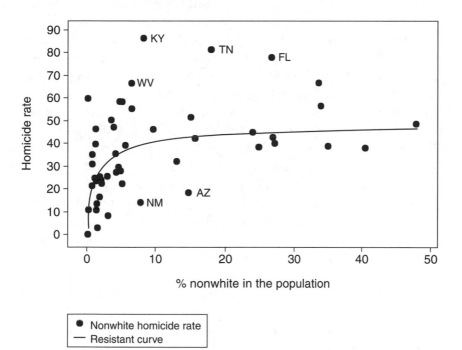

Figure 9.3 Nonwhite homicide rate in the United States versus percent nonwhite in the population, 1937–1941 (per 100,000 adults per year).

median rate for nonwhites was 45 percent higher in urban states than in the most rural states (South Carolina, Arkansas, and Mississippi): 55 per 100,000 adults per year versus 38 per 100,000. Outside the South the median rate for nonwhites was 67 percent higher in urban states: 30 per 100,000 versus 18 per 100,000. Nonwhites were the primary victims of unemployment, vice-ridden neighborhoods, poor schools, and poor policing in the late nineteenth and early twentieth centuries, and in urban areas the very numerousness of people like themselves reinforced their perception of their situation as hopeless.[26]

Despite these differences, homicide rates declined between 1933 and 1941 for nonwhites and whites in every region and in every type of community. The federal government loomed so large in people's lives and in their consciousness during the Great Depression that it created a national polity whose attitudes toward government moved more or less in unison, and those attitudes, as always, correlated perfectly with the homicide rate. The integration of individual voters and local institutions into a broader national community—a phenomenon reflected in the development of national opinion polls and in the expanded role of the federal government—did not eliminate local, regional, or racial differences—far from it; but those differences no longer overshadowed differences over national issues, such as the state of the economy, the size of the federal government, or foreign policy. It was the federal government that people had in mind when they considered whether or not they had faith in government, its officials, and its laws. And to the degree that faith in the federal government increased or decreased across the nation, the homicide rate responded accordingly, as it has from the Great Depression to this day.

The decline in homicide in the United States continued through World War II and the Cold War, when patriotic fervor and hatred of fascism and communism were most intense. In 1957–58, at the height of the Cold War, the homicide rate hit its lowest point in the twentieth century—4.5 per 100,000 persons per year (Figure I.1). The Eisenhower administration helped to foster national unity by governing from the center and by avoiding partisan rhetoric. Although Eisenhower did not intervene in defense of leftists who were being blacklisted, he did repudiate the anticommunist extremists when they turned their attention to the army, an institution that mainstream America cared about. He thereby reinforced Americans' perceptions of themselves as decent and fair-minded. And he embraced what he hoped would be a consensus-building approach to the civil rights movement, which began in earnest with the Supreme Court's ruling against segregated schools in 1954 and the Montgomery, Alabama, bus boycott of 1955. Like most leaders in both political parties, Eisenhower favored a gradual approach to integration. He wanted to give anxious whites, especially in the South, time to accept change, tried to persuade civil rights leaders to move slowly, and supported only legislation, like the Civil Rights Acts of 1957 and 1960, that would not be unduly burdensome for whites. When white supremacists beat and jailed civil rights activists, he was reluctant to intervene, fearing that federal action would only intensify white resistance. But on occasion he did take a firm hand against racist violence, as in 1957, when he took over the Arkansas National Guard and sent the 101st Airborne to Little Rock to protect black students trying to integrate an all-white high school; and he was committed over the long run to creating a color-blind society.[27]

President Kennedy found it more difficult to maintain national unity because of the growing impatience of civil rights activists and the militance of white supremacists. Opponents of the civil rights movement hated Kennedy not so much for what he did as for who he was: a wealthy Roman Catholic from Massachusetts who represented change—the Peace Corps, the race to the moon, the Alliance for Progress. He was an enemy of their faith, their religion, their traditions, their racial privileges, and their way of life. But Kennedy, like Eisenhower, was a centrist on civil rights. He supported gradual progress toward an integrated society, and he temporized on new civil rights legislation. He asked civil rights leaders to be patient, and he, too, was initially reluctant to send federal troops or law-enforcement officers to the South to defend civil rights leaders or to enforce federal laws. His policies disappointed civil rights leaders, but he held the nation together by occupying the middle ground. And when it came to unifying Americans by appealing to their better nature and building consensus on the economy and foreign policy, Kennedy had no peer. He inspired a generation of activists and volunteers when he called upon Americans to ask what they could do for their country, and he won even more hearts and minds by stimulating the economy with tax cuts and by facing down the Soviet Union during the Cuban missile crisis.[28]

The popularity of Eisenhower and Kennedy was not the ultimate cause of the continuing decline in the homicide rate. Homicide rates and presidential approval ratings have correlated weakly since the Gallup poll first sought in 1937 to determine how many Americans approved of the job their president was doing. The homicide rate declined in 1937–38, for example, when Roosevelt's poll numbers were declining, and fell again in the late 1940s and early 1950s, when Truman's ratings bottomed out at 22 percent.[29] The lower homicide rates correlated with factors that were much less volatile than presidential popularity, which could plummet on the basis of a single bill or a bad week on Wall Street. Those factors included patriotism and fellow feeling, which grew out of the successful struggle against fascism in World War II and the ongoing struggle against communism; trust in government, which now provided a safety net for the elderly, the sick, and the unemployed; and satisfaction with the opportunities for prosperity and a respected position in the community, reinforced in this era by

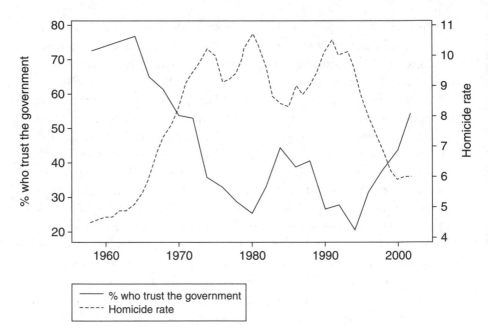

Figure 9.4 Percentage of Americans who "trust the government to do what is right" most of the time versus the homicide rate in the United States, 1958–2002 (per 100,000 persons per year). R-squared = 66 percent. *Sources:* LaFree (1998: 100–104); Sapiro, Rosenstone, and the National Election Studies (2004).

strong labor unions and a booming wartime and postwar economy.
Conservatives' embrace of New Deal programs and liberals' embrace
of anticommunism forged a strong political consensus in the United
States, especially from 1954 to 1962, when divisions over the Korean
War and the persecution of alleged communist sympathizers were be-
ginning to heal, and when continued prosperity seemed assured.[30]

In 1958 the proportion of Americans who reported feeling that they
could trust the federal government was high: 52 percent among African Americans in the South, 66 percent among African Americans in
the North and West, 69 percent among white southerners, and 75 percent among white northerners and westerners. Only 30 percent of
Americans believed that many or most public officials were corrupt
(Figures 9.4 and 9.5). Trust in government held steady among both
whites and blacks outside the South through the early years of the civil

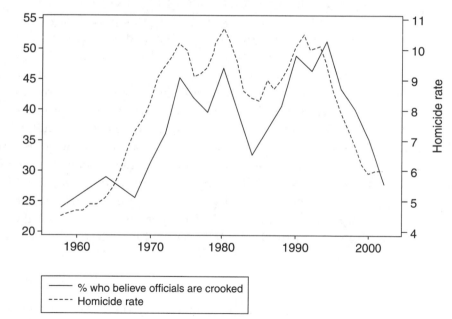

Figure 9.5 Percentage of Americans who believe that "quite a few people
running the government are crooked" versus the homicide rate in the
United States, 1958–2002 (per 100,000 persons per year). R-squared = 63
percent. *Sources:* LaFree (1998: 100–104); Sapiro, Rosenstone, and the
National Election Studies (2004).

rights movement and soared among blacks in the South, from 52 percent in 1958 to 83 percent in 1964. While that trust lasted, it was a powerful deterrent to homicide.[31]

Between 1955 and 1962 the homicide rate for African Americans, which stood at 23 per 100,000 persons per year, was still high by global standards—so high, in fact, that it doubled the nation's homicide rate. But the rate for whites—only 2 per 100,000 persons per year—was low by historic standards; for them, all the correlates of lower homicide rates were in place. The United States was nearly as nonhomicidal for white Americans in the late 1950s and early 1960s as the North and the mountain South had been in the 1820s and 1830s. Whites who remember the postwar years as a tranquil time when people were not afraid to leave their doors unlocked or to stroll down the street at night are right: for whites the United States was, for a brief moment, a nonhomicidal society.[32]

Homicide rates fell much faster, however, in western Europe, where the citizens of war-torn nations like France, Germany, and Italy rallied in support of democratic governments. When their homicide rates reached historic lows in the 1950s and early 1960s, the homicide gap between the United States and other Western nations reappeared. Because of its legacy of political strife and racial oppression from the nineteenth and early twentieth centuries, the United States produced five to six times as many murders per capita as those countries did.

Homicide rates rose in nearly every Western nation at some point after the mid-1960s. The rate doubled in the United States between 1964 and 1975 to 9 per 100,000 persons per year and remained high through the early 1990s (Figure I.1). The rates in most other Western nations seldom rose above 2 per 100,000 persons per year, but they were much higher by the 1990s than they had been in the 1950s, tripling, for instance, in Sweden, Switzerland, Italy, and Canada, quadrupling in Belgium and Denmark, and quintupling or more in Ireland, the Netherlands, Greece, and Spain.[33]

The underlying problems were the same everywhere. The decline in employment in farming, mining, forestry, and manufacturing hit unskilled and semiskilled workers hard, reducing their wages or leaving them underemployed or unemployed. Women entered the workforce in great numbers, shrinking the job pool even further. The "disappearance of work," as William J. Wilson has termed it, had a number of causes, but its consequences for homicide rates were clear. In the last forty years of the twentieth century many young men had a hard time finding steady work, forming independent households, and providing for their families, while those with good jobs in the new economy saw their incomes soar.[34] In Memphis, the gains that workers had made since the beginning of World War II were nullified when Firestone, International Harvester, and other firms closed their factories in the early 1980s and moved production to low-wage countries like Mexico or to more mechanized, less labor-intensive plants. "Every time you looked," said Evelyn Bates, a retired factory worker and union activist, "there was a factory going out of business. . . . This is pitiful how you can go by all of these factories, and the windows are all broke out. The building just sitting there, just going to waste. *No jobs.* Nothing to look forward to." North Memphis, once a prosperous working-class neighborhood, became a blighted area, with abandoned homes or businesses on nearly every block and a growing share of its population on welfare. Similar losses occurred in the rural counties surrounding Memphis, where the furniture industry closed plant after plant. Most of those factories had been unionized and integrated in the late 1960s and early 1970s by labor and civil rights activists, who had braved violence, intimidation, and economic hardship to improve the wages, benefits, and treatment of workers. These job losses, which occurred nationwide, devastated the union movement. Unions had represented a third of all nonagricultural workers between 1945 and 1960, but only 20 percent by 1983 and 13 percent by 2008. The disappearance of unions contributed to the stagnation of working-class wages and the loss of health-care and retirement plans. As a result it became increasingly difficult for poorly educated Americans to move themselves and their children out of poverty.[35]

These deep-seated changes made it hard for many young men in the industrialized world to achieve a satisfactory place in their societies. It is not surprising that those who lived in economically depressed neighborhoods turned to violence. Evelyn Bates, who had lived in North Memphis all her life, described the changes her neighborhood experienced in the 1980s and linked them to the factory closings in the community. "There's no jobs out there for young people today. . . . So now there's crime, that's what it's doing. Youngsters breaking into your house, killing, selling dope. You're afraid to let your windows up or your door stay open." The homicide rate rose in Memphis and other deindustrialized cities and rural communities as young people, deprived of access to socially approved methods of earning the respect of their peers, found ways to make money in criminal enterprises and fought—and sometimes killed—to exact deference from friends and family in the streets or in their homes.[36]

The changes of the second half of the twentieth century, together with the arrival of poor immigrants from nonindustrial or industrializing nations, also led to the segregation of the workforce and of neighborhoods along ethnic lines. Many affluent nations saw homicide and other violent crimes become more common among minorities that have been the targets of prejudice: Afro-Caribbean immigrants in England and Canada, North Africans in France, Finns in Sweden, Koreans in Japan, Aborigines in Australia, and Turks and eastern Europeans in Germany. The marginalization of these people led to resentment and a sense of hopelessness and abandonment. Many of them could not become citizens and did not have equal rights or good economic prospects. The homicide rates that appeared in the United States in the nineteenth century among members of ethnic and racial groups that were driven to the bottom of the social hierarchy became a common problem throughout the industrialized world.[37]

Yet these changes did not lead to high or even moderately high homicide rates in Canada or western Europe. Most of these nations were politically stable, and their native-born inhabitants had strong national feeling. Popular uprisings in the late 1960s by leftists, union members, and college students in France, the Low Countries, and several other European nations coincided with a brief rise in homicide, as did the provincial separatist movements in Canada in the late 1970s. But only Northern Ireland, trapped in an extended civil war, saw its homicide rate spike dramatically, from less than 1 per 100,000 persons per year in the 1960s to 14 per 100,000 in 1974–1977. (It has since fallen to between 4 and 6 per 100,000.) In most nations, the rise in homicide was slow and steady from the mid-1960s on. Immigration and the loss of high-paying jobs made homicide a chronic problem in nearly all Western societies, but in the absence of political crises, homicide rates did not reach catastrophic levels.[38]

In the United States, however, the arrival of millions of immigrants from Asia and Latin America and the disappearance of well-paid work in factories and industries such as mining and logging coincided with a political crisis that shattered faith in the central government and put an end to the rise in fellow feeling that had been building since the New Deal. Divisions over race relations and the Vietnam War polarized the nation and left many Americans angry, bitter, and hostile toward each other. Trust in government and faith in public officials nearly evaporated between 1963 and 1974, and the homicide rate doubled, from 2.6 per 100,000 persons per year to 5.8 for whites (including Hispanics), from 2.2 per 100,000 to 5.2 for Asian Americans, and from 23.1 per 100,000 to 43.1 for African Americans (Figures 9.1, 9.4, and 9.5).[39]

Most Americans associate the homicide boom of the late 1960s and early 1970s with sensational cases like the Manson murders, or with radical activism, or with national tragedies, like the assassinations of Martin Luther King Jr. and Robert Kennedy. But the homicides of that era were not sui generis. They had much in common with the homicides of the mid-nineteenth century and, more broadly, with the homicides that occur whenever a state loses legitimacy, fellow feeling diminishes, and men lose hope of winning respect by legitimate means. There was a rash of political murders, motivated by ideology or by a desire to maintain the status quo. White supremacists like James Earl Ray and Byron De La Beckwith, who murdered civil rights leaders, killed to maintain the upper hand politically and economically; and people who considered themselves idealists, like the Symbionese Liberation Army, killed to further their idea of human progress. There were deadly riots and gang violence. There were predatory murders by robbers, rapists, and serial killers.

However, as in every homicide surge, the bulk of the deaths stemmed from everyday murders by ordinary citizens who killed friends, acquaintances, or strangers over insults or property. Law-enforcement officers were once again caught in the middle. They died by the hundreds and killed an even greater number of civilians, not merely when they tried to stop riots, but when they tried to arrest thieves or pulled people over in traffic stops. The New York City police department killed ninety-three civilians in the line of duty in 1971 alone—a number that the FBI does not include in its standard count of homicides.[40]

The feelings and beliefs behind the soaring homicide rates emerged suddenly and unexpectedly in the mid-1960s. The progress that blacks had made through the union movement, nonviolent protests, and mainstream politics, and the willingness of the majority of white southerners to relinquish legal disfranchisement and segregation peacefully appeared at first to vindicate the political consensus of the 1950s and early 1960s. Most Americans thought that the United States would gradually become an egalitarian society. Similarly, most Americans initially believed that the Vietnam War was yet another instance of the United States trying to support a fragile democracy against communist aggression. In 1965 and 1966 support for the war was nearly unanimous in opinion polls and in Congress. But the political peace was shattered when the war began to go badly and when the civil rights movement foundered on the question of how far, how fast, and at whose cost African Americans would move toward "equality as a fact and equality as a result."[41]

Ironically, for African Americans the success of the civil rights movement and the passage of the Civil Rights Act of 1964 and the Voting Rights Act of 1965 made the inequality that remained all the more intolerable. They were angry about discrimination and police brutality and impatient with poor schools, segregated neighborhoods, high unemployment, and poverty. James Farmer, a founder of the Congress on Racial Equality, was fed up with the pace of progress and disgusted by the subtle racism of white liberals, which he had borne patiently while the struggle for legal equality was under way. "We are sick to death of being analyzed, mesmerized, bought, sold, and slobbered over, while the same evils that are the ingredients of our oppression go unattended." Young men were especially impatient. As Martin Luther King Jr. delivered his "I Have a Dream" speech on the steps of the Lincoln Memorial in 1963, one youth yelled out, "Fuck that dream, Martin! Now, goddamit, now!"[42]

Militance spread rapidly through the black community, and community leaders strove to channel it in productive ways. They preached black pride, power, self-determination, enterprise, and community control. In cities like Boston, African Americans took those words to heart and tried to remake their schools and neighborhoods. Gil Caldwell, pastor of Union United Methodist Church in the South End, despaired at times and confessed to a friend, "God help me, I hate white people so much!" But he and his congregation worked tirelessly with public officials to build a church-sponsored housing project and commercial center in his neighborhood, which Caldwell hoped would serve as a model for redevelopment. Black parents protested against conditions in the Boston schools: demoralized teachers, broken desks and windows, outdated books, basement classrooms that smelled of urine and coal dust, discipline with bamboo whips, racist graffiti on the walls, and segregated seating in the classrooms of some white teachers. They demanded clean facilities, better teachers, more minority faculty, parental oversight boards, and an end to corporal punishment. They organized boycotts and sued for an end to gerrymandered districts that assigned black students to inferior, minority-dominated schools. But self-help and protest did not always bring improvements. The housing project sponsored by the Union United Methodist Church went bankrupt, and under new management it became dangerous, drug-ridden, and dilapidated. Its commercial center failed, except for a small grocery and a music store that became a gang hangout. The parents' movement changed little in the schools because of opposition from the city's school committee, most of whose members were openly racist. Such failures only intensified black anger.[43]

That anger often erupted into violence, some of it political. Young militants found inspiration in the words of Malcolm X: "Be peaceful, be courteous, obey the law, respect everyone; but if someone puts his hand on you, send him to the cemetery." Stokely Carmichael, H. Rap Brown, and other leaders in the Black Power movement declared that they had had enough of nonviolent protest: they would fight back against the violence that blacks had previously endured in silence. Incidents of police brutality sparked deadly riots from the Watts neighborhood in Los Angeles to Detroit and led to shootouts between the police and radical groups like the Black Panthers. For the most part, however, the anger, alienation, and disillusionment of young black men were channeled into violent crimes such as robberies, rapes, and murders. A few incidents were racially motivated. In Boston, for instance, three young blacks confronted René Wagler, a twenty-four-year-old white woman, on the street in Roxbury, a predominantly black neighborhood, and told her, "Honky, get out of this part of town." She ignored them. Later that week they spotted her as she was walking to her car with a can of gasoline. They dragged her into an alley, forced her to pour the gasoline on herself, and set her on fire.[44]

There were very few such killings, however. Most black murderers, robbers, and rapists selected their victims without regard to race. They felt so disconnected, disempowered, and disrespected that they were willing to attack anyone, friend or stranger, who crossed them or presented a target of opportunity. For that reason, most of their victims were black.

Anger also intensified among whites in the mid-1960s and 1970s, especially among opponents of integration. Hatred of the federal government, of blacks, and of their white allies was intense. White supremacists were by no means reconciled to the end of legal segregation in the South or de facto segregation in the North. Their champions, like George Wallace, the governor of Alabama, denounced the "low-down, carpetbaggin', scalawaggin', race-mixin'" liberals who supported the civil rights movement in the South. Elvira "Pixie" Palladino and John "Bigga" Kerrigan, members of Boston's school committee and militant supporters of neighborhood schools, were equally blunt. Palladino said, "I don't believe in integration. God made people of different colors and once we lose our identity, we have nothing." She had no interest in sending her children to school with "jungle bunnies" or "pickaninnies" or, as Kerrigan called them, "savages."[45]

But anger among whites was not confined to white supremacists. A far larger group of whites believed that although the United States should and eventually would be an integrated society, the speed with which black leaders and their white liberal allies were trying to reshape America was injurious to the nation. They had no quarrel with the slogan of the March on Washington—"jobs, jobs, jobs"—but they were not convinced that blacks were willing to work as hard as other Americans, and they bristled at increased spending on welfare, which in their minds transferred their hard-earned wealth to the indolent and irresponsible. A Chicago construction worker from Croatia said he had no quarrel with people who worked as hard as he did, but he was tired of "feeding the Niggers." Many whites who believed in the goals of integration and equal opportunity were also irate about affirmative action, which in their opinion gave less-qualified minorities the jobs of deserving whites. That feeling was especially strong among working-class whites, who lost their preferential access to employment at a time when high-paying jobs with minimal educational requirements were disappearing. And whites who believed in quality schools for all were outraged by court-ordered busing. In their opinion, shuttling students from one ill-equipped, underperforming urban school to another did nothing to improve education; it only undermined neighborhoods and sent children where they were not welcome and would be subjected to violence. By 1971 three out of four white Americans opposed court-ordered busing (as did a narrow majority of African Americans). Alice McGoff, a grassroots leader of Boston's antibusing organization, ROAR (Restore Our Alienated Rights), wondered why politicians and suburban liberals were eager to bus the children of a widowed working mother like herself into dangerous neighborhoods in Roxbury and Dorchester, but were unwilling to send their own children into such neighborhoods or to contribute financially to the education of poor and working-class children.[46]

Conservative politicians drew upon that anger to build a formidable, nonviolent political movement that opposed not only busing, affirmative action, and welfare, but all threats to America's "values." They denounced the kind of behavior that they believed mired people of all races in poverty—drugs, crime, violence, truancy, sexual promiscuity—and emphasized the need for personal responsibility. George Wallace was the most incendiary spokesperson for the movement. He demanded "law and order," harsh punishment of criminals, taxpayer support for private and parochial schools (so that whites could opt out of integrated public schools), and strict eligibility requirements for welfare mothers, who were "breeding children as a cash crop." Together, Wallace and Richard Nixon, who campaigned on the same issues, won two-thirds of the white vote in the presidential election of 1968.[47]

White anger led not only to a revival of political conservatism but also to higher levels of violence. Aggrieved whites poured out their anger against minorities, liberals, the courts, the press, and the federal government. In Boston, antibusing protestors assaulted black students, threw rocks and bottles at the police, bombed the homes of opponents, fired shots into the offices of the *Boston Globe,* beat up a black attorney who happened by during a demonstration at City Hall, terrorized black families who integrated white neighborhoods, and retaliated against black neighborhoods for the murders of whites. Young men in predominantly Irish neighborhoods in Charlestown, South Boston, and the South End were especially violent, angry not only at blacks but at all their perceived enemies, old and new. The graffiti in

Wainwright Park spelled it out: "Gays Suck, Liberals Suck, Brits Suck, Niggers Suck." Alienated from the government, their neighbors, and most of their fellow Americans, all too many turned like their black counterparts to gangs, drugs, crime, and violence, most of which was visited upon other whites.[48]

Indignation about the government's racial policies was not the only emotion that underlay the rise in homicide in the 1960s and 1970s. The Cold War consensus on foreign policy, which had united Americans in support of their government's fight against fascism and communism, collapsed. Although the war in Vietnam was supported by the vast majority of Americans through 1967 (the AFL-CIO, the umbrella organization for most American unions, rejected an antiwar resolution at its 1967 convention by a vote of 2,000 to 6), the young and the poor, who bore the brunt of the fighting, began to reject it, and civil rights leaders, including Martin Luther King Jr., denounced it as immoral, costly, and a diversion from more important national and international concerns. It was least popular among African Americans, who suffered 24 percent of battle deaths in 1965 (a percentage that dropped to 13 percent by 1968 as the army eliminated racial disparities in combat deployments).[49]

As it became apparent in 1967–68 that the war was not going well and that the government had not been honest about its purpose or its progress, a substantial minority of Americans turned against the war, and many of those who supported it lost faith in the way it was being fought, favoring a more aggressive approach that would include an invasion of or a nuclear strike against North Vietnam. Trust in the government and in political leaders eroded, and the war's most ardent opponents and supporters began to demonize one another. Americans on the right mobilized the faithful with slogans such as "My country right or wrong" and "America, love it or leave it"; Americans on the left shouted back, "Babykillers" and "Fascist warmongers." Most people expressed their views through petitions, votes, and nonviolent demonstrations, but some chose violence, turning their wrath against the institutions that supported the war or the protestors who opposed it. In 1968–69 nearly 150 antiwar demonstrations on college campuses ended in rock throwing, window smashing, or clashes with authorities. In 1970 the National Guard and the police shot 26 demonstrators and bystanders at Kent State and Jackson State, and afterward police in

New York City stood idly by as 200 construction workers savagely beat a group of mourners who had gathered to remember the dead and wounded. Both radicals and conservatives incited violence. George Wallace declared that "if any demonstrator ever lays down in front of my car, it'll be the *last* car he'll ever lay down in front of." The violence soon spread to the army, where division, disillusionment, and poor morale led to desertion (7 of every 100 soldiers), racial violence, and the "fragging" of over 1,000 officers. But the greatest contribution the war made to the nation's violence was indirect—the erosion of fellow feeling and unity in the face of external threats that had deterred everyday homicides among unrelated adults during World War II and the Cold War.[50]

The scandals that culminated in the Watergate hearings and the resignation of Richard Nixon were the last straw. Law enforcement was well financed, prisons were full, the poverty rate was declining, and the economy was robust until the oil embargo of 1973, but these and other alleged deterrents to homicide did not matter very much once political anger and alienation rose to heights that had not been seen since the 1920s and early 1930s. Once again, a loss of government legitimacy and growing political divisions in the nation correlated with rising homicide rates.[51]

Presidents Ford and Carter realized that their most important task was to heal the nation, revitalize the political center, and restore trust in government. But there was only so much they could do, despite their personal integrity, to revive confidence. Americans were so suspicious of public officials in the wake of the Watergate scandals, the forced resignation of Vice President Spiro Agnew on corruption charges, and the falsehoods told by the Johnson and Nixon administrations about the Vietnam War that they suspected foul play when President Ford pardoned Richard Nixon and when President Carter's closest confidant, Burt Lance, was charged with influence-peddling. Lance was eventually found innocent, and Ford had not made a corrupt bargain with Nixon in exchange for the vice presidency. But so deep was the public distrust of government that Ford's and Carter's reputations were irrevocably damaged and Lance was forced to resign as director of the Office of Management and Budget.[52]

Yet Ford and Carter contributed to the distrust of government by speaking against government as often as they spoke for it. Echoing the spirit of the times, they declared themselves skeptical of the motives of Washington insiders. To show his opposition to congressional spending habits, Ford vetoed sixty-six bills passed by Congress—a new record. Carter campaigned for the presidency as an outsider and promised to clean up the "mess" in Washington, which he attributed to corruption, influence-peddling, pork-barrel projects, and wasteful spending—the very problems that his friend Burt Lance was appointed to rectify.[53]

Ford and Carter also found it difficult to reunite the American people politically. Whenever they tried to build consensus or tacked to the center on an issue, foreign or domestic, they faced opposition, Ford from the conservative wing of his party, Carter from the liberal wing of his. Whenever they spoke out about busing, affirmative action, welfare, détente, alliances with authoritarian regimes, or human rights, they stirred up a hornets' nest of angry voters. Both faced serious challenges with the economy, which entered a period of "stagflation"— high inflation, high unemployment, and slow economic growth. They were generally right about the causes of the economic malaise—deficit spending to finance the Vietnam War and an eightfold increase in oil prices—and about the painful remedies—higher interest rates, fiscal discipline, and higher energy prices to promote production and conservation. But because of the anger, distrust, and polarization generated in the 1960s and early 1970s, it was difficult to win Americans' support to do anything, and it proved impossible to restore the confidence, unity, and sense of purpose that had prevailed during World War II and the Cold War. President Carter observed in July 1979 that the American psyche had been deeply wounded by the upheaval of the 1960s and 1970s:

> We were sure that ours was a nation of the ballot, not the bullet, until the murders of John Kennedy, Robert Kennedy, and Martin Luther King, Jr. We were taught that our armies were always invincible and our causes always just, only to suffer the agony of Vietnam. We respected the Presidency as a place of honor until the shock of Watergate. We remember when the phrase "sound as a dollar" was an expression of absolute dependability, until the years of inflation began to shrink our dollar and our savings. We believed that our nation's resources were limitless until 1973, when we had to face a growing dependence on

foreign oil. The wounds are still very deep. They have never been healed.[54]

Carter's analysis of what the media called "the national malaise" was astute, but a cure would require more than accurate analysis, intelligent policies, or inspirational leadership. It would require a change of feelings and beliefs among the American people—a difficult feat, given that many political leaders believed they had to increase suspicion of government and risk polarizing the nation in order to capture the presidency and seize control of Congress.

Black and white Americans viewed the Ford and Carter years somewhat differently, and homicide rates responded accordingly. Anger toward the federal government declined slightly among blacks after the war ended; black men did not view the American flight from Vietnam with the shame and outrage that many white males felt. And President Carter, with his appointments of black judges and cabinet members, his urban development program, and his earnest efforts toward inclusion in his personal life, was a source of inspiration for black Americans in the first two years of his administration. The proportion of blacks who trusted the government rose from a low of 18 percent in 1974 to 29 percent in 1978, and the homicide rate for nonwhites fell from its peak of 44 per 100,000 persons per year to 34 per 100,000 (a rate that was still 50 percent higher than it had been in 1963). Like other Americans, however, blacks were dismayed by the problems that afflicted Carter's last years in office—11 percent inflation, rising unemployment, the humiliation in Iran—and disappointed by his failure to commit himself wholeheartedly to a new fair housing bill. Their trust in government declined between 1978 and 1980, and their homicide rate rose again, to 40 per 100,000 persons per year (Figure 9.1).[55]

The defeat in Vietnam and the temporizing of Ford and Carter on welfare, crime, and civil rights were problematic for militant whites. Neither Ford nor Carter, despite their fiscal conservatism, was willing to make deep cuts in welfare benefits, and they refused to ban court-ordered busing, repeal affirmative-action laws, abandon détente with the Soviet Union, or make "law and order" a focal point of their administrations. The proportion of whites who trusted the government fell from 38 percent in 1974 to 25 percent in 1980, and the homicide rate for whites rose from 5.8 per 100,000 persons per year to 7.0 per

100,000—nearly three times what it had been in 1963 (Figure 9.1). As a result, the overall homicide rate in 1980 was the highest recorded since World War I—10.7 per 100,000 persons per year.[56]

The homicide rate improved dramatically during President Reagan's first term. It fell as rapidly each year as it had during the first four years of Roosevelt's presidency, from a high of 10.7 per 100,000 persons per year in 1980 to 8.3 per 100,000 in 1985 (Figure I.1). The rate fell by 20 to 25 percent for people of every race: for whites (including Hispanic Americans), African Americans, Native Americans, and Asian Americans. It did so despite the recession of 1981–82, when unemployment reached 10 percent and Reagan's approval rating dropped below 50 percent. Trust in government increased for the first time since the early 1960s. The increase was not overwhelming. In 1984 only 46 percent of whites and 32 percent of blacks said that they trusted the government to do the right thing most of the time—a far smaller percentage than in the 1950s and early 1960s. And a third believed many public officials were corrupt—50 percent more than when the poll was first taken in 1958. But that was still an improvement over the late 1960s and 1970s (Figures 9.4 and 9.5).[57]

Tax cuts apart, President Reagan's policies were never widely popular among Americans. But before the scandals of his second term, he and his staff had a solid reputation for personal integrity, and his optimism and confidence in a "new morning in America" inspired trust, even among minorities and the poor. Most Americans shared his commitment to traditional values, families, and communities, which were under siege in a "permissive" society. They also shared his faith in free enterprise, innovation, investment, and hard work. He believed that everyone would be able to prosper if they lived responsibly and that government's responsibility was to crack down on criminals and radical agitators, keep taxes and regulations to a minimum, and otherwise stay out of the way. Those beliefs, and their appeal to a broad section of Americans, were the ultimate reason why homicide rates fell during his first term.[58]

But Reagan was at the same time a polarizing figure. He spoke for whites who were angry about defeat in Vietnam and the direction the civil rights movement had taken since the early 1960s. The gap between Democrats and Republicans in his approval rating was in the range of 50 percent—one of the highest ever recorded—because he ran against the New Deal and for the war in Vietnam and wars like it. He shared the outrage of conservatives who felt that they had been betrayed by liberals and antiwar protestors during the Vietnam War. He called the war a "noble cause" and promised that he would never "break faith with those who are risking their lives—on every continent, from Afghanistan to Nicaragua—to defy Soviet-supported aggression." And he campaigned against big government (except in military and foreign affairs), calling government "the problem" rather than the solution. Reagan also opposed affirmative action, court-ordered busing, welfare, and most federal aid to education. He appointed judges and administrators who shared his opposition to "reverse discrimination," and he cut public assistance, food stamps, and other means-tested programs. He decreased federal support for education, expanded the federal prison system, stepped up enforcement of drug laws, and dropped 300,000 people from federal job-training programs. His solution to poverty, crime, urban unrest, and racial inequality was simple—get tough on criminals, increase opportunities for those who wanted to work, and let those who did not want to work suffer the consequences.[59]

Reagan's conservative policies and pronouncements resonated with militant whites through his second term, but they did not have the same appeal for minorities and for moderate and liberal whites. The proportion of Americans who believed that many public officials were corrupt rose to where it had been in the 1970s in the wake of the Iran-Contra scandal, the savings-and-loan scandal, and the Housing and Urban Development scandal, in which low-income-housing funds were used to build golf courses and luxury apartments. And although between 40 and 45 percent of white Americans still reported that they trusted their government, that share fell to between 20 and 25 percent among black Americans and remained low among moderate and liberal whites, who were troubled by an epidemic of homelessness, record budget deficits, and out-of-control covert operations in Iran, Nicaragua, and El Salvador. Whether these feelings were justified is a matter for partisan debate, but they made it impossible for Reagan and his supporters to forge the new political consensus they had hoped for, and that failure had an impact on homicide rates during Reagan's second term. The rate for non-Hispanic whites held steady through 1988–89, but the rates for Asian Americans, Hispanic Americans, and African Africans started to rise again after 1985. By the end of Reagan's second term the homicide rate stood at 9 per 100,000. The crack-cocaine epidemic certainly played a role in the increase, but a larger factor was the renewed erosion of confidence in government among all but the most partisan supporters of the Reagan revolution (Figure I.1).[60]

The homicide rate inched up to 10 per 100,000 persons per year during the administration of George H. W. Bush and the first two years of the Clinton administration as trust in government decreased to 21 percent. Homicide rates rose for people of every race, peaking at 10.5 per 100,000 persons per year in 1991, the second-highest rate in the twentieth century (Figures I.1, 9.4, and 9.5). Why trust fell among both whites and minorities after President Reagan left office is much debated, but there is little doubt that Presidents Bush and Clinton alienated militant whites, in both cases by raising taxes and, in Clinton's case, by pushing a liberal agenda that included universal health insurance and protection for gays in the military. At the same time, both presidents failed to restore the confidence of Americans who had felt left out during Reagan's presidency, especially African Americans. The American people were still too polarized in the early 1990s to build the kind of political consensus that could change their collective feelings toward the government and one another.

But a semblance of that consensus, or at least a wider political center, began to emerge after the Republicans gained control of the House and Senate in 1994. Trust in government increased, and the homicide rate fell from 10 per 100,000 in 1994 to 6 per 100,000 in 2000—as rapidly as it had fallen during Roosevelt's presidency and during Reagan's first term (Figures I.1, 9.4, and 9.5). The homicide rate for non-Hispanic whites fell 29 percent, and those for Hispanic Americans, African Americans, and other minorities fell 40–50 percent. A politically divided government went some way toward satisfying Americans on both the left and the right by balancing the budget, reforming welfare, increasing the minimum wage, doubling funding for child care and Head Start, and putting more police on the streets. A strong economy promised to make capitalism work for everyone. President Clinton's leadership style appealed both to minorities and to a substantial portion of whites, and once the missteps and bold liberal initiatives of his first years in office were behind him, Clinton became a less polarizing figure than President Reagan had been. His approval rating differed between Republicans and Democrats by only 30–35 percent, as opposed to 50 percent for Reagan. That broader appeal helped him to survive impeachment and to pursue bipartisan initiatives through the end of his term.[61] He believed that he had revitalized "the vital American center." But divided government, a popular president, and centrist policies did not restore the level of trust, hope, or fellow feeling that had existed in the 1950s and early 1960s, nor did it solve the challenges posed by the continued loss of skilled and semi-skilled jobs and the influx of undocumented workers, despite massive, bipartisan spending on education and welfare programs.

In the early years of the twenty-first century, trust in government began to decline once again. Scandals, intelligence failures, record budget deficits, protracted wars in Afghanistan and Iraq, and the divisive debate over undocumented workers left many Americans, even conservative Republicans, disillusioned. The gap between rich and poor widened, and, despite a robust economy, high-paying jobs for working people continued to disappear, especially in manufacturing. As the strain on the nation's social hierarchy and frustration with the government intensified, the homicide rate began to rise in 2005, especially among African Americans, most of whom reported feeling abandoned by the government. There was an abrupt decline in the number of African Americans volunteering for service in the army, far steeper than the decline among other Americans. Opinion polls had already revealed growing skepticism about the war in Iraq, but there had to be serious alienation to disrupt the historical relationship between African Americans and the military. It was a sign that homicide rates were about to go up, especially among the poor and among blacks.

The federal government's belated response to Hurricane Katrina only deepened the alienation of African Americans. So did the willingness of some whites to blame poor blacks in New Orleans for the problems they faced. By December 2005 homicide was on the rise. In New Orleans itself the rate soared, reaching 96 per 100,000 persons in 2006.[62] The nation's homicide rate would remain above 6 per 100,000 persons per year through the elections of 2006, when the American people gave the Democrats a majority in Congress and repudiated the

Bush administration's rationale for the war in Iraq. Whether the homicide rate would continue to rise would depend on whether Americans could come up with a set of policies and a style of leadership that could reunify the nation, restore faith in government, and renew hope that the economy could work for everyone.

Conclusion

Can America's Homicide Problem Be Solved?

High homicide rates are not inevitable. In countries where the government is stable and where legal and judicial institutions are capable of redressing wrongs and protecting life and property, homicide rates usually range from 6 to 10 per 100,000 persons per year. In countries where citizens have confidence in government and the social hierarchy and are bound to one another with a feeling of patriotism, empathy, or kinship, homicide rates can fall to 1 to 2 per 100,000 persons per year. If conditions are right, human beings will feel protected, respected, empowered, and connected with their fellow citizens in ways that check the hostile, defensive, and predatory emotions that cause killings.

It is difficult to create those conditions, because they involve feelings and beliefs that throughout history have been shaped more readily by the flow of events than by social or political policies. The history of homicide in the United States confronts us with some of the grimmer realities of human nature. Nothing depresses homicide rates more effectively than a race war (for the winning side, at least). Nothing increases homicide rates more surely, at least in the short term, than an effort by a dedicated minority to create a more just society, as happened during the Revolution and in the struggle against slavery in the mid-nineteenth century.

In the search for policies that could help to address America's homi-

469

cide problem, some unpleasant truths about human nature resurface, and history may look like sociobiology writ large. However, some efforts to decrease specific forms of homicide seem to have borne fruit. For example, although the FBI data are incomplete, there appears to have been a steady decline in spousal homicide in recent decades, from roughly 1.5 per 100,000 adults per year to 0.5 per 100,000. To some extent this trend reflects changes in the way domestic violence is treated. Better police work, automatic arrests of domestic violence suspects, restraining orders, and shelters for victims of marital abuse have helped to deter spousal murders, as have improved therapies for depression. Spousal homicides are not as rare as they were before the 1830s and 1840s, but they are far less common than they were in the late 1960s and early 1970s, even when we take into account the smaller percentage of adults who are married or in common-law relationships.[1]

Reducing the spousal homicide rate further will not be easy. Americans certainly have more realistic expectations of marriage and romance than they did in the nineteenth century, and they are much more willing to move on after relationships fail. The rate at which wives kill husbands has declined faster than the rate at which husbands kill wives, probably because women have been more willing and able to leave violent relationships.[2] But the loss of mutual dependence between wives and husbands appears to be permanent. Will men at risk of committing spousal murders come to accept the independence of their wives and respect their decisions to leave? Will they stop demanding the deference from their wives that they cannot get from society? For many men, the answers to those questions will always be no, and those answers cannot be changed easily by cultural or social engineering.

Difficult as it is to deter intimate violence, it will be much harder to reduce the homicide rate among unrelated adults. That rate is also dependent upon forces that are hard to engineer: political stability, the legitimacy of the government, the degree of unity and fellow feeling in the nation, and men's prospects for achieving a satisfactory place in society. It will be difficult to reverse the problems that have been caused by the decline of manufacturing, logging, and mining and the disappearance of family-owned shops and farms in small-town and rural America. Although a majority of Americans are now able to purchase goods that were once unavailable to the poor and even to the middle class, it is the character of the work that people do, not their possessions, that ultimately shapes their self-image and assigns them their status in society. If the "disappearance of work" cannot be stopped, people will have to find other avenues to status.

Of course, satisfaction can be nurtured in other ways. Certain kinds of patriotism, faith, and pride in a particular social, religious, or cultural group can be enormously satisfying, but they can also be divisive. They often pit Americans against one another by proclaiming, implicitly or explicitly, the superiority of some people to others—a problematic form of building esteem, where homicide is concerned. Hip-hop artists may fire up fans when they attack conservative politicians, and conservative Christians may generate religious fervor in their children when they teach them that the government is evil, but both groups contribute to the homicide problem by encouraging people to hate their fellow Americans and American institutions. Wealth and property ownership can also be sources of satisfaction, but to play a part in reducing homicide rates they have to be available to a significant majority of people, as they were in the North and the mountain South in the early nineteenth century. Since the early 1990s, most Democrats and Republicans have said the right things about building people's faith in capitalism and creating an ownership society. But given the surge in economic inequality since the 1970s and the loss of secure jobs and of health and retirement benefits—often caused by circumstances beyond the government's control—the ownership society may never become a reality for many Americans.[3]

Given that both the proximate and the ultimate causes of killings among unrelated adults involve emotions and beliefs, policy-driven solutions will always be inadequate. It is difficult to see how much more could be done to preserve law and order. The "broken windows" method of policing—citing people for minor crimes to prevent the commission of more serious ones—and greater attention to the upkeep of urban neighborhoods—tearing down abandoned buildings, ordering landlords to repair rental units, and fixing streets and sidewalks—may have helped to restore order in some neighborhoods since the 1980s.[4] Increased spending on police and prisons may have made gang and drug wars less homicidal than they might otherwise have been, and such measures have prevented a return to the extreme homicide rates that prevailed on contested frontiers or in areas that experienced guerrilla warfare during the Revolution, the Mexican War, and the Civil War. But more spending will not lead to a low homicide rate. There is only so much that code enforcement, law enforcement, and incarceration can do, and in some instances citing people for minor crimes may only increase the likelihood that they will commit more serious crimes. Witness, for example, the behavior of Willie Meeks, who conspired to kill Lamont Galloway. Meeks had never committed a major crime, but he was cited repeatedly by the Columbus police for minor infractions in the months before he and Mike Saunders ambushed Galloway. Imprisoning felons for nonviolent offenses can also lead to more serious crimes, because ex-convicts often become hardened to violence, and their records make it hard for them to find work in the legitimate economy. Emergency services will continue to improve, but their ability to save the lives of assault victims has also reached the point of diminishing returns.

Political leadership may be the area in which there is the greatest potential for improvement. Political leaders bear the greatest responsibility for the nation's political life and for the homicide problem it has caused. But given the polarization of politics in the United States today and the divisiveness of the issues that Americans face, it will be difficult for leaders of either party to unify the nation and to rebuild faith in government, especially in the eyes of the poor, who are most at risk of committing murder and of being murdered. The statistics make it clear that in the twentieth century, homicide rates have fallen during the terms of presidents who have inspired the poor or have governed from the center with a popular mandate, and they have risen during the terms of presidents who presided over political and economic crises, abused their power, or engaged in unpopular wars. The most disastrous increase occurred while Richard Nixon was in office. The most substantial decreases occurred under Roosevelt, Eisenhower, and Clinton. But it is not always clear whether the decreases were related to specific policies or whether they were due to the appearance of legitimacy that a particular administration achieved in the eyes of the poor.

One of the problems for politicians is that if they do nothing the homicide rate may still drop, and it may rise even if they make a determined effort to lower it. But if they recognize the role that emotions and beliefs play in homicide, and the importance of legitimate government and national unity, they may be able to act in more constructive ways. The difficulty will be to help the American people find common ground, an objective that might best be accomplished by pursuing widely shared goals by practical means. Welfare reform, one of the great political successes of the 1990s, is a case in point. By setting a time limit on welfare and by trying to facilitate the movement of the poor from welfare to work, Republicans and Democrats made the welfare system more legitimate in the eyes of all Americans, including the poor, even though it will take years to determine whether the reformed system actually helps the poor work their way out of poverty.

Sometimes even the greatest leaders can do very little to deter homicide. Abraham Lincoln spoke eloquently of the need for a government that would live up to the promise of the American Revolution. He tried to build a consensus behind centrist policies on slavery and Reconstruction, and, more important, he called for sympathy and understanding for all Americans, even those who were feared or hated by most members of his own party: immigrants, Catholics, the drinking poor, slaveowners, slaves, Confederates, and freed people. Looking beyond the war, he exhorted all Americans to move forward "with malice toward none, with charity for all" and to try to "do all which may achieve and cherish a just and lasting peace, among ourselves, and with all nations."[5] But the hatreds coursing through the nation were much too strong for him to overcome, and, like so many of his compatriots, he too became a victim of murder.

Neither the drop in homicide during the Great Depression and the Cold War nor the rise in homicide in the 1960s and 1970s makes sense if we try to ascribe them to changes in law enforcement, the recent performance of the economy, or other time-honored explanations. However, when we think about similar events from the past and weigh the emotions and beliefs that we encounter in the media, in opinion polls, and in everyday life, the latest movements in homicide rates do make sense. History cannot predict the future of homicide ten or twenty years from now—there are too many unforeseeable events and trends. And the latest movements in homicide rates must be studied thoroughly before we know exactly how the character and incidence of homicide changed. But knowing the past can help us to understand the present by teaching us what to look for, especially where people's feelings are concerned, and by telling us what happened in similar situations in the past.

It would have been nice to be able to end this book on a hopeful note. But we humans are, as primatologist Frans de Waal observes, a "bipolar" species.[6] Our capacity for cooperation, teamwork, friendship, empathy, kindness, forbearance, forgiveness, compromise, and reconciliation is unparalleled, because our happiness and survival depend on the strength of our social groups and on our commitment to them. But we also have an unparalleled capacity for competition, factionalism, hostility, sadism, cruelty, intransigence, and domination. If we feel that our social groups are threatened, if a power struggle is under way within them, or if we have no social group to protect us, we can be violent—perhaps more ruthlessly and willfully violent than any other species. Which side of our nature prevails depends on historical circumstances. It is a hopeful sign that so many affluent nations have had low homicide rates since World War II, at least until recently, when religious violence and domestic terrorism began to take the lives of so many of their citizens. It is also a good sign that most of the leading candidates in the American elections of 2008 recognized that divisive rhetoric is capable of inciting violence and deliberately stepped back from the worst excesses of partisanship. But as America's experience in the mid-nineteenth century reminds us, events can overtake even the best political leaders, and there is no certainty that any nation, however low its murder rate, will remain nonhomicidal forever.

Sources

The data on homicides are drawn from a variety of sources: newspaper articles, diaries, letters, local histories, coroners' reports, vital records, government documents, court records, and court case files. Some important documents have not survived, but thanks to the overlap of various records, enough information remains in most jurisdictions to offer a fairly complete count of the homicides and suspected homicides that drew public notice. Murders of adults were difficult to conceal, and, once suspected, they attracted the attention of relatives, neighbors, coroners, reporters, and magistrates. Homicides thus left more traces in the historical record than did other violent assaults.

The goal has been to gather evidence on deaths that resulted, intentionally or unintentionally, from assaults. The data thus include homicides resulting from assaults that were legally justified (that is, committed in self-defense or in the execution of official duties) and from assaults that caused death indirectly (for example, by inducing a fatal coronary seizure or chasing an assault victim into water, where he drowns). However, the data do not include all cases in which persons were indicted or convicted of homicide, because the surviving evidence reveals in some cases that the deaths were the result of suicide, accident, or natural causes. Those cases are included in the data files archived in the Historical Violence Database at the Criminal Justice Research Center of Ohio State University (http://cjrc.osu.edu/

researchprojects/hvd/), so that scholars can make their own decisions about how to classify them. Uncertain cases, in which homicide was possible but the cause of death was unclear, are not included in the homicide data, but they too are included in the archived data files.[1] Most uncertain cases concern victims of drowning, who may have suffered severe bodily injuries before or after they drowned, or victims of poisoning, who may have killed themselves. The number of uncertain cases is small compared with the number of probable and certain homicides. Their exclusion does not alter the trends in the data.

New England

The most important sources for studying homicides in New Hampshire and Vermont are court records, case files, and inquests. The records of Hillsboro, Grafton, Merrimack, Rockingham, Strafford, and Sullivan counties in New Hampshire are at the New Hampshire State Archives, Concord; the records of Addison and Orange counties in Vermont are at the Department of Public Records, Middlesex; and some records of Chittenden County, Vermont, are in the Special Collections of the University of Vermont Library. The records of the Council of Safety of Vermont are in Walton (1873). The other surviving records are at their respective county courthouses in New Hampshire and Vermont.

New York courts had jurisdiction in Vermont from 1764 to 1774. The records of Albany County are at the Albany County Hall of Records, Albany, New York; the records of Cumberland County are at the Windham County courthouse, Newfane, Vermont. The records of Gloucester County are published in Vermont Historical Society (1926: 141–192). The records of Charlotte County, which were deposited at the New York State Library, Albany, were misplaced after being used by Goebel and Naughton (1944: 765) and D. Greenberg (1976: 239) and were therefore not available for this study.

Several court records are incomplete. The early records of Bennington County, Vermont, were destroyed by fire in 1850, and the early records of Coös County, New Hampshire, burned in 1885. The early records of Washington County, Vermont, were poorly kept, and the records of Carroll County, New Hampshire, 1840–1861, have been lost. Most of these deficits can be addressed through other sources, such as the annual journals of the General Assembly of Vermont, which in the early nineteenth century reported the charge and the defendant in every felony case that was brought before a grand jury during the preceding year, whether or not the grand jury handed down an indictment. The loss of the Coös County records, however, cannot be made up from other sources until after the Civil War, so the data do not include homicides in Coös County from the county's founding in 1805 through 1865. Gaps of two to eight years during the Revolution appeared in the records of all but one county court. These gaps, too, cannot be made up, because other sources from the revolutionary period neglected all but politically motivated homicides.

Coroners' inquests did not survive systematically in Vermont after 1793 and in New Hampshire after 1824. Complete or near-complete runs survive thereafter for brief periods for Rutland County, Vermont, and Strafford County, New Hampshire. The surviving inquests reveal that they were seldom the sole surviving record of homicides, and that when they were, the homicide was invariably a neonaticide or the murder of an adult by a relative who was mentally ill.

The court records, inquests, and case files of colonial Connecticut and Massachusetts are described in Dayton (1995) and in Hoffer and Hull (1981). Some of the records have been lost for Massachusetts, 1644–1692, but substantial evidence remains from even that period. The data on Connecticut were compiled by Cornelia Hughes Dayton, and the data on Massachusetts by the author and Cornelia Hughes Dayton, with the assistance of Robb Haberman, Brian Carroll, Alexis Antracoli, and Eliza Clark.

Newspapers were the other important source of data on homicides. I have relied on a systematic reading of the surviving issues of the following newspapers:

Boston Gazette, 1719–1797
Boston News-Letter, 1704–1776
Burlington Free Press (Vermont), 1822–1900
Concord Monitor (New Hampshire), 1898–1900
Connecticut Courant (Hartford), 1764–1797
Connecticut Gazette (New Haven), 1755–1790
Connecticut Journal (New Haven), 1767–1797
Farmer's Cabinet (Amherst, New Hampshire), 1803–1820

Farmer's Museum (Walpole, New Hampshire), 1793–1810
New Hampshire Gazette (Portsmouth), 1756–1820
New Hampshire Patriot (Concord), 1818–1897
The Phoenix (Dover, New Hampshire) (various titles), 1793–1829
Rutland Herald (Vermont), 1792–1900
Vermont Gazette (Bennington) (various titles), 1783–1820

Additional newspapers from Vermont and New Hampshire were consulted in the search for more information on specific cases; this undertaking more than doubled the number of newspapers read systematically from the mid-1790s to 1900. Newspapers were the best sources for studying homicide, particularly after 1840, when they replaced courts as the primary recorders of suspicious or violent deaths, in almost every case with the full cooperation of legal authorities, including coroners, prosecutors, and attorneys for the defense. More than half of all households in northern New England subscribed to a weekly newspaper by 1830.[2] Such newspapers employed a large number of informants and correspondents to report on local events and to correct erroneous reports. Some newspaper accounts of homicide proved to be sensationalized or false, but contemporaries recognized with some humor that nearly every one of those reports came from a single source—the *Boston Globe,* whose correspondents were paid by the piece.

Vital records proved to be the most disappointing sources for locating homicides. The fact that every homicide identified in the vital records was already identified in another source made it impossible to generate an independent list of homicides to complement those drawn from court papers and from newspapers. The vital records for New Hampshire, 1850–1900, are at the Bureau of Health Statistics, Department of Health, Concord. The vital records for Vermont, 1857–1900, are at the Department of Public Records, Middlesex.

Virginia and Maryland

The most important sources for studying homicides in Virginia are county court records. County order books or books of wills and deeds recorded the proceedings of each county's monthly courts. The order books and wills and deeds for the following counties are included in the study:

Tidewater and Piedmont Region

Amelia, 1735–1900
Charles City, 1655–1665, 1677–1679, 1688–1695
Lancaster, 1652–1900
Lower Norfolk, 1652–1666
Middlesex, 1679–1725, 1745–1782, 1784–1797, 1799–1800
Richmond, 1700–1753
Spotsylvania, 1724–1765, 1768–1798
Surry, 1662–1718, 1741–1776, 1782, 1786–1900
Sussex, 1754–1800
Westmoreland, 1663–64, 1671–1673, 1677–1688, 1698–1710
York, 1657–1662

Shenandoah Valley

Augusta, 1745–1800
Botetourt, 1770–1800
Rockbridge, 1778–1900
Rockingham, 1778–1784, 1786–1800

On occasion the clerks of Richmond, Surry, and Sussex counties recorded the examinations of felony suspects in special books. These examination books are available in Hoffer and Scott (1984), Surry County (1742–1822), and Haun (1993). Additional order books, case files, judgments, inquests, and court papers are available for Amelia, Lancaster, Rockbridge, and Surry counties, 1780–1900. They are located at the Library of Virginia, Richmond, or at the appropriate county courthouses. The other county order books used in this study are available on microfilm at the Library of Virginia.

Felony examinations for homicide took place whenever a coroner's inquest found probable cause that a person, slave or free, had been murdered and a suspect had been taken into custody.[3] Order and examination books do not include homicides in which suspects fled, committed suicide, or were never identified. The books thus fall short of a complete record of publicly recognized homicides. They do include, however, a number of examinations that did not result in criminal indictments, either because the evidence against the suspect was inadequate, because the homicide was committed in self-defense, or because the court was uncertain whether the death in question was the result of homicide. Order and examination books may thus include some cases that were not homicides.

Order books kept a record of another class of homicides: the killings of outlawed slaves—that is, slaves who were fugitives from justice and who had been found guilty in absentia of committing a felony. Public authorities and private citizens were permitted to take outlawed slaves into custody dead or alive. The owners of outlawed slaves were eligible for compensation if their slaves died trying to elude or resist authorities. Owners of outlawed slaves submitted claims for compensation at annual or semiannual county courts of claims.

Masters had reason to conceal homicide suspects whom they owned, because they usually received only partial compensation for slaves who were executed for felonies. County courts and the Virginia House of Burgesses routinely valued condemned slaves below market value, because they were "troublesome." When, however, a slave murdered a slave owned by another master, or a free person murdered a slave owned by someone else, the victim's owner had reason to prosecute. Owners had to lay the legal groundwork before they could seek financial compensation for the murdered slave from either the murderer or the murderer's owner.[4]

The records of most counties are incomplete, usually because order or examination books have been lost or because courts failed to meet, a particular problem during the Revolution. Some records, however, are incomplete because county clerks failed to record felony examinations alongside other business. The problem was acute in the seventeenth century. Some county clerks saw no need to record proceedings against felony suspects who were slaves, until legislative acts of 1692 and 1705 formalized slave trials. Some clerks failed to copy the case files of freeborn and freed felony suspects and simply forwarded them to Virginia's General Court, whose records were almost entirely lost during the Civil War. Each county's record of felony examinations has been checked against the county's financial accounts (where such accounts are itemized) to determine if an examination was recorded for every examination paid for by the county. Counties are included in the study only during periods when their examinations and accounts matched. Where itemized accounts are not available, order books are considered complete only if they recorded at least one felony examination every five years.

The quality of most county records improved dramatically after the Revolution, when county clerks and magistrates came under the supervision of the new district courts. Amelia and Surry counties have complete series of inquests and case files after the mid-1780s, and Lancaster and Rockbridge counties have complete series of criminal judgments. Newspapers in Rockbridge County and in adjacent counties reported systematically in the late eighteenth and the nineteenth centuries on felonies and inquests. I have relied on a systematic reading of the surviving issues of newspapers published in Fincastle, Lexington, and Staunton, Virginia, 1790–1821 (available at the Library of Virginia in the Valley of Virginia newspaper collection), and of the following newspapers:

Lexington Gazette, 1835–1900
Republican Farmer (Staunton), 1822–23
Rockbridge Intelligencer (Lexington), 1823–1832
Union (Lexington), 1832–1835

Similar newspaper coverage is not available for Amelia, Lancaster, or Surry counties, but as the Shenandoah Valley newspapers demonstrate, Virginia courts held examinations or inquests into nearly every suspicious death (including lynchings) and preserved a record of nearly every homicide proceeding. It is therefore possible to construct comprehensive lists of publicly recognized homicides for the four Virginia counties studied intensively from the mid-1780s to 1900.

It is impossible to create such comprehensive lists for the colonial and revolutionary periods. Early county court records can be supplemented, however, with data from other sources. Most records of Virginia's General Court have been lost, so it is impossible to trace from year to year the number of homicide indictments returned by county courts against free persons.[5] It is possible, however, using early histories (J. Smith 1986; Percy 1922), executive papers (McIlwaine, Hall, and Hillman 1925–1966, 2: 154–155), the surviving issues of the

Virginia Gazette, and the surviving volumes of General Court records (Kingsbury 1906–1935; McIlwaine 1924), to construct a list from 1607 to 1632 of homicides of European colonists by other colonists, and lists from 1670–1675, 1751–52, 1755, and 1766–1777 of criminal indictments for homicides of European colonists by other colonists.

It is possible to construct a similar list of criminal indictments for early Maryland.[6] The records of the Provincial Court of Maryland, 1637–1672, 1683–1687, and 1692–93, are available in Browne et al. (1883–1972: vols. 4, 10, 41, 49, 57, 65). Changes in Maryland's court system and the loss of district court records make it impossible to extend the series into the eighteenth century, but the series can be supplemented with the list of homicides that appeared in the *Maryland Gazette* (Annapolis), 1749–1756, when the newspaper's editors took a keen interest in crimes committed in the colony.

The records on homicide in colonial and revolutionary Virginia were supplemented further. Cappon and Duff (1950) and Headley (1987) indexed Virginia's eighteenth-century newspapers for homicide. McIlwaine, Hall, and Hillman (1925–1966) compiled the proclamations issued by Virginia's colonial governors for the arrest of homicide suspects who remained at large, 1750–1775. And Kennedy and McIlwaine (1905–1915) listed petitions to the Virginia House of Burgesses, 1736–1775, including petitions from slaveowners who sought compensation for the death of runaway slaves who had been outlawed. Some of those slaves had committed murder, and a number had been killed by authorities while resisting arrest or trying to escape.

None of these sources except the early histories of Virginia take careful note of homicides committed by or against Native Americans. It is thus impossible to estimate the homicide rates for Native Americans or the rates at which Native Americans committed homicide.

The data on homicides in Virginia and Maryland were gathered by the author and by James Watkinson, who researched Lancaster, Lower Norfolk, and Rockbridge counties, Virginia.

New Netherlands

The data on New Netherlands, 1638–1656, are from published sources. They include minutes of the colonial council (Scott and Stryker-Rodda 1974; Gehring 1983, 1995), minutes of the courts at Fort Orange and Rensselaerswyck (Van Laer 1922; Gehring 1990), government documents (O'Callaghan 1853–1887), and historical accounts by contemporaries (Jameson 1909).

Georgia and South Carolina

The data on homicides in Franklin, Gilmer, Jasper, Rabun, and Wilkes counties, Georgia, were gathered by the author and by Kenneth Wheeler. The most important sources are county court records, case files, and inquests, which are located at the Georgia Department of History and Archives in Atlanta or at the appropriate county courthouses. Additional Wilkes County records are located in Davidson (1992) and R. S. Davis (1979). The records are complete for each county, but the case files and inquests are not. Those for Jasper are nearly complete, those for Franklin nearly complete before the Civil War, and those for Gilmer, Rabun, and Wilkes mostly lost. The records of slave trials for Elbert County, 1837–1849, and of the Inferior Court of Putnam County, 1813–1843, contain information on felony trials of slaves. The records are available respectively at the Elbert County courthouse, Elberton, and at the Georgia Department of History and Archives.

The court records and the surviving case files and inquests were supplemented by an examination of Tad Evans' superb indexes of the Baldwin County, Georgia, newspapers (Hartz, Hartz, and Evans 1990–1995; T. Evans 1994–1997, 1995–1997). Surviving issues of the following newspapers were also examined:

Augusta Chronicle, 1785–1815
Carnesville Advance, 1899–1900
Friend and Monitor (Washington), 1814–15
Georgia Journal (Milledgeville), 1809–1840
Jasper County and Monticello News, 1882–1884, 1892–1900
Monitor and Impartial Observer (Washington), 1802–1809
Southern Recorder (Milledgeville), 1820–1872
Union Recorder (Milledgeville), 1830–1887
Washington Gazette, 1868–1876
Washington News, 1816–1840

Other sources examined include the Mortality Schedules of the Bureau of Census for 1850, 1860, 1870, and 1880; the proclamations issued by Georgia governors for the apprehension of fugitive homicide suspects (R. S. Davis 1982–1987, 3–14, 135–164, 307–374); reports to Georgia governors during Reconstruction on racial and political violence (R. S. Davis 1982–1987, 1: 227–270 and 2: 137–156); and the records of the Georgia Penitentiary (at the Georgia Department of History and Archives).

Typescripts by Flora B. Searles of the coroners' books of Edgefield County, South Carolina, 1844–1885, and Horry County, South Carolina, 1849–1874, were also studied. The books are incomplete, but they contain transcripts of homicide inquest testimony. The typescripts are located at the South Caroliniana Library at the University of South Carolina.

Ohio and Illinois

For Ohio, the data on homicides in Ross and Holmes counties, 1798–1900, were gathered by Kenneth Wheeler, with assistance from the author for 1881–1900. The sources are described in Wheeler (1997). Ross Bagby collected census and genealogical information on the victims and suspects and examined Ross County newspapers, 1881–1900. The data on Cuyahoga County, 1840–1876, are from homicide cases reported in the abstracts of newspaper articles in Cleveland Works Progress Administration Project (1936–1939) and from the Coroner Files at the Cuyahoga County Archives, Cleveland. The Cuyahoga County data were compiled by students in History 598 at Ohio State University for a class project.

For Illinois, the data on homicides in Calhoun, Henderson, and Williamson counties were gathered by Carpenter (1981), Allaman (1989), and Erwin (1914). Carpenter listed murder and manslaughter indictments in Calhoun County. Allaman and Erwin drew on court records, newspapers, and local tradition for their respective lists of homicides in Henderson and Williamson counties. Chicago data, 1879–1920, are from the Chicago Historical Homicide Project (http://homicide.northwestern.edu), directed by Leigh Beinen, which includes information on homicides recorded in the logs of Chicago homicide detectives (Bienen 2004). They are supplemented by reports of homicides in the *Chicago Tribune,* 1879–1885, compiled by the author and by students in History 375 at Ohio State University for a research assignment.

Philadelphia, New York City, Florida, and the Trans-Mississippi West

The data on indictments for homicide in Philadelphia, 1839–1901, were gathered by Roger Lane. The sources are described in Lane (1979). The data on homicides in New York City, 1797–1900, were gathered by Eric Monkkonen. The New York City data, which are described in Monkkonen (2001), are from coroners' inquests, indictments, newspapers, and annual reports of the New York City Department of Health. The data on homicides in Los Angeles, 1830–1900, were also gathered by Monkkonen. The sources are described in Monkkonen (2005). The data on homicides in Florida, 1821–1861, were collected by James M. Denham. The sources are listed in Denham (1997). The data on indictments and coroners' inquests from Douglas County, Nebraska, Gila County, Arizona, and Las Animas County, Colorado, 1880–1900, are from McKanna (1997). The data on homicides in San Francisco, 1846–1900, are from Mullen (1989 and 2005); and the data from seven additional counties in California, 1850–1899, are from McKanna (2002). All of these data sets are available from the Historical Violence Database at the Criminal Justice Research Center of Ohio State University.

Methods

Homicide Estimates

The surviving evidence on homicides in New England, New Nether-lands, Ohio, Georgia, Florida, and Rockbridge County, Virginia, is sufficient to estimate the number of probable murders that came to the attention of authorities or the public. Two lists of homicides were created, one drawn from legal records (inquests, case files, docket books, minute books, and prison records) and the other from nonlegal sources (newspapers, diaries, oral tradition recorded in early town histories, etc.). The lists were matched to determine the number of homicides that appeared on both lists (C), on the list from legal records only (N_L), and on the list from nonlegal records only (N_{N-L}). Following the method of Chandra Sekar and Deming (1949), as adapted by Eckberg (2001), the proportion of homicides missed by both lists (X) can be estimated thus:

$$X = (N_L * N_{N-L}) / C$$

The result can be used to estimate the number of publicly recognized homicides (N) that occurred: the sum of the number found only in legal records (N_L), the number found only in nonlegal records (N_{N-L}), the number found in both kinds of records (C), and the number missed by both lists (X):

$$N = N_L + N_{N-L} + C + X$$

The standard error of the estimate (which measures, in practical terms, the reliability of the estimate) is equal to the square root of

$$(N * q_L * q_{N-L}) / (p_L * p_{N-L})$$

where q and p are the proportions used to calculate the standard error:

$$p_L = C / (C + N_{N-L})$$

$$p_{N-L} = C / (C + N_L)$$

$$p_L + q_L = p_{N-L} + q_{N-L} = 1$$

The matching-list method has been used successfully to estimate death rates for young children in Egypt (Becker et al. 1996), HIV infection rates among drug addicts in Thailand (Mastro et al. 1994), and other vital or epidemiological rates in societies that lack effective means of registration or reporting (e.g., Crimmins 1980; Hook and Regal 1995).

The method is robust. It does not require that the evidence from which the lists are drawn be comprehensive or complete, so long as the loss of records and the omissions of recordkeepers are random. The method requires, however, that the matched lists be statistically independent, an assumption that does not hold for homicides as a whole. The requirement for independence can be largely met by disaggregating the homicides on the lists into homogeneous groups based on geography, period, etc., and by estimating the number of homicides separately for each group. What interdependence between the lists remains after disaggregation will probably bias the estimates downward in the range of 10–15 percent, but that bias should be consistent over time and is far too small to account for the historical trends that appear in the homicide rates.

Estimates of the proportions of publicly recognized homicides that appear in the surviving records for each jurisdiction are in American Homicide Supplemental Volume (AHSV 2009: Homicide Estimates). The estimates vary, depending on the degree of record loss, the effectiveness of the criminal justice system, the availability of local news in periodicals, diaries, or town histories, and the race of the victim. For instance, the surviving records from New Hampshire and Vermont contain evidence on an estimated 98 percent of homicides, 1794–

1880, but on only 72 percent of homicides during the revolutionary period, 1775–1793, when courts were disrupted and newspapers lost touch with local correspondents. The estimates for European Americans in colonial and revolutionary New England range from a low of 55 percent, 1650–1669 (the years for which the minutes of the Massachusetts Court of Assistants are missing), to a high of 95 percent, 1784–1797. The estimates for Native Americans and African American, 1670–1797, are generally lower, because their murders were less likely to be recorded.

Homicide Counts

The homicide totals for New York City, Philadelphia, Illinois, Maryland, South Carolina, the trans-Mississippi West, and most of Virginia are not estimates. They are counts drawn from single lists of homicide examinations, indictments, inquests, or reports, or from multiple lists that are unsuitable for matching-list analysis because they are not statistically independent. For instance, the accounts of homicides in the *Chicago Tribune* are not independent of the homicide reports compiled by the Chicago Police Department, because the reporters for the *Tribune* spoke directly with homicide detectives and knew about every homicide reported by the police. Similarly, where both indictments and inquests are available, they cannot be used to estimate the number of homicides that legal authorities failed to record. They can be used together only to count the number of homicides investigated by the authorities.

The indictment totals here for Philadelphia differ from those in Lane (1979). They enumerate the victims of persons indicted for homicide, rather than the persons indicted for homicide. The homicide totals here for the trans-Mississippi West also differ from those in McKanna (1997 and 2002). They enumerate the victims noted in indictments or inquests, rather than the persons indicted.

The data from other quantitative studies of homicide are not yet available, so their homicide counts must be used as published. Nearly all these studies rely on a single source, so they undercount the actual number of homicides; and few distinguish between homicides of children and adults or among various kinds of adult homicide, so homicides cannot be sorted by type. Such partial, aggregate counts are used here as proxies for the number of homicides among unrelated adults, because the overwhelming majority of homicides usually involve unrelated adults and because there is little chance that the resulting counts will be greater than the actual number of homicides among unrelated adults. Homicide counts based on inquests or newspapers are usually more complete than counts based on indictments, which understate the number of homicides by a third or more where estimates are possible. That is why it is important to distinguish indictment series from other homicide series. As a general rule, increasing a homicide indictment count by 50 percent will approximate more closely the number of homicides among unrelated adults.

Population Estimates and Counts

To calculate homicide rates, it is necessary to determine not only the number of homicides but also the number of persons at risk. In jurisdictions where it is possible to use the matching-list technique to estimate the number of homicides that came to the attention of the public, it is necessary to estimate the population as well, rather than accept undercounts from official sources. In these instances, the population figures from the federal censuses, 1790–1900, were supplemented by data from the Integrated Public Use Microdata Series (IPUMS, Minnesota Population Center, University of Minnesota). The data, 1850–1900, were corrected for underenumeration using the method outlined in AHSV (2009: Population Estimates). The underenumeration figures for whites are from Hacker (1999) and for blacks from Coale and Rives (1973). Record-linkage studies were used to estimate variations in undercounting by race, nativity, and region (Adams and Kasakoff 1991; Davenport 1985; Ginsburg 1988; Knights 1991; Pleck 1979: 215). Techniques for estimating the ethnic composition of European American populations are discussed in AHSV (2009: Ethnicity Estimates).

It is important to note, however, that the same historic trends would appear if the homicide rates were based on raw population figures from the Bureau of the Census. Historical rises and declines in homicide rates are too large to attribute to enumeration errors.

The raw U.S. Census figures, 1790–1900, are used for the populations of the other jurisdictions included in the study. Because the homicide totals for those jurisdictions are based on counts from primary sources rather than on matching-list estimates, they understate the number of homicides. The decision was made to understate the populations as well, to avoid understating the homicide rates.

Population figures for the years before 1790 were gathered from a variety of sources.

New Hampshire and Vermont

Population totals for New Hampshire and Vermont before 1790 are from Holbrook (1981: 10; 1982: xii). Totals for the black population before 1790 are from Bureau of the Census (1975, 2: Series Z 1–19). The age and gender distribution of the population before 1790 is determined by extrapolation and interpolation using the 1800 census for the white population and the 1820 census for the black population, together with the Vermont census of 1771 (Holbrook 1982: xviii) and the New Hampshire censuses of 1767 and 1773 (Bureau of the Census 1909: 149–154).

New England

The estimates of the white population of colonial New England, 1630–1780, are modified from Bureau of the Census (1909: 9), following Thomas and Anderson (1973), which finds that growth rates did not vary as widely from decade to decade as assumed in Bureau of the Census (1975, 2: Series Z 1–8). The estimates were further modified from 1700 to 1780, so that New England's white population would by 1790 and 1800 match the totals for the federal censuses of those years, corrected for underenumeration. The age and gender distribution of the population is interpolated between the distributions for 1690 (Thomas and Anderson 1973: 654) and 1800 (the federal census corrected for underenumeration). The interpolated age and gender distributions match those in the colonial censuses of the 1760s and 1770s (corrected for underenumeration) to within .1 percent. The age distribution between 1630 and 1690 is interpolated between the distributions for 1620–1649 (R. Archer 1990: 480) and 1690 (Thomas and Anderson 1973: 654). The gender distribution of the population cannot be calculated precisely before 1690, however, because the male/female ratios in R. Archer (1990: 480) are 1.5 or higher at all ages.

The estimates of the black and Native American populations of colonial New England are also imprecise. The estimates for the black population are from Bureau of the Census (1975, 2: Series Z 1–8), multiplied by 1.213 to correct for underenumeration (based on the level of underenumeration of nonwhites in the 1820 census, the first to report age-specific populations for nonwhites). The estimates for the Native American population are from Snow (1980: 31–42), Snow and Lanphear (1988), Cronon (1983), Ghere (1997: 257), and the colonial censuses of the 1750s, 1760s, and 1770s (Bureau of the Census 1909: 150–183). The colonial censuses for the Native American population were also multiplied by 1.213, and their population loss during King Philip's War, 1675–76, was estimated at 25 percent. The data are too sparse to attempt reliable estimates of the age and gender distributions of the black and Native American populations.

Virginia and Maryland

Estimates of the white and black populations of Virginia and Maryland in the colonial and revolutionary period are from McCusker and Menard (1985: 136), supplemented by Menard (1980: 116–123, 157–166; 1981), Kulikoff (1977: 415–428), Earle (1979), and Bureau of Census (1975, 2: Series Z 13–14). The estimates understate the total populations of Maryland and Virginia by probably 5–10 percent by the end of the eighteenth century, because they rely on raw U.S. Census figures for 1790 and 1800. Judicial examination rates for homicide in Maryland and Virginia are thus probably overstated by 5–10 percent in the 1750s, 1760s, and 1770s. The overstatement is negligible, however, relative to the magnitude of interregional differences and changes over time in examination rates.

Estimates of the changing age and gender distributions of the white and black populations in Virginia and Maryland in the colonial and revolutionary period are from Menard (1975; 1980: 121) and P. D. Morgan (1998: 82–83). The estimates are supplemented by estimates of the age and gender distributions of the white population in 1800 and of the black population in 1820, which are based on U.S. Census figures adjusted for underenumeration.

See AHSV (2009: Population Estimates) for the methods used to estimate the white and black populations of specific counties in Virginia during the colonial and revolutionary periods.

The raw data from other quantitative studies of homicide are not available. In these cases, the population estimates are used as is or are taken from other scholars' improved population estimates. Where possible, homicide rates per 100,000 persons per year are recalculated as homicide rates per 100,000 persons aged sixteen and older per year. In most populations from the sixteenth through the nineteenth centuries, the proportion of adults in the population ranged from 63 percent to 70 percent. Only frontiers showed significantly higher proportions of adults. So, as a general rule, the adult population was historically about 65 percent of the total population. Homicide rates per capita can be translated roughly into adult homicide rates by dividing by .65, and adult homicide rates can be roughly translated into per capita rates by multiplying by .65.

Notes

Preface

1. Roth (2007).
2. Lieberson (1985: 14–43, 120–151).
3. Lieberson (1985: 200–217) defends this approach to nonexperimental empirical research.

Introduction

1. The account here is based on my personal observation of the trial, but see also the *Columbus Dispatch*, 27 November 1995: 5C; the obituary for Lamont Galloway, 29 November 1995: 6B; and the indictments from the case: 2001 CR A 016760 City of Columbus v. Michael A. Saunders, and 2001 CR A 021503 City of Columbus v. Willie Meeks, Franklin County Clerk of Courts, Columbus, Ohio.
2. Hackney (1969: 908).
3. Rosenberg and Mercy (1986).
4. Bureau of the Census (1937–1993) for 1965–1992 and Federal Bureau of Investigation (1998–). The homicide rate per 100,000 persons per year was 5.5 for whites and 31.8 for nonwhites. It was 4.0 for females and 14.5 for males.
5. From 1965 to 1992 the homicide rate per 100,000 persons per year was 9.1 for all persons, 2.7 for white females, 8.4 for white males, 11.7 for nonwhite females, and 54.2 for nonwhite males. Life expectancies in

2005 are from the Centers for Disease Control: 77.6 years for all persons, 80.5 for white females, 75.4 for white males, 76.1 for nonwhite females, and 69.2 for nonwhite males. See National Center for Health Statistics (2005). The formula for converting homicide rates into "risks" is: risk = 100,000 / (homicide rate × years of exposure).

6. Data on homicide rates during the second half of the twentieth century are available in Archer and Gartner (1984), Gartner (1990), World Health Organization (1950–), and United Nations Office on Drugs and Crime (1970–). LaFree (1999b: 126–135) discusses the quality of the available data. The estimates here of the homicide rates in the United States and other nations in the late 1990s are from World Health Organization (2002). Nations with extreme homicide rates raised the average world homicide rate dramatically, to 8.8 per 100,000 persons per year, so the rate in the United States (6.9 per 100,000 persons per year) fell below the average world rate. However, the rate in the United States was well above the median rate for the world's nations.

7. Exemplary works include Messner and Rosenfeld (1994), Zimring and Hawkins (1997), LaFree (1998, 1999a), and Blumstein and Wallman (2000).

8. On the conceal-carry hypothesis, see Lott (2000). On the abortion hypothesis, see Donohue and Levitt (2001). See A. R. Harris et al. (2002) for an attempt to measure the impact of medical improvements on homicide rates. The magnitude of the impact remains a matter of debate, but not the decline in death rates.

9. See LaFree (1998: 81–83, 120–123) and J. Q. Wilson (1975: 3) on the weak relationship between the violent crime rate and the level of unemployment or average income. On violence during the crack epidemic, see Blumstein and Wallman (2000: 164–206). On the relationship between substance abuse and violence, see S. Walker (1994), M. Marshall (1979), Fagan (1990), R. N. Parker (1998), and Pernanen (1991). On the history of alcohol consumption, see Rorabaugh (1979) and Roberts (1995).

10. On the percentage of homicides cleared by arrest in recent years, see Bureau of Justice Statistics (2002–2006), table 4.19. The proportion of known homicides that ended in conviction or a verdict of not guilty by reason of insanity ranged from 40 percent in New Hampshire and Vermont, 1775–1900, to 27 percent in the counties studied in Georgia, 1790–1900. See AHSV (2009: Criminal Justice).

Levitt (1996) estimates that a 10 percent increase in a state's prison population correlates with decreases of 2.5 percent in rape, 3 percent in auto theft and larceny, 4 percent in burglary and assault, and 7 percent in robbery. But it correlates with only a 1.5 percent decrease in murder. Clearly, the correlation between homicide and incarceration is weak. See Blumstein and Wallman (2000: 97–129, 207–265) and LaFree (1998: 10, 85–86, 154–155, 164–171) on the limited ability of prisons and the police to deter homicide and other violent crimes. From 1948 to 1992 per-capita spending on police increased sevenfold and on corrections twelvefold. On the failure of potential violent offenders to respond rationally to deterrents and incentives, see LaFree (1998: 58–61).

11. On the limited ability of such measures to deter homicide, see LaFree (1998: 152–172; 1999a). On employment in law enforcement and incarceration rates, see Federal Bureau of Investigation (1998–) 2003: 364–365; and Schlosser (1998: 51–52).

12. On the ethnic hypothesis, see Mullen (2005) and McWhiney (1988). Immigration has itself been cited as a cause of higher homicide rates because of its power to overwhelm local institutions (especially law enforcement and social services), depress wages, and strain relations between natives and immigrants. The same has been said of other kinds of mass migration, including the demobilization of armies and the movement of workers from the countryside to cities. But higher homicide rates are not a necessary consequence of mass movements of people. Migration can have a divisive impact on communities if newcomers are perceived as a threat and if that hatred is politicized, as happened when Irish Catholics moved to England and the United States during the potato famine. Migration can also have a divisive impact if former soldiers are alienated from the national government and from their fellow citizens, as was true of many former Confederates in the American South after the Civil War and of many veterans of England's continental wars in the late sixteenth and early seventeenth centuries. But most mass migrations associated with immigration, urbanization, or demobilization have had little or no impact on homicide rates, because they were not associated with breakdowns in law and order, destabilizations of governments, erosions of fellow feeling, or disruptions of status hierarchies. Migration contributes to higher homicide rates in some historical circumstances but not in others, and periods of low migration can be homicidal.

13. For an introduction to frontier violence, see Hollon (1974).

14. Studies that address the relationship between gender and violence include Rotundo (1993), Pleck (1987), Bynum (1992), and Peterson del Mar (2002).

15. Elias (1982), Gurr (1981), Stone (1983), Spierenburg (1994, 1996,

1998), Österberg (1996), Karonen (2001), Ylikangas (2001), and Eisner (2001). Americans have contributed to this theory with discussions of the civilizing influence of schools, factories, and police forces (Lane 1979; Monkkonen 2001).

16. On the impact of improved trauma care, see Eckberg (2007). See Roth (2001) and AHSV (2009: Civilization Thesis) for a critique of the quantitative argument of the civilization theorists.

17. Wyatt-Brown (1982), Ayers (1984), K. S. Greenberg (1985, 1996), and Denham (1997). On honor in Europe, see Pitt-Rivers (1966), M. E. James (1986), Neuschel (1989), and Spierenburg (1994).

18. Ayers (1984), Butterfield (1995), Lane (1997), and Clarke (1998).

19. In England, for example, women were the primary assailants in 4.6 percent of the homicides that occurred among unrelated adults outside the household in rural Essex and Surrey Counties, 1559–1625, and 4.9 percent in urban Middlesex County, 1549–1632 (Cockburn 1975–1982; Jeaffreson 1886–1892; AHSV 2009: European Homicides, table 1). In the United States, 1976–2003, women were the primary assailants in 6.4 percent of the homicides that occurred among unrelated adults, including homicides that occurred among unrelated adults within households (Fox 2005; AHSV 2009: Gender and Homicide). Future research may reveal historical circumstances in which women were the primary assailants in a substantial proportion of homicides among unrelated adults outside the household, and it is possible too that the proportion will increase if societies achieve genuine gender equality. It is possible, however, that the propensity to violence against unrelated acquaintances and strangers will prove to be gendered to a degree that violence against children, relatives, spouses, romantic partners, and unrelated members of households is not.

20. On the relationship between perceptions of political legitimacy and violent crime, see LaFree (1998: 75–81, 91–113) and Tyler (1990). On definitions and measures of political trust, see Hetherington (2005: 8–35).

21. H. Brown (2006: 3–13) articulates and defends this theory persuasively in his analysis of homicide and political violence during the French Revolution. See also Gould (2003: 147–166).

22. For an introduction to the years of turmoil, 1348–1415, see M. Jones (2000: 17–41, 82–154).

23. For an excellent discussion of the relationship between "the degree of popular consensus about a nation's identity, core values, and mission" and the ability of citizens to engage in "peaceful bargaining and compromise" in national and international politics, see Citrin et al. (1994:

2–5). That ability to compromise, I believe, translates to the local level as well, and affects everyday relationships among friends, acquaintances, and strangers.

24. For instance, the homicide rate was low in the caste-stratified rural Sinhalese areas of Sri Lanka from the end of the nineteenth century into the 1970s, except in the 1940s, during the political crisis that led to independence (A. L. Wood 1961; Rogers 1987).

1. "Cuttinge One Anothers Throates"

1. AHSV (2009: American Homicides [AH], tables 1–4) and Lachance (1984: 25–41, 71–87). On warfare in colonial America, see A. Taylor (2001: 23–274) and Richter (2001: 1–150).

2. No one has made precise estimates of homicide rates in England, but indictment rates were highest in suburban neighborhoods on the outskirts of London and in Cheshire, a pastoral county in northwestern England: 15 to 20 per 100,000 adults per year. Rates were also high in the predominantly agricultural counties in southern and eastern England from which most New England settlers came. The actual adult homicide rate in those counties was probably in the same range as New England's estimated rate for European colonists in the mid-seventeenth century: 8 to 10 per 100,000 adults per year. Actual homicide rates were probably half again to twice as high as indictment rates (Roth 2001: 33–35, 44–45, 52–57).

3. Le Roy Ladurie (1971: 23–79, 129–226, 288–308), Walter and Schofield (1989: 21–25), Lawson (1986: 107–109), and Bowden (1976: 621).

4. Bourne (1990: 24), Roth (2001: 49, 46), Beier (1974), Emmison (1976), Slack (1974), Walter (1989), Wrightson (1996: 18–22), Wrightson and Levine (1979), Fogel (1992; 2000: 144–145, 153–156, 158–159), and Jeaffreson (1886–1892, 1: 94–96, 101–103, 109, 221).

5. According to inquests and indictments, fewer than 5 percent of homicides among unrelated men were formal duels. Most duels were spontaneous, the result of quarrels or sudden attacks, so the best proxy for counting them is the use of swords or rapiers. Fourteen percent of nonhousehold, nonfamily homicides among men were committed with swords or rapiers in rural Essex County, 1559–1625 (17 of 119); 35 percent in suburban Surrey County, 1559–1625 (51 of 147); and 53 percent in suburban Middlesex County, 1549–1632 (94 of 178). Four percent of all nonhousehold, nonfamily homicides with male assailants in rural Essex County were connected to robberies or burglaries (5 of

139), and 7 percent in suburban Sussex County (10 of 151). Probably 30 percent of female homicide victims of nonhousehold, nonfamily homicides in Essex County (6 of 20) and 45 percent in suburban Surrey and Middlesex Counties (9 of 20) were victims of sexual assaults. (Cockburn 1975–1982; Jeaffreson 1886–1892).

6. Cockburn (1975–1982), Essex Indictments, James I, cases 634 and 740; and G. Walker (2003: 121–122). Such murders were most common in rural counties, like Essex. Inquests and indictments do not mention motive or circumstance in 75 percent of the 119 nondomestic homicides perpetrated by men in Essex, 1559–1625, but at least 13 percent (16) stemmed from quarrels at work or social gatherings; 4 percent (5) from trespassing, poaching, or property disputes; and 3 percent (4) from resisting arrest for debt or riot.

7. Cockburn (1975–1982), Sussex Indictments, Elizabeth I, cases 1399, 1593, and 1822; and Kent Indictments, Elizabeth I, cases 2987 and 2988. In Essex and Surrey Counties, 1559–1625, women were the principal assailants in 5 percent of the nonfamily, nonhousehold homicides that led to inquests or indictments (14 of 304), but they made up 8 percent of the accomplices who were indicted (6 of 80) (Cockburn 1975–1982). On nonlethal assaults, see Gowing (1996: 59–138), Fletcher (1985), Sharpe (1980), Ingram (1985, 1987), Foyster (1999), and Emmison (1976: 233–237).

8. Jeaffreson (1886–1892, 1: 78, 73–74) and G. Walker (2003: 125). In Essex and Surrey, gentlemen were the assailants in 23 percent of the 69 nonfamily, nonhousehold homicides that involved swords or rapiers, and yeomen were the assailants in 50 percent. Gentlemen used swords or rapiers 60 percent of the time, yeomen 50 percent of the time, and tradesmen, clerks, husbandmen, and laborers only 12 percent of the time. The latter preferred knives and blunt weapons. Daggers were the only weapons that were as likely to be used by the wealthy as by the poor—11 percent of the time (Cockburn 1975–1982). On dueling, see Kiernan (1988), Anglo (1990), Billaçois (1990), Spierenburg (1994), and J. Kelly (1995).

9. Jeaffreson (1886–1892, 1: xliii), Barber (1957), and C. B. Watson (1960). In Essex, 1559–1625, 38 of 119 nonhousehold, nonfamily homicides among men were committed with daggers, rapiers, swords, or pikes (32 percent); 99 of 147 in Surrey, 1559–1625 (67 percent); and 114 of 178 (64 percent) in Middlesex, 1549–1632 (Cockburn 1975–1982; Jeaffreson 1886–1892). On carrying arms, see Cockburn (1991: 83–84) and Emmison (1976: 132–137).

10. The point is made by Spierenburg (1998: 119–124) in his discussion of

pietists in Amsterdam. The same practices were in force among Puritans in England (Spufford 1974: 223–352; Hill 1964).

11. Helgerson (1992), McEachern (1996), Claydon and McBride (1998: 3–29), T. H. Breen (1980: 3–24), Collinson (1988), and Cressy (1989: 152–153, 162, 181).

12. Tallett (1992: 103–104, 138–146) and M. S. Anderson (1998: 24).

13. Lawson (1986: 114–117), Hay (1982: 117–160), Childs (1997), McLynn (1989: 320–340), Cockburn (1977: 61), and Tallett (1992: 88, 90–104, 138–147). Cockburn (1991: 85–86) cautions against exaggerating the impact of demobilized soldiers on the homicide rate.

14. Carlton (1998), Underdown (1985), and Everitt (1966).

15. Everitt (1966: 127–128, 185–187, 190, 244, 244n2, 276–277), Carlton (1998), Morrill (1994; 1999: 104–122, 127–166), and Underdown (1985: 146–270). On poor relief, see Slack (1988: 38–40, 48–55).

16. Faller (1987: ix–x, 6–20) and *Complete Newgate Calendar* (1926).

17. AHSV (2009: European Homicides [EH], fig. 1). Cities in Sweden and Finland also experienced a surge in homicide in the late sixteenth and early seventeenth centuries and were more homicidal than England (AHSV 2009: EH, fig. 2).

18. Dupâquier (1988, 2: 60, 179–219), Moote (1971), Ranum (1993), Muchembled (1989: 9–15, 105–118), G. Parker (1977: 169–178), and Greenshields (1994: 45–62, 123–171). The annual reports of the Maréchaussée show a homicide rate double that of England's in the late sixteenth and early seventeenth centuries, as do the proceedings of the Grands Jours, an extraordinary royal court commissioned in 1665 to suppress feuding, tax evasion, and corruption in the church and local government. The records of the mounted police and of the Grands Jours contain evidence of only a small fraction of the homicides that occurred in Haute Auvergne. The mounted police alone handled 3 or 4 homicides per 100,000 persons per year, 1587–1664. For the thirty-seven years for which records are available, there were 185 homicides reported, a rate of 3.35 cases per 100,000 persons per year. The Grands Jours heard 1,350 cases from September 1665 to January 1666 in the provinces of the Massif Central. The cause was recorded for 282 cases; 107 were for murder. The Grands Jours heard cases that had occurred since 1655 (the last time it heard cases in Haute Auvergne), for a rate of 5.72 cases per 100,000 persons per year (Greenshields 1994: 68, 224n76; Lebigre 1976: 139; Cameron 1981: 193–207). In Artois the number of pardons granted to convicted killers shows a homicide rate at least twice as high as England's; 97 percent of the pardons granted were for homicides (Muchembled 1989: 19–23).

In Geneva, an independent city-state on France's eastern border, the homicide rate was as high as in England's most homicidal counties: at least 14 per 100,000 persons per year (Watt 2001: 53–62).

19. That figure includes villagers who died in murders committed to avenge the killing of a friend or relative and villagers who jumped into a fight to protect a friend. Fifty-five percent of homicides occurred in taverns and another 17 percent in streets and alleys, where men most often socialized. Festival days were also deadly (Muchembled 1989: 29–39, 43–45, 70–118). On everyday violence see Muchembled (1989: 23–105, 143–168), Greenshields (1994: 70–90, 100–120), and Castan (1974).

20. Greenshields (1994: 70–90, 92n90, 93, 105–113, 158–171).

21. Van der Wee (1978), de Vries (1974, 1978), and Egmond (1993). Only 34 trial transcripts survive for Amsterdam, 1651–1700. Seventy-one percent of the assailants were not born in Amsterdam, and 53 percent had been arrested before on a criminal charge. Inquests show that 499 of 623 male homicide victims (80 percent) for whom the weapon was known were stabbed to death, 1667–1729 (Spierenburg 1994: 707–710). On knife fighting, see Spierenburg (1998: 103–119). In Leiden the rate at which suspects were tried for homicide reached 13 per 100,000 persons per year, 1590–1620; it was 7 per 100,000 in 1620–1650 (Diederiks 1980, 1989, 1990).

22. Spierenburg (1996; 1998: 119–124), Diederiks (1989), Egmond (1993), and G. Parker (1977). The second war between Spain and the Netherlands, 1621–1648, witnessed fewer atrocities (Israel 1986: 97, 100, 105; M. P. Gutmann 1980: 32–36, 52–58, 61–62, 163–164).

23. Estimated rates among colonists of the same nationality were 30 per 100,000 adults per year in New England, 1630–1636, and New Netherlands, 1638–1656. The rate was probably 50 per 100,000 adults in Virginia, 1607–1632, and 400 per 100,000 in Maryland, 1635–1655. Including homicides among people of different nationalities, the rate in Virginia was probably 250 per 100,000 adults per year, 1607–1646, and in Maryland 500 per 100,000, 1635–1651. That rate was also high in New Netherlands through 1645 (AHSV 2009: AH, tables 1–4). It is impossible to know how high homicide rates rose among Native Americans, but their rates were probably higher than those of European colonists, considering the number of Indians murdered by Europeans. On colonial warfare see Leach (1973), Cave (1996), Washburn (1957), and Richter (2001: 62–67).

24. For example, Philbrick (2006: 103) and J. Smith (1986, 2: 240).

25. Robbery, vigilante, and revenge murders accounted for 6 of the 19 known murders of colonists in Virginia, 1607–1622; 2 of 12 in Mary-

land, 1635–1651; 10 of 29 in New Netherlands, 1638–1656; and 12 of 30 in New England, 1630–1637. All but 2 of these 30 homicides were committed by Native Americans. Robbery, vigilante, and terrorist murders accounted for 15 of the 25 known murders of Native Americans in these years. Nine were committed by colonists.

26. Courtwright (1996).
27. Campeau (1972: 40–47) and Thwaites (1896–1901, 2: 251–265). Politically motivated homicides accounted for 10 of the 19 known murders of colonists in Virginia, 1607–1622; 7 of 12 in Maryland, 1635–1651; 2 of 29 in New Netherlands, 1638–1656; and 12 of 30 in New England, 1630–1637. Nineteen of those 31 murders were committed by Native Americans. Politically motivated murders accounted for 8 of the 25 known murders of Native Americans in these years. Two were committed by colonists.
28. Winthrop (1996: 103, 140) and J. G. Reid (1981: 84–85).
29. J. Smith (1986, 2: 256–257), Hale (1951: 195–206, 225–226, 233–234), and Browne et al. (1883–1972, 4: 21–23).
30. Gehring (1983: 8–9), Bradford (1970: 262–268), and Winthrop (1996: 114–115, 122–125, 131).
31. Cave (1996: 57–61). Of 31 homicides over trade and territory, three-fifths (19) were committed by Native Americans in Virginia, 1607–1622; Maryland, 1635–1651; New Netherlands, 1638–1656; and New England, 1630–1637. The others were committed by colonists.
32. Winthrop (1996: 58, 87) and Noble (1901–1928, 2, pt. 1: 25–26).
33. Percy (1922: 265).
34. Morton (1947: 75–76), Bradford (1970: 100–110, 113–120), Salisbury (1982: 125–140), and Winslow (1910: 289–290, 313–332).
35. On the murder of Finch, see Morton (1947: 18), who conflates the two incidents. On the murder of Penowanyanquis, see Bradford (1970: 299–301) and Winthrop (1996: 260–262). On other homicides, see J. Smith (1996, 2: 293), Beverley (1947: 53), Kingsbury (1906–1935, 4: 10–11); Noble (1901–1928, 2, pt. 1: 69), Winthrop (1996: 235–266), and Jameson (1909: 275–276).
36. J. Smith (1986, 2: 264–265, 256–257) and Jameson (1909: 213–214, 274–275).
37. Winthrop (1996: 70, 84–85). See also Jameson (1909: 216–217, 276).
38. C. C. Hall (1910: 54, 88–90, 183–184) and S. M. Ames (1954: lx–lxi, 57–58). For examples in New Netherlands and New England, see Jameson (1909: 215–216, 276), Bradford (1970: 299–301), Chapin (1916: 81–89), Gardener (1833: 154), Shurtleff (1855–1861, 9: 50), and Underhill (1971: 82).
39. Kingsbury (1906–1935, 3: 242), J. Smith (1986, 2: 266), and A. Brown

(1898: 582). Harrison died fourteen days after receiving a wound in his thigh. The cause of his death was disputed because he was severely ill at the time of the duel, so his death has not been included in the calculation of early Virginia's homicide rate, although it was probably caused by the wound and subsequent infection.

40. Scott and Stryker-Rodda (1974: 24–25, 51–53, 189–192, 292, 351–352), Winthrop (1996: 626–627, 491–492), Bradford (1970: 345–346), Jameson (1909: 275–276), and O'Callaghan (1853–1887, 1: 412–413).

41. Jameson (1909: 275–276), Scott and Stryker-Rodda (1974: 189–192, 292, 351–352), and O'Callaghan (1853–1887, 1: 184–185, 413–414 and 13: 12–13). The surviving records report only one incident before the mid-1670s in which a woman colonist may have killed someone outside her family or household (Lower Norfolk County [Va.] Wills and Deeds, C: 1651/52–1656: 20a–21). It is possible that the victim was her servant, however, given that the suspect was the wife of a planter and that she killed her alleged victim with "violent Stroakes & bloes."

42. Cave (1996: 46–47) and Salisbury (1982: 125–140). For homicides, 1602–1620, see Champlain (1922–1936, 1: 349–355, 415–423, 427–432, 449), Lescarbot (1907–1914, 2: 277–278, 332–338), Levermore (1912, 1: 580), Bradford (1970: 81–84), Baxter (1890, 2: 29); Salisbury (1982: 106–188), Heath (1963: 52), and Morton (1947: 18).

43. J. G. Reid (1981: 83–102).

44. Cave (1996) and Rountree (1990: 87–96).

45. On Maryland, see Rountree and Davidson (1997: 89–91, 112–116); Browne et al. (1883–1972, 2: 53, 195, 570; 10: 293–296; 49: 481–484, 489, 491; 53: 609, 616; 54: 402; and 60: 92–93). On New Netherlands, see Haefeli (1999) and Otto (1995: 209–214, 233–240).

46. AHSV (2009: AH, table 1). On typical postfrontier homicides, see Bradstreet (1855: 46); Hubbard (1677: front matter, n.p.); Suffolk Files 1035, Massachusetts Archives, Boston; and Gehring (1983: 97). On the murder by Busshege, see Winthrop (1996: 534–535) and Hoadly (1857: 135, 146); by Mesapano, Trumbull (1850, 1: 294), Hull (1857: 180), and Hubbard (1677: front matter, n.p.); and by Punneau, Newport Court Book, A: 11, Rhode Island Judicial Archives, Pawtucket.

47. Lancaster County (Va.) Deeds and Wills, 1652–1657: 95, 163; Lancaster County Court Order Book, 3: 125–126; and Rountree (1990: 92–93).

48. AHSV (2009: AH, tables 1–4).

49. See Norton (2002: 17–18, 46–47, and passim), for example; and Benton (1911).

50. On the conflict, see Washburn (1957), E. S. Morgan (1975: 250–270), and Wertenbaker (1940).

51. Andrews (1943: 35, 67–71, 89–92, 130–136), Washburn (1957: 86), and Sainsbury (1893: 453–454).

52. On Maryland, see Hale (1951: 285–290) and C. C. Hall (1910: 141–142, 204, 242–244, 262–265, 304–305). On Baxter's rebellion, see Hoadly (1858: 52–67, 76–77, 92–95) and Trumbull (1850, 1: 253–254).

53. Gilje (1996: 17–20); Chapin (1916: 192–199); Billings, Selby, and Tate (1986: 106–108); E. S. Morgan (1975: 286–287); and Daniell (1981: 90–92).

54. McIlwaine (1924: 190–192). See also Lower Norfolk County Wills and Deeds, 1656–1666, D: 386–388; and Browne et al. (1883–1972, 57: 352–355, 363–364). Motive and circumstance are unknown in 13 of the 34 known nonfamily, nonhousehold homicides that occurred among colonists in New England, 1639–1692; 3 of the 9 in New Netherlands, 1638–1656; 11 of the 18 in Virginia; and 13 of the 48 in Maryland. Excluding the 42 known cases of political homicide, motive and circumstance are unknown in 40 of 67 nonfamily, nonhousehold homicides. These data must be interpreted with caution. The 27 cases of nonfamily, nonhousehold, nonpolitical homicides in which motive and circumstance are known include 3 sexual assaults, 1 case of resisting arrest, 1 case of a colonist mistaken for an Indian, and 20 quarrels, property disputes, or ethnic or religious confrontations.

55. Browne et al. (1883–1972, 49: 10–17). See also McIlwaine (1924: 183–184).

56. On the murder of House, see Rhode Island Court Records (1920–1922, 2: 97–98); of Bedford, Libby, Moody, and Allen (1928–1947, 3: xxxix–xli, 22, 86); and of Sherburne, Libby, Moody, and Allen (1928–1947, 1: 90–91, 628–629) and Hammond (1943: 369–370, 377–378, 404).

57. Gehring (1983: 200–201), Bradford (1970: 147–163, 234), and Morton (1947: 80–81).

58. Block (2006), M. D. Smith (2001), Dayton (1995: 157–284), Lindemann (1984), Marietta and Rowe (2006: 137–146), Hurl-Eamon (2005: 32–48), and G. Walker (2003: 55–60).

59. Winthrop (1996: 712, 236–238) and Noble (1901–1928, 2, pt. 1: 70). Seven female colonists were known to have been murdered in nonfamily, nonhousehold homicides, 1607–1692. Three were probably sexually assaulted. The character of the other four homicides is unknown.

60. Connecticut Archives, Crimes and Misdemeanors, Ser. 1, I: 109–113, Connecticut State Library, Hartford; and Hearn (1999: 53–54).

61. Roth (2002) and Lindgren and Heather (2002). Only 5 of 204 non-

family, nonhousehold homicides were committed with guns in Middlesex, 1549–1632 (2 percent); 2 of 161 in Sussex, 1559–1625 (1 percent); and 0 of 143 in Essex, 1559–1625 (Jeaffreson 1886–1892; Cockburn 1975–1982). The proportions in Kent were 8 of 305 (3 percent), 1560–1639; and 23 of 200 (12 percent), 1640–1689; but those proportions included accidental deaths caused by firearms (Cockburn 1991: 81, 83–88, 94). Excluding accidental deaths, only 1 gun was used in the 46 nonfamily, nondomestic homicides that occurred in Kent, 1676–1688 (2 percent); and none in the 5 household or family homicides (Cockburn 1997). In Amsterdam, 1667–1729, only 15 of 623 male homicide victims (2 percent) for whom the murder weapon was known were killed with guns (Spierenburg 1994). Guns are not mentioned as murder weapons in Artois (Muchembled 1989: 33–39).

In New England and New Netherlands, 1630–1675, 11 of the 29 homicides among unrelated colonists in which the weapons are known were committed with guns. In Maryland, 1635–1675, 17 of the 42 homicides among unrelated colonists in which the weapons are known were committed with guns, but that number may have been as high as 27 (64 percent) if all twenty victims of the Battle of the Severn were killed with guns, rather than half (AHSV 2009: Weapons).

62. Horn (1994: 210–212, 268–276).
63. Quoted in Billings, Selby, and Tate (1986: 52–53). On revenge by indentured servants, see Trumbull (1850: 124) and Hoadly (1857: 26, 35, 46, 61; 1858: 169–172, 187–189, 384–387, 504–510). On attitudes toward indentured servants, see E. S. Morgan (1975: 295, 308–309, 320–326) and K. M. Brown (1996: 75–104). For the rates at which indentured servants killed or were killed by their masters, mistresses, or overseers, see AHSV (2009: AH, tables 1–4).
64. On the murder by Grammar, see Browne et al. (1883–1972, 49: 307–312, 351); by the Bradnoxes, Browne et al. (1883–1972, 41: 482, 500–506); and by Alvey, Browne et al. (1883–1972, 49: 167–168, 230, 233, 235, 539–545). On the sadism of some masters and mistresses, see Libby, Moody, and Allen (1928–1947, 1: 262, 272, 286); Westmoreland County (Va.) Deeds, Patents, Etc., 1665–1677: 215–216; Browne et al. (1883–1972, 10: 524–525, 534–541); and McIlwaine (1924: 22–24). On homicides by overwork, see Suffolk Files 830; Browne et al. (1883–1972, 54: 360–362); Charles City County (Va.) Order Book, 1661–1664: 357; and McIlwaine (1924: 22–24). On illness, see Grob (2002: 48–69) and Rutman and Rutman (1984, 1: 130–134, 179).
65. In New England, 1637–1675, homicides between indentured servants and their owners or overseers took the lives of European American

men at a rate of 2 per 100,000 per year and of European American women at a rate of 0.5 per 100,000. In Virginia, 1652–1676, the comparable rates were 12 per 100,000 and 28 per 100,000; and in Maryland, 1656–1672, 20 per 100,000 and 18 per 100,000. European American women in the Chesapeake were murdered by nonrelatives at the same rate as men through the first decade of the eighteenth century because of the high proportion of women who worked as indentured servants (AHSV 2009: AH, tables 5–6).

66. On the murder by Ward, see Browne et al. (1883–1972, 54: 9); and by Nevell, Browne et al. (1883–1972, 41: 467, 470–471, 475, 478–480).

67. AHSV (2009: AH, table 7).

68. On the murder of Williams, see Hammond (1943: 318, 329, 337); New Hampshire Court Papers, 3: 7, 297, New Hampshire State Archives, Concord; S. Sewall (1973, 1: 10); and Suffolk Files 1349 and 1363; and of Emeritt, Maryland Provincial Court Judgments, 1682–1702, Liber T. G. 2: 88–90, Maryland State Archives, Annapolis.

69. On the murder of Hawkins, see Browne et al. (1883–1972, 65: 2–8). See also Lower Norfolk County Wills and Deeds, 1656–1666, D: 398; and York County (Va.) Deeds, Wills, and Orders 3: 46, 50, 97.

70. Billings, Selby, and Tate (1986: 80); E. S. Morgan (1975: 295, 246, 216–218); and Horn (1994: 157, 416).

2. "All Hanging Together"

1. AHSV (2009: American Homicides [AH], tables 1, 3–4).

2. R. Thompson (1986: 19–33) and Godbeer (2002: 19–51, 227–236). On gun ownership, see Roth (2002) and Lindgren and Heather (2002). King Philip's War claimed the lives of perhaps a tenth of all adult male colonists and two-fifths of all Native Americans, and it devastated trade and economic production. A third of the colonists' towns were destroyed at a loss of about £150,000, and the war effort itself cost another £100,000. King William's War (1689–1699) and Queen Anne's War (1702–1713) took the lives of 5 percent of European adult males and roughly half of all Native Americans in northern New England. Those two wars largely depopulated Maine, New Hampshire, and the upper Connecticut River Valley. Taxes had to be increased to pay for the wars and to provide relief for displaced colonists. New towns appeared in the less fertile areas of Connecticut and Rhode Island, but New England's northern boundary receded. A few sectors of the economy benefited from the later wars as Great Britain geared up for naval campaigns against France and demanded masts, ships, and naval

stores, but fishing and farming suffered. J. D. Drake (1999: 4, 42, 168–169), Allegro (1997: 35–36), Puglisi (1991: 31–83), and R. R. Johnson (1981: 129, 197–198, 274–277, 379–380, 413).

The damage from Bacon's Rebellion and the Indian war that provoked it was largely confined to plantations on the upper James and Rappahannock and to the estates of prominent rebels and loyalists in the Tidewater, but King William's War affected the entire region. For contrasting assessments of the cost of the rebellion, see Wertenbaker (1940: 83–84, 90–91, 103–138) and Washburn (1957: 24–25, 32–33, 77–91, 102, 105–109). King William's War depressed demand for farm commodities by disrupting the Caribbean trade, although it strengthened demand for ships, sailors, and naval stores. Planters who grew sweet-scented tobacco on Virginia's Lower and Middle Neck prospered in the 1680s and 1690s, but planters who grew the less desirable Oronoco tobacco in Maryland and on Virginia's Eastern Shore and South Side faced declining prices (Bradburn and Coombs 2006: 137–144, 148–149; K. Kelly 1989: 166–180; Walsh 1999; A. H. Rutman 1987: 3–7). The opening of new counties in the Piedmont, new settlement on the Lower and Middle Necks, and the continued growth of domestic and coastal trade offset these difficulties to a degree, but the economy slowed, as did immigration from Europe (Bradburn and Coombs 2006: 139, 144–150).

3. On the growing diversity of the colonists, see Butler (1990).

4. Galenson (1981) and Coombs (2003: 211–223).

5. See Berlin (1998: 17–63), E. S. Morgan (1975: 180–292), and W. D. Jordan (1969: 66–82).

6. J. D. Drake (1999: 16–56, 197–201).

7. Leach (1973: 50–56, 69–75) and J. G. Reid (1981: 127–163).

8. Individual Puritans were responsible for several of the household murders and political murders that occurred in New England in the seventeenth century, but to date no perpetrator of a homicide of an unrelated adult has been identified through genealogical research as a member of a Puritan church, although several, such as John Billington and William Schooler, have been identified as antagonists of the Puritans.

9. In addition to the hangings in chapter 1, see, for example, the executions carried out by Virginia during and after Bacon's Rebellion (Washburn 1957: 119) and by Maryland during the Glorious Revolution (Lovejoy 1972: 308–310). On New England, see Hearn (1999: 5–102).

10. Lovejoy (1972: 263–264, 340–353, 364–377).

11. J. D. Drake (1999: 54–74), Lepore (1998: 21–47), and Bourne (1990).
12. Folger (1725: 6) and Puglisi (1991: 178).
13. J. D. Drake (1999: 4, 42, 168–169) and Cook (1973).
14. Puglisi (1991: 35–38), Lepore (1998: 137–138), and Pulsipher (1996).
15. J. D. Drake (1999: 144), Puglisi (1991: 36), and Lepore (1998: 43–44).
16. Norton (2002: 95–98, 143–146, 185–192).
17. J. D. Drake (1999: 8–9, 118–119, 132–133, 146–147), Puglisi (1991: 202), and Bourne (1990: 156–158, 182–189, 195–205).
18. Roetger (1984: 251–252), R. Thompson (1986: 8), Pope (1969), and P. Miller (1961: 229).
19. Puglisi (1991: 14–26, 175–178) and Norton (2002: 17–18, 46–47).
20. E. S. Morgan (1975: 250–292), Washburn (1957), and S. S. Webb (1984: 3–163).
21. E. S. Morgan (1975: 295–315), Galenson (1981: 117–168), and Berlin (1998: 109–141).
22. AHSV (2009: AH, tables 3–4).
23. W. D. Jordan (1969: 71–82, 91–98).
24. E. S. Morgan (1975: 331–337) and Coombs (2003: 171–172, 177–179, 245–250).
25. E. S. Morgan (1975: 331–333, 344–345), K. M. Brown (1996: 179–186, 207–211), and Coombs (2003: 177–179).
26. E. S. Morgan (1975: 338–362) and D. W. Jordan (1987: 84–89, 168).
27. E. S. Morgan (1975: 328–337) and Zelinsky (1988: 124–125).
28. Allegro (1997: 62–113).
29. P. Miller (1961: 156).
30. Lovejoy (1972: xiii–xiv, 1–159).
31. R. R. Johnson (1981: 50–83) and Lovejoy (1972: 160–219).
32. Lovejoy (1972: 350–353) and R. R. Johnson (1981: 121–135, 242–246).
33. On William's policies, see Claydon and McBride (1998: 75–104).
34. Lovejoy (1972: 340–353, 370–374), R. R. Johnson (1981: 242–305), Haffenden (1974), and Pencak (1981: 35–113).
35. R. R. Johnson (1981: 327) and Norton (2002: 10–11, 311–312).
36. R. R. Johnson (1981: 412–413) and P. Miller (1961: 173–190, 209–225).
37. P. Miller (1961: 163), Claydon (1996), Allegro (1997: 30–33), R. R. Johnson (1981: 130–133), and Pincus (1999).
38. Zelinsky (1988: 124–125) and Cressy (1989: 205).
39. Carr and Jordan (1974: 215–217) and Hoffman (2000: 67).
40. Norton (2002: 180, 104) and Allegro (1997: 16, 34–43).
41. Puglisi (1991: 190–193, 179–180).
42. According to Gilje (1996: 24–34), land disputes between New Yorkers and New Englanders, and between Marylanders and Pennsylvanians,

claimed five lives between 1700 and 1765. On the homicide involving the Protestant and the Catholic, see *Maryland Gazette*, 15 September 1747; and Lee (1994: 79).

43. AHSV (2009: AH, tables 1, 3–4). Table 3 prorates the 20 deaths in Bacon's Rebellion over the years 1607–1676. Eight of 28 known homicides among unrelated colonists in New England, 1630–1675, were known to have had political motives, and 31 of 57 in Maryland, 1635–1675. On the conflict between the proprietary and antiproprietary forces in Maryland, see Maryland Provincial Court Judgments, 1692–93, Liber D. S. No. C 4: 41–42, Maryland State Archives, Annapolis; and Lovejoy (1972: 308–310).

44. For examples of robbery murders, see *Maryland Gazette*, 27 February, 30 March, and 1 May 1751, 4 and 25 April and 9 May 1754; *Massachusetts Gazette* (Boston), 29 June 1769; *Virginia Gazette*, 10 June and 16 September 1737, 18 and 25 August 1738, and 30 May 1751; *Boston Newsletter*, 22 March and 11 October 1744; Spotsylvania County (Va.) Court Order Book, 1738–49: 18; Massachusetts Superior Court of Judicature records, 1743–1748: 119, Massachusetts Archives, Boston; Suffolk Files 16737, 58364, 59403, 59428, 89210, and 169145, Massachusetts Archives, Boston; and Hoffer and Scott (1984: 148–152).

45. AHSV (2009: AH, tables 5 and 6).

46. See, for example, the unintended homicide of Andrew Gardiner, Pike (1875–76: 139) and J. Marshall (1884: 24); of Grace Wentworth, Pike (1875–76: 146) and *Boston Newsletter*, 22 September 1707; of Stephen Swazey, Suffolk Files 2915; and of William Conner and John Briant, Suffolk Files 26099 and *Boston Newsletter*, 21 and 28 November 1745. Riots against press-gangs claimed at least ten lives in the colonies between 1700 and 1765 (Gilje 1996: 24–26).

47. On the murders in Portsmouth, see McIlwaine, Hall, and Hillman (1925–1966, 6: 240–242, 244, 247–249); and in Newport, *Connecticut Journal*, 13 May 1768. See also *Maryland Gazette*, 30 January 1751; and *Boston Newsletter*, 9 August 1770. The homicide rate in Halifax, Nova Scotia, a major British port, was 19.7 per 100,000 persons per year from 1749 to 1765, and 13.1 per 100,000 from 1766 to 1784. Half of the homicides were committed by sailors or soldiers (Phillips and May 2001).

48. For an example of a nonhousehold murder among unrelated women, see Noble (1901–1928, 1: 358) and Massachusetts Superior Court of Judicature records, 1686–1700: 129–130. Ten of the 77 homicides among unrelated colonists in New England in which the weapons are known were committed with guns, 1676–1769, and 8 of 71 in Maryland, 1676–1762. Nine of 24 were committed with guns in New England, 1630–

1675, and probably 17 of 42 in Maryland, 1635–1675. AHSV (2009: Weapons).

49. McWhiney (1988), Fischer (1989: 621–632, 639, 667–668, 675–680, 687–690, 740–743, 765–771), Wormald (1980), Goldie (1996: 227–229), Withers (1988: 76–86), Mitchison (1996: 24–46; 2002: 179–356), Whetstone (1981: 38–39), and Kenyon and Ohlmeyer (1998: 3–72).

50. AHSV (2009: European Homicides [EH], fig. 3) and Garnham (1996: 1, 174–209, 220–224). The adult rate here assumes that roughly 65 percent of the population was age sixteen or older. On Ireland, see Somerset Fry and Somerset Fry (1988: 104–188); Leyburn (1962); Kenyon and Ohlmeyer (1998: 3–40, 73–102); Moody, Martin, and Byrne (1976: 20–29, 115–141); Moody and Vaughan (1986: 66–69, 78–82); Connolly (1992: 198–262); Garnham (1996: 1–132, 174–182, 256–280); Henry (1994: 77–99); Griffin (2001); Barnard (1998); and McBride (1998).

51. Beames (1983), T. D. Williams (1973), Garnham (1996: 178–209), and AHSV (2009: EH, fig. 3). Garnham (1996: 174–184, 220–224) determined the probable proportion of homicide defendants who were Protestant in Armagh, 1730–1800. Catholics in Armagh, 1730–1800, were indicted for murder at three or four times the rate that Protestants were. The indictment rate for Catholics had been 20 per 100,000 adults per year in the 1730s and 11 per 100,000 in the 1740s. It was about 8 per 100,000 in the 1750s and 1760s. The rate for Protestants had been 5 per 100,000 adults per year in the 1730s. It was about 2 per 100,000 in the 1750s and 1760s. Comparable data are not available for Tyrone.

In most counties where Catholics were in the majority, they may not have been more homicidal than Protestants. Data from the early nineteenth century, 1805–1814, drawn from House of Commons (1980–1982), show that the homicide indictment rate in central Ireland (5.4 per 100,000 adults per year) was not much higher than it was in Ulster (4.3 per 100,000). However, the rate was much higher in predominantly Catholic southwest Ireland (13.8 per 100,000). These data may not be a reliable guide to homicide rates in Ireland in the mid-eighteenth century, since the homicide rate appears to have fallen markedly in Ireland between 1780 and 1805. The data are, however, consistent with the data from Armagh, Tyrone, and the city of Dublin in the 1790s.

52. Daniell (1981: 141) and AHSV (2009: AH, tables 8 and 9). The only certain cases of homicides in New England by Scots were committed in 1757. John Clark of Casco Bay, Maine, a suspected thief, shot a member of the posse that had come to arrest him; and Alexander Frazer, a

sergeant in the British army stationed in Stratford, Connecticut, killed another sergeant with whom he had quarreled. Suffolk Files 75438 and 76728; *New Hampshire Gazette,* 18 March 1757; Connecticut Superior Court records, 16: 385, Connecticut State Library, Hartford; and *Boston Gazette,* 2 January 1758.

53. AHSV (2009: AH, tables 8 and 9). According to county court records for Augusta, Botetourt, Rockbridge, and Rockingham counties, at least six men had ears bitten off in fights that occurred in the southern Shenandoah Valley in the years before the Revolution, but only three were assaulted by Scots. Augusta County (Va.) Court Order Book, 4: 413; 6: 336; 7: 204; and 8: 213; Botetourt County (Va.) Court Order Book, 1770–1777: 120; and A. P. Scott (1930: 206).

54. AHSV (2009: AH, tables 8 and 9). Eighty percent of the 100,000 Ulster Presbyterians who migrated to British North America between 1718 and 1775 paid their own passage, and most emigrated as families. In contrast, many of the Irish were too poor to pay their own way, and many emigrated alone (Griffin 2001: 79). On Irish culture, see Barnard (1998), McBride (1998), and Kenny (1998: 18–24).

On homicides by the Irish, see the murder by Terence Connors, *Maryland Gazette,* 28 September and 26 October 1752; by Thomas Murray, Augusta County Court Order Book, 7: 150–151; by Samuel Corkerin, *Boston Newsletter,* 15 November 1739; and by Maurice Cavenaugh, *Massachusetts Gazette,* 7 September 1769.

55. AHSV (2009: AH, tables 1 and 3–6). In Virginia, 1607–1675, and in Maryland, 1635–1675, masters, mistresses, and overseers murdered 21 servants, and servants mudered 6 masters, mistresses, and overseers. In Virginia, 1676–1774, and in Maryland, 1683–1693 and 1749–1756, the corresponding numbers were 9 and 12.

56. Ekirch (1987: 135–138, 166–177, 185–193) and, for example, *Virginia Gazette,* 30 May 1751.

57. AHSV (2009: AH, table 6) and Hoffer and Scott (1984: 195–198).

58. On the murder by Wortham, see Middlesex County (Va.) Deeds, 1703–1720: 277–283. See also the four election-day murders in Maryland in *Maryland Gazette,* 19 April and 3 May 1749, 23 October 1751, and 23 April 1752; and Maryland Provincial Court Judgments, Liber E. I. 14: 216, 231–232. See also New Hampshire Provincial Court files 28451, New Hampshire State Archives, Concord; Gloucester County Court Records (1926: 169); and Wells (1902: 501, 510).

59. AHSV (2009: AH, tables 6 and 10). On colonial military involvement in King George's War and the French and Indian War, and the increase in patriotic and racial feeling among colonists, see Leach (1973: 206–

261, 307–485), F. Anderson (1984, 2000), and Daniell (1981: 139–140).

60. On the emergence of British national identity, see Pincus (1999), Colley (1992: 1–100), Claydon and McBride (1998), M. Cohen (1996), and K. Wilson (1998, 2003). On faith in the British monarchy and political system, see Bushman (1985: 11–132) and Haffenden (1974). On the British public, see Pincus (1995, 1999) and Shields (1997). The Bill of Rights of 1689 can be viewed at http://www.constitution.org/eng/eng_bor.htm.

61. See especially Colley (1992: 1–100).

62. Roeber (1981) and G. Morgan (1989). The rates per 1,000 white adult males per year in Amelia County, 1756–1762, were 10.7 for civil assault prosecutions, 1.4 for state assault prosecutions, and 0.9 for civil slander prosecutions. The corresponding rates in Richmond County, 1732–1746, were 10.3, 1.3, and 0.9. See the court order books for the respective counties.

Of the 329 civil suits for assault that occurred in Amelia County, 1735–1762, and in Richmond County, 1692–1721 and 1732–46, 2 involved slaves as plaintiffs and masters as defendants, 2 involved gentlemen as plaintiffs and two as defendants, 12 involved husbands and wives as plaintiffs and 3 as defendants, and 5 involved women as plaintiffs and 4 as defendants. The rest—94 percent of plaintiffs and 98 percent of defendants—involved men who were not described as gentlemen.

63. Rockbridge County (Va.) Court judgments, 1782. The court fined Thompson a surprisingly large sum—£20—plus costs. My thanks to James Watkinson for bringing this story to my attention.

64. Baird (1999: 90–92), A. P. Scott (1930: 164–174, 181–185), Horn (1994: 363–368), and Norton (1987). In Amelia and Richmond counties, damages in slander suits ranged from 1 shilling to £20, with an average of 29.5 shillings and a median of £2. Damages in assault suits ranged from 1 shilling to £75, with an average of 24.1 shillings and a median of £2. There were 20 shillings in each pound sterling. Fourteen of 54 slander suits (26 percent) ended in damage awards for the plaintiffs, as did 64 of 329 assault and battery suits (19 percent). See the court order books for Amelia and Richmond counties.

65. Shields (1997), Pincus (1995), M. Cohen (1996), and Bushman (1992). On the growing importance of civility, genteel manners, and the control of anger in the late seventeenth and early eighteenth centuries, see Stearns and Stearns (1986: 28–35), L. E. Klein (1994), M. B. Becker (1994), and Braddick (2000).

66. Connecticut Archives, Crimes and Misdemeanors, Ser. 1, 1: 248–255,

Connecticut State Library, Hartford. My thanks to Cornelia Hughes Dayton for bringing this case to my attention.

67. P. Miller (1961: 324–344) and Daniell (1981: 170).

68. Comprehensive homicide data are not yet available for North Carolina. The available data on homicide indictments against free persons, 1720–1769, are from Spindel (1989: 57). The data are incomplete because the court records of 14 of 35 counties are missing (Spindel 1989: xv–xvii, 147–161). The rates do not take missing records into account, so they understate the actual indictment rate. Reliable estimates of the free black population of colonial North Carolina are not yet available, so estimates of the white population from Bureau of the Census (1975, 2: 1168) are used as proxies for the total free population. On early North Carolina's troubled political history, see Lefler and Newsome (1973: 32–75) and Spindel (1989: 16, 140).

69. The homicide accusation data, 1682–1800, are from Marietta and Rowe (1999: 26–29). The rates take into account missing court records. They include accusations against African Americans, European Americans, and Native Americans. The rate for 1776–1783 greatly understates the actual homicide rate because of the disruption of the criminal justice system during the Revolution. These are rough estimates of homicide rates, based on the fact that about a third of the population was under the age of sixteen and that a significant number of homicides found in inquests or newspapers did not lead to formal accusations of homicide in court.

Some indentured servants died of abuse in early Pennsylvania, but on the whole, indentured servants received better treatment in Pennsylvania than in the Chesapeake, because it was primarily a system for helping poorer friends and relatives with marketable skills to migrate to the New World, at least until the late 1720s (Salinger 1987: 2–4, 18–46).

70. Marietta and Rowe (2006: 63–80), Nash (1979: 93–128), and Wendel (1968). See also the homicide committed by Nichols Hentwerk, *American Weekly Mercury* (Philadelphia), 3–10 April 1730; by John Murry, *American Weekly Mercury,* 16 February 1725; by William Battin, *American Weekly Mercury,* 11 November 1721 and 16 August 1722; by a man named Bourk, *Boston Gazette,* 10 August 1730; and by Hugh Pugh and a man named Lazaras, *Boston News-Letter,* 5 May 1718; and Lokken (1959: 198–199).

71. Lokken (1959: 214–224).

72. Wendel (1968), Lokken (1959: 208–235), Nash (1979: 148–157), and Marietta and Rowe (2006: 63–80).

73. Smolenski (2004: 104, 115–116, 122–124) and the homicides by Robert and Walter Winter, *Boston Gazette,* 15 July 1728.
74. Starna (2004), Preston (2004), and Wendel (1968: 304–305).
75. Pencak (2002: 109–115), F. Anderson (2000: 160–165, 205–207), and Marietta and Rowe (2006).
76. On New France, see Lachance (1984: 82, 129, 132). The data include examinations for neonaticide as well as homicide. The annual rate at which suspects in Quebec were examined on suspicion of homicide fell from 9.42 per 100,000 persons, 1650–1699, to 2.97 per 100,000, 1712–1759. Homicides involving Native Americans, however, seldom came under the jurisdiction of Quebec's courts (Grabowski 1996). On European rates, see AHSV (2009: EH, figs. 1–3) and Eisner (2001).
77. AHSV (2009: AH, table 11). Note that Figure 2.1 is per 100,000 persons per year—not per 100,000 adults per year. Because more than two-thirds of the black population in New England was age sixteen or older, the rate for adults was at least 15 per 100,000. Accurate estimates of the age distribution of the African American population in New England have yet to be developed, which is why the rates are reported per 100,000 persons.

    For examples of cases in which slaves were beaten to death, see the murders of Andrew and Fortier, Massachusetts Superior Court of Judicature records, 1700–1714: 265 and 1715–1721: 25–26; and Suffolk Files 13190. See also McIlwaine, Hall, and Hillman (1925–1966, 4: 111–112, 206–207); Rankin (1965: 207); Richmond County (Va.) Court Order Book, 1704–1708: 302–306; Hoffer and Scott (1984: 218–219); and *Virginia Gazette,* 2 and 23 November 1739 and 21 April and 13 May 1775.
78. Suffolk Files 12068.
79. Suffolk Files 15551; and *Boston Gazette,* 8 September 1735.
80. *Boston Newsletter,* 23 July 1741; and Suffolk Files 61453.
81. *Maryland Gazette,* 8 February 1770; and Kennedy and McIlwaine (1905–1915, 12: 92).
82. Schwarz (1988: 79–80, 140). The rate of 2 per 100,000 black adults per year is calculated from claims for compensation for deceased fugitive slaves that were submitted to the House of Burgesses in Virginia, 1736–1775 (Kennedy and McIlwaine 1905–1915). Homicides of fugitive slaves are included in the homicide totals for the counties in this study, but not suicides or negligent manslaughters.
83. See also AHSV (2009: AH, table 12). All but 3 of the 21 known homicides of African Americans in New England by unrelated adults were committed by whites, so the rate at which blacks were murdered by

whites was roughly the same as the rate at which they were murdered by all persons. On homicides of blacks, see Suffolk Files 147139; and *Boston Gazette,* 12 October 1761. One master turned an aged, infirm slave out of the house on Christmas Day in 1784 and left him to freeze to death, but that case stands alone in the surviving record (Suffolk Files 160036).

84. See, for example, Schwarz (1988: 79) on the views of Lieutenant Governor Spotswood of Virginia; *Virginia Gazette,* 21 April 1775; Piersen (1988: 3–61); and P. D. Morgan (1998: 257–300, 662–663). P. Wood (1974: 218–238) argues that white anxiety about slave rebellion and fear of blacks increased in the mid-eighteenth century in South Carolina, as did legal coercion against slaves. Whether white fears translated into an increase in lethal violence against blacks is uncertain, but South Carolina may have followed a different path from New England and the Chesapeake when it came to homicides of blacks by whites.

85. Schwarz (1988: 89–91, 154), Harms (1981: 36–37, 84, 97, 137, 149–154, 188, 208–209), Manning (1990: 111–113, 117–118), M. A. Klein (1997: 71–72), and Keim (1997: 152).

86. Schwarz (1988: 92–113) and Coombs (2003: 105–107). Witches were held responsible for most deaths, illnesses, and other reversals of fortune (Harms 1981: 84–85, 201–202, 207–208; Keim 1997: 147).

87. AHSV (2009: AH, tables 12–14). On the murder of Poro, see Suffolk Files 67369 and 68150.

88. McIlwaine, Hall, and Hillman (1925–1966, 6: 254 and 8: 260–261, 271); and *Connecticut Gazette,* 16 May 1761.

89. Schwarz (1988: 64–65), Kulikoff (1986), Egerton (1993), Sidbury (1997), and Coombs (2003: 230–245).

90. Piersen (1988: 14–22, 74–86, 96–140).

91. AHSV (2009: AH, tables 12, 15–16).

92. In New England, see the murder of Jemima Beacher, Connecticut Superior Court files, drawer 325, Connecticut State Library, Hartford; of Tabitha Sandford, *Boston Newsletter,* 20 September 1745; of John Codman, Suffolk Files 147038 and Massachusetts Superior Court of Judicature records, 1763–64: 193; and of Elizabeth McKinstry, *Boston Gazette,* 13 June 1763. For similar cases in Virginia, see *Boston Newsletter,* 12 May 1729; *Virginia Gazette,* 4 and 25 February and 10 June 1737; and *Massachusetts Gazette,* 5 and 19 September 1754. On conspiracies, see Ellefson (1963: 308n255); *Maryland Gazette,* 6 and 13 December 1753; *Virginia Gazette,* 15 June and 20 July 1769; *Massachusetts Gazette,* 6 and 13 December 1753; *Connecticut Journal,* 13 June 1770; and Oates (1975: 15).

93. *Boston Gazette,* 9 April 1739 and 9 and 23 January 1753. See also *Boston Newsletter,* 9 July 1741; and P. Wood (1974: 286).

94. Schwarz (1988: 114–136) and P. Wood (1974: 288–301).

95. AHSV (2009: AH, tables 1, 3–4, and 10). For examples, see the murder of the Rowley family, Richmond County Court Order Book 3 (1699–1704): 361–364; of Moses Cook, *Connecticut Journal,* 27 December 1771; and of John Rogers, *Boston Newsletter,* 14 September 1732. Native Americans were not always tried or found guilty, however, for killing whites in self-defense. See, for example, the killing of John Everise, Connecticut Archives, Crimes and Misdemeanors, Ser. 1, 1: 384–387; and Lacy (1937: 472–479); and the killing of a French trader, *Boston Newsletter,* 1 August 1734.

    On homicides away from the colonists' settlements, see McIlwaine, Hall, and Hillman (1925–1966, 4: 327, 330–331); *Virginia Gazette,* 7 April, 30 June, and 21 July 1738; Kennedy and McIlwaine (1905–1915, 10: xx–xxiv); *Connecticut Courant,* 17 June 1765; E. Ames et al. (1869–1922, 7: 523–530); Massachusetts Archives, 1622–1799, 30: 378–412, Massachusetts Archives, Boston; and Massachusetts Council, Executive Records, 2: 419, Massachusetts Archives. For an excellent analysis of the cycle of war and peace on the New England frontier in the late seventeenth and the eighteenth centuries, see Calloway (1990).

96. AHSV (2009: AH, tables 15–16). On hunting homicides, see *New Hampshire Gazette,* 26 July 1765; and Wells (1902: 44). On the murder of Seepat, see Suffolk Files 62925; of the Abenakis, *Boston Gazette,* 19 and 26 December 1749; and of the Penobscots, *Connecticut Gazette,* 19 July 1755. See also *Boston Gazette,* 26 March 1754.

97. On the homicide of Sam, see *Boston Gazette,* 26 May 1735. On homicides in ritual combat, see Morton (1947: 27), Bradford (1970: 69–70), and R. Williams (1936: 186–189).

98. Morton (1947: 36, 44–45) and Lepore (1998: xx).

99. Morton (1947: 36), R. Williams (1936: 186–187), and W. Wood (1977: 88–93).

100. On the murder by Deerskins, see Massachusetts Superior Court of Judicature records, 1721–1725: 38–39; and Suffolk Files 15438; by Quasson, Suffolk Files 19323 and *Boston Gazette,* 16 May 1726; and by the whalers, *Boston Newsletter,* 22 October 1767; and *Connecticut Courant,* 22 February 1768. For further examples, see the homicides by David Stevens, *Boston Newsletter,* 11 March 1736; and by John Comfort, Suffolk Files 49602 and *Boston Newsletter,* 9 November 1738. On the relationship between alcohol consumption and violence among Native Americans, see Mancall (1995: 63–96).

3. Family and Intimate Homicide in the First Two Centuries

1. AHSV (2009: American Homicides [AH], table 17). The estimated number of family and intimate homicides are for blacks and whites in New England, 1630–1797.

2. The data available for whites in Virginia, 1607–1827, and in Maryland, 1635–1762, and for victims of all races in New England, 1630–1797, and in New Hampshire and Vermont, 1798–1827, show that 51 of 64 known victims of marital homicides were women (80 percent), as were 16 of 38 known victims of homicides of other adult relatives (42 percent) and 2 of 3 victims of romance homicide (67 percent). The proportions persisted and were similar elsewhere through the nineteenth century. The proportions are slightly lower today. In the United States, 1976–2003, 64 percent of spouses, 70 percent of ex-spouses, 65 percent of lovers, and 33 percent of adult relatives who were victims of homicide were female. See AHSV (2009: Gender and Homicide).

3. AHSV (2009: AH, tables 17–19; European Homicides [EH], table 2). The homicide rates in England for spouses and other adult relatives are based on indictments or inquests. The rates in the Chesapeake are based on examinations of homicide suspects and in New England on homicide estimates.

   The rate in southeastern England ranged from about 0.4–0.5 per 100,000 adults per year in the early seventeenth century to 0.2–0.3 per 100,000 in the late eighteenth century. The data for England are from the Home Counties, 1559–1625 (Cockburn 1975–1982); Kent, 1626–1800 (Cockburn 1991: 94); and Wiltshire, 1753–1796 (Hunnisett 1981). In Essex the homicide rate for family members and relatives (including children) was 0.44 per 100,000 adults per year for 1560–1609, 0.64 for 1610–1659 (when murders of newborn children peaked), and 0.38 for 1660–1709 (Sharpe 1981: 34).

   The rates for European Americans and African Americans in New England stood at only 0.2 and 0.3 per 100,000 adults per year for most of the seventeenth and eighteenth centuries, and dropped to 0.1 per 100,000 after the Revolution.

   Rates in the Chesapeake stood at about 0.8 per 100,000 adults per year for European Americans and 0.4–0.5 per 100,000 for African Americans. The data for England and the Chesapeake are not directly comparable with the data from New England. The data from England are from indictments or inquests only, and the data from Maryland and Virginia are primarily from examinations of homicide suspects (which determine whether there is enough evidence to bring an indictment).

The data from England and the Chesapeake thus understate the number of homicides compared with the data from New England, which were used to estimate the actual number of publicly recognized homicides. Also, family relationships among African American homicide victims and suspects are not indicated in the Chesapeake records, so intergender violence among African Americans must stand as a proxy for family and intimate violence. The fact that the indictment, inquest, and examination rates from England and the Chesapeake were as high as or higher than New England's homicide rates indicates that their family homicide rates were higher than New England's. Too few counties have been studied, however, to allow us to draw comparisons with certainty, and the fragmentary data from Maryland court records, 1635–1693, and Maryland newspapers, 1749–1756, reveal higher levels of family violence than the data from Virginia's court records. The comparative analysis presented here is thus tentative, pending further study of criminal records in the Chesapeake and in England.

4. For efforts to understand the character and frequency of marital violence in early America, see Roth (1999: 65–71), Pleck (1987), K. M. Brown (1996: 334–342), Peterson del Mar (1996), and Main (2001: 87–91). On England, see Hunt (1992), Foyster (2005), Hurl-Eamon (2005: 49–61), and G. Walker (2003: 63–74). Court records and divorce records reveal, for instance, that at least 1–2 percent of all marriages in Vermont and 3 percent of marriages in New Hampshire in the nineteenth century were violent.

5. Rockingham County (N.H.) Court files 15395; and Browne et al. (1883–1972, 10: 109–112). See also Hoffer and Scott (1984: 113).

6. Rockingham County Court files 14012, 14373, and 14064. For examples in New England, see Roth (1999: 69–70), Hammond (1943: 20, 83, 115, 161, 166), and Shurtleff (1855–1861, 3: 75). For examples in the Chesapeake and in England, see Browne et al. (1883–1972, 53: 628), Jeaffreson (1886–1892, 1: 212 and 2: 185), Foyster (1999: 181–193), Gowing (1996: 206–231), Amussen (1994), and Hunt (1992).

7. Ulrich (1982: 35–50), Berkin (1996: 26–33), and McCusker and Menard (1985: 91–111, 258–276). On Quaker and Puritan marriages, see Levy (1988: 69–75, 132–133, 227–229), Fischer (1989: 75–86, 485–498), L. Wilson (1998), and Main (2001: 92–93).

8. L. Wilson (1998), Roth (1987: 286–288), Gilmore (1989: 114–134), and AHSV (2009: AH, table 20).

9. Bandel (1978), Dayton (1995: 105–156), and Cott (1976b). Peterson del Mar (1996: 9–14, 28–31) finds that in Oregon in the 1850s, abusive husbands (most of whom had migrated from Missouri and central Illi-

nois) used physical force primarily to enforce patriarchal authority. Abusive husbands in postrevolutionary New England seem to have asserted such authority far less often; they fought more often, as did abusive wives, over what they considered to be the failure of their spouses to fulfill their end of the marital bargain. Regional contrasts in nonlethal marital violence, as well as changes in nonlethal marital violence over time, require further study.

10. Parrella (1983: 129–131) finds the same instrumental violence and low marital homicide rate in northern France in the early nineteenth century. Eltis (2000: 85–113) argues for the similarity of marriage and gender relations across Europe, especially northwestern Europe. People in those areas shared a belief in the right of women to decide when and whom they would marry. Eltis feels that belief was rooted more in a spiritual and political commitment to individual rights rather than in any concern about the economic productivity of women.

11. One deliberate murder was committed under extraordinary circumstances and is not included here. An unknown Englishman killed his wife in Virginia during the "starving time" of 1609–10 because, he said, he "martoally hated" her. He then cut her to pieces and ate her. See *True Declaration* (1947, 3: 16) and J. Smith (1986, 2: 232–233).

12. On the murder by Newdale, see Fleet (1988, 1: 275–278); by Spooner, *Connecticut Journal*, 18 and 25 March and 6 May 1778; and Navas (1999). See also the murder by Cornish in Maine, Winthrop (1996: 563–564); by Kemble in Maryland, McIlwaine, Hall, and Hillman (1925–1966, 1: 271); and by Barclay in Georgia, *Augusta Chronicle*, 22 March, 17 May, and 7 June 1806. For examples in England, see G. Walker (2003: 118).

13. *Boston Newsletter*, 28 May 1715. For other examples of murders committed by spouses who were mentally ill, see *Virginia Gazette*, 6 July 1769; inquest into the death of Sarah Wallingford, 5 May 1815, Strafford County (N.H.) Court files; *Rutland Herald*, 20 and 27 August 1792; Old Vermont Supreme Court Files 1626, Clerk's Office, Rutland County Superior Court; and *Farmer's Museum*, 5 May 1800.

14. *Connecticut Journal*, 23 February and 23 November 1785.

15. Surry County (Va.) Criminal Proceedings, 30 April 1802; and inquest on Margaret Dunbar Campbell, 25 April 1802, Surry County Court files. On the slave conspiracy of 1802, see Egerton (1993: 119–146).

16. *Woodstock Observer* (Vt.), 30 June 1829 and 19 October 1830; *New Hampshire Patriot*, 29 June 1829; and *Farmer's Museum*, 19 April 1803 and 27 April and 4 May 1805. See also *Farmer's Cabinet*, 11 June 1805, on the case of an elderly man in Brookfield, Vermont. Colaizzi (1983: 32, 256–

258, 333–334) and Grob (1994: 5–21) discuss the difficulty of caring for the mentally ill, especially those prone to violence, in the pre-asylum era.

17. On the murder by Thomson, see Lacy (1937, 2: 485–493); and by Steadman, *Maryland Gazette,* 6 March and 17 April 1751. Only 5 known cases of marital homicide in New England, 1630–1797, could be positively attributed to mental illness, and none of the known cases in early Maryland and in the counties studied in Virginia, 1607–1800. Between 1790 and 1827, 2 of the known marital homicides in the counties studied in Virginia, Georgia, Ohio, Vermont, and New Hampshire could be attributed positively to mental illness.

18. On the murder by Ford, see Suffolk Files 12601, Massachusetts Archives, Boston; by Duty, Grafton County (N.H.) Superior Court of Judicature records, 9: 538; by Maxfield, *Farmer's Museum,* 7 September 1805; by Cook, *Maryland Gazette,* 1 February and 26 April 1753; and by Lamphier, *Post-Boy* (Windsor, Vt.), 11 November 1806.

19. Only 4 of the 44 family and intimate homicides among European Americans in New England, 1630–1797, for which the weapon is known were committed with guns. None of the 9 family and intimate homicides in Maryland, 1635–1762, for which the weapon is known were committed with guns. AHSV (2009: Weapons).

20. Inquest on Eliza Ann Ferguson, 2 October 1840, Rockingham County Court files B19140; and inquest on Nancy Smart, 27 November 1836, Merrimack County (N.H.) Court files.

21. Shurtleff (1855–1861, 3: 75). On the willingness of colonists in New England, the Chesapeake, and elsewhere in British North America to interfere in violent marriages, see Wall (1990), Pleck (1987: 17–33), and Siegel (1996: 2131).

22. McIlwaine (1924: 108, 116) and Hammond (1943: 242).

23. Roth (1999: 74).

24. For instance, the records of Windsor County, Vermont, 1793–1861, show that only four of the 134 spouses accused of intolerable severity in divorce petitions were prosecuted for assault (Roth 1999: 74).

25. On divorce and separation in early modern England, see Gowing (1996: 30–58, 180–231) and Foyster (1999: 164–177, 181–198); and in Virginia and Maryland, see McIlwaine (1924: 452, 516, 518, 520) and K. M. Brown (1996: 335–336).

26. Dayton (1995: 105–156), S. S. Cohen (1980, 1985, 1986), Cott (1976a, 1976b), Bandel (1978), Koehler (1980: 49–50, 152–153, 320–321, 362–363, 453–459), and Main (2001: 65–67).

27. Bandel (1978: 222–223) and Metcalf (1916: 732–733).

28. Dayton (1995: 105–156), Cott (1976a, 1976b), and S. S. Cohen (1980). On Rhode Island, see S. S. Cohen (1985).
29. Foyster (2005: 8), G. Walker (2003: 63–74), Hurl-Eamon (2005: 49–61), and Roth (1999: 77).
30. McIlwaine (1924: 70). See also Browne et al. (1883–1972, 53: 628).
31. J. Parker (1830). See also inquest on Eliza Ann Ferguson, 2 October 1840, Rockingham County Court files B19140; and Roth (1999: 77).
32. Dayton (1995: 110) and Powell (1972: 66–100).
33. Gowing (1996: 180–231).
34. Bandel (1978) and *Vermont Gazette*, 6 March 1809. See also *Vermont Gazette*, 2 January 1796; and *Vermont Republican* (Windsor), 4 September 1815.
35. Sword (2002).
36. Old Vermont Supreme Court Files 1921, 2209, 3075.
37. David Brooks v. Azuba Brooks, August 1813 Term, Windham County (Vt.) Court files, box 20.
38. *Burlington Free Press*, 12 June 1846.
39. Ibid.; and Old Vermont Supreme Court Files 2209.
40. On Cloyes, see Lacy (1937, 1: 58–59); and on Hanno, *Boston Newsletter*, 29 May 1721; and Mather (1721: 31–40).
41. Hoffer and Scott (1984: 88–89); Middlesex County (Va.) Court Order Book, 1769–1772, 18 October 1771; ibid., 1794–1796, 28 September 1795; and *Virginia Gazette*, 14 July 1768. See also *Virginia Gazette*, 20 October 1774, on a murder by a jealous husband; and Schwarz (1988: 153–154) on the possible murder in 1746 of a woman and her lover by her estranged husband in Louisa County.
42. Greene (1942: 191–198, 201–210) and Cottrol (1998: 76–77).
43. Piersen (1988: 87–95) and Stevenson (1996: 207–222, 230–232, 235–236, 239).
44. Greene (1942: 201–207) and Piersen (1988: 90).
45. Piersen (1988: 93) and Cottrol (1998: 12–20).
46. C. Spear (1832: 52–57).
47. P. D. Morgan (1998: 503–511, 519–540, 548–558), Kulikoff (1986: 358–371), and Stevenson (1996: 207–208, 250–252). On the diversity of the forms of marriage in colonial South Carolina, see P. Wood (1974: 97–99, 139–141). For examples of murders of romantic rivals, see *Virginia Gazette*, 20 October 1774; and Schwarz (1988: 149, 153). Most evidence of murders of romantic rivals comes from the early nineteenth century, when the murder rate among African Americans went up generally. See Schwarz (1988: 230, 249–250) and P. D. Morgan (1998: 410–412).

48. Manfra and Dykstra (1985: 32) and Stevenson (1996: 244).
49. AHSV (2009: AH, table 17), Bureau of the Census (1909: 158–162, 166–169), Mandell (1996), and Plane (2000: 105–113, 123–127).
50. Plane (2000: 6–7, 14–32, 129–177) and Main (2001: 13, 63–64).
51. Thwaites (1896–1901, 3: 99–103). See also Plane (2000: 26–32, 67–68, 149–151).
52. Winship (1905: 279) and W. Wood (1977: 114–116).
53. Seventeen known victims of marital homicide among Native Americans in New England were women. The exception was Great Harry, who was murdered by his wife Betty in Plymouth Colony in 1685. She threw a rock at him and hit him in the head. Shurtleff (1855–1861, 6: 153–154). For examples of wife murders, see *Boston Newsletter,* 8 March 1733 and 5 August 1736; *Boston Gazette,* 21 July 1752; *Connecticut Journal,* 28 February 1776; Suffolk Files 41304, 41307, 41568, 42140; and inquest on Samuel and Mary Sawes, 12 July 1752, Connecticut Superior Court files, New London County, Papers by Subject, Inquests, c. 1711–1875, N–Z, box 135, Connecticut State Library, Hartford. On Combs, see Suffolk Files 133562 and *Connecticut Journal,* 7 June 1786 and 3 January 1787.
54. On the murder in Roxbury, see Bradstreet (1855: 45); by Josiah, Massachusetts Superior Court of Judicature records, 1700–1714: 242, Massachusetts Archives, Boston; and Danforth (1710); and of Ompatawin, see Suffolk Files 16065. See also the murder of Betty David, Suffolk Files 70864.
55. On the murder of Peorowarrow, see Lyford (1903, 1: 87–98); of Cayes, *Connecticut Courant,* 30 December 1793.
56. Axtell (1981: 71–102), Russell (1980: 51, 96–103), and Plane (2000: 1–4, 26–32).
57. Bragdon (1996), Plane (2000: 67–95), Axtell (1981: 103–170), Russell (1980: 51, 96–103), and Haviland and Power (1994: 158–168). The colonial court on the island of Nantucket heard domestic cases brought by Native Americans for a brief period, 1677–1689; but otherwise colonial courts took an interest only when Indians committed major crimes or were involved in interracial sex, whether voluntary or coerced.
58. Greene (1942: 198–201), Mandell (1996: 182–196), Plane (2000: 143–149), Main (2001: 197–198), Hearn (1999: 190), and Cottrol (1998: 79).
59. On the murder by Hull, see *Boston Newsletter,* 4 May and 14 September 1719; and by Paschal, New Hampshire Provincial Court files 20613, New Hampshire State Archives, Concord. Elizabeth Fales of Dedham, Massachusetts, was also the victim of a suitor, but there is no firm evi-

dence that she had rejected Jason Fairbanks before he murdered her in 1801. It is more likely that she was killed for resisting a sexual assault. Hearn (1999: 187–188).

60. *Virginia Herald and Fredericksburg Advertiser,* 2 May 1793; and *Connecticut Courant,* 29 October 1792.

61. For an example of romance murder in early modern England and of the public reaction to such murders, see Brewer (2004). See also Gowing (1996: 176–177), Thompson (1986: 37–38), MacDonald and Murphy (1990: 291–292), and Foyster (1999: 44–45, 55–58).

62. R. Thompson (1986: 37–39, 95–96), Gowing (1996: 153–154, 157–158), K. M. Brown (1996: 259, 299), and E. K. Rothman (1984: 44–55). See also Foyster (1999: 57).

63. Gowing (1996: 141–142, 148–159, 164) and Main (2001: 70–83).

64. Foyster (1999: 44–45), Gowing (1996: 179), and R. Thompson (1986: 37–38, 69–70).

65. Lantz et al. (1968: 419–421) and Lantz, Schmitt, and Herman (1973: 577–579). Emotions were glorified in 59 of 328 references to romantic relationships in the articles that were surveyed for 1741–1794 and in 437 of 761 references for 1795–1825.

66. AHSV (2009: AH, table 20), E. K. Rothman (1984: 38–40), and R. Thompson (1986: 38).

67. E. K. Rothman (1984: 38, 33, 42–44) and Gowing (1996: 179).

68. Cottrol (1998: 22, 44–47).

69. Stevenson (1996: 226–229) and Gutman (1976: 72–75, 158–159).

70. Schwarz (1988: 153–154, 153n39, 249). There is evidence of romance murders among African Americans in the mid-Atlantic colonies. See the murders of Caesar, *Connecticut Gazette,* 7 February 1761; and of a slave of Mr. Marston, *New London Gazette* (Conn.), 12 September 1766.

71. Powers (1841: 175–184), Z. Thompson (1842: 206), and Wells (1902: 61–63, 88).

72. AHSV (2009: AH, tables 17–18; EH, table 2). The rates in England and the Chesapeake were in the range of 0.2 per 100,000 per year and in New England 0.1 per 100,000 per year.

73. On the Hill case, see Suffolk Files 3897, 162421, and 162471. My thanks to John Lund for bringing this case to my attention. The analysis follows his. See also the murder of Joseph Junin, *New Hampshire Gazette,* 9 April 1791; and of Nathaniel Smith, *Strafford Recorder* (Dover, N.H.), 5 August 1790; and *Connecticut Journal,* 18 August 1790.

74. *Maryland Gazette,* 27 November and 25 December 1751.

75. On the murder by Baker, see S. Sewall (1973) 1: 288; and by Frost, *Connecticut Journal,* 8 October 1783. See also the murder by Roger Humphrey, *Boston Newsletter,* 10 February 1759; by Mr. Hutchinson, *New Lon-*

don Gazette, 10 February 1764; by Ebenezer Turrel, *Connecticut Courant,* 6 October 1766; by Israel Wilkins Jr., *New Hampshire Gazette,* 4 December 1772; and by Thomas Goode, *American Constellation* (Petersburg, Va.), 14 August 1834.

76. Connecticut Archives, Crimes and Misdemeanors, Ser. 1, 1: 80–84, 146–148, Connecticut State Library, Hartford.

77. *Middlesex Gazette,* 5 and 19 August 1796; and Huntington (1797).

78. Ploux (2002: 19–54), Parrella (1992: 645–651), and Chesnais (1982: 118–122).

79. Ben-Amos (1994: 165–170, 180) and Beier (1985: 29–69).

80. AHSV (2009: AH, tables 18–19).

81. Cayton (2002: 32).

82. Kulikoff (1986: 354) and Piersen (1988: 87, 90–92).

83. AHSV (2009: AH, table 18), P. D. Morgan (1998: 503–511, 519–540, 548–558), Kulikoff (1986: 358–371), and Stevenson (1996: 207–208, 250–252).

84. All five known cases occurred between 1726 and 1769. See *Boston News-letter,* 3 March 1726; *Connecticut Journal,* 30 June 1768; inquest on unknown Indian man, Colchester, Connecticut, 31 January 1726, Connecticut Superior Court files, New London County, Papers by Subject, Inquests, c. 1711–1875, A–M, box 134; State v. Moses Sesuch, Connecticut Superior Court records, September 1754 term, New London, Connecticut State Library, Hartford; and Suffolk Files 24567, 24576, 25015, and 144112.

4. "A Sense of Their Rights"

1. H. Brown (2006: 16–19, 98–105, 361). The number of homicides was probably three or four times the number tried in criminal courts.

2. Eisner (2001: 623–624, 628–630, 633), Emsley (1996: 41–49), Watt (2001: 55–57, 192), Diederiks (1980, 1990), Kossmann (1978: 92–100), Phillips and May (2001), and Oliver (1998: 31).

3. Nash (1979: 233–384) and B. G. Smith (1990).

4. On North Carolina, see Lefler and Newsome (1973: 173–215) and Ekirch (1981: 86–202). On Pennsylvania, see Pencak (2002: 112–115), Camenzind (2004), Moyer (2004), Frantz and Pencak (1998: 133–152), and F. S. Fox (2000: xiv–xv). The homicide indictment rate fell in Pennsylvania, 1776–1783, because courts closed and law enforcement broke down in many counties (Frantz and Pencak 1998: 12). Future research will probably show that the homicide rate in Pennsylvania was higher in 1776–1783 than it was in 1765–1775 or 1784–1794.

It is not yet possible to determine the proportion for Virginia pre-

cisely, because the political homicides identified to date occurred outside the eleven counties studied intensively (AHSV 2009: American
Homicides [AH], table 21).

5. F. Anderson (1984: 110–141; 2000: 286–293).
6. Merritt (1966: 78–81, 122–130, 179–182) and Zelinsky (1988: 124–
125). Merritt (1996: 127) notes, however, that the proportion of references in American-datelined articles that described the colonies implicitly as British declined only slightly, from 38 percent, 1745–1754, to
34 percent, 1765–1775.
7. On the Boston Massacre, see *Boston Newsletter,* 8 and 15 March 1770;
and Hoerder (1977: 216–234). On the homicide by Richardson, see
Connecticut Journal, 9 March 1770; and of Taylor, Cheshire County
(N.H.) Superior Court of Judicature records, 1: 84–86; inquest on
John Taylor, 3 April 1774, Cheshire County Court files; and Sanger
(1987: 6).
8. *Connecticut Journal,* 1 July 1776, 4 April 1777, and 24 May 1781; *Boston
Gazette,* 7 April 1777, 9 March 1778, and 14 August 1780; Massachusetts
Superior Court of Judicature records, 1778–1780: 210, Massachusetts
Archives, Boston; Suffolk Files 102574, 102630a, and 102707, Massa-
chusetts Archives; Rockingham County (N.H.) Court files 4258; and
Nathaniel P. Sargent Court Minutes, Sargent Family Papers, box 1,
folder 11, Peabody Essex Museum, Salem, Mass.
9. On loyalist and Tory raids, see *Connecticut Journal,* 28 January 1778;
Boston Gazette, 4 September 1780; and Leamon (1993: 126–127). On
Irish and Mallory, see Hemenway (1868–1891, 1: 129–130) and Walton
(1873: 167–168); and on Prindle, *Connecticut Courant,* 17 June 1776.
10. On Vermont, see Walton (1873: 314n2, 315n2, 316n1, 330–338); *Connecticut Courant,* 27 March 1775 and 19 February 1776; Sanger (1987:
31–32); *Vermont Gazette,* 13 March 1784; and Town of Guilford, Vermont (1961: 93–94). On Shays' Rebellion, see Szatmary (1980: 102–
103, 111); Feer (1988: 363–368, 402–404); *Connecticut Journal,* 13, 20,
and 27 September and 18 October 1786, 31 January, 28 February, and
7 and 14 March 1787; and *Boston Gazette,* 5 March 1787.
11. F. S. Fox (2000: xiv–xv), Pencak (2002: 109–115), Hutson (1972: 41–
243), and Nash (1979: 282–290).
12. Frantz and Pencak (1998: 134–135, 171–193); F. S. Fox (2000: 59–60);
Pencak (2002: 114); Pencak and Richter (2004: 201–220, 238–257);
Connecticut Courant, 28 July and 8 September 1766; and *Connecticut Journal,* 19 February 1768.
13. Frantz and Pencak (1998: 112–113). See also the murder of J. Smith,
Connecticut Journal, 6 and 13 October 1769.

14. Frantz and Pencak (1998: 133–170), Pencak and Richter (2004: 221–237), and Pencak (2002: 146). See also the murder of Nathan Ogden, *Connecticut Journal,* 26 July 1771.

15. Pencak (2002: 121–133).

16. Rosswurm (1987: 205–222), Frantz and Pencak (1998: xix–xxiv, 18–19, 46–132), F. S. Fox (2000: 14–31), and Pencak (2002: 121–133). Even the conflict between Federalists and anti-Federalists over the constitution in 1787–88 led to political homicides in the mid-Atlantic states (Waldstreicher 1997: 12, 95, 97).

17. Eckenrode (1916: 240–241, 246–248) and Palmer, McRae, and Colston (1875–1893, 1: 534 and 2: 40, 285).

18. Hast (1982: 140–141) and Palmer, McRae, and Colston (1875–1893, 2: 339–340 and 3: 161–162).

19. On Philips, see Hast (1982: 96–99, 115), Eckenrode (1916: 180–184, 257–258, 282), and McIlwaine (1926–1929, 1: 267–268, 282–283, 300, 308). On Tory gangs in Pennsylvania, see Palmer, McRae, and Colston (1875–1893, 2: 151, 189–190); Frantz and Pencak (1998: 19, 38–39, 42–43); and *Connecticut Journal,* 17 September 1783. On Connecticut, see inquest on John Baker Otis and John Bowen, 24 December 1775, Connecticut Superior Court files, Litchfield County, Papers by Subject, Inquests, box 300, Connecticut State Library, Hartford; *Connecticut Courant,* 27 October 1772; *Boston Newsletter,* 29 October 1772; *Connecticut Journal,* 1 January and 3 September 1773 and 25 August 1779; Connecticut Archives, Crimes and Misdemeanors, Ser. 1, 5: 408, Connecticut State Library; and Connecticut Superior Court files, New London County, Papers by Subject, Inquests, c. 1711–1875, N–Z, box 135, Connecticut State Library.

20. On the Davenports, see *Connecticut Journal,* 16 February 1780; and Hearn (1999: 162–164). See also the killing of a man named Sympson, Suffolk Files 158161; and of unknown men, *Boston Newsletter,* 5 March 1772; and *Connecticut Journal,* 27 October 1779. On robbery homicides, see *Connecticut Journal,* 3 May, 3 September, and 21 November 1787 and 17 September 1788; *Connecticut Courant,* 1 October 1792; *Potowmac Guardian and Berkeley Advertiser* (Martinsburg, Va.), 28 August 1796; and *Norfolk Herald* (Va.), 1 June 1799. Between 1770 and 1797, 42 of the 81 homicides among unrelated European Americans for which the weapon was known were committed with guns. AHSV (2009: Weapons).

21. Amelia County (Va.) Court Order Book, 13: 28 and 14: 41, 279–281; and *Connecticut Courant,* 1 October 1792.

22. Frantz and Pencak (1998: 42). See also the murder of David Mussel-

man, *Connecticut Journal*, 18 July and 8 August 1787; of Henry Hamilton, *Connecticut Gazette*, 3 December 1763; of John Coulton, *Connecticut Journal*, 29 July 1768; of Timothy McAuliffe, *Connecticut Journal*, 22 September 1784; of an unknown person, *Connecticut Journal*, 25 April 1785; of Andrew Pollard, *Connecticut Journal*, 3 August 1785; and of Joseph Dudley, *Connecticut Journal*, 20 August 1788. On deadly brawls, see *Connecticut Journal*, 1 March 1775 and 24 August 1785.

23. Rosswurm (1987: 36) and Fenn (2001: 41–42).

24. Waldstreicher (1997: 1–245).

25. W. D. Jordan (1969: 315–569).

26. Zelinsky (1988: 124–125), Waldstreicher (1997: 246–348), Onuf (1996), and Cayton (2000).

27. Gallay (2002: 160 and 388n16) and Coleman (1976: 234). Gamble (1923: 1–8) notes that duels also occurred among British officers in Savannah during King George's War. See Stevens (1940: 9–14) on the rarity of duels in colonial America. On the Phillips duel, see Suffolk Files 21897; *Boston Newsletter*, 4 July 1728; and J. Sewall (1728).

28. J. Sewall (1728).

29. Baird (1999: 96).

30. Baird (1999: 88–90) and Steward (2000: 10–12).

31. *Boston Newsletter*, 3 October 1765. See also Stevens (1940: 16–17).

32. Hughes (2006), J. Kelly (1995: 94, 97, 128, 139–147, 167–173), Freeman (2001), Baird (1999: 95–97, 101–102), and Steward (2000).

33. Baird (1999: 98), Freeman (2001: 169), and *Farmer's Library* (Rutland, Vt.), 4 November and 2 and 23 December 1793. See also Freeman (2001: xiii, 32–34, 158, 167–171, 181–187), Steward (2000: 10–12, 21–22, 24–40, 75–78), and K. S. Greenberg (1996: 16–23).

34. Coleman (1976: 280), Fleming (1999: 7–9, 283–331), and Chernow (2004: 650–656, 680–709). McIntosh worried about extending voting rights to poor white men and giving too much power to frontier counties, but he, unlike Gwinnett, was an opponent of slavery. See Frey (1991: 54), W. D. Jordan (1969: 301), and Gamble (1923: 9–22).

35. Beeman (1985), Ekirch (1981: 161–202), Lefler and Newsome (1973: 217–239), R. N. Klein (1990: 9–77), R. M. Brown (1963: 36–37), and Cashin (1985).

36. E. G. Evans (1985: 188, 194, 196, 202), L. P. Summers (1966: 273–278, 292–294), and Eckenrode (1916: 234–236).

37. Cashin (1985) and Writers' Program of the Works Progress Administration (1941: 23–24).

38. Chapman (1897: 13, 31–34, 67–70), Lambert (1987), Pancake (1985), Weigley (1970), R. N. Klein (1990: 78–108), and Dann (1980: 174–233).

39. Chapman (1897: 39–41).

40. Writers' Program of the Work Projects Administration (1941: 31–32, 36) and *Augusta Chronicle,* 14 June 1794.

41. R. S. Davis (1979: 172) and *Georgia State Gazette* (Augusta), 26 May 1787.

42. Wilkes County (Ga.) Superior Court minutes, 1795–1798: 37, 117; *Augusta Chronicle,* 8 July 1787; and State v. John Neal and Julian Neal, October 1800 term, Franklin County (Ga.) Court files, 159-1-41, box 1, and 159-1-59, box 5, Georgia Department of History and Archives, Atlanta.

43. Faragher (1992: 249–250), Bonner (1978: 1–9), Green (1982: 29–36), and Saunt (1999: 67–110).

44. Harrison and Klotter (1997: 55–64) and Abernethy (1932: 64–102).

45. Abernethy (1961: 136–168; 1932: 1–143, 164–193).

46. Faragher (1992: 106–140, 238–242, 245–249, 263) and Harrison and Klotter (1997: 16–17, 24–29, 52–55).

47. On the homicide by Allen, see *Augusta Chronicle,* 18 January and 1 and 15 March 1794; and Chapman (1897: 290–291); and of Thomas, *Augusta Chronicle,* 26 September 1795. On antigovernment feeling, see *Augusta Chronicle,* 23 August and 6, 13, and 30 September 1794; 21 March and 4 July 1795; and 27 February 1796.

48. On homicides in Georgia, see Bonner (1978: 9). On the murder of Benjamin Townsend, see *Georgia State Gazette,* 26 July 1788; of John London, *Augusta Chronicle,* 5 and 12 April 1806; of Frederick Snider, *Georgia State Gazette,* 22 December 1787 and 19 January 1788; and of William Dobey, *Augusta Chronicle,* 12 and 26 August 1797. On homicides in Ohio, see inquest on Robert Shaw, 26 July 1813, Ross County (Ohio) coroner's inquests; *Western Spy and Hamilton Gazette* (Cincinnati), 3 June 1801; *Scioto Gazette and Chillicothe Advertiser* (Ohio), 21 and 28 May 1801; 2 January and 7 and 21 May 1804; and 5 September 1810.

49. Newton (1889: 87–88, 90).

50. Mason (1915: 26–27) and Erwin (1914: 15–16, 92–97).

51. *Georgia State Gazette,* 1 and 22 March and 2 August 1788.

52. Rothert (1924: 60, 136).

53. Rothert (1924: 157–171).

54. A. Taylor (1990: 115–121, 188–203, 264–270).

55. Dean Trial (1808); *Farmer's Cabinet,* 20 January 1812 and 4 December 1813; Dutcher (1872: 293–296); *Green Mountain Farmer* (Bennington), 7 October 1812 and 17 July 1813; *Vermont Mirror* (Middlebury), 15 September 1813; *Dover Sun* (N.H.), 20 November 1813; inquest on John Dennett, 9 October 1813, Caledonia County (Vt.) Court files; and Stratton (1984: 51–55).

56. Hemenway (1868–1891, 2: 370–372, 375–376).

57. AHSV (2009: AH, table 21) and Hart (1942: 102–113).

58. Hart (1942: 83–101) and McIlwaine (1926–1929, 3: 157–158). Hart reports that the county enlisted 868 men in the Continental army to meet government levies, not including men enlisted by recruiting officers.

59. Hart (1942: 180–187).

60. On murders of blacks, see Connecticut Superior Court records, 22: 300–301, Connecticut State Library; Suffolk Files 106227 and 160036; *Boston Gazette*, 1 July 1793; *Boston Newsletter*, 8 and 15 March 1770; and *Connecticut Journal*, 15 August 1787.

61. AHSV (2009: AH, table 12). See, for example, inquest on Jack, 11 March 1786, Surry County (Va.) Court files; and Henrico County (Va.) Court Order Book, 1794–1796: 217–218.

62. Sweet (1995: 303–304); Frey (1991: 51–53, 57–65); Hadden (2001: 137, 142); Schwarz (1988: 165–190); P. D. Morgan (2002: 159); Crow (1980: 93–94); and *Georgia State Gazette*, 28 October 1786 and 13 January, 19 May, and 16 June 1787.

63. Dann (1980: 183, 240, 244–245) and D. O. White (1973: 28–29).

64. Quarles (1961: ix, 94) and D. O. White (1973: 7–8).

65. W. D. Jordan (1969: 260–304, especially 276, 281, 293) and Schwarz (1988: 11, 24–26, 61–65).

66. Sweet (1995: 193–204) and Crow (1980: 79–80).

67. Frey (1991: 51), Sweet (1995: 343), and Dann (1980: 26–28).

68. Frey (1991: 45–107) and Crow (1980: 86–89).

69. On New England, see Plummer (1795) and *Salem Gazette* (Mass.), 17 February and 11 August 1795. On Virginia, see AHSV (2009: AH, table 14); *Virginia Gazette*, 6 November 1778; and Schwarz (1988: 146–149).

70. Frey (1991: 81–107) and Egerton (1993).

5. The Emergence of Regional Differences

1. In New York City the rate declined to 6 per 100,000 adults per year, in Cincinnati to 4 per 100,000, in Boston and Cleveland to 2 per 100,000, and in the rural Midwest to 2 to 3 per 100,000. Nondomestic homicide rates between the War of 1812 and the late 1840s ranged from 0.6 per 100,000 adults per year in Holmes County, Ohio; to 2.2 per 100,000 in Henderson County, Illinois; 2.7 per 100,000 in Ross County, Ohio; 3.3 per 100,000 in Williamson County, Illinois; and 6.1 per 100,000 in Calhoun County, Illinois. In northern New England the rate fell to less than 1 per 100,000.

2. AHSV (2009: American Homicides [AH], tables 22–25). In mountain

counties, nondomestic homicide rates between the War of 1812 and the late 1840s ranged from zero per 100,000 adults in Gilmer and Rabin counties in Georgia (once the removal of the Cherokees was complete) to 4.3 per 100,000 in Taney County, Missouri. Homicide rates have not yet been determined for any slaveholding counties in the Mississippi Valley or along the Gulf Coast, except for Florida.

3. On duels, see, for example, Lloyd (1807) and Selfridge (1807). On homicides in ports, see Gilje (1996: 65); *Boston Gazette,* 27 September 1779 and 10 November 1783; *Connecticut Journal,* 11 January 1781; Suffolk Files 103257, Massachusetts Archives, Boston; and Genealogical Committee, Georgia Historical Society (1983–1989), 1: the deaths of Johannes Marten and Richard Caryer; 2: the deaths of Nathaniel Putnam, Jonathan Cox, Michael Kellock, Laurence Nelson; and 3: the deaths of Jacob R. Taylor, John Collins, Pierre Scipion, Cherie Shaddock, Timothy Lewis, James Morris, and Daniel Mason.

4. Cayton (2002: 5–6, 39), S. Williams (1794: vii–viii), and Lemon (2002: xxiii).

5. S. White (1991: 207) and G. R. Hodges (1999: 187–189).

6. Zelinsky (1988: 119–143).

7. F. S. Fox (2000: xvii–xviii).

8. Montgomery (1967: 25–31), Wilentz (1984: 61–103), and Roth (1987: 117–141).

9. *New York Tribune,* 19 July 1841; and inquest on Margaret Dix, Adlow Manuscripts, 110, Boston Public Library. See also the murder of Johanna Sweeney, *New York Tribune,* 29 May 1844; and of James Cloudsley, *New York Tribune,* 29 July 1844. On life in tenement neighborhoods, see Anbinder (2002: 14–140).

10. Gorn (1986: 34–97), Gilje (1987: 260–264), Asbury (1998: 1–56), Wilentz (1984: 259–263, 269–270, 300), Anbinder (2002: 30–31), and Tager (2001: 120–124). See the murder of James Doyle, *New York Tribune,* 10 October 1843; of Daniel McNeil, *New York Tribune,* 5 and 6 April 1844; of Daniel Carman, *New York Tribune,* 21 June 1844; and of William Deshayes, *New York Tribune,* 28 and 29 April 1846.

11. Gilje (1987: 95–264; 1996: 64–84, 87–91) and Grimsted (1998: 3–82). See also Melish (1998: 201–208), Gilje (1996: 66–67, 71–72, 76), and Anbinder (2002: 7–13, 145–158).

12. Gilje (1996: 60–64, 68; 1987: 3–92), Ignatiev (1995: 125–133, 151–153), Feldberg (1975), Nash (1988: 273–274), and Grimsted (1998: 203–204).

13. Hearn (1997: 38, 40; 1999: 217–218) and Diary of Arthur Bennett, 20 and 21 May 1844, American Antiquarian Society, Worcester, Mass.

For murders by felony convicts, see Reynolds (1834: 33–48); Godfrey (1818); Savage (1873: 61, 81); Hearn (1999: 208–209, 224–225); *Rutland Herald,* 29 June 1824; and Hemenway (1868–1891, 2: 298).

14. Whitcher (1909).

15. See the murder of Briggs, J. C. Williams (1869: 216–217) and *Rutland Herald,* 13 January 1824; and of Small, *Farmer's Cabinet,* 11 September 1840. See also Hearn (1997: 38, 40, 43–44; 1999: 217–219, 224–226).

16. See the murder by Wheeler, Thorpe (1911: 185–188); and by Hall, *Rutland Herald,* 27 October 1835.

17. AHSV (2009: Weapons); Erwin (1914: 97–98); *New Hampshire Patriot,* 3 November 1834; and *Farmer's Cabinet,* 26 September 1834.

18. Montgomery (1967: 25–31), Wilentz (1984: 107–142), and Roth (1987: 117–141).

19. Roth (1987), H. Watson (1990), and Pessen (1978).

20. P. E. Johnson (1978), Ryan (1981), and Roth (1987: 80–116, 187–264).

21. W. B. Parker (1924: 14) and Vermont Historical Society (1984).

22. Ira Hoffman to Henry Hoffman, 28 February 1848, Vermont Historical Society Library, Barre.

23. Gilje (1996: 24–59).

24. Black (1912: 165, 172–175).

25. Black (1912: 172–175), Brumbaugh (1927: 28–65), and Rose (1906).

26. Blacks were victimized at a rate of 6.7 per 100,000 adults per year in New York City, 1815–1843, and whites at a rate of 6.5 per 100,000. According to less complete data on individual homicides, 1823–1843, blacks committed homicide at a rate of 4.7 per 100,000 adults per year versus 4.3 for whites. In Philadelphia, according to indictments, blacks were victimized at a rate of 3.7 per 100,000 adults per year, 1839–1846, and whites at a rate of 2.9 per 100,000. On drunken quarrels, see Philadelphia indictments, March 1841 term, no. 4; November 1843 term, no. 4; March 1845 term, no. 1, Philadelphia City Archives; on robbery homicides, Philadelphia indictments, November 1840 term, no. 4; March 1844 term, no. 12; on interracial homicides, Philadelphia indictments, March 1844 term, no. 15, and November 1841 term, no. 11; and on the Flying Horse Riot, Ignatiev (1995: 125–133), Nash (1988: 273–274), and Grimsted (1998: 203–204).

27. *Rutland Herald,* 30 November 1819 and 1 February 1820; and Hemenway (1868–1891, 2: 298). It may prove that blacks accounted for a greater proportion of homicide perpetrators than victims in Philadelphia, but determining that will require more data, including a tally of blacks and whites killed in riots. Blacks committed homicide there at over twice the rate whites did, 1839–1846, according to indictment records (6.5 per 100,000 adults per year versus 2.7), because they were

more likely to commit both intraracial and interracial homicide. It may be that Philadelphia's antiblack riots, the disfranchisement of blacks in Pennsylvania, and increased competition with whites for unskilled jobs were beginning to take their toll.

28. Ignatiev (1995: 34–59). For an estimate of the proportions of homicide victims and assailants in northern New England who were Irish, see AHSV (2009: Ethnicity Estimates). In Calhoun, Henderson, and Williamson counties in Illinois, 1812–1853, none of the 7 known homicide assailants or victims were Irish. In Ross and Holmes Counties in Ohio, only 2 of 39 known homicide victims were Irish, 1798–1846, and none of the assailants. The homicide rate in Ireland, 1805–1814, was at least 4 per 100,000 adults per year in Ulster, 5 per 100,000 in central Ireland, 6 per 100,000 in Dublin, and 14 per 100,000 in southwestern Ireland. However, Ireland's homicide rate probably fell in the 1830s and early 1840s to about 3 or 4 per 100,000 adults per year on the eve of the famine of 1845–1850. AHSV (2009: European Homicides [EH], figs. 3 and 8).

29. Gilje (1996: 66) and Conley (1999: 20–24).

30. *Burlington Free Press,* 1 October 1841 and 27 March 1846; *Vermont Chronicle* (Windsor), 18 March 1846; and Conley (1999: 17–50).

31. K. A. Miller (1985: 169–279, especially 202–204) and Miller et al. (2003: 536–627).

32. K. A. Miller (1985: 203).

33. On the Irish homicide rate in New York City, 1823–1846, see AHSV (2009: Ethnicity Estimates); Philadelphia indictments, September term 1844, nos. 2, 7, 8, and 11; and Feldberg (1975). On the homicide rate in contemporary Ireland, see AHSV (2009: EH, fig. 8).

34. Ignatiev (1995).

35. Ward (1965: 197, 207) and R. S. Davis (1982–1987, 1: 146). The mountain South, as defined here, does not include all of Appalachia, as most historians define it. It includes only the most mountainous regions, which Salstrom (1995: 77–78) defines as "intermediate" and "newer" Appalachia, and J. A. Williams (2002: 13) defines as the Blue Ridge or the Allegheny/Cumberland region. It excludes areas in the southern highlands where plantation slavery was firmly established, such as the Great Valley, which extended from the Shenandoah Valley to northwestern Georgia. See Inscoe (1989, 1995) on the importance of slavery in the larger towns and more fertile valleys of Appalachia. In Georgia, the mountain South includes Fannin, Gilmer, Pickens, Rabun, Town, and Union counties, which were 97 percent white in 1850 and 96 percent white in 1860.

The mountain counties considered in this study include Gilmer and

Rabun Counties in Georgia, where no homicides were reported among black or white settlers from the pioneer period to the late 1840s; Cabell County, West Virginia, 1816, 1826–1835, and Greenbriar County, West Virginia, 1817–1822, 1827–1838, where only 2 examinations for homicide were held (Stinson 1988; Eldridge 1994, 1995)—a rate of 2 per 100,000 adults per year; Taney County, Missouri, where only 3 homicides were reported by McConkey (1887: 38) between 1832 and 1860—a rate of 4 per 100,000 adults per year; and a four-county area on the Kentucky-Tennessee border studied by Montell (1986: 8–9), where no homicides were reported before the 1850s.

36. Dunaway (1995, 1996), Mann (1995: 132–146), J. A. Williams (2002: 68–77, 109–118), R. B. Drake (2001: 68–74, 80–92), Salstrom (1994, 1995), Waller (1988: 19–29), and Montell (1986: 8–9). J. A. Williams (2002: 134–153) notes, however, that slaveholders who lived in towns or on plantations near the mountains dominated politics and the economy in the backcountry.

37. Komlos and Coclanis (1997), Steckel (1991), J. A. Williams (2002: 157–168), and R. B. Drake (2001: 85–95). The data on land ownership are from the samples of the free population in counties in northern Georgia in 1850 and 1860 in the Integrated Public Use Microdata Series, Minnesota Population Center, University of Minnesota. The mountain counties included Fannin, Gilmer, Pickens, Rabun, Towns, and Union. See J. A. Williams (2002: 125–134) on opportunities outside agriculture.

38. Ayers (1984: 34–72), Rousey (1996: 11–39), Hadden (2001: 1–166), and AHSV (2009: AH, tables 22–25). The rates for plantation counties varied widely. The data on homicide indictments in Granville, Montgomery, and Orange counties in North Carolina, 1830–1860, are from Bynum (1992: 82). Montgomery County was different from every other southern county studied to date: it had only one indictment for homicide in the period, for a rate of 1 per 100,000 adults per year. Granville had 23 indictments against free persons, for a rate of 12 per 100,000 adults per year; and Orange had 20 indictments, for a rate of 8 per 100,000. Together the rate for the three counties was comparable to those in Virginia and in Franklin, Jasper, and Wilkes Counties in Georgia.

Data on indictments in Greene and Whitfield counties in Georgia, 1850–1860, are from Ayers (1984: 115). Greene had a homicide indictment rate of 17 per 100,000 adults per year and Whitfield a rate of 21 per 100,000. Horry County, a rice-growing county on the South Carolina coast, had a homicide rate of at least 23 per 100,000 adults per year for blacks and 30 per 100,000 for whites, 1849–1863 (Horry

County [S.C.] Inquest Book, 1849–1874, South Caroliniana Library, University of South Carolina). It may prove that rice-growing counties were more violent than grain-, tobacco-, and cotton-growing counties. Much remains to be learned about variation in homicide rates within regions and between blacks and whites.

The data on homicide examinations in Frederick County, Maryland, are from Rice (1994: 34, 100). The data cover the years 1748–1837 rather than the period after the Revolution, but the rate over the entire period is comparable to those in plantation counties in Virginia and North Carolina, which is why it is reported here.

39. Abernethy (1961: 427) and Sydnor (1948: ix).
40. Egerton (1993: 163) and W. D. Jordan (1969: 561).
41. Schwarz (1988: 267), Mathews (1977: 136–184), Crow (1980: 90–91), Peterson (1975: 567–569), J. A. Williams (2002: 155), and Jefferson (1904, 16: 8–13).
42. Franklin (1961: 76).
43. W. D. Jordan (1969: 491–494, 573–582) and Fredrickson (1971: 43–70).
44. On evangelical churches, see Mathews (1965: 3–29; 1977: 66–80). Antislavery sentiment remained strong among Quakers and evangelicals in a few places, like northern Southampton County, Virginia (Crofts 1992: 90–96). On the political crusade to defend slavery, see W. D. Jordan (1969: 347–349, 399–422), Sidbury (1997: 32–35), Crow (1980: 91–93), Hinks (1997: xiv–xvi), Mathews (1977: 185–236), and D. B. Davis (1975: 326–342). Legislators from nonslaveholding areas in western Virginia opposed many of the initiatives of the defenders of slavery, including their efforts to block voluntary emancipations and to restrict the rights of free blacks (V. B. Hall 1991). On measures to improve slave patrols and increase surveillance over free blacks, see W. D. Jordan (1969: 399, 403–406), Egerton (1993: 163–173), Hadden (2001: 17–66), and Rousey (1996: 11–39).
45. Egerton (1993: 69–94, 119–146; 1999: 229–232), Sidbury (1997: 118–147), Schwarz (1988: 257–260, 269, 271–272, 324–330), Strickland (1982), Wyatt-Brown (1982: 427–434), Aptheker (1969: 256n31), and M. P. Johnson (2001).
46. D. Walker (1965: 70), Hinks (1997: 116–172), and Grimsted (1998: 138–139).
47. Grimsted (1998: 136–144) and Oates (1975: 96, 98–101, 106–107).
48. Shore (1982) and Grimsted (1998: 144–156).
49. Denham and Roth (2007: 225) and AHSV (2009: AH, tables 22 and 24).
50. AHSV (2009: Weapons).

51. Amelia County (Va.) Court Order Book, 27 July 1815 and 24 March 1825; and inquest on the body of Tom, 20 June 1815, Amelia County Court files. See also Amelia County Court Order Book, 25 September and 1 October 1823.

52. Rockbridge County (Va.) Court Order Book, 1804–1805: 415–421.

53. Rockbridge County Court Order Book, 1846–1848: 212; and *Lexington Gazette,* 3 June 1847.

54. Edgefield County (S.C.) Coroner's Book of Inquisitions, 1859–1868: 39–40, South Caroliniana Library; Oates (1975: 132–133); and Grimsted (1998: 122).

55. AHSV (2009: AH, tables 23 and 25).

56. Wyatt-Brown (1982), Ayers (1984), K. S. Greenberg (1996), Longstreet (1992: 35), Denham and Huneycutt (2004: 126), and Denham and Brown (2000: 46).

57. Rockbridge County Court Order Book, 1840–1843, 28 October and 3 November 1842; and Amelia County Court Order Book, 2 December 1828.

58. State v. Richard V. Gregory, October 1836 term, Jasper County (Ga.) Court files; and State v. Turner Horton, October 1838 term, ibid.

59. On homicides over games of chance or strength, see inquest on Thomas Shelly, 17 March 1814, Surry County (Va.) Court files; *New Hampshire Patriot,* 30 July 1821; *Lexington Gazette,* 9 October 1835 and 23 November 1854; State v. Samuel McDaniel, April 1834 term, Jasper County Court files; State v. David V. Palmer, October 1838 term, ibid.; State v. Jefferson Clay et al., April 1843 term, ibid.; State v. John Hoard, October 1844 term, ibid.; *Union Recorder,* 17 January 1854; and Edgefield County Coroner's Book of Inquisitions, 1851–1859: 2–5, 121–122; 1859–1868: 35–36. On homicides over property, see Grimsted (1998: 88); Edgefield County Coroner's Book of Inquisitions, 1844–1850: 17–20, 25–28, 49–52; 1851–1859: 34–36, 152–158; and 1859–1868: 51–52; Rockbridge County Court Order Book, 1802–03, 22 November 1802, and 1807–1809, 9 and 10 November 1807; Amelia County Court Order Book, 1825–1827, 28 July and 25 August 1825; and *Lexington Gazette,* 24 August 1838.

60. Longstreet (1992: 224–229).

61. Steward (2000), J. K. Williams (1980), Bruce (1979), and Gamble (1923).

62. Writers' Program of the Works Progress Administration (1941: 47–48) and Franklin (1961: 50).

63. Shade (1996: 222), Stevens (1940: 84–86), Franklin (1961: 57–58), Oates (1975: 136–139), Crofts (1992: 118–119), and Ayers (1984: 114).

See also *Augusta Chronicle*, 11 September 1802; *Virginia Telegraphe* (Lexington), 26 April 1803; and *Lexington News-Letter* (Va.), 20 March 1819.

64. K. S. Greenberg (1985).

65. *Lexington News-Letter*, 17 April 1819; and *American Constellation* (Petersburg, Va.), 22 July 1834. See also *Daily Republican* (Petersburg, Va.), 2, 5, 12, and 26 April 1843; and Franklin (1961: 55–56).

66. *Burlington Free Press*, 29 March 1839.

67. Franklin (1961: 36–39), Stevens (1940: 111–128), and Wyatt-Brown (1982: 359–360).

68. Longstreet (1992: 61, 197).

69. MacIntyre (1923, 1: 8–9), Morris (1995: 121–131), Gilje (1996: 82), and Grimsted (1998: 103).

70. For interregional comparisons of the number of deaths that resulted from collective violence, see Grimsted (1998) and R. M. Brown (1975).

71. Ignatiev (1995: 125–133).

72. G. W. Harris (1987: 20–28, 134–148), Mayfield (2000), and Grimsted (1998: 105–107).

73. Grimsted (1998: 87–88, 92–93).

74. Stevens (1940: 38–41, 46, 79, 90–91), Cramer (1999: 57, 60, 79, 105, 113–114, 117), and Steward (2000: 79–99).

75. AHSV (2009: Weapons).

76. Cramer (1999: 76, 84, 111, 121, 132) and Jasper County Superior Court minutes, Grand Jury presentments, March 1808, October 1833, April 1834.

77. Cramer (1999: 1–8, 47–142). The South Carolina legislature did not pass a concealed-weapons law, but it received numerous petitions on behalf of such a law (Grimsted 1998: 97).

78. Wyatt-Brown (1982: 364–365), Franklin (1961: vii, ix, xi), and Ayers (1984: 17).

79. Cusick (2003: 174–177, 303–304).

80. Baptist (2002: 46–47, 53–58, 91–96, 111–119, 159–165) and Doherty (1949). These political practices and their economic consequences were not uncommon on the postrevolutionary frontier (Abernethy 1932).

81. Denham and Roth (2007); *St. Joseph Times* (Fla.), 21 April 1840; *Jacksonville Florida News*, 3 and 10 October 1846; and *Tallahassee Florida Sentinel*, 11 and 18 August 1846.

82. Denham and Roth (2007). On property disputes, see the murder of Wildman Hines, Jefferson County (Fla.) Court files, 1838, Jefferson County Circuit Court, Monticello, Fla.; of Felix Livingston, *Jacksonville*

Florida News, 14 April 1855; and of Peter Alba, *St. Augustine Florida Herald,* 31 October 1833. On fights among political leaders, see Doherty (1961: 16–92) and Baptist (2002: 120–125, 151–153). The same pattern of violence appeared among political leaders in Missouri during the territorial period. The violence abated, as it did in Florida, when a two-party system developed (Steward 2000: 41–78, 116–132).

83. AHSV (2009: Weapons).

84. Baptist (2002: 158, 154–190), Mahon (1967), and Doherty (1961: 93–117).

85. Doherty (1959) and A. W. Thompson (1961).

86. Oates (1975: 55–56).

87. AHSV (2009: AH, tables 23 and 25). On stealth murders, see *Augusta Chronicle,* 13 June and 4 July 1807; *Virginia Telegraphe,* 10 February 1820; and Schwarz (1988: 237).

88. *Augusta Chronicle,* 2 and 9 August 1806; Lancaster County (Va.) Court Order Book, 14 May 1804; and Wilkes County (Ga.) Superior Court minutes, September 1851 term. See also Bynum (1992: 114–116); Horry County Inquest Book, 1849–1874: 5; Jasper County Superior Court minutes, July 1854 term; and Edgefield County Coroner's Book of Inquisitions, 1851–1859: 82.

89. Schwarz (1988: 46, 237, 239). See also inquisition on William Woodram, 8 February 1820, Henrico County (Va.) coroner's inquests, Library of Virginia, Richmond.

90. Denham and Roth (2007: 225) and AHSV (2009: AH, tables 22 and 24).

91. State vs. Bill, April 1860 term, Jasper County Court files. See also *Rockbridge Intelligencer,* 22 March 1827; Edgefield County Coroner's Book of Inquisitions, 1851–1859: 10–12, 33–34; 1859–1868: 60–61; and Butterfield (1995: 32).

92. *Lexington News and Gazette,* 27 December 1865.

93. Schwarz (1988: 250–251). See also Rockbridge County Court Order Book, 1852–1854: 189, 196–202.

94. Hodges (1999: 190–191) and Hadden (2001: 162–165).

95. Wyatt-Brown (1982: 398–399), MacIntyre (1923, 1: 14–15), and *Augusta Chronicle,* 24 January and 9 and 16 May 1807. See also Henrico County coroner's inquests, 17 August 1807, 2 September 1810, 25 March 1812, and 22 March and 26 December 1822.

96. Franklin County (Ga.) Superior Court minutes, September 1853 term; State v. Lank, Jerry, and Daniel, September 1853 term, Franklin County Court files, Record Group 159-1-41, boxes 9, 14, and 18, Georgia Department of History and Archives, Atlanta. See also Simmons

(1984: 3893–3895) and Lancaster County Court Order Book, 15 May 1828.

97. AHSV (2009: AH, tables 22 and 23). In addition to the data on Amelia, Lancaster, Rockbridge, and Surry counties, data on homicide trials of slaves are available for Henry, Southampton, and Spotsylvania counties, courtesy of Philip Schwarz.

98. Shade (1996: 194–203, 297–298), Crofts (1992: 108–110), French (2004: 51–60), and Freehling (1982).

99. Perdue, Barden, and Phillips (1976: 74–77); M. K. Davis (2003); Crofts (1992: 17); Oates (1975: 55–56, 82); Parramore (2003: 61–62); and P. H. Breen (2003).

100. J. A. Williams (2002: 126) and Oates (1975: 105, 109).

101. French (2004: 85).

102. Oates (1975: 134).

103. French (2004: 81–86) and Perdue, Barden, and Phillips (1976: 74–77).

104. Oates (1975: 113).

105. Surry County (Va.) Court Minute Book, 5 September 1831; and deposition of Dick, 26 September 1831, Surry County Court files.

106. French (2004: 60–64).

107. *Lexington Gazette*, 7 January 1841.

108. Weber (1982, 1992), Hamnett (1986), and Van Young (2001).

109. The data on homicides are from Langum (1987: 56–96) and Monkkonen (2005). In Monterey, Langum found 6 homicides among unrelated adults, 1841–1846. On the basis of an assumed adult population of 2,100, the homicide rate in Monterey was at least 48 per 100,000 adults per year. In Los Angeles, Monkkonen found 26 homicides among unrelated adults, 1830–1846. On the basis of an assumed adult population of 2,100, the homicide rate in Los Angeles was at least 73 per 100,000 adults per year, 1830–1846. On the Sacramento Valley, see G. H. Phillips (1993: 117–134) and Hurtado (1988: 47–71).

110. See Mocho (1997) on homicides that came before the territorial courts in New Mexico. Fewer homicides appear to have reached the territorial court in New Mexico than reached the local courts in California, but the rate at which cases appeared rose at the same rate in New Mexico's territorial court as in local courts in Monterey and Los Angeles, California. Mocho reports no trials for murders among unrelated adults in 1830–1835, 2 in 1836–1840, and 6 in 1841–1846. Langum (1987: 56–96) reports no murders among unrelated adults in Monterey in 1830–1835, 1 in 1836–1840, and 7 in 1841–1846. Monkkonen (2005) reports 4 murders among unrelated adults in 1830–1835, 7 in 1836–1840, and 15 in 1841–1846. The estimate for south

Texas is an educated guess based on the abundant anecdotal evidence of homicide. A precise rate has not yet been determined.

111. Weber (1992: 326–333), O. L. Jones (1979: 51, 148, 164–165, 238, 246–248), and Tijerina (1994: 5–24).

112. Mocho (1997: ix–xii, 4–6), Griswold del Castillo (1979: 10–13), Hurtado (1988: 14–31, 55–71), and Weber (1992: 304–308; 1982: 188–190).

113. Mocho (1997: ix–xii, 4–6).

114. Weber (1982: 207–241).

115. Mocho (1997: 98–106, 84–96). See also Langum (1987: 65).

116. Mocho (1997: 40–49).

117. Langum (1987: 79–80), Bancroft (1884–1890, 3: 638), and Weber (1992: 303).

118. McKanna (1997: 56–57), Mocho (1997: 74–83), and G. H. Phillips (1980: 438–439). M. C. Gutmann (2007: 221–242) cautions against attributing such violent behavior to *machismo,* a cultural concept that appeared belatedly in the 1940s and 1950s. As Gutmann notes, *machismo* is a stereotype, not an explanation of violent behavior or of its incidence over time.

119. Langum (1987: 80), Bancroft (1884–1890, 4: 629–630), and Mocho (1997: 122–156).

120. Weber (1982: 15–42) and Tijerina (1994: 125–136).

121. Weber (1982: 40–42) and Tijerina (1994: 130–132).

122. Weber (1982: 255–260).

123. Lecompte (1985) and Weber (1982: 261–266).

124. Campbell (2003: 131–133), Weber (1982: 242–255), and Tijerina (1994: 113–136; 1996: 33–47).

125. Horsman (1981), Crisp (1976), Campbell (2003: 132), Weber (1992: 337–341), and De León (1983: 1–13).

126. Tijerina (1994: 124; 1996: 43–46) and S. L. Hardin (1996).

127. Campbell (2003: 131–133, 170, 177–181), Weber (1982: 245–255), and Utley (2002: 39–40, 52–56).

128. Lack (1996: 94).

129. On homicides related to slavery, see Campbell (2003: 166, 171, 175, 182) and Grimsted (1998: 105, 107–111, 309n53, 310n61). On violence involving Native Americans, see G. H. Phillips (1993: 76–134), Lecompte (1985: 3–11), Weber (1982: 97), Campbell (2003: 169–173), F. T. Smith (2000: 111–134), and Himmel (1999: 3–92).

130. Eisner (2001: 629), H. Brown (2006: 303–358), Chesnais (1982: 76), Gould (2003: 155–158), and AHSV (2009: EH, figs. 4 and 5). On politi-

cal homicides and the contest between revolutionary and counterrevolutionary forces, see Cobban (1965, 2: 71–227).

131. On enfranchisement rates for voting for lower houses of representative institutions in Europe, 1815–1914, see Goldstein (1983: 4–5).

132. Oliver (1998: 31). On the different ways in which nations could build a sense of nationality, see Potter (1968).

133. Bumsted (1992, 1: 231–257, 317–327).

134. Bumsted (1992, 1: 317–319, 326–327).

135. Emsley (1996: 41–44), Philips (1977: 253–261), and Conley (1991: 49, 53–54, 55–56, and 60). In Figure 5.11 the number of known homicides, 1810–1867, is extrapolated from the number of committals for homicide. For the period 1868–1914, figures for both known homicides and homicide committals are available. The mean and median difference between the former and the latter is 0.33, with a range from 0.10 to 0.50. Homicide committals, 1810–1867, were therefore multiplied by 1.33 to approximate the number of known homicides in each year.

Beginning in 1878, the British government reported known infanticides separately from other known homicides, so it is possible to approximate more closely the number of known homicides among adults. Note that the rate of all known homicides and the rate of known homicides without infanticides parallel each other. On the limitations of official British government data on homicides, see J. E. Archer (2008).

136. Colley (1992: 283–363), Emsley (1996: 36–40), and R. K. Webb (1970: 152–252).

137. Colley (1992: 321–334, 350–375).

138. Hoffman et al. (2000: table B.1), W. R. Miller (1999), R. K. Webb (1970: 160–163, 174–176, 184–185), Emsley (1996: 21–32, 36–40), and Colley (1992: 321–322).

6. The Rise in Family and Intimate Homicide in the Nineteenth Century

1. See M. C. Gutmann (2007: 4, 198–215, 223–230, 236, 239, 243–244) for a similar explanation of an increase in intimate violence in poor neighborhoods in contemporary Mexico City.

2. For instance, only 1 of 15 stealth murders of wives in New Hampshire, Vermont, Holmes and Ross counties in Ohio, and Calhoun, Henderson, and Williamson counties in Illinois, 1828–1900, were committed by French, German, or Irish husbands, in contrast to 26 of 72 nonstealth murders.

3. The rates are understated for California because the data do not include third parties killed in marital disputes. In the nine counties that have been studied so far, the spousal homicide rates, 1849–1900, were 0.7 per 100,000 per year for husbands and 2.8 per 100,000 for wives. In San Francisco the romance homicide rates, 1849–1900, were 0.7 per 100,000 for men and 1.1 per 100,000 for women. Romance homicide rates are not yet available for the other eight counties, but the rates were probably higher than in San Francisco, as were spousal homicide rates and nondomestic homicide rates for women. Rates for men and women are best stated separately for California because it had far fewer women than men in its population through the nineteenth century; but the composite rates for women and men, without adjusting for the inability of many men to be involved in marriages or romantic relationships, were 1.5 per 100,000 per year for spousal homicides and 0.9 per 100,000 per year in San Francisco for romance homicides.

4. The rates ranged from 0.4 to 0.9 per 100,000 in the rural North, 0.6 to 1.2 per 100,000 in the rural South, and 1.1 to 1.7 per 100,000 in northern and southern cities. For adult relatives, the numbers were 0.3 to 0.6 per 100,000 per year in the rural North, 0.4 to 1.8 per 100,000 in the rural South, and 0.6 to 1 per 100,000 in northern and southern cities.

5. The increase in marital murders was most evident in northern New England, for which the best data are available. There the marital homicide rate jumped more than fivefold, from less than 0.1 per 100,000 adults per year to 0.5 per 100,000. Only five or six such murders occurred in New Hampshire and Vermont between 1775 and 1827, but there were more than 131 between 1828 and 1900, far more than would be expected from the growth of the population. The increase in the marital murder rate was just as dramatic in the rural Midwest. It rose from zero in the early nineteenth century to 0.5 per 100,000 by midcentury in Holmes and Ross counties in Ohio, and from zero to 0.9 per 100,000 in Calhoun, Henderson, and Williamson counties in Illinois. It doubled to 1.3 per 100,000 in New York City and to 1.6 per 100,000 in Cleveland. The indictment rate for marital murder also rose in Philadelphia to 0.5 per 100,000 by century's end.

6. Hearn (1997: 44–45) and Allaman (1989: 170–173). For further examples of brutal spousal homicides, see De Beck (1867: 8–9); the murder by Roxy Druse in Tippetts (1885); by Richard Bean, Rockingham County (N.H.) Court files 19516 and 19732; by Joseph Burch, *Mercer County Standard* (Celina, Ohio), 14 April 1887; of Frances Curry, 4 January 1875, Ross County (Ohio) coroner's inquests; by Peter Lavalle,

Cleveland Herald, 23 December 1843; and by Daniel Keefe, *Cleveland Leader,* 23 May 1859.

7. State v. Brewster Young, September 1863 term, Grafton County (N.H.) Court files. See also the murder of Samuel Armstrong, *Keene Sentinel,* 20 April 1848; of George Claypole, 12 September 1830, Ross County coroner's inquests; of Charles Hammond, 29 December 1853, ibid.; and of Lewis Ritter, *Holmes County Farmer* (Millersburg, Ohio), 13 January 1870.

8. Roth (1999: 72–73).

9. Of 44 murders of wives at home by abusive husbands in New Hampshire, Vermont, and the counties studied intensively in rural Ohio and Illinois, 3 were committed with guns, 3 with knives, and 21 by husbands who were French, German, Irish, or of other foreign nationalities. The 22 murders involving abusive husbands and estranged wives include 15 homicides of wives by estranged husbands, 3 of estranged husbands by intervening parties, and 3 of intervening parties by estranged husbands. In the final case, an intervening party accidentally shot the estranged wife while trying to shoot the estranged husband.

10. Roth (1987: 117–141, 220–246, 265–279).

11. Ross County coroner's inquests, 15 February 1864. See also Complete Record of the Ross County Court of Common Pleas, 3: 386–388; inquest on Catherine Elvin, 17 October 1859, Ross County coroner's inquests; and *Holmes County Farmer,* 6 October 1859.

12. State v. Sophia Damon, April 1833 term, Rutland County (Vt.) Court files; and *Rutland Herald,* 9 October 1838. See also *Burlington Free Press,* 9 and 10 January 1862; *Rutland Herald,* 11 January 1862; and Chittenden County (Vt.) Court files 71, September 1862 term.

13. Bushman (1992); Larkin (1988); Roth (1987: 284–290); Lantz, Keyes, and Schultz (1975: 24–28); and AHSV (2009: American Homicides [AH], table 20).

14. *Holmes County Farmer,* 17 and 24 February and 4 May 1876.

15. *Burlington Free Press,* 28 August 1862; and Chittenden County Court files 66, September 1862 term.

16. State v. Brewster Young, September 1863 term, Grafton County Court files.

17. For example, see *Mountain Democrat* (Fayetteville, Vt.), 11 March 1836; *Spirit of the Age* (Woodstock, Vt.), 4 September, 9 October, and 18 December 1840; State v. Sylvester Corbet, September 1852 term, Rutland County Court files; and Roth (1987: 254–255; 1991: 208–209).

18. *Burlington Free Press,* 28 August 1862; Rockingham County Court files 19516 and 19732; State v. Brewster Young, September 1863 term, Graf-

ton County Court files; and Roth (1999: 68). In Rutland and Windham Counties, 1791–1815, 33 of the 89 men who petitioned for divorce on known grounds cited intolerable severity. In Windsor County the number was 17 of 37, 1793–1827, but only 5 of 78, 1828–1861. In all Vermont, 1862–1866, the number was 17 of 256.

19. Peterson del Mar (1996: 5, 47–71) discovers a decrease in nonlethal marital violence in Oregon somewhat later in the nineteenth century. The evidence from northern New England suggests, however, that the decline in female marital violence was greater than the decline in male violence.

20. Roth (1999: 68).

21. *Manchester Mirror* (N.H.), 6 June 1871, and *New Hampshire Patriot*, 7 and 14 June 1871. See also Dean (1885) and the murder by Patrick Walsh, *New Hampshire Patriot*, 20 January 1881; by Frederick Eastwood, *Burlington Free Press*, 14 and 19 December 1899; and by Clark Sanders, *Vermont Watchman* (Montpelier), 27 August 1884.

22. Lane (1979: 13–34), Kushner (1991), and O. Anderson (1987). Nine of the eighteen estranged husbands who killed their wives or third parties in New Hampshire, Vermont, Ross and Holmes Counties in Ohio, and Calhoun, Henderson, and Williamson Counties in Illinois committed or attempted suicide.

23. *New Hampshire Patriot*, 4 February 1874; *Berlin Reporter* (N.H.), 6 May 1898; and *New Hampshire Sentinel* (Keene), 31 May 1899.

24. Five of the 18 homicides by estranged husbands were committed with knives or razors, 10 with revolvers, 1 with a shotgun, 1 with an ax, and 1 resulted from a beating.

25. *New Hampshire Patriot*, 18 March 1857; *St. Albans Messenger* (Vt.), 18 September 1890; Basch (1982); Grossberg (1985); Hartog (1997); and P. N. Stearns (1989). By the mid-nineteenth century the American legal system had also repudiated the right of husbands to chastise their wives physically (Siegel 1996: 2129–2134).

26. *Manchester Mirror,* 6 June 1871; and *Burlington Free Press,* 28 December 1889.

27. Craig (1993), Craig and Field-Hendrey (1993), Goldin and Sokoloff (1982, 1984), and Goldin (1990).

28. De Beck (1867: 26–29), Howard Trial (1849), and *Concord Evening Monitor,* 1–4 February 1899.

29. *New Hampshire Patriot*, 22 December 1869.

30. *New Hampshire Patriot*, 15 March 1824 and 3 July 1879. See also *New Hampshire Patriot*, 29 May 1837; *Burlington Free Press*, 9 February 1863; and *Rutland Herald*, 19 August 1875.

31. *New Hampshire Sentinel,* 1 July 1885. See also the murder of Jacob McIntire, *New Hampshire Patriot,* 24 November 1852; of Frederick Merrill, *Manchester Mirror,* 8–17 April 1873; and of Edgar Beckman, *Portsmouth Chronicle,* 7 and 8 January 1891.

32. *New Hampshire Patriot,* 30 May 1877. See also the murder of Samuel Roberts, *New Hampshire Patriot,* 9 February 1853; of George Dusham, *New Hampshire Argus* (Newport), 15 September 1865; of Alvin Glover, *Burlington Free Press,* 17 February 1871; of Ransom Tilton, *New Hampshire Patriot,* 3 May 1883; of Edgar Hayes, *St. Johnsbury Caledonian* (Vt.), 31 December 1885; and of Lewis Ritter, *Holmes County Farmer,* 13 January 1870.

33. See the murder of Angell, *New Hampshire Argus,* 7, 21, and 28 February 1879; and of Smith, *Burlington Free Press,* 24 and 25 October 1879. See also the murder of Levi Stone, *New Hampshire Patriot,* 27 November and 4 December 1879; of James Durgin, *Granite State News* (Wolfborough, N.H.), 13 September 1886; of Carlos Grant, *Concord Evening Monitor,* 10 and 16 September 1898; and of James Bochard, *Chillicothe Leader Gazette* (Ohio), 13 January 1900.

34. Twelve of 17 in the counties studied intensively.

35. Seven of 23 in the counties studied intensively.

36. Peake Trial (1836).

37. *St. Johnsbury Caledonian,* 25 May 1866.

38. For possible killings of disabled spouses, see the alleged murder by Newell Leathers, *Granite State Whig* (Lebanon, N.H.), 25 May and 8 and 29 June 1849; by Stephen Harris, *Keene Sentinel,* 30 September 1847; and by Thomas Arnoux, *Manchester Daily Mirror,* 6 September 1884. See also the murder by Ragan, *Celina Western Standard* (Ohio), 12 April 1855; and of Lucy Ricker, 18 December 1855, Strafford County (N.H.) coroner's inquests; and *Dover Gazette* (N.H.), 22 December 1855. Sixteen of twenty-three alleged stealth murderers were adulterers.

39. For examples of marital homicides in cities, see Adler (1997: 258–261; 1999a: 3, 7, 11–13). According to murder and manslaughter indictments, there were at least 0.5 marital murders per 100,000 adults per year in Philadelphia after the Civil War, and according to newspaper and police reports, there were 1.5 per 100,000 per year in Chicago, 1879–1885. The marital homicide rate was at least 0.7 per 100,000 in Omaha, 1.3 per 100,000 in New York City, and 1.6 per 100,000 in Cleveland.

40. Adler (1999a; 1997: 264–268).

41. Adler (1999b: 300–309), Lane (1986), McKanna (1997), and A. H. Spear (1967). Marital murder rates among African Americans reached

at least 2 per 100,000 adults per year in Philadelphia in the 1890s, 3.9 per 100,000 in Omaha, and 7.1 per 100,000 in Chicago.

42. Adler (1999b: 307).

43. Philadelphia indictments, August 1892 term, no. 377; May 1888 term, no. 443; November 1900 term, no. 185; October 1900 term, no. 46, Philadelphia City Archives; Adler (2006: 143–155); and Lane (1986: 155–157; 1979: 108–111).

44. The rate in Louisiana was at least 1.1 per 100,000 white adults and 1.4 per 100,000 black adults per year in the city of New Orleans, and 0.6 per 100,000 white adults and 0.4 per 100,000 black adults elsewhere in the state (Vandal 2000: 28). In rural Virginia the annual rate was 0.6 per 100,000 white adults, 1790–1900, and 1.1 per 100,000 black adults, 1864–1900.

45. Inquests from Horry and Edgefield counties in South Carolina yield rates of 1.1 per 100,000 adults per year for blacks and whites. Estimates from multiple sources for Franklin, Jasper, and Wilkes counties in Georgia show annual rates of 1.4 or 1.5 per 100,000 adults for whites during the nineteenth century and 1.1 per 100,000 adults for blacks in the late nineteenth century. See Buckley (2002) and Wyatt-Brown (1982: 117–324) on the distinctiveness of southern marriages and the slow progress of the South toward an acceptance of a companionate ideal of marriage and of divorce.

46. Schwarz (1988: 239–240); Perdue, Barden, and Phillips (1976: 117); P. D. Morgan (1998: 411); State v. Pearson, April 1868 term, Jasper County (Ga.) Court files; and J. D. Rothman (2003: 133–163).

47. For examples of homicides prompted by adultery or allegations of adultery, see Horry County (S.C.) Inquest Book, 1849–1874: 39–40; Surry County (Va.) Criminal Proceedings, 21 January 1807; inquest on Abram, 13 January 1807, Surry County Court files; Schwarz (1988: 249); Wyatt-Brown (1982: 246, 298–307, 462–493); and Edgefield County Coroner's Book of Inquisitions, 1859–1868: 57–60.

48. See, for example, Rockbridge County (Va.) Court Order Book, 1827–1831: 149–151; State v. Craddock, April 1848 term, Amelia County (Va.) Court files; State v. Lipscomb, May 1870 term, ibid.; State v. Dexter, March 1841 term, Jasper County Inferior Court minutes; State v. Jones and Orr, April 1826 term, Jasper County Court files; State v. Kirk and Kirk, October 1829 term, Franklin County (Ga.) Court files, box 20, 159-1-41, Georgia Department of History and Archives, Atlanta; and Vandal (2000: 113, 120). For stealth murders, see *Carnesville Enterprise* (Ga.), 20 and 27 March 1891; and State v. Waters and Bebee, June 1891 term, Jasper County Court files. For murders of estranged

spouses, see Edgefield County Coroner's Book of Inquisitions, 1859–1868: 99; *Washington Gazette,* 6 February 1885; *Washington Chronicle* (Ga.), 30 January 1893; State v. Bryant, May 1869 term, Jasper County Court files; and Moore (2006: 135–136). On the rates at which black and white women murdered their husbands, see Vandal (2000: 129).

49. In California the marital murder rate among persons ages sixteen and older was 1.4 per 100,000 men and 3.9 per 100,000 women, but between 1850 and 1865 the rate for women was at least 6 per 100,000 per year. The rate declined by the last two decades of the nineteenth century, but it was still high compared to rates in the North and South: 0.7 per 100,000 men and 2.6 per 100,000 women. The spousal murder rate was similarly high for non–Native Americans in Gila County, Arizona, and Las Animas County, Colorado, even though the number of spousal murders was small: 0.5 per 100,000 men per year and 1.9 per 100,000 women between 1881 and 1900.

50. In the counties studied intensively in California, the ratio of men to women among adults was 3.15 in 1850–1865, 1.76 in 1866–1880, and 1.35 in 1881–1900. The ratio was 1.29 in 1881–1900 among non–Native American adults in Gila County, Arizona, and Las Animas County, Colorado.

51. Mullen (1989: 260) and McKanna (1997: 103–104; 2002: 57–60).

52. Hurtado (1988: 149–168). The annual marital homicide rate in California for adult women, 1849–1900, was 3.8 per 100,000 for Asians and 5.9 per 100,000 for Native Americans, compared to 2.7 per 100,000 for non-Hispanic whites.

53. McKanna (2002: 27–28; 1997: 135–137) and G. H. Phillips (1997: 131, 148). Six Apache wives were known victims of spouse murder, 1881–1900: a rate of 98 per 100,000 adult females per year. The male-female ratio was 3 to 2, as it was among Native Americans in California. On marital violence among the Pueblo Indians in New Mexico, see Mocho (1997: 51–58, 61–62).

54. McKanna (1997: 56–57). The annual marital homicide rate for persons ages sixteen and older in California, 1849–1900, was 2.5 per 100,000 for Hispanics and 1.5 per 100,000 for non-Hispanic whites. The rate was 4.2 per 100,000 for Hispanic women and 2.7 for non-Hispanic white women, and 1.1 per 100,000 for Hispanic men and 0.7 for non-Hispanic white men. In the Mixteca Alta of south-central Mexico, the rate at which adults were killed in spousal homicides was at least 2.3 per 100,000 per year, and probably 3.1 per 100,000 in central Mexico, assuming a total adult homicide rate of 33 per 100,000 per year (W. B. Taylor 1979: 85–88, 94–95). W. B. Taylor (1979: 81–83, 109–110) finds

evidence of the same legal practices and cultural attitudes in central and south-central Mexican peasant villages in the late eighteenth and early nineteenth centuries. High rates of spousal homicide persist in central Mexico today, as does jealous behavior by husbands (M. C. Gutmann 2007; Azaola Garrido 1997: 37–39, 64–67).

55. Mocho (1997: 23–38). See also Boessenecker (1999: 23, 135, 152–156) and Mullen (1989: 153).

56. Eifler (2002: 215–224), Rohrbough (1997), and Boessenecker (1999: 179).

57. On trials for wife murder in England and Wales, see Wiener (2004: 146–147, 166–167) and Conley (2007: 126). Wiener discusses the same transition from manslaughter killings by abusive husbands (172–173, 175–176) to the kinds of marital murders that occurred in the northern United States (127–131, 144–279). According to Foyster (2005: 6–8, 168–204), neighbors tried to prevent marital violence, but like their counterparts in the United States they were unable to prevent the increase in marital murders. The homicide totals for England, Wales, and Scotland from court records and newspapers are from a personal communication from Carolyn Conley; population totals are from Mitchell (1988).

On northern France, see Parrella (1992: 647–651). According to official government statistics, rates of marital homicides related to adultery and rates of other domestic homicides declined in France, 1852–1909 (Gillis 1996: 1282–83). Parrella's detailed study of the Nord shows, however, that those statistics are misleading. In the Nord, nonmarital domestic homicides were declining as marital homicides were rising, and adultery-related homicides accounted for a small share of marital homicides. Furthermore, by the early twentieth century a third of all marital homicides in the Nord occurred in common-law relationships; they were not listed as domestic homicides in the official statistics, but they were in fact marital murders.

58. Parrella (1983: 129–155), Conley (1991: 47, 57–59, 66–67, 72–81; 1999: 52; 2007: 124–128), Emsley (1996: 42–49), and Philips (1977: 254–255, 265). Population totals for Ireland are from Vaughan and Fitzpatrick (1978).

59. After midcentury in Ross and Holmes counties in Ohio and in Calhoun, Henderson, and Williamson counties in Illinois, 0.1 per 100,000 adults per year died as a result of a romance murder, and in New Hampshire and Vermont, 0.05 per 100,000. The rate was higher in post–Civil War Cleveland; lovers and romantic rivals were killed at a

rate of 0.3 per 100,000 per year. In Chicago, 1879–1885, whites committed romance homicides at an annual rate of 0.4 per 100,000, and blacks at a rate of 4.7 per 100,000. Adler (1999a: 5; 1999b: 300–301), who relies on police reports alone, finds a similar difference between black and white rates for the period 1875–1909. The data for Philadelphia are from homicide indictments (Lane 1979). The victim-based homicide indictment rates per 100,000 adults per year for romance homicides in Philadelphia are, for whites: .02 for 1839–1874 and .05 for 1875–1901; for nonwhites: .18 for 1839–1874 and .98 for 1875–1901. Two of the 9 black victims of romance homicides that led to indictments were lovers and 7 were rivals. Six of the 10 white victims of romance homicides that led to indictments were lovers and 4 were rivals. The actual rates of romance homicide were probably closer to Chicago's than to northern New England's or rural Ohio's, since romance homicides were more likely than other kinds of homicide to end in the suicide of the murderer rather than in criminal prosecution. The data for San Francisco are from 1849–1900. The number of victims was small: 5 Asians, 4 Hispanics, and 48 Anglos.

60. *Holmes County Farmer,* 1 August 1878. The annual jealousy murder rate in Louisiana in 1866–1884 was 0.9 per 100,000 white adults and 1.2 per 100,000 black adults in the countryside, and 0.6 per 100,000 whites and 0.4 per 100,000 blacks in the city of New Orleans (Vandal 2000: 28).

61. *Toccoa News* (Ga.), 5 September 1895; *Rutland Herald,* 28 February 1878; and Adler (1999a: 12).

62. *Burlington Free Press,* 16 and 18 August 1894; and Adler (1999b: 301). See also Philadelphia indictments, May 1895 term, no. 46, and April 1892 term, no. 178; Hearn (1997: 73); Complete Record of the Ross County Court of Common Pleas, 34: 188–226 and 35: 555–556; and *Ross County Register* (Chillicothe, Ohio), 25 March 1871.

63. E. K. Rothman (1984: 40, 103–110) and AHSV (2009: AH, table 20).

64. Nochlin (1971: 13–101), Binion (1986: 25–27), and J. H. Miller (2000: 13–14).

65. E. K. Rothman (1984: 87–93, 108, 110, 125), Lystra (1989: 6–55), and Seidman (1991: 13–61).

66. Lystra (1989: 49), Shelley (1904: 466), and AHSV (2009: AH, table 20).

67. *Vermont Watchman,* 21 June 1831; *New Hampshire Patriot,* 14 June and 19 December 1831.

68. Philadelphia indictments, August 1898 term, no. 100, and November 1901 term, no. 19; and *Washington Chronicle* (Ga.), 27 May 1895. On the

difficulties of sustaining interracial romances, see Alexander (1991: 67–98, 114–130, 156–159), K. A. Leslie (1995: 57–58, 64–75, 87–97), Madden (1992: 2–5, 97–101, 131, 142), Moran (2001: 17–28), and J. D. Rothman (2003).

69. That pattern was typical for suitors in the mid-nineteenth century: men were more likely to have left home by the time they began courting women (E. K. Rothman 1984: 68).

70. E. K. Rothman (1984: 73) and Wahl (1986: 402).

71. Webster (1913: 389–390) and *New Hampshire Patriot,* 18 June 1873. See also Elbert County (Ga.) Superior Court, Criminal Evidence, 1873–74: 59–76; and *Cleveland Leader,* 9 March 1874.

72. *Manchester Daily Mirror and American,* 14 and 17 January 1867; and *Nashua Gazette* (N.H.), 3 October 1872. See also *Haverhill Courier* (N.H.), 19 May 1893; and Hearn (1999: 282–283, 289; 1997: 73, 75).

73. Eleven of 18 men who murdered or attempted to murder lovers committed or attempted suicide. The data are from New Hampshire; Vermont; Cuyahoga, Holmes, and Ross counties, Ohio; and Calhoun, Henderson, and Williamson counties, Illinois. All the attempted murders are from New Hampshire and Vermont. On Louisiana, see Vandal (2000: 121).

74. Thirteen of 18 cases of murder or attempted murder of lovers by men in the counties studied intensively in northern New England and the Midwest were committed with guns. In Philadelphia, 10 of 19 romance homicides were committed with guns. In San Francisco, 33 of 52 romance homicides with known weapons were committed with guns. Five others were committed with unknown weapons. See AHSV (2009: Weapons).

75. Conley (1991: 61, 46–47, 56–57), Philips (1977: 264), and Wiener (2004: 126–127, 132–134, 136–144). According to Carolyn Conley's data on homicide trials and murder-suicides in Great Britain, 1867–1892, murders of lovers occurred at a rate of at least 0.3 per 100,000 adults per year, but the real rate was probably much higher. She has to date found evidence of 115 trials and 40 murder-suicides involving lovers or former lovers, even though only 7 percent of all homicides that came to trial in England were committed with guns and only 3 percent in Scotland. Conley found few murders of lovers or former lovers in Ireland, however, "perhaps because Irish marriages were still usually arranged" (Conley 2007: 62–67, 113). Wiener (2004: 143) finds little evidence after 1860 of "lover-killings," but his study is confined to criminal trials. It excludes murder-suicides and does not examine newspapers, inquests, or other sources in which most romance homicides are

found. On gun use in contemporary romance homicides, see Milroy (1995: 118) and Lund and Smorodinsky (2001: 455–456).

76. See the murder by Alphonse Chaquette, *Vermont Watchman,* 3 September 1890; by James Caswell, *Vermont Watchman,* 11 September 1889; by Charles Doherty, *Burlington Free Press,* 20–22 February 1899; and Hearn (1999: 251–252).

77. *Rutland Herald,* 11 October 1897; *Lexington Gazette,* 1 December 1887; and *Burlington Free Press,* 20–22 September 1899.

78. Mullen (1989: 191); *Lexington Gazette,* 9 February 1838; Boessenecker (1999: 206, 214–216); Ward (1965: 374); *Dahlonega Signal* (Ga.), 12 October 1894; Stanley (1984: 31–33); and Hearn (1999: 229–230).

79. Boessenecker (1999: 136) and Mullen (1989: 251–252).

80. *Rutland Herald,* 31 May and 1 June 1897.

81. *Manchester Mirror,* 30 July and 3 August 1870; and *New Hampshire Patriot,* 6 April 1870. See also Boessenecker (1999: 156–158) and the murder by Jennie Droz in *Cleveland Leader,* 17 and 18 February 1871.

82. *Concord Monitor,* 13 and 14 November 1899. See also Philadelphia indictments, September 1900 term, no. 97; Boessenecker (1999: 137–139, 148–152); and Mullen (1989: 257).

83. In New Hampshire and Vermont the rate tripled by the 1880s and 1890s to 0.3 per 100,000 adults per year. In Ross and Holmes counties in Ohio, it rose from zero to 0.5 per 100,000, and in Calhoun, Henderson, and Williamson counties in Illinois, from zero to 0.6 per 100,000. The indictment rate in Philadelphia for murders of adult relatives reached only 0.2 per 100,000 per year for whites and 0.3 per 100,000 for blacks after the Civil War, but those rates were 50 percent higher than before the war. In Chicago the rate reached 0.6 per 100,000 and in Cleveland 0.7 per 100,000. The data are not as complete or consistent for the South or the Southwest, but it appears that murder rates among adult relatives were higher than rates in the rural North but probably not higher than in northern cities. The four counties studied intensively in Virginia had no murders of adult relatives in the mid- and late nineteenth century, but the annual rates in New Orleans during Reconstruction were roughly 0.7 per 100,000 for blacks and 1.0 per 100,000 for whites. In Edgefield and Horry counties in South Carolina the annual rates were 0.2 per 100,000 for blacks and 0.6 per 100,000 for whites between 1844 and 1885, and in rural Louisiana during Reconstruction they were 0.2 per 100,000 for whites and 0.4 per 100,000 for blacks. In the Georgia plantation counties of Franklin, Jasper, and Wilkes, the annual rate was at least 0.7 per 100,000 for blacks and 2.3 per 100,000 for whites between 1880 and 1900. In the predominantly

white Georgia mountain counties of Gilmer and Rabun, it was at least 1.8 per 100,000. In California the annual rate was only 0.4 per 100,000 in San Francisco, but 0.8 per 100,000 among in-laws in ranching, farming, and mining counties.

84. Twelve of 89 murders of adult relatives in the counties studied intensively in northern New England and the Midwest, 1828–1900, were committed by German, Irish, or French Canadian immigrants or their descendants; and 4 of 9 in urban, heavily immigrant Cuyahoga County, Ohio. As already noted, a number of fathers and brothers killed or were killed trying to protect their married daughters or sisters from abusive husbands. If those homicides were included here among homicides of adult relatives, rather than among marital homicides, they would push the homicide rate for adult relatives higher.

85. In the counties studied intensively in northern New England and the Midwest (including Cuyahoga County, Ohio), where the motives for the murders of 91 adult relatives are known, 15 were to secure an inheritance and 7 were over debts or property.

86. *Keene Sentinel,* 3 May 1849. See also Boessenecker (1999: 183–187); the murder by Archibald Bates, *Rutland Herald,* 9 and 16 October 1838; by Perley Beck, *New Hampshire Patriot,* 6 and 13 February 1890 and 18 June 1891; by George Peck, *Burlington Free Press,* 8 September and 4 October 1894; by Alfred Jones, *Concord Evening Monitor,* 3–5 January 1898; and by Isaac Sawtell, Sawtell (n.d.).

87. On the murder by Pelham, see *Burlington Free Press,* 16 May 1861; and by Nichols, *New Hampshire Patriot,* 5 June 1851. See also the murder by John Wolley, *Rutland Herald,* 27, 30, and 31 October 1876; by Lyman Clark, *Vermont Watchman,* 26 November and 3 December 1890; by John Carlton, *Bellows Falls Times* (Vt.), 21 June 1872; and by Silas Wilder, *St. Johnsbury Caledonian,* 4 February 1876.

88. See the murder of Deborah Jane Galligan, 24 July 1876, Ross County coroner's inquests; and *Ross County Register,* 29 July 1876; by Lovejoy, *Jasper County News* (Monticello, Ga.), 14 April 1898; by Tyler, *Jasper County News,* 17 May 1900; by Sarah Maria Victor, *Cleveland Leader,* 6 and 7 February and 11 June 1867; by John Coole, *Cleveland Leader,* 29 and 30 June and 7 July 1868; by John Kennedy, *Cleveland Leader,* 29 April 1871; and Hearn (1997: 243–244, 253–257, 279; 1999: 68). See also *Holmes County Farmer,* 12 February 1863; Edgefield County Coroner's Book of Inquisitions, 1859–1868: 123–124; R. S. Davis (1982–1987, 1: 241); Papers of Governor Rufus Brown Bullock, 1868–1871, Record Group 1-1-5, box 56: 2740-12: 22 July 1868, Thomas County,

Georgia Department of History and Archives; State v. Armisted T. Stokes, March 1853 term, Wilkes County (Ga.) Superior Court minutes; Philadelphia indictments, June 1872 term, no. 530; June 1873 term, no. 420; March 1875 term, no. 262; March 1894 term, no. 380; April term 1895, no. 127; and June 1900 term, nos. 393 and 394; Horry County Inquest Book, 1849–1874: 1–2; and *Lexington Gazette*, 6 January 1853.

89. See the murder of Thomas, *New Hampshire Patriot*, 22 February 1849; of Pinkham, *Dover Gazette*, 7 July 1865; of Van Buskirk, *Bennington Banner* (Vt.), 31 October 1872; and of Dillingham, *New Hampshire Patriot*, 12 February 1880. See also *Rutland Herald*, 4 May 1874; Elbert County Superior Court, Criminal Evidence, 1873–1874: 3–8; *Holmes County Whig*, 27 July 1849; inquest on Thomas Hughes, 10 May 1852, Ross County coroner's inquests; *Union Recorder*, 31 December 1873; State v. James M. Campbell, September 1896 term, Jasper County Court files; Bynum (1992: 97); and Philadelphia indictments, February 1852 term, no. 240; June 1875 term, no. 606; April 1895 term, no. 127; and September 1898 term, no. 191. In the counties studied intensively in northern New England and the Midwest (including Cuyahoga County, Ohio), where the motives for the murders of 91 adult relatives are known, 30 were caused by quarrels, 11 by abuse, and 2 by sexual assaults.

90. Nineteen percent of homicides of adult relatives were committed with guns in New York City, 1847–1874 (6 of 32), 30 percent in the counties studied intensively in northern New England and the Midwest (including Cuyahoga County, Ohio), 1865–1900 (21 of 71), and 65 percent in nine counties in California (including San Francisco and Los Angeles), 1847–1900 (40 of 62). Handguns were the preferred weapons in cities, but in rural areas more gun homicides of adult relatives were committed with rifles and shotguns than with handguns. See AHSV (2009: Weapons).

91. Sixty-five of 97 in the counties studied intensively in northern New England and the Midwest (including Cuyahoga County, Ohio). The total includes 15 brothers, 9 mothers, 2 stepmothers, 15 fathers, 4 stepfathers, 9 brothers-in-law, 9 mothers-in-law, and 2 fathers-in-law. Four sons, 4 stepsons, and 4 sons-in-law were murdered.

92. The data on homicide trials in Great Britain, 1867–1892, are courtesy of Carolyn Conley. On France, see Ploux (2002: 19–54), Parrella (1992: 645–651), and Chesnais (1982: 118–122).

93. Conley (1999: 51–59; 2007: 95–97). In Scotland the rate at which persons were tried for murdering adult relatives was 0.2 per 100,000 per

year, 1867–1892. The actual rate at which adult relatives were murdered in Scotland probably fell between England's and Ireland's, but it will require additional research to be certain and to explain why.

7. "All Is Confusion, Excitement and Distrust"

1. In 1867 the homicide rate in England and Wales fell from roughly 4.5 per 100,000 adults per year to 3 per 100,000. After 1884 it fell abruptly again to 2 per 100,000. On the Reform Acts, see R. K. Webb (1970: 323–327, 395–396, 400–402). The Ballot Act of 1872, which made voting secret, also played an important role in building confidence in the political system by making it difficult to intimidate voters at the polls.

2. The research on homicide in Canada is fragmentary. Weaver (1995: 217–223) found only 12 homicides in the Gore District, Upper Canada, 1869–1900. The homicide indictment rate for Canada, 1879–1929, is calculated from Urquhart and Buckley (1965: Series Y14 and Y61). The homicide rate for Canada, 1926–1929, is calculated from ibid., Series Y14 and Y67. See Peterson del Mar (2002: 51) for the homicide rates in British Columbia, 1859–1871; Oregon, 1850–1865; and Washington, 1860. On homicide by and of Native Americans in the Northwest, see Peterson del Mar (2002: 13–45) and J. R. Reid (1999).

3. AHSV (2009: European Homicides [EH], figs. 4–7). The homicide rate in Italy fell from roughly 20 per 100,000 adults per year in the mid-nineteenth century to 8.5 per 100,000 in the late nineteenth century and 6 per 100,000 in the early twentieth century (Eisner 2001: 629). Chesnais (1982: 86–90) reports higher figures for the late nineteenth and early twentieth centuries, but they show the same downward trend. As in Canada, homicide rates were lower in the core provinces in northern Italy than in outlying provinces, particularly in the south, where poverty and illiteracy prevented most adult males from voting. The voting law of 1882 extended the franchise to adult males who paid a certain amount each year in direct taxes or who had had at least four years of primary schooling, but only 16 percent of adults in southern Italy were literate, as opposed to 46 percent in northern Italy. The voting law of 1912 established universal male suffrage (Goldstein 1983: 8–9).

   On Germany, see Chesnais (1982: 70–73); and on France, see Cobban (1965, 2: 133–227 and 3: 9–108), Chesnais (1982: 73–79), and Gould (2003: 155–156).

4. In New York City, where the Irish were responsible for a majority of homicides in the mid-nineteenth century, the proportional difference be-

tween their homicide rate and that of other whites barely changed, because the homicide rate increased so rapidly among non-Irish whites. The proportion of Irish in the city's white population rose from 25 percent to 40 percent with the influx of refugees from the potato famine of 1845–1850, which made it appear that the Irish were responsible for the sudden rise in the city's homicide rate; but the homicide rate for Irish assailants rose only from 2.7 to 3.1 times that of white non-Irish assailants. The homicide rate for Irish assailants rose more substantially in New Hampshire and Vermont, from 1.9 to 2.7 times that of white non-Irish assailants. At midcentury, therefore, the homicide rate for the Irish in both the countryside and the cities of the North was higher than in contemporary Ireland. See (AHSV 2009: Ethnicity Estimates and EH, fig. 8).

By midcentury the nondomestic homicide rate for assailants of English, Scots, and Welsh descent in New Hampshire and Vermont was 71 percent as high as the rate for all whites, in rural Ohio and Illinois 94 percent, and in San Francisco 113 percent. The percentages for victims of English, Scots, and Welsh descent in these places were 79, 90, and 97 respectively (AHSV 2009: American Homicides [AH], tables 26–28).

5. On the American response to the revolutions of 1848, see Higham (2001). On government corruption, see M. W. Summers (1987).

6. Sectional parties (like the Free Soil and Republican parties) and special-interest parties (such as the nativist American Party) had a strong appeal for many voters, but such parties were part of the problem as far as homicide was concerned. They expressed the divisions among Americans, but they could not overcome them (Altschuler and Blumin 2000: 152–183).

7. Rates for all homicides in the urban North jumped from 2 to 10 per 100,000 adults per year in Boston, from 3 to 10 per 100,000 in Cleveland, from 6 to 15 per 100,000 in New York City, and from 4 to 20 per 100,000 in Cincinnati. The homicide totals in Cincinnati are from Dannenbaum (1978: 127) and the Boston totals from Ferdinand (1967). Indictment rates in Philadelphia rose from 3.6 to 5.6 per 100,000 adults per year. Rates rose from 1 to 2 per 100,000 in Vermont and New Hampshire; from 0.5 to 2.5 per 100,000 in Amish- and Mennonite-dominated Holmes County, Ohio; and from 2.5 to 8 per 100,000 in Ross County, Ohio, and Henderson County, Illinois. In Williamson and Calhoun counties in Illinois, which were populated predominantly by white migrants from the South, homicide rates rose from 3 to 27 per 100,000 and from 6 to 33 per 100,000, respectively.

8. McPherson (1988: 28) and Montgomery (1967: 26–31). See also Grierson (1909: 7–8).

9. On violence in coal mining and railroading, see Gilje (1996: 117–119, 140–141), Lane (1997: 156–165), Broehl (1964: 210–266), Kenny (1998: 73–212), and Taft and Ross (1978: 218–226, 242–247). On workplace homicides, see the murders by Wilson in 1855 and Stockley in 1881 in Hearn (1997: 56–57, 72); see also the murder of Alexander Dunlop, *New York Tribune,* 30 October and 1 November 1847; of Dennis Mahegan, *New Hampshire Patriot,* 30 December 1847; of Michael Kelley, *Granite State Whig* (Lebanon, N.H.), 26 November 1847; and of Mariam Berry, *Dover Enquirer* (N.H.), 17 January 1878.

10. McPherson (1988: 32, 40).

11. On the economy, see Fogel (1989: 354–362). On nativism, see Billington (1938: 323, 325–326, 338) and Grimsted (1998: 218–245).

12. McPherson (1988: 32, 141), Billington (1938: 422), Gilje (1996: 67, 69, 83–84), and Grimsted (1998: 227–229).

13. On nativist riots, see Ignatiev (1995: 155), Gilje (1996: 69), and Gordon (1993). Grimsted (1998: 226) attributes at least five deaths in the North in the mid-1850s to political riots involving nativists.

14. See the murder of the Englishman, *New York Tribune,* 20 November 1848; of an Irish boy in Rollinsford, *Dover Gazette* (N.H.), 11 June 1853; of Shears, *Scioto Gazette* (Chillicothe, Ohio), 3 February 1863; and Ross County (Ohio) coroner's inquests, 1 February 1863; and by McHaney, Erwin (1914: 99).

15. D. B. Davis (1971: 124, 120), McPherson (1988: 55, 42), and Etcheson (2004: 24–25). On the Mexican War, see Bauer (1974) and McPherson (1988: 47–52).

16. McPherson (1988: 51).

17. McPherson (1988: 84). On violent resistance to the return of fugitive slaves, see Black (1912: 209) and Grimsted (1998: 75–82).

18. See the murders of two black workers, *New York Tribune,* 3 May and 20 August 1847; and by Philadelphia paupers, Philadelphia indictments, October 1858 term, no. 749, Philadelphia City Archives. See also the murder of Daniel Routt, Cuyahoga County (Ohio) coroner's inquests 49, Cuyahoga County Archives, Cleveland. On the lynching of a rape suspect in Ohio, see *Ironton Register* (Ohio), 4 December 1856; and on the California House Riot, Ignatiev (1995: 155–156). On the decline in economic opportunity and health for blacks, see Barney (1987: 64–73) and Costa and Steckel (1997).

19. See the murder by Diehl, *Cleveland Leader,* 19 July 1864; and by

Thorner, *Scioto Gazette,* 23 June 1880. See also the murder of Israel Freeman, *Burlington Free Press,* 26 and 27 October 1871.

20. When homicides by whites alone are counted, 5 per 100,000 adult blacks per year were murdered in the rural Midwest and northern New England, 25 per 100,000 in New York City, and 30 per 100,000 in Cleveland. AHSV (2009: AH, table 29).

21. See the murders by Raymond and Nokes, Philadelphia indictments, December 1850 term, no. 403, and June 1851 term, no. 213; and AHSV (2009: AH, table 29). See also Hearn (1997: 51).

22. McPherson (1988: 146–147, 152) and Etcheson (2004: 38–39). On the violence in Kansas, see Etcheson (2004), McPherson (1988: 145–153), Fellman (1989: 11–22), and Grimsted (1998: 246–265, 347n4).

23. On the murder in Henderson County, see Allaman (1989: 99–101); on Tally, see Black (1912: 210–212). See also R. M. Brown (1975: 9–11) and Klement (1960: 79, 92).

24. Erwin (1914: 99–230). See also R. M. Brown (1991: 11–14).

25. Broehl (1964: 90–95). The homicide statistics are for Schuylkill County, 1863–1867. Schuylkill is adjacent to Carbon County.

26. Ayers (2003: 230–231). On antiblack riots, see Gilje (1996: 91–94) and Ignatiev (1995: 170–171).

27. For boasts or teasing that led to homicides, see the murders by Max Geisenberger and Benjamin Welsh, Philadelphia indictments, December 1858 term, no. 679, and December 1858 term, no. 677; the murder by Peter McDonald, *Burlington Free Press,* 23 and 24 May 1859; by Peter Kane and Frank Wentworth, inquest on William H. Davis, 20 October 1860, Strafford County (N.H.) Court files; by John Smith, *New York Tribune,* 1 July 1847; and by John Johnson, *Cleveland Leader,* 23 December 1874. For homicides over quarrels in the workplace, see the murder by Charles McCarty, *New York Herald,* 17 March 1849; and by John Kilpatrick and William Hamilton, Philadelphia indictments, December 1857 term, no. 357, and August 1854 term, no. 349.

On competitions that led to homicides, see the card games in *New Hampshire Patriot,* 16 June 1852 and 7 September 1870; the horse races and dogfights in Erwin (1914: 98); *New Hampshire Patriot,* 17 September 1856; and *Exeter Newsletter* (N.H.), 15 September 1856; fights and wrestling matches in Philadelphia indictments, August 1851 term, no. 446; *New Hampshire Patriot,* 8 August 1855; and Allaman (1989: 115–117); a race to set up bowling pins in Philadelphia indictments, October 1854 term, no. 465; a raffle in ibid., no. 467; and Hearn (1997: 64–66).

28. See the murder of Perry, *New Hampshire Patriot,* 26 June 1851; by Hayes,

Philadelphia indictments, August 1860 term, no. 848; by Johnson, *New Hampshire Patriot,* 13 June 1855; and by Hersnnel, *Cleveland Leader,* 25 August 1862. For killings over debts, see the murder of Erastus Cross, *St. Johnsbury Caledonian* (Vt.), 19 June 1856; of John Somers, 7 September 1848, Ross County coroner's inquests; of Edmond Fuller, *Cleveland Daily True Democrat,* 8 February 1853; of August Rude, *Cleveland Leader,* 22 July 1872; and of James Spellman, *Burlington Free Press,* 21 and 22 July 1878.

29. See the murder by Snow, *St. Johnsbury Caledonian,* 4 July 1873; and of Gambs, 26 May 1878, Ross County coroner's inquests. See also Hearn (1997: 66).

30. On killings of clerks, bouncers, etc., see the murder of John Eichel, Philadelphia indictments, April 1859 term, no. 608; of James Hoban, *Cleveland Leader,* 30 September and 1 October 1868; of Cyrus Gonyear Jr., *Northern Sentinel* (Colebrook, N.H.), 2 January 1874; and Hearn (1997: 68). On killings of unruly customers, see the murder by Charles Cady, *Holmes County Farmer,* 22 April 1880; by Sarah Webber, *New Hampshire Patriot,* 30 November 1864; by Mike Helfrich, *Ross County Register,* 8 July 1871; and by Franklin Farwell and Sherrod Lawrence, *Rutland Daily Herald,* 27 and 28 December 1871.

31. See, for example, State v. Martin Deveney, October 1872 term, Merrimack County (N.H.) Court files; and the murder of Charles Herring, *Cleveland Leader,* 3–6 June 1868.

32. See the murder by Maloney, Philadelphia indictments, August 1856 term, no. 342; and by Foster in 1871 and Rodgers in 1857 in Hearn (1997: 66, 58). See also the murder of Patrick Fitzgibbons, *Vermont Watchman* (Montpelier), 30 April 1867; Allaman (1989: 156–158); and Hearn (1997: 66).

33. Asbury (1998: 46–48). For examples of nicknames, see *New Hampshire Patriot,* 12 and 19 December 1878.

34. On fights between fire companies, see Philadelphia indictments, June 1849 term, no. 227; June 1850 term, no. 3; and June 1850 term, no. 167. On fights between gang members, see Asbury (1998: 79–91) and Anbinder (2002: 274–296).

35. Rorabaugh (1979: 7–10) and AHSV (2009: Weapons).

36. For homicides over property disputes, see the murder of David P. Williams, *St. Johnsbury Caledonian,* 28 October 1848; of Abial Chase, *Burlington Free Press,* 14 September 1855; of W. H. H. Niles, *New Hampshire Patriot,* 7 August 1861; of Simon Ortman, 22 October 1848, Ross County coroner's inquests; of John G. Eichorn, *Cleveland Daily True Democrat,* 23 and 26 August 1853; of Ferdinand Gesser, *Cleveland Leader,*

17 November 1869; of Patrick Finnegan, *Burlington Free Press,* 21 January 1867; of Michael Callin, *New Hampshire Patriot,* 14 June 1854; Hearn (1997: 70); and Allaman (1989: 96–98).

37. *Rutland Daily Herald,* 3–6 August 1868.

38. *Granite State Free Press* (Lebanon, N.H.), 3 and 10 August 1860. See also the murder by J. Q. Adams, *St. Johnsbury Caledonian,* 7 July 1871.

39. See the murder by McCann in 1878 in Hearn (1997: 70); and by Cone, *New Hampshire Patriot,* 9 and 16 August 1876. See also the murder by John Harris, *Scioto Gazette,* 24 December 1867; and by William Wheeler, inquest on Samuel Jones, 18 September 1862, Ross County coroner's inquests.

40. On Cone, see Carroll County (N.H.) Court files, A-277; and on Davenport, State v. Jesse C. Davenport, December 1863 term, Bennington County (Vt.) Court, typescript, Vermont Historical Society Library, Barre.

41. R. M. Brown (1991: 3–37).

42. Black (1912) argues that the outbreak of vigilantism in Iowa was triggered by the economic recession of 1857. There is no evidence, however, that the Panic of 1857 had a profound impact on Iowa's economy, and during recessions in the 1870s and 1890s, which did have a profound impact there, there were few vigilante killings. In Iowa deadly vigilantism coincided with political events, not with economic events.

43. Black (1912: 188–190, 224). See also Mott (1859) and F. Allen (2004) on similar vigilante movements in northern Indiana and Montana. On the tolerant attitude of the law and the criminal justice system toward vigilantism in the 1850s and afterward, see R. M. Brown (1975: 144–179).

44. R. M. Brown (1975: 22–25, 98–112, 309–311) and Black (1912: 238–240). Vigilantes took at least 20 lives in Indiana and Illinois in the 1850s and 1860s.

45. For cases in New England in which citizens threatened to lynch criminals, see Hearn (1999: 234–235, 255–256). On capital punishment in New Hampshire and Vermont, see Roth (1997: 20–21).

46. Mott (1859: 19–22) and Broehl (1964: 236–237).

47. See the murder by Capie and Enos, Philadelphia indictments, February 1853 term, no. 3; by Bresnahan in 1878 in Hearn (1997: 70); and by the Benders in 1872–73 in J. T. James (1913).

48. On the murder by Williams, see *Rutland Daily Herald,* 15–18 May 1877. On killings of jewelers, peddlers, etc., see the murder of Christiana Sigsby, *Cleveland Daily True Democrat,* 29 April 1853; and *Cleveland Plain Dealer,* 2 May 1853; of David Skinner, *Cleveland Leader,* 14–17 September

1868; of James Swing, *Cleveland Leader,* 22 and 27 November 1871; by Felix Burns, Philadelphia indictments, June 1852 term, no. 298; by John Phair, *Rutland Daily Herald,* 10, 15, and 16 June 1874; Allaman (1989: 101–108); and Hearn (1997: 51, 53, 55–56, 67–68; 1999: 246–247, 255–257). On murders of farmers and the elderly, see Hearn (1997: 49–50, 63, 71; 1999: 233).

49. *Circleville Democrat & Watchman* (Ohio), 2 November 1877. See also the murder of E. Anderson, *Forest City Democrat* (Cleveland), 12 December 1853; of Perry Russell, *Burlington Free Press,* 5–8 October 1868; and Hearn (1997: 60–61, 67–68, 70–71; 1999: 234–235, 260–261).

50. *Burlington Free Press,* 26 July 1867. For other killings by hired hands, see the murder by Alexander McConnell, *Cleveland Leader,* 11 July 1866; by Samuel Mills, *Burlington Free Press,* 20 December 1866; and Hearn (1997: 50, 54, 63).

51. *Rutland Daily Herald,* 26 July 1865. See also the murder by Henry Carnel, *New York Herald,* 4–6 March 1851; by Peter Johnson, *Dover Enquirer,* 22 January 1874; by Francisco Creboni, *Burlington Free Press,* 8 and 9 August 1871; by John Kain, *Cleveland Leader,* 7 July 1876; and Hearn (1997: 58, 60–62, 67, 70).

52. See the murder in Sandgate, inquest on Frances Kenyon, 13 March 1861, Bennington County Court files; of Annie Morrison, *Manchester Daily Union,* 21 September 1871; and by Scudder in 1852 and Fee and Muldoon in 1859 in Hearn (1997: 54, 58–59). See also Hearn (1997: 69; 1999: 232–233, 240–241, 248–249).

53. Necrophilia, mutilation, sadism, and compulsive killing have occurred throughout recorded history, but there is no evidence of serial sexual homicide—that is, killings involving female victims who were targeted systematically in a particular geographic area and sexually mutilated—in the United States before the mid-nineteenth century. See Masters and Lea (1963: 56–94, 96–99, 144–154) on serial sexual murders in Europe. Some nineteenth-century serial killers in the United States and in Europe did not target or attack women exclusively, even though sexual fantasies drove many or all of their murders. See the murders by James Brown in Masters and Lea (1963: 109) and by H. H. Mudgett (Larson 2003).

54. *New Hampshire Patriot,* 14 November 1850 and 6 November 1872. See also Hearn (1999: 257–258).

55. Lapage Trial (1876). See also Masters and Lea (1963: 79–94, 96–99, 144) and the murder of Mrs. Griffes, *San Francisco Chronicle,* 28 February 1893.

56. On the character of sexual homicide, see Ressler, Burgess, and Douglas

(1988); Ressler and Schachtman (1992); and Schechter and Everitt (1996). There is evidence that some of the North's serial sexual killers were preoccupied with commercialized sex. Sexuality was more commercialized in the North than in the South, with the difference most apparent in small towns and rural areas, and the sexual underworld was more highly developed. Thomas Piper, a necrophile from the Boston area who bludgeoned his victims to death before raping them, was well acquainted with the sex trade: he hired prostitutes, bought sexual stimulants, and owned a variety of sexual devices. The availability of such products and services may have nurtured his obsession (Hearn 1999: 257–258). It may prove that serial sexual murder was less common in the South than in the North or in Europe. A serial killer mutilated a number of prostitutes in Texas in 1887, but that is the only notice to date of such killings in the South (Masters and Lea 1963: 93).

57. See the murder of Laker in 1866 in Hearn (1997: 62); of Berry, *Dover Enquirer,* 17 January 1878; and of the wife of the Confederate sympathizer, Carpenter (1981: n.p.). Twenty-six of the 35 nondomestic homicides of women that occurred in New Hampshire, Vermont, Cleveland, and the counties studied in rural Ohio and Illinois, 1847–1880, had known causes. Seven were robberies and 5 were sexual assaults.

58. See the murder by Rickman, *Scioto Gazette,* 12 November 1861; by Margaret Kelly, *Cleveland Leader,* 17 and 24 December 1859; and by Hennessey, *New Hampshire Patriot,* 11 February 1857. Of the 11 nondomestic homicides committed by women in New Hampshire, Vermont, Cleveland, and the counties studied in rural Ohio and Illinois, 1847–1880, 3 involved proprietors of bowling alleys or brothels who killed unruly customers, and 3 were brawls in which women supported friends or relatives.

59. On killings of or by police officers or militiamen, see W. R. Miller (1999: especially 21–22, 145–146), Asbury (1998: 57–78), M. S. Johnson (2003: 12–56), and Hearn (1997: 54, 60, 63–64, 66, 68, 72; 1999: 233–234). On homicides of officers in Philadelphia, see Philadelphia indictments, December 1850 term, nos. 318 and 333; February 1851 term, no. 158; August 1852 term, no. 440; December 1853, no. 240; October 1854 term, no. 466; and August 1857 term, no. 1255. On killings of or by law-enforcement officials in New England and the Midwest, see the murder of Willie Young, *Burlington Free Press,* 31 August 1874; of Nicholas Cox, *Coos County Republican* (Lancaster, N.H.), 21 June 1870; by Andrew Smith, *New Hampshire Patriot,* 19 April 1876; by Thomas Johnson, inquest on James H. Boggs, 25 and 26 July 1873, Ross

County coroner's inquests; by John Hamley, *Daily True Democrat* (Cleveland), 28 November and 2 December 1853; by William McKenna, *Cleveland Leader,* 21 and 22 June 1855; by James Cowell, *Cleveland Leader,* 14 May 1875; Allaman (1989: 92–96, 105–106, 111–115); and Hearn (1999: 233–234, 271–272).

60. On collaboration with vigilantes, see inquest on Stephen Parker, 10 December 1860, Ross County coroner's inquests; Allaman (1989: 83–84); and Broehl (1964: 239–242). On homicides of or by officers, see Lane (1967: especially 104, 139), Savage (1873: 64–65, 87, 98), and Gilje (1996: 116–130, 138–142).

61. AHSV (2009: AH, tables 24–25).

62. Rousey (1996: 66–101) and Gleeson (2001: 94–120).

63. Billington (1938: 266, 273, 291, 300–302), Gilje (1996: 67, 69, 83–84), and Grimsted (1998: 107, 110–111, 227–242, 247). Grimsted (1998: 226) attributes at least 72 deaths in the South in the 1850s to political riots involving nativists.

64. On violence in southeastern Louisiana, see Hyde (1996). Throughout the rural South the rates at which blacks committed homicide remained steady, reflecting a lack of change in their condition. On political divisions within the South, see Hyde (1996: 63–91) and M. P. Johnson (1977: xx–xxi, 79–101).

65. On the appeal of the proslavery movement in the rural South, see Hyde (1996: 63–91), Blair (1998: 11–32), and M. P. Johnson (1977: 28–58, 105–187).

66. On Texas, see Marten (1990: 6–12), Pickering and Falls (2000: 3, 11–13, 44), McCaslin (1994: 22–27, 51–52), and Grimsted (1998: 174–178). On Florida, see Denham and Roth (2007), C. Brown (1991; 1997: 81–120; 1999), Denham (1997: 185–204), and Baptist (2002: 265–275). See also Mohr (1986: 3–67) on Georgia.

67. Grimsted (1998: 118–128, 174–175), Marten (1990: 7, 59), and Pickering and Falls (2000: 49–50).

68. Grimsted (1998: 119), Marten (1990: 9), and Pickering and Falls (2000: 38).

69. Pickering and Falls (2000: 3–27).

70. Pickering and Falls (2000: 15, 40) and Campbell (2003: 261).

71. Pickering and Falls (2000: 22–23, 28–67, 92) and McCaslin (1994: 31–32).

72. On Cooke County, see Smallwood, Crouch, and Peacock (2003: 19, 22); and McCaslin (1994). On Hart's raiders, see Pickering and Falls (2000: 68–101).

73. Fellman (1989: 133); E. E. Leslie (1996); Schultz (1996); and Small-

wood, Crouch, and Peacock (2003: 22–24). On murders by regular Confederate soldiers, see Marten (1990: 86); Smallwood, Crouch, and Peacock (2003: 21–24, 31–35); and McCaslin (1994: 84–150).

74. On Missouri and Arkansas, see Fellman (1989) and Mackey (1999).

75. Fellman (1989: 199–214) and McCaslin (1994: 57). See also Fellman (1989: 24, 27–28, 193–215); Pickering and Falls (2000: 21, 85–86, 102–104); and Smallwood, Crouch, and Peacock (2003: 7, 33–36, 42, 53, 55, 63–64, 85, 96, 109, 126).

76. J. A. Williams (2002: 171–179); Williams, Williams, and Carlson (2002); Paludan (1981: 30, 59–61); and Groce (1999: 21–67).

77. Montell (1986: 9–10, 164); Waller (1988: 1–33); Williams, Williams, and Carlson (2002: 173–174); and Noe (1997).

78. Noe and Wilson (1997: xxiii–xiv), Sarris (1993), Montell (1986: 164), and AHSV (2009: AH, table 30).

79. Paludan (1981: 60–61).

80. Ward (1965: 345), J. A. Williams (2002: 178), Paludan (1981: 5, 98, 116), and Sarris (1993). See also Ward (1965: 96–97, 287, 325–326, 341–347); Montell (1986: 9–13); and Williams, Williams, and Carlson (2002: 167 168, 172 179).

81. On the homicide rate in the Cumberland Plateau, see AHSV (2009: AH, table 30).

82. Paludan (1981: 23–25, 109) and Montell (1986: 12).

83. Montell (1986: 11) and McKinney (1978: 30–204).

84. Montell (1986: 18–19). Studies of feuds in the post-Reconstruction period point to a wide array of causes for specific feuds and for feuding in general (e.g., Montell 1986; Waller 1988). Those feuds are discussed in chapter 8. In the immediate postwar period, however, government instability was the ultimate cause.

85. Montell (1986: 14, 19); Ward (1965: 219); the murder by Anthony Goble, *Signal and Advertiser* (Dahlonega, Ga.), 25 May 1877; and Waller (1988: 53–76).

86. Montell (1986: 14). See also Ward (1965: 34–39); the murder by William O'Grady, *Ellijay Courier* (Ga.), 26 January 1876; of Lt. McIntyre, *Washington Gazette*, 16 February 1877; and Holmes (1980).

87. State v. Joel Arrendale and State v. David McClain, Rabun County (Ga.) Superior Court, Record of Testimony, 1877–1888.

88. Thelen (1986: 65–66, 70–77); Brant (1992); Smallwood, Crouch, and Peacock (2003: 27–39); and P. B. Nolan (1987: 128, 146, 151–170). Bob Lee made a similar effort to portray himself as a defender of the Confederacy and the white race (Smallwood, Crouch, and Peacock 2003: 44, 51, 65). On revenge killings, see Fellman (1989: 231–234).

89. Smallwood, Crouch, and Peacock (2003: 41, 47, 51, 94–95).
90. Smallwood, Crouch, and Peacock (2003: 55–58, 73–79, 82, 97–99, 101–104) and Fellman (1989: 210–214).
91. Smallwood, Crouch, and Peacock (2003: 3–5, 116, 130). On the toll from the fighting, see Fellman (1989: 65–73, 238–242) and Smallwood, Crouch, and Peacock (2003: 40–116).
92. The data on Richmond are from Monkkonen (1981: 65–85; 1994).
93. Blair (1998: 4–6, 46, 81–107) and Sutherland (1999: 86). On the impact of military defeats on civilian morale elsewhere in the Confederacy, see Fellman (1989: 102, 109–110) and Marten (1990: 86).
94. Sutherland (1999: 77) and Blair (1998: 51, 92).
95. Blair (1998: 108).
96. Aptheker (1938: 24), Wiley (1943: 82), and E. L. Jordan (1995: 49–90, 177, 267). On killings of black soldiers and spies, see Perdue, Barden, and Phillips (1976: 150, 159, 259–260); and E. L. Jordan (1995: 277–281, 286–287).
97. Kerr-Ritchie (1999: 31–91, especially 82–88) and Crofts (1992: 230–231). On interracial killings, see E. L. Jordan (1995: 180, 292), Engs (1979: 87–88, 102, 114–119), and the murder by Isaac Cheney, *Lexington News and Gazette* (Va.), 4 January 1866. On the Norfolk march, see Engs (1979: 88).
98. Blair (1998: 151) and Maddex (1980: 114–120).
99. On politics in postwar Virginia, see Maddex (1970, 1980) and Lowe (1991: 25–182).
100. Maddex (1980: 113–114) and Hahn (2003: 367–369).
101. On homicide rates in Virginia, see AHSV (2009: AH, tables 22–23). On the Ku Klux Klan in Virginia, see Trelease (1971: 66–68, 114). Only one lynching occurred in Amelia, Lancaster, Rockbridge, and Surry counties between 1864 and 1880, of a black man who had raped and murdered a white woman. In Amelia, Lancaster, Rockbridge, and Surry counties, 1785–1880, 8 percent of 38 black homicide assailants for whom the weapon is known used guns, and 36 percent of 72 white homicide assailants (ASHV: Weapons).
102. AHSV (2009: AH, tables 22–23).
103. The motive was known in 18 of the 29 known nonfamily, nonintimate homicides that occurred in Amelia, Lancaster, Rockbridge, and Surry counties, 1864–1880. Ten of the 18 were provoked by insults and 4 by feuds over property. The other 4 were the consequence of 2 predatory crimes, a robbery, and a rape. For examples of homicides provoked by insults, see Rockbridge County (Va.) Court Order Book, 1865–1867: 181, 191–205; *Lexington Gazette*, 7 July 1871, 2 January and 22 May 1874;

State v. Smith Grandison, May 1879 term, Amelia County (Va.) Court files; and Perdue, Barden, and Phillips (1976: 52). On feuds over property, see Rockbridge County Court Order Book, 1861–1865: 373–378; and *Lexington Gazette,* 3 October 1873, 15 January and 14 May 1875, and 8 February 1878.

104. Maddex (1980: 140–150), Lowe (1991: 183–195), Kerr-Ritchie (1999: 125–180), Dailey (2000: 15–102), and Hahn (2003: 373–384, 400–411).

105. D. Williams (1998); Williams, Williams, and Carlson (2002: 151–177); Hyde (1996: 102–138); and Bynum (2001).

106. Vandal (2000: 50–52); D. Williams (1998: 144–150); Hyde (1996: 102–138); Williams, Williams, and Carlson (2002: 168); State v. Riley S. Fears and Robert Letson, October 1865 term, Jasper County (Ga.) Court files; Franklin County (Ga.) Superior Court minutes, October 1863–October 1875: 29–30; and *Union Recorder,* 3 January 1865.

107. AHSV (2009: AH, tables 31 [Louisiana], 24–25 [South Carolina], and 21–22 [Virginia]). The data from Franklin, Jasper, and Wilkes counties in Georgia are not directly comparable with the data from Vandal (2000) on Louisiana because of the difficulty in determining the identity and race of victims in Franklin and Wilkes. Comparable data are available from Edgefield County, South Carolina, a piedmont plantation county on the Georgia border; but they do not include the most violent years of Reconstruction in South Carolina, 1870–1876. In Edgefield County, 1864–1869, 6 blacks and 2 whites were killed in interracial confrontations, and whites killed one another at three times the rate blacks did (15 per 100,000 versus 5 per 100,000). In Jasper County, 1864–1873, 5 blacks and 1 white were killed in interracial confrontations, and whites killed one another at six times the rate blacks did (54 per 100,000 versus 9 per 100,000).

108. Cimbala (1997: 204–208), Drago (1982: 112), and Vandal (2000: 67, 71). Considering only those homicides for which the motive is known, Vandal (2000: 28) finds that 51 percent of nonfamily homicides by whites in rural Louisiana were motivated by politics and 7 percent by economic disputes. In Franklin, Jasper, and Wilkes counties in Georgia and in Edgefield County, South Carolina, 1864–1873, the motive was known in 14 of 20 known murders of blacks by whites: 5 political, 3 economic, 4 in defense of personal reputation, and 2 robbery. The motive was known in 16 of 23 known murders of whites by whites: 3 political, 7 economic, 4 in defense of personal reputation, and 2 robbery.

109. Trelease (1971: xx). See also Drago (1982: 153–154).

110. R. S. Davis (1982–1987, 1: 255); inquest on Emanuel Trippe, 17 October 1868, Jasper County Court files; and letters from John W. Cheek,

15 and 22 May and 24 August 1870, and depositions from George Wallace and Thomas M. Allen, 21 October 1868, Papers of Governor Rufus Brown Bullock, 1868–1871, Record Group 1-1-5, box 58: 2740-13: Jasper County, Georgia Department of History and Archives, Atlanta. See also Drago (1982: 145–156) and Cimbala (1997: 75).

111. Trelease (1971: 73–79, 127–136, 226–242, 318–335) and Vandal (2000: 90–109).

112. On deadly quarrels and murders over insults, see inquest on Jarret McGinnis, 31 May 1868, Jasper County Court files; inquest on John Jenkins, 3 September 1874, ibid.; and *Washington Gazette,* 3 March 1871. On murders caused by property disputes, see *Washington Gazette,* 23 May 1873; Elbert County (Ga.) Superior Court, Criminal Evidence, 1873–1874: 1–2, 20–32; and Edgefield County (S.C.) Coroner's Book of Inquisitions, 1859–1868: 77–79. On predatory murders, see Edgefield County Coroner's Book of Inquisitions, 1859–1868: 72, 108–110; and Vandal (2000: 76–78).

In rural Louisiana, 17 percent of the nonfamily, nonintimate homicides with known causes committed by whites were criminal (including robberies, rapes, and arson murders), 24 percent were quarrels (including honor murders), and 7 percent were economic (including feuds) (Vandal 2000: 28). In Franklin, Jasper, and Wilkes counties in Georgia and Edgefield County, South Carolina, 1864–1873, the motive was known in 16 of 24 murders of whites by whites, including 8 property-dispute murders, 4 murders in defense of personal reputations, 1 robbery, and 3 from miscellaneous causes.

113. See the murder by a black Union soldier, Edgefield County Coroner's Book of Inquisitions, 1859–1868: 94; by Ashley and of Garrett, Vandal (2000: 147, 162); and by Jefferson, Trelease (1971: 228–230). On robbery, rape, and revenge murders against whites, see Vandal (2000: 76–78, 140–141); the murder by Robert Arnold, *Washington Gazette,* 9 April 1869; and Inquests in Oglethorpe County, letter from F. R. Robinson to Governor Rufus Bullock, 11 June 1869, Papers of Governor Rufus Brown Bullock, 1868–1871, Record Group 1-1-5, box 57: 2740-13, Georgia Department of History and Archives.

114. Trelease (1971: 228–230).

115. Vandal (2000: 174–191).

116. Edgefield County Coroner's Book of Inquisitions, 1859–1868: 71–72 and 1877–1885: 17–27. See also the murder by James Nelson, *Southern Recorder,* 13 June 1871; Elbert County Superior Court, Criminal Evidence, 1873–1874: 9–15, 51–59; and inquest on Anna Freeman, 20 March 1869, Jasper County Court files.

117. ASHV (2009: AH, tables 22–25 and 31). The data from Georgia are

from Jasper County, the only county studied intensively in Georgia where it was possible to determine the race of a significant proportion of assailants and victims.

118. AHSV (2009: Weapons).

119. Vandal (2000: 27–37, 93–105) and Rousey (1996: 129).

120. Vandal (2000: 46–58, 63–64, 144).

121. Vandal (2000: 27–37) and Rousey (1996: 126–158). Whites killed blacks at a rate of 33 per 100,000 adults per year; blacks killed whites at a rate of 2 per 100,000. Whites killed one another at a rate of 22 per 100,000 adults; blacks killed one another at a rate of 11 per 100,000 (AHSV 2009: AH, table 31).

122. Vandal (2000: 35, 46–58, 63–64, 180–191, 184–186), Rousey (1996: 126–158), and Blassingame (1973: 174). On the Irish, see Gleeson (2001: 121–194).

123. The mortality tables in the federal censuses of 1860, 1870, and 1880 badly undercount the number of homicides, and they exclude homicides of Native Americans not under federal jurisdiction. For the year before June 1870, the tables list 44 homicides of persons ages fifteen and older in Arizona (31 committed by Native Americans), 37 in Colorado, 19 in Nevada, 51 in New Mexico, and 109 in Texas south and west of the Colorado River. For the years before June 1860 and June 1880 the mortality tables list 129 and 158 homicides, respectively, in New Mexico. On the basis of those counts alone, the homicide rate in 1869–70 was 60 per 100,000 persons ages fifteen and older per year in Nevada, 171 per 100,000 in Arizona (577 if homicides by Native Americans are included), 137 per 100,000 in Colorado, 55 per 100,000 in Nevada, and 268 per 100,000 in south and west Texas. The rates in New Mexico were 235 per 100,000 in 1859–60, 93 per 100,000 in 1869–70, and 210 per 100,000 in 1879–80. See Bureau of the Census (1866: 3–43; 1872: 17–205; 1885: 43–497).

124. Of the 450 known homicides in San Francisco, 1849–1880, the character of 280 is known. Of those, 146 involved personal quarrels (68 of which occurred in brothels, dance halls, or taverns), 57 involved predatory or gang assaults, 45 involved economic disputes, and 18 involved vigilantes, mobs, or politically or racially motivated killers. Ten victims were killed by law enforcement officers and 4 by persons who were mentally ill.

125. AHSV (2009: AH, table 32, and Weapons).

126. E. H. Adams (1887: 55–56).

127. Samora, Bernal, and Peña (1979: 27–31); and Utley (2002: 63, 73, 77–79).

128. Chamberlain (1956: 83–84, 86–90, 144–146, 173–178); Bauer (1974:

84–85, 204, 208–209, 218, 220–222); Samora, Bernal, and Peña (1979: 30–31); and Utley (2002: 83).

129. Chamberlain (1956: 69, 71–73, 145–155, 186–191, 208–217, 236–238) and Bauer (1974: 224).

130. Bauer (1974: 139–141).

131. Chamberlain (1956: 39–40, 267–297).

132. Pitt (1971: 26–36) and Bauer (1974: 164–200).

133. Aarim-Heriot (2003: 15); Bauer (1974: 363); and, on interracial homicide rates, AHSV (2009: AH, table 33). The figures on homicides by Anglos include homicides committed by unknown persons, most of whom were probably Anglos.

The rates in California in 1848 and 1854–55 are based on newspaper reports alone. See Boessenecker (1999: 323–325) and Bancroft (1887–1890, 1: 131). The rate in Los Angeles (including Native Americans) rose from 100 before the Mexican War to 240 after it; for Monterey those figures were 100 before the war and 600 after (Monkkonen 2005; Boessenecker 1999: 323–325). For nine of the most populous counties in California, including San Francisco, Sacramento, and Los Angeles, the homicide rate from 1849 to 1865 was at least 67 per 100,000 adults per year, based on indictments and inquests. The rates for migrants from China, Europe, and the eastern United States were probably between 55 and 65 per 100,000 adults per year, and the rate for Hispanics (immigrant and native-born) was at least 161 per 100,000. The corresponding rate for Native Americans was at least 75 per 100,000 adults per year, the same as the rate (based on newspaper reports) for Native Americans in northern and central California who were not yet under state or federal jurisdiction (AHSV 2009: AH, table 34). Those rates are deceptively low, however. If Native Americans killed in massacres were included, their homicide rate would quintuple. In the late 1860s and the 1870s, when most Indians lived under the jurisdiction of county courts, their homicide rate was still at least 81 per 100,000 adults per year, based on indictments and inquests.

134. Pitt (1971: 48–68) and Carrigan and Webb (2003: 51).

135. Pitt (1971: 50–59). On violence against Native Americans, see G. H. Phillips (1975: 53–55, 71–110), Carranco and Beard (1981: 46–83), McKanna (2002: 17–28), Cook (1976: 255–361), Heizer (1993: 219–265, 277–283), Hollon (1974: 62–63), Pitt (1971: 150–152), and Hurtado (1988: 93–96, 107–108, 114, 118–119, 122, 134–135, 180–187).

136. Pitt (1971: 56–59) and Rohrbough (1997: 220–226).

137. Pitt (1971: 60–61).

138. Pitt (1971: 60–68) and Boessenecker (1999: 299).

139. Clappe (1970: 146–148, 150–152), Boessenecker (1999: 51–52, 139–145), Pitt (1971: 71, 73–74), and Hollon (1974: 66).

140. Mullen (1989: 245–247, 257, 53–71). On the wider involvement of New York Volunteers in early San Francisco homicides, see Mullen (1989: 29–30, 45).

141. Pitt (1971: 83–103) and Boessenecker (1999: 68–69).

142. Pitt (1971: 69–82, 149, 167–180, 256–262), Camarillo (1979: 20–21), and Boessenecker (1999: 68).

143. Boessenecker (1999: 52–58).

144. Camarillo (1979: 6–32) and Pitt (1971: 106–107).

145. Camarillo (1979: 6–32) and Pitt (1971: 174–175).

146. Camarillo (1979: 16–17) and Pitt (1971: 195–213).

147. Pitt (1971: 200–210).

148. Boessenecker (1999: 70–71) and Pitt (1971: 172–173).

149. Camarillo (1979: 21–22), Boessenecker (1999: 70–71), and Carrigan and Webb (2003: 47).

150. S. L. Johnson (2000: 248), Boessenecker (1999: 136), and Mullen (1989: 261). Tax collectors killed six miners in 1855 (Bancroft 1887–1890, 1: 131).

151. Hollon (1974: 93–95) and Chan (1986: 372). See also Barth (1964: 129–156), Pitt (1971: 74–82), and Heizer (1993: 299).

152. Barth (1964: 9–31) and Chan (1986: 16–26).

153. Barth (1964: 50–108), Chan (1986: 7–78), and Hollon (1974: 86–89).

154. McKanna (2002: 32–51); the murder by Ah Sin, *San Francisco Chronicle*, 17 October 1874; and AHSV (2009: AH, table 35).

155. AHSV (2009: AH, table 33).

156. Heizer (1993: 277–283), Hurtado (1988: 93–94, 107–108, 114, 118–119, 122, 180–187), and AHSV (2009: AH, tables 33 and 36). In the late 1860s and the 1870s, when most surviving Native Americans came under the jurisdiction of California authorities, the homicide rate among Natives was at least 33 per 100,000 adults per year. The statistics from the 1850s and early 1860s are less reliable, because American authorities did not have (or in some cases want) jurisdiction over homicides among Indians. They show nonetheless that Native Americans living under Anglo jurisdiction killed one another at an annual rate of at least 25 per 100,000 in that period and that those living outside Anglo jurisdiction killed one another at a rate of at least 41 per 100,000.

　　Cook (1976: 358–361) found articles in California's major newspapers on 139 homicides of Indians by Indians in northern and central California, 1852–1865. The articles noted the cause of 97 of those homicides. Fifty-six involved "intertribal feuds."

157. G. H. Phillips (1975: 58), McKanna (2002: 28), and Mullen (1989:

246–247). Cook (1976: 358–361) also found articles on 41 homicides among Native Americans of the same tribe in northern and central California, 1852–1865. Thirty-eight involved alcohol.

158. AHSV (2009: AH, table 33).

159. Mullen (1989: 253–256, 260).

160. AHSV (2009: AH, table 33). On bandits and vigilantes, see Pitt (1971: 120–129, 149, 153–160, 168) and Boessenecker (1999: 251–252). On community formation, see Camarillo (1979: 41–51) and Griswold del Castillo (1979: 30–61, 150–160).

161. Boessenecker (1999: ix, 8–9) and AHSV (2009: AH, table 33). On law enforcement and recreation in mining towns, see also McGrath (1984). On the popularity of revolvers, see Hollon (1974: 109–112).

162. Boessenecker (1999: 204–224) and Lotchin (1974: 217–230, 245–249). See also the duels in Boessenecker (1999: 13–14), Clappe (1970: 156), and Mullen (1989: 81, 245–261).

163. AHSV (2009: AH, table 33).

164. Utley (2002: 212–216, 294–295).

165. Marten (1990: 30) and De León (1983: 15).

166. De León (1983: 55–56, 96–97, 49–53), Marten (1990: 13, 30), and Utley (2002: 188–206).

167. Utley (2002: 161–167, 243–246, 294–295); Marten (1990: 148–150); Samora, Bernal, and Peña (1979: 48–53, 55–56); and Abbott and Smith (1939: 57–58). On lynchings, see Carrigan and Webb (2003) and De León (1983: 68, 80, 87–92, 98).

168. Utley (2002: 160, 106–119); Samora, Bernal, and Peña (1979: 33–37); R. White (1991: 335); and Carrigan and Webb (2003: 54). See also De León (1983: 92–94, 98–99).

169. De León (1983: 90, 96–97).

170. Dykstra (1968: 11–73), R. White (1991: 344–346), Hine and Faragher (2000: 304–308), and Campbell (2003: 296–299). Wyoming and Montana were as homicidal as cattle states in the Southwest. According to the mortality tables of the 1870 census, there were at least 37 homicides in Montana (24 killed by Native Americans) and 15 in Wyoming (11 killed by Natives). The rate for Montana was 212 per 100,000 adults per year and for Wyoming 167 per 100,000. When homicides by Native Americans are excluded, the homicide rate in Montana and Wyoming was at least 67 per 100,000 adults per year. See Bureau of the Census (1872: 17–205).

171. R. White (1991: 344) and Dykstra (1968: 293–354).

172. Kupper (1945: 12–13, 64, 82–83, 107–116), Utley (1987: 21–22), R. White (1991: 344–345), Hine and Faragher (2000: 322–323), De

León (1983: 97), Rosenbaum (1981: 93–94), and F. W. Nolan (1992: 48–55).

173. Utley (1987: 17–20; 2002: 168–170, 233–239), Sonnichsen (1957: 185–199), Campbell (2003: 300–304), and Hollon (1974: 170–171). On other range wars in Texas and New Mexico, see Utley (2002: 180–183), Sonnichsen (1951: 97–132), Lamar (1970: 136–155), and Rosenbaum (1981: 68–90).

174. Utley (1987; 2002: 239–243) and R. M. Brown (1994: 394–396).

175. R. M. Brown (1994: 394–396).

176. Abbott and Smith (1939: 29–35, 47–48) and Siringo (1966: 2 and passim).

177. Dykstra (1968: 112–148). Homicide totals are from Dykstra (1968: 113, 142–148). The rates assume that the effective population of each cattle town was 50 percent higher than the population listed in the census, because of the number of cattlemen passing through.

178. Utley (1987: 112–117, 129–131).

179. J. W. Hardin (1961: 37–42).

180. Utley (1987: 10), Hollon (1974: 184–185), and Abbott and Smith (1939: 38–39). See also Dykstra (1968: 130).

181. R. M. Brown (1991: 49–58).

182. Rosa (1974: 10–71; 1996: 4–6). Hickok came from an abolitionist family in Indiana that had helped fugitive slaves, but he does not seem to have been an abolitionist, and when a black woman annoyed him in Kansas in 1856, he was quick to call her a "damn niger" (Rosa 1974: 19–20). R. M. Brown (1991: 49–58) may be wrong to call him a Radical Republican.

183. R. M. Brown (1991: 39–86) and Rosa (1974: 172–203).

184. R. M. Brown (1994: 409–410).

185. Abbott and Smith (1939: 27–28).

8. The Modern Pattern Is Set

1. Keller (1977: 4–5).

2. Keller (1977: 35–53, 162, 285–287) and M. W. Summers (1993).

3. Mullen (2005: 63–81).

4. In Boston the rate for all homicides fell from a peak of 12 per 100,000 adults per year during Reconstruction to 6 per 100,000 in the 1880s and 1890s, and in New York from 6 per 100,000 to 4 per 100,000. In Philadelphia the indictment rate for homicides among unrelated adults dropped from 3.4 per 100,000 per year to 2.3 per 100,000. In Calhoun County, Illinois, the annual rate among unrelated adults fell

from 19 per 100,000 to 5, and in Henderson County from 11 per 100,000 to 2. In Ross County, Ohio, it dropped from 4 per 100,000 to 2; in Holmes County, Ohio, from 1.1 to 0.4; and in New Hampshire and Vermont, from 1.4 per 100,000 to 1.1. The arrest rate for homicide—a less reliable measure of homicide—also reached lows in the 1880s and 1890s in fifteen northern cities studied by Monkkonen (1981: 65–85; 1994). The average polished median arrest rate was 2.3 per 100,000 persons per year, 1877–1887, and 3.1 per 100,000, 1888–1905. For an explanation of polished medians and the method of calculating them, see Roth (1998: 18–24).

Rates appear to have increased in most jurisdictions in the late 1890s or early 1900s. No homicide estimates based on multiple sources are yet available for the North in the early twentieth century, so rates must be determined provisionally from official data—homicide detective reports, arrest records, and mortality statistics. The average polished median arrest rate in fifteen northern cities rebounded to 4.7 per 100,000 persons per year, 1906–1915. The same pattern appeared in industrial states in the Northeast and Midwest, from the Atlantic coast to Illinois and Wisconsin. According to mortality statistics compiled by the Bureau of the Census (1906–1938), the median homicide rate in those states climbed steadily from 5.6 to 5.9 per 100,000 adults per year, 1907–1910, to 8.1 by 1914. In Chicago, according to detective reports, the turning point was the mid-1890s; in New York City, according to mortality statistics, the late 1890s; and in Philadelphia, according to arrest records and detective reports, the early 1900s. But the pattern—a steep decline at the end of Reconstruction followed by a steady rise in the late nineteenth or early twentieth century—was common. Boston was an exception. Its homicide arrest rate fell from 6.6 per 100,000 adults per year in 1901–1903 to 3.1 in 1914–1916 (AHSV 2009: American Homicides [AH], figs. 1–3). But Massachusetts as a whole saw its homicide mortality rate rise from 2.5 per 100,000 adults per year in 1907 to 5.9 in 1914, following the general trend. On state-level homicide mortality rates, 1907–1914, see Bureau of the Census (1906–1938) and AHSV (2009: American Homicides Twentieth Century [AHTC], figs. 1–3).

5. On labor violence, see Gilje (1996: 116–143). On robbery homicides, see Adler (2006: 236–271).

6. See the murder by Poe, *Scioto Gazette* (Chillicothe, Ohio), 29 April 1899; and by McDuffee, *Dover Enquirer* (N.H.), 24 April 1891.

7. In Chicago, 1879–1885, 40 of 188 known homicides among unrelated adults stemmed from robberies or burglaries. In New Hampshire and Vermont, robbery homicides accounted for 17 percent of 197 homi-

cides among unrelated adults with known motives, 1847–1880, and 10 percent of 116, 1881–1900. In the five counties studied intensively in rural Ohio and Illinois, they comprised 8.4 percent of 87, 1847–1880, and 10 percent of 27, 1881–1900.

8. Gilje (1996: 116–143).

9. AHSV (2009: AH, tables 26–27). The rate at which the Irish committed nondomestic homicides fell in New Hampshire and Vermont from 3.3 per 100,000 adults per year, 1847–1880, to 1.9 per 100,000, and in rural Ohio and Illinois from 1.4 per 100,000 to zero per 100,000. On race consciousness among European Americans, see Roediger (1991, 2005), Jacobson (1998), and Foner and Fredrickson (2004).

10. See, for example, the obituaries of Francis Henry, *Rutland Herald*, 17 August 1880; John L. Davis, *New Hampshire Patriot*, 10 February 1881; and George Beauman, *Vermont Watchman* (Montpelier), 15 July 1885.

11. See the murders by Fred Stockwell and James Palmer, *New Hampshire Patriot*, 24 May 1895 and 31 May 1888.

12. Lane (1979: 53–114; 1986: 6–16), Rosenzweig (1983), and Adler (2006: 6–44).

13. On trends in education, see AHSV (2009: Time Trends). Rural children were as likely to attend school as urban children, but they spent fewer months in school. Among whites in 1900, only a fifth of farm children and two-fifths of rural nonfarm children spent nine or more months in school each year, but four-fifths of urban children did.

14. On the size of police forces, see Monkkonen (1981) and Rousey (1996: 24, 163–164). On the character of policing, see Lane (1967: 157–224), Monkkonen (1981: 74–75, 83, 129–147), and D. R. Johnson (1979: 122–146, 182–188). Twenty-five of 188 known homicides among unrelated adults in Chicago, 1879–1885, involved police officers: 16 as assailants and 9 as victims. See especially the murders of John Ebert, John Marzek, and John Shea, *Chicago Tribune*, 18 and 19 January 1885, 10 and 11 January 1883, 19 June 1882. Homicides by law-enforcement officers accounted for a smaller proportion of homicides in northern New England and the rural Midwest, but the victims there were also nonviolent offenders. See, for example, the homicides of Dean McVoy, *Mercer County Observer* (Celina, Ohio), 3 November 1892; and Henry Burnham, *Burlington Free Press*, 21 May 1894.

15. Adler (2006: 161–170, 179–196). In Chicago, 1911–1915, the homicide rates among unrelated adults were 38.3 per 100,000 adults per year for Italians and 7.7 for other European Americans. In Philadelphia, the rates were 10.3 per 100,000 adults per year for Italians and 1.7 for other European Americans in 1902, 15.5 and 2.8 respectively in 1908,

and 21.1 and 3.2 respectively in 1914. And in Omaha, 1880–1919, the rates were 23.3 per 100,000 adults per year for Italians and 5.6 for other European Americans. The pattern was not uniform, however. For instance, Italians were more likely than other whites to commit nondomestic homicides in Vermont and New Hampshire and in San Francisco, 1881–1900, but not in rural Ohio and Illinois (AHSV 2009: AH, tables 26–28 and 37). On homicide rates in Italy, see Chesnais (1982: 85–90).

16. See the murder of Dazane, *New Hampshire Patriot,* 1 March 1895; by Buno, Philadelphia indictments, September 1895 term, no. 595, Philadelphia City Archives; and of Gentile, *Chicago Tribune,* 2 November 1897. For examples of labor camp and gang homicides, see the murder by Giuseppe Mancera, *Laconia Democrat* (N.H.), 30 September 1892; of Salvatori di Giovanni, *Chicago Tribune,* 22 February 1901; and Adler (2006: 180–196).

17. See the murder by Dominito, *Chicago Tribune,* 10 November 1899; and Adler (2006: 175–179).

18. See the murders by Nolan and Varra, Philadelphia indictments, May 1896 term, no. 392, and October 1889 term, no. 17; and by Sienni, *Chicago Tribune,* 5 August 1899. On the nativist campaign against Italian immigrants, see Higham (1965).

19. The homicide rate for non-Italians of southern or eastern European descent varied from place to place, but on average it was about the same as the rate for other whites. In Philadelphia, 1902–1920, it was lower—1.6 per 100,000 adults per year versus 3.8 for other whites (and 18.3 for Italians). In Omaha, 1880–1919, it was higher—8.3 per 100,000 adults per year versus 5.4 for other whites (and 23.0 for Italians). In Chicago, 1911–1920, it was roughly the same—6.9 per 100,000 adults versus 8.2 for other whites (and 35.7 for Italians). Adler (2006: 169–170, 197–199) finds that non-Italian migrants from southern and eastern Europe were less than a sixth as likely as Italians to be murdered in Chicago. He also finds that homicide rates for Greeks and Hungarians in Chicago were higher than those of other southern and eastern Europeans, but lower than those of Italians.

20. On nativist feeling and political conflict between immigrants from southern and eastern Europe and the native-born or older immigrants, see Higham (1965).

21. See the murder of Isaac Cunningham, *Chillicothe Advertiser* (Ohio), 10 July 1891; and of Perley Baker, *Chillicothe Advertiser,* 3 April 1891.

22. Quigley (2004: 71–89) and Kousser (1991: 220–226, 233–239; 2002a; 2002b: 181–183, 195–198).

23. Lane (1986: 45–81). On similar political developments in New York City and Boston, see Osofsky (1971: 159–161) and Lukas (1985: 55–58).

24. Lane (1986; 1997: 187–188), McKanna (1997), Monkkonen (2001: 136–141), and Adler (2006: 120–158). On school attendance, see AHSV (2009: Time Trends).

25. AHSV (2009: AH, table 38); and Philadelphia indictments, March 1890 term, no. 401, and September 1895 term, no. 766. See also Philadelphia indictments, October 1895 term, no. 447, and September 1898 term, no. 648.

26. Lane (1986: 137–139) and AHSV (2009: AH, table 38). See also Philadelphia indictments, January 1895 term, no. 378, and July 1900 term, no. 241.

27. Philadelphia indictments, December 1901 term, no. 346, and August 1893 term, no. 212. See also ibid., June 1901 term, no. 184, and November 1901 term, no. 421.

28. Philadelphia indictments, March 1899 term, no. 437; July 1900 term, no. 30; November 1900 term, nos. 186 and 187; and AHSV (2009: AH, table 38). According to indictment records, 23 whites and 15 blacks were killed in interracial homicides in Philadelphia, 1881–1901.

29. Philadelphia indictments, August 1892 term, no. 354; April 1896 term, nos. 491 and 492; February 1898 term, no. 168; and April 1898 term, no. 432.

30. Philadelphia indictments, October 1895 term, no. 193; October 1899 term, no. 389; and September 1892 term, no. 919. See also ibid., January 1894 term, no. 109.

31. AHSV (2009: AH, table 39). Seven whites and 9 blacks were killed in interracial homicides in Chicago, 1879–1885; and 31 whites and 43 blacks, 1911–1915.

32. McKanna (1997: 45–77) and AHSV (2009: AH, table 40). Three whites and 5 blacks were killed in interracial homicides in Omaha in the 1890s.

33. AHSV (2009: AH, table 40). Twenty-one whites and 9 blacks were killed in interracial homicides in Omaha, 1901–1919.

34. Angle (1992: 102–116).

35. Lane (1986: 82–94), McKanna (1997: 61–64), and AHSV (2009: Criminal Justice).

36. AHSV (2009: AH, tables 38–41).

37. A. H. Spear (1967: 181–200).

38. A. H. Spear (1967: 184–189), AHSV (2009: AH, table 39, and AHTC, figs. 4–5). The nonwhite homicide rates for Maryland and Kentucky

are for 1913–14. On black politics in Boston and New York City, see Lukas (1985: 55–60) and Osofsky (1971: 159–178). According to Weiss (1983: 227–229), 61 percent of the potential black electorate in Chicago voted in the presidential election of 1932, compared to 52 percent in Cleveland, 41 percent in Detroit, and 29 percent in Harlem. Only 46 percent of potential black voters were registered in Philadelphia in that year.

39. AHSV (2009: AHTC, figs. 6–8). Mortality statistics are not available for Arizona before 1926 and for New Mexico and Nevada before 1929, so the estimate here is an extrapolation based on homicide trends in California, Colorado, and other western states. Rates were comparable to those in other western states on the eve of World War I: 10 per 100,000 adults per year in Washington, 17 per 100,000 in Montana and Colorado, and probably 20–30 per 100,000 in Wyoming.

40. Lamar (1970: 432–459), Ball (1992: 11–16, 28–36, 41–43, 50–74, 108–127, 225–255), and McKanna (1997: 117–139). Similar conditions had prevailed in territorial Florida.

41. Gila County data are from McKanna (1997).

42. Woody and Schwartz (1977) and Forrest (1984).

43. McKanna (1997: 117–154).

44. Gila County data are from McKanna (1997).

45. McKanna (1997: 90–92).

46. Las Animas County data are from McKanna (1997). On the history of mining towns in southern Colorado, see J. B. Allen (1966), Deutsch (1987), Papanikolas (1991), and McKanna (1997: 78–94). On labor violence, see McKanna (1997: 78–116).

47. AHSV (2009: AH, table 28).

48. On rates of interracial homicides, see AHSV (2009: AH, table 33).

49. AHSV (2009: AH, tables 33–34). Paciotti (2005: 238) finds that 69 percent of homicides among the Chinese in Seattle, 1900–1940, were gang related. He finds the same high homicide rates among the Chinese in Seattle in the early twentieth century that Mullen (2005: 63–81) finds in San Francisco.

50. AHSV (2009: AH, table 33). The Hispanic intraracial homicide rate fell from 37 per 100,000 adults per year in the late 1860s and 1870s to 17 per 100,000 in the 1880s and 1890s.

51. Pitt (1971: 262–276), Camarillo (1979: 104, 117–141), and Griswold del Castillo (1979: 124–170).

52. The Hispanic rate was 20 (versus 17 for Anglos) per 100,000 adults per year in mining, ranching, and farming counties, and 6 (versus 9) per 100,000 adults in San Francisco. In San Francisco and Los Angeles the

Chinese killed one another at a rate of 28 per 100,000 adults per year, while Anglos killed one another at rates of 9 per 100,000 in San Francisco and 11 per 100,000 in Los Angeles.

53. AHSV (2009: AH, tables 33–34).

54. AHSV (2009: AH, tables 24–25 [South Carolina] and 31 [Louisiana]). The annual rate at which blacks were murdered by whites fell from 6 to 3 per 100,000 in Edgefield County, South Carolina; from 33 to 7 per 100,000 in New Orleans; and from 78 to 12 in rural Louisiana. The rate at which whites murdered one another fell from 15 to 8 per 100,000 per year in Edgefield County, South Carolina; from 22 to 13 per 100,000 in New Orleans; and from 34 to 22 per 100,000 in rural Louisiana.

   The average polished median arrest rate for homicide in seven southern and border cities fell from 9.4 per 100,000 persons per year, 1866–1876, to 6.5 per 100,000, 1877–1887 (Monkkonen 1981: 65–85; 1994). The seven cities include Baltimore, Louisville, Richmond, St. Louis, and Washington, D.C. Cincinnati is also included. Its native-born population was predominantly southern, and after the Civil War its homicide arrest rate paralleled the rates of cities in the southern and border states, not the rates of cities in the North. The drop in northern cities was from 3.3 per 100,000 to 2.3 per 100,000. Monkkonen's data include fifteen northern cities.

55. AHSV (2009: AH, tables 24–25 [South Carolina] and 31 [Louisiana]). On the disfranchisement of black and poor white voters, see Kousser (1974; 1999: 12–68) and Perman (2001).

56. See the murder by Hopkins, *Atlanta Constitution*, 1 August 1885; and by Jones, Edgefield County (S.C.) Coroner's Book of Inquisitions, 1877–1885: 51–52. See also the murder of Jeff Nickles, *Jasper County News* (Monticello, Ga.), 6 December 1884.

57. Edgefield County Coroner's Book of Inquisitions, 1877–1885: 52–57.

58. Waller (1995: 364–367).

59. See the murder by Dyer, *Atlanta Constitution*, 18 September 1885; by Findley and Woody, *Dahlonega Signal* (Ga.), 10 October 1884; and Stanley (1975: 138–143).

60. See the murder of Hammond, *Ellijay Courier* (Ga.), 28 June 1883; and of the Swillings, *Toccoa News* (Ga.), 17 and 24 December 1886.

61. AHSV (2009: AH, tables 24 [South Carolina] and 31 [Louisiana]). According to the annual reports of the coroner of Savannah, Georgia, 1895–1898, the homicide rate among blacks was one and a half times the rate among whites: 23 per 100,000 adults per year versus 14 per 100,000 (Ayers 1984: 336n16; AHSV 2009: AH, table 42).

62. Rousey (1996: 159–196).

63. Rousey (1996: 167, 186, 160).

64. Butterfield (1995: 35–45) and Chapman (1897: 104, 261). On the exodus of blacks from the South, see Painter (1976), Hair (1969: 83–99), and Hahn (2003: 317–363).

65. See the murder by Dorn in 1881, Edgefield County Coroner's Book of Inquisitions, 1877–1885: 63–64.

66. See the murders by Harris in 1882 and by Butler in 1878, ibid., 29–33, 83–85.

67. Butterfield (1995: 35–45) and Du Bois (1965: 257–258).

68. *Jasper County News,* 28 July 1883 and 16 August 1884.

69. J. D. Anderson (1988: 4–32).

70. McKinney (1978: 110–194). Electoral data are from University of Maryland (1991).

71. On southern populism, see Woodward (1951: 175–263; 1963: 129–277), Hahn (1983; 2003: 412–425, 431–440), Hair (1969: 107–233), Ayers (1992: 187–282), and J. D. Anderson (1988: 26–27).

72. Woodward (1951: 188). Electoral data are from University of Maryland (1991).

73. Ayers (1992: 34–54) and Woodward (1951: 107–174).

74. The rates for lynching, 1889–1903, are for the ten southern states studied by Tolnay and Beck (1995: 271). On South Carolina, 1887–1914, see Moore (2006: 130–131); on the upper Cumberland, see Montell (1986: 146) and AHSV (2009: AH, table 30). The data for South Carolina include indictments for murder and manslaughter. After 1900, however, they include not only homicides but also automobile accidents that led to manslaughter charges.

    The polished median homicide arrest rate in seven southern and border cities rose from 6.5 per 100,000 persons per year, 1877–1887, to 9.0 per 100,000, 1888–1911, and 14.2 per 100,000, 1912–1920 (Monkkonen 1981: 65–85; 1994). On homicide rates in the South in the 1920s and 1930s, see AHSV (2009: AHTC, figs. 4–5).

75. Holmes (1980) and Rabun County (Ga.) Superior Court, Record of Testimony, 1873–1888: 142–149.

76. Holmes (1980: 607–609, 604–605, 601–602) and Ward (1965: 643–644). Holmes finds that of the sixty-six known vigilante attacks in northwestern Georgia, 1889–1894, 42 percent opposed revenue laws, 20 percent enforced moral standards, 11 percent attacked blacks on racial grounds, and 27 percent had no identified purpose.

77. *Toccoa Times,* 19 February 1896.

78. Transcript of State v. J. A. Kimmons and Bunyan Kimmons, January 1911 Special Term, Gilmer County (Ga.) Superior Court, Ellijay.

79. On backcountry homicides, see Montell (1986: 23–64); the murder by John Fowler, *Toccoa Times,* 8 April 1896; by Tobe Chastain, *Dahlonega Nugget* (Ga.), 21 October 1898; by Oscar Griggs, *Monticello News* (Ga.), 3 July 1914; and Transcript of State v. J. Hershel Charles, October 1918 Term, Gilmer County Superior Court. On Cumberland County, see Montell (1970: 86–91).

80. Montell (1970: 81–83, 91–101).

81. Montell (1970: 101–105).

82. Montell (1970: 122–146).

83. Montell (1970: 106–109).

84. Tolnay and Beck (1995) and Brundage (1993).

85. Tolnay and Beck (1995) and Brundage (1993). From 1889 to 1903, lynchings claimed the lives of 0.3 per 100,000 adults per year in Virginia, 0.7 per 100,000 in Kentucky, at least 0.8 per 100,000 in Texas, and 1 per 100,000 in the rest of the South. The data for Virginia are from Brundage (1993: 281–283), for Kentucky from Wright (1990: 71, 307–323), for Texas from National Association for the Advancement of Colored People (1969: 95–99), and for the rest of the South from Tolnay and Beck (1995: 271–272).

86. Utley (2002: 246–248), R. M. Brown (1975: 258–260), and Sonnichsen (1951: 186–226).

87. Woodward (1963: 216–243; 1951: 264–290) and Utley (2002: 260–263, 271–273).

88. Goodwyn (1971) and Hahn (2003: 398–399, 439–440).

89. Kousser (1991: 219; 1999: 12–68) and Hahn (2003: 379–380).

90. Hahn (2003: 440–451), Perman (2001), Kousser (1974; 1999: 12–68), and Williamson (1984).

91. Kousser (1999: 12–68), Woodward (1951: 321–349), Hair (1969: 234–267), and Ayers (1992: 283–338).

92. Butterfield (1995: 46–67) and Du Bois (1965: 258).

93. Montell (1970: 71–74).

94. Montell (1970: 160–162).

95. Montell (1970: 110–121).

96. Butterfield (1995: 54); Rousey (1996: 194); and the murder of Dan Barber, *Monticello News,* 15 and 22 January 1915. See also the murder of John Ware, *Carnesville Advance,* 23 September 1904.

97. See the murder by Orange Rucker, *Carnesville Advance,* 11 March 1910; and State v. Tink Thompson and Irwin Johnson, September 1893 term,

Jasper County (Ga.) Court files. Tink Thompson's friends told a different story, but the court and the other witnesses did not believe them. Their story, too, however, involved a thrown bottle and affronts to honor. See also the murder by Willie Shannon, *Monticello News*, 12 October 1906; and by Lou Phillips, *Monticello News*, 15 November 1907.

98. State v. Fred Nolley, March 1905 term, Jasper County Court files. For murders at church or at social events, see State v. Stephen Malone, September 1888 term, and State v. Greene Maxey, March 1892 term, Jasper County Court files; State v. Tom Shirley, March 1916 term, Franklin County (Ga.) Court files; the murder by Charles Shepperd, *Washington Chronicle* (Ga.), 30 October 1893; by Frank Coleman, *Jasper County News*, 17 May 1894; by George Kelly, *Jasper County News*, 15 December 1898; by Barry Epps, *Jasper County News*, 7 March 1901; and by Rufe Tomlin and Sam Jones, *Jasper County News*, 24 July 1902.

99. State v. Teasley, March 1917 term, Franklin County Court files.

9. The Problem Endures

1. According to the FBI's Supplementary Homicide Reports (Fox 2005), the proportion of homicides in which the relationship between the victim and offender is "unknown" rose from 23 percent in 1976 to 43 percent in 2003. But local authorities are confident that they know the relationship between the victim and the offender in over 90 percent of homicides; they are just reluctant to share that knowledge with anyone, including the FBI, until arrests are made. Homicides by strangers probably account for no more than a quarter of all homicides in the United States, but without access to information on individual cases, scholars cannot be certain. Newspapers are no longer a reliable source for that information, because police officers, coroners, prosecutors, defense attorneys, witnesses, and defendants are not as willing as they once were to speak with reporters. The result has been an information blackout that has made it difficult to understand individual homicides and to chart the course of various kinds of homicide. AHSV (2009: American Homicides Twentieth Century [AHTC], fig. 9), K. Williams and Flewelling (1987), Decker (1993), and M. D. Smith and Zahn (1999: 31–52).

2. AHSV (2009: European Homicides [EH], figs. 8–11). On Ireland, see O'Donnell (2005: 673), Somerset Fry and Somerset Fry (1988: 295–320), and R. K. Webb (1970: 493–496); on Russia, Stickley (2006: 16–25); on Belgium, Rousseaux, Vesentini, and Vrints (2004); and on

France, Chesnais (1982: 79–81). The homicide rate in France was at least 2.03 per 100,000 persons per year in 1943 and 1.99 per 100,000 in 1945: 2.4 times the prewar rate.

3. Gould (2003: 150–161), Chesnais (1982: 75, 81–85), and AHSV (2009: EH, fig. 6). The statistical correlations that Gould found between regime change and homicide in Italy, France, and Finland, do not hold for the United States or for most other Western nations, because regime change does not correlate in many instances with political instability, loss of legitimacy, or diminution of national feeling.

4. AHSV (2009: EH, fig. 7) and Chesnais (1982: 70–73).

5. AHSV (2009: AHTC, figs. 10–11).

6. AHSV (2009: AHTC, figs. 1–8). The rates in the industrial states of the Northeast and Midwest rose from 3 to 8 per 100,000 adults per year on the eve of World War I to 6 to 13 per 100,000 on the eve of the Great Depression, with a spike in 1917–1919 that drove the homicide rate in Illinois to 22 per 100,000, in New Jersey to 37 per 100,000, and in New York to 42 per 100,000.

7. Tuttle (1970).

8. Higham (1965), Roediger (2005: 3–130), Tindall (1984: 987), and *Chicago Daily Tribune,* 7 May 1919.

9. Tindall (1984: 980) and Lane (1997: 216).

10. Terkel (1970: 13–16) and Kennedy (1999: 92).

11. Kennedy (1999: 137, 245–248, 379–380).

12. Kennedy (1999: 153, 243–248, 363–380), Weiss (1983: 289–291), Bakke (1940: 52–54), and McElvaine (1983: 3–16, 157–229).

13. AHSV (2009: AHTC, tables 1 and 2).

14. Weiss (1983: 53–57, 163–168, 173–174).

15. Honey (1999: 15–85).

16. The homicide rate in Memphis fell from 117.0 per 100,000 persons per year for blacks in 1930–1934 to 57.9 per 100,000 in 1939–1941 (51 percent), and for whites from 18.8 per 100,000 to 6.4 per 100,000 (66 percent). The figures for the South as a whole were 13 percent for nonwhites and 53 percent for whites. The Memphis data are available through the courtesy of Douglas Eckberg.

17. Leuchtenburg (1963: 141) and Weiss (1983: 51–53, 237).

18. Weiss (1983: 211–214, 218–221).

19. Weiss (1983: 286–295).

20. Franklin (1980: 437–440) and Honey (1999: 86–212).

21. Sitkoff (1981: 3–39) and Franklin (1980: 450–455).

22. On Asian and Native American homicide rates, see AHSV (2009: AHTC, table 1). The Asian homicide rate in the late 1950s and early

1960s is an average from 1954–1963, because the relatively small population of Asian Americans allowed the rate to fluctuate substantially from year to year.

23. The homicide data are from Bureau of the Census (1937–1993: 1937–1941). The population data are from the U.S. Census of 1940 and from the sample of that census in the Integrated Public Use Microdata Series, Minnesota Population Center, University of Minnesota, which identifies people with Spanish surnames. Most citizens with Hispanic surnames (97 percent) were listed as white in the census of 1940. They accounted for 1.4 percent of the white population. It is probable that most Hispanic homicide victims were listed as white in the vital statistics of 1940, but it is impossible to know definitively without a sample from the original vital records.

The curve is a resistant "line," based on the cube root of the proportion of Hispanics, Asians, Native Americans, and African Americans in the population. For the method of calculating resistant lines, see Roth (1998: 11–17). The only state with a higher-than-expected homicide rate that could not trace its problem to the mid-nineteenth century was Nevada, which was plagued in 1937–1941 by homicides related to gambling, prostitution, and organized crime.

24. The curve is a resistant line, based on the negative inverse of the proportion of Asians, Native Americans, and African Americans in the population raised to the .4 power. The white homicide rate is not correlated as closely at the state level with urbanization as it is with the proportion of Asians, Hispanics, Native Americans, and African Americans in the population, but it is statistically significant and strongly negative, even when white urbanization and the ethnic and racial composition of the population are regressed simultaneously on the white homicide rate. The data on lynching are from Tolnay and Beck (1995: 271–272).

25. AHSV (2009: AHTC, fig. 12). Urban states are those in which 50 percent or more of the white population lived in communities of 2,500 persons or more.

26. AHSV (2009: AHTC, fig. 13). Urban states are those in which 25 percent or more of the nonwhite population lived in communities of 2,500 persons or more.

27. Tindall (1984: 1217–1259) and Patterson (1996: 243–310, 380–433).

28. Tindall (1984: 1266–1276) and Patterson (1996: 433–441, 458–523).

29. A regression of the mean annual presidential approval rating in Gallup polls on the annual homicide rate, 1937–2006, yields an R-square of only 14.3 percent. The homicide rate correlates far more strongly with

measures of trust in government. The Gallup polls are from Roper Center Public Opinion Archives at http://www.ropercenter.uconn .edu/data_access/data/presidential_approval.html.

30. On the political consensus of the postwar years, see Hodgson (1976: 17–18, 67–98).

31. AHSV (2009: AHTC, tables 14 and 15). According to a survey of scholars of American history and politics, national integration and government legitimacy were considerably higher in 1950 than in 1930, 1970, or 1990 (Citrin et al. 1994: 3–5). LaFree (1998: 100–104) first observed the connection between homicide rates in the United States and the level of trust in government (as measured by opinion polls).

32. The United States as a whole was probably more homicidal for whites in the late 1950s and early 1960s than the North and the mountain South were for their inhabitants in the 1820s and 1830s, once improvements in medical care are considered. Still, the homicide rate for whites in the late 1950s and early 1960s was remarkably low.

33. LaFree (2005: 199) and LaFree and Drass (2002).

34. W. J. Wilson (1996), Schneider (1999: xv–xx, 27–50, 106–136, 164–187), and LaFree (1998: 114–134).

35. Honey (1999: 237–368) and Patterson (1996: 739–740; 2005: 63–65).

36. Honey (1999: 324–330).

37. Tonry (1997); Chilton, Teske, and Arnold (1995); Jackson (1995); and LaFree (1998: 188–191).

38. The statistics are from the World Health Organization (1950–).

39. See AHSV (2009: AHTC, table 1). The Native American homicide rate since 1960 is difficult to interpret because of the rapid increase in the number of Americans who were previously classified as white but now identify themselves as Native American. According to the Bureau of the Census, the Native American population rose from 524,000 in 1960 to 793,000 in 1970, to 1,420,000 in 1980, and to 1,904,000 in 1990, far faster than the birth rate would allow. Only 165,000 Hispanic Americans identified themselves as Native American in 1990, so the increase has come primarily from Americans who are fully assimilated into white society and have changed their racial identification from white to Native American. Because of this increase in the reported Native American population, the homicide rate for Native Americans rose only 29 percent from 1963 to 1974, from 14.9 per 100,000 persons per year to 20.9 per 100,000, and has fallen steadily since.

40. M. S. Johnson (2003: 278).

41. Hodgson (1976: 153–499). The quote is from Lyndon Johnson. See Patterson (1996: 586).

42. Patterson (1996: 579–588) and Lukas (1985: 16).
43. Patterson (1996: 585–588) and Lukas (1985: 100–104, 112–139, 186–187).
44. Patterson (1996: 655–662), Breitman (1965: 12), Lukas (1985: 110–111, 156–157, 414–423, 528–531, 567–575), and Sitkoff (1981: 199–221).
45. Patterson (1996: 583) and Lukas (1985: 137–138, 452–455).
46. Lukas (1985: 252–276, 288) and Patterson (1996: 732–741).
47. Patterson (1996: 668–677, 697–709) and Sitkoff (1981: 221–225).
48. Lukas (1985: 256–258, 323–326, 455–462, 473–474, 509–535).
49. Patterson (1996: 593–619).
50. Patterson (1996: 620–636, 752–757).
51. LaFree (1998: 91–113).
52. Patterson (2005: 92–94) and Wilentz (2008: 76, 80).
53. Wilentz (2008: 26–32, 69–80) and Patterson (2005: 81–94, 105–110).
54. Patterson (2005: 76–151), Wilentz (2008: 26–126), and Hodgson (2004: 8–22). For the quote from Jimmy Carter, see Hodgson (2004: 15).
55. Patterson (2005: 113–114, 121–128).
56. Patterson (2005: 92–128). However, the white homicide rate included homicides committed by Hispanics, and the nonwhite homicide rate included homicides committed by Asian Americans. Reliable homicide rates for Hispanic and Asian Americans were not available before 1985, but they were probably much higher for Hispanics than for non-Hispanic whites and lower for Asians than for African Americans. Thus, the growing number of Hispanics and Asian Americans in the population contributed to the rise of the white homicide rate and the decline in the nonwhite homicide rate in the late 1970s.
57. See Wilentz (2008: 147–148) on the recession. The annual rates fell from 7.0 per 100,000 persons to 5.6 per 100,000 for whites (including Hispanic Americans), from 39.6 per 100,000 to 29.9 per 100,000 for African Americans, from 15.4 per 100,000 to 11.9 per 100,000 for Native Americans, and from 5.7 per 100,000 to 4.3 per 100,000 for Asian Americans (AHSV 2009: AHTC, table 1).
58. Wilentz (2008: 127–138, 207–208).
59. Wilentz (2008: 176, 180–182) and Patterson (2005: 131, 145–148, 153–165).
60. The homicide rate in 1989 was 4.0 per 100,000 for non-Hispanic whites, 5.4 per 100,000 for Asian Americans, 12.1 per 100,000 for Native Americans, 16.1 per 100,000 for Hispanic Americans, and 37.3 per 100,000 for African Americans (AHSV 2009: AHTC, table 1).

61. Wilentz (2008: 278, 355–381), Patterson (2005: 346–386), and AHSV (2009: AHTC, table 1).
62. *New York Times,* 12 February 2006: 1, 28. As I had anticipated, the murders were caused by petty disputes among friends, acquaintances, and strangers. FBI statistics for 2005 and 2006 confirm the increase. See Federal Bureau of Investigation (1998–). The revised homicide rate for New Orleans in 2006 was calculated by Professor Mark VanLandingham of Tulane University (*New Orleans Times-Picayune,* 12 March 2006).

Conclusion

1. Blumstein and Wallman (2000: 134, 137–143, 152–159) and J. A. Fox and Zawitz (2004: 79–93). The FBI data are incomplete because in an increasing number of cases state and local agencies have been reluctant to specify the relationship between victim and suspect before those cases are completely resolved.
2. Blumstein and Wallman (2000: 134).
3. In 2008 the rapper Ludacris put out a song titled "Politics as Usual," in which he says, "McCain don't belong in any chair unless he's paralyzed / Yeah I said it, 'cause Bush is mentally handicapped." In the documentary *Jesus Camp* (2006) a Pentecostal minister is shown instructing children at a summer camp to smash mugs labeled "government" with hammers.
4. Kelling and Coles (1996), Silverman (1999), and Skogan (1990). For critiques of the "broken window" theory, see Harcourt (2001), R. Taylor (2001), and Sampson and Raudenbush (1999).
5. Lincoln (1989, 2: 687).
6. de Waal (2005: 227–250).

Sources

1. AHSV (2009: Distinguishing Homicides from Natural Deaths, Accidental Deaths, or Suicides).
2. Gilmore (1989: 193–195, 447n11).
3. A. P. Scott (1930: 41–49), Rankin (1965: 1–42), and Schwarz (1988: 3–45).
4. Schwarz (1988: 3–45).
5. A. P. Scott (1930: 41–49) and Rankin (1965: 1–42).
6. Semmes (1938: 21–40).

References

Aarim-Heriot, N. 2003. *Chinese Immigrants, African Americans, and Racial Anxiety in the United States, 1848–1882*. Urbana: University of Illinois Press.

Abbott, E. C., and H. H. Smith. 1939. *We Pointed Them North: Recollections of a Cowpuncher.* New York: Farrar and Rinehart.

Abernethy, T. P. 1932. *From Frontier to Plantation in Tennessee: A Study in Frontier Democracy.* Chapel Hill: University of North Carolina Press.

———. 1961. *The South in the New Nation, 1789–1819*. Baton Rouge: Louisiana State University Press.

Adams, E. H. 1887. *To and Fro in Southern California*. In the collection California As I Saw It: First-Person Narratives of California's Early Years, 1849–1900. Washington, D.C.: General Collections and Rare Book and Special Collections Division, Library of Congress, 1997. Available at http://memory.loc.gov/ammem/cbhtml/cbhome.html.

Adams, J. W., and A. B. Kasakoff. 1991. "Estimates of Census Underenumeration Based on Genealogies." *Social Science History* 15: 527–543.

Adler, J. S. 1997. "'My Mother-in-Law Is to Blame, but I'll Walk on Her Neck Yet': Homicide in Late Nineteenth-Century Chicago." *Journal of Social History* 31: 253–276.

———. 1999a. "'If We Can't Live in Peace, We Might as Well Die': Homicide-Suicide in Chicago, 1875–1910." *Journal of Urban History* 26: 3–21.

———. 1999b. "'The Negro Would Be More than an Angel to Withstand Such Treatment': African-American Homicide in Chicago, 1875–1910."

In *Lethal Imagination: Violence and Brutality in American History*, ed. M. Bellesiles, 295–314. New York: New York University Press.

———. 2006. *First in Violence, Deepest in Dirt: Homicide in Chicago, 1875–1920*. Cambridge: Harvard University Press.

AHSV. 2009. American Homicide Supplemental Volume. Computer file. Available through Historical Violence Database (http://cjrc.osu.edu/researchprojects/hvd/).

Alexander, A. L. 1991. *Ambiguous Lives: Free Women of Color in Rural Georgia, 1789–1879*. Fayetteville: University of Arkansas Press.

Allaman, J. L. 1989. "Nineteenth Century Homicide in Henderson County, Illinois: A Study of Court Records and the Press Media as Reliable Sources for Writing Local History." Ph.D. diss., Illinois State University.

Allegro, J. J. 1997. "Law, Politics, and Slavery in Massachusetts Bay Colony, 1686–1738." M.A. thesis, Tufts University.

Allen, F. 2004. *A Decent, Orderly Lynching: The Montana Vigilantes*. Norman: University of Oklahoma Press.

Allen, J. B. 1966. *The Company Town in the American West*. Norman: University of Oklahoma Press.

Altschuler, G. C., and S. M. Blumin. 2000. *Rude Republic: Americans and Their Politics in the Nineteenth Century*. Princeton: Princeton University Press.

Ames, E., et al., eds. 1869–1922. *The Acts and Resolves, Public and Private, of the Province of the Massachusetts Bay*. 21 vols. Boston: Wright and Potter.

Ames, S. M., ed. 1954. *County Court Records of Accomack-Northampton, Virginia, 1632–1640*. Vol. 7 of *American Legal Records*. Washington, D.C.: American Historical Association.

Amussen, S. D. 1994. "'Being Stirred to Much Unquietness': Violence and Domestic Violence in Early Modern Europe." *Journal of Women's History* 6: 70–89.

Anbinder, T. 2002. *Five Points: The Nineteenth-Century New York City Neighborhood That Invented Tap Dance, Stole Elections, and Became the World's Most Notorious Slum*. New York: Plume.

Anderson, F. 1984. *A People's Army: Massachusetts Soldiers and Society in the Seven Years' War*. Chapel Hill: University of North Carolina Press.

———. 2000. *Crucible of War: The Seven Years' War and the Fate of Empire in British North America, 1754–1766*. New York: Alfred A. Knopf.

Anderson, J. D. 1988. *The Education of Blacks in the South, 1860–1935*. Chapel Hill: University of North Carolina Press.

Anderson, M. S. 1998. *War and Society in Europe of the Old Regime, 1618–1789*. Stroud: Sutton.

Anderson, O. 1987. *Suicide in Victorian and Edwardian England.* New York: Oxford University Press.

Andrews, C. M. 1943. *Narratives of the Insurrections, 1675–1690.* New York: Barnes and Noble.

Angle, P. M. 1992. *Bloody Williamson: A Chapter in American Lawlessness.* Urbana: University of Illinois Press.

Anglo, S. 1990. "'How to Kill a Man at Your Ease': Fencing Books and the Duelling Ethic." In *Chivalry in the Renaissance,* ed. S. Anglo, 1–12. Woodbridge: Boydell.

Aptheker, H. 1938. *The Negro in the Civil War.* New York: International Publishers.

———. 1969. *American Negro Slave Revolts.* New York: International Publishers.

Archer, D., and R. Gartner. 1984. *Violence and Crime in Cross-National Perspective.* New Haven: Yale University Press.

Archer, J. E. 2008. "Mysterious and Suspicious Deaths: Missing Homicides in North-West England, 1850–1900." *Crime, History, and Societies* 12: 45–63.

Archer, R. 1990. "New England Mosaic: A Demographic Analysis for the Seventeenth Century." *William and Mary Quarterly,* 3d. ser., 47: 477–502.

Asbury, H. 1998. *The Gangs of New York: An Informal History of the Underworld.* New York: Thunder's Mouth Press.

Axtell, J., ed. 1981. *The Indian Peoples of Eastern America: A Documentary History of the Sexes.* New York: Oxford University Press.

Ayers, E. L. 1984. *Vengeance and Justice: Crime and Punishment in the Nineteenth-Century American South.* New York: Oxford University Press.

———. 1992. *The Promise of the New South: Life after Reconstruction.* New York: Oxford University Press.

———. 2003. *In the Presence of Mine Enemies: War in the Heart of America, 1859–1863.* New York: W. W. Norton.

Azaola Garrido, E. 1997. *El delito de ser mujer: Hombres y mujeres homicidas en la Ciudad de México: Historias de vida.* México: Plaza y Valdes Editores.

Baird, B. 1999. "The Social Origins of Dueling in Virginia." In *The Lethal Imagination: Violence and Brutality in American History,* ed. M. Bellesiles, 87–112. New York: New York University Press.

Bakke, E. W. 1940. *Citizens without Work.* New Haven: Yale University Press.

Ball, L. D. 1992. *Desert Lawmen: The High Sheriffs of New Mexico and Arizona, 1846–1912.* Albuquerque: University of New Mexico Press.

Bancroft, H. H. 1884–1890. *History of California.* 7 vols. San Francisco: History Company.

———. 1887–1890. *Popular Tribunals.* 2 vols. San Francisco: History Company.

Bandel, B. 1978. "What the Good Laws of Man Hath Put Asunder . . ." *Vermont History* 46: 221–233.

Baptist, E. E. 2002. *Creating an Old South: Middle Florida's Plantation Frontier before the Civil War.* Chapel Hill: University of North Carolina Press.

Barber, C. L. 1957. *The Idea of Honour in the English Drama, 1591–1700.* Göteborg: Elanders.

Barnard, T. 1998. "Protestantism, Ethnicity and Irish Identities, 1660–1760." In *Protestantism and National Identity: Britain and Ireland, c. 1650–c. 1850,* ed. T. Claydon and I. McBride, 206–235. Cambridge: Cambridge University Press.

Barney, W. L. 1987. *The Passage of the Republic: An Interdisciplinary History of Nineteenth-Century America.* Lexington, Mass.: D. C. Heath.

Barth, G. P. 1964. *Bitter Strength: A History of the Chinese in the United States, 1850–1870.* Cambridge: Harvard University Press.

Basch, N. 1982. *In the Eyes of the Law: Women, Marriage, and Property in Nineteenth-Century New York.* Ithaca: Cornell University Press.

Bauer, K. J. 1974. *The Mexican War, 1846–1848.* New York: Macmillan.

Baxter, J. P. 1890. *Sir Ferdinando Gorges and His Province of Maine.* 3 vols. Boston: Prince Society.

Beames, M. R. 1983. *Peasants and Power: The Whiteboy Movements and Their Control in Pre-Famine Ireland.* New York: St. Martin's Press.

Becker, M. B. 1994. *The Emergence of Civil Society in the Eighteenth Century: A Privileged Moment in the History of England, Scotland, and France.* Bloomington: Indiana University Press.

Becker, S., et al. 1996. "Estimating the Completeness of Under-5 Death Registration in Egypt." *Demography* 33: 329–339.

Beeman, R. R. 1985. "The Political Response to Social Conflict in the Southern Backcountry: A Comparative View of Virginia and the Carolinas during the Revolution." In *An Uncivil War: The Southern Backcountry during the American Revolution,* ed. R. Hoffman, T. W. Tate, and P. J. Albert, 213–239. Charlottesville: University Press of Virginia.

Beier, A. L. 1974. "Vagrants and the Social Order in Elizabethan England." *Past and Present* 64: 3–29.

———. 1985. *Masterless Men: The Vagrancy Problem in England, 1560–1640.* London: Methuen.

Ben-Amos, I. K. 1994. *Adolescence and Youth in Early Modern England.* New Haven: Yale University Press.

Benton, J. H. 1911. *Warning Out in New England, 1656–1817.* Boston: W. B. Clarke.

Berkin, C. 1996. *First Generations: Women in Colonial America.* New York: Hill and Wang.

Berlin, I. 1998. *Many Thousands Gone: The First Two Centuries of Slavery in North America*. Cambridge: Belknap Press of Harvard University Press.

Beverley, R. 1947. *The History and Present State of Virginia* [1705]. Ed. L. B. Wright. Chapel Hill: University of North Carolina Press.

Bienen, L. 2004. Homicide in Chicago, 1870–1930. Computer file. Northwestern University School of Law. Available at http://homicide.northwestern.edu.

Billaçois, F. 1990. *The Duel: Its Rise and Fall in Early Modern France*. Trans. and ed. T. Selous. New Haven: Yale University Press.

Billings, W. M., J. E. Selby, and T. W. Tate. 1986. *Colonial Virginia: A History*. White Plains, N.Y.: KTO Press.

Billington, R. A. 1938. *The Protestant Crusade, 1800–1860: A Study of the Origins of American Nativism*. New York: Macmillan.

Binion, R. 1986. *After Christianity: Christian Survivals in Post-Christian Culture*. Durango, Colo.: Logbridge-Rhodes.

Black, P. W. 1912. "Lynchings in Iowa." *Iowa Journal of History and Politics* 10: 151–254.

Blair, W. A. 1998. *Virginia's Private War: Feeding Body and Soul in the Confederacy, 1861–1865*. New York: Oxford University Press.

Blassingame, J. W. 1973. *Black New Orleans, 1860–1880*. Chicago: University of Chicago Press.

Block, S. 2006. *Rape and Sexual Power in Early America*. Chapel Hill: University of North Carolina Press.

Blumstein, A., and J. Wallman, eds. 2000. *The Crime Drop in America*. New York: Cambridge University Press.

Boessenecker, J. 1999. *Gold Dust and Gunsmoke: Tales of Gold Rush Outlaws, Gunfighters, Lawmen, and Vigilantes*. New York: John Wiley.

Bonner, J. C. 1978. *Milledgeville: Georgia's Antebellum Capital*. Athens: University of Georgia Press.

Bourne, R. 1990. *The Red King's Rebellion: Racial Politics in New England, 1675–1678*. New York: Atheneum.

Bowden, P. J. 1976. "Agricultural Prices, Farm Profits and Rents." In *The Agrarian History of England and Wales*, ed. J. Thirsk, 4: 593–695. Cambridge: Cambridge University Press.

Bradburn, D. M., and J. C. Coombs. 2006. "Smoke and Mirrors: Reinterpreting the Society and Economy of the Seventeenth-Century Chesapeake." *Atlantic Studies* 3: 131–157.

Braddick, M. J. 2000. *State Formation in Early Modern England, c. 1550–1700*. New York: Cambridge University Press.

Bradford, W. 1970. *Of Plymouth Plantation, 1620–1647*. Ed. S. E. Morison. New York: Alfred A. Knopf.

Bradstreet, S. 1855. "Simon Bradstreet's Journal, 1664–1683." *New England Historical and Genealogical Register* 9: 43–51.

Bragdon, K. 1996. "Gender as a Social Category in Native Southern New England." *Ethnohistory* 43: 573–592.

Brant, M. 1992. *The Outlaw Youngers: A Confederate Brotherhood.* Lanham, Md.: Madison Books.

Breen, P. H. 2003. "A Prophet in His Own Land: Support for Nat Turner and His Rebellion within Southampton's Black Community." In *Nat Turner: A Slave Rebellion in History and Memory,* ed. K. S. Greenberg, 103–118. New York: Oxford University Press.

Breen, T. H. 1980. *Puritans and Adventurers: Change and Persistence in Early America.* New York: Oxford University Press.

Breitman, G. 1965. *Malcolm X Speaks.* New York: Grove Press.

Brewer, J. 2004. *A Sentimental Murder: Love and Madness in the Eighteenth Century.* New York: Farrar, Straus and Giroux.

Broehl, W. G., Jr. 1964. *The Molly Maguires.* Cambridge: Harvard University Press.

Brown, A. 1898. *The First Republic in America.* Boston: Houghton Mifflin.

Brown, C., Jr. 1991. *Florida's Peace River Frontier.* Orlando: University of Central Florida Press.

———. 1997. *Ossian Bingley Hart: Florida's Loyalist Reconstruction Governor.* Baton Rouge: Louisiana State University Press.

———. 1999. *Tampa before the Civil War.* Tampa: University of Tampa Press.

Brown, H. 2006. *Ending the Revolution: Violence, Justice, and Repression from the Terror to Napoleon.* Charlottesville: University Press of Virginia.

Brown, K. M. 1996. *Good Wives, Nasty Wenches, and Anxious Patriarchs: Gender, Race, and Power in Colonial Virginia.* Chapel Hill: University of North Carolina Press.

Brown, R. M. 1963. *The South Carolina Regulators.* Cambridge: Belknap Press of Harvard University Press.

———. 1975. *Strain of Violence: Historical Studies of American Violence and Vigilantism.* New York: Oxford University Press.

———. 1991. *No Duty to Retreat: Violence and Values in American History and Society.* New York: Oxford University Press.

———. 1994. "Violence." In *The Oxford History of the American West,* ed. C. A. Milner II, C. A. O'Connor, and M. A. Sandweiss, 393–425. New York: Oxford University Press.

Browne, W. H., et al., eds. 1883–1972. *Archives of Maryland.* 72 vols. Baltimore: Maryland Historical Society.

Bruce, D. D., Jr. 1979. *Violence and Culture in the Antebellum South.* Austin: University of Texas Press.

Brumbaugh, A. L. 1927. "The Regulator Movement in Illinois." M. A. thesis, University of Illinois.

Brundage, W. F. 1993. *Lynching in the New South: Georgia and Virginia, 1880–1930*. Urbana: University of Illinois Press.

Buckley, T. E. 2002. *The Great Catastrophe of My Life: Divorce in the Old Dominion*. Chapel Hill: University of North Carolina Press.

Bumsted, J. M. 1992. *The Peoples of Canada*. 2 vols. Toronto: Oxford University Press.

Bureau of Justice Statistics. 2002–2006. Sourcebook of Criminal Justice Statistics Online. Available at http://www.albany.edu/sourcebook/index.html.

Bureau of the Census. 1866. *Eighth Census of the United States*. Vol. 4: *Statistics of the United States*. Washington, D.C.: Government Printing Office.

———. 1872. *Ninth Census of the United States*. Vol. 2: *The Vital Statistics of the United States*. Washington, D.C.: Government Printing Office.

———. 1885. *Tenth Census of the United States*. Vol. 11, pt. 1: *Report on the Mortality and Vital Statistics of the United States*. Washington, D.C.: Government Printing Office.

———. 1906–1938. *Mortality Statistics, 1900–1936*. Washington, D.C.: Government Printing Office.

———. 1909. *A Century of Population Growth*. Washington, D.C.: Government Printing Office.

———. 1937–1993. *Vital Statistics of the United States*. Multiple vols. Washington, D.C.: Government Printing Office.

———. 1975. *Historical Statistics of the United States, Colonial Times to 1970*. 2 vols. Washington, D.C.: Government Printing Office.

Bushman, R. L. 1985. *King and People in Provincial Massachusetts*. Chapel Hill: University of North Carolina Press.

———. 1992. *The Refinement of America: Persons, Houses, Cities*. New York: Alfred A. Knopf.

Butler, J. 1990. *Awash in a Sea of Faith: Christianizing the American People*. Cambridge: Harvard University Press.

Butterfield, F. 1995. *All God's Children: The Bosket Family and the American Tradition of Violence*. New York: Alfred A. Knopf.

Bynum, V. E. 1992. *Unruly Women: The Politics of Social and Sexual Control in the Old South*. Chapel Hill: University of North Carolina Press.

———. 2001. *The Free State of Jones: Mississippi's Longest Civil War*. Chapel Hill: University of North Carolina Press.

Calloway, C. G. 1990. *The Western Abenakis of Vermont, 1600–1800: War, Migration, and the Survival of an Indian People*. Norman: University of Oklahoma Press.

Camarillo, A. 1979. *Chicanos in a Changing Society: From Mexican Pueblos to*

American Barrios in Santa Barbara and Southern California, 1848–1930. Cambridge: Harvard University Press.

Camenzind, K. 2004. "Metonymy, Violence, Patriarchy, and the Paxton Boys." In *Friends and Enemies in Penn's Woods: Indians, Colonists, and the Racial Construction of Pennsylvania*, ed. W. A. Pencak and D. K. Richter, 201–220. University Park: Pennsylvania State University Press.

Cameron, I. A. 1981. *Crime and Repression in the Auvergne and the Guyenne, 1720–1790*. Cambridge: Cambridge University Press.

Campbell, R. B. 2003. *Gone to Texas: A History of the Lone Star State*. New York: Oxford University Press.

Campeau, L. 1972. *La première mission des Jésuites en Nouvelle-France, 1611–1613*. Cahiers d'Histoire des Jésuites, vol. 1. Montreal: Les Éditions Bellarmin.

Cappon, L. J., and S. F. Duff. 1950. *Virginia Gazette Index, 1736–1780*. 2 vols. Williamsburg: Institute of Early American History and Culture.

Carlton, C. 1998. "Civilians." In *The Civil Wars: A Military History of England, Scotland, and Ireland, 1638–1660*, ed. J. P. Kenyon, J. H. Ohlmeyer, and J. S. Morrill, 272–305. New York: Oxford University Press.

Carpenter, G. W. 1981. *"I Want to See a Lawyer": Murder in Calhoun, 1821–1981, and the Story of Our Calhoun Court Systems in the Past 160 Years*. Hardin, Ill.: Privately published.

Carr, L. G., and D. W. Jordan. 1974. *Maryland's Revolution of Government, 1689–1692*. Ithaca: Cornell University Press.

Carranco, L., and E. Beard. 1981. *Genocide and Vendetta: The Round Valley Wars of Northern California*. Norman: University of Oklahoma Press.

Carrigan, W. D., and C. Webb. 2003. "Muerto por Unos Desconocidos (Killed by Persons Unknown): Mob Violence against Blacks and Mexicans." In *Beyond Black and White: Race, Ethnicity, and Gender in the U.S. South and Southwest*, ed. S. Cole and A. M. Parker, 35–74. College Station: Texas A & M University Press.

Cashin, E. J. 1985. "'But Brothers, It Is Our Land We Are Talking About': Winners and Losers in the Georgia Backcountry." In *An Uncivil War: The Southern Backcountry during the American Revolution*, ed. R. Hoffman, T. W. Tate, and P. J. Albert, 240–275. Charlottesville: University Press of Virginia.

Castan, Y. 1974. *Honnêteté et relations sociales en Languedoc, 1715–1780*. Paris: Plon.

Cave, A. A. 1996. *The Pequot War*. Amherst: University of Massachusetts Press.

Cayton, A. R. L. 2000. "'Separate Interests' and the Nation-State: The Washington Administration and the Origins of Regionalism in the Trans-Appalachian West." *Journal of American History* 79: 39–67.

———. 2002. *Ohio: The History of a People*. Columbus: Ohio State University Press.

Chamberlain, S. E. 1956. *My Confession*. New York: Harper and Brothers.

Champlain, S. de. 1922–1936. *The Works of Samuel de Champlain*. Ed. H. P. Biggar. 6 vols. Toronto: Champlain Society.

Chan, S. 1986. *This Bitter-Sweet Soil: The Chinese in California Agriculture, 1860–1910*. Berkeley: University of California Press.

Chandra Sekar, C., and W. E. Deming. 1949. "On a Method of Estimating Birth and Death Rates and the Extent of Registration." *Journal of the American Statistical Association* 44: 101–115.

Chapin, H. M. 1916. *Documentary History of Rhode Island: Being the History of the Towns of Providence and Warwick to 1649 and of the Colony to 1647*. Providence: Preston and Rounds.

Chapman, J. A. 1897. *History of Edgefield County from the Earliest Settlements to 1897*. Newberry, S.C.: Elbert H. Aull.

Chernow, R. 2004. *Alexander Hamilton*. New York: Penguin.

Chesnais, J.-C. 1982. *Histoire de la violence en Occident de 1800 à nos jours*. Rev. ed. Paris: Robert Laffont.

Childs, J. 1997. "War, Crime Waves, and the English Army in the Late Seventeenth Century." *War and Society* 15: 1–17.

Chilton, R., R. Teske, and H. Arnold. 1995. "Ethnicity, Race, and Crime: German and Non-German Suspects, 1960–1990." In *Ethnicity, Race, and Crime: Perspectives across Time and Place*, ed. D. F. Hawkins, 323–340. Albany: State University of New York Press.

Cimbala, P. A. 1997. *Under the Guardianship of the Nation: The Freedmen's Bureau and the Reconstruction of Georgia, 1865–1870*. Athens: University of Georgia Press.

Citrin, J., E. B. Haas, C. Muste, and B. Reingold. 1994. "Is American Nationalism Changing? Implications for Foreign Policy." *International Studies Quarterly* 38: 1–31.

Clap, N. 1715. *The Lord's Voice, Crying to His People: in Some Extraordinary Dispensations Considered in a Sermon . . . Occasioned by the Terrible Tragedies of a Man Barbarously Murdering his Wife and Her Sister, and then Burning his House, March 22, 1715*. Boston: B. Green.

Clappe, L. A. K. S. 1970. *The Shirley Letters: Being Letters Written in 1851–1852 from the California Mines*. Santa Barbara, Calif.: Peregrine Smith.

Clarke, J. W. 1998. *The Lineaments of Wrath: Race, Violent Crime, and American Culture*. New Brunswick, N.J.: Transaction Books.

Claydon, T. 1996. *William III and the Godly Revolution*. New York: Cambridge University Press.

Claydon, T., and I. McBride, eds. 1998. *Protestantism and National Identity:*

Britain and Ireland, c. 1650–c. 1850. Cambridge: Cambridge University Press.

Cleveland Works Progress Administration Project. 1936–1939. *Annals of Cleveland.* 59 vols. Cleveland: Distributed by the Cleveland Public Library.

Coale, A. J., and N. W. Rives. 1973. "A Statistical Reconstruction of the Black Population of the United States, 1880–1970." *Population Index* 39: 3–36.

Cobban, A. 1965. *A History of Modern France.* 2d ed. 3 vols. Harmondsworth: Penguin.

Cockburn, J. S., ed. 1975–1982. *Calendar of Assize Records.* 10 vols. London: Her Majesty's Stationery Office.

———. 1977. "The Nature and Incidence of Crime in England, 1559–1625: A Preliminary Survey." In *Crime in England, 1550–1800,* ed. J. S. Cockburn, 49–71. Princeton: Princeton University Press.

———. 1991. "Patterns of Violence in English Society: Homicide in Kent, 1560–1985." *Past and Present* 130: 70–106.

———. 1997. *Calendar of Assize Records: Kent Indictments: Charles II, 1676–88.* London: Public Record Office.

Cohen, M. 1996. *Fashioning Masculinity: National Identity and Language in the Eighteenth Century.* London: Routledge.

Cohen, S. S. 1980. "'To Parts of the World Unknown': The Circumstances of Divorce in Connecticut, 1750–1797." *Canadian Review of American Studies* 11: 275–293.

———. 1985. "The Broken Bond: Divorce in Providence County, 1749–1809." *Rhode Island History* 44: 67–79.

———. 1986. "What Man Hath Put Asunder: Divorce in New Hampshire, 1681–1784." *Historical New Hampshire* 41: 118–141.

Colaizzi, J. 1983. "Predicting Dangerousness: Psychiatric Ideas in the United States, 1800–1983." Ph.D. diss., Ohio State University.

Coleman, K. 1976. *Colonial Georgia: A History.* New York: Charles Scribner's Sons.

Colley, L. 1992. *Britons: Forging the Nation, 1707–1837.* New Haven: Yale University Press.

Collinson, P. 1988. *The Birthpangs of Protestant England: Religious and Cultural Change in the Sixteenth and Seventeenth Centuries.* Basingstoke: Macmillan.

The Complete Newgate Calendar. 1926. Vol. 1. London: Navarre Society. Available at http://tarlton.law.utexas.edu/lpop/etext/newgate/howard .htm.

Conley, C. A. 1991. *The Unwritten Law: Criminal Justice in Victorian Kent.* New York: Oxford University Press.

————. 1999. *Melancholy Accidents: The Meaning of Violence in Post-Famine Ireland.* Lanham, Md.: Lexington Books.

————. 2007. *Certain Other Countries: Homicide, Gender, and National Identity in Late Nineteenth-Century England, Ireland, Scotland, and Wales.* Columbus: Ohio State University Press.

Connolly, S. J. 1992. *Religion, Law, and Power: The Making of Protestant Ireland, 1660–1760.* Oxford: Clarendon Press.

Cook, S. F. 1973. "Interracial Warfare and Population Decline among the New England Indians." *Ethnohistory* 20: 1–24.

————. 1976. *The Conflict between the California Indian and White Civilization.* Berkeley: University of California Press.

Coombs, J. C. 2003. "Building 'The Machine': The Development of Slavery and Slave Society in Early Colonial Virginia." Ph.D. diss., College of William and Mary.

Costa, D. L., and R. H. Steckel. 1997. "Long-Term Trends in Health, Welfare, and Economic Growth in the United States." In *Health and Welfare during Industrialization,* ed. R. H. Steckel and R. Floud, 47–89. Chicago: University of Chicago Press.

Cott, N. F. 1976a. "Divorce and the Changing Status of Women in Eighteenth-Century Massachusetts." *William and Mary Quarterly,* 3d ser., 33: 586–614.

————. 1976b. "Eighteenth-Century Family and Social Life Revealed in the Massachusetts Divorce Records." *Journal of Social History* 10: 20–43.

Cottrol, R. J. 1998. *From African to Yankee: Narratives of Slavery and Freedom in Antebellum New England.* Armonk, N.Y.: M. E. Sharpe.

Courtwright, D. T. 1996. *Violent Land: Single Men and Social Disorder from the Frontier to the Inner City.* Cambridge: Harvard University Press.

Craig, L. A. 1993. *To Sow One Acre More: Childbearing and Farm Productivity in the Antebellum North.* Baltimore: Johns Hopkins University Press.

Craig, L. A., and E. Field-Hendrey. 1993. "Industrialization and the Earnings Gap: Regional and Sectoral Tests of the Goldin-Sokoloff Hypothesis." *Explorations in Economic History* 30: 60–80.

Cramer, C. E. 1999. *Concealed Weapon Laws of the Early Republic: Dueling, Southern Violence, and Moral Reform.* Westport, Conn.: Praeger.

Cressy, D. 1989. *Bonfires and Bells: National Memory and the Protestant Calendar in Elizabethan and Stuart England.* London: Weidenfeld and Nicholson.

Crimmins, E. 1980. "The Completeness of 1900 Mortality Data Collected by Registration and Enumeration for Rural and Urban Parts of States: Estimates Using the Chandra Sekar-Deming Technique." *Historical Methods* 13: 163–169.

Crisp, J. E. 1976. "Anglo Texan Attitudes toward the Mexican, 1821–1845." Ph.D. diss., Yale University.

Crofts, D. W. 1992. *Old Southampton: Politics and Society in a Virginia County, 1834–1869*. Charlottesville: University Press of Virginia.

Cronon, W. 1983. *Changes in the Land: Indians, Colonists, and the Ecology of New England*. New York: Hill and Wang.

Crow, J. J. 1980. "Slave Rebelliousness and Social Conflict in North Carolina, 1775 to 1802." *William and Mary Quarterly*, 3d ser., 37: 79–102.

Cusick, J. G. 2003. *The Other War of 1812: The Patriot War and the American Invasion of Spanish East Florida*. Gainesville: University Press of Florida.

Dailey, J. E. 2000. *Before Jim Crow: The Politics of Race in Postemancipation Virginia*. Chapel Hill: University of North Carolina Press.

Danforth, S. 1710. *The Woful Effects of Drunkenness. A Sermon Preached at Bristol Octob. 12, 1709, When Two Indians, Josias and Joseph, Were Executed for Murther, Occasioned by the Drunkenness Both of the Murthering and Murthered Parties*. Boston: B. Green.

Daniell, J. R. 1981. *Colonial New Hampshire: A History*. Millwood, N.Y.: KTO Press.

Dann, J. C., ed. 1980. *The Revolution Remembered: Eyewitness Accounts of the War for Independence*. Chicago: University of Chicago Press.

Dannenbaum, J. 1978. "Immigrants and Temperance: Ethnocultural Conflict in Cincinnati, 1845–1860." *Ohio History* 87: 125–139.

Davenport, D. P. 1985. "Duration-of-Residence in the 1855 Census of New York State." *Historical Methods* 18: 5–12.

Davidson, G. G. 1992. *Early Records of Georgia, Wilkes County*. 2 vols. Greenville, S.C.: Southern Historical Press.

Davis, D. B., ed. 1971. *The Fear of Conspiracy: Images of Un-American Subversion from the Revolution to the Present*. Ithaca: Cornell University Press.

———. 1975. *The Problem of Slavery in the Age of Revolution, 1770–1823*. Ithaca: Cornell University Press.

Davis, M. K. 2003. "What Happened in This Place?: In Search of the Female Slave in the Nat Turner Slave Insurrection." In *Nat Turner: A Slave Rebellion in History and Memory*, ed. K. S. Greenberg, 162–176. New York: Oxford University Press.

Davis, R. S., Jr. 1979. *Wilkes County Papers, 1773–1833*. Easley, S.C.: Southern Historical Press.

———. 1982–1987. *The Georgia Black Book: Morbid, Macabre, & Sometimes Disgusting Records of Genealogical Value*. 2 vols. Easley, S.C.: Southern Historical Press.

Dayton, C. H. 1995. *Women before the Bar: Gender, Law, and Society in Connecticut, 1639–1789*. Chapel Hill: University of North Carolina Press.

Dean, N. F. 1885. *Trial of Daniel Giddings for Shooting Benjamin Wiltshire, August 5, 1882 near Chillicothe, Ohio*. Hillsboro, Ohio: n.p.

Dean Trial. 1808. *The Trial of Cyrus B. Dean for the Murder of Jonathan Ormsby and Asa Marsh.* Burlington, Vt.: Samuel Mills.

De Beck, W. L. 1867. *Murder Will Out: The First Step in Crime Leads to the Gallows; The Horrors of the Queen City.* Cincinnati: n.p.

Decker, S. H. 1993. "Exploring Victim-Offender Relationships in Homicide: The Role of Individual and Event Characteristics." *Justice Quarterly* 10: 585–612.

De León, A. 1983. *They Called Them Greasers: Anglo Attitudes toward Mexicans in Texas, 1821–1900.* Austin: University of Texas Press.

Denham, J. M. 1997. *"A Rogue's Paradise": Crime and Punishment in Antebellum Florida, 1821–1861.* Tuscaloosa: University of Alabama Press.

Denham, J. M., and C. Brown Jr. 2000. *Cracker Times and Pioneer Lives: The Florida Reminiscences of George Gillett Keen and Sarah Pamela Williams.* Columbia: University of South Carolina Press.

Denham, J. M., and K. L. Huneycutt, eds. 2004. *Echoes from a Distant Frontier: The Brown Sisters' Correspondence from Antebellum Florida.* Columbia: University of South Carolina Press.

Denham, J. M., and R. Roth. 2007. "Why Was Antebellum Florida Murderous?: A Quantitative Analysis of Homicide in Florida, 1821–1861." *Florida Historical Quarterly* 86: 216–239.

Deutsch, S. 1987. *No Separate Refuge: Culture, Class, and Gender on an Anglo-Hispanic Frontier in the American Southwest, 1880–1940.* New York: Oxford University Press.

de Vries, J. 1974. *The Dutch Rural Economy in the Golden Age, 1500–1700.* New Haven: Yale University Press.

———. 1978. "An Inquiry into the Behavior of Wages in the Dutch Republic and the Southern Netherlands, 1580–1800." *Acta Historiae Neerlandicae* 10: 79–97.

de Waal, F. 2005. *Our Inner Ape: A Leading Primatologist Explains Why We Are Who We Are.* New York: Riverhead Books.

Diederiks, H. 1980. "Patterns of Criminality and Law Enforcement during the Ancien Regime: The Dutch Case." *Criminal Justice History* 1: 157–174.

———. 1989. "Criminality and Its Repression in the Past: Quantitative Approaches: A Survey." *Economic and Social History in the Netherlands* 1: 67–86.

———. 1990. "Quality and Quantity in Historical Research in Criminality and Criminal Justice." *Historical Social Research* 15: 57–76.

Doherty, H. J., Jr. 1949. "Political Factions in Territorial Florida." *Florida Historical Quarterly* 28: 131–142.

———. 1959. *The Whigs of Florida, 1845–54.* Gainesville: University of Florida Press.

———. 1961. *Richard Keith Call: Southern Unionist.* Gainesville: University of Florida Press.

Donohue, J. J., and S. D. Levitt. 2001. "The Impact of Legalized Abortion on Crime." *Quarterly Journal of Economics* 116: 379–420.

Drago, E. L. 1982. *Black Politicians and Reconstruction in Georgia.* Baton Rouge: Louisiana State University Press.

Drake, J. D. 1999. *King Philip's War: Civil War in New England, 1675–1676.* Amherst: University of Massachusetts Press.

Drake, R. B. 2001. *A History of Appalachia.* Lexington: University Press of Kentucky.

Du Bois, W. E. B. 1965. *The Souls of Black Folk.* In *Three Negro Classics,* ed. J. H. Franklin, 207–389. New York: Avon Books.

Dunaway, W. A. 1995. "Speculators and Settler Capitalists: Unthinking the Mythology about Appalachian Landholding, 1790–1860." In *Appalachia in the Making: The Mountain South in the Nineteenth Century,* ed. M. B. Pudup, D. B. Billings, and A. L. Waller, 50–75. Chapel Hill: University of North Carolina Press.

———. 1996. *The First American Frontier: Transition to Capitalism in Southern Appalachia, 1700–1860.* Chapel Hill: University of North Carolina Press.

Dupâquier, J., ed. 1988. *Histoire de la population français: De la Renaissance à 1789.* 4 vols. Paris: Presses Universitaires de France.

Dutcher, L. L. 1872. *The History of St. Albans, Vermont.* St. Albans, Vt.: Stephen E. Royce.

Dykstra, R. R. 1968. *The Cattle Towns.* New York: Alfred A. Knopf.

Earle, C. V. 1979. "Environment, Disease, and Mortality in Early Virginia." In *The Chesapeake in the Seventeenth Century: Essays on Anglo-American Society,* ed. T. W. Tate and D. L. Ammerman, 96–125. Chapel Hill: University of North Carolina Press.

Eckberg, D. L. 1995. "Estimates of Early Twentieth-Century U.S. Homicide Rates: An Econometric Forecasting Approach." *Demography* 32: 1–16.

———. 2001. "Stalking the Elusive Homicide: A Capture-Recapture Approach to the Estimation of Post-Reconstruction South Carolina Killings." *Social Science History* 25: 67–91.

———. 2007. "Coroner's Records and Estimates of 'Excessive' Homicide Deaths in Charleston, South Carolina, 1879–1912." Paper presented at the annual meeting of the Social Science History Association, Chicago, 16 November.

Eckenrode, H. J. 1916. *The Revolution in Virginia.* Boston: Houghton Mifflin.

Egerton, D. R. 1993. *Gabriel's Rebellion: The Virginia Slave Conspiracies of 1800 and 1802.* Chapel Hill: University of North Carolina Press.

Egmond, F. 1993. *Underworlds: Organized Crime in the Netherlands, 1650–1800.* Cambridge, Mass.: Polity Press.

Eifler, M. A. 2002. *Gold Rush Capitalists: Greed and Growth in Sacramento.* Albuquerque: University of New Mexico Press.

Eisner, M. 2001. "Modernization, Self-Control, and Lethal Violence: The Long-Term Dynamics of European Homicide Rates in Theoretical Perspective." *British Journal of Criminology* 41: 618–638.

Ekirch, A. R. 1981. *"Poor Carolina": Politics and Society in Colonial North Carolina, 1729–1776.* Chapel Hill: University of North Carolina Press.

———. 1987. *Bound for America: The Transportation of British Convicts to the Colonies, 1718–1775.* Oxford: Clarendon Press.

Eldridge, C. 1994. *Cabell County, West Virginia: Minute Book E-3, 1826–1835.* Athens, Ga.: Iberian Publishing.

———. 1995. *Cabell County, West Virginia: Minute Book 1, 1809–1815.* Athens, Ga.: Iberian Publishing.

Elias, N. 1982. *The Civilizing Process.* Trans. E. Jephcott. 2 vols. New York: Pantheon.

Ellefson, C. A. 1963. "The County Courts and the Provincial Court in Maryland, 1733–1763." Ph.D. diss., University of Maryland.

Eltis, D. 2000. *The Rise of African Slavery in the Americas.* New York: Cambridge University Press.

Emmison, F. G. 1976. *Elizabethan Life: Home, Work, and Land from Essex Wills and Sessions and Manorial Records.* Chelmsford, U.K.: Essex Court Council.

Emsley, C. 1996. *Crime and Society in England, 1750–1900.* 2d ed. Harlow: Longman.

Engs, R. F. 1979. *Freedom's First Generation: Black Hampton, Virginia, 1861–1890.* Philadelphia: University of Pennsylvania Press.

Erwin, M. 1914. *History of Williamson County, Illinois, from the Earliest Times Down to the Present.* Herrin, Ill.: Herrin News.

Etcheson, N. 2004. *Bleeding Kansas: Contested Liberty in the Civil War Era.* Lawrence: University Press of Kansas.

Evans, E. G. 1985. "Trouble in the Backcountry: Disaffection in Southwest Virginia during the American Revolution." In *An Uncivil War: The Southern Backcountry during the American Revolution,* ed. R. Hoffman, T. W. Tate, and P. J. Albert, 179–212. Charlottesville: University Press of Virginia.

Evans, T. 1994–1997. *Baldwin County, Georgia, Newspaper Clippings (Union Recorder), 1830–1887.* 12 vols. Savannah: T. Evans.

———. 1995–1997. *Milledgeville, Georgia, Newspaper Clippings (Southern Recorder), 1820–1872.* 12 vols. Savannah: T. Evans.

Everitt, A. 1966. *The Community of Kent and the Great Rebellion, 1640–1660.* Leicester: Leicester University Press.

Fagan, J. 1990. "Intoxication and Aggression." In *Crime and Justice: A Review of Research*, ed. M. Tonry and J. Q. Wilson, 13: 241–320. Chicago: University of Chicago Press.

Faller, L. B. 1987. *Turned to Account: The Forms and Functions of Criminal Biography in Late Seventeenth- and Early Eighteenth-Century England*. Cambridge: Cambridge University Press.

Faragher, J. M. 1992. *Daniel Boone: The Life and Legend of an American Pioneer*. New York: Henry Holt.

Federal Bureau of Investigation. 1998–. *Crime in the United States*. Multiple vols. Available at http://www.fbi.gov/ucr/ucr.htm.

Feer, R. A. 1988. *Shays's Rebellion*. New York: Garland.

Feldberg, M. 1975. *The Philadelphia Riots of 1844: A Study of Ethnic Conflict*. Westport, Conn.: Greenwood.

Fellman, M. 1989. *Inside War: The Guerrilla Conflict in Missouri during the American Civil War*. New York: Oxford University Press.

Fenn, E. A. 2001. *Pox Americana: The Great Smallpox Epidemic of 1775–82*. New York: Hill and Wang.

Ferdinand, T. N. 1967. "The Criminal Patterns of Boston since 1849." *American Journal of Sociology* 73: 84–99.

Fischer, D. H. 1989. *Albion's Seed: Four British Folkways in America*. New York: Oxford University Press.

Fleet, B. 1988. *Virginia: Colonial Abstracts*. 3 vols. Baltimore: Genealogical Publishing.

Fleming, T. J. 1999. *The Duel: Alexander Hamilton, Aaron Burr, and the Future of America*. New York: Basic Books.

Fletcher, A. J. 1985. "Honour, Reputation and Local Officeholding in Elizabethan and Stuart England." In *Order and Disorder in Early Modern England*, ed. A. J. Fletcher and J. Stevenson, 92–115. Cambridge: Cambridge University Press.

Fogel, R. W. 1989. *Without Consent or Contract: The Rise and Fall of American Slavery*. New York: W. W. Norton.

——. 1992. "Second Thoughts on the European Escape from Hunger: Famines, Chronic Malnutrition, and Mortality Rates." In *Nutrition and Poverty*, ed. S. R. Osmani, 243–286. Oxford: Clarendon Press.

——. 2000. *The Fourth Great Awakening and the Future of Egalitarianism*. Chicago: University of Chicago Press.

Folger, P. 1725. *A Looking Glass for the Times*. Boston: n.p.

Foner, N., and G. M. Fredrickson, eds. 2004. *Not Just Black and White: Historical and Contemporary Perspectives on Immigration, Race, and Ethnicity in the United States*. New York: Russell Sage Foundation.

Forrest, E. R. 1984. *Arizona's Dark and Bloody Ground*. Tucson: University of Arizona Press.

Fox, F. S. 2000. *Sweet Land of Liberty: The Ordeal of the American Revolution in Northampton County, Pennsylvania*. University Park: Pennsylvania State University Press.

Fox, J. A. 2005. Uniform Crime Reports [United States]: Supplementary Homicide Reports, 1976–2005. Computer file. Inter-University Consortium for Political and Social Research, Ann Arbor.

Fox, J. A., and M. W. Zawitz. 2004. *Homicide Trends in the United States*. Washington, D.C.: Bureau of Justice Statistics. Available at http://www.ojp.usdoj.gov/bjs/homicide/homtrnd.htm#contents.

Foyster, E. 1999. *Manhood in Early Modern England: Honour, Sex, and Marriage*. London: Longman.

———. 2005. *Marital Violence: An English Family History, 1660–1857*. Cambridge: Cambridge University Press.

Franklin, J. H. 1961. *The Militant South, 1800–1861*. Cambridge: Belknap Press of Harvard University Press.

———. 1980. *From Slavery to Freedom: A History of Negro Americans*. 5th ed. New York: Alfred A. Knopf.

Frantz, J. B., and W. Pencak, eds. 1998. *Beyond Philadelphia: The American Revolution in the Pennsylvania Hinterland*. University Park: Pennsylvania State University Press.

Fredrickson, G. M. 1971. *The Black Image in the White Mind: The Debate on Afro-American Character and Destiny, 1817–1914*. New York: Harper and Row.

Freehling, A. G. 1982. *Drift toward Dissolution: The Virginia Slavery Debate of 1831–1832*. Baton Rouge: Louisiana State University Press.

Freeman, J. B. 2001. *Affairs of Honor: National Politics in the New Republic*. New Haven: Yale University Press.

French, S. 2004. *The Rebellious Slave: Nat Turner in American Memory*. Boston: Houghton Mifflin.

Frey, S. R. 1991. *Water from the Rock: Black Resistance in a Revolutionary Age*. Princeton: Princeton University Press.

Galenson, D. 1981. *White Servitude in Colonial America: An Economic Analysis*. New York: Cambridge University Press.

Gallay, A. 2002. *The Indian Slave Trade: The Rise of the English Empire in the American South, 1670–1717*. New Haven: Yale University Press.

Gamble, T. 1923. *Savannah Duels and Duelists, 1733–1877*. Savannah: Review Publishing and Printing.

Gardener, L. L. 1833. "Leift Lion Gardener his relation of the Pequot Warres." *Collections of the Massachusetts Historical Society*, 3d ser., 3: 131–160.

Garnham, N. 1996. *The Courts, Crime and Criminal Law in Ireland, 1692–1760*. Dublin: Irish Academic Press.

Gartner, R. 1990. "The Victims of Homicide: A Temporal and Cross-National Comparison." *American Sociological Review* 55: 92–106.

Gatrell, V. A. C. 1980. "The Decline of Theft and Violence in Victorian and Edwardian England." In *Crime and the Law: The Social History of Crime in Western Europe since 1500,* ed. V. A. C. Gatrell, B. Lenman, and G. Parker, 238–370. London: Europa Publications.

Gehring, C. T., ed. and trans. 1983. *New York Historical Manuscripts: Dutch.* Vol. 5: *Council Minutes, 1652–1654.* Baltimore: Genealogical Publishing.

———. 1990. *New Netherland Documents Series.* Vol. 16, pt. 2: *Fort Orange Court Minutes, 1652–1660.* Syracuse: Syracuse University Press.

———. 1995. *New Netherland Documents Series.* Vol. 6: *Council Minutes, 1655–1656.* Syracuse: Syracuse University Press.

Genealogical Committee, Georgia Historical Society. 1983–1989. *Register of Deaths in Savannah, Georgia, 1803–1853.* 6 vols. Savannah: Georgia Historical Society.

Ghere, D. L. 1997. "Myths and Methods of Abenaki Demography: Abenaki Population Recovery, 1725–1750." *Ethnohistory* 44: 511–534.

Gilje, P. A. 1987. *The Road to Mobocracy: Popular Disorder in New York City, 1763–1834.* Chapel Hill: University of North Carolina Press.

———. 1996. *Rioting in America.* Bloomington: Indiana University Press.

Gillis, A. R. 1996. "So Long as They Both Shall Live: Marital Dissolution and the Decline of Domestic Homicide in France, 1852–1909." *American Journal of Sociology* 101: 1273–1305.

Gilmore, W. J. 1989. *Reading Becomes a Necessity of Life: Material and Cultural Life in Rural New England, 1780–1835.* Knoxville: University of Tennessee Press.

Ginsburg, C. A. 1988. "Estimates and Correlates of Enumeration Completeness: Censuses and Maps in Nineteenth-Century Massachusetts." *Social Science History* 12: 71–86.

Gleeson, D. T. 2001. *The Irish in the South, 1815–1877.* Chapel Hill: University of North Carolina Press.

Gloucester County Court Records. 1926. *Proceedings of the Vermont Historical Society for the Years 1923, 1924, 1925.* Bellows Falls, Vt.: P. H. Gobie Press: 141–192.

Godbeer, R. 2002. *Sexual Revolution in Early America.* Baltimore: Johns Hopkins University Press.

Godfrey, S. 1818. *A Sketch of the Life of Samuel Godfrey.* Windsor, Vt.: n.p.

Goebel, J. N., Jr., and T. R. Naughton. 1944. *Law Enforcement in Colonial New York: A Study in Criminal Procedure, 1664–1776.* New York: Commonwealth Fund.

Goldie, M. 1996. "Divergence and Union: Scotland and England, 1660–1707." In *The British Problem, c. 1534–1707: State Formation in the Atlantic*

Archipelago, ed. B. Bradshaw and J. S. Morrill, 220–246. New York: St. Martin's Press.

Goldin, C. D. 1990. *Understanding the Gender Gap: An Economic History of American Women.* New York: Oxford University Press.

Goldin, C., and K. Sokoloff. 1982. "Women, Children, and Industrialization in the Early Republic: Evidence from the Manufacturing Censuses." *Journal of Economic History* 42: 741–774.

———. 1984. "The Relative Productivity Hypothesis of Industrialization." *Quarterly Journal of Economics* 99: 461–488.

Goldstein, R. J. 1983. *Political Repression in Nineteenth-Century Europe.* London: Croom Helm.

Goodwyn, L. C. 1971. "Populist Dreams and Negro Rights: East Texas as a Case Study." *American Historical Review* 76: 1435–1456.

Gordon, M. A. 1993. *The Orange Riots: Irish Political Violence in New York City, 1870 and 1871.* Ithaca: Cornell University Press.

Gorn, E. J. 1986. *The Manly Art: Bare-Knuckle Prize Fighting in America.* Ithaca: Cornell University Press.

Gould, R. V. 2003. *Collision of Wills: How Ambiguity about Social Rank Breeds Conflict.* Chicago: University of Chicago Press.

Gowing, L. 1996. *Domestic Dangers: Women, Words, and Sex in Early Modern London.* Oxford: Clarendon Press.

Grabowski, J. 1996. "French Criminal Justice and Indians in Montreal, 1670–1760." *Ethnohistory* 43: 405–429.

Green, M. D. 1982. *The Politics of Indian Removal: Creek Government and Society in Crisis.* Lincoln: University of Nebraska Press.

Greenberg, D. 1976. *Crime and Law Enforcement in the Colony of New York, 1691–1776.* Ithaca: Cornell University Press.

Greenberg, K. S. 1985. *Masters and Statesmen: The Political Culture of American Slavery.* Baltimore: Johns Hopkins University Press.

———. 1996. *Honor and Slavery.* Princeton: Princeton University Press.

Greene, L. J. 1942. *The Negro in Colonial New England.* New York: Columbia University Press.

Greenshields, G. 1994. *An Economy of Violence in Early Modern France: Crime and Justice in the Haute Auvergne, 1587–1664.* University Park: Pennsylvania State University Press.

Grierson, F. 1909. *The Valley of Shadows.* London: Archibald Constable.

Griffin, P. 2001. *The People with No Name: Ireland's Ulster Scots, America's Scots Irish, and the Creation of a British Atlantic World, 1689–1764.* Princeton: Princeton University Press.

Grimsted, D. 1998. *American Mobbing, 1828–1861: Toward Civil War.* New York: Oxford University Press.

Griswold del Castillo, R. 1979. *The Los Angeles Barrio, 1850–1890: A Social History.* Berkeley: University of California Press.

Grob, G. N. 1994. *The Mad among Us: A History of the Care of America's Mentally Ill.* New York: Free Press.

———. 2002. *The Deadly Truth: A History of Disease in America.* Cambridge: Harvard University Press.

Groce, W. T. 1999. *Mountain Rebels: East Tennessee Confederates and the Civil War, 1860–1870.* Knoxville: University of Tennessee Press.

Grossberg, M. 1985. *Governing the Hearth: Law and the Family in Nineteenth-Century America.* Chapel Hill: University of North Carolina Press.

Gurr, T. R. 1981. "Historical Trends in Violent Crime: A Critical Review of the Evidence." In *Crime and Justice: An Annual Review of Research,* ed. M. Tonry and N. Morris, 3: 295–353. Chicago: University of Chicago Press.

Gutman, H. G. 1976. *The Black Family in Slavery and Freedom, 1750–1925.* New York: Pantheon.

Gutmann, M. C. 2007. *The Meanings of Macho: Being a Man in Mexico City.* Berkeley: University of California Press.

Gutmann, M. P. 1980. *War and Rural Life in the Early Modern Low Countries.* Princeton: Princeton University Press.

Hacker, J. D. 1999. "The Human Cost of War: White Population in the United States, 1850–1880." Ph.D. diss., University of Minnesota.

Hackney, S. 1969. "Southern Violence." *American Historical Review* 74: 906–925.

Hadden, S. E. 2001. *Slave Patrols: Law and Violence in Virginia and the Carolinas.* Cambridge: Harvard University Press.

Haefeli, E. 1999. "Kieft's War and the Cultures of Violence in Colonial America." In *Lethal Imagination: Violence and Brutality in American History,* ed. M. Bellesiles, 17–40. New York: New York University Press.

Haffenden, P. S. 1974. *New England in the English Nation, 1689–1713.* Oxford: Clarendon Press.

Hahn, S. 1983. The *Roots of Southern Populism: Yeoman Farmers and the Transformation of the Georgia Upcountry, 1850–1890.* New York: Oxford University Press.

———. 2003. *A Nation under Our Feet: Black Political Struggles in the Rural South from Slavery to the Great Migration.* Cambridge: Belknap Press of Harvard University Press.

Hair, W. I. 1969. *Bourbonism and Agrarian Protest: Louisiana Politics, 1877–1900.* Baton Rouge: Louisiana State University Press.

Hale, N. C. 1951. *Virginia Venturer: A Historical Biography of William Claiborne, 1600–1677.* Richmond, Va.: Dietz Press.

Hall, C. C. 1910. *Narratives of Early Maryland, 1633–1684.* New York: Barnes and Noble.

Hall, V. B. 1991. "The Politics of Appalachian Virginia, 1790–1830." In *Appalachian Frontiers: Settlement, Society, and Development in the Preindustrial Era,* ed. R. D. Mitchell, 166–186. Lexington: University Press of Kentucky.

Hammond, O. G. 1943. *New Hampshire Court Records, 1640–1692: Court Papers, 1652–1668.* New Hampshire State Papers Series, No. 40. Concord: State of New Hampshire.

Hamnett, B. R. 1986. *Roots of Insurgency: Mexican Regions, 1750–1824.* Cambridge: Cambridge University Press.

Harcourt, B. E. 2001. *Illusion of Order: The False Promise of Broken Windows Policing.* Cambridge: Harvard University Press.

Hardin, J. W. 1961. *The Life of John Wesley Hardin as Written by Himself.* 1896; reprint, Norman: University of Oklahoma Press.

Hardin, S. L. 1996. "Efficiency in the Cause." In *Tejano Journey, 1770–1850,* ed. G. E. Poyo, 49–71. Austin: University of Texas Press.

Harms, R. 1981. *River of Wealth, River of Sorrow: The Central Zaire Basin in the Era of the Slave and Ivory Trade, 1500–1891.* New Haven: Yale University Press.

Harris, A. R., S. H. Thomas, G. A. Fisher, and D. J. Hirsch. 2002. "Murder and Medicine: The Lethality of Criminal Assault, 1960–1999." *Homicide Studies* 6: 128–166.

Harris, G. W. 1987. *Sut Lovingood Yarns.* Ed. M. T. Inge. Memphis: St. Lukes Press.

Harrison, L. H., and J. C. Klotter. 1997. *A New History of Kentucky.* Lexington: University Press of Kentucky.

Hart, F. H. 1942. *The Valley of Virginia in the American Revolution, 1763–1789.* Chapel Hill: University of North Carolina Press.

Hartog, H. 1997. "Lawyering, Husbands' Rights, and 'the Unwritten Law' in Nineteenth-Century America." *Journal of American History* 84: 67–96.

Hartz, F. R., E. K. Hartz, and T. Evans. 1990–1995. *Genealogical Abstracts from the Georgia Journal (Milledgeville) Newspaper, 1809–1840.* 5 vols. Savannah: T. Evans.

Hast, A. 1982. *Loyalism in Revolutionary Virginia: The Norfolk Area and the Eastern Shore.* Ann Arbor: UMI Research Press.

Haun, W. P. 1993. *Sussex County, Virginia, Court Records, 1754–1801: Book 1. Court of Oyer & Terminer, 1754–1801; Order Book, 1754–1756.* Durham, N.C.: Privately published.

Haviland, W. A., and M. W. Power. 1994. *The Original Vermonters: Native Inhab-*

itants, Past and Present. Rev. ed. Hanover, N.H.: University Press of New England.

Hay, D. 1982. "War, Dearth, and Theft in the Eighteenth Century: The Record of English Courts." *Past and Present* 95: 117–160.

Headley, R. K., Jr. 1987. *Genealogical Abstracts from 18th-Century Virginia Newspapers.* Baltimore: Genealogical Publishing.

Hearn, D. A. 1997. *Legal Executions in New York State: A Comprehensive Reference, 1639–1963.* Jefferson, N.C.: McFarland.

———. 1999. *Legal Executions in New England: A Comprehensive Reference, 1623–1960.* Jefferson, N.C.: McFarland.

Heath, D. B., ed. 1963. *A Journal of the Pilgrims at Plymouth: Mourt's Relation.* New York: Corinth Books.

Heizer, R. F., ed. 1993. *The Destruction of California Indians.* Lincoln: University of Nebraska Press.

Helgerson, R. 1992. *Forms of Nationhood: The Elizabethan Writing of England.* Chicago: University of Chicago Press.

Hemenway, A. M. 1868–1891. *The Vermont Historical Gazetteer.* 5 vols. Burlington, Vt.: A. M Hemenway.

Henry, B. 1994. *Dublin Hanged: Crime, Law Enforcement, and Punishment in Late Eighteenth-Century Dublin.* Dublin: Irish Academic Press.

Hetherington, M. J. 2005. *Why Trust Matters: Declining Political Trust and the Demise of American Liberalism.* Princeton: Princeton University Press.

Higham, J. 1965. *Strangers in the Land: Patterns of American Nativism, 1860–1925.* New York: Atheneum.

———. 2001. "From Boundlessness to Consolidation: The Transformation of American Culture, 1848–1860." In *Hanging Together: Unity and Diversity in American Culture,* ed. C. J. Guarneri, 149–165. New Haven: Yale University Press.

Hill, C. 1964. *Society and Puritanism in Pre-Revolutionary England.* New York: Schocken.

Himmel, K. F. 1999. *The Conquest of the Karankawas and the Tonkawas, 1821–1859.* College Station: Texas A & M University Press.

Hine, R. V., and J. M. Faragher. 2000. *The American West: A New Interpretive History.* New Haven: Yale University Press.

Hinks, P. P. 1997. *To Awaken My Afflicted Brethren: David Walker and the Problem of Antebellum Slave Resistance.* University Park: Pennsylvania State University Press.

Hoadly, C. J., ed. 1857. *Records of the Colony and Plantation of New Haven, 1638–1649.* Hartford: Case, Lockwood.

———. 1858. *Records of the Colony and Plantation of New Haven from May 1653 to the Union.* Hartford: Case, Lockwood.

Hodges, G. R. 1999. *Root and Branch: African Americans in New York and East Jersey, 1613–1863.* Chapel Hill: University of North Carolina Press.

Hodgson, G. 1976. *America in Our Time.* New York: Random House.

———. 2004. *More Equal than Others: America from Nixon to the New Century.* Princeton: Princeton University Press.

Hoerder, D. 1977. *Crowd Action in Revolutionary Massachusetts, 1765–1780.* New York: Academic Press.

Hoffer, P. C., and N. E. H. Hull. 1981. *Murdering Mothers: Infanticide in England and New England, 1558–1803.* New York: New York University Press.

Hoffer, P. C., and W. B. Scott, eds. 1984. *Criminal Proceedings in Colonial Virginia: [Records of] Fines, Examination of Criminals, Trials of Slaves, etc., from March 1710 [1711] to [1754] [Richmond County, Virginia].* Athens: University of Georgia Press.

Hoffman, P. T., D. Jacks, P. A. Levin, and P. H. Lindert. 2000. "Prices and Real Inequality in Europe since 1500." Working Paper Series, No. 102. Agricultural History Center, University of California at Davis.

Hoffman, R., with S. D. Mason. 2000. *Princes of Ireland, Planters of Maryland: A Carroll Saga, 1500–1782.* Chapel Hill: University of North Carolina Press.

Holbrook, J. M. 1981. *New Hampshire 1732 Census.* Oxford, Mass.: Holbrook Research Institute.

———. 1982. *Vermont 1771 Census.* Oxford, Mass.: Holbrook Research Institute.

Hollon, W. E. 1974. *Frontier Violence: Another Look.* New York: Oxford University Press.

Holmes, W. F. 1980. "Moonshining and Collective Violence: Georgia, 1889–1895." *Journal of American History* 67: 589–611.

Honey, M. K. 1999. *Black Workers Remember: An Oral History of Segregation, Unionism, and the Freedom Struggle.* Berkeley: University of California Press.

Hook, E. B., and R. R. Regal. 1995. "Capture-Recapture Methods in Epidemiology: Methods and Limitations." *Epidemiological Reviews* 17: 243–264.

Horn, J. 1994. *Adapting to a New World: English Society in the Seventeenth-Century Chesapeake.* Chapel Hill: University of North Carolina Press.

Horsman, R. 1981. *Race and Manifest Destiny: The Origins of American Racial Anglo-Saxonism.* Cambridge: Harvard University Press.

House of Commons. 1980–1982. Parliamentary Papers, 1801–1900. Ed. Peter Cockton. Microfiche. Cambridge: Chadwyck-Healey.

Howard Trial. 1849. *Trial of Mrs. Margaret Howard, for the Murder of Miss Mary Ellen Smith, Her Husband's Paramour, in Cincinnati, on the 2nd of February Last.* Cincinnati: E. E. Barclay.

Hubbard, W. 1677. *A Narrative of the Troubles with the Indians in New England.* Boston: John Foster.

Hughes, S. 2006. "Comparative Histories of Violence: Dueling." Paper presented at the annual meeting of the Social Science History Association, Minneapolis, 2 November.

Hull, J. 1857. "The Diaries of John Hull, Mint-Master and Treasurer of the Colony of Mass Bay." *Transactions and Collections of the American Antiquarian Society* 3: 117–265.

Hunnisett, R. F., ed. 1981. *Wiltshire Coroners' Bills, 1752–1796.* Devizes: Wiltshire Record Society.

Hunt, M. 1992. "Wife Beating, Domesticity and Women's Independence in Eighteenth-Century London." *Gender and History* 4: 10–33.

Huntington, E. 1797. *A Sermon Preached at Haddam, June 14, 1797, on the Day of the Execution of Thomas Starr, Condemned for the Murder of His Kinsman, Samuel Cornwell.* Middletown, Conn.: Moses H. Woodward.

Hurl-Eamon, J. 2005. *Gender and Petty Violence in London, 1680–1720.* Columbus: Ohio State University Press.

Hurtado, A. L. 1988. *Indian Survival on the California Frontier.* New Haven: Yale University Press.

Hutson, J. H. 1972. *Pennsylvania Politics, 1746–1770: The Movement for Royal Government and Its Consequences.* Princeton: Princeton University Press.

Hyde, S. C., Jr. 1996. *Pistols and Politics: The Dilemma of Democracy in Louisiana's Florida Parishes, 1810–1899.* Baton Rouge: Louisiana State University.

Ignatiev, N. 1995. *How the Irish Became White.* New York: Routledge.

Ingram, M. 1985. "Ridings, Rough Music and Mocking Rhymes in Early Modern England." In *Popular Culture in Seventeenth-Century England,* ed. B. Reay, 166–197. London: Croom Helm.

———. 1987. *Church Courts, Sex and Marriage in England, 1570–1640.* Cambridge: Cambridge University Press.

Inscoe, J. C. 1989. *Mountain Masters, Slavery, and the Sectional Crisis in Western North Carolina.* Knoxville: University of Tennessee Press.

———. 1995. "Race and Racism in Nineteenth-Century Southern Appalachia: Myths, Realities, Ambiguities." In *Appalachia in the Making: The Mountain South in the Nineteenth Century,* ed. M. B. Pudup, D. B. Billings, and A. L. Waller, 103–131. Chapel Hill: University of North Carolina Press.

Israel, J. I. 1986. *The Dutch Republic and the Hispanic World, 1606–1661.* Oxford: Clarendon Press.

Jackson, P. I. 1995. "Minority Group Threat, Crime, and the Mobilization of Law in France." In *Ethnicity, Race, and Crime: Perspectives across Time and*

Place, ed. D. F. Hawkins, 341–360. Albany: State University of New York Press.

Jacobson, M. F. 1998. *Whiteness of a Different Color: European Immigrants and the Alchemy of Race.* Cambridge: Harvard University Press.

James, J. T. 1913. *The Benders in Kansas.* Wichita: Kansas-Oklahoma Publishing.

James, M. E. 1986. "English Politics and the Concept of Honour, 1485–1642." In *Society, Politics, and Culture: Studies in Early Modern England,* ed. M. E. James, 308–415. Cambridge: Cambridge University Press.

Jameson, J. F., ed. 1909. *Narratives of New Netherland, 1609–1664.* New York: Barnes and Noble.

Jeaffreson, J. C., ed. 1886–1892. *Middlesex County Records.* 4 vols. London: Middlesex County Records Society.

Jefferson, Thomas. 1904. *The Writings of Thomas Jefferson.* 20 vols. Washington, D.C.: Thomas Jefferson Memorial Association.

Johnson, D. R. 1979. *Policing the Urban Underworld: The Impact of Crime on the Development of the American Police, 1800–1887.* Philadelphia: Temple University Press.

Johnson, M. P. 1977. *Toward a Patriarchal Republic: The Secession of Georgia.* Baton Rouge: Louisiana State University Press.

———. 2001. "Denmark Vesey and His Co-Conspirators." *William and Mary Quarterly,* 3d ser., 58: 915–976.

Johnson, M. S. 2003. *Street Justice: A History of Police Violence in New York City.* Boston: Beacon Press.

Johnson, P. E. 1978. *A Shopkeepers' Millennium: Society and Revivals in Rochester, New York, 1815–1837.* New York: Hill and Wang.

Johnson, R. R. 1981. *Adjustment to Empire: The New England Colonies, 1675–1715.* New Brunswick, N.J.: Rutgers University Press.

Johnson, S. L. 2000. *Roaring Camp: The Social World of the California Gold Rush.* New York: W. W. Norton.

Jones, M., ed. 2000. *The New Cambridge Medieval History.* Vol. 6: *C. 1300–c. 1415.* New York: Cambridge University Press.

Jones, O. L. 1979. *Los Paisanos: Spanish Settlers on the Northern Frontier of New Spain.* Norman: University of Oklahoma Press.

Jordan, D. W. 1987. *Foundations of Representative Government in Maryland, 1632–1715.* New York: Cambridge University Press.

Jordan, E. L. 1995. *Black Confederates and Afro-Yankees in Civil War Virginia.* Charlottesville: University Press of Virginia.

Jordan, W. D. 1969. *White over Black: American Attitudes toward the Negro, 1550–1812.* Baltimore: Penguin.

Karonen, P. 2001. "A Life for a Life versus Christian Reconciliation: Violence and the Process of Civilization in the Kingdom of Sweden, 1540–1700." In *Five Centuries of Violence in Finland and the Baltic Area*, ed. H. Ylikangas, P. Karonen, and M. Lehti, 85–132. Columbus: Ohio State University Press.

Keim, C. A. 1997. "Women in Slavery among the Mangbetu, c. 1800–1910." In *Women and Slavery in Africa*, ed. C. C. Robertson and M. A. Klein, 144–159. Portsmouth, N.H.: Heinemann.

Keller, M. 1977. *Affairs of State: Public Life in Late Nineteenth Century America*. Cambridge: Belknap Press of Harvard University Press.

Kelling, G. L., and C. M. Coles. 1996. *Fixing Broken Windows: Restoring Order and Reducing Crime in Our Communities*. New York: Simon and Schuster.

Kelly, J. 1995. *"That Damn'd Thing Called Honour": Duelling in Ireland, 1570–1860*. Cork: Cork University Press.

Kelly, K. 1989. *Economic and Social Development of Seventeenth-Century Surry County, Virginia*. New York: Garland.

Kennedy, D. M. 1999. *Freedom from Fear: The American People in Depression and War, 1929–1945*. New York: Oxford University Press.

Kennedy, J. P., and H. R. McIlwaine, eds. 1905–1915. *Journals of the House of Burgesses of Virginia*. 13 vols. Richmond: Colonial Press, Everett Waddey.

Kenny, K. 1998. *Making Sense of the Molly Maguires*. New York: Oxford University Press.

Kenyon, J. P., and J. H. Ohlmeyer, eds. 1998. *The Civil Wars: A Military History of England, Scotland, and Ireland, 1638–1660*. New York: Oxford University Press.

Kerr-Ritchie, J. R. 1999. *Freedpeople in the Tobacco South: Virginia, 1860–1900*. Chapel Hill: University of North Carolina Press.

Kiernan, V. G. 1988. *The Duel in European History: Honour and the Reign of the Aristocracy*. Oxford: Oxford University Press.

Kingsbury, S. M. 1906–1935. *The Records of the Virginia Company of London*. 4 vols. Washington, D.C.: Government Printing Office.

Klein, L. E. 1994. *Shaftesbury and the Culture of Politeness: Moral Discourse and Cultural Politics in Early Eighteenth-Century England*. New York: Cambridge University Press.

Klein, M. A. 1997. "Women in Slavery in the Western Sudan." In *Women and Slavery in Africa*, ed. C. C. Robertson and M. A. Klein, 67–92. Portsmouth, N.H.: Heinemann.

Klein, R. N. 1990. *Unification of a Slave State: The Rise of the Planter Class in the South Carolina Backcountry, 1760–1808*. Chapel Hill: University of North Carolina Press.

Klement, F. L. 1960. *The Copperheads in the Middle West*. Chicago: University of Chicago Press.

Knights, P. R. 1991. "Potholes in the Road of Improvement?: Estimating Census Underenumeration by Longitudinal Tracing: U.S. Censuses, 1850–1880." *Social Science History* 12: 517–526.

Koehler, L. 1980. *A Search for Power: The "Weaker Sex" in Seventeenth-Century New England*. Urbana: University of Illinois Press.

Komlos, J., and P. Coclanis. 1997. "On the Puzzling Cycle in the Biological Standard of Living: The Case of Antebellum Georgia." *Explorations in Economic History* 34: 433–459.

Kossmann, E. H. 1978. *The Low Countries, 1780–1940*. Oxford: Clarendon Press.

Kousser, J. M. 1974. *The Shaping of Southern Politics: Suffrage Restriction and the Establishment of the One-Party South, 1880–1910*. New Haven: Yale University Press.

———. 1991. "Before *Plessy*, Before *Brown*: The Development of the Law of Racial Integration in Louisiana and Kansas." In *Toward a Useable Past: Liberty under State Constitutions*, ed. P. Finkleman and S. C. Gottlieb, 213–270. Athens: University of Georgia Press.

———. 1999. *Colorblind Injustice: Minority Voting Rights and the Undoing of the Second Reconstruction*. Chapel Hill: University of North Carolina Press.

———. 2002a. "*Cumming* and *Giles*, Meet *Jenkins* and *Shaw*: Voting Rights and Education in the Two Reconstructions." Paper presented at the Conference on Constitutional Law, sponsored by the Association of American Law Schools and the American Political Science Association, Washington, D.C., 5–8 June.

———. 2002b. "'The Onward March of Right Principles': State Legislative Actions on Racial Discrimination in Schools in Nineteenth-Century America." *Historical Methods* 35: 177–204.

Kulikoff, A. 1977. "A 'Prolifick' People': Black Population Growth in the Chesapeake Colonies, 1700–1790." *Southern Studies* 16: 391–428.

———. 1986. *Tobacco and Slaves: The Development of Southern Cultures in the Chesapeake, 1680–1800*. Chapel Hill: University of North Carolina Press.

Kupper, W. 1945. *The Golden Hoof: The Story of the Sheep of the Southwest*. New York: Alfred A. Knopf.

Kushner, H. I. 1991. *American Suicide*. New Brunswick, N.J.: Rutgers University Press.

Lachance, A. 1984. *Crimes et Criminels en Nouvelle-France*. Montreal: Boréal Express.

Lack, P. D. 1996. "The Córdoba Revolt." In *Tejano Journey, 1770–1850*, ed. G. E. Poyo, 89–109. Austin: University of Texas Press.

Lacy, N. B. 1937. *Records of the Court of Assistants of Connecticut, 1665–1701*. 2 vols. M.A. thesis, Yale University.

LaFree, G. 1998. *Losing Legitimacy: Street Crime and the Decline of Social Institutions*. Boulder: Westview.

———. 1999a. "Declining Violent Crime Rates in the 1990s: Predicting Crime Booms and Busts." *Annual Review of Sociology* 25: 145–168.

———. 1999b. "A Summary and Review of Cross-National Comparative Studies of Homicide." In *Homicide: A Sourcebook of Social Research*, ed. M. D. Smith and M. A. Zahn, 125–145. Thousand Oaks, Calif.: Sage.

———. 2005. "Evidence for Elite Convergence in Cross-National Homicide Victimization Trends, 1956 to 2000." *Sociological Quarterly* 46: 191–211.

LaFree, G., and K. A. Drass. 2002. "Counting Crime Booms among Nations: Evidence for Homicide Victimization Rates, 1956 to 1998." *Criminology* 40: 769–800.

Lamar, H. R. 1970. *The Far Southwest, 1846–1912: A Territorial History*. New York: W. W. Norton.

Lambert, R. S. 1987. *South Carolina Loyalists in the American Revolution*. Columbia: University of South Carolina Press.

Lane, R. 1967. *Policing the City: Boston, 1822–1885*. Cambridge: Harvard University Press.

———. 1979. *Violent Death in the City: Suicide, Accident, and Murder in Nineteenth-Century Philadelphia*. Cambridge: Harvard University Press.

———. 1986. *Roots of Violence in Black Philadelphia, 1860–1900*. Cambridge: Harvard University Press.

———. 1997. *Murder in America: A History*. Columbus: Ohio State University Press.

Langum, D. J. 1987. *Law and Community on the Mexican California Frontier: Anglo-American Expatriates and the Clash of Legal Traditions, 1821–1846*. Norman: University of Oklahoma Press.

Lantz, H. R., R. L. Schmitt, M. Britton, and E. C. Snyder. 1968. "Pre-Industrial Patterns in the Colonial Family in America: A Content Analysis of Colonial Magazines." *American Sociological Review* 33: 413–426.

Lantz, H. R., R. L. Schmitt, and R. Herman. 1973. "The Pre-Industrial Family in America: A Further Examination of Early Magazines." *American Journal of Sociology* 79: 566–588.

Lantz, H. R., J. Keyes, and M. Schultz. 1975. "The American Family in the Pre-Industrial Period: From Base Lines in History to Change." *American Sociological Review* 40: 21–36.

Lapage Trial. 1876. *The Trial of Joseph Lapage the French Monster, for the Murder of the Beautiful School Girl, Miss Josie Langmaid. Also the Account of the Mur-*

der of Miss Marietta Ball, the School Teacher, in the Woods, in Vermont. Philadelphia: Old Franklin Publishing House.

Larkin, J. 1988. *The Reshaping of Everyday Life, 1790–1840.* New York: Harper and Row.

Larson, E. 2003. *The Devil in the White City: Murder, Magic, and Madness at the Fair That Changed America.* New York: Crown.

Lawson, P. 1986. "Property Crime and Hard Times in England, 1559–1624." *Law and History Review* 4: 95–127.

Leach, D. E. 1973. *Arms for Empire: A Military History of the British Colonies in North America, 1607–1763.* New York: Macmillan.

Leamon, J. S. 1993. *Revolution Downeast: The War for American Independence in Maine.* Amherst: University of Massachusetts Press.

Lebigre, A. 1976. *Les grands jours d'Auvergne: Désordres et répression au XVIIe siècle.* Paris: Hachette.

Lecompte, J. 1985. *Rebellion in Río Arriba, 1837.* Albuquerque: University of New Mexico Press.

Lee, J. B. 1994. *The Price of Nationhood: The American Revolution in Charles County.* New York: W. W. Norton.

Lefler, H. T., and A. R. Newsome. 1973. *North Carolina: The History of a Southern State.* 3d ed. Chapel Hill: University of North Carolina Press.

Lemon, J. T. 2002. *The Best Poor Man's Country: Early Southeastern Pennsylvania.* Baltimore: Johns Hopkins University Press.

Lepore, J. 1998. *The Name of War: King Philip's War and the Origins of American Identity.* New York: Alfred A. Knopf.

Le Roy Ladurie, E. 1971. *Times of Feast, Times of Famine: A History of Climate since the Year 1000.* Trans. B. Bray. New York: Doubleday.

Lescarbot, M. 1907–1914. *The History of New France.* Ed. and trans. W. L. Grant. 3 vols. Toronto: Champlain Society.

Leslie, E. E. 1996. *The Devil Knows How to Ride: The True Story of William Clarke Quantrill and His Confederate Raiders.* New York: Random House.

Leslie, K. A. 1995. *Woman of Color, Daughter of Privilege: Amanda America Dickson, 1849–1893.* Athens: University of Georgia Press.

Leuchtenburg, W. E. 1963. *Franklin Delano Roosevelt and the New Deal, 1932–1940.* New York: Harper and Row.

Levermore, C. H., ed. 1912. *Forerunners and Competitors of the Pilgrims and Puritans.* 2 vols. Brooklyn: New England Society of Brooklyn.

Levitt, S. D. 1996. "The Effect of Prison Population Size on Crime Rates: Evidence from Prison Overcrowding Litigation." *Quarterly Journal of Economics* 111: 319–351.

Levy, B. 1988. *Quakers and the American Family: British Settlement in the Delaware Valley.* New York: Oxford University Press.

Leyburn, J. G. 1962. *The Scotch-Irish: A Social History*. Chapel Hill: University of North Carolina Press.

Libby, C. T., R. E. Moody, and N. W. Allen, Jr., eds. 1928–1947. *Province and Court Records of Maine*. 4 vols. Portland: Maine Historical Society.

Lieberson, S. 1985. *Making It Count: The Improvement of Social Research and Theory*. Berkeley: University of California Press.

Lincoln, A. 1989. *Abraham Lincoln: Speeches and Writings*. Ed. D. E. Fehrenbacher. 2 vols. New York: Library of America.

Lindemann, B. S. 1984. "'To Ravish and Carnally Know': Rape in Eighteenth-Century Massachusetts." *Signs: Journal of Women in Culture and Society* 10: 63–82.

Lindgren, J., and J. L. Heather. 2002. "Counting Guns in Early America." *William and Mary Law Review* 43: 1777–1841.

Lloyd, T. 1807. *Trial of Thomas O. Selfridge, Attorney at Law, Before the Hon. Isaac Parker, Esquire, for Killing Charles Austin*. Boston: Russell and Cutler, Belcher and Armstrong, and Oliver and Munroe.

Lokken, R. N. 1959. *David Lloyd: Colonial Lawmaker*. Seattle: University of Washington Press.

Longstreet, A. B. 1992. *Georgia Scenes, Characters, Incidents &c. in the First Half Century of the Republic*. Savannah: Beehive Press.

Lotchin, R. W. 1974. *San Francisco, 1846–1856: From Hamlet to City*. New York: Oxford University Press.

Lott, J. R., Jr. 2000. *More Guns, Less Crime: Understanding Crime and Gun-Control Laws*. 2d ed. Chicago: University of Chicago Press.

Lovejoy, D. S. 1972. *The Glorious Revolution in America*. New York: Harper and Row.

Lowe, R. G. 1991. *Republicans and Reconstruction in Virginia, 1856–1870*. Charlottesville: University Press of Virginia.

Lukas, J. A. 1985. *Common Ground: A Turbulent Decade in the Lives of Three American Families*. New York: Alfred A. Knopf.

Lund, L. E., and S. Smorodinsky. 2001. "Violent Death among Intimate Partners: A Comparison of Homicide and Homicide Followed by Suicide in California." *Suicide and Life-Threatening Behavior* 31: 451–459.

Lyford, J. O., ed. 1903. *History of Concord, New Hampshire*. 2 vols. Concord: Rumford Press.

Lystra, K. 1989. *Searching the Heart: Women, Men, and Romantic Love in Nineteenth-Century America*. New York: Oxford University Press.

MacDonald, M., and T. R. Murphy. 1990. *Sleepless Souls: Suicide in Early Modern England*. Oxford: Clarendon Press.

MacIntyre, W. I. 1923. *History of Thomas County, Georgia*. 2 vols. Thomasville, Ga.: Privately published.

Mackey, R. R. 1999. "Bushwhackers, Provosts, and Tories: The Guerrilla War in Arkansas." In *Guerrillas, Unionists, and Violence on the Confederate Home Front,* ed. D. E. Sutherland, 171–185. Fayetteville: University of Arkansas Press.

Madden, T. O., Jr., with A. L. Miller. 1992. *We Were Always Free: The Maddens of Culpeper County, Virginia; A Two-Hundred-Year Family History.* New York: W. W. Norton.

Maddex, J. P. 1970. *The Virginia Conservatives, 1867–1879: A Study in Reconstruction Politics.* Chapel Hill: University of North Carolina Press.

———. 1980. "Virginia: The Persistence of Centrist Hegemony." In *Reconstruction and Redemption in the South,* ed. O. H. Olsen, 113–155. Baton Rouge: Louisiana State University Press.

Mahon, J. K. 1967. *History of the Second Seminole War, 1835–1842.* Gainesville: University of Florida Press.

Main, G. L. 2001. *Peoples of a Spacious Land: Families and Cultures in Colonial New England.* Cambridge: Harvard University Press.

Mancall, P. C. 1995. *Deadly Medicine: Indians and Alcohol in Early America.* Ithaca: Cornell University Press.

Mandell, D. R. 1996. *Behind the Frontier: Indians in Eighteenth-Century Eastern Massachusetts.* Lincoln: University of Nebraska Press.

Manfra, J., and R. Dykstra. 1985. "Serial Marriage and the Origins of the Black Stepfamily: The Rowanty Evidence." *Journal of American History* 72: 18–44.

Mann, R. 1995. "Diversity in the Antebellum Appalachian South: Four Farm Communities in Tazewell County, Virginia." In *Appalachia in the Making: The Mountain South in the Nineteenth Century,* ed. M. B. Pudup, D. B. Billings, and A. L. Waller, 132–162. Chapel Hill: University of North Carolina Press.

Manning, P. 1990. *Slavery and African Life: Occidental, Oriental, and African Slave Trades.* New York: Cambridge University Press.

Marietta, J. D., and G. S. Rowe. 1999. "Violent Crime, Victims, and Society in Pennsylvania, 1682–1800." *Explorations in Early American Culture* 66: 24–54.

———. 2006. *Troubled Experiment: Crime and Justice in Pennsylvania, 1682–1800.* Philadelphia: University of Pennsylvania Press.

Marshall, J. 1884. "Diary, 1697–1711." *Proceedings of the Massachusetts Historical Society,* ser. 2., 1: 148–161.

Marshall, M., ed. 1979. *Beliefs, Behaviors, and Alcoholic Beverages: A Cross-Cultural Survey.* Ann Arbor: University of Michigan Press.

Marten, J. A. 1990. *Texas Divided: Loyalty and Dissent in the Lone Star State, 1856–1874.* Lexington: University Press of Kentucky.

Mason, R. L. 1915. *Narrative of Richard Lee Mason in the Pioneer West, 1819.* New York: Charles Frederick Heartman.

Masters, R. E. L., and E. Lea. 1963. *Sex Crimes in History: Evolving Concepts of Sadism, Lust-Murder, and Necrophilia from Ancient to Modern Times.* New York: Julian Press.

Mastro, T. D., et al. 1994. "Estimating the Number of HIV-Infected Injection Drug Users in Bangkok: A Capture-Recapture Method." *American Journal of Public Health* 84: 1094–1099.

Mather, C. 1721. *Tremenda: The Dreadful Sound with which the Wicked are to be Thunderstruck.* Boston: B. Green.

Mathews, D. G. 1965. *Slavery and Methodism: A Chapter in American Morality, 1780–1845.* Princeton: Princeton University Press.

———. 1977. *Religion in the Old South.* Chicago: University of Chicago Press.

Mayfield, J. 2000. "George Washington Harris: The Fool from the Hills." In *The Human Tradition in Antebellum America,* ed. M. A. Morrison, 229–243. Wilmington, Del.: SR Books.

McBride, I. 1998. "'The Common Name of Irishman': Protestantism and Patriotism in Eighteenth-Century Ireland." In *Protestantism and National Identity: Britain and Ireland, c. 1650–c. 1850,* ed. T. Claydon and I. McBride, 236–261. Cambridge: Cambridge University Press.

McCaslin, R. B. 1994. *Tainted Breeze: The Great Hanging at Gainesville, Texas, 1862.* Baton Rouge: Louisiana State University Press.

McConkey, F. 1887. *The Bald Knobbers or Citizens' Committee of Taney and Christian Counties, Missouri.* Forsyth, Mo.: Groom and McConkey.

McCusker, J. J., and R. R. Menard. 1985. *The Economy of British America, 1607–1789.* Chapel Hill: University of North Carolina Press.

McEachern, C. E. 1996. *The Poetics of English Nationhood, 1590–1612.* Cambridge: Cambridge University Press.

McElvaine, R. S., ed. 1983. *Down and Out in the Great Depression: Letters from the Forgotten Man.* Chapel Hill: University of North Carolina Press.

McGrath, R. D. 1984. *Gunfighters, Highwaymen, and Vigilantes: Violence on the Frontier.* Berkeley: University of California Press.

McIlwaine, H. R., ed. 1924. *Minutes of the Council and General Court of Colonial Virginia, 1622–1632, 1670–1676, with Notes and Excerpts from Original Council and General Court Records, into 1683, Now Lost.* Richmond: Colonial Press, Everett Waddey.

———. 1926–1929. *Official Letters of the Governors of the State of Virginia.* 3 vols. Richmond: Virginia State Library.

McIlwaine, H. R., W. L. Hall, and B. J. Hillman, eds. 1925–1966. *Executive Journals of the Council of Colonial Virginia.* 6 vols. Richmond: Virginia State Library.

McKanna, C. V. 1997. *Homicide, Race, and Justice in the American West, 1880–1920.* Tucson: University of Arizona Press.

——. 2002. *Race and Homicide in Nineteenth-Century California.* Reno: University of Nevada Press.

McKinney, G. B. 1978. *Southern Mountain Republicans, 1865–1900: Politics and the Appalachian Community.* Chapel Hill: University of North Carolina Press.

McLynn, F. 1989. *Crime and Punishment in Eighteenth-Century England.* London: Routledge.

McPherson, J. M. 1988. *Battle Cry of Freedom: The Civil War Era.* New York: Oxford University Press.

McWhiney, G. 1988. *Cracker Culture: Celtic Ways in the Old South.* Tuscaloosa: University of Alabama Press.

Melish, J. P. 1998. *Disowning Slavery: Gradual Emancipation and "Race" in New England, 1780–1860.* Ithaca: Cornell University Press.

Menard, R. R. 1975. "The Maryland Slave Population, 1658–1730: A Demographic Profile of Blacks in Four Counties." *William and Mary Quarterly,* 3d. ser., 32: 29–54.

——. 1980. "The Tobacco Industry in the Chesapeake Colonies, 1617–1730: An Interpretation." *Research in Economic History* 5: 109–177.

——. 1981. "The Growth of Population in the Chesapeake Colonies: A Comment." *Explorations in Economic History* 18: 399–410.

Merritt, R. L. 1966. *Symbols of American Community, 1735–1775.* New Haven: Yale University Press.

Messner, S. F., and R. Rosenfeld. 1994. *Crime and the American Dream.* Belmont, Calif.: Wadsworth.

Metcalf, H. H. 1916. *Laws of New Hampshire: First Constitutional Period, 1784–1792.* Concord: Rumford Press.

Miller, J. H. 2000. *The Disappearance of God: Five Nineteenth-Century Writers.* Urbana: University of Illinois Press.

Miller, K. A. 1985. *Emigrants and Exiles: Ireland and the Irish Exodus to North America.* New York: Oxford University Press.

Miller, K. A., A. Schrier, B. D. Boling, and D. N. Doyle, eds. 2003. *Irish Immigrants in the Land of Canaan: Letters and Memoirs from Colonial and Revolutionary America, 1675–1815.* New York: Oxford University Press.

Miller, P. 1961. *The New England Mind: From Colony to Province.* Boston: Beacon Press.

Miller, W. R. 1999. *Cops and Bobbies: Police Authority in New York and London, 1830–1870.* 2d ed. Columbus: Ohio State University Press.

Milroy, C. M. 1995. "The Epidemiology of Homicide-Suicide (Dyadic Death)." *Forensic Science International* 71: 117–122.

Mitchell, B. R. 1988. *British Historical Statistics.* Cambridge: Cambridge University Press.

Mitchison, R. 1996. "The Government and the Highlands, 1707–1745." In *Scotland in the Age of Improvement,* ed. N. T. Phillipson and R. Mitchison, 24–46. Edinburgh: Edinburgh University Press.

———. 2002. *A History of Scotland.* 3d ed. London: Routledge.

Mocho, J. 1997. *Murder and Justice in Frontier New Mexico, 1821–1846.* Albuquerque: University of New Mexico Press.

Mohr, C. L. 1986. *On the Threshold of Freedom: Masters and Slaves in Civil War Georgia.* Athens: University of Georgia Press.

Monkkonen, E. H. 1981. *Police in Urban America, 1860–1920.* Cambridge: Cambridge University Press.

———. 1994. Police Departments, Arrests, and Crime in the United States, 1860–1920. Computer file. Inter-University Consortium for Political and Social Research, Ann Arbor.

———. 2001. *Murder in New York City.* Berkeley: University of California Press.

———. 2005. Los Angeles Homicides, 1830–2001. Computer file. Historical Violence Database, Criminal Justice Research Center, Ohio State University.

Montell, W. L. 1970. *The Saga of Coe Ridge: A Study in Oral History.* Knoxville: University of Tennessee Press.

———. 1986. *Killings: Folk Justice in the Upper South.* Lexington: University Press of Kentucky.

Montgomery, D. 1967. *Beyond Equality: Labor and the Radical Republicans, 1862–1872.* New York: Alfred A. Knopf.

Moody, T. W., F. X. Martin, and F. J. Byrne, eds. 1976. *A New History of Ireland.* Vol. 3: *Early Modern Ireland, 1534–1691.* Oxford: Clarendon Press.

Moody, T. W., and W. E. Vaughan, eds. 1986. *A New History of Ireland.* Vol. 4: *Eighteenth-Century Ireland, 1691–1800.* Oxford: Clarendon Press.

Moore, J. H. 2006. *Carnival of Blood: Dueling, Lynching, and Murder in South Carolina, 1880–1920.* Columbia: University of South Carolina Press.

Moote, A. L. 1971. *The Revolt of the Judges: The Parlement of Paris and the Fronde, 1643–1652.* Princeton: Princeton University Press.

Moran, R. F. 2001. *Interracial Intimacy: The Regulation of Race and Romance.* Chicago: University of Chicago Press.

Morgan, E. S. 1975. *American Slavery, American Freedom: The Ordeal of Colonial Virginia.* New York: W. W. Norton.

Morgan, G. 1989. *The Hegemony of the Law: Richmond County, Virginia, 1692–1776.* New York: Garland.

Morgan, P. D. 1998. *Slave Counterpoint: Black Culture in the Eighteenth-Century*

Chesapeake and Low Country. Chapel Hill: University of North Carolina Press.

———. 2002. "Conspiracy Scares." *William and Mary Quarterly,* 3d ser., 59: 159–166.

Morrill, J. S. 1994. *Cheshire, 1630–1660: County Government and Society during the English Revolution.* Oxford: Oxford University Press.

———. 1999. *Revolt in the Provinces: The People of England and the Tragedies of War, 1630–1648.* 2d ed. New York: Longman.

Morris, C. 1995. *Becoming Southern: The Evolution of a Way of Life, Warren County and Vicksburg, Mississippi, 1770–1860.* New York: Oxford University Press.

Morton, T. 1947. "New English Canaan" (1632). In *Tracts and Other Papers Relating Principally to the Origin, Settlement, and Progress of the Colonies of North America,* ed. P. Force, 2: 1–128. New York: Peter Smith.

Mott, M. H. 1859. *History of the Regulators of Northern Indiana.* Indianapolis: Indianapolis Journal.

Moyer, P. 2004. "'Real' Indians, 'White' Indians, and the Contest for the Wyoming Valley." In *Friends and Enemies in Penn's Woods: Indians, Colonists, and the Racial Construction of Pennsylvania,* ed. W. A. Pencak and D. K. Richter, 221–237. University Park: Pennsylvania State University Press.

Muchembled, R. 1989. *La violence au village: Sociabilité et comportements populaires en Artois du XVe au XVIIe siècle.* Turnhout: Editions Brepols.

Mullen, K. J. 1989. *Let Justice Be Done: Crime and Politics in Early San Francisco.* Reno: University of Nevada Press.

———. 2005. *Dangerous Strangers: Minority Newcomers and Criminal Violence in the Urban West, 1850–2000.* New York: Palgrave Macmillan.

Nash, G. B. 1979. *The Urban Crucible: Social Change, Political Consciousness, and the Origins of the American Revolution.* Cambridge: Harvard University Press.

———. 1988. *Forging Freedom: The Formation of Philadelphia's Black Community, 1720–1840.* Cambridge: Harvard University Press.

National Association for the Advancement of Colored People. 1969. *Thirty Years of Lynching in the United States, 1889–1918.* New York: Negro Universities Press.

National Center for Health Statistics. 2005. "Life Expectancy Hits Record High." Available at http://www.cdc.gov/nchs/pressroom/05facts/lifeexpectancy.htm.

Navas, D. 1999. *Murdered by His Wife.* Amherst: University of Massachusetts Press.

Neuschel, K. B. 1989. *Word of Honor: Interpreting Noble Culture in Sixteenth-Century France.* Ithaca: Cornell University Press.

Newton, G. F. 1889. "History of Holmes County, Ohio." Manuscript. Ohio Historical Society, Columbus.

Noble, J., ed. 1901–1928. *Records of the Court of Assistants of the Colony of the Massachusetts Bay.* 3 vols. Boston: County of Suffolk.

Nochlin, L. 1971. *Realism.* New York: Penguin.

Noe, K. W. 1997. "Exterminating Savages: The Union Army and Mountain Guerrillas in Southern West Virginia, 1861–1862." In *The Civil War in Appalachia,* ed. K. W. Noe and S. H. Wilson, 104–130. Knoxville: University of Tennessee Press.

Noe, K. W., and S. H. Wilson, eds. 1997. *The Civil War in Appalachia.* Knoxville: University of Tennessee Press.

Nolan, F. W. 1992. *The Lincoln County War: A Documentary History.* Norman: University of Oklahoma Press.

Nolan, P. B. 1987. *Vigilantes on the Middle Border: A Study of Self-Appointed Law Enforcement in the States of the Upper Mississippi from 1840 to 1880.* New York: Garland.

Norton, M. B. 1987. "Gender and Defamation in Seventeenth-Century Maryland." *William and Mary Quarterly,* 3d ser., 44: 3–39.

———. 2002. *In the Devil's Snare: The Salem Witchcraft Crisis of 1692.* New York: Alfred A. Knopf.

Oates, S. B. 1975. *The Fires of Jubilee: Nat Turner's Fierce Rebellion.* New York: Harper and Row.

O'Callaghan, E. B., ed. 1853–1887. *Documents Relative to the Colonial History of the State of New York.* 15 vols. Albany: Weed, Parsons.

O'Callaghan, M. 2000. *The "Shepheards Nation": Jacobean Spenserians and Early Stuart Political Culture, 1612–1625.* Oxford: Clarendon Press.

O'Donnell, I. 2005. "Lethal Violence in Ireland, 1841–2003: Famine, Celibacy and Parental Pacification." *British Journal of Criminology* 45: 671–695.

Oliver, P. 1998. *"Terror to Evil-Doers": Prisons and Punishments in Nineteenth-Century Ontario.* Toronto: University of Toronto Press.

Onuf, P. S. 1996. "Federalism, Republicanism, and the Origins of American Sectionalism." In *All Over the Map: Rethinking American Regions,* ed. E. L. Ayers et al., 11–37. Baltimore: Johns Hopkins University Press.

Osofsky, G. 1971. *Harlem: The Making of a Ghetto; Negro New York, 1890–1930.* 2d ed. New York: Harper and Row.

Österberg, E. 1996. "Criminality, Social Control, and the Early Modern State: Evidence and Interpretations in Scandinavian Historiography." In *The Civilization of Crime: Violence in Town and Country since the Middle Ages,* ed. E. A. Johnson and E. H. Monkkonen, 35–62. Urbana: University of Illinois Press.

Otto, P. A. 1995. "New Netherland Frontier: Europeans and Native Americans along the Lower Hudson River, 1524–1664." Ph.D. diss., Indiana University.

Paciotti, B. 2005. "Homicide in Seattle's Chinatown, 1900–1940: Evaluating the Influence of Social Organizations." *Homicide Studies* 9: 229–255.

Painter, N. I. 1976. *Exodusters: Black Migration to Kansas after Reconstruction.* New York: Alfred A. Knopf.

Palmer, W. P., S. McRae, and R. Colston, eds. 1875–1893. *Calendar of Virginia State Papers.* 11 vols. Richmond: R. F. Walker.

Paludan, P. S. 1981. *Victims: A True Story of the Civil War.* Knoxville: University of Tennessee Press.

Pancake, J. S. 1985. *This Destructive War: The British Campaign in the Carolinas, 1780–1782.* Tuscaloosa: University of Alabama Press.

Papanikolas, Z. 1991. *Buried Unsung: Louis Tikas and the Ludlow Massacre.* Lincoln: University of Nebraska Press.

Parker, G. 1977. *The Dutch Revolt.* London: Allen Lane.

Parker, J. 1830. *Report of the Trial of Daniel H. Corey, on an Indictment for the Murder of Mrs. Matilda Nash.* Newport, N.H.: French and Brown.

Parker, R. N. 1998. "Alcohol, Homicide, and Cultural Context: A Cross-National Analysis of Gender-Specific Homicide Victimization." *Homicide Studies* 2: 6–30.

Parker, W. B. 1924. *The Life and Public Services of Justin Smith Morrill.* Boston: Houghton Mifflin.

Parramore, T. C. 2003. "Covenant in Jerusalem." In *Nat Turner: A Slave Rebellion in History and Memory,* ed. K. S. Greenberg, 58–76. New York: Oxford University Press.

Parrella, A. 1983. "Violence in Northern France: A Social Historical Analysis of Murder, 1815–1909." Ph.D. diss., University of Virginia.

———. 1992. "Industrialization and Murder: Northern France, 1815–1904." *Journal of Interdisciplinary History* 22: 627–654.

Patterson, J. T. 1996. *Grand Expectations: The United States, 1945–1974.* New York: Oxford University Press.

———. 2005. *Restless Giant: The United States from Watergate to Bush v. Gore.* New York: Oxford University Press.

Peake Trial. 1836. *Trial of Mrs. Rebecca Peake, Indicted for the Murder of Ephraim Peake.* Montpelier, Vt.: E. P. Walton and Son.

Pencak, W. 1981. *War, Politics, and Revolution in Provincial Massachusetts.* Boston: Northeastern University Press.

———. 2002. "The Promise of Revolution, 1750–1800." In *Pennsylvania: A History of the Commmonwealth,* ed. R. M. Miller and William Pencak, 101–152. University Park: Pennsylvania State University Press.

Pencak, W. A., and D. K. Richter, eds. 2004. *Friends and Enemies in Penn's*

Woods: Indians, Colonists, and the Racial Construction of Pennsylvania. University Park: Pennsylvania State University Press.

Percy, G. 1922. "A Trewe Relacyon of the Procedinges and Ocurrentes of Momente wch have hapned in Virginia from the Tyme Sr Thomas Gates was shippwrackte uppon the Bermudes ano 1609 untill my departure outt of the Country wch was in ano Dñi 1612." *Tyler's Quarterly Historical and Genealogical Magazine* 3: 259–282.

Perdue, C. L., Jr., T. E. Barden, and R. K. Phillips, eds. 1976. *Weevils in the Wheat: Interviews with Virginia Ex-Slaves.* Charlottesville: University Press of Virginia.

Perman, M. 2001. *Struggle for Mastery: Disfranchisement in the South, 1888–1908.* Chapel Hill: University of North Carolina Press.

Pernanen, K. 1991. *Alcohol in Human Violence.* New York: Guilford.

Pessen, E. 1978. *Jacksonian America: Society, Personality, and Politics.* Rev. ed. Homewood, Ill.: Dorsey Press.

Peterson, M. D., ed. 1975. *The Portable Thomas Jefferson.* New York: Viking.

Peterson del Mar, D. 1996. *What Trouble I Have Seen: A History of Violence against Wives.* Cambridge: Harvard University Press.

———. 2002. *Beaten Down: A History of Interpersonal Violence in the West.* Seattle: University of Washington Press.

Philbrick, N. 2006. *Mayflower: A Story of Courage, Community, and War.* New York: Viking.

Philips, D. 1977. *Crime and Authority in Victorian England: The Black Country, 1835–1860.* London: Croom Helm.

Phillips, G. H. 1975. *Chiefs and Challengers: Indian Resistance and Cooperation in Southern California.* Berkeley: University of California Press.

———. 1980. "Indians in Los Angeles, 1781–1875: Economic Integration, Social Disintegration." *Pacific Historical Review* 49: 427–451.

———. 1993. *Indians and Intruders in Central California, 1769–1849.* Norman: University of Oklahoma Press.

———. 1997. *Indians and Indian Agents: The Origins of the Reservation System in California, 1849–1852.* Norman: University of Oklahoma Press.

Phillips, J., and A. May. 2001. "Homicide in Nova Scotia, 1749–1815." *Canadian Historical Review* 82: 625–661.

Pickering, D., and J. Falls. 2000. *Brush Men and Vigilantes: Civil War Dissent in Texas.* College Station: Texas A & M University Press.

Piersen, W. D. 1988. *Black Yankees: The Development of an Afro-American Subculture.* Amherst: University of Massachusetts Press.

Pike, J. 1875–76. "Journal of the Reverend John Pike, 1678–1709." *Proceedings of the Massachusetts Historical Society,* ser. 1, 14: 117–152.

Pincus, S. C. A. 1995. "'Coffee Politicians Does Create': Coffeehouses and Restoration Political Culture." *Journal of Modern History* 67: 807–834.

———. 1999. "Nationalism, Universal Monarchy, and the Glorious Revolution." In *State/Culture: State-Formation after the Cultural Turn*, ed. George Steinmetz, 182–210. Ithaca: Cornell University Press.

Pitt, L. 1971. *The Decline of the Californios: A Social History of the Spanish-Speaking Californians, 1846–1890*. Berkeley: University of California Press.

Pitt-Rivers, Julian. 1966. "Honour and Social Status." In *Honour and Shame: The Values of Mediterranean Society*, ed. J. G. Péristiany, 19–77. Chicago: University of Chicago Press.

Plane, A. M. 2000. *Colonial Intimacies: Indian Marriage in Early New England*. Ithaca: Cornell University Press.

Pleck, E. H. 1979. *Black Migration and Poverty: Boston, 1865–1900*. New York: Academic.

———. 1987. *Domestic Tyranny: The Making of Social Policy against Family Violence from Colonial Times to the Present*. New York: Oxford University Press.

Ploux, F. 2002. *Guerres paysannes en Quercy: Violences, conciliations et répression pénale dans les campagnes du Lot (1810–1860)*. Paris: Boutique de l'Histoire.

Plummer, J. 1795. *Dying Confession of Pomp, A Negro Man, Who Was Executed at Ipswich, on the 6th of August, 1795, for Murdering Capt. Charles Furbush, of Andover*. Newburyport, Mass.: Blunt and March.

Pope, R. G. 1969. *The Half-Way Covenant: Church Membership in Puritan New England*. Princeton: Princeton University Press.

Potter, D. M. 1968. "The Historian's Use of Nationalism and Vice Versa." In *The South and the Sectional Conflict*, ed. D. M. Potter, 34–83. Baton Rouge: Louisiana State University Press.

Powell, C. L. 1972. *English Domestic Relations, 1487–1653*. New York: Russell and Russell.

Powers, G. 1841. *Historical Sketches of the Discovery, Settlement, and Progress of Events in the Coos Country . . . 1754–1785*. Haverhill, N.H.: J. F. C. Hayes.

Preston, D. L. 2004. "Squatters, Indians, Proprietary Government, and Land in the Susquehanna Valley." In *Friends and Eenemies in Penn's Woods: Indians, Colonists, and the Racial Construction of Pennsylvania*, ed. W. A. Pencak and D. K. Richter, 167–179. University Park: Pennsylvania State University Press.

Puglisi, M. J. 1991. *Puritans Besieged: The Legacies of King Philip's War in the Massachusetts Bay Colony*. Lanham, Md.: University Press of America.

Pulsipher, J. H. 1996. "Massacre at Hurtleberry Hill: Christian Indians and English Authority in Metacom's War." *William and Mary Quarterly*, 3d ser., 53: 459–486.

Quarles, B. 1961. *The Negro in the American Revolution*. Chapel Hill: University of North Carolina Press.

Quigley, D. 2004. *Second Founding: New York City, Reconstruction, and the Making of American Democracy.* New York: Hill and Wang.

Rankin, H. F. 1965. *Criminal Trial Proceedings in the General Court of Colonial Virginia.* Williamsburg: Colonial Williamsburg.

Ranum, O. 1993. *The Fronde: A French Revolution, 1648–1652.* New York: W. W. Norton.

Reid, J. G. 1981. *Acadia, Maine, and New Scotland: Marginal Colonies in the Seventeenth Century.* Toronto: University of Toronto Press.

Reid, J. R. 1999. *Patterns of Vengeance: Crosscultural Homicide in the North American Fur Trade.* Pasadena, Calif.: Ninth Judicial Circuit Historical Society.

Ressler, R. K., A. W. Burgess, and J. E. Douglas. 1988. *Sexual Homicide: Patterns and Motives.* Lexington, Mass.: Lexington Books.

Ressler, R. K., and T. Schachtman. 1992. *Whoever Fights Monsters.* New York: St. Martin's Press.

Reynolds, J. 1834. *Recollections of Windsor Prison.* Boston: A. Wright.

Rhode Island Court Records. 1920–1922. *Records of the Court of Trials of the Colony of Providence Plantations.* 2 vols. Providence: Rhode Island Historical Society.

Rice, J. D. 1994. "Crime and Punishment in Frederick County and Maryland, 1748–1837: A Study in Culture, Society, and Law." Ph.D. diss., University of Maryland at College Park.

Richter, D. K. 2001. *Facing East from Indian Country: A Native History of Early America.* Cambridge: Harvard University Press.

Roberts, J. S. 1995. "Long-Term Trends in the Consumption of Alcoholic Beverages." In *The State of Humanity,* ed. J. L. Simon, 114–121. Oxford: Blackwell.

Roeber, A. G. 1981. *Faithful Magistrates and Republican Lawyers: Creators of Virginia Legal Culture, 1680–1810.* Chapel Hill: University of North Carolina Press.

Roediger, D. R. 1991. *The Wages of Whiteness: Race and the Making of the American Working Class.* London: Verso.

———. 2005. *Working toward Whiteness: How America's Immigrants Became White: The Strange Journey from Ellis Island to the Suburbs.* New York: Basic Books.

Roetger, R. W. 1984. "Transformation of Sexual Morality." *Canadian Review of American Studies* 15: 243–257.

Rogers, J. D. 1987. *Crime, Justice, and Society in Colonial Sri Lanka.* London: Curzon Press.

Rohrbough, M. J. 1997. *Days of Gold: The California Gold Rush and the American Nation.* Berkeley: University of California Press.

Rorabaugh, W. J. 1979. *The Alcoholic Republic: An American Tradition.* New York: Oxford University Press.

Rosa, J. G. 1974. *They Called Him Wild Bill: The Life and Adventures of James Butler Hickok.* 2d ed. Norman: University of Oklahoma Press.

———. 1996. *Wild Bill Hickok: The Man and His Myth.* Lawrence: University Press of Kansas.

Rose, J. A. 1906. "The Regulators and Flatheads in Southern Illinois." *Illinois State Historical Society Transactions for 1906* 11: 108–121.

Rosenbaum, R. J. 1981. *Mexicano Resistance in the Southwest: "The Sacred Right of Self-Preservation."* Austin: University of Texas Press.

Rosenberg, M. L., and J. A. Mercy. 1986. "Homicide: Epidemiologic Analysis at the National Level." *Bulletin of the New York Academy of Medicine* 62: 376–399.

Rosenzweig, R. 1983. *Eight Hours for What We Will: Workers and Leisure in an Industrial City, 1870–1920.* Cambridge: Cambridge University Press.

Rosswurm, S. 1987. *Arms, Country, and Class: The Philadelphia Militia and the "Lower Sort" during the American Revolution, 1775–1783.* New Brunswick, N.J.: Rutgers University Press.

Roth, R. 1987. *The Democratic Dilemma: Religion, Reform, and the Social Order in the Connecticut River Valley of Vermont, 1791–1850.* New York: Cambridge University Press.

———. 1991. "Why Are We Still Vermonters? Vermont's Identity Crisis and the Founding of the Vermont Historical Society." *Vermont History* 59: 197–211.

———. 1997. "'Blood Calls for Vengeance!' The History of Capital Punishment in Vermont." *Vermont History* 65: 10–25.

———. 1998. "Did Class Matter in American Politics? The Importance of Exploratory Data Analysis." *Historical Methods* 31: 5–25.

———. 1999. "Spousal Murder in Northern New England, 1776–1865." In *Over the Threshold: Intimate Violence in Early America,* ed. C. Daniels and M. V. Kennedy, 65–93. New York: Routledge.

———. 2001. "Homicide in Early Modern England, 1549–1800: The Need for a Quantitative Synthesis." *Crime, History, and Societies* 5: 33–67.

———. 2002. "Guns, Gun Culture, and Homicide: The Relationship between Firearms, the Uses of Firearms, and Interpersonal Violence in Early America." *William and Mary Quarterly,* 3d ser., 59: 223–240.

———. 2007. "Guns, Murder, and Probability: How Can We Decide Which Figures to Trust?" *Reviews in American History* 35: 165–175.

Rothert, O. A. 1924. *The Outlaws of Cave-in-Rock.* Cleveland: Arthur H. Clark.

Rothman, E. K. 1984. *Hands and Hearts: A History of Courtship in America.* New York: Basic Books.

Rothman, J. D. 2003. *Notorious in the Neighborhood: Sex and Families across the Color Line in Virginia, 1787–1861.* Chapel Hill: University of North Carolina Press.

Rotundo, E. A. 1993. *American Manhood: Transformations in Masculinity from the Revolution to the Modern Era.* New York: Basic Books.

Rountree, H. C. 1990. *Pocahontas's People: The Powhatan Indians of Virginia through Four Centuries.* Norman: University of Oklahoma Press.

Rountree, H. C., and T. E. Davidson. 1997. *Eastern Shore Indians of Virginia and Maryland.* Charlottesville: University Press of Virginia.

Rousey, D. C. 1996. *Policing the Southern City: New Orleans, 1805–1889.* Baton Rouge: Louisiana State University Press.

Rousseaux, X., F. Vesentini, and A. Vrints. 2004. "Statistics of Homicide in Belgium: A Preliminary Analysis." Paper presented at the CEGES Congress on "Violence in History: Long-Term Trends and the Role of Wars," Brussels, 3–4 December.

Russell, H. S. 1980. *Indian New England before the Mayflower.* Hanover, N.H.: University Press of New England.

Rutman, A. H. 1987. "Still Planting the Seeds of Hope: The Recent Literature of the Early Chesapeake Region." *Virginia Magazine of History and Biography* 95: 3–24.

Rutman, D. B., and A. H. Rutman. 1984. *A Place in Time.* 2 vols. New York: W. W. Norton.

Ryan, M. P. 1981. *Cradle of the Middle Class: The Family in Oneida County, New York, 1790–1865.* New York: Cambridge University Press.

Sainsbury, W. N., ed. 1893. *Calendar of State Papers, Colonial Series, America and West Indies, 1675–1676.* London: Her Majesty's Stationery Office.

Salinger, S. V. 1987. *"To Serve Well and Faithfully": Labor and Indentured Servants in Pennsylvania, 1682–1800.* New York: Cambridge University Press.

Salisbury, N. 1982. *Manitou and Providence: Indians, Europeans, and the Making of New England, 1500–1643.* New York: Oxford University Press.

Salstrom, P. 1994. *Appalachia's Path to Dependency: Rethinking a Region's Economic History, 1730–1940.* Lexington: University Press of Kentucky.

———. 1995. "New Appalachia as One of America's Last Frontiers." In *Appalachia in the Making: The Mountain South in the Nineteenth Century,* ed. M. B. Pudup, D. B. Billings, and A. L. Waller, 76–102. Chapel Hill: University of North Carolina Press.

Samora, J., J. Bernal, and A. Peña. 1979. *Gunpowder Justice: A Reassessment of the Texas Rangers.* Notre Dame: University of Notre Dame Press.

Sampson, R. J., and S. W. Raudenbush. 1999. "Systematic Social Observation of Public Spaces: A New Look at Disorder in Urban Neighborhoods." *American Journal of Sociology* 105: 603–651.

Sanger, A. 1987. *Very Poor and of a Lo Make: The Journal of Abner Sanger.* Ed.

L. K. Stabler. Portsmouth, N.H.: P. E. Randall for the Historical Society of Cheshire County.

Sapiro, V., S. J. Rosenstone, and the National Election Studies. 2004. American National Election Studies Cumulative Data File, 1948–2002. Computer file. Inter-University Consortium for Political and Social Research, Ann Arbor.

Sarris, J. D. 1993. "Anatomy of an Atrocity: The Madden Branch Massacre and Guerrilla Warfare in North Georgia, 1861–1865." *Georgia Historical Quarterly* 77: 679–710.

Saunt, C. 1999. *A New Order of Things: Property, Power, and the Transformation of the Creek Indians, 1733–1816*. New York: Cambridge University Press.

Savage, E. H. 1873. *Police Records and Recollections; or, Boston by Daylight and Gaslight for Two Hundred and Forty Years*. Boston: John P. Dale.

Sawtell, I. N.d. *The History of the Murder of Hiram Sawtell by His Brother Isaac Sawtell*. Laconia, N.H.: John J. Lane.

Schechter, H., and D. Everitt. 1996. *The A–Z Encyclopedia of Serial Killers*. New York: Pocket Books.

Schlosser, E. 1998. "The Prison-Industrial Complex." *Atlantic Monthly*, December: 51–77.

Schneider, E. C. 1999. *Vampires, Dragons, and Egyptian Kings: Youth Gangs in Postwar New York*. Princeton: Princeton University Press.

Schultz, D. 1996. *Quantrill's War: The Life and Times of William Clarke Quantrill, 1837–1865*. New York: St. Martin's Press.

Schwarz, P. J. 1988. *Twice Condemned: Slaves and the Criminal Laws of Virginia, 1705–1865*. Baton Rouge: Louisiana State University Press.

Scott, A. P. 1930. *Criminal Law in Colonial Virginia*. Chicago: University of Chicago Press.

Scott, K., and K. Stryker-Rodda, eds. 1974. *New York Historical Manuscripts: Dutch*. Vol. 4: *Council Minutes, 1638–1649*. Trans. A. J. F. Van Laer. Baltimore: Genealogical Publishing.

Seidman, S. 1991. *Romantic Longings: Love in America, 1830–1980*. New York: Routledge.

Selfridge, T. O. 1807. *A Correct Statement of the Whole Preliminary Controversy between Thomas O. Selfridge and Benj. Austin*. Charlestown, Mass.: Samuel Etheridge.

Semmes, R. 1938. *Crime and Punishment in Early Maryland*. Baltimore: Johns Hopkins University Press.

Sewall, J. 1728. *He that Would Keep God's Commandments Must Renounce the Society of Evil Doers: A Sermon Preach'd at the Publick Lecture in Boston, July 18th, 1728, after a Bloody and Mortal Duel*. Boston: D. Henchman.

Sewall, S. 1973. *The Diary of Samuel Sewall, 1674–1729*. Ed. M. H. Thomas. 2 vols. New York: Farrar, Straus and Giroux.

Shade, W. G. 1996. *Democratizing the Old Dominion: Virginia and the Second Party System, 1824–1861*. Charlottesville: University Press of Virginia.

Sharpe, J. A. 1980. *Defamation and Sexual Slander in Early Modern England: The Church Courts at York*. Heslington: University of York.

———. 1981. "Domestic Homicide in Early Modern England." *Historical Journal* 24: 29–48.

Shelley, P. B. 1904. "Epipsychidion." In *The Complete Poetical Works of Shelley*, ed. T. Hutchinson, 453–467. Oxford: Clarendon Press.

Shields, D. S. 1997. *Civil Tongues and Polite Letters in British America*. Chapel Hill: University of North Carolina Press.

Shore, L. 1982. "Making Mississippi Safe for Slavery: The Insurrectionary Panic of 1835." In *Class, Conflict, and Consensus: Antebellum Southern Community Studies*, ed. O. V. Burton and R. C. McMath Jr., 96–127. Westport, Conn.: Greenwood.

Shurtleff, N. B., ed. 1855–1861. *Records of the Colony of New Plymouth in New England*. 10 vols. Boston: W. White.

Sidbury, J. 1997. *Ploughshares into Swords: Race, Rebellion, and Identity in Gabriel's Virginia, 1730–1810*. New York: Cambridge University Press.

Siegel, R. B. 1996. "'The Rule of Love': Wife Beating as Prerogative and Privacy." *Yale Law Journal* 105: 2117–2207.

Silverman, E. B. 1999. *NYPD Battles Crime: Innovative Strategies in Policing*. Boston: Northeastern University Press.

Simmons, C. J. 1984. "Twenty-Five Decades of Court History in Lancaster County." *Northern Neck of Virginia Historical Magazine* 34: 3878–3900.

Siringo, C. A. 1966. *A Texas Cowboy*. Lincoln: University of Nebraska Press.

Sitkoff, H. 1981. *The Struggle for Black Equality, 1954–1980*. New York: Hill and Wang.

Skogan, W. G. 1990. *Disorder and Decline: Crime and the Spiral of Decay in American Neighborhoods*. New York: Free Press.

Slack, P. 1974. "Vagrants and Vagrancy in England, 1598–1664." *Economic History Review*, 2d ser., 27: 360–379.

———. 1988. *Poverty and Policy in Tudor and Stuart England*. London: Longman.

Smallwood, J. M., B. A. Crouch, and L. Peacock. 2003. *Murder and Mayhem: The War of Reconstruction in Texas*. College Station: Texas A & M University Press.

Smith, B. G. 1990. *The "Lower Sort": Philadelphia's Laboring People, 1750–1800*. Ithaca: Cornell University Press.

Smith, F. T. 2000. *The Wichita Indians: Traders of Texas and the Southern Plains, 1540–1845*. College Station: Texas A & M University Press.

Smith, J. 1986. *The Complete Works of Captain John Smith*. Ed. P. L. Barbour. 3 vols. Chapel Hill: University of North Carolina Press.

Smith, M. D., ed. 2001. *Sex without Consent: Rape and Sexual Coercion in America.* New York: New York University Press.

Smith, M. D., and M. A. Zahn, eds. 1999. *Studying and Preventing Homicide: Issues and Challenges.* Thousand Oaks, Calif.: Sage.

Smolenski, J. 2004. "The Death of Sawantaeny and the Problem of Justice on the Frontier." In *Friends and Enemies in Penn's Woods: Indians, Colonists, and the Racial Construction of Pennsylvania,* ed. W. A. Pencak and D. K. Richter, 104–128. University Park: Pennsylvania State University Press.

Snow, D. R. 1980. *The Archaeology of New England.* New York: Academic Press.

Snow, D. R., and K. M. Lanphear. 1988. "European Contact and Indian Depopulation in the Northeast: The Timing of the First Epidemics." *Ethnohistory* 35: 15–33.

Somerset Fry, P., and F. Somerset Fry. 1988. *A History of Ireland.* London: Routledge.

Sonnichsen, C. L. 1951. *I'll Die before I'll Run: The Story of the Great Feuds of Texas.* New York: Harper.

———. 1957. *Ten Texas Feuds.* Albuquerque: University of New Mexico Press.

Spear, A. H. 1967. *Black Chicago: The Making of a Negro Ghetto, 1890–1920.* Chicago: University of Chicago Press.

Spear, C. 1832. *Memoir of Mrs. Chloe Spear, A Native of Africa, Who was Enslaved in Childhood, and Died in Boston, January 3, 1815. . . . Aged 65 Years.* Boston: James Loring.

Spierenburg, P. 1994. "Faces of Violence: Homicide Trends and Cultural Meanings: Amsterdam, 1431–1816." *Journal of Social History* 27: 701–716.

———. 1996. "Long-Term Trends in Homicide: Theoretical Reflections and Dutch Evidence, Fifteenth to Twentieth Centuries." In *The Civilization of Crime: Violence in Town and Country since the Middle Ages,* ed. E. A. Johnson and E. H. Monkkonen, 63–105. Urbana: University of Illinois Press.

———. 1998. "Knife Fighting and Popular Codes of Honor in Early Modern Amsterdam." In *Men and Violence: Gender, Honor, and Rituals in Modern Europe and America,* ed. P. Spierenburg, 103–127. Columbus: Ohio State University Press.

Spindel, D. J. 1989. *Crime and Society in North Carolina, 1663–1776.* Baton Rouge: Louisiana State University Press.

Spufford, M. 1974. *Contrasting Communities: English Villagers in the Sixteenth and Seventeenth Centuries.* Cambridge: Cambridge University Press.

Stanley, L. L. 1975. *A Little History of Gilmer County.* Ellijay, Ga.: L. L. Stanley.

———. 1984. *Cherokee Georgia: The Enchanted Land.* Ellijay, Ga.: L. L. Stanley.

Starna, W. A. 2004. "The Diplomatic Career of Canasatego." In *Friends and Enemies in Penn's Woods: Indians, Colonists, and the Racial Construction of*

Pennsylvania, ed. W. A. Pencak and D. K. Richter, 144–163. University Park: Pennsylvania State University Press.

Stearns, C. Z., and P. N. Stearns. 1986. *Anger: The Struggle for Emotional Control in America's History.* Chicago: University of Chicago Press.

Stearns, P. N. 1989. *Jealousy: The Evolution of an Emotion in American History.* New York: New York University Press.

Steckel, R. H. 1991. Confederate Amnesty Records for the United States Civil War, 1863–1866. Computer file. Inter-University Consortium for Political and Social Research, Ann Arbor.

Stevens, W. O. 1940. *Pistols at Ten Paces: The Story of the Code of Honor in America.* Boston: Houghton Mifflin.

Stevenson, B. E. 1996. *Life in Black and White: Family and Community in the Slave South.* New York: Oxford University Press.

Steward, D. 2000. *Duels and the Roots of Violence in Missouri.* Columbia: University of Missouri Press.

Stickley, A. 2006. "On Interpersonal Violence in Russia in the Present and the Past: A Sociological Study." Ph.D. diss., Stockholm University.

Stinson, H. S. 1988. *Greenbrier County, West Virginia, Court Orders, 1780–1850.* Moorpark, Calif.: Privately published.

Stone, L. 1983. "Interpersonal Violence in English Society, 1300–1980." *Past and Present* 101: 22–33.

Stratton, A. L. 1984. *History of the Town of Isle La Motte, Vermont.* Barre: Northlight Studio Press.

Strickland, J. S. 1982. "The Great Revival and Insurrectionary Fears in North Carolina: An Examination of Antebellum Southern Society and Slave Revolt Panics." In *Class, Conflict, and Consensus: Antebellum Southern Community Studies,* ed. O. V. Burton and R. C. McMath Jr., 57–95. Westport, Conn.: Greenwood.

Summers, L. P. 1966. *History of Southwest Virginia, 1746–1786, Washington County, 1777–1870.* Baltimore: Genealogical Publishing.

Summers, M. W. 1987. *The Plundering Generation: Corruption and the Crisis of the Union, 1849–1861.* New York: Oxford University Press.

———. 1993. *The Era of Good Stealings.* New York: Oxford University Press.

Surry County. 1742–1822. "Criminal Proceedings against Free Persons, Slaves, Etc." Microfilm. Library of Virginia, Richmond.

Sutherland, D. E. 1999. "The Absence of Violence: Confederates and Unionists in Culpeper County, Virginia." In *Guerrillas, Unionists, and Violence on the Confederate Home Front,* ed. D. E. Sutherland, 75–87. Fayetteville: University of Arkansas Press.

Sweet, J. W. 1995. "Bodies Politic: Colonialism, Race, and the Emergence of the American North: Rhode Island, 1730–1830." Ph.D. diss., Princeton University.

Sword, K. 2002. "Wayward Wives, Runaway Slaves, and the Limits of Patriarchal Authority in Early America." Ph.D. diss., Harvard University.

Sydnor, C. S. 1948. *The Development of Southern Sectionalism, 1819–1848*. Reprint, Baton Rouge: Louisiana State University Press, 1968.

Szatmary, D. P. 1980. *Shays' Rebellion: The Making of an Agrarian Insurrection*. Amherst: University of Massachusetts Press.

Taft, P., and P. Ross. 1978. "American Labor Violence: Its Causes, Character, and Outcome." In *Riot, Rout, and Tumult: Readings in American Social and Political Violence*, ed. R. Lane and J. J. Turner Jr., 218–250. Westport, Conn.: Greenwood.

Tager, J. 2001. *Boston Riots: Three Centuries of Social Violence*. Boston: Northeastern University Press.

Tallett, F. 1992. *War and Society in Early Modern Europe, 1495–1715*. London: Routledge.

Taylor, A. 1990. *Liberty Men and Great Proprietors: The Revolutionary Settlement on the Maine Frontier, 1760–1820*. Chapel Hill: University of North Carolina Press.

———. 2001. *American Colonies*. New York: Viking.

Taylor, R. 2001. *Breaking Away from Broken Windows*. Boulder: Westview Press.

Taylor, W. B. 1979. *Drinking, Homicide, and Rebellion in Colonial Mexican Villages*. Stanford: Stanford University Press.

Terkel, S. 1970. *Hard Times*. New York: Pantheon.

Thelen, D. P. 1986. *Paths of Resistance: Tradition and Dignity in Industrializing Missouri*. New York: Oxford University Press.

Thomas, R. P., and T. L. Anderson. 1973. "White Population, Labor Force, and Extensive Growth of the New England Economy in the Seventeenth Century." *Journal of Economic History* 33: 634–661.

Thompson, A. W. 1961. *Jacksonian Democracy on the Florida Frontier*. Gainesville: University of Florida Press.

Thompson, R. 1986. *Sex in Middlesex: Popular Mores in a Massachusetts County, 1649–1699*. Amherst: University of Massachusetts Press.

Thompson, Z. 1842. *History of Vermont: Natural, Civil, and Statistical*. Burlington: Chauncey Goodrich.

Thorpe, W. 1911. *History of Wallingford, Vermont*. Rutland: Tuttle.

Thwaites, R. G., ed. 1896–1901. *Jesuit Relations and Allied Documents: Travels and Explorations of the Jesuit Missionaries in New France, 1610–1791*. 73 vols. Cleveland: Burrows Brothers.

Tijerina, A. 1994. *Tejanos and Texans under the Mexican Flag, 1821–1836*. College Station: Texas A & M University Press.

————. 1996. "Under the Mexican Flag." In *Tejano Journey, 1770–1850,* ed. G. E. Poyo, 33–47. Austin: University of Texas Press.

Tindall, G. B. 1984. *America: A Narrative History.* New York: W. W. Norton.

Tippetts, W. H. 1885. *Herkimer County Murders.* Herkimer, N.Y.: H. P. Witherstine.

Tolnay, S. E., and E. M. Beck. 1995. *A Festival of Violence: An Analysis of Southern Lynchings, 1882–1930.* Urbana: University of Illinois Press.

Tonry, M., ed. 1997. *Ethnicity, Crime, and Immigration: Comparative and Cross-National Perspectives.* Chicago: University of Chicago Press.

Town of Guilford, Vermont. 1961. *Official History of Guilford, Vermont, 1678–1961.* Brattleboro: Vermont Printing Company for the Town of Guilford and Broad Brooks Grange No. 151.

Trelease, A. W. 1971. *White Terror: The Ku Klux Klan Conspiracy and Southern Reconstruction.* New York: Harper and Row.

A True Declaration of the Estate of the Colonie in Virginia, with a Confutation of Such Scandalous Reports as Have Tended to the Disgrace of So Worthy an Enterprise. Published by advise and direction of the Councell of Virginia [1610]. 1947. In *Tracts and Other Papers Relating Principally to the Colonies in North America,* ed. P. Force, 3: 3–27. New York: Peter Smith.

Trumbull, J. H. 1850. *The Public Records of the Colony of Connecticut Prior to the Union with New Haven Colony.* 2 vols. Hartford: Brown and Parsons.

Tuttle, W. M., Jr. 1970. *Race Riot: Chicago in the Red Summer of 1919.* New York: Atheneum.

Tyler, T. R. 1990. *Why People Obey the Law.* New Haven: Yale University Press.

Ulrich, L. T. 1982. *Good Wives: Image and Reality in the Lives of Women in Northern New England, 1650–1750.* New York: Alfred A. Knopf.

Underdown, D. 1985. *Revel, Riot, and Rebellion: Popular Politics and Culture in England, 1603–1660.* Oxford: Clarendon Press.

Underhill, J. 1971. *Newes from America* [1638]. New York: Da Capo Press.

United Nations Office on Drugs and Crime. 1970–. *United Nations Survey on Crime Trends and Operations of Criminal Justice Systems.* Multiple vols. Vienna.

University of Maryland. 1991. *The Great American History Machine.* College Park: Academic Software Development Group.

Urquhart, M. C., and K. A. H. Buckley. 1965. *Historical Statistics of Canada.* Toronto: Macmillan.

Utley, R. M. 1987. *High Noon in Lincoln: Violence on the Western Frontier.* Albuquerque: University of New Mexico Press.

————. 2002. *Lone Star Justice: The First Century of the Texas Rangers.* New York: Oxford University Press.

Van der Wee, H. 1978. "Prices and Wages as Development Variables: A Comparison between England and the Southern Netherlands, 1400–1700." *Acta Historiae Neerlandicae* 10: 58–78.

Van Laer, A. J. F., ed. and trans. 1922. *Minutes of the Court of Rensselaerswyck, 1648–1652*. Albany: University of the State of New York.

Van Young, E. 2001. *The Other Rebellion: Popular Violence, Ideology, and the Mexican Struggle for Independence, 1810–1821*. Stanford: Stanford University Press.

Vandal, G. 2000. *Rethinking Southern Violence: Homicides in Post–Civil War Louisiana, 1866–1884*. Columbus: Ohio State University Press.

Vaughan, W. E., and A. J. Fitzpatrick, eds. 1978. *Irish Historical Statistics: Population, 1821–1971*. Dublin: Royal Irish Academy.

Vermont Historical Society. 1926. *Proceedings of the Vermont Historical Society for the Years 1923, 1924, 1925*. Bellows Falls: P. H. Gobie Press.

———. 1984. "Anecdote." *Vermont History News* 35: 118.

Wahl, J. B. 1986. "New Results on the Decline in Household Fertility in the United States from 1750 to 1900." In *Long-Term Factors in American Economic Growth*, ed. S. L. Engerman and R. E. Gallman, 391–425. Chicago: University of Chicago Press.

Waldstreicher, D. 1997. *In the Midst of Perpetual Fetes: The Making of American Nationalism, 1776–1820*. Chapel Hill: University of North Carolina Press.

Walker, D. 1965. *David Walker's Appeal*. Ed. C. M. Wiltse. New York: Hill and Wang.

Walker, G. 2003. *Crime, Gender, and Social Order in Early Modern England*. Cambridge: Cambridge University Press.

Walker, S. 1994. *Sense and Nonsense about Crime and Drugs*. 3d ed. Belmont, Calif.: Wadsworth.

Wall, H. M. 1990. *Fierce Communion: Family and Community in Early America*. Cambridge: Harvard University Press.

Waller, A. L. 1988. *Feud: Hatfields, McCoys, and Social Change in Appalachia, 1860–1900*. Chapel Hill: University of North Carolina Press.

———. 1995. "Feuding in Appalachia: Evolution of a Cultural Stereotype." In *Appalachia in the Making: The Mountain South in the Nineteenth Century*, ed. M. B. Pudup, D. B. Billings, and A. L. Wallers, 347–376. Chapel Hill: University of North Carolina Press.

Walsh, L. S. 1999. "Summing the Parts: Implications for Estimating Chesapeake Output and Income Subregionally." *William and Mary Quarterly*, 3d ser., 56: 53–94.

Walter, J. 1989. "The Social Economy of Dearth in Early Modern England." In *Famine, Disease and the Social Order in Early Modern Society*, ed. J. Walter and R. S. Schofield, 75–128. Cambridge: Cambridge University Press.

Walter, J., and R. Schofield. 1989. "Famine, Disease and Crisis Mortality in

Early Modern Society." In *Famine, Disease and the Social Order in Early Modern Society,* ed. Walter and Schofield, 1–74. Cambridge: Cambridge University Press.

Walton, E. P., ed. 1873. *Records of the Council of Safety and Governor and Council of the State of Vermont.* Montpelier: J. and J. M. Poland.

Ward, G. G. 1965. *The Annals of Upper Georgia: Centered in Gilmer County.* Carrollton, Ga.: Thomasson.

Washburn, W. E. 1957. *The Governor and the Rebel: A History of Bacon's Rebellion in Virginia.* Chapel Hill: University of North Carolina Press.

Watson, C. B. 1960. *Shakespeare and the Renaissance Concept of Honor.* Princeton: Princeton University Press.

Watson, H. 1990. *Liberty and Power: The Politics of Jacksonian America.* New York: Noonday.

Watt, J. R. 2001. *Choosing Death: Suicide and Calvinism in Early Modern Geneva.* Kirksville, Mo.: Truman State University Press.

Weaver, J. C. 1995. *Crimes, Constables, and Courts: Order and Transgression in a Canadian City, 1816–1970.* Montreal: McGill–Queen's University Press.

Webb, R. K. 1970. *Modern England: From the Eighteenth Century to the Present.* New York: Dodd, Mead.

Webb, S. S. 1984. *1676: The End of American Independence.* New York: Alfred A. Knopf.

Weber, D. J. 1982. *The Mexican Frontier, 1821–1846: The American Southwest under Mexico.* Albuquerque: University of New Mexico Press.

———. 1992. *The Spanish Frontier in North America.* New Haven: Yale University Press.

Webster, K. 1913. *History of Hudson, New Hampshire.* Manchester: Granite State Publishing.

Weigley, R. F. 1970. *The Partisan War: The South Carolina Campaign of 1780–1782.* Columbia: University of South Carolina Press.

Weiss, N. J. 1983. *Farewell to the Party of Lincoln: Black Politics in the Age of FDR.* Princeton: Princeton University Press.

Wells, F. P. 1902. *History of Newbury, Vermont.* St. Johnsbury: Caledonian Press.

Wendel, T. 1968. "The Keith-Lloyd Alliance: Factional and Coalition Politics in Colonial Pennsylvania." *Pennsylvania Magazine of History and Biography* 92: 289–305.

Wertenbaker, T. J. 1940. *Torchbearer of the Revolution: The Story of Bacon's Rebellion and Its Leader.* Princeton: Princeton University Press.

Wheeler, K. H. 1997. "Infanticide in Nineteenth-Century Ohio." *Journal of Social History* 31: 407–418.

Whetstone, A. E. 1981. *Scottish County Government in the Eighteenth and Nineteenth Centuries*. Edinburgh: J. Donald.

Whitcher, W. F. 1909. *Josiah Burnham: His Trial and Execution for Murder*. Woodsville, N.H.: News Book and Job Print.

White, D. O. 1973. *Connecticut's Black Soldiers, 1775–1783*. Chester, Conn.: Pequot Press.

White, R. 1991. *"It's Your Misfortune and None of My Own": A New History of the American West*. Norman: University of Oklahoma Press.

White, S. 1991. *Somewhat More Independent: The End of Slavery in New York City, 1770–1810*. Athens: University of Georgia Press.

Wiener, M. J. 2004. *Men of Blood: Violence, Manliness, and Criminal Justice in Victorian England*. Cambridge: Cambridge University Press.

Wilentz, S. 1984. *Chants Democratic: New York City and the Rise of the American Working Class, 1788–1850*. New York: Oxford University Press.

———. 2008. *The Age of Reagan: A History, 1974–2008*. New York: HarperCollins.

Wiley, B. I. 1943. *The Plain People of the Confederacy*. Baton Rouge: Louisiana State University Press.

Williams, D. 1998. *Rich Man's War: Class, Caste, and Confederate Defeat in the Lower Chattahoochee Valley*. Athens: University of Georgia Press.

Williams, D., T. C. Williams, and D. Carlson. 2002. *Plain Folk in a Rich Man's War: Class and Dissent in Confederate Georgia*. Gainesville: University Press of Florida.

Williams, J. A. 2002. *Appalachia: A History*. Chapel Hill: University of North Carolina Press.

Williams, J. C. 1869. *The History and Map of Danby, Vermont*. Rutland: McLean and Robbins.

Williams, J. K. 1980. *Dueling in the Old South: Vignettes of Social History*. College Station: Texas A & M University Press.

Williams, K., and R. L. Flewelling. 1987. "Family, Acquaintance, and Stranger Homicide: Alternative Procedures for Rate Calculations." *Criminology* 25: 543–560.

Williams, R. 1936. *A Key into the Language of America*. 5th ed. Providence: Rhode Island and Providence Plantations Tercentenary Committee.

Williams, S. 1794. *The Natural and Civil History of Vermont*. Walpole, N.H.: Isaiah Thomas and David Carlisle.

Williams, T. D., ed. 1973. *Secret Societies in Ireland*. New York: Barnes and Noble.

Williamson, J. 1984. *The Crucible of Race: Black/White Relations in the American South since Emancipation*. New York: Oxford University Press.

Wilson, J. Q. 1975. *Thinking about Crime*. New York: Basic Books.

Wilson, K. 1998. *The Sense of the People: Politics, Culture, and Imperialism in England, 1715–1785.* New York: Cambridge University Press.

———. 2003. *The Island Race: Englishness, Empire, and Gender in the Eighteenth Century.* London: Routledge.

Wilson, L. 1998. "A Marriage 'Well Ordered': Love, Power, and Partnership in Colonial New England." In *A Shared Experience: Men, Women, and the History of Gender,* ed. L. McCall and D. Yacavone, 78–97. New York: New York University Press.

Wilson, W. J. 1996. *When Work Disappears: The World of the New Urban Poor.* New York: Alfred A. Knopf.

Winship, G. P., ed. 1905. *Sailors' Narratives of Journeys along the Coast of New England, 1524–1624.* New York: Burt Franklin.

Winslow, E. 1910. "Winslow's Relation." In *Chronicles of the Pilgrim Fathers,* ed. J. Masefield, 267–357. New York: E. P. Dutton.

Winthrop, J. 1996. *The Journal of John Winthrop, 1630–1649.* Ed. R. S. Dunn, J. Savage, and L. Yeandle. Cambridge: Belknap Press of Harvard University Press.

Withers, C. W. J. 1988. *Gaelic Scotland: The Transformation of a Culture Region.* London: Routledge.

Wood, A. L. 1961. *Crime and Aggression in Changing Ceylon: A Sociological Analysis of Homicide, Suicide, and Economic Crime. Transactions of the American Philosophical Society,* n.s., 51: pt. 8.

Wood, P. 1974. *Black Majority: Negroes in Colonial South Carolina from 1670 through the Stono Rebellion.* New York: W. W. Norton.

Wood, W. 1977. *New England's Prospect.* Ed. A. T. Vaughan. Amherst: University of Massachusetts Press.

Woodward, C. V. 1951. *Origins of the New South, 1877–1913.* Baton Rouge: Louisiana State University Press.

———. 1963. *Tom Watson: Agrarian Rebel.* New York: Oxford University Press.

Woody, C. T., and M. L. Schwartz. 1977. "War in Pleasant Valley: The Outbreak of the Graham-Tewksbury Feud." *Journal of Arizona History* 18: 43–68.

World Health Organization. 1950–. *World Health Statistics Annual.* Multiple vols. Geneva.

———. 2002. *World Report on Violence and Health.* Geneva.

Wormald, J. 1980. "Bloodfeud, Kindred and Government in Early Modern Scotland." *Past and Present* 87: 54–97.

Wright, G. C. 1990. *Racial Violence in Kentucky, 1865–1940: Lynchings, Mob Rule, and "Legal Lynchings."* Baton Rouge: Louisiana State University Press.

Wrightson, K. 1996. "The Politics of the Parish in Early Modern England."

In *The Experience of Authority in Early Modern England*, ed. P. Griffiths, A. Fox, and S. Hindle, 10–46. New York: St. Martin's Press.

Wrightson, K., and D. Levine. 1979. *Poverty and Piety in an English Village: Terling, 1525–1700*. New York: Academic Press.

Writers' Program of the Works Progress Administration. 1941. *The Story of Washington-Wilkes*. Athens: University of Georgia Press.

Wyatt-Brown, B. 1982. *Southern Honor: Ethics and Behavior in the Old South*. New York: Oxford University Press.

Ylikangas, H. 2001. "What Happened to Violence? An Analysis of the Development of Violence from Medieval Times to the Early Modern Era Based on Finnnish Source Material." In *Five Centuries of Violence in Finland and the Baltic Area*, ed. H. Ylikangas, P. Karonen, and M. Lehti, 1–83. Columbus: Ohio State University Press.

Zelinsky, W. 1988. *Nation into State: The Shifting Symbolic Foundations of American Nationalism*. Chapel Hill: University of North Carolina Press.

Zimring, F. E., and G. Hawkins. 1997. *Crime Is Not the Problem: Lethal Violence in America*. New York: Oxford University Press.

Acknowledgments

The one good thing about taking a long time to research a book is that it has given me an opportunity to visit old friends and make new ones as I traveled around the country to visit archives and libraries. I would like to thank first and foremost my friends and relatives who invited me to stay with them while I worked in the archives, including Barney and Darryl Bloom, Nina Dayton and Jim Bolster, Mary and Steve Fortado, Bob Fuss, Cindy Low and Dan McGraw, Duane Mellor and Lee Carlson, Steve Michaels, Reidun and Andy Nuquist, Jeff and Jane Potash, Greg and Ondis Sanford, Dan and Tracey Sweeney, the late Allan and Dorothy Sweeney, Andy and Kate Taylor, and Jim and Pat Watkinson. I know that I must have appeared to their friends and neighbors to be the Kato Kaelin of homicide studies (who is that guy living in the spare room, and what does he do all day?). I also owe an enormous debt to my parents, Paula Roth and the late Albert Roth. Thank you, everyone, for your kindness and your faith that I would finish the book someday.

I would also like to thank the county clerks, archivists, librarians, and historical society members who helped me find and understand the records I needed, especially Gay Johnson, Clerk of Court, Rutland County, Rutland, Vermont; Don Goodnow, Clerk of Court, Strafford County, Dover, New Hampshire; Karen Forgrave, Family History Center, Dublin, Ohio; Frank Mevers, New Hampshire State Archives, Concord; Edward Horton, New Hampshire State Library, Concord; Barney Bloom, Kevin Graffagnino, Reidun Nuquist, and Michael Sherman, Vermont Historical Society, Montpelier; Paul Donovan, Vermont State Library, Montpelier; Connie Gallagher and Jeff Marshall, Wilbur Collection, University of Vermont Library, Burlington; Jim and Pat Watkinson, Library of Virginia, Richmond; Dale Couch and Andy Taylor, Georgia Department of History and Archives, Atlanta; and Edward Patterson, Franklin County Historical Society, Carnesville, Georgia.

I am grateful to the scholars who commented on the papers I delivered on homicide, particularly before the Society for Historians of the Early Republic and the Social Science History Association; to my students in criminal justice history at Ohio State University who researched the history of violence in Chicago and Cleveland; and to students and colleagues who responded to my lectures at Chicago, Harvard, Miami of Ohio, Northern Illinois, Northwestern, Ohio State–Newark, Penn, Stanford, SUNY–Buffalo, SUNY–Binghampton, Vermont, and Yale. I'd like to thank scholars who helped me with their particular expertise, including Dan Cohen, Robert Davis Jr., David Hacker, Fritz Hafer, and Tad Evans, who gave me access to his wonderful indexes of Georgia newspapers.

My greatest scholarly debts are to my friends in the Criminal Justice Network of the Social Science History Association ("the Crime Gang"), who are working together to create the Historical Violence Database; and to friends who read all or part of the manuscript for *American Homicide*. Thanks to my data-dredging colleagues, especially Ross Bagby Jr., Carolyn Conley, Nina Dayton, Mike Denham, Manuel Eisner, Doug Eckberg, Robb Haberman, Barbara Hanawalt, Roger Lane, Bud McKanna, Jack Marietta, Kevin Mullen, Phil Schwarz, Pieter Spierenburg, Frédéric Vesentini, Ken Wheeler, Marty Wiener, and the late Eric Monkkonen. And thanks to friends and colleagues who helped me shape the manuscript: Ken Andrien, Manse Blackford, Howard Brown, Rachel Cleves, Norman Dupont, Robert Dykstra, Barbara Hanawalt, Brian Hansen, Lara Heimert, Dick Holway, Hasan Jeffries, Morgan Kousser, Jim Lindgren, Stephanie Shaw, Laurel Ulrich, and especially Jeff Adler, Roger Lane, Bertram Wyatt-Brown, Jim Bartholomew, and Tamara Thornton, who read the penultimate draft.

I am grateful for the financial support I received from the National Science Foundation, the National Endowment for the Humanities, the

Harry Frank Guggenheim Foundation, and the College of Humanities and Criminal Justice Research Center at Ohio State University. Thanks as well to Michael Aronson and Hilary Jacqmin of Harvard University Press and to my copyeditor, Ann Hawthorne, for their excellent editorial advice, and to Marie Martin, Ron McLean, and Jim Bach of Ohio State, for their help with the figures.

And thanks above all to my spouse, Allison Sweeney, and to our son, Alex, for putting up with this project for so long. It has been a fixture of Alex's life since the day he was born, but it hasn't been without its benefits. When Alex and his friends troop through the basement, he points to me working and says, "My dad studies murder," to which his friends always say, "Cool." Alas, for Allison the benefits haven't been all that clear, but she never lost faith in the project.

Index

Abbott, Teddy Blue, 380, 384
Abenakis, 41–42, 47, 68, 79, 173
Abilene, Kansas, 382–383
Abolition. *See* Antislavery movement
Abortion, 8–9
Adams, John Quincy, 306
Africa: homicide rates in, 7, 100; witchcraft in, 100
African Americans: homicide estimates for, xii; homicide rates of, 13, 25–26, 39, 94–95, 98, 101, 147, 175, 180, 195–196, 206, 224, 225, 226, 309, 330, 387–388, 395, 397–401, 403, 410–411, 441, 445–448, 452, 455, 463–464, 466, 534n26, 547n41, 548nn44,45, 550n59, 551n60, 553n83, 559n20, 567n107, 569n121, 586nn57,60; marital homicide among, 23, 123–127, 271–275; free, 25–26, 71–72, 205; and revolutionary ideas, 25, 103, 177–179, 182, 224; in colonial New England, 95–96, 99; in colonial Chesapeake, 96–97, 99; and law enforcement, 96, 178, 432; homicide among unrelated, 99–102, 177, 195–196, 226–227, 346, 348, 351–352, 387–388, 395–403, 410, 414–418, 432–434; and racial solidarity, 101–102, 127, 177, 227, 231–232, 432–434; family and intimate homicide among, 108; romance homicide among, 135–137, 279–280, 282–283; relative homicide among, 142–143, 553n83; in

American Revolution, 175–176; and legal equality, 181–182, 395–396, 410–411; in plantation South, 224–233, 415–418; and the Great Migration, 271, 402; and loss of political power in 1880s and 1890s, 271, 396–397, 402–403, 418, 428–430; and the Great Depression, 441–445; and civil rights movement, 456–458. *See also* Interracial homicide
Agnew, Spiro, 461
Alcohol, 9, 106, 128, 257, 315
Alden, John, 68
Allen, Ira, 160
American Homicide Supplemental Volume (AHSV), xv
American Revolution, 11, 13–14, 19, 146–179; and homicide rates, 146–149; in New England, 149–151, 172–173; and political homicide, 149–154, 164, 166, 169, 172–173; and frontier homicide, 151–152, 155–156, 161–173; in Pennsylvania, 151–153, 155; in Virginia, 153–155, 163–164, 173–175; patriotism during, 156–157; in Georgia and South Carolina, 164–169
Andros, Edmund, 68
Anglos. *See* European Americans
Anne (queen of England), 82
Anti-Catholicism, 63, 76, 77, 78–79, 197–198, 304–305, 393–394
Antislavery movement, 157, 176–177; in

644